Applying Data Science and Learning Analytics Throughout a Learner's Lifespan

Goran Trajkovski
Western Governors University, USA

Marylee Demeter
Western Governors University, USA

Heather Hayes
Western Governors University, USA

IGI Global
PUBLISHER of TIMELY KNOWLEDGE

A volume in the Advances in Educational Technologies and Instructional Design (AETID) Book Series

Published in the United States of America by
IGI Global
Information Science Reference (an imprint of IGI Global)
701 E. Chocolate Avenue
Hershey PA, USA 17033
Tel: 717-533-8845
Fax: 717-533-8661
E-mail: cust@igi-global.com
Web site: http://www.igi-global.com

Library of Congress Cataloging-in-Publication Data

Names: Trajkovski, Goran, 1972- editor. | Demeter, Marylee, 1972- editor. | Hayes, Heather, 1978- editor.
Title: Applying data science and learning analytics throughout a learner's lifespan / Goran Trajkovski, Marylee Demeter, Heather Hayes editors.
Description: Hershey, PA : Information Science Reference, 2022. | Includes bibliographical references and index. | Summary: "This publication examines novel and emerging applications of data science and sister disciplines in gaining insights from data to inform interventions into the learners' journey and interactions with an academic or training institution, covering topics such as building models of learners for success, using data to inform courseware and assessmentware development"-- Provided by publisher.
Identifiers: LCCN 2021060930 (print) | LCCN 2021060931 (ebook) | ISBN 9781799896449 (hardcover) | ISBN 9781799896456 (paperback) | ISBN 9781799896463 (ebook)
Subjects: LCSH: Education--Data processing. | Data mining.
Classification: LCC LB1028.43 .A64 2022 (print) | LCC LB1028.43 (ebook) | DDC 371.33/4--dc23/eng/20211223
LC record available at https://lccn.loc.gov/2021060930
LC ebook record available at https://lccn.loc.gov/2021060931

This book is published in the IGI Global book series Advances in Educational Technologies and Instructional Design (AETID) (ISSN: 2326-8905; eISSN: 2326-8913)

British Cataloguing in Publication Data
A Cataloguing in Publication record for this book is available from the British Library.

For electronic access to this publication, please contact: eresources@igi-global.com.

Advances in Educational Technologies and Instructional Design (AETID) Book Series

Lawrence A. Tomei
Robert Morris University, USA

ISSN:2326-8905
EISSN:2326-8913

Mission

Education has undergone, and continues to undergo, immense changes in the way it is enacted and distributed to both child and adult learners. In modern education, the traditional classroom learning experience has evolved to include technological resources and to provide online classroom opportunities to students of all ages regardless of their geographical locations. From distance education, Massive-Open-Online-Courses (MOOCs), and electronic tablets in the classroom, technology is now an integral part of learning and is also affecting the way educators communicate information to students.

The **Advances in Educational Technologies & Instructional Design (AETID) Book Series** explores new research and theories for facilitating learning and improving educational performance utilizing technological processes and resources. The series examines technologies that can be integrated into K-12 classrooms to improve skills and learning abilities in all subjects including STEM education and language learning. Additionally, it studies the emergence of fully online classrooms for young and adult learners alike, and the communication and accountability challenges that can arise. Trending topics that are covered include adaptive learning, game-based learning, virtual school environments, and social media effects. School administrators, educators, academicians, researchers, and students will find this series to be an excellent resource for the effective design and implementation of learning technologies in their classes.

Coverage

- Web 2.0 and Education
- Digital Divide in Education
- K-12 Educational Technologies
- Adaptive Learning
- Online Media in Classrooms
- Curriculum Development
- Educational Telecommunications
- Bring-Your-Own-Device
- Higher Education Technologies
- Instructional Design Models

IGI Global is currently accepting manuscripts for publication within this series. To submit a proposal for a volume in this series, please contact our Acquisition Editors at Acquisitions@igi-global.com or visit: http://www.igi-global.com/publish/.

The Advances in Educational Technologies and Instructional Design (AETID) Book Series (ISSN 2326-8905) is published by IGI Global, 701 E. Chocolate Avenue, Hershey, PA 17033-1240, USA, www.igi-global.com. This series is composed of titles available for purchase individually; each title is edited to be contextually exclusive from any other title within the series. For pricing and ordering information please visit http://www.igi-global.com/book-series/advances-educational-technologies-instructional-design/73678. Postmaster: Send all address changes to above address.

Titles in this Series

For a list of additional titles in this series, please visit: www.igi-global.com/book-series/advances-educational-technologies-instructional-design/73678

Technology-Supported Interventions for Students With Special Needs in the 21st Century
Xiongyi Liu (Cleveland State University, USA) and Patrick Wachira (Cleveland State University, USA)
Information Science Reference • © 2022 • 289pp • H/C (ISBN: 9781799888741) • US $195.00

Cases on Practical Applications for Remote, Hybrid, and Hyflex Teaching
Valerie Harlow Shinas (Lesley University, USA) Chu N. Ly (Framingham State University, USA) and Sule Yilmaz Ozden (Sakarya Üniversitesi, Turkey)
Information Science Reference • © 2022 • 355pp • H/C (ISBN: 9781799891680) • US $195.00

Affordances of Film for Literacy Instruction
Jason D. DeHart (Appalachian State University, USA)
Information Science Reference • © 2022 • 277pp • H/C (ISBN: 9781799891369) • US $195.00

Applications of Machine Learning and Artificial Intelligence in Education
Seda Khadimally (North American University, USA)
Information Science Reference • © 2022 • 271pp • H/C (ISBN: 9781799877769) • US $195.00

Handbook of Research on Promoting Global Citizenship Education
Jared Keengwe (University of North Dakota, USA)
Information Science Reference • © 2022 • 371pp • H/C (ISBN: 9781799895428) • US $265.00

Assistive Technologies for Differently Abled Students
Sangeeta Dhamdhere-Rao (Modern College of Arts, Science and Commerce, India) and Frederic Andres (National Insitute of Informatics, Japan)
Information Science Reference • © 2022 • 305pp • H/C (ISBN: 9781799847366) • US $195.00

Impact of Digital Transformation in Teacher Training Models
Ana Afonso (LE@D, Universidade Aberta, Portugal & CISUC, University of Coimbra, Portugal) Lina Morgado (Universidade Aberta, Portugal) and Licínio Roque (University of Coimbra, Portugal)
Information Science Reference • © 2022 • 313pp • H/C (ISBN: 9781799895381) • US $195.00

Enhancing Teaching and Learning With Socratic Educational Strategies Emerging Research and Opportunities
Frank G. Giuseffi (William Woods University, USA)
Information Science Reference • © 2022 • 172pp • H/C (ISBN: 9781799871729) • US $175.00

IGI Global
PUBLISHER of TIMELY KNOWLEDGE

701 East Chocolate Avenue, Hershey, PA 17033, USA
Tel: 717-533-8845 x100 • Fax: 717-533-8661
E-Mail: cust@igi-global.com • www.igi-global.com

Table of Contents

Preface xv

Section 1
Perspectives on Data

Chapter 1
Mind the Gap: From Typical LMS Traces to Learning to Learn Journeys 1
Carmel Kent, The Open University, UK
Abayomi Akanji, EDUCATE Ventures Research, UK
Benedict du Boulay, EDUCATE Ventures Research, UK
Ibrahim Bashir, EDUCATE Ventures Research, UK
Thomas G. Fikes, Arizona State University, USA
Sue A. Rodríguez De Jesús, Arizona State University, USA
Alysha Ramirez Hall, Arizona State University, USA
Paul Alvarado, Arizona State University, USA
Jennifer E. Jones, Arizona State University, USA
Mutlu Cukurova, University College London, UK
Varshita Sher, EDUCATE Ventures Research, UK
Canan Blake, University College London, UK
Arthur Fisher, EDUCATE Ventures Research, UK
Juliet Greenwood, Arizona State University, USA
Rosemary Luckin, University College London, UK

Chapter 2
Relationships Between Out-of-School-Time Lessons and Academic Performance Among Adolescents in Four High-Performing Education Systems 27
David R. Litz, University of Northern British Columbia, Canada
Shaljan Areepattamannil, Emirates College for Advanced Education, UAE
Scott H. Parkman, New Mexico Highlands University, USA

Chapter 3
An Assessment of Self-Service Business Intelligence Tools for Students: The Impact of Cognitive Needs and Innovative Cognitive Styles 56
Mohammad K. Daradkeh, University of Dubai, UAE & Yarmouk University, Jordan

Section 2
Applications

Chapter 4
Univariate and Multivariate Filtering Techniques for Feature Selection and Their Applications in Field of Machine Learning 73
Dharmendra Trikamlal Patel, Smt .Chandaben Mohanbhai Patel Institute of Computer Applications, CHARUSAT, India
Nirali Honest, Smt .Chandaben Mohanbhai Patel Institute of Computer Applications, CHARUSAT, India
Pranav Vyas, Smt .Chandaben Mohanbhai Patel Institute of Computer Applications, CHARUSAT, India
Atul Patel, Smt .Chandaben Mohanbhai Patel Institute of Computer Applications, CHARUSAT, India

Chapter 5
Scalable Personalization for Student Success: A Framework for Using Machine Learning Methods in Self-Directed Online Courses 94
Thomas Wagner, Western Governors University, USA
Morgan Diederich, Western Governors University, USA

Chapter 6
User Sentiment Analysis and Review Rating Prediction for the Blended Learning Platform App.... 113
Md Shamim Hossain, Hajee Mohammad Danesh Science and Technology University, Bangladesh
Md. Kutub Uddin, Hajee Mohammad Danesh Science and Technology University, Bangladesh
Md. Kamal Hossain, Széchenyi István University, Hungary
Mst Farjana Rahman, Hajee Mohammad Danesh Science and Technology University, Bangladesh

Chapter 7
Analyzing and Predicting Learner Sentiment Toward Specialty Schools Using Machine Learning Techniques 133
Md Shamim Hossain, Hajee Mohammad Danesh Science and Technology University, Bangladesh
Mst Farjana Rahman, Hajee Mohammad Danesh Science and Technology University, Bangladesh
Md. Kutub Uddin, Hajee Mohammad Danesh Science and Technology University, Bangladesh

Section 3
Advancing the Profession

Chapter 8
Working Towards a Data Science Associates Degree Program: Impacts, Challenges, and Future Directions 160
Wendy Chin, Community College of Baltimore County, USA
James Braman, Community College of Baltimore County, USA
Hanks Melissa, Community College of Baltimore County, USA
Paulette Comet, Community College of Baltimore County, USA

Chapter 9
A Storied Approach to Learning Data Analytics in a Graduate Data Analytics Program........ 176
Brandon Vaughn, Western Governors University, USA

Chapter 10
Identifying Structure in Program-Level Competencies and Skills: Dimensionality Analysis of Performance Assessment Scores From Multiple Courses in an IT Program........ 193
Heather Hayes, Western Governors University, USA
Goran Trajkovski, Western Governors University, USA

Section 4
Considerations

Chapter 11
Don't @ Me: A Study of the Perception of Twitter Users of Educational Offerings 220
Goran Trajkovski, Western Governors University, USA
Eduard Fabregat, Universitat Abat Oliba, Spain

Chapter 12
The Secret Lives of ePortfolios: Text Network Analysis and the Future of Algorithmic Hiring 239
Samuel Collins, Towson University, USA

Chapter 13
Do We Need a Digital Data Exorcism? End of Life Considerations of Data Mining Educational Content........ 260
James Braman, Community College of Baltimore County, USA
Alfreda Dudley, Towson University, USA

Compilation of References 276

About the Contributors 306

Index 313

Detailed Table of Contents

Preface xv

Section 1
Perspectives on Data

Chapter 1
Mind the Gap: From Typical LMS Traces to Learning to Learn Journeys 1
Carmel Kent, The Open University, UK
Abayomi Akanji, EDUCATE Ventures Research, UK
Benedict du Boulay, EDUCATE Ventures Research, UK
Ibrahim Bashir, EDUCATE Ventures Research, UK
Thomas G. Fikes, Arizona State University, USA
Sue A. Rodríguez De Jesús, Arizona State University, USA
Alysha Ramirez Hall, Arizona State University, USA
Paul Alvarado, Arizona State University, USA
Jennifer E. Jones, Arizona State University, USA
Mutlu Cukurova, University College London, UK
Varshita Sher, EDUCATE Ventures Research, UK
Canan Blake, University College London, UK
Arthur Fisher, EDUCATE Ventures Research, UK
Juliet Greenwood, Arizona State University, USA
Rosemary Luckin, University College London, UK

Many universities aim to improve students' 'learning to learn' (LTL) skills to prepare them for post-academic life. This requires evaluating LTL and integrating it into the university's curriculum and assessment regimes. Data is essential to provide evidence for the evaluation of LTL, meaning that available data sources must be connected to the types of evidence required for evaluation. This chapter describes a case study using an LTL ontology to connect the theoretical aspects of LTL with a university's existing data sources and to inform the design and application of learning analytics. The results produced by the analytics indicate that LTL can be treated as a dimension in its own right. The LTL dimension has a moderate relationship to academic performance. There is also evidence to suggest that LTL develops at an uneven pace across academic terms and that it exhibits different patterns in online as compared to face-to-face delivery methods.

Chapter 2
Relationships Between Out-of-School-Time Lessons and Academic Performance Among Adolescents in Four High-Performing Education Systems 27
David R. Litz, University of Northern British Columbia, Canada
Shaljan Areepattamannil, Emirates College for Advanced Education, UAE
Scott H. Parkman, New Mexico Highlands University, USA

Research into the effects of out-of-school-time mathematics and science lessons on academic performance has thus far proved inconclusive. The relationship between the two requires investigation to elucidate the benefits of these lessons or lack thereof. Using data from the 2009 Program for International Student Assessment (PISA), this study examined the relationship between out-of-school-time mathematics and science lessons and academic performance among 15-year-olds in Hong Kong, China; Korea; Shanghai, China; and Singapore. In light of different cultural contexts, educational standards, and societal norms, and after accounting for gender and family socioeconomic status, which takes into consideration parents' occupational status, years of education, and home possessions, regression analyses revealed inconsistent results across these countries. The study concludes with the implications of the findings and scope for future research, underscoring the need for further investigation that addresses educational disparities in Asia and globally.

Chapter 3
An Assessment of Self-Service Business Intelligence Tools for Students: The Impact of Cognitive Needs and Innovative Cognitive Styles 56
Mohammad K. Daradkeh, University of Dubai, UAE & Yarmouk University, Jordan

While previous research has mainly focused on improving the technical capabilities of self-service business intelligence (SSBI) tools, very little is known about how students evaluate different self-service BI tools, especially if they have different levels of experience. The goal of this chapter is to understand how students' characteristics influence their evaluation of different self-service BI tools. In this chapter, the authors focus specifically on two important student characteristics: need for cognition (NFC) and innovative cognitive style (ICS). These end-user characteristics were incorporated into a research model developed based on the elaboration likelihood model (ELM). To test the model, a laboratory experiment was conducted with undergraduate students for data analysis and reporting tasks, and the resulting data were analyzed using the partial least squares (PLS) approach. The results showed that the effect of NFC and ICS on the evaluation of SSBI tools varied depending on students' experience and familiarity with the tool.

Section 2
Applications

Chapter 4
Univariate and Multivariate Filtering Techniques for Feature Selection and Their Applications in Field of Machine Learning 73
Dharmendra Trikamlal Patel, Smt .Chandaben Mohanbhai Patel Institute of Computer Applications, CHARUSAT, India
Nirali Honest, Smt .Chandaben Mohanbhai Patel Institute of Computer Applications, CHARUSAT, India
Pranav Vyas, Smt .Chandaben Mohanbhai Patel Institute of Computer Applications, CHARUSAT, India
Atul Patel, Smt .Chandaben Mohanbhai Patel Institute of Computer Applications, CHARUSAT, India

Machine learning's feature selection technique aids in the selection of a subset of original features in order to decrease high-dimensional data space. As per the literature, there are two basic strategies for feature selection: supervised and unsupervised. This chapter will focus on supervised filtering approaches only. Filter, intrinsic, and wrapper are the three types of supervised filtering algorithms. Filtering strategies are the subject of this chapter. The chapter covers the most popular univariate filtering algorithms with examples, advantages and downsides, and R implementation. The chapter compares univariate filtering techniques with number of parameters. The chapter also depicts two popular multivariate filtering techniques: minimum redundancy and maximum relevance (mRMR) and correlation-based feature selection (CFS) using appropriate example and implementation with R programming. Finally, the chapter deals with prominent applications of filtering techniques in context to machine learning.

Chapter 5
Scalable Personalization for Student Success: A Framework for Using Machine Learning Methods in Self-Directed Online Courses 94
Thomas Wagner, Western Governors University, USA
Morgan Diederich, Western Governors University, USA

Most online courses are self-directed, "navigate anywhere" in their design. Personalization in those courses involve drawing students' attention to the modules where they need additional study time. Using an example from an online, competency-based institution, the authors explore the steps necessary to use machine-learning-directed personalization in a way that can scale to hundreds of courses. This process is broken down into eight steps: feature selection, clustering, identification of targeted behaviors, identifying the most important modules, determining the student's location in the course, assessing what the student understands at a point in time, understanding where they are in their assessment cycle, and then using all that information to create business rules that can be coded into software to produce recommendations.

Chapter 6
User Sentiment Analysis and Review Rating Prediction for the Blended Learning Platform App.... 113
Md Shamim Hossain, Hajee Mohammad Danesh Science and Technology University, Bangladesh
Md. Kutub Uddin, Hajee Mohammad Danesh Science and Technology University, Bangladesh
Md. Kamal Hossain, Széchenyi István University, Hungary
Mst Farjana Rahman, Hajee Mohammad Danesh Science and Technology University, Bangladesh

Understanding how to assess the learners' evaluation has become an essential topic for both academics and practitioners as blended mobile learning applications have proliferated. This study examines users' sentiment and predicts the review rating of the blended learning platform app using machine learning (ML) techniques. The data for this study came from Google Play Store reviews of the Google Classroom app. The VADER and AFINN sentiment algorithms were used to determine if the filtered summary sentences were positive, neutral, or negative. In addition, five supervised machine learning algorithms were used to differentiate user evaluations of the Google Classroom app into three sentiment categories in the current study. According to the results of this investigation, the majority of reviews for this app were negative. While all five machine learning algorithms are capable of correctly categorizing review text into sentiment ratings, the random logistic regression outperforms in terms of accuracy.

Chapter 7
Analyzing and Predicting Learner Sentiment Toward Specialty Schools Using Machine Learning Techniques 133
Md Shamim Hossain, Hajee Mohammad Danesh Science and Technology University, Bangladesh
Mst Farjana Rahman, Hajee Mohammad Danesh Science and Technology University, Bangladesh
Md. Kutub Uddin, Hajee Mohammad Danesh Science and Technology University, Bangladesh

The objective of the research is to use machine learning techniques to evaluate and predict learners' sentiment toward specialty school. The current study used the Yelp website's reviews to obtain data on specialty schools after filtering. Following cleaning, the filtered summary sentences were rated as positive, neutral, or negative sentiments using the AFINN and VADER sentiment algorithms. In addition, to split learner ratings of specialty schools into three sentiment categories, the current study also used four supervised machine learning techniques. The majority of ratings for specialty schools were favorable, according to the findings of the present study. Furthermore, while all of the techniques (decision tree, K-neighbors classifier, logistic regression, and SVM) can accurately classify review text into sentiment class, and SVM outperforms in terms of high accuracy. Specialty educational institutes will be able to better understand learners' psychological sentiments based on the findings of the study, allowing them to improve and adjust their services.

Section 3
Advancing the Profession

Chapter 8
Working Towards a Data Science Associates Degree Program: Impacts, Challenges, and Future Directions 160
Wendy Chin, Community College of Baltimore County, USA
James Braman, Community College of Baltimore County, USA
Hanks Melissa, Community College of Baltimore County, USA
Paulette Comet, Community College of Baltimore County, USA

As data science continues to grow and become intertwined into many domains, its application becomes increasingly relevant. Data science is becoming a part of an interdisciplinary web of methodologies that can be used to extract essential insights from many types of data and are used in numerous occupations. Due to the rising importance of this emerging field, additional educational opportunities to learn data science will be beneficial in the future. In this chapter, the authors discuss the development of an associate's degree program in data science that provides students with specific coursework required to transfer to other institutions that offer bachelor's degrees in data science. Alternatively, students could also use this program to learn new skills in data science to change career paths or to continue their education. First, the general development of the data science program is discussed, followed by development challenges and opportunities, specific courses, and future directions.

Chapter 9
A Storied Approach to Learning Data Analytics in a Graduate Data Analytics Program.................. 176
Brandon Vaughn, Western Governors University, USA

This study considers the construction and application of a storied approach to teaching graduate level data analytics. Although some research stresses replacing traditional lectures with more active learning methods, the approach of this study is to construct an entire data analytics program around a "story" idea of active learning and projects. The results of this study indicate that such a storied approach to learning not only improves student cognition of course material, but student morale as well. An instructional approach that combines active-learning activities in a progressive, storied approach appears to be a better approach than traditional lecturing alone for teaching graduate-level students.

Chapter 10
Identifying Structure in Program-Level Competencies and Skills: Dimensionality Analysis of Performance Assessment Scores From Multiple Courses in an IT Program..................................... 193
Heather Hayes, Western Governors University, USA
Goran Trajkovski, Western Governors University, USA

Programs in an online competency-based higher education (OCBHE) institute will focus on a set of skills and competencies that form a theme throughout multiple courses, where one course builds upon another in terms of increasing the strength or depth of competency. Thus, for students within a given program or major, it is ideal for scores from course assessments with overlapping content to correlate and indicate higher-order skills or competencies. The purpose of this study was to use factor analysis to test the internal and structural validity of course-level performance assessment scores for a group of courses taken as part of a data analytics program in an OCBHE institution. Moreover, the presence of program-level competencies was investigated using hierarchical factor analysis for two groups: a faster, shorter course track and a slow, longer course track. Results supported validity at the course level as well as the presence of a higher-order factor (program-level competency) for the fast course track but not the slow track.

Section 4
Considerations

Chapter 11
Don't @ Me: A Study of the Perception of Twitter Users of Educational Offerings 220
Goran Trajkovski, Western Governors University, USA
Eduard Fabregat, Universitat Abat Oliba, Spain

With the changes in societies and economies, new formats and packaging of educational products have been emerging as alternatives to the traditional degrees and certificates. Most of these offerings emerge outside higher education institutions and aim to alleviate the gap between the supply of skills and the needs of industries which had a big impact on the educational space. The authors studied approximately four hundred thousand tweets discussing educational offerings. They used a combination of topic modeling and network analysis to group topics into wider themes over the topic network. They also used word embeddings to measure semantic similarity of words related to specific educational packagings and further understand the discussion carried out on Twitter. The results of this study show how public opinion on Twitter discussed formal and non-formal educational offerings in ways that stress economic and professional advancement. Finally, the results from the word embeddings analysis revealed a need for common and clear taxonomy that differentiates between educational formats.

Chapter 12
The Secret Lives of ePortfolios: Text Network Analysis and the Future of Algorithmic Hiring 239
Samuel Collins, Towson University, USA

This chapter looks at student ePortfolios as a potential resource for graduate careers through text network analysis. The chapter begins with a critical examination of the current state of applicant tracking systems (ATS) and the way they utilize ranking algorithms to reduce graduates to a bundle of fungible skills. As a complementary corrective to these systems, the essay suggests text network analysis of ePortfolios, arguing that this would be one way to hire graduates for the future by opening the possibility for latent networked skills and meanings to re-define jobs. Network applications allow for prospective employers to quickly analyze ePortfolio content and see potential connections and innovations. Moreover, a text network analysis would be one way to develop more team-based approaches that would focus less on the individual than on the way that graduates might combine with each other in innovative teams. ePortfolios emerge here as a way of bringing back complexity into what is fast becoming an entirely automated hiring process.

Chapter 13
Do We Need a Digital Data Exorcism? End of Life Considerations of Data Mining Educational Content... 260
James Braman, Community College of Baltimore County, USA
Alfreda Dudley, Towson University, USA

Considering the many interactions we have with technology over our lifetime, many data points, records, files, and other content are recorded in many digital forms. We inevitably construct a narrative of various life events in a digital format that often lasts well beyond the expiration date of our physical form. This construction of a digital narrative is especially true regarding education records and their use for data mining as our files can be used for analysis. In this chapter, the authors discuss the idea of a digital data exorcism as the potential ability to purge educational records if it is the desire of the individual. A data exorcism can be seen as the needed process for removing or expelling data, done so to protect those from which it was derived. Many forms of data will be discussed in this chapter; however, the focus will be on educational records related to end-of-life considerations. The main theme of this chapter is that facet that we have the right to be forgotten. The right to be deleted or, in other words, "exorcised" from the various systems in which our data resides.

Compilation of References 276

About the Contributors 306

Index 313

Preface

Research in the domains of learning analytics and educational data mining has prototyped an approach where methodologies from data science and machine learning are used to gain insights into the learning process by using large amounts of data. Various experiments have been piloted across learning and training institutions with various degrees of success limited largely to the interest of individuals or small groups in affecting academic and business operations supporting learning activities. As many training and academic institutions are maturing in their data-driven decisioning, useful, scalable, and interesting trends may start emerging, and organizations can benefit from sharing information on those efforts. While training and academic institutions may vary in definition, approach, size, and mission, learning about the learner and providing services that are as closely aligned to their behaviors as needs is the essence of their existence.

This book examines novel and emerging applications of data science and sister disciplines in gaining insights from data to inform interventions into the learners' journey and interactions with an academic or training institution. Topics will focus on building models of learners for success, using data to inform courseware and assessmentware development, and planning services supporting the learning process, including capturing, understanding, impacting, and implementing changes in learning, teaching, and assessment. Data are collected at various times and places throughout the learners' lifecycles, and the learners and the institution should benefit from the insights and knowledge gained from those data.

The primary target audience for this volume are leaders at academic and training organizations interested in putting the data they have been collecting into action via insights and prescriptions enabled by the application of various methods from data science, machine learning, business intelligence, Big Data, data mining, statistics, and other related disciplines. Product design and development professionals, including instructional designers, assessment developers, instructional technologists, and psychometricians, will use the topics covered in the publication to develop environments for data-driven decision-making in their respective domains. Data scientists will contribute and benefit from the publication by reviewing the application of methodologies in the domain of learning.

PERSPECTIVES ON DATA

Chapter 1: Mind the Gap – From Typical LMS Traces to Learning to Learn Journeys

Carmel Kent, Abayomi Akanji, Benedict du Boulay, Ibrahim Bashir, Thomas Fikes, Sue Rodríguez De Jesús, Alysha Ramirez Hall, Paul Alvarado, Jennífer Jones, Mutlu Cukurova, Varshita Sher, Canan Blake, Arthur Fisher, Juliet Greenwood, Rosemary Luckin

Many universities aim to improve students' 'learning to learn' (LTL) skills to prepare them for post-academic life. This requires evaluating LTL and integrating it into the university's curriculum and assessment regimes. Data is essential to provide evidence for the evaluation of LTL, meaning that available data sources must be connected to the types of evidence required for evaluation. This chapter describes a case study using an LTL ontology to connect the theoretical aspects of LTL with a university's existing data sources and to inform the design and application of learning analytics. The results produced by the analytics indicate that LTL can be treated as a dimension in its own right. The LTL dimension has a moderate relationship to academic performance. There is also evidence to suggest that LTL develops at an uneven pace across academic terms and that it exhibits different patterns in online as compared to face-to-face delivery methods.

Chapter 2: Relationships Between Out-of-School-Time Lessons and Academic Performance Among Adolescents in Four High-Performing Education Systems

David Litz, Shaljan Areepattamannil, Scott Parkman

Research into the effects of out-of-school-time mathematics and science lessons on academic performance has thus far proved inconclusive. The relationship between the two requires investigation to elucidate the benefits of these lessons or lack thereof. Using data from the 2009 Program for International Student Assessment (PISA), this study examined the relationship between out-of-school-time mathematics and science lessons and academic performance among 15-year-olds in Hong Kong-China, Korea, Shanghai-China, and Singapore. In light of different cultural contexts, educational standards, and societal norms, and after accounting for gender and family socioeconomic status, which takes into consideration parents' occupational status, years of education, and home possessions, regression analyses revealed inconsistent results across these countries. The study concludes with the implications of the findings and scope for future research, underscoring the need for further investigation that addresses educational disparities in Asia and globally.

Chapter 3: An Assessment of Self-Service Business Intelligence Tools for Students – The Impact of Cognitive Needs and Innovative Cognitive Styles

Mohammad Daradkeh

While previous research has mainly focused on improving the technical capabilities of self-service business intelligence (SSBI) tools, very little is known about how students evaluate different self-service BI tools, especially if they have different levels of experience. The goal of this chapter is to understand how students' characteristics influence their evaluation of different self-service BI tools. In this chapter, we focus specifically on two important student characteristics: need for cognition (NFC) and innovative cognitive style (ICS). These end-user characteristics were incorporated into a research model developed based on the Elaboration Likelihood Model (ELM). To test the model, a laboratory experiment was conducted with undergraduate students for data analysis and reporting tasks, and the resulting data were analyzed using the partial least squares (PLS) approach. The results showed that the effect of NFC and ICS on the evaluation of SSBI tools varied depending on students' experience and familiarity with the tool.

APPLICATIONS

Chapter 4: Univariate and Multivariate Filtering Techniques for Feature Selection and Their Applications in the Field of Machine Learning

Dharmendra Patel, Nirali Honest, Pranav Vyas, Atul Patel

Machine Learning's feature selection technique aids in the selection of a subset of original features in order to decrease high-dimensional data space. As per the literature, there are two basic strategies for feature selection are: Supervised and Unsupervised. This chapter will focus on supervised filtering approaches only. Filter, Intrinsic, and Wrapper are the three types of supervised filtering algorithms. Filtering strategies are the subject of this chapter. The chapter covers the most popular univariate filtering algorithms with examples, advantages and downsides, and R implementation. The chapter compares univariate filtering techniques with number of parameters. The chapter also depicts two popular multivariate filtering techniques: Minimum Redundancy and Maximum Relevance (mRMR) and Correlation based feature selection (CFS) using appropriate example and implementation with R programming. Finally, the chapter deals with prominent applications of filtering techniques in context to Machine Learning.

Chapter 5: Scalable Personalization for Student Success – A Framework for Using Machine Learning Methods in Self-Directed Online Courses

Thomas Wagner, Morgan Diederich

Most online courses are self-directed, "navigate anywhere" in their design. Personalization in those courses involve drawing students' attention to the modules where they need additional study time. Using an example from an online, competency-based institution, we explore the steps necessary to use machine-learning-directed personalization in a way that can scale to hundreds of courses. This process is broken down into eight steps: feature selection, clustering, identification of targeted behaviors, identifying the most important modules, determining the student's location in the course, assessing what the student understands at a point in time, understanding where they are in their assessment cycle, and then using all that information to create business rules that can be coded into software to produce recommendations.

Chapter 6: User Sentiment Analysis and Review Rating Prediction for the Blended Learning Platform App

Md Shamim Hossain, Md. Kutub Uddin, Md. Kamal Hossain, Mst Farjana Rahman

Understanding how to assess the learners' evaluation has become an essential topic for both academics and practitioners as blended mobile learning applications have proliferated. This study examines users' sentiment and predicts the review rating of the blended learning platform app using machine learning

(ML) techniques. The data for this study came from Google Play Store reviews of the Google Classroom app. The VADER and AFINN sentiment algorithms were used to determine if the filtered summary sentences were positive, neutral, or negative. In addition, five supervised machine learning algorithms were used to differentiate user evaluations of the Google Classroom app into three sentiment categories in the current study. According to the results of this investigation, the majority of reviews for this app were negative. While all five machine learning algorithms are capable of correctly categorizing review text into sentiment ratings, the random logistic regression outperforms in terms of accuracy.

Chapter 7: Analyzing and Predicting Learners' Sentiment Toward Specialty Schools Using Machine Learning Techniques

Md Shamim Hossain, Mst Farjana Rahman, Md. Kutub Uddin

The objective of the research is to use machine learning techniques to evaluate and predict learners' sentiment toward specialty school. The current study used the Yelp website's reviews to obtain data on specialty schools after filtering. Following cleaning, the filtered summary sentences were rated as positive, neutral, or negative sentiments using the AFINN and VADER sentiment algorithms. In addition, to split learner ratings of specialty schools into three sentiment categories, the current study also used four supervised machine learning techniques. The majority of ratings for specialty schools were favorable, according to the findings of the present study. Furthermore, while all of the techniques (decision tree, K Neighbors Classifier, logistic regression, and SVM) can accurately classify review text into sentiment class, and SVM outperforms in terms of high accuracy. Specialty educational institutes will be able to better understand learners' psychological sentiments based on the findings of the study, allowing them to improve and adjust their services.

ADVANCING THE PROFESSION

Chapter 8: Working Towards a Data Science Associates Degree Program – Impacts, Challenges, and Future Directions

Wendy Chin, James Braman, Melissa Hanks, Paulette Comet

As data science continues to grow and become intertwined into many domains, its application becomes increasingly relevant. Data science is becoming a part of an interdisciplinary web of methodologies that can be used to extract essential insights from many types of data and are used in numerous occupations. Due to the rising importance of this emerging field, additional educational opportunities to learn data science will be beneficial in the future. In this chapter, the authors discuss the development of an associate's degree program in data science that provides students with specific coursework required to transfer to other institutions that offer bachelor's degrees in data science. Alternatively, students could also use this program to learn new skills in data science to change career paths or to continue their education. First, the general development of the data science program is discussed, followed by development challenges and opportunities, specific courses, and future directions.

Chapter 9: A Storied Approach to Learning Data Analytics in Graduate Data Analytics Program

Brandon Vaughn

This study considers the construction and application of a storied approach to teaching graduate-level data analytics. Although some research stresses replacing traditional lectures with more active learning methods, the approach of this study is to construct an entire data analytics program around a "story" idea of active learning and projects. The results of this study indicate that such a storied approach to learning not only improves student cognition of course material, but student morale as well. An instructional approach that combines active-learning activities in a progressive, storied approach appears to be a better approach than traditional lecturing alone for teaching graduate-level students.

Chapter 10: Identifying Structure in Program-Level Competencies and Skills – Dimensionality Analysis of Performance Assessment Scores From Multiple Courses in an IT Program

Heather Hayes, Goran Trajkovski

Programs in an online competency-based higher education (OCBHE) institute will focus on a set of skills and competencies that form a theme throughout multiple courses, where one course builds upon another in terms of increasing the strength or depth of competency. Thus, for students within a given program or major, it is ideal for scores from course assessments with overlapping content to correlate and indicate higher-order skills or competencies. The purpose of this study was to use factor analysis to test the internal and structural validity of course-level performance assessment scores for a group of courses taken as part of a data analytics program in an OCBHE institution. Moreover, the presence of program-level competencies was investigated using hierarchical factor analysis for two groups: a faster, shorter course track and a slow, longer course track. Results supported validity at the course level as well as the presence of a higher-order factor (program-level competency) for the fast course track but not the slow track.

CONSIDERATIONS

Chapter 11: Don't @ Me – A Study of the Perception of Twitter Users of Educational Offerings

Goran Trajkovski, Eduard Fabregat

With the changes in societies and economies, new formats and packaging of educational products have been emerging as alternatives to the traditional degrees and certificates. Most of these offerings emerge outside higher education institutions and aim to alleviate the gap between the supply of skills and the needs of industries which had a big impact on the educational space. We studied approximately four hundred thousand tweets discussing educational offerings. We used a combination of topic modeling and network analysis to group topics into wider themes over the topic network. We also used word embeddings to measure semantic similarity of words related to specific educational packagings and further understand the discussion carried out on Twitter. The results of this study show how public opinion on Twitter discussed formal and non-formal educational offerings in ways that stress economic and professional advancement. Finally, the results from the word embeddings analysis revealed a need for common and clear taxonomy that differentiates between educational formats.

Chapter 12: The Secret Lives of ePortfolios – Text Network Analysis and the Future of Algorithmic Hiring

Samuel Collins

This chapter looks at student ePortfolios as a potential resource for graduate careers through text network analysis. The chapter begins with a critical examination of the current state of Applicant Tracking Systems (ATS) and the way they utilize ranking algorithms to reduce graduates to a bundle of fungible skills. As a complementary corrective to these systems, the essay suggests text network analysis of ePortfolios, arguing that this would be one way to hire graduates for the future by opening the possibility for latent, networked skills and meanings to re-define jobs. Network applications allow for prospective employers to quickly analyze ePortfolio content and see potential connections and innovations. Moreover, a text network analysis would be one way to develop more team-based approaches that would focus less on the individual than on the way that graduates might combine with each other in innovative teams. Eportfolios emerge here as a way of bringing back complexity into what is fast becoming an entirely automated hiring process.

Chapter 13: Do We Need a Digital Data Exorcism? End of Life Considerations of Data Mining Educational Content

James Braman, Alfreda Dudley

Considering the many interactions we have with technology over our lifetime, many data points, records, files, and other content are recorded in many digital forms. We inevitably construct a narrative of various life events in a digital format that often lasts well beyond the expiration date of our physical form. This construction of a digital narrative is especially true regarding education records and their use for data mining as our files can be used for analysis. In this chapter, we discuss the idea of a digital data exorcism as the potential ability to purge educational records if it is the desire of the individual. A data exorcism can be seen as the needed process for removing or expelling data, done so to protect those from which it was derived. Many forms of data will be discussed in this chapter; however, the focus will be on educational records related to end-of-life considerations. The main theme of this chapter is that facet that we have the right to be forgotten. The right to be deleted or, in other words, "exorcised" from the various systems in which our data resides.

IMPACT ON THE FIELD

This book contributes to the field of learning analytics in an educational context by providing state-of-the-art data science methodology for the purpose of evaluating and improving both student-level and program-level aspects of the educational journey. Perspectives on data introduce the importance of evaluating the usefulness of alternative learning strategies both in and outside the classroom as well as matching self-service business tools to the cognitive needs and styles of the students. Data science methods such as machine learning can be applied in novel ways to help guide students toward areas in need of improvement at a large scale as well as predict learner sentiment toward, and thus propensity for, a variety of competing teaching methodologies. Moreover, this book contributes to the understanding of how to best develop educational programs and evaluate program-level skills to meet the needs of both the students and their future employers, thus advancing the profession itself. Finally, this book introduces additional considerations in data analytics and education such as scouring and interpreting data from open source social media to identify trends or patterns of interest in non-traditional, alternative degree programs and certificates, network analysis of ePortfolios for potential employers, and underscore the delicacy and sensitivity of handling and protecting identity data such as demographics as well as the collection of digital data points that provide a narrative for a given student. The coordination of data science with educational theory and goals detailed in this book equip educators and students with the tools they need to succeed not only in education but in the workplace.

Section 1
Perspectives on Data

Chapter 1
Mind the Gap:
From Typical LMS Traces to Learning to Learn Journeys

Carmel Kent
The Open University, UK

Abayomi Akanji
EDUCATE Ventures Research, UK

Benedict du Boulay
EDUCATE Ventures Research, UK

Ibrahim Bashir
EDUCATE Ventures Research, UK

Thomas G. Fikes
Arizona State University, USA

Sue A. Rodríguez De Jesús
https://orcid.org/0000-0002-1710-3167
Arizona State University, USA

Alysha Ramirez Hall
Arizona State University, USA

Paul Alvarado
Arizona State University, USA

Jennifer E. Jones
Arizona State University, USA

Mutlu Cukurova
https://orcid.org/0000-0001-5843-4854
University College London, UK

Varshita Sher
EDUCATE Ventures Research, UK

Canan Blake
University College London, UK

Arthur Fisher
EDUCATE Ventures Research, UK

Juliet Greenwood
Arizona State University, USA

Rosemary Luckin
University College London, UK

ABSTRACT

Many universities aim to improve students' 'learning to learn' (LTL) skills to prepare them for post-academic life. This requires evaluating LTL and integrating it into the university's curriculum and assessment regimes. Data is essential to provide evidence for the evaluation of LTL, meaning that available

DOI: 10.4018/978-1-7998-9644-9.ch001

data sources must be connected to the types of evidence required for evaluation. This chapter describes a case study using an LTL ontology to connect the theoretical aspects of LTL with a university's existing data sources and to inform the design and application of learning analytics. The results produced by the analytics indicate that LTL can be treated as a dimension in its own right. The LTL dimension has a moderate relationship to academic performance. There is also evidence to suggest that LTL develops at an uneven pace across academic terms and that it exhibits different patterns in online as compared to face-to-face delivery methods.

INTRODUCTION

This study was initiated to explore how, and to what degree, students at Arizona State University (ASU) acquire skills in Learning to Learn (LTL).

Helping students learn to learn is a worthwhile aim, but it needs to be actioned through explicit teaching and reflective assessment. If LTL is one of the aims of higher education, it also needs to be assessed at various stages to ensure its growth. Just as the students routinely get transcripts that reflect their performance grades, there needs to be some validation about their increasing effectiveness as learners (Molenaar et al., 2019). However, most learning management systems (LMSs) record students' actions largely as 'users' of the university rather than as learners. For example, LMSs often record students watching a video or submitting an assignment, rather than activities that offer more evidence about LTL, such as reacting to feedback (Suraworachet et al., 2021) and self-reflecting on their learning activity (Lau et al., 2017).

A Working Definition for LTL

The concept of LTL is derived from the definition of learning. Scholars continually debate the definition of learning, but most of them would agree that learning is a process, that it involves change that follows experience (Schunk, 2012), and that, for the most part, it is internal and so invisible (Lefrançois, 2019). These characteristics - all have direct consequences on how learning can be evaluated.

In this chapter, LTL was conceptualized as a process of improvement in self-regulated learning (SRL). Self-regulated learners are *"meta-cognitively, motivationally, and behaviourally active participants in their own learning process"* (Zimmerman,1989, p. 4).

LTL depends on each learner's ability and willingness to reflect on and thus improve their self-regulated learning capability (Education Council, 2006; Hautamäki et al., 2002). To measure this process, it is necessary to adopt a temporal viewpoint of the progress learners make in their ability to understand (and adapt) their own learning strategies, strengths, and motivation as learners (The Campaign for Learning, 2007). In the current study, the researchers operationalized the LTL journeys of university students as a temporal sequence of "snapshots", each of which might contain some evidence about students' SRL (or SRL-related) capabilities. Examples of the types of snapshots, along with the process of suggesting which moments should be captured as snapshots are given in the 'LTL Ontology' section. The temporal order of these snapshots and their individual strengths of evidence about students' SRL capability were used to create an overall view of their LTL journeys.

Learning to Learn in the Literature

Being aware of one's learning processes, one's inclinations and then improving them is a crucial educational objective for many learners in the 21st century. Learners live in a constantly changing environment and must adapt to its changing demands. These uncertainties call for the need to make it easier for learners to transition across disciplines and become independent learners. In fact, LTL is mentioned as one of the eight critical competencies in the recommendations for lifelong learning, which were adopted by the Education Council and the European Parliament in December 2006 and revised in 2018 (Education Council, 2006, 2018).

As LTL is defined in this study as an improvement in students' SRL capabilities, other related constructs such as expectations, motivation, goals, and self-regulatory learning strategies immediately come into play (Eccles & Wigfield, 2002; Robbins et al., 2004). These constructs related to LTL are both malleable and highly context-sensitive (e.g., Carver & Scheier, 1981; Richardson, 2012; Wolters et al., 2003). This raises the question as to how an academic institution can know how well its students are able to self-regulate their learning processes? The indicators are far from being straightforward and directly observable.

SRL is based on students' self-awareness, regulatory skills, and their ability to then transfer those *learning skills* to domains other than those in which they were originally developed (Epstein, 2019; Halpern, 1998). Note that the authors are not referring to the transfer of problem-solving skills or conceptual understanding from one domain to another, for example, from arithmetic to algebra, but to the *transfer of the learning skills themselves* from one context to another. For instance, learning to self-explain effectively in one context to choosing to self-explain in an unrelated context because it is an effective learning strategy is an example of such a transfer (see, for example, Chi et al., 1989). Awareness of one's own learning focuses on knowing what one knows, what one does not know, what are the skills one has gained, and what are one's attitudes and desires with regards to learning. Regulatory skills comprise individuals' ability to organize their actions to achieve their learning goals (Matrić, 2018). They include learning management skills such as planning what to do next, setting goals, monitoring progress, and then reflecting on it all (Zimmerman, 2002).

Research has shown that the observable outcomes related to LTL, such as improved academic performance and retention, are also closely related to constructs such as SRL, engagement, motivation, and self-efficacy (Richardson, 2012). LTL is also related to personality traits, which are widely studied in the learning literature (e.g., conscientiousness, openness, agreeableness, emotional stability, extraversion; Poropat, 2009). Nevertheless, it was hypothesized in this work that, despite these interrelations between these related pedagogic constructs, LTL represents a unique dimension of learning.

The research reported here is concerned with the challenge of how the gap between the desired and the existing data can be bridged when exploring LTL. Specifically, two research questions were explored:

Research Question 1 (RQ1): Is LTL, specifically the SRL sub-construct, a distinct dimension from other, well-researched dimensions, such as academic performance and engagement?

Research Question 2 (RQ2): How does LTL, specifically the SRL sub-construct, change over time, in particular across academic terms?

Table 1. Main datasets used

Data	Granularity	Description
Academic performance, enrolment data and socio-demographic data	One record per student, course, year, and term	See bullet points *o*, *p* and *q* in Figure 2 below. These are the contextual data of the students, containing information such as each student's admission, courses taken, term, academic performance and loans.
Assignment dataset from the LMS	Daily	See bullet point *s* in Figure 2. These are records of assignments that were either submitted or not. The same student could submit several assignments each week, which would result in several records. The data contain the student's anonymized ID, the contextual assignment information, dates associated with the submission, their grade etc.
Clickstream data from the LMS	Weekly	See bullet point *r* in Figure 2. These contain students' digital footprints of their engagement, such as sessions, clicks, and duration.

METHODS

As described above, LTL is considered as an improvement in students' SRL, which is a mental attribute. Researchers have tried to study various observable approximations to it, such as heart-rate variability (Spann et al., 2017), question-asking and engagement in online discussions (Pardo et al., 2016), and the association of learning strategies with teachers' feedback (Matcha et al., 2019). Some researchers have used self-reporting mechanisms, such as interviews or questionnaires (Pintrich et al., 1991). While there are questionnaires which measure LTL-related constructs, they do not capture the external signifiers of LTL ecologically as they take place and are harder to scale to a large number of students. To overcome these shortcomings, some researchers have used clickstream data from LMSs (Cicchinelli et al., 2018; Motz et al., 2019). LMS clickstreams are themselves limited since they are rarely developed to reveal the contextual complexity and multi-dimensionality of constructs such as SRL (Boulton et al., 2018). Other researchers have used other approaches to assess LTL-related constructs. For example, Henderson (2018) employed a phenomenological approach to study the engagement of history students with a simulation. He collected memos and diagrams throughout the students' learning process, following Corbin and Strauss's (2014) memos and diagrams protocol, and complemented it with semi-structured interviews with some of the students. Another example is the use of the Baker Rodrigo Cumpaugh Monitoring Protocol (BROMP), a well-validated protocol for quick and time-synchronized quantitative field observations of students' affect and behaviour (Baker et al., 2018). BROMP has been used to evaluate different teacher practices (Hymavathy et al., 2014), and students' regulatory skills and engagement (Downer et al., 2010; Hymavathy et al., 2014).

Data Sets and Cohort

This section describes the data sources the researchers used in the analysis, as well as the details of the observed cohort of students. This study was conducted using data from two courses at ASU. The raw data included students' demographic information, their enrolment and learning context information such as courses, scholarships and grades, details about the submission of assignments and the digital footprints of their work in the LMS. The observed cohort consisted of students who took one or other of two courses: BIO181 (the most basic course in the Biology programme) and PSY101 (the most basic course in the Psychology programme). The students were enrolled in two different study delivery modalities (online

Table 2. Cohort data

Courses	Description	Number of students
BIO181	Biology's typical first course	2,056
PSY101	Psychology's typical first course	1,895
Terms	**Description**	**Number of students**
Spring of 2019		520
Summer of 2019		298
Fall of 2019		979
Spring of 2020		924
Summer of 2020		454
Fall of 2020		950
Sessions	**Description**	**Number of students**
A	Seven and a half weeks of online learning.	1,872
B	Seven and a half weeks of online learning.	1,653
C	Fifteen weeks of F2F learning (runs in parallel with Sessions A and B).	467

or face-to-face – F2F) during 2019 and 2020. Each of these two academic years consisted of three terms (Fall, Spring, Summer). In each term, students could study in one of the three possible sessions: Session A, which typically spanned the first seven and a half weeks of the term; Session B, typically the last seven and a half weeks of the term; or Session C, which was fifteen weeks long and ran in parallel with A and B. Students learning in the online provision (called ASU Online – ASUO) were enrolled in Sessions A and/or B, while students enrolled on the F2F provision took the longer Session C. In some instances, especially in the F2F sessions, students were still active in the LMS even after the end of their session.

Tables 1 and 2 below show detailed information about the data sources used and the cohort of students observed, respectively. The numbers in Table 2 do not always match up since there were intersections

Figure 1. An ontology as a bridge

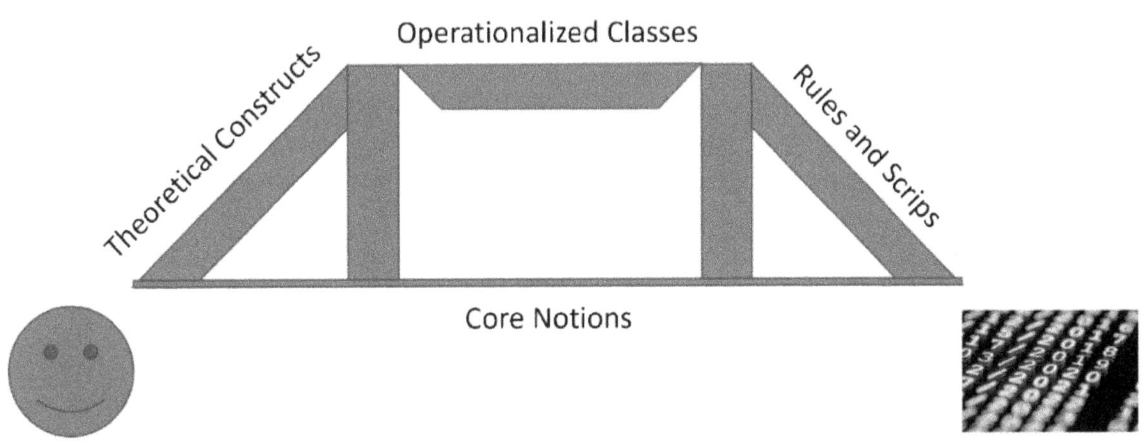

among the elements in the categories. For example, a specific student might be participating in both courses in the same term and session. In that case, the student's instance would be counted twice in the courses (once in each course) but would be counted just once for the term and session.

The LTL Ontology

Most LMSs are designed to provide 'institutional analytics' and are missing a layer of semantics needed to provide any sense of the students' behavioural and emotional points of view. To build this semantic bridge, the authors developed an LTL ontology, which expresses the complexities of the LTL concepts, along with their relationships and properties. As mentioned earlier, there is a gap between the data sources which are typically found in higher educational institutions, and data that would be helpful for analyzing LTL. Here the authors address this gap and how they designed the required bridge.

Connecting Theoretical and Operationalized Constructs

Most LMSs use concepts such as courses, assignments and grades, rather than theoretical concepts such as engagement and SRL. The LTL ontology was designed to distinguish between theoretical constructs and observable bits of behaviour (see Figure 1 below).

At the left-hand end of this bridge are the **theoretical constructs** of LTL, such as SRL, attention, reflection, motivation and so on. Along the ground are the **core notions**, such as a course, a session and programme. The main span of the bridge is made up of what the researchers have called **operationalized classes**. These describe observable "bits of behaviour" that students engage in, such as taking part in a group assignment or undertaking some peer review tasks. At the right-hand end of the bridge is the data.

The ontology expresses the associations between theoretical constructs and their possible operationalizations and represents the fact that a theoretical construct might be operationalized in more than one way. For example, to operationalize student engagement, one might want to collect data about their interactions in class discussions, as well as their engagement with the course materials. The other way round is also possible. Namely, a single observable behaviour might contribute to the operationalization of more than one theoretical construct. For example, a student attending their instructor's office hours might operationalize a behaviour of help-seeking but might also indicate their engagement and motivation in the course.

Connecting Temporal and Static Information

To capture the notion of LTL as a process, the authors built the ontology around the concepts of a *snapshot* and a *sequence of snapshots*. A snapshot is a time-stamped event capturing data about a student's behaviour. The snapshot includes properties such as the snapshot's type (e.g., submitting an assignment) and its granularity (e.g., occurring at a specific instant in time or across a whole week). A sequence of snapshots captures the order and frequency of individual snapshots and thus encapsulates the essence of an LTL journey.

Figure 2. Analytic architecture to bridge between the desired and existing data. The circled bullet point annotations are used in the body of the text to further explain each component. Bullet point k is planned for future research

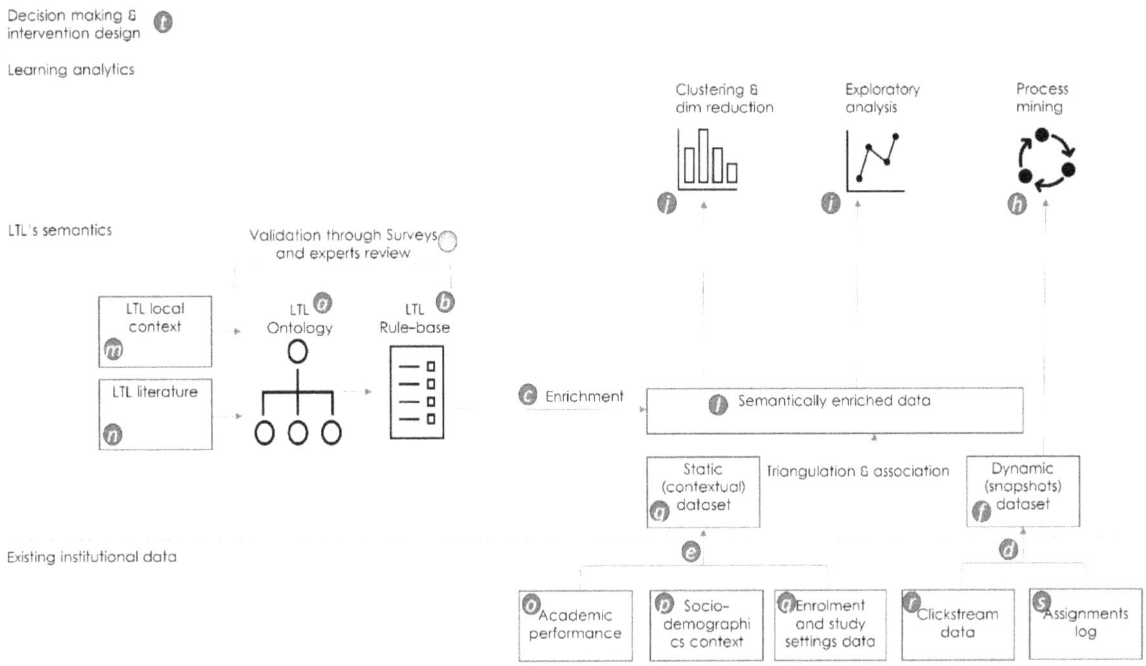

Connecting Existing and Desired Data Points

To bridge between the semantics of the existing data and LTL, the researchers derived a set of features, represented via a coding system that classified those snapshots providing some evidence of LTL together with a score indicating the degree of relevance of its evidence to LTL. The LTL coding system was validated, both by experienced tertiary educators (who are among the authors of this chapter) and by identifying significant correlations with well-established metrics, such as the Grade Point Average (GPA). To do that, an LTL rule-base was designed (seen at the righthand end of the bridge in Figure 1, and some of which is shown in Appendix 1). This set of rules was designed to enrich the existing evidence as collected from the raw dataset (see bullet points *o, p, q, r* and *s* in Figure 2).

Two of the engineered features that were created using the LTL rule-base were an LTL Classification scheme and a measure of the strength of the LTL Evidence. Each LTL Classification feature assigned an LTL-related annotation to the activities described in the snapshots. The classification types were Analysis, Assessment, Engagement, Feedback, Motivation, Practice, Reflection and Review. The LTL evidence strength used a numerical scale from –3 to 3, which indicated the strength and valence of the evidence related to LTL that was associated with different snapshots. Negative values (from –3 to –1) were assigned if the evidence was considered to be associated negatively with LTL, 0 if the evidence was considered to be independent of LTL, or positive (from 1 to 3) if the evidence was considered to be associated positively with LTL.

The above engineered features provided an insight into how different snapshots (such as interactions with the LMS) and outcomes (such as assignment grades) contributed to each student's LTL evidence base. The researchers could now quantify how the LTL evidence strength for different LTL types changed across each term/session. Since these features were computed for each snapshot, the researchers could compare the LTL evidence of an individual student's particular snapshot with the average value of all snapshots for that student. Similarly, they could also juxtapose each student's LTL evidence against the average of all students in the same course during a specific term or session.

The Analytic Architecture

The semantic layer described above (see bullet point *c* in Figure 2 below) was created by the LTL rule-base (see bullet point *b* in Figure 2 below). It was built based on experts' pedagogical knowledge and based on a literature review about LTL, both of which were described by the ontology (see bullet point *a* in figure 2).

The way the LTL ontology was designed informed both a temporal view of the data (to capture behavioural trends, see bullet point *f* in Figure 2) and a static view of the data (to capture the rich contextual characteristics of the students' LTL journeys, see bullet point *g* in Figure 2). To analyse the temporal nature of LTL, while not neglecting the rich context ASU maintained for their students, the researchers opted for a hybrid analytical approach, as described below, involving process mining (bullet point *h* in Figure 2), exploratory analysis (bullet point *i*) and dimension reduction & clustering (bullet point *j*). They also tried validating the whole approach using survey data (bullet point *k*). However, they could not complete this due to a low response rate (see more in the Limitations and future work section).

Process mining

Process mining (Van Der Aalst, 2012) (bullet point *h* in Figure 2) is a commonly used technique for analyzing and monitoring the processes of students' behaviour (Saint, 2021). The researchers used it to model the LTL journeys, which were operationalized by the students' sequences of snapshots. Those sequences exhibit the order and frequency of various LTL related snapshots throughout an academic term. The researchers employed Heuristic Miner (HM), a commonly used process mining algorithm to model the snapshots data (Weijters et al., 2006), which creates heuristic nets, implemented by using the pm4py Python library (Berti et al., 2019). HM's aim is to generalize the process models. It seeks generic rules or patterns that the sequences of snapshots most frequently follow, which makes it more robust with respect to noise and outliers compared to other algorithms.

The HM nets were modelled with nodes representing snapshots, annotated by the combination of their corresponding LTL classification and the strength of LTL evidence. To make the models more interpretable the researchers decided to reduce the number of possible nodes. For that, they merged some of the combinations of LTL classification and evidence strength and reduced the number of possible nodes to 13. The merging was based on the semantics of those classifications, separately merging all the positive and negative evidence levels together. Then, the researchers chose a threshold of 0.05% and filtered out all nodes appearing with a lower frequency than that (See the filtered list in Appendix 2).

The directed edges between the nodes corresponded to temporal relationships between the snapshot nodes. For instance, an edge connecting snapshots *s1* and *s2* corresponds to the observation that snapshot *s1* was followed by snapshot *s2*. The edge connecting the two snapshots could be embellished with extra

Table 3. Principal Component Analysis, rotation converged in 5 iterations. Only loadings above 0.3 are shown. The bolded numbers suggest a simple solution

Behavioural feature	Component 1 - Engagement	Component 2 – Academic performance	Component 3 - LTL
The average number of cursor clicks (transformed by square root)	**0.825**		
The average time (number of minutes) spent on the LMS's section of each course (transformed by square root).	**0.793**		0.316
An average LTL evidence level of the Practice category (as seen in assignments like lab works, simulations, case studies, problem sets and quizzes).	**0.735**		
The average number of sessions a student spent on the LMS (transformed by square root).	**0.707**		0.356
The average submission earliness (how early a student submits a course' assessment, before the due date) (transformed by log10).	**0.661**		
The average percentage of grade points a student earned for their course' assessment.	0.661	**0.409**	0.371
The number of grades a student has gained that are higher than their personal average grade.		**0.897**	
The number of grades a student has gained that are lower than their personal average grade.			
The number of grades a student has gained that are higher than the average of all students' grades (transformed by square root).	0.613	**0.657**	
The number of grades a student has gained that are lower than the average of all students' grades (square root).		**0.721**	
Average LTL evidence level of assessment (as seen in events such as final examinations and assignment).	0.598		**0.463**
Average LTL evidence level of engagement (seen through the number of clicks, sessions, and minutes spent online).			**0.782**
The percentage of assignments not submitted out of all assignments that should have been submitted (transformed by log10).			**-0.684**

information, such as how many instances were found to follow this edge, or the average time taken per instance to go from *s1* to *s2*.

Dimension reduction and clustering

Dimension reduction and clustering were carried out to complement the process mining approach with the context of the data. The researchers carried out a factor analysis to identify whether LTL features formed a unified dimension and whether this was a distinct dimension from other, well-researched dimensions, such as academic performance and engagement.

Using the dimensions identified, they clustered (Trivedi et al., 2015) the semantically enriched aggregated dataset to identify various learner profiles (del Valle & Duffy, 2007). In future work, the authors suggest that these clusters should be validated on a larger cohort of students and that learning interventions are designed to be tailored for each of them.

In the next section, the results of the hybrid approach to learning analytics are detailed to answer both the research questions.

RESULTS

In this section, the authors present the models that resulted from their ontology-informed analysis.

RQ1: Is LTL Indeed a Distinct Dimension?

A principal components analysis (PCA) was run on the 13 variables aggregated from the dynamic dataset (after removing five variables as they were not adequate for a PCA) and 4,208 cases (after removing eight outliers). Each case represented a unique combination of a student, a term, a session within the term, and a course. The 13 variables, along with the transformations that were applied to them to make them adequate for a PCA, are shown in Table 3 below.

To inspect the suitability of the PCA, the correlation matrix showed that all variables had at least one correlation coefficient greater than 0.3. Variables with a correlation above 0.85 were considered as too highly correlated and some were therefore removed. The overall Kaiser-Meyer-Olkin (KMO) (Kaiser, 1974) measure was 0.809, with individual KMO measures all greater than 0.7 (except for the number of low course-standardized grades, transformed by square root, which the researchers decided to leave in since it was semantically important). Bartlett's test of sphericity was statistically significant ($p < .001$), indicating that the data was likely to be factorizable.

The PCA revealed three components that had eigenvalues greater than one and explained 69.15% of the total variance (out of which component 1 explained 46.69%, component 2 explained 13.66% and component 3 explained 8.79% of the total variance). Visual inspection of the scree plot indicated that three components should be retained (Cattell, 1966). In addition, a three-component solution met the interpretability criterion. A Varimax orthogonal rotation was employed to aid interpretability, which exhibited a 'simple structure' (Thurstone, 1947). The interpretation of the data was consistent with the theoretical assumptions about LTL with strong loadings of engagement items on component 1, grades on component 2, and LTL evidence items on component 3. Component loadings and communalities of the rotated solution are presented in Table 3 above.

It is interesting to note that the engagement component included the LTL evidence for practice, which might suggest that practice and engagement were strongly related. It is also interesting to note that the percentage of points earned (a standardized calculated feature) had a loading larger than 0.3 on all three components. For interpretability reasons, the researchers decided to base their analysis on associating it with the academic performance component, although statistically, it bears on all three components. It is shown already that academic performance and engagement are moderately related and yet still signify different dimensions (Kent et al., 2016), and as it will be shown later in this section, academic performance was also moderately related, yet signified a different dimension than LTL. The number of assignments that were not submitted was negatively loading onto the LTL component, which also suggests that LTL goes hand in hand with staying on track with the academic workload.

Once the researchers had gained some understanding of how students' behaviour could be explored, they turned to clustering the students. For that, they added to the three components already revealed (see Figure 3) the five LTL evidence variables, which were excluded from the PCA beforehand to create a

Figure 3. A component plot of the PCA solution. It appears that grades (text without an outline), engagement (text with an outline but no fill) and LTL (text with outline and grey fill) were three distinct dimensions, which strengthens the hypothesis that LTL was a distinct dimension and should be evaluated separately

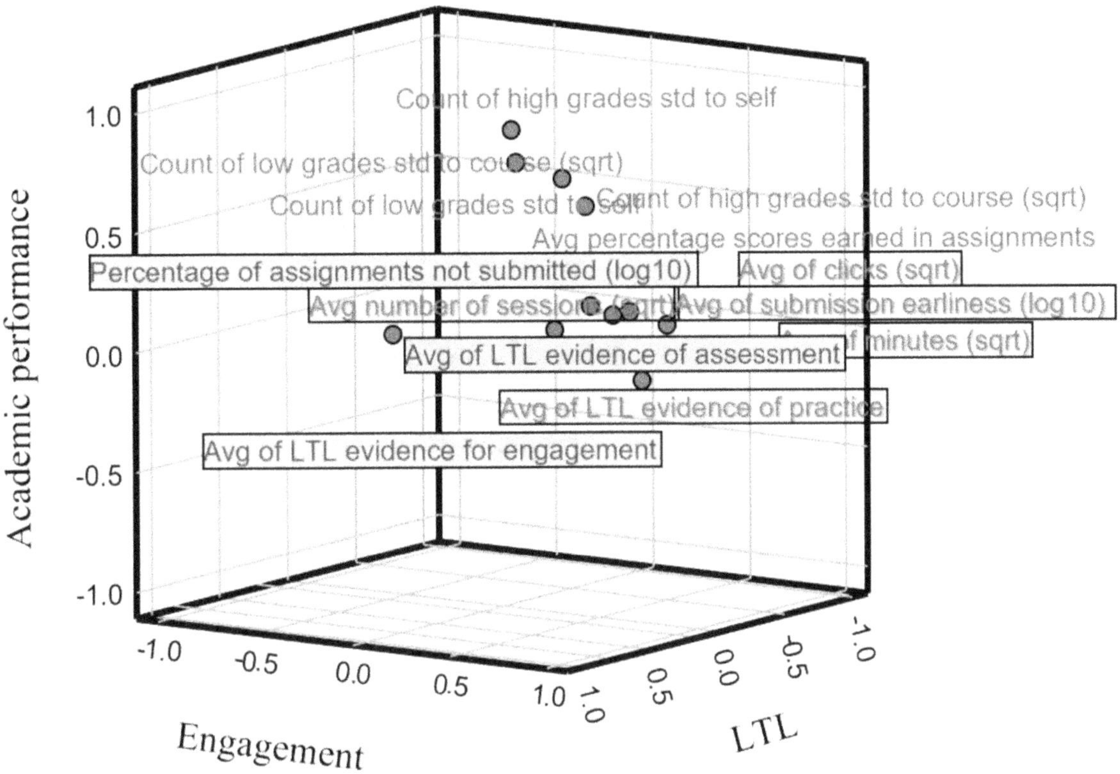

distribution that was appropriate for a PCA. These five variables were namely – the LTL classifications of reflection, motivation, review, unclassified and analysis.

The researchers then carried a K-means cluster analysis (Lloyd, 1982) to explore various clustering solutions, used after various sorting options. They considered standardizing the eight variables but decided against it because they used completely different scales, and the solution on the standardized version was weaker. Finally, the chosen solution converged after 11 iterations.

Three clusters of students were identified: cluster 1 with 267 cases, cluster 2 with 2,818 cases, and cluster 3 with 1123 cases (see Figure 4 below). The proportions were not ideal, with cluster 1 being very small. However, further analysis showed that cluster 1 was more distant from clusters 2 & 3 (3.35 and 3.61 respectively in the 8-dimensional space of the 8 variables) than they were from each other (1.82). This was deemed potentially interesting (taking into account the other variables) and was therefore further explored.

It seems from the analysis below that the three clusters could be characterized roughly as:

- Cluster 1 (in dots in Figure 4), which the researchers termed as **'The Versatile (Adaptable) Achievers'**: is the smallest cluster, which contains students exhibiting relatively high grades and high LTL levels;

Figure 4. Percentage of cases in each cluster. Eight cases were not clustered due to missing values

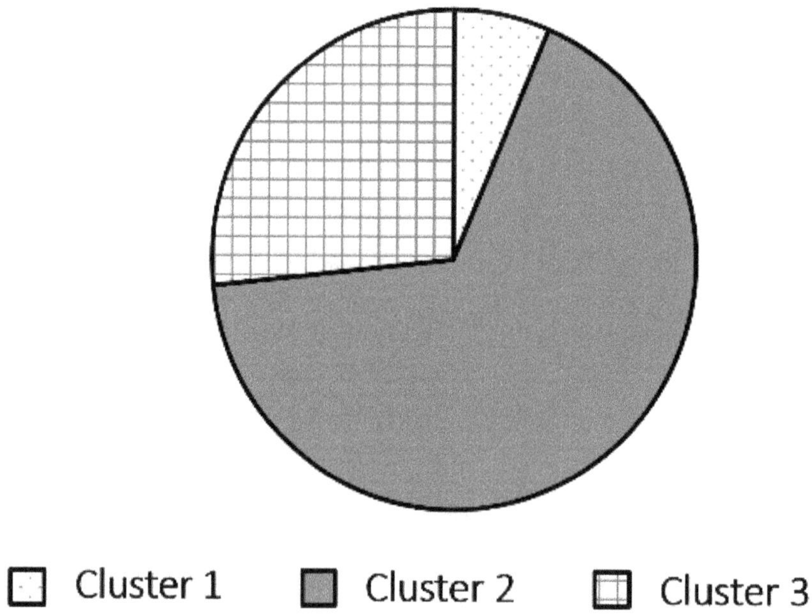

Figure 5. The three clusters using a final centres profiling (i.e., the mean of each variable within the various clusters): cluster 1 in dots, cluster 2 with solid fill and cluster 3 with a grid fill

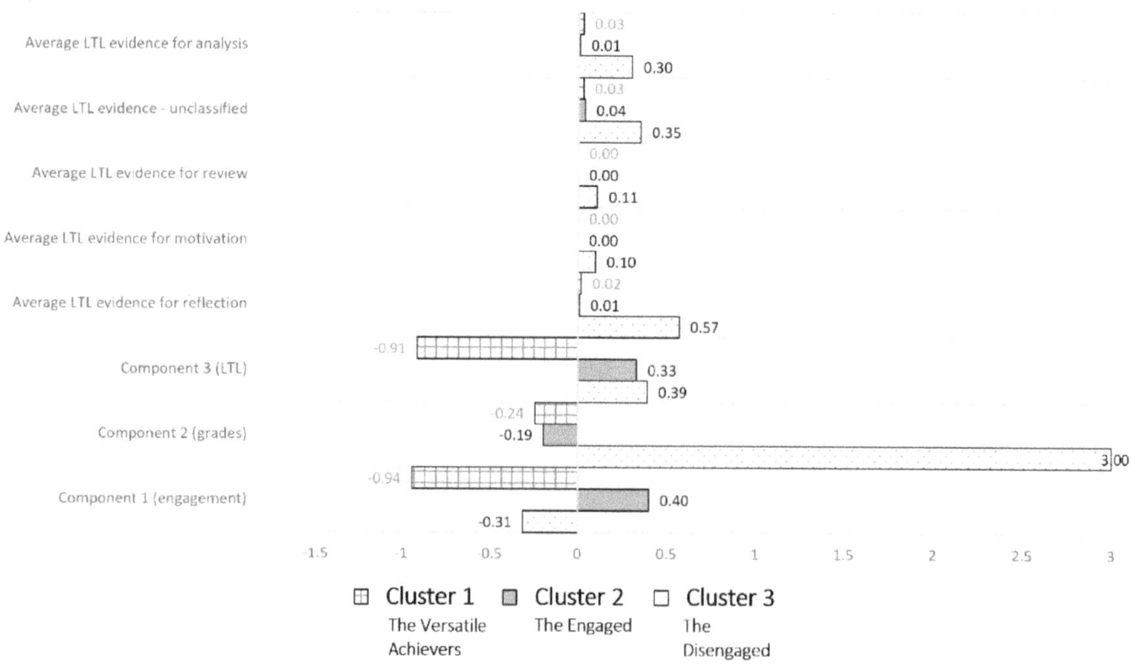

Figure 6. The clusters' Heuristic nets: (a: left top): cluster 1 (the Versatile Achievers); (b: right top): cluster 2 (the Engaged); and (c: bottom): cluster 3 (the Disengaged)

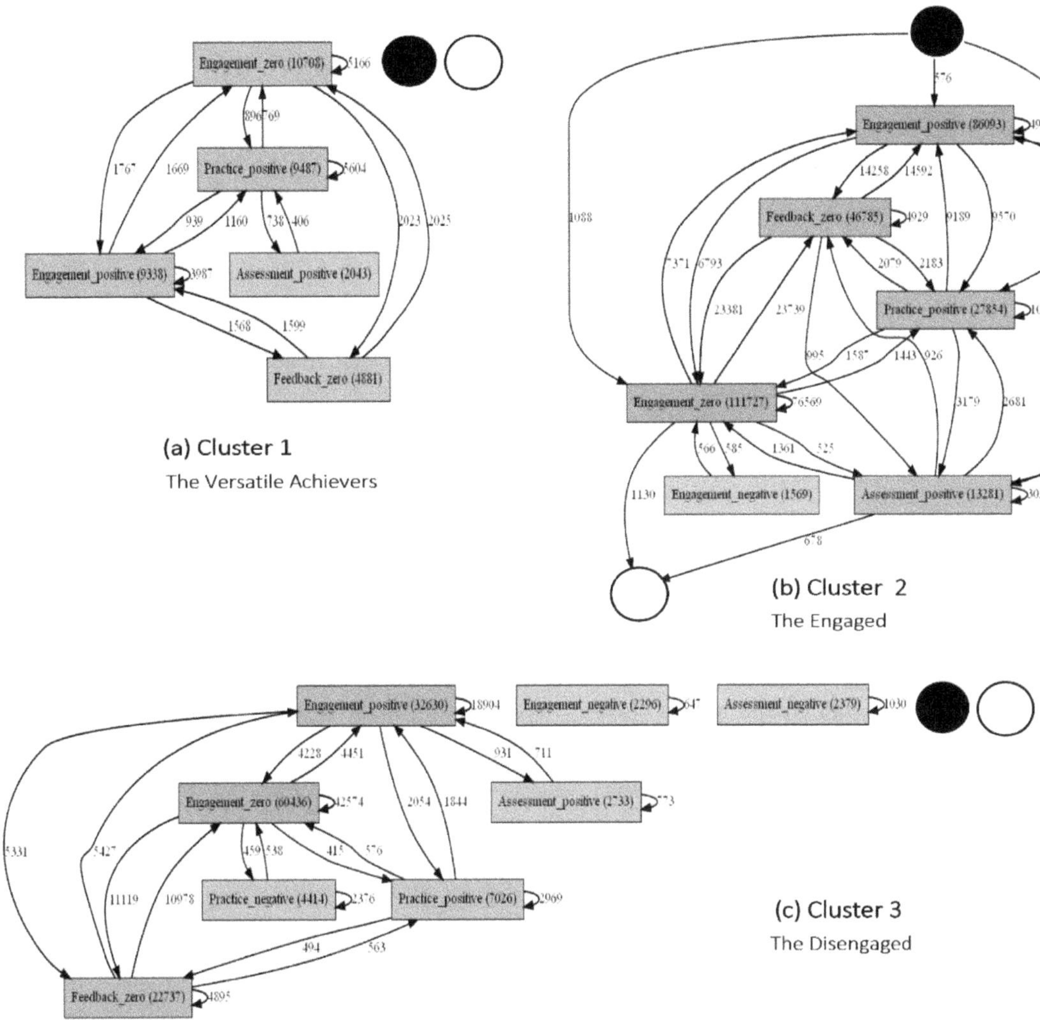

- Cluster 2 (with solid fill in Figure 4), termed '**The Engaged**': was by far the largest cluster, with the most engaged students in it;
- Cluster 3 (with grid fill in Figure 4), termed as '**The Disengaged**': is the cluster that might require the most attention in designing interventions, since the students in it are characterized with relatively low levels of engagement, low grades, and low LTL levels.

As shown in Figure 5 below and in the post hoc analysis shown in Appendix 3: (i) the differences between cluster 1 (the *Versatile Achievers)* and the other two clusters in terms of LTL evidence and grades were statistically significant, (ii) both clusters 1 (the *Versatile Achievers)* & 2 (the *Engaged)* had a statistically significantly higher level of the LTL component as compared to cluster 3 (the *Disengaged),* and (iii) cluster 2 (the *Engaged*) had a statistically significantly higher level of the engagement compo-

Figure 7. (a: left) Relationship of the strength of average LTL evidence (Y axis) against the cumulative GPA (X axis); (b: right) The relationship between the strength of evidence of LTL (Y axis) and the grade awarded (X axis)

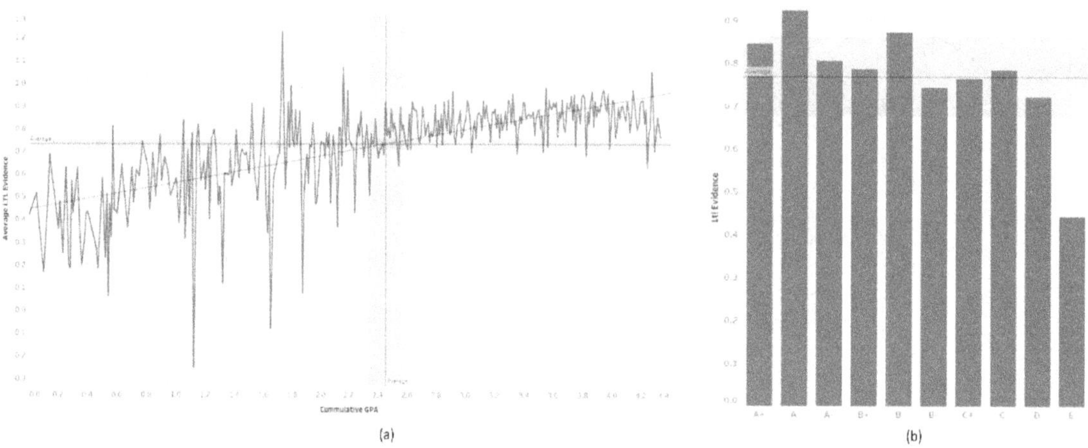

nent over cluster 1 (the *Versatile Achievers)*, which was statistically significantly higher than cluster 3 (the *Disengaged).*

The clusters were chosen to maximize the differences among cases in different clusters. All variables had a significant impact on determining the clusters, as shown in the ANOVA table in Appendix 3.

To further strengthen the observations from the ANOVA analyses, the researchers decided to investigate the process models from the three students' clusters using HM (see Figure 6 below). The black and the white discs indicate the start and the end state nodes of those process models respectively. In two of the HMs they seem disconnected as the edges connecting them to the rest of the model were not manifested frequently enough. As can be seen in Figure 6, the HM of the *Disengaged* cluster showed the highest number of instances of negative engagement snapshots and subsequent negative assessment snapshots when compared to the remaining two clusters. These observations support the hypothesis that poor academic performance is associated with this cluster. Surprisingly, even though the *Versatile Achievers* cluster was characterized as the group with the highest grades, their engagement levels were lower when compared to the *Engaged* cluster and they registered fewer instances of positive practice snapshots following positive engagement snapshots. In other words, even though the *Engaged* cluster students' engagement level with the course curriculum was higher and they were more likely to transform their positive engagement levels into positive practice, their grades were not reflective of their efforts. Recently, Suraworachet et al. (2021) have shown that high SRL students react to their feedback faster than low SRL students. Similarly, these findings are supported to some extent by the three process models, shown below, where the ratio of positive to zero LTL snapshots which directly follow being given feedback was 79%, 61% and 49% for clusters 1, 2 and 3 respectively.

To further understand the relationship between academic performance and LTL, the researchers examined how the average value of students' LTL (across all LTL types) changed in relation to their cumulative GPA (Figure 7(a)) and their cumulative grades (Figure 7(b)).

As can be seen, higher academic performance corresponds to higher average values of LTL evidence. Figure 7(a) shows that when the cumulative GPAs are below average, there is a much higher variance

Figure 8. The average LTL evidence (Y axis) throughout the term weeks (X axis), for online students (ASUO in black, attending shorter sessions A and B) and F2F students (F2F in grey, attending 15 weeks sessions C)

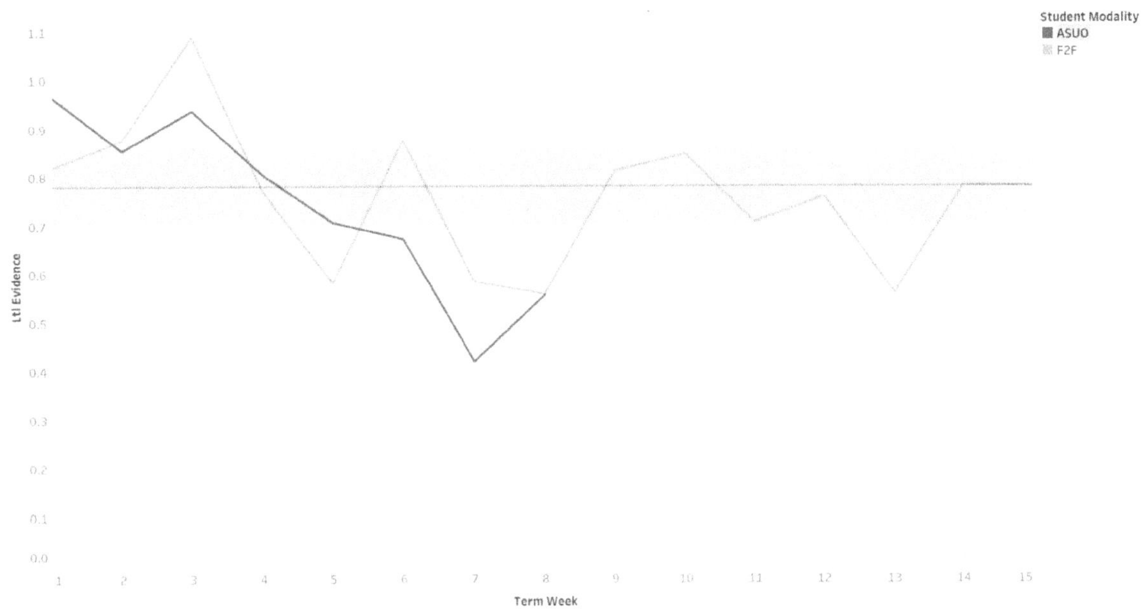

and inconsistency in the average LTL evidence, with most values of LTL evidence levels also lying below the average. However, for above-average cumulative GPAs, a tighter spread of LTL evidence can be seen, with almost all the values consistently lying above the average. A Spearman's rho correlation coefficient was used to assess the relationship between a student's cumulative GPA and the strength of their LTL evidence (as the examined data were not normally distributed). There was a moderate positive relationship between the two, i.e., a student's cumulative GPA and their LTL evidence, r=0.46, p<0.001. Since the LTL evidence was not normally distributed, Mann-Whitney U test was used to show that the average LTL evidence was significantly higher for students with A grades (including A+, A & A-) than those with C grades (including C & C+), U=251755.50, p<0.001.

RQ2: How Does LTL Change throughout the Term?

Next, the researchers explored how LTL levels changed throughout the term (see Figure 8 below).

Both teaching modalities (online and F2F) show a clear pattern of decrease in the LTL evidence across the term. Finer grained interpretations, which are more descriptive and should be taken more cautiously might suggest other similar trends. For example, both the online and F2F samples show higher than median LTL evidence before the middle of the term (week 4 for online, week 7 for F2F) followed by a steep drop at the middle of the term (which might be around the half-term evaluations), followed by a decelerating drop thereafter. Interestingly, the F2F students are showing a partial "bounce back" after the mid-term slump, which does not seem to happen for the online students. However, even when the F2F students do recover their LTL levels, the LTL evidence generally stays below the median. For both teaching modalities, there is another local dip near the end of the session (possibly around the time of

Figure 9. (a: above) the Heuristic Net for BIO181; (b: below): the Heuristic net for PSY101. Within each of the figures, the authors have added a magnified image of weeks 5-10 to show the details of the patterns

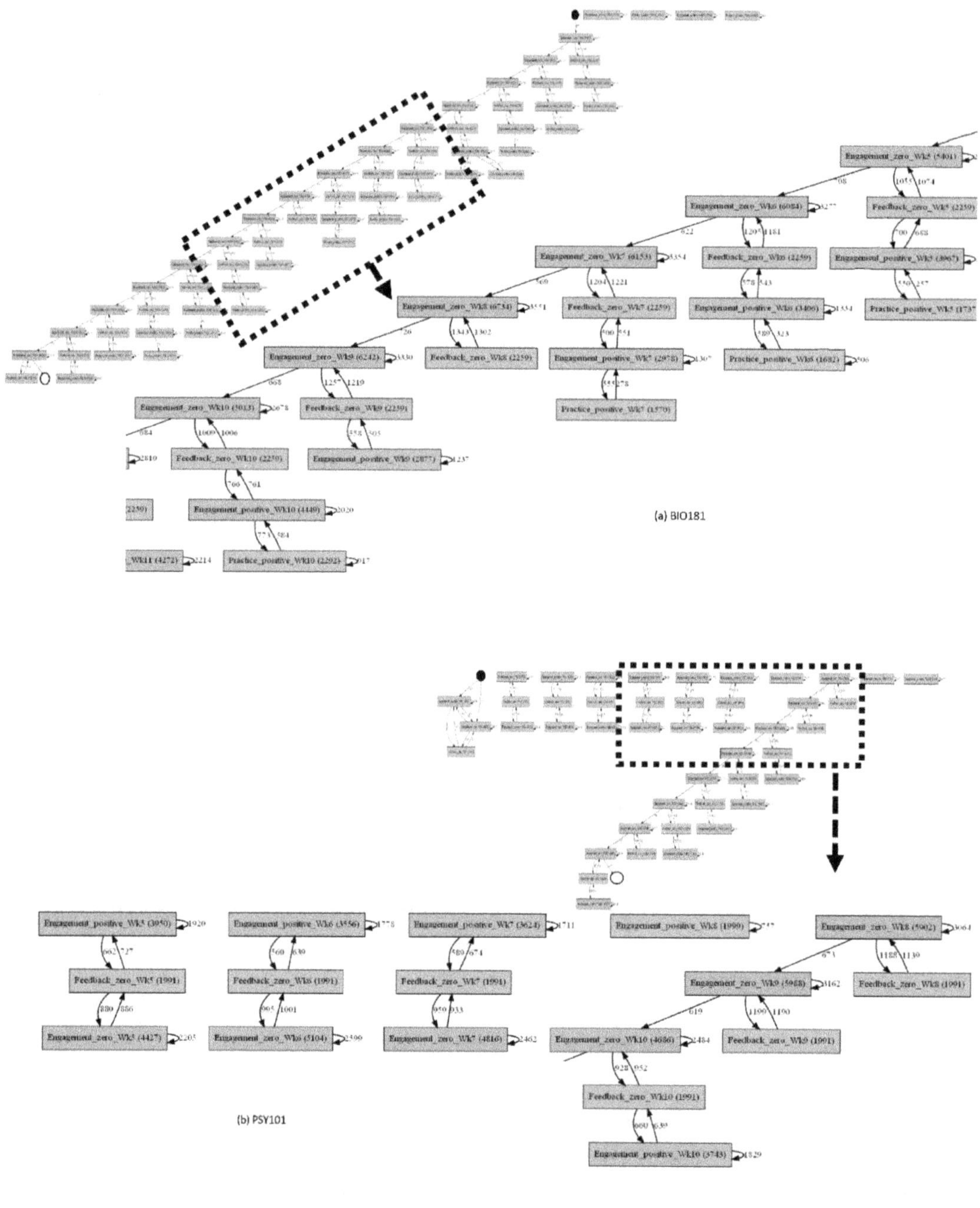

the final evaluations). Note that the assumption underlying this analysis was that the behavioural patterns of sessions A and B were similar and were therefore combined. Future analysis, however, should look into potential differences between them.

To further examine whether the learning design or the content might have an impact on the pattern of change of the LTL evidence levels throughout the term, the researchers compared the heuristic nets from the biology course BIO181 (in Figure 9(a)) with that of the psychology course PSY101 (Figure 9(b)). Given that the two courses differ widely based on factors such as instructional design, overall learning goals, content, criteria, and evaluation methods, they hypothesized there would be a visible difference in the process flows in the two courses. On the contrary, both the heuristic models were shown to be quite similar in their design. This might be due to LTL's factors being relatively resilient or not affected by the learning design. However, it might also be that the process models or the LTL classifications are not sensitive enough to those differences and validating it with other courses could shed some light on it.

Within each week, the researchers observed patterns of learners transitioning from zero engagement to positive engagement through feedback (whereas in the biology course it has also transferred to positive practice). This pattern is presumably signalling an effective LTL process flow. However, the patterns during weeks 8 and 9 were strikingly different from the rest of the weeks, where a lower translation rate to LTL evidence of practice and engagement were found. This is consistent with the findings shown in Figure 8, where there are dips in LTL levels in the middle of both the long and short sessions and another dip towards their end.

Summary of the Results

RQ1: A dimension reduction analysis has shown that academic performance, engagement, and LTL are three distinct dimensions, although the standardized assignment scores (which are a strong proxy for academic performance) also loaded on all three components. Although the LTL component contributed the least to the variation in the data, to answer the first research question the researchers suggest that LTL can be referred to as a dimension on its own with a moderate relationship to academic performance. It was also interesting to note that, similarly to the moderate relationship between engagement and academic outcome in higher education (Kent et al., 2016), the data also provide evidence for a moderate relationship between academic outcome and LTL. This was more evident for students with above-average academic performance, which is consistent with evidence about the relationship between academic performance and engagement (Boulton et al., 2018). It might suggest that for students on the below-average side, academic performance might be also affected by factors other than LTL.

The cluster analysis identified three distinct clusters based on three components (engagement, academic performance, and LTL). The clusters were characterized as the Versatile Achievers (cluster 1), the Engaged (cluster 2) and the Disengaged (cluster 3). From a process mining perspective, the Disengaged cluster registered the highest number of instances of negative engagement and subsequent negative assessment. These observations align with the poor academic performance and engagement levels associated with this cluster, but also might suggest that low engagement precedes low academic performance. Clearly, the researchers do not have evidence of a causal relationship, but future research could look to validate that. Also, the Versatile Achievers cluster was characterized as the group with the highest grades. This is despite the fact that students in the Versatile Achievers cluster showed significantly lower engagement levels compared to the Engaged cluster students, and they registered fewer instances of positive practice levels following positive engagement. Even though the Engaged cluster students' engagement levels were higher and they were more likely to transform their positive engagement into positive practice, the evidence shows that they were not able to transform it into higher academic performance. Their grades were not reflective of their efforts. Interestingly, their LTL evidence was lower than the Versatile Achievers, which might explain this inability to translate engagement into performance.

RQ2: Both the online and F2F modalities exhibited similar LTL levels patterns across the weeks of the term, regardless of the content. They both exhibited a general decline and a further local decline during the middle of the term. However, the F2F students showed a partial recovery pattern after the half-term, which was not exhibited by online students. Given the small number of observations for F2F, the noise in the time series, and the limited number of courses in the sample, it is hard to know whether the recovery is real or whether the 15 week F2F time series is simply decreasing at a lower rate. Even if the recovery pattern were real, it is hard to hypothesize why this difference would be observed. It might be due to the modality or due to the different length of the sessions, as the online courses are half as long as the F2F courses; or it could be due to subject matter or instructional design differences (the longer, F2F course was just in biology). Regardless, it is apparent that LTL levels were generally in a decline throughout the term, both for online and F2F students.

CONCLUSION

In this chapter, the authors have discussed the process of implementing a practical operationalization of a pedagogical construct (such as LTL), which usually remains largely theoretical or is explored in a qualitative manner. For universities to base students' assessment and feedback on those meaningful constructs, a semantic bridge must be used to connect the selected theoretical concepts with the actual data that is typically collected to assess students' progress. The case study reported here was carried out on an initial cohort of more than 4,000 students who took one of two undergraduate courses during 2019-2020. It undertook an end-to-end process that began from the university's decision to focus on the concept of LTL, through the development of an ontology, and on to a modeling and analysis framework dedicated to LTL.

LIMITATIONS AND FUTURE RESEARCH

Data from further courses and departments should be added, for ecological and internal validity and to enrich the framework with the contexts of various instructional designs, assignment types, content domains, reflection mechanisms, and an enlarged cohort of students. To better understand if there are significant differences in students' LTL patterns between online and F2F teaching provisions, data from students participating in equal-length sessions would need to be obtained, which the researchers did not have. Furthermore, enriching the raw data layer with additional data sources to be transformed into both the dynamic and static datasets is crucial to further refine the LTL models. Specifically, enriching the dynamic dataset with further levels of granularity (such as daily and even per millisecond) could give us a more accurate understanding of students' behavioural patterns. Enriching the static (contextualized) dataset with data sources bearing more LTL-related semantics, such as students' reflection journals, could reduce the theory-practice gap even further.

An additional expert review process should be undertaken to review the rule-base, extending the initial review carried out internally by the researchers and via the literature review.

To validate the relevance of the findings about students' SRL progress, the researchers suggest that a set of standardized questionnaires be administered to validate students' SRL levels. Ideally, these could be administered to a sample of the students, at specific points in time during their studies to establish a longitudinal baseline. For example, the researchers suggest basing those questionnaires on the findings of a well-validated meta-analysis of adults' SRL and educational attainment (Sitzman & Ely, 2011) to emphasize the following dimensions: goal setting (Bernard et al., 2009), self-efficacy (Pintrich, 1991), effort and persistence (Elliot et al., 1999). In this work, the researchers did try to conduct this external validation, however not enough responses were obtained to enable the validation to take place, so this remains as a limitation and a future research opportunity (see bullet point *k* in Figure 2).

Reflecting on possible future research on LTL, the researchers suggest looking at questions such as - do students in different programs and/or different delivery methods (such as online vs. F2F) make different amounts of progress in LTL throughout their learning journey? Do they show different kinds of SRL capability by the time of their graduation? Do the identified clusters lead to differences in either the overall progress or kind of LTL? Further, future research should explore the association between LTL and SRL through the diversity, equity, and inclusion lenses, given that there might be significant variations across different groups (e.g., gender, ethnicity). The diversities that exist amongst the student population across universities may have important implications in how LTL and SRL may be conceptualized and studied.

Practically, this study's findings could suggest interventions, all of which should be closely validated. For example, the finding that LTL manifests a separate outcome dimension calls for a new outlook on the implementation of evaluation-feedback cycles. The finding that LTL levels were generally in a decline throughout the term might call for a half-term intervention to refresh and boost students' reflective capabilities.

To close the theoretical-practical gap, educational institutions must address bridging three main gaps between: (1) evaluating LTL *vs.* explicitly fostering it in the curriculum; (2) assessing LTL *vs.* universities' more traditional assessment regimes, and (3) the data that is typically collected about students *vs.* the data that is required to evaluate LTL. This chapter has been very much focused on the third gap (i.e., the data collection gap). However, addressing the data collection gap reveals an opportunity to also address the instructional design gap and the assessment gap. Although many studies have investigated the self-regulation processes of academic learning and the personal and contextual factors involved, it is still a challenge *"to build and test instructional models that support and promote SRL within contexts that are full of new information technologies"* (Nuñez, et al., 2011, p.275). Some classroom-based methods that can be used by instructors, such as paying attention to students' prior knowledge, providing clear feedback, helping students organize concepts and terminology for the particular discipline that they are studying, as well as explicitly getting students to reflect on their learning as distinct from the subject that they are learning, can help learners make sense of their learning. Instructors may need to be reminded that students might have difficulty deploying their metacognitive skills and that this difficulty might manifest itself in different ways and at different stages of learning and level. This is sometimes even more the case when using technology-enhanced learning environments, as these environments sometimes add extra difficulties due to their open nature and students not knowing how to deploy self-regulating processes while learning (Azevedo, 2005).

Finally, the use of ontologies as the basis of any analysis framework also opens the possibility of using semantic technologies to integrate publicly available ontologies and data sources, semantic search and analysis, and semantically enriched decision support systems (Sabou et al., 2005).

ACKNOWLEDGMENT

The authors wish to thank the School of Life Sciences and the School of Social and Behavioral Sciences' Department of Psychology at ASU for their participation in workshops that lead to the ontologies and questions addressed in this paper. The authors also wish to thank the Office of the Provost at ASU and the Office of the Dean at ASU's EdPlus for their support and creative input.

REFERENCES

Baker, R., Ocumpaugh, J., & Andres, A. (2018). BROMP Quantitative Field Observations: A Review. In R. Feldman (Ed.), Learning Science: Theory, Research, and Practice. Academic Press.

Berti, A., van Zelst, S. J., & van der Aalst, W. (2019). *Process mining for python (PM4Py): bridging the gap between process and data science.* arXiv preprint arXiv:1905.06169.

Boulton, C. A., Kent, C., & Williams, H. T. (2018). Virtual learning environment engagement and learning outcomes at a 'bricks-and-mortar' university. *Computers & Education, 126*, 129–142. doi:10.1016/j.compedu.2018.06.031

Carver, C. S., & Scheier, M. F. (1981). A control-systems approach to behavioral self regulation. In L. Wheeler (Ed.), Vol. 2, pp. 107–140). Review of personality and social psychology. Sage.

Cattell, R. B. (1966). The scree test for the number of factors. *Multivariate Behavioral Research, 1*(2), 245–276. doi:10.120715327906mbr0102_10 PMID:26828106

The Campaign for Learning. (2007). *What is learning to learn?* https://www.campaign-for-learning.org.uk/Handlers/Download.ashx?IDMF=07f4cb7b-6f5f-42d2-8831-842c5f189797

Chi, M. T. H., Bassok, M., Lewis, M. W., Reimann, P., & Glaser, R. (1989). Self-explanations: How students study and use examples in learning to solve problems. *Cognitive Science, 13*(2), 145–182. doi:10.120715516709cog1302_1

Cicchinelli, A., Veas, E., Pardo, A., Pammer-Schindler, V., Fessl, A., Barreiros, C., & Lindstädt, S. (2018). Finding traces of self-regulated learning in activity streams. In *Proceedings of the 8th International conference on learning analytics and knowledge (LAK)* (pp. 191-200). 10.1145/3170358.3170381

Corbin, J., & Strauss, A. (2014). *Basics of Qualitative Research.* Sage.

Downer, J. T., Booren, L. M., Lima, O. K., Luckner, A. E., & Pianta, R. C. (2010). The Individualized Classroom Assessment Scoring System (inCLASS): Preliminary reliability and validity of a system for observing preschoolers' competence in classroom interactions. *Early Childhood Research Quarterly, 25*(1), 1–16. doi:10.1016/j.ecresq.2009.08.004 PMID:23175598

del Valle, R., & Duffy, T. M. (2007). Online learning: Learner characteristics and their approaches to managing learning. *Instructional Science, 37*(2), 129–149. doi:10.100711251-007-9039-0

Eccles, J. S., & Wigfield, A. (2002). Motivational beliefs, values, and goals. *Annual Review of Psychology, 53*(1), 109–132. doi:10.1146/annurev.psych.53.100901.135153 PMID:11752481

Education Council. (2006) Recommendation of the European Parliament and the Council of 18 December 2006 on key competencies for lifelong learning. Official Journal of the European Union, 30.

Education Council. (2018). *Council Recommendation on key competences for lifelong learning.* ST/9009/2018/INIT, 1–13

Elliot, A. J., & McGregor, H. A. (2001). A 2 × 2 achievement goal framework. *Journal of Personality and Social Psychology*, *80*(3), 501–519. doi:10.1037/0022-3514.80.3.501 PMID:11300582

Halpern, D. F. (1998). Teaching Critical Thinking for Transfer Across Domains. *The American Psychologist*, *53*(4), 449–455. doi:10.1037/0003-066X.53.4.449 PMID:9572008

Hautamäki, J., Arinen, P., Eronen, S., Hautamäki, A., Kupiainen, S., Lindblom, B., Niemivirta, M., Pakaslahti, L., Rantanen, P., & Scheinin, P. (2002). *Assessing learning-to-learn: a framework*. National Board of Education.

Henderson, S. A. (2018). Pedagogical contraband: A phenomenological approach to understanding student engagement during simulations. *Dissertations and Theses @ UNI*. 936. https://scholarworks.uni.edu/etd/936

Hymavathy, C., Krishnamani, V., & Sumathi, C. P. (2014). Analyzing learner engagement to enhance the teaching-learning experience. In *Proceedings of the International Conference on MOOC, Innovation and Technology in Education (MITE)*. IEEE. 10.1109/MITE.2014.7020243

Kaiser, H. F. (1974). An index of factorial simplicity. *Psychometrika*, *39*(1), 31–36. doi:10.1007/BF02291575

Kent, C., Laslo, E., & Rafaeli, S. (2016). Interactivity in online discussions and learning outcomes. *Computers & Education*, *97*, 116–128. doi:10.1016/j.compedu.2016.03.002

Lau, C., Sinclair, J., Taub, M., Azevedo, R., & Jang, E. E. (2017). Transitioning self-regulated learning profiles in hypermedia-learning environments. In *Proceedings of the 7th International Learning Analytics & Knowledge Conference (LAK)* (pp. 198-202). 10.1145/3027385.3027443

Lloyd, S. (1982). Least squares quantization in PCM. *IEEE Transactions on Information Theory*, *28*(2), 129–137. doi:10.1109/TIT.1982.1056489

Matcha, W., Gašević, D., Uzir, N. A. A., Jovanović, J., & Pardo, A. (2019, March). Analytics of learning strategies: Associations with academic performance and feedback. In *Proceedings of the 9th International Conference on Learning Analytics & Knowledge* (pp. 461-470). 10.1145/3303772.3303787

Motz, B., Quick, J., Schroeder, N., Zook, J., & Gunkel, M. 2019. The validity and utility of activity logs as a measure of student engagement. In *Proceedings of the 9th International Conference on Learning Analytics & Knowledge (LAK)*. Association for Computing Machinery. 10.1145/3303772.3303789

Matrić, M. (2018). Self-regulatory systems: Self-regulation and learning. Journal of Process Management. *Nuclear Technology*, *6*(4), 79–84. doi:10.5937/jouproman6-19338

Molenaar, I., Horvers, A., Dijkstra, R., & Baker, R. (2019). Designing Dashboards to support learners' Self-Regulated Learning. *Proceedings 9th International Conference on Learning Analytics & Knowledge*, 1-12.

Motz, B., Quick, J., Schroeder, N., Zook, J., & Gunkel, M. 2019. The validity and utility of activity logs as a measure of student engagement. In *Proceedings of the 9th International Conference on Learning Analytics & Knowledge (LAK)*. Association for Computing Machinery. 10.1145/3303772.3303789

Pardo, A., Han, F., & Ellis, R. A. (2016, April). Exploring the relation between self-regulation, online activities, and academic performance: A case study. In *Proceedings of the 6th International Conference on Learning Analytics & Knowledge (LAK)* (pp. 422-429). 10.1145/2883851.2883883

Pintrich, P., Smith, D., Garcia, T., & McKeachie, W. (1991). *A manual for the use of the motivated strategies for learning questionnaire (MSLQ)*. National Center for Research to Improve Postsecondary Teaching and Learning.

Poropat, A. E. (2009). A meta-analysis of the five-factor model of personality and academic performance. *Psychological Bulletin, 135*(2), 322–338. doi:10.1037/a0014996 PMID:19254083

Richardson, M., Abraham, C., & Bond, R. (2012). Psychological correlates of university students' academic performance: A systematic review and meta-analysis. *Psychological Bulletin, 138*(2), 353–387. doi:10.1037/a0026838 PMID:22352812

Sabou, M., Wroe, C., Goble, C., & Stuckenschmidt, H. (2005). Learning domain ontologies for semantic web service descriptions. *Journal of Web Semantics*, *3*(4), 340–365. doi:10.1016/j.websem.2005.09.008

Saint, J., Fan, Y., Singh, S., Gasevic, D., & Pardo, A. (2021, April). Using process mining to analyze self-regulated learning: a systematic analysis of four algorithms. In *Proceedings of the 11th International Learning Analytics and Knowledge Conference (LAK)* (pp. 333-343). 10.1145/3448139.3448171

Schunk, D. H. (2012). *Learning Theories–An Educational Perspective* (6th ed.). Pearson Education.

Spann, C. A., Schaeffer, J., & Siemens, G. (2017, March). Expanding the scope of learning analytics data: Preliminary findings on attention and self-regulation using wearable technology. In *Proceedings of the 7th international learning analytics & knowledge conference (LAK)* (pp. 203-207). 10.1145/3027385.3027427

Suraworachet, W., Villa-Torrano, C., Zhou, Q., Asensio-Pérez, J. I., Dimitriadis, Y., & Cukurova, M. (2021). Examining the relationship between reflective writing behaviour and self-regulated learning competence: A time-series analysis. In *European Conference on Technology Enhanced Learning* (pp. 163-177). Springer. 10.1007/978-3-030-86436-1_13

Thurstone, L. L. (1947). *Multiple-factor analysis: A development and expansion of The Vectors of Mind*. Academic Press.

Trivedi, S., Pards, Z. A., & Heffernan, N. T. (2015). The utility of clustering in prediction tasks. *arXiv*, (September), 1–11.

Van Der Aalst, W. (2012). Process mining. *Communications of the ACM*, *55*(8), 76–83. doi:10.1145/2240236.2240257

Wolters, C. A., Pintrich, P. R., & Karabenick, S. A. (2005). Assessing academic self-regulated learning. In *What do children need to flourish?* (pp. 251–270). Springer. doi:10.1007/0-387-23823-9_16

Weijters, A. J. M. M., van Der Aalst, W. M., & De Medeiros, A. A. (2006). Process mining with the heuristics miner-algorithm. *Technische Universiteit Eindhoven. Tech. Rep. WP*, *166*, 1–34.

Zimmerman, B. J. (1989). A social cognitive view of self-regulated academic learning. *Journal of Educational Psychology*, *81*(3), 329–339. doi:10.1037/0022-0663.81.3.329

Zimmerman, B. (2002). Becoming a Self-Regulated Learner: An Overview. *Theory into Practice*, *41*(2), 64–70. doi:10.120715430421tip4102_2

KEY TERMS AND DEFINITIONS

Clickstream: Data are traces of users' operations within digital systems, such as which objects users clicked on and when and the duration through which they engaged with them.

Cluster Analysis: Is a common statistical analysis technique, focused on grouping a set of entities (e.g., students' data) in such a way that entities clustered together are concerned as more similar to each other than to those in other clusters.

Learning Management System (LMS): Is a software application used by educational institutions to plan, implement and assess students' learning process.

Learning to Learn (LTL): Is conceptualized as a process of improvement in the self-regulated learning (SRL) abilities of students.

Ontology: Is a formal, machine-readable representation of a specific body of knowledge. The ontology would typically include the definition of the relevant concepts, categories, properties and the relationships between them.

Process Mining: Is a data science technique used to analyze and identify common process-based patterns, based on event logs.

Self-Regulated Learning (SRL): Refers to students' abilities to use their metacognition, planning, monitoring, and evaluating their own learning process.

APPENDIX 1: EXAMPLES FOR THE LTL RULE BASE

Table 4. a list of the LTL engineered features and examples of the rules applied to compute them

Engineered Features	Descriptions	Examples rules
LTL classification	This feature classifies the snapshots with the type of LTL activity. The possible classification types are: Analysis, Assessment, Engagement, Feedback, Motivation, Practice, Reflection and Review.	A snapshot will be classified as Engagement if it's about students' engagement with their study (using indications such as the number of sessions, clicks, duration etc); Motivation if a student submits a bonus assignment; Reflection if a student engages with a reflective journal; Analysis if a student is involved in research; Assessment if a student submits a final exam; Feedback if the instructor has inputted on a student's assignment; Practice if the student has submitted a lab work and; Review if their assignment is related to the lecture.
LTL evidence	The LTL evidence is on a numerical scale, with values from –3 to 3, which indicates the strength of the evidence related to LTL that is associated with different snapshots. Values from –3 to –1 would be assigned if the evidence is considered to be associated negatively with LTL, 0 if they are not considered indicative of LTL at all, or 1 to 3 if the evidence is considered to be associated positively with LTL.	For example, LTL evidence would be assigned as -2 when the snapshot is about an assignment that was not submitted. In contrast, when a snapshot indicates a submission of an assignment that is classified as a Reflection snapshot, the LTL evidence would be assigned +3, as this is a strong positive indication for LTL.
Course-standardized grade	For an assignment submission snapshot, it compares a student's *grade* to all *students' average grades* (in a course/term/session)	HIGH: if the student's grade is equal to or higher than the average course grade. LOW: if the student's grade is lower than the average course grade.
Self-standardized grade	For an assignment submission snapshot, it compares a student's grade to that student's average grade in all assignments (in a course/term/session)	HIGH: if a student's grade is equal to or higher than the student's average grade. LOW: if a student's grade is lower than the student's average grade.
Course-standardized LTL evidence	For an engagement snapshot, it compares the student's engagement level to all students' average engagement levels (within a course/term/session).	+2: if the student's engagement count is equal to or higher than the course average engagement count. -2: if the student's engagement count is lower than the course average engagement count.
Self-standardized LTL evidence	For an engagement snapshot, it compares the *student's engagement* level to their *average engagement* level (in a course/term/session).	+2: if the student's engagement count is equal to or higher than their average engagement count. -2: if the student's engagement count is lower than their average engagement count.

APPENDIX 2: THE MERGED AND FILTERED LIST OF NODES USED IN THE PROCESS MODELS

All the merged combinations which do not appear below, did not cross the 0.05% frequency threshold.

1. LTL classification Feedback, LTL evidence level zero
2. LTL classification Assessment, LTL evidence level negative

3. LTL classification Assessment, LTL evidence level positive
4. LTL classification Analysis, LTL evidence level positive
5. LTL classification Motivation, LTL evidence level positive
6. LTL classification Practice, LTL evidence level negative
7. LTL classification Practice, LTL evidence level positive
8. LTL classification Reflection, LTL evidence level positive
9. LTL classification Review, LTL evidence level positive
10. LTL classification Unclassified, LTL evidence level positive
11. LTL classification Engagement, LTL evidence level zero
12. LTL classification Engagement, LTL evidence level negative
13. LTL classification Engagement, LTL evidence level positive

APPENDIX 3: FURTHER DETAILS ABOUT THE CLUSTERING ANALYSIS

Table 5. ANOVA table for the clustering solution, all the variables contributed significantly to the solution

	Mean Square	F	Significance
Component 1 (engagement)	735.36	1130.06	0.00
Component 2 (grades)	1288.45	3323.67	0.00
Component 3 (LTL)	634.81	908.75	0.00
reflection Average LTL evidence for	38.23	267.10	0.00
Average LTL evidence for motivation	1.20	175.60	0.00
Average LTL evidence for review	1.36	110.73	0.00
Average LTL evidence - unclassified	12.69	147.41	0.00
Average LTL evidence for analysis	10.10	156.88	0.00

Post-Hoc Comparisons Between the Clusters

A Games-Howell post hoc test was used because the homogeneity of variance was violated. The main significant results are detailed below:

Significant differences in Component 1 (engagement)

- The Engaged cluster had a statistically significant higher level of Comp1 (engagement) than the Versatile Achievers cluster (mean increase of 0.72), 95% CI [0.62, 0.81] ($p<0.001$) and than the Disengaged cluster (mean increase of 1.34), 95% CI [1.27, 1.41], ($p<0.001$).
- The Versatile Achievers cluster had a statistically significant higher level of Comp1 (engagement) than the Disengaged cluster (mean increase of 0.62), 95% CI [0.51, 0.73], ($p<0.001$).

Significant differences in Component 2 (grades)

- The Versatile Achievers cluster had a statistically significant higher level of Comp2 (grades) than the Engaged cluster (mean increase of 3.19), 95% CI [3.04, 3.35], (p<0.001), and than the Disengaged cluster (mean increase of 3.24), 95% CI [3.08, 3.40], (p<0.001).

A significant difference in Component 3 (LTL)

- The Versatile Achievers cluster had a statistically significant higher level of Comp3 (LTL) than the Disengaged cluster (mean increase of 1.29), 95% CI [1.16, 1.43], (p<0.001).
- The Engaged cluster had a statistically significant higher level of Comp3 (LTL) than the Disengaged cluster (mean increase of 1.24), 95% CI [1.15, 1.32], (p<0.001).

Significant differences in LTL evidence for reflection

- The Versatile Achievers cluster had a statistically significant higher level of LTL evidence for reflection than the Engaged cluster (mean increase of 0.56), 95% CI [0.39, 0.72], (p<0.001) and than the Disengaged cluster (mean increase of 0.54), 95% CI [0.37, 0.71], (p<0.001).

Significant differences in LTL evidence for motivation

- The Versatile Achievers cluster had a statistically significant higher level of LTL evidence for motivation than the Engaged cluster (mean increase of 0.098), 95% CI [0.05, 0.14], (p<0.001) and than the Disengaged cluster (mean increase of 0.097), 95% CI [0.05, 0.14], (p<0.001).

Significant differences in LTL evidence for review

- The Versatile Achievers cluster had a statistically significant higher level of LTL evidence for review than the Engaged cluster (mean increase of 0.10), 95% CI [0.05, 0.16], (p<0.001).

Significant differences in LTL evidence for unclassified LTL

- The Versatile Achievers cluster had a statistically significant higher level of evidence for unclassified LTL than the Engaged cluster (mean increase of 0.31), 95% CI [0.23, 0.40], (p<0.001) and than the Disengaged cluster (mean increase of 0.32), 95% CI [0.24, 0.41], (p<0.001).

Significant differences in LTL evidence for LTL classification of analysis

- The Versatile Achievers cluster had a statistically significant higher level of evidence for LTL analysis than the Engaged cluster (mean increase of 0.29), 95% CI [0.20, 0.37], (p<0.001), and than the Disengaged cluster (mean increase of 0.27), 95% CI [0.18, 0.35], (p<0.001).

Chapter 2
Relationships Between Out-of-School-Time Lessons and Academic Performance Among Adolescents in Four High-Performing Education Systems

David R. Litz
https://orcid.org/0000-0001-7893-133X
University of Northern British Columbia, Canada

Shaljan Areepattamannil
Emirates College for Advanced Education, UAE

Scott H. Parkman
New Mexico Highlands University, USA

ABSTRACT

Research into the effects of out-of-school-time mathematics and science lessons on academic performance has thus far proved inconclusive. The relationship between the two requires investigation to elucidate the benefits of these lessons or lack thereof. Using data from the 2009 Program for International Student Assessment (PISA), this study examined the relationship between out-of-school-time mathematics and science lessons and academic performance among 15-year-olds in Hong Kong, China; Korea; Shanghai, China; and Singapore. In light of different cultural contexts, educational standards, and societal norms, and after accounting for gender and family socioeconomic status, which takes into consideration parents' occupational status, years of education, and home possessions, regression analyses revealed inconsistent results across these countries. The study concludes with the implications of the findings and scope for future research, underscoring the need for further investigation that addresses educational disparities in Asia and globally.

DOI: 10.4018/978-1-7998-9644-9.ch002

INTRODUCTION

The Program for International Student Assessment (PISA) focuses on students' preparedness for life (OECD, 2010c). "PISA underlines, in particular, the need for many advanced countries to tackle educational underperformance so that as many members of their future workforces as possible are equipped with at least the baseline competencies that enable them to participate in social and economic development" OECD, p. 3). Shanghai-China and Singapore took part in PISA for the first time in 2009, while Hong Kong and Korea had begun to participate from 2000 (OECD, 2011a).

The exemplary performance of 15-year-olds from all these four countries on the 2009 PISA placed these education systems on the list of strong performers and successful reformers in education (OECD, 2010b). Moreover, Hong Kong, Korea, Shanghai-China, and Singapore have continuously served as nations with some of the highest-performing education systems in the world (OECD, 2010b; OECD, 2018; Jensen, 2012). According to the OECD (2010b), countries are high-performing educationally if almost all of their students are in high school at the appropriate age; average school performance is high; the top quarter of performers are among the best performers in the world (with respect to their mastery of the complex knowledge and skills needed in advanced economies as well their ability to apply that knowledge and those skills to problems with which they are not familiar); student performance is minimally related to socio-economic background; and spending per pupil is comparatively low. Thus, high-performing education systems place importance on high participation, high quality, high equity, and high efficiency (OECD, 2010b).

The average scores of 15-year-olds in Hong Kong, Korea, Shanghai-China, and Singapore on the PISA 2009 reading, mathematics, and science assessments showcase their excellent performance. The average scores of Shanghai-China's adolescents in reading, mathematics, and science were 556, 600, and 575, respectively (OECD, 2010c), and they outscored their counterparts from more than 70 countries/economies in all three assessments (Walker, 2011). Korea ranked second in reading (fourth and fifth in mathematics and science, respectively), Singapore ranked second in mathematics (fourth and fifth in science and reading, respectively), and Hong Kong ranked third in mathematics and science and fourth in reading (OECD, 2010c). To contextualize literacy in science, a considerable percentage of students in these societies can identify the scientific components of many complex life situations, apply scientific concepts and knowledge to these situations, and reflect on the appropriate scientific evidence when responding to life situations (OECD, 2011a).

Given the continued superior performance of 15-year-olds in Hong Kong, Korea, Shanghai-China, and Singapore over the last decade on the PISA reading, mathematics, and science assessments, it is crucial to examine the factors that influence these adolescents' academic performance. Although several such factors may influence the academic performance of adolescents (Winne & Nesbit, 2010), one of the sparsely explored elements influencing the academic performance of adolescents is out-of-school-time lessons; that is, school subject lessons and academic supports held outside of normal school hours (OECD, 2011a). Specifically, there is scarcity of research on the influence of out-of-school-time lessons in mathematics and science on adolescents' mathematical and scientific literacy in the high-performing East Asian education systems of Hong Kong, Korea, Shanghai-China, and Singapore.

Out-of-school-time instruction is both an openly accepted method and rapidly expanding service in most developed and hyper-competitive East-Asian societies as many families increasingly seek out comprehensive tutoring services to suit their children's academic needs and future aspirations. The instruction may occur outside the classroom or school and may be planned for enrichment or remedial purposes, particularly in contexts that are characterized by examination-oriented systems, the commodification of education, and socio-economic disparities of household wealth (Pallegedara & Mottaleb, 2018; Yung, 2020). As the OECD (2011b) posited, secondary school students are often encouraged to take after-school classes and/or tutoring in subjects already taught in school to help them improve their performance in key subjects. Students can take part in after-school lessons in the form of remedial 'catch-up' classes or enrichment courses, with individual tutors or in-group lessons provided by schoolteachers, or other independent courses. These lessons are sometimes financed publicly, but most often they are funded by students and their families (p. 382).

Exploring the relationships between participation in out-of-school-time programmes and student performance in mathematics and science may shed light on the influence of such programmes on adolescents' academic performance and greater well-being in these countries. Hence, the purpose of the present study is to examine the relationship between out-of-school-time lessons in mathematics and science and academic performance in these subjects among adolescents in four high-performing Asian education systems. Specifically, the study addressed the following research question:

- *To what extent do out-of-school-time lessons in mathematics and science predict mathematical and scientific literacy among adolescents in Hong Kong, Korea, Shanghai-China, and Singapore?*

LITERATURE REVIEW

As mentioned previously, out-of-school time instruction is quite common in many Asian countries. Figure 1 provides an overview of the percentages of children enrolled in enrichment and remedial lessons in Singapore, Korea, Hong Kong, Shanghai, as well as the overall OECD average. More specifically, in Singapore, 48% of 15-year-olds attend out-of-school-time enrichment lessons in mathematics, while 34% of 15-year-olds undertake such lessons in science. Further, over 48% and 41% of 15-year-olds in Singapore attend out-of-school-time remedial lessons in mathematics and science, respectively. In Korea, over 36% and 16% of 15-year-olds are enrolled in out-of-school-time enrichment lessons in mathematics and science, respectively; whereas 60% and 44% of 15-year-olds attend out-of-school-time remedial lessons in mathematics and science, respectively. Meanwhile, approximately 30% and 17% of 15-year-olds in Hong Kong attend out-of-school-time enrichment lessons in mathematics and science, respectively, and over 22% and 12% of 15-year-olds attend out-of-school-time remedial lessons in mathematics and science, respectively. In Shanghai-China, more than 27% and 9% of 15-year-olds attend out-of-school-time enrichment lessons in mathematics and science, respectively, while 38% and 7% of 15- year-olds attend out-of-school-time remedial lessons in mathematics and science, respectively. The OECD noted the averages for out-of-school-time lessons in mathematics and science as enrichment lessons in mathematics (17%), enrichment lessons in science (9%), remedial lessons in mathematics (18%), and remedial lessons in science (8%), and stated, "The higher proportion of students attending out-of-school-time classes in mathematics as compared to science is only partly due to the lower proportion of students taking regular science classes. Some 38% of students who take regular classes in science attend out-of-school-time lessons for science and 48% of students who take regular classes in mathematics attend out-of-school-time lessons in mathematics. Students not only attend more mathematics and language of instruction classes in regular hours when compared to science, they are also more likely to attend classes in mathematics and the language of instruction after school" (OECD, 2011a, p. 2)

Figure 1. Out-of-school-time lessons in mathematics and science
Source: Authors, based on OECD PISA 2009 database (http://pisa2009.acer.edu.au/interactive.php)

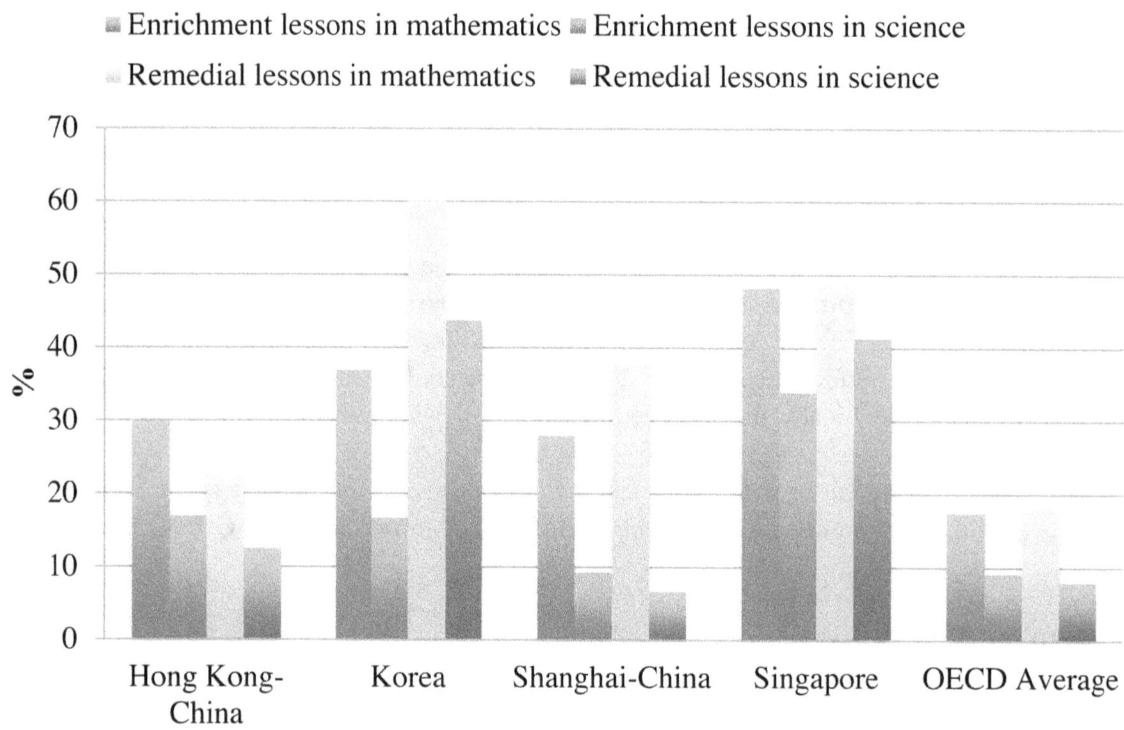

Given the extent of out-of-school-time lessons in mathematics and science across these four high-performing education systems, it is critical to investigate the relationship between out-of- school-time lessons in mathematics and science and adolescent academic performance in these subjects among these four high-performing education systems. A deeper understanding of the relationship between the quantity and quality of out-of-school-time lessons in mathematics and science and academic performance may help us gauge whether or not investing in out-of-school-time instruction in mathematics and science is ultimately beneficial. It might also bolster arguments to enhance opportunities for students living in societies in which educational systems do not customarily or actively endorse these types of supplemental learning programmes.

Out-of-School-Time Lessons and Academic Performance

The findings of current research on the impact of out-of-school-time lessons in mathematics and science on student achievement have been inconsistent; studies have found both a positive and a negative association between participation in out-of-school-time lessons in mathematics/science and student performance in these subject areas. For example, a two-year intervention and random assignment evaluation of adapted models of regular-school-day mathematics instruction in US after-school settings for 1,961 students in grades 2 through 5 revealed that students in the enhanced mathematics programmes experienced more targeted instruction, resulting in significant gains in mathematics (Black et al., 2008). These students were provided with 30% more hours of math instruction over the school year than students in the regular after-school programme group and, as measured by the SAT 10, this intervention helped to increase their average test score by 35.8 scaled score points (Black et al., 2008).

Similarly, a two-year longitudinal study that examined the effects of participation in high-quality after-school programmes among 2,914 US students—1,796 elementary and 1,118 middle school students—found that regular participation in high-quality after-school programmes combining recreational, arts-based, and other enrichment activities with trained professionals was linked to significant improvements in standardised mathematics test scores (Vandell, Reisner, & Pierce, 2007).

This study, which was largely centered around low-income students of color from immigrant families, noted that programmatic initiatives encompassed tutoring and games to support students in their math and reading development, recreational engagements, service opportunities in the community, and more. It was determined that this type of programme also yielded improved work habits, mitigation in behavior problems among underprivileged students, and positive interpersonal relationships among students. These multifaceted academic benefits are significant, demonstrating that high quality programmes can stifle the negative academic outcomes that many disadvantaged children otherwise face because of minimal after school supervision.

Meta-analyses of the effectiveness of out-of-school-time educational interventions have also found the positive effects of out-of-school-time instruction in mathematics on students' performance. For instance, meta-analyses of 35 out-of-school-time educational outcome studies indicated small but statistically significant positive effects of out-of-school-time programmes on low-achieving and at-risk students' performance in mathematics (Lauer et al., 2006). In their meta-analysis of after-school programmes that seek to enhance the personal and social skills of children and adolescents, Durlak, Weissberg, and Pachan (2010) indicated that, compared to controls, participants demonstrated significant increases in their school grades and levels of academic achievement. In some cases, when the programmes included specific tutoring, not just enrichment activities, the positive effects on student achievement were even greater (Lauer et al., 2006).

It should also be considered that not all programmes of out-of-school-time enrichment are the same: they may many vary in quality, and they also differ from culture to culture. Lee (2007) noted the prevalence of after-school mathematics tutoring in Korea and the United States but observed that this tutoring is used for different purposes and, thus, has differing results. In the United States, tutoring is mostly reserved for low-achieving students who need remediation, while in Korea many of the students being tutored in mathematics seek enrichment in hopes of being prepared for success in high-ranking universities. These subtle differences in the prevalence, type, and goals of after-school or out-of-school-time tutoring, even when that tutoring is effective, make correlations with positive achievement harder to generalize.

Studies have also documented the negative effects of out-of-school-time programmes on student performance in mathematics. Firstly, it is not entirely clear that out-of-school-time academic programmes are a net positive for student development, regardless of educational achievement or demographic. Despite the success of the enhanced math programme highlighted in the 2008 study by Black et al., there were no statistically significant impacts on the behavioral measures of student engagement, behavior, or homework completion. These are important considerations, as they broaden the scope through which student performance and achievement are defined, in turn painting a more holistic picture of remedial programmes and their advantages. Cosden et al. (2004) also raise important concerns, highlighting that too much homework or structured academic activity might not be propitious for students. Understanding the importance of maintaining a balance between academic activities and unstructured time, they recommend free play for younger children, or time to explore non-academic interests and enrichment activities for older students.

Indeed, while Dettmers, Trautwein, and Lüdtke's (2009) meta-analysis of data from 231,759 students in 9,791 schools and 40 countries from the 2003 PISA cycle did find a positive association between school-average homework time and mathematics achievement in almost all countries, the size of the association decreased considerably once socio-economic background and school track were controlled. Additionally, at the student level, no clear-cut relationship was established between homework time and achievement across the 40 countries. More recently, the OECD (2011a), drawing on data from the 2006 PISA cycle, examined the relationship between time spent in deliberate learning activities in and out of school and academic performance among 15-year-olds in 57 countries. The study found that students in most of the OECD-member countries who spent more time learning mathematics in out-of-school-time lessons tended to perform poorly in mathematics. Specifically, it was found that students who spent less than 2 hours per week in mathematics performed more poorly than students who did not spend any time learning mathematics in out-of-school-time lessons, while students who spent 2 to less than 4 hours per week in out-of-school-time mathematics lessons tended to perform 31 score points lower in this subject. Furthermore, students who spent 4 to less than 6 hours per week in out-of-school-time lessons in mathematics tended to perform 46 score points lower in mathematics than students who did not spend any time learning mathematics in out-of-school-time lessons, and students who spent 6 or more hours per week in out-of-school-time lessons in mathematics tended to perform 47 score points lower in mathematics.

Discrepancies of this kind may be rooted in a few issues. First, outcomes for those receiving out-of-school-time lessons from a schoolteacher and those from a non-school teacher are not equitable (OECD, 2011a). Group lessons with a non-school teacher seem to be related to high performance, but they might reinforce educational inequity given socio-economically advantaged students are more likely to be involved in this type of out-of-school-time lesson and consequently achieve higher scores (OECD, 2011a). Furthermore, students who spend long hours in individual study are often those who need more time than others, resulting in a use of time that does not necessarily put them at an advantage (OECD, 2011a).

In Korea and Taiwan, however, there was a positive relationship between learning time in out-of-school-time lessons and performance in mathematics, as students who spent time learning mathematics in out-of-school-time lessons tended to achieve higher scores than those who did not. Zehr (2009), on the other hand, found mixed results for after-school programmes featuring specific subjects: while one particular mathematics programme was helpful for students, others were not, underscoring the fact that such enrichment is not consistently helpful for all students when compared to regular, non-academic after-school programmes that do not include additional instruction.

Some studies, however, have not uncovered a significant relationship between participation in out-of-school-time programmes and student performance in mathematics. For example, Lauver (2002) investigated whether an after-school programme administered by an urban, public middle school could induce meaningful improvements in academic and social outcomes for young adolescents aged 10 to 14 years in the United States and did not find any measurable benefits of the after-school programme on academic grades or standardized mathematics test scores. Prenovost (2001) also revealed similar results in a quasi-experimental study conducted among 620 middle school students in the United States.

Although there is a growing body of research examining the effects of out-of-school-time instruction on students' achievement in mathematics, only a small number of studies have focused on the association between out-of-school-time instruction and student performance in science (Schwartz & Noam, 2007). The OECD study (2011a) demonstrated that students in most of the OECD-member countries who spent less than two hours per week in out-of-school-time lessons in science tended to perform 19 score points lower in science than students who did not spend any time learning science in such lessons, while students who spent between two and six hours per week in out-of-school-time lessons in science tended to perform 28 score points lower. However, in the OECD partner economies—Hong Kong and Taiwan, students who spent time learning science in out-of-school-time lessons tended to achieve higher scores than students who did not. Nevertheless, even here the association is not entirely straightforward. Suter (2016) found that in many countries, the longer students attended science-focused after-school programmes, the lower their standardised test scores became (as described above); however, *their interest in science careers and science activities, in fact, increased, despite the reductions in their test-score achievements.*

Specifically, in Hong Kong, Lam and Lau (2014) found that interest in science careers and self-efficacy in science had higher impacts on student achievement in science than many other more traditional predictors, such as parental involvement. These findings offer a broader understanding of the kinds of benefits engendered because of supplemental academic supports, including those of the professional and socio-economic realm. Although these utilities are not seen immediately, students in various countries who receive out-of-school-time instruction can often identify and work towards their professional goals sooner, as well as profit from the eventual financial gains acquired from potential work in the STEM fields.

In short, prior research on the association between participation in out-of-school-time lessons and student performance in mathematics and science has produced a myriad of findings. Divergent results concerning the relationship between participation in out-of-school-time programmes and student performance may be due to variability in research designs, sample characteristics, or programme features (Mahoney, Parente, & Zigler, 2010). However, the majority of studies examining the effects of out-of-school-time programmes on student performance have been conducted in Western countries, and in the United States in particular, because "stakeholders [there] have a growing interest in knowing if these programmes are attracting those most in need of services and if youth are acquiring the intended benefits of programme participation, such as improved school performance" (Harvard Family Research Project, 2003, p. 1).

Instructional Design Model and Theoretical Framework

Instructional design (ID) is at the core of planning lessons and the method of instruction. Out-of-school lessons are also a part of instructional design. Instructional design (ID) is also known as instructional systems design (ISD). It is the practice of systematically designing, developing, and delivering instructional materials, such as lessons, and creating teaching and learning experiences that can be done both digitally and physically, in a consistent manner. Instructional design interventions help in creating efficient, effective, and engaging ways of acquiring knowledge.

Additionally, instructional design models show how the instructional design process can be planned to conduct the process of teaching and help educators to plan the overall teaching process. Gustafson & Branch (2002) have suggested the following characteristics should be present in all effective instructional design models:

- Instructional design is learner-centered as learner performance is the most important factor.
- Instructional design must be guided by well-defined goals.
- Instructional design focuses on improving performance of learners.

- Instructional design focuses on measurable outcomes of instructions through performance.
- Instructional design is based on data and empirical evidence.
- Instructional design is based on team effort of teachers and students.

Likewise, Branch and Kopcha (2014) have stated that "instructional design is intended to be an iterative process of planning outcomes, selecting effective strategies for teaching and learning, choosing relevant technologies, identifying educational media and measuring performance" (p. 77). Moreover, according to Reigeluth (1999), instructional design theories offer guidance on how students can learn better and how to improve the learning process. The learning process could be cognitive, emotional, social, physical, and spiritual. In the case of cognitive learning, the instructional process must involve clear information, thoughtful practice with opportunity given to learners to engage actively, extrinsic and extrinsic motivation of students, as well as informative feedback and/or counselling as part of the learning process.

Instructional Intervention Framework

There are several frameworks that are applicable to instructional design. For instance, out of school lessons or teaching interventions can be explained with data analytics and the instructional intervention model or framework. Instructional interventions are focused on supporting underachieving students and help to measure or monitor their progress. Instructional interventions can use specific educational programs or a set of goals to steps to meet the special needs of these students. These steps or methods of teaching are based on specialized, out of school or other methods of instruction that are meant to support the students who may be struggling in the classroom. Instructional interventions are used to help students who struggle with science, maths or reading (Andreas and Stylianides, 2014). Instruction interventions are based on continuous monitoring, assessing, and updating the instructions to fit the needs of the students. After the scores of the lessons are obtained and progress is monitored, a feedback loop is created with the data that helps to assess whether the instructional interventions are effective (Boudett, City, & Murname, 2013).

Figure 2 illustrates how the diagnostic data from an intervention can aid in monitoring the progress of the student's learning (NCII, n.d.). Using this theoretical framework, an out-of-school lesson programme or instructional intervention can only be effective if there is constant feedback on whether the students are making responsive and significant progress in their learning. Out of school interventions can be leveraged and used globally to support students from different cultures, nations, and educational systems. However, for such interventions to be effective, it is necessary to use a theoretical framework and the relevant data to understand where or in which educational systems, out of school interventions are likely to be most effective, and in which systems such interventions are likely to fail or remain ineffective (Tennyson et al.,1997).

The ADDIE Instructional Model

Another applicable framework is the ADDIE Model. ADDIE stands for the 5 phases contained in the model (Analyze, Design, Develop, Implement, and Evaluate). The first phase of instruction is content development for the instruction, and this requires analysis. Analysis is the act of gathering and sorting information that can be used for the students, and how the learners view the content, considering the

Figure 2. Diagram of instructional intervention framework
Image Credit: National Center on Intensive Intervention

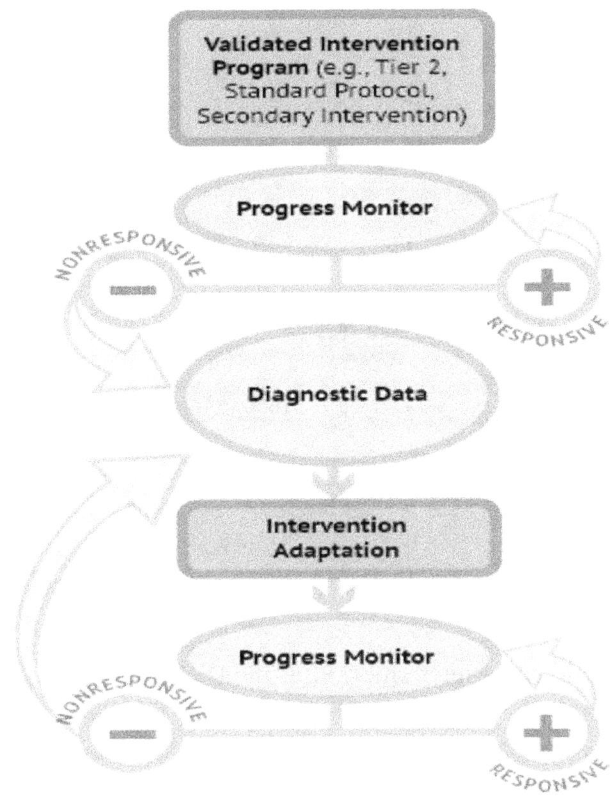

overall goals of the project. The instructional material must then be designed and classified, and the project must be created using theories and models on how the learning process will occur. The design phase specifies a learning objective and tasks are identified and the learning activities are specified. In the third phase of development, the activities that will be implement are created. The fourth phase of the model involves implementation, and all materials are tested to determine whether they are functional. The final phase is the evaluation of the materials acquired and the desired outcomes. There is a also a formative and summative assessment process. Since the model is iterative, it allows the designer to assess and update or revise every stage of the instructional design process. In the final stage of evaluation, the instructor or educator can change, enhance, or revise the design.

The ADDIE model is efficient as it allows a continuous feedback, update, and revise opportunity to enhance the instructions. Revisions to the method of teaching can be done at all phases for improvements. Many current educational models are based on the ADDIE model, as continuous teacher and student feedbacks help to enhance and update the learning process. Figure 3 provides a depiction of the ADDIE Model.

Figure 3. The ADDIE Model
Image Credit: International Society for Educational Technology

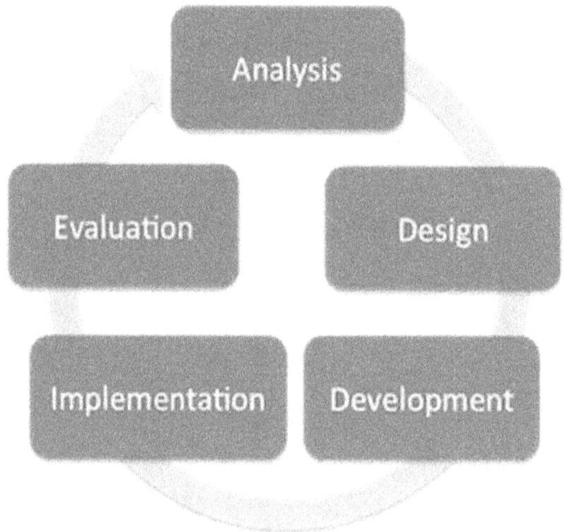

The Systems Approach Framework

Another well-known instructional design framework is the Dick and Carey Systems Approach Model. This model was initially proposed by Walter Dick and Lou Carey in 1978 in their book "The Systematic Design of Instruction". Dick and Carey (2005) provide a systems approach methodology of instruction, focusing on a holistic approach to teaching. The model emphasizes the interrelationships of context, content, instructions, and learning, and suggested that the components like instructors, learners, learning materials, activities, delivery of instructions, and performance tend to interact and provide continuous feedback to result in desired learning outcomes (Dick & Carey, 2005).

According to Dick & Carey (2005), the Systems Approach model indicates the following steps for instructional effectiveness:

1. *Instructional Goal(s):* the teacher or educator must first identify the goals of learning and the skills or knowledge that the learner is expected to acquire at the end of the learning process.
2. *Instructional Analysis*: this step specifies what activities the learner must perform to acquire certain skills.
3. *Learners and Contexts*: the learners' attributes such as prior skills, experience, performance, and characteristics directly related to the skills will be identified and analyzed at this stage.
4. *Performance Objectives*: in this stage, the educator must specify the performance objectives with the description of ideal behavior and the objectives that will be used to judge the learners' performance.
5. *Assessment Instruments*: the learning assessment process must be elaborate, objective with assessment instruments that would test entry behavior, and learning behaviors with practice problems.
6. *Instructional Strategy*: the instructional strategy must include pre-instructional activities, content presentation, learner participation and assessment.
7. *Instructional Materials*: once the strategy is finalized, it would be necessary to select and develop the most appropriate instructional materials.

8. *Formative Evaluation of Instruction*: in this stage designers would evaluate the instructional materials and processes and identify areas that need improvement.
9. *Instruction Revision*: this stage identifies ineffective instructional materials and methods,
10. *Summative Evaluation of Instructions*: in this stage designers would evaluate the learning processes of students and identify areas that need improvement.

Figure 4 provides a graphical representation of the Systems Approach model.

Figure 4. The Systems Approach model
Image Credit: Educational Technology

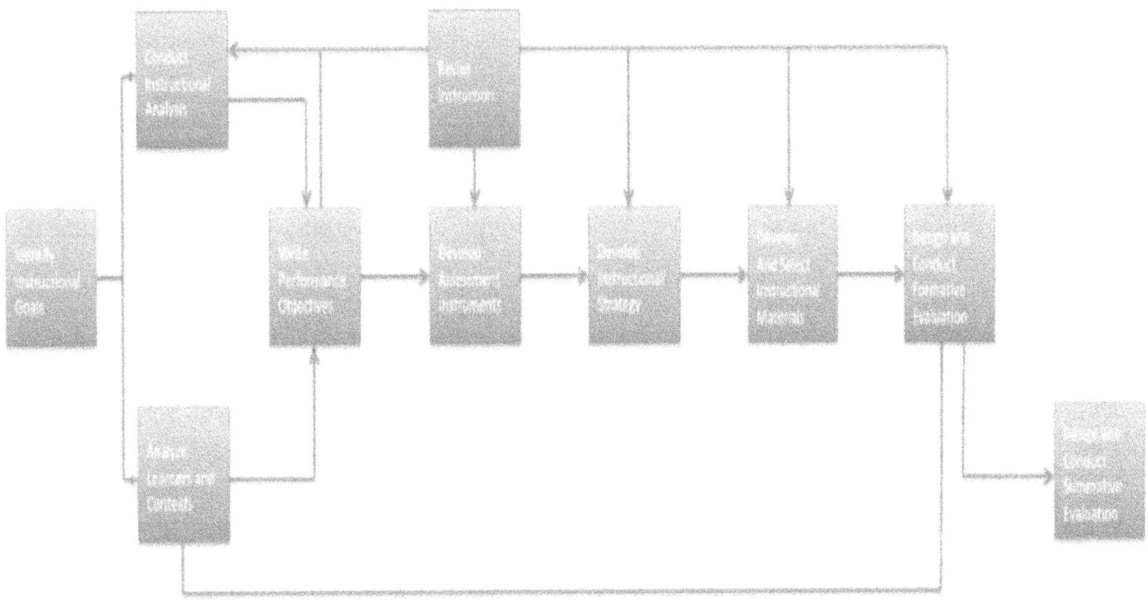

Like the other two models described here, the learning process and evaluation of materials and methods, are all done iteratively, and parallelly, rather than in a linear manner, so that there is continuous change, and improvement of the learning methods and instructional activities.

METHOD

Sample

Data for the study were drawn from the OECD's 2009 PISA results. PISA assesses the knowledge and life skills of 15-year-old students as they approach the end of their compulsory period of schooling (OECD, 2010b). Approximately 475,000 15-year-olds from 65 countries/economies took part in PISA 2009. Of these, 20,224 adolescents were from Hong Kong (*N* = 4837; male = 2557, female = 2280), Korea (*N*

= 4989; male = 2590, female = 2399), Shanghai-China (N = 5115; male = 2528, female = 2587), and Singapore (N = 5283; male = 2626, female = 2657).

Outcome Measures

Mathematical literacy

Although the focus of PISA 2009 was reading literacy, paper-and-pencil tests were also conducted to assess 15-year-olds' mathematical literacy (35 test items; see OCED, 2010b). According to the OECD (2010d), mathematical literacy is an individual's capacity "to formulate, employ, and interpret mathematics in a variety of contexts". It includes mathematical reasoning and the use of mathematical concepts, procedures, facts, and tools to describe, explain, and predict phenomena. It assists individuals to recognise the role that mathematics plays in the world and to make the well-founded judgments and decisions required of constructive, engaged, and reflective citizens (p. 4).

PISA generally reports achievement scores in the form of plausible values, which are multiple estimates of individual student performance that enable group-level estimates. PISA 2009 computed five plausible values for each student's mathematical literacy. The IEA International Database (IDB) Analyzer for PISA (IEA, 2009), a plug-in for SPSS, was used to combine these five plausible values, produce their average values, and correct standardized errors.

Scientific literacy

In addition to paper-and-pencil tests to assess 15-year-olds' mathematical literacy, PISA 2009 also included paper-and-pencil assessments of 15-year-olds' scientific literacy (53 test items; see OCED, 2010c). According to the OECD (2010c), scientific literacy is an individual's scientific knowledge and use of that knowledge to identify questions, acquire new knowledge, explain scientific phenomena, and draw evidence-based conclusions about science-related issues; their understanding of the characteristic features of science as a form of human knowledge and inquiry; their awareness of how science and technology shape our material, intellectual, and cultural environments; and their willingness to engage in science-related issues, and with the ideas of science, as a reflective citizen (p. 137). Again, PISA 2009 computed five plausible values for each student's scientific literacy. The IEA IDB Analyzer for PISA (IEA, 2009) was once more used to combine these five plausible values, to produce their average values, and correct standard errors.

Predictor Variables

The PISA 2009 questionnaire asked students to identify the type of out-of-school-time mathematics and science lessons they attended and to report how many hours they spent attending these out-of-school-time lessons. Such lessons could be held at school, home, or elsewhere, and might be taught by school or non-schoolteachers, tutors, or staff. The types of out-of-school-time lessons in mathematics and science were enrichment lessons in mathematics (1 = yes, 0 = no), enrichment lessons in science (1 = yes, 0 = no), remedial lessons in mathematics (1 = yes, 0 = no), and remedial lessons in science (1 = yes, 0 = no). The amount of learning time spent in out-of-school-time mathematics and science lessons was rated on a 5-point Likert scale ranging from 1 (*I do not attend out-of-school-time lessons*) to 5 (*6 or more*

Table 1. Descriptive statistics for outcome measures and predictor variables

	Hong Kong-China		Korea		Shanghai-China		Singapore	
	M	*SE*	*M*	*SE*	*M*	*SE*	*M*	*SE*
Mathematical literacy	554.53	2.73	546.23	4.02	600.08	2.82	562.02	1.44
Scientific literacy	549.03	2.75	537.99	3.44	574.62	2.30	541.70	1.36
Gender	0.47	0.02	0.47	0.02	0.50	0.01	0.49	0.00
Economic, social, and cultural status	-0.80	0.04	-0.15	0.03	-0.49	0.04	-0.43	0.01
Enrichment lessons in mathematics	0.30	0.01	0.38	0.01	0.28	0.01	0.49	0.01
Enrichment lessons in science	0.17	0.01	0.17	0.01	0.09	0.01	0.34	0.01
Remedial lessons in mathematics	0.22	0.01	0.61	0.02	0.38	0.01	0.49	0.01
Remedial lessons in science	0.13	0.01	0.45	0.02	0.07	0.01	0.42	0.01
Learning time in OST lessons in mathematics	1.88	0.02	2.82	0.04	2.56	0.02	2.51	0.02
Learning time in OST lessons in science	1.56	0.03	2.03	0.05	1.52	0.03	2.16	0.02

Note. OST = out-of-school-time

hours a week). In addition to these predictors, control variables such as gender (0 = male, 1 = female) and socio-economic status (SES) were also included in the study. The PISA 2009 index of economic, social, and cultural status (ESCS), an index of SES derived from parental occupations, parental education, and home possessions (see OECD, 2010b), was used as an SES measure.

RESULTS

The descriptive statistics and correlation between outcome measures and predictor variables are presented in Tables 1 and 2. To address the purpose of the study, regression analyses were conducted and presented in Tables 3 and 4. The dependent variables were mathematical literacy and scientific literacy.

Predicting Mathematical Literacy

In the first step of the regression analysis, the control variables of gender and ESCS were entered into the regression model, producing an adjusted R^2 = 0.07, 0.13, 0.11, and 0.15 in Hong Kong, Korea, Shanghai-China, and Singapore, respectively. In the second step of the regression analysis, the main independent variables—out-of-school-time lessons in mathematics and science and learning time in those lessons—were entered into the regression model, and they explained an additional 5%, 5%, and 2% of variability in the students' mathematical literacy in Hong Kong, Korea, and Shanghai-China, respectively. However, the addition of these variables to the regression equation did not result in a statistically significant increment in explained variance in Singapore.

Statistically speaking, out-of-school-time enrichment lessons in mathematics were significantly positively associated with mathematical literacy in Korea and Shanghai-China, while such lessons in mathematics were significantly negatively associated with mathematical literacy in Hong Kong. How-

Table 2. Correlation between outcome variable and predictor variables

	Hong Kong-China		Korea		Shanghai-China		Singapore	
	ML	SL	ML	SL	ML	SL	ML	SL
Gender	-0.08***	-0.02	-0.06***	-0.02	-0.01	-0.01	-0.07***	-0.04**
Economic, social, and cultural status	0.26***	0.22***	0.34***	0.30***	0.33***	0.33***	0.36***	0.38***
Enrichment lessons in mathematics	-0.02	-0.05***	0.23***	0.18***	0.11***	0.13***	-0.01	0.03*
Enrichment lessons in science	0.14***	0.09***	0.09***	0.08***	0.09***	0.11***	0.07***	0.05***
Remedial lessons in mathematics	-0.11***	-0.10***	0.15***	0.15***	-0.05***	-0.03*	-0.14***	-0.13***
Remedial lessons in science	0.07***	0.04**	0.10***	0.11***	0.01	0.02	-0.05***	-0.06***
Learning time in OST lessons in mathematics	-0.03*	-0.02	0.29***	0.25***	0.04**	0.06***	-0.08***	-0.07***
Learning time in OST lessons in science	0.18***	0.15***	0.13***	0.13***	0.06***	0.07***	-0.02	-0.03*

Note. ML = mathematical literacy. SL = scientific literacy. OST = out-of-school-time.
$^*p < 0.05$. $^{**}p < 0.01$. $^{***}p < 0.001$.

ever, out-of-school-time enrichment lessons in mathematics were not significantly associated in either direction with mathematical literacy in Singapore. Interestingly, out-of-school-time enrichment lessons in science were significantly positively associated with mathematical literacy in Hong Kong and Sin-

Table 3. Regression analyses predicting mathematical literacy

	Hong Kong-China		Korea		Shanghai-China		Singapore	
	B	*SE*	*B*	*SE*	*B*	*SE*	*B*	*SE*
Model 1								
Gender	-13.98	4.75	-5.97	6.25	0.05	3.37	-7.05	2.57
Economic, social, and cultural status	23.52**	2.25	38.72**	3.15	33.38**	2.85	49.30**	1.95
Model 2								
Gender	-11.11*	4.57	-13.81*	5.49	0.50	3.57	-14.10***	2.68
Economic, social, and cultural status	22.95***	2.03	28.93***	3.64	30.43***	2.70	42.09***	2.14
Enrichment lessons in mathematics	-13.34*	4.30	19.24**	4.38	19.11***	3.61	-10.66	4.76
Enrichment lessons in science	13.77*	5.92	-6.17	7.25	11.34	6.96	16.60*	5.00
Remedial lessons in mathematics	-26.02***	4.68	2.68	6.35	-25.66***	4.10	-20.99***	4.01
Remedial lessons in science	4.36	6.78	5.81	6.57	-3.19	8.08	8.36	4.30
Learning time in OST lessons in mathematics	-4.80	2.24	11.90**	2.72	1.43	1.43	-4.40	1.97
Learning time in OST lessons in science	12.93**	2.69	-2.40	4.69	1.98	2.58	-1.35	1.99
R^2 (Model 1)	0.07		0.13		0.11		0.15	
R^2 (Model 2)	0.12		0.18		0.13		0.15	
ΔR^2	0.05		0.05		0.02		0.00	
f^2	0.06		0.06		0.02		0.00	

Note. OST = out-of-school-time
$^*p < 0.05$. $^{**}p < 0.01$. $^{***}p < 0.001$.

gapore, whereas such lessons in science were not significantly associated with mathematical literacy in Korea or Shanghai-China.

Out-of-school-time remedial lessons in mathematics were significantly negatively associated with mathematical literacy in Hong Kong, Shanghai-China, and Singapore, while such remedial mathematics lessons were not significantly associated with mathematical literacy in Korea. In addition, out-of-school-time remedial science lessons were not significantly associated with mathematical literacy in Hong Kong, Korea, Shanghai-China, or Singapore.

Learning time spent in out-of-school-time lessons in mathematics was significantly positively associated with mathematical literacy in Korea. In contrast, learning time spent in out-of-school-time mathematics lessons was not significantly associated with mathematical literacy in Hong Kong, Shanghai-China, or Singapore. Whereas learning time in out-of-school-time lessons in science was significantly positively associated with mathematical literacy in Hong Kong, it was not statistically significantly associated with mathematical literacy in Korea, Shanghai-China, or Singapore.

Predicting Scientific Literacy

In the first step of the regression analysis, the control variables of gender and ESCS were entered into the regression model, producing an adjusted R^2 = 0.05, 0.10, 0.12, and 0.16 in Hong Kong, Korea, Shanghai-China, and Singapore, respectively. In the second step of the regression analysis, the main independent variables—out-of- school-time lessons in mathematics and science and learning time in those lessons—were entered into the regression model, and they explained an additional 14%, 3%, and 1% of variability in the students' scientific literacy in Hong Kong, Korea, and Shanghai- China, respectively. However, the addition of these variables to the regression equation did not result in a statistically significant increment in explained variance in Singapore.

Out-of-school-time enrichment lessons in mathematics were significantly positively associated with scientific literacy in Korea and Shanghai-China, while such enrichment lessons in mathematics were significantly negatively associated with scientific literacy in Hong Kong. However, out-of-school-time enrichment lessons in mathematics were not significantly associated with scientific literacy in Singapore. Out-of-school-time enrichment lessons in science were significantly positively associated with scientific literacy in Shanghai-China alone; such enrichment lessons in science were not significantly associated with scientific literacy in Hong Kong, Korea, or Singapore.

Out-of-school-time remedial mathematics lessons were significantly negatively associated with scientific literacy in Hong Kong, Shanghai-China, and Singapore. They were not, however, significantly associated with scientific literacy in Korea. Out-of-school-time remedial science lessons were also not significantly associated with scientific literacy in Hong Kong, Korea, Shanghai-China, or Singapore.

Learning time spent in out-of-school-time mathematics lessons was significantly positively associated with scientific literacy in Korea, whereas it was significantly negatively associated with scientific literacy in Singapore. In Hong Kong or Shanghai-China, learning time spent in out-of-school-time mathematics lessons was not significantly associated with scientific literacy. Furthermore, learning time spent in out-of-school-time lessons in science was significantly positively associated with scientific literacy in Hong Kong, while it was not significantly associated with scientific literacy in Korea, Shanghai-China, or Singapore.

Table 4. Regression analyses predicting scientific literacy

	Hong Kong-China		Korea		Shanghai-China		Singapore	
	B	*SE*	*B*	*SE*	*B*	*SE*	*B*	*SE*
Model 1								
Gender	-2.76	3.98	0.26	5.31	-0.34	2.47	-0.85	2.39
Economic, social, and cultural status	18.62*	2.28	31.89***	2.78	26.81**	2.20	51.80***	1.66
Model 2								
Gender	-1.02	3.80	-6.65	4.84	-0.42	2.51	-8.54**	2.37
Economic, social, and cultural status	18.13***	2.08	23.48***	3.05	23.57***	2.11	44.92***	2.05
Enrichment lessons in mathematics	-17.36**	4.36	11.57*	3.89	16.56***	2.72	0.88	4.66
Enrichment lessons in science	9.69	5.24	-2.20	6.27	14.35*	5.47	4.43	4.13
Remedial lessons in mathematics	-22.14***	3.79	5.90	5.23	-18.07***	3.19	-15.48**	3.63
Remedial lessons in science	0.50	6.01	4.38	5.85	-1.21	5.66	3.71	4.67
Learning time in OST lessons in mathematics	-1.64	2.10	8.64**	2.53	2.18	1.12	-5.16*	1.85
Learning time in OST lessons in science	10.04**	2.37	-1.05	4.03	1.22	1.80	-0.69	1.89
R^2 (Model 1)	0.05		0.10		0.12		0.16	
R^2 (Model 2)	0.09		0.13		0.13		0.16	
ΔR^2	0.04		0.03		0.01		0.00	
f^2	0.04		0.03		0.01		0.00	

Note. OST = out-of-school-time.
*$p < 0.05$, **$p < 0.01$, ***$p < 0.001$.

DISCUSSION

The present study examined the influences of out-of-school-time lessons in mathematics and science, as well as on mathematical and scientific literacy among adolescents in four high-performing education systems: Hong Kong, Korea, Shanghai-China, and Singapore. In accordance with previous research on the effects of out-of-school-time programmes on student performance (e.g., OECD, 2011a), the current study yielded mixed results.

Firstly, as PISA's focal point of reference is the student's role within society (i.e., successful education should achieve the goal of helping students engage with their social surroundings and learn about and actively contribute to life in both their local and global community) (OECD, 2009), some of the results may be, as expected, influenced by students' immediate psychological needs in their process of learning within their wider socio-cultural and educational context (Yung, 2020). As such, it is important not to overlook the notion of students' varying levels of self-concept. As noted by Lam and Lau (2014), while self-efficacy shows students' perception of their abilities in specific subject-matter topics, self-concept takes into consideration students' perceptions more broadly; that is, their beliefs about their abilities in a subject in its entirety. In this instance, adolescents in Korea and Shanghai-China who attended out-of-school-time enrichment lessons in mathematics tended to perform significantly better in mathematics than their peers who did not attend such lessons. Out-of-school-time enrichment programmes are often offered to students who seek further enrichment; thus, adolescents in Korea and Shanghai-China who attended out-of-school-time lessons in mathematics for enrichment purposes might be more interested in mathematics and have a greater sense of self-concept in the subject than peers who did not attend these lessons. After all, a substantial body of research has demonstrated the positive relationship between an interest in mathematics and mathematical achievement among school children (e.g., Heinze, Reiss, & Franziska, 2005; Koller, Baumert, & Schnabel, 2001).

In contrast, adolescents in Hong Kong who attended out-of-school-time enrichment lessons in mathematics tended to perform significantly worse in mathematics than their peers who did not; therefore, out-of-school-time enrichment lessons in mathematics offered in Hong Kong may not be conducive to enhancing mathematical literacy among adolescents there who seek further enrichment in mathematics. In Singapore, however, no significant relationship was found between out-of-school-time enrichment lessons in mathematics and mathematical literacy among adolescents. Nonetheless, no data in this study considered the type and quality of tutoring programmes that students might participate in outside of school and outside of the formal out-of-school-time programmes discussed here. As noted by Vandell et al. (2004) positive developmental settings encompass appropriate structure, physical and psychological safety, supportive relationships, opportunities for belonging, positive social norms, support for the development of self-concept/efficacy, skill building opportunities, and the integration of family, school, and community.

Research (e.g., OECD, 2011a) also shows that variations in educational outcomes within the context of industrialised nations are more likely explained by the quality of human resources (i.e., teachers and school leadership) than by material and financial resources. Because information and analyses were lacking regarding the exact nature of these initiatives, specific student needs and demographics, and instructor qualifications were largely absent, it is difficult to make definitive conclusions. However, taking into consideration the extent to which programmes and people align with the aforementioned aspects in Hong Kong and in Singapore, these factors might well make a difference in achievement, and the same, of course, is true in the other areas of the world discussed in this study (e.g., Lauer et al., 2006).

Interestingly, however, adolescents who attended out-of-school-time remedial lessons in mathematics in Hong Kong, Shanghai-China, and Singapore tended to perform significantly worse in mathematics than their peers who did not engage in such remedial mathematics lessons. This finding is unsurprising since out-of-school-time remedial lessons in mathematics are often organized to help at-risk and underperforming students successfully complete their classes alongside their peers. Therefore, the student population is, generally speaking, lower-achieving, or they would not be attending programmes of this type in the first place. Based on these findings, these populations may need to be considered separately in further analyses: despite living and receiving education in the same location, it is likely that they do not have a high enough level of homogeneity, to yield defensible data leading to real-world evidence.

The findings pinpoint the ineffectiveness of out-of-school-time remedial mathematics lessons to enhance at-risk and underperforming adolescents' mathematical literacy in Hong Kong, Shanghai-China, and Singapore. At the same time, no significant relationship was also found between out-of-school-time remedial lessons in mathematics and mathematical literacy among adolescents in Korea. This might be due to curricular differences between the countries, attitudes toward remedial lessons, the use of tutoring (as discussed in the literature review on Korea in particular), or several other factors, all of which might provide directions for future research. It is, however, worth noting that overcoming socio-economic barriers in academic settings is indeed possible for disadvantaged students (OECD, 2011b). A disadvantaged student is marked resilient if their residual performance as shown in PISA is found to be among the top quarter of students' residual performance from all countries. In fact, 72% of disadvantaged students in Hong Kong and 76% of students in Shanghai-China were deemed resilient.

Consistent with previous research (e.g., OECD, 2011a), learning time in out-of-school- time lessons in mathematics were significantly positively related to adolescents' mathematical literacy in Korea, suggesting that adolescents who spent more time in out-of-school-time mathematics lessons tended to perform significantly better in mathematics than their peers who spent less out-of-school time learning mathematics. However, learning time in out-of-school-time mathematics lessons was not significantly related to mathematical literacy among adolescents in Hong Kong, Shanghai-China, and Singapore. Discrepancies between these countries suggest that it is worth looking further at the use of time in out-of-school learning as it pertains to mathematics. According to a U.S. based study (Black et al., 2008), access to an enhanced academic after-school math programme improved the mathematical performance of the students in attendance. While 15% of students in the regular after-school programme group were offered academic instruction in the subject, the enhanced programme offered academic instruction to all students. This differed from the students in the regular programme who primarily received homework help and/or tutoring. Furthermore, 97% of staff members providing instruction to the enhanced group students were certified educators, compared with 62% of those instructing the regular after-school programme. Enhanced programme staff also received considerably more training, suggesting the relevance of the presence of skilled and more knowledgeable adults in the learning process. In summation, students in the enhanced programme group received roughly 30% more robust academic instruction in math over the course of the school year. Even though educational standards and goals are not always aligned in different regions of the world, assessing the types of educational support that students are receiving is of great significance. Because out-of-school-time mathematics lessons were not significantly related to mathematical literacy among adolescents in Hong Kong, Shanghai-China, and Singapore, it could be suggested that the quality of instruction needs re-examining in these countries. After all, the way in which instruction time is spent and who it is led by does seem to matter in some contexts.

Regarding learning time, it is important to note that, according to research findings (OECD, 2011a), students are likely to perform better if much of their total learning time, including regular school lessons, out-of-school-time lessons, and individual study, is devoted to regular school lessons. Furthermore, some research (e.g., Vandell et al., 2004) postulates that the frequency at which students engage in high-quality programmes is significant, as those who receive a higher "dosage" of programming will see greater benefits than those who do not, putting into question the quality of such programmes in Hong Kong, Shanghai-China, and Singapore. Furthermore, it is important to consider that in both learning time spent in regular school lessons and in individual study, female students tend to spend more time than male students, socio-economically advantaged students tend to spend more time than disadvantaged students, students in private schools tend to spend more time than those in public schools, students in academic schools tend to spend more time than those in vocational schools, and students in urban schools tend to spend more time than those residing in rural areas (OECD, 2011a). However, knowing that females, for example, spend more time than males, yet perform worse overall (Lam & Lau, 2014) in some contexts (e.g., Hong Kong) raises important questions surrounding why this is the case. *Is learning time of a better quality for male students in Hong Kong because, historically, more focus has been put towards males when it comes to the STEM subjects? Are remnants of these gendered academic structures the reason behind females' lower success rates?*

Additionally, the present study found an interesting significant positive association between out-of-school-time enrichment lessons in science and the mathematical literacy of adolescents in Hong Kong and Singapore. In other words, adolescents in Hong Kong and Singapore who attended out-of-school-time enrichment lessons in science tended to perform better in mathematics than their peers who did not. This unexpected correlation between science and math discovered within the data provides interesting avenues for future exploration. Perhaps, for example, adolescents who attend out-of-school-time enrichment lessons in science are already performing well in science, rather than requiring remedial help. Prior research has documented the positive relationship between scientific achievement and mathematical achievement based on adolescents' standardised science and mathematics test scores (e.g., Wang, 2005). Nevertheless, no significant relationship has been found between out-of-school-time enrichment lessons in science and mathematical literacy in Korea and Shanghai-China.

However, the results of the study did not present a significant relationship between out-of-school-time remedial science lessons and mathematical literacy among adolescents in Hong Kong, Korea, Shanghai-China, and Singapore. Learning time in out-of-school-time lessons in science was significantly positively related to mathematical literacy among adolescents in Hong Kong, suggesting that adolescents who spent more time in out-of-school-time lessons in science tended to perform significantly better in mathematics than their peers who spent less time in such lessons. However, learning time spent in out-of-school-time lessons in science was not significantly related to adolescents' mathematical literacy in Korea, Shanghai-China, and Singapore.

Regarding adolescents' scientific literacy, only in Shanghai-China were out-of-school-time enrichment lessons in science significantly positively related to scientific literacy: adolescents who attended out-of-school-time enrichment lessons in science tended to perform significantly higher in science than their peers who did not. The study did not find, however, a significant relationship between out-of-school-time enrichment lessons in science and scientific literacy among adolescents in Hong Kong, Korea, and Singapore, suggesting that out-of-school-time enrichment lessons in science offered in these countries may not influence their adolescents' scientific literacy. Likewise, no significant relationship was found between out-of-school-time remedial lessons in science and scientific literacy among adolescents in Hong Kong, Korea, Shanghai-China, and Singapore. It is also interesting to note that Hong Kong and Korea are examples of high-performing Asian countries/regions with low self-efficacy and self-concept in science learning. Lam and Lau (2014) note that this phenomenon may be explained "partly by the Asian cultures that emphasize modesty, but the sense of failure caused by the highly competitive exam cultures in these regions is likely one of the main causes" (p. 14). Regardless, studies indicate that these attitudinal factors are significantly associated with science performance, particularly for Hong Kong students.

Moreover, as it pertains to learning time, only in Hong Kong out-of-school-time lessons in science were significantly positively related to scientific literacy among adolescents. Adolescents from Hong Kong who spent more time learning science in out-of-school-time science lessons tended to perform significantly better in science than their peers who spent less time engaging in these lessons. No such relationship, however, existed between learning time in out-of-school-time science lessons and scientific literacy in Korea, Shanghai-China, or Singapore.

Furthermore, the study found significant relationships between out-of-school-time enrichment lessons in mathematics and the scientific literacy of adolescents in Hong Kong Korea, and Shanghai-China. In Korea and Shanghai-China in particular, out-of-school-time enrichment lessons in mathematics were significantly positively related to scientific literacy, suggesting that adolescents who attended such lessons in these countries tended to perform significantly better in science than peers who did not attend lessons of this type. Conversely, out-of-school-time enrichment lessons in mathematics were significantly negatively related to scientific literacy in Hong Kong, indicating that adolescents who attended out-of-school-time enrichment lessons in mathematics tended to perform noticeably more poorly in science than their peers who did not.

No significant relationship was found between out-of-school-time remedial lessons in mathematics and scientific literacy among adolescents in Korea, but the results of the present study did indicate a significant negative relationship between out-of-school-time remedial mathematics lessons and scientific literacy in Hong Kong-China, Shanghai-China, and Singapore. Adolescents who attended out-of-school-time remedial lessons in mathematics tended to perform significantly lower in science than peers who did not attend out-of-school-time remedial lessons in mathematics; thus, adolescents who attend out-of-school-time remedial lessons in mathematics might be at risk of underperforming in science.

Finally, learning time in out-of-school-time lessons in mathematics was significantly related to adolescents' scientific literacy in Korea and Singapore, but was not significantly related to adolescents' scientific literacy in Hong Kong and Shanghai-China. Adolescents in Korea who spent more time in out-of-school-time mathematics lessons tended to perform significantly better in science than peers who spent less time in these mathematics lessons, while, in contrast, adolescents in Singapore who spent more time in out-of-school-time mathematics lessons tended to perform significantly worse in science than peers who spent less time in out-of-school-time mathematics lessons.

Wang's (2005) research demonstrates that students who tend to perform well in mathematics are more likely to do better in science as well, and vice versa. He also suggests that, regardless of context, including the country or curriculum setting, evidence supports the idea that mathematics and science instructions should be linked in some way. It is evident that these ideas both align and conflict with the findings of the present study, clarifying that the ways in which after-school and other out-of-school-time programmes influence math and science achievements are complex and made more so by the many hard-to-control variables that they encompass. As such, conflicting data underscores the need for further investigation surrounding this topic, including why some countries showcase positive correlations and why others illustrate the opposite, and the ways in which these two curricula can best be integrated.

SIGNIFICANCE OF FINDINGS

The present study evaluated the significance of out-of-school lessons in science and mathematics on the scientific and mathematical literacy of adolescent students as found in the four countries with advanced educational systems. The study suggests mixed results in overall school performance of the students in these countries. The target audience of this research are the academics, educational policy makers, teachers, and school administrators. From the findings of this study, several insights can be extrapolated to aid the decision-making process regarding educational policies that can be most effective. The results suggest that students who took out-of-school enrichment programs in mathematics, tended to perform better and scored higher in mathematics in Korea and Shanghai-China.

In Singapore, there was no significant difference between mathematical scores of students who attended out-of-school-time enrichment lessons and students who did not attend out-of-school-time lessons. In Hong Kong, the opposite effect was seen, so students who attended out-of-school-time enrichment lessons in mathematics scored lower in mathematics than students who did not attend such lessons. From these findings, it can be suggested that out-of-school-time enrichment programs in mathematics are only effective in Korea and Shanghai-China, but not in Singapore and Hong Kong. The findings also show that students who attended out-of-school-time remedial lessons in mathematics in Hong Kong,

Shanghai-China and Singapore performed poorly in mathematics suggesting that out-of-school-time remedial lessons are probably not effective in any cultural context. There was no significant difference noted between students who attended remedial mathematics lessons in Korea and students who did not attend these remedial out-of-school-time lessons. Learning time in out-of-school lessons improved mathematical literacy for students in Korea but not for students in Hong Kong, Shanghai, and Singapore.

Additionally, students in Shanghai and Korea who attended out-of-school-time lessons in mathematics scored better in scientific literacy. In Hong Kong, the learning time of out-of-school science lessons significantly improved scientific literacy of students. Out-of-school-time enrichment lessons in mathematics significantly improved scientific literacy in students in Hong Kong, Shanghai, and Korea.

The overall findings from this study suggest that enrichment lessons in science are generally more effective in improving both mathematical and scientific literacy among students in Korea, Hong Kong, and Shanghai. Remedial lessons are generally not effective among students in Hong Kong and Shanghai. Learning time of these lessons improved scores for students in Korea, but not for students in Hong Kong, Shanghai, and Singapore. For the most part, lessons in mathematics and scientific literacy were correlated as students who attended out of school lessons in mathematics showed improvement in scientific literacy, and this was especially true in Korea and Shanghai, although not in Hong Kong. From these results, educators and policy makers can plan educational curricula that would have implications for student performance in science and mathematics, in these countries. Generally, mathematics lessons should help students with scientific literacy and vice versa, although in Hong Kong and Singapore, this trend was not noted. It could be suggested from the findings that in all these educational systems, enrichment lessons, whether in mathematics or in science would be effective and the effectiveness would depend on learning time, rather than the remedial lessons, which did not bring about significant improvement in scores, either in science or in mathematics. For educational programs and initiatives in these educational systems, several measures can be suggested, based on the findings. Table 5 is provided to show which methods of education are most effective in which specific countries in addition to advancing the understanding of the mechanisms by which out-of-school programs successfully improve student learning and success. Out of school programs can work only in specific contexts and have different impacts in different regions, as seen from this table. For instance, enrichment lessons in mathematics are clearly effective in Shanghai and Korea, but not in Hong Kong and Singapore. So, to improve mathematical literacy, enrichment lessons could be recommended in Shanghai and Korea. Remedial lessons in mathematics need reconsideration in all these countries, as generally they are not effective. Increased learning time in mathematics improved mathematical literacy, only in Korea, so in Korea, students should be encouraged to spend more time in participating in these types of instructional programs.

Enrichment lessons in science improved mathematical literacy in Hong Kong and Singapore, so enrichment lessons should be considered in these countries. Likewise, although not effective in mathematics, in Hong Kong, enrichment lessons in science clearly improved mathematical literacy among students. This suggests that to improve mathematical literacy, out of school enrichment mathematics lessons must be given in Shanghai and Korea, and out of school enrichment science lessons must be given in Hong Kong and Singapore. Out of school remedial mathematics and science lessons have no impact on improving mathematical literacy and are not recommended to improve maths performance. Learning time in science positively influenced mathematical literacy only in Hong Kong students, and not among others. This can be compared with the fact that increased learning time in mathematics improved mathematical literacy among students in Korea.

Table 5. Summary of impact of out-of-school lessons

	Hong Kong	Shanghai-China	Singapore	Korea
Enrichment lessons in mathematics and mathematical literacy	Negative	Positive	No relationship	Positive
Remedial lessons in mathematics and mathematical literacy	Negative	Negative	Negative	No relationship
Learning time in mathematics and mathematical literacy	No relationship	No relationship	No relationship	Positive
Enrichment lessons in science and mathematical literacy	Positive	No relationship	Positive	No relationship
Remedial science lessons and mathematical literacy	No relationship	No relationship	No relationship	No relationship
Learning time in science and mathematical literacy	Positive	No relationship	No relationship	No relationship
Enrichment lessons in science and scientific literacy	No relationship	Positive	No relationship	No relationship
Remedial lessons in mathematics and scientific literacy	Negative	Negative	Negative	No relationship
Learning time in mathematics and scientific literacy	No relationship	No relationship	Positive	Positive

So, as the data shows, increased learning time is suggested for out of school science programs in Hong Kong and out of school maths lessons in Korea. Enrichment lessons in science improved scientific literacy of students only in Shanghai. So, in Shanghai, out of school enrichment lessons are recommended, both in science and in mathematics. Remedial lessons in science or maths seem to have no impact or negative impact on both scientific and mathematical literacy and are not recommended in any of these countries. Learning time in mathematics improved scientific literacy for students in Singapore and Korea. In Korea, learning time significantly improved both scientific and mathematical literacy among students and is highly recommended. In Hong Kong learning time must be increased in out of school science classes to improve mathematical literacy and in Singapore, learning time should be increased in mathematics to improve scientific literacy and understanding among students. Insights from the data are crucial in understanding the overall significance of the findings (Hamilton et al., 2009).

Learning time, enrichment and remedial lessons, and the overall design of instructional programs can be done in accordance with the theoretical frameworks already presented here - the instructional interventional approach, the ADDIE model of instructions and the Systems Approach model. All these models or frameworks are iterative or have feedback control loops for continuous updating, change and improvement of the instructional process, and all are applicable to the educational contexts of the countries examined in this study. However, these frameworks differ in terms of steps or stages or the methods that are used in the learning process.

As a comparison of these three models, the instructional intervention model is perhaps the simplest, as there is diagnostic data based on learner scores, and there is a progress monitor that helps to assess whether the learning protocols must be changed to fit the needs of the students. Instructional interventions can be out of school programs or even increased contact hours of formal teaching provided to all types of students and can be focused on improving science, maths, etc., skills of underachieving students, as well as those who enrolled in enrichment programs.

The ADDIE model is one of the most common models in instructional design and being based on the five stages of instruction, it is a more formal and a rigorous method used to improve learning (Branch & Kopcha, 2014). It is largely used by educators for instruction in all subjects but was originally used for training in the armed forces. Since the model is rigorous, objective, and methodical with stages clearly identified, it is also preferred as a learning method for university courses. However, the model can be adopted to suit the specific needs of underachievers, special needs, as well as high achieving students.

The final theoretical framework discussed is the Systems Approach model by Dick and Carey (2005). This framework is like the interventions model and is iterative with feedback loops, although there are more detailed stages all the stages in the model are connected and there are interrelationships between elements, stages, and activities, suggesting a holistic approach to instruction. This framework considers all aspects of the learning process from instructional goals and strategy to learner characteristics and performance objectives, so this is very well laid out, providing a comprehensive picture on all aspects of learning and how the learning objectives can be attained. There are formative evaluations of the instructional program with continuous opportunities for revision. Using this framework in out-of-school programs would be effective, only if there is continuous feedback and evaluation of learner performance at every stage and instructional goals are clearly specified after evaluation of learner characteristics. In fact, if this framework is applied to the instructional program(s) given to students, it can be most comprehensive and most effective, despite being sufficiently time consuming.

To sum up, regarding future educational planning, evaluation, and policy considerations, if sufficient information and data are available, the systems approach model of instruction can be most effective. However, for a simple and quick instructional feedback model, the interventions model can be used to improve the learning process of underachieving students.

LIMITATIONS AND DIRECTIONS FOR FURTHER RESEARCH

The limitations of this study can yield fruitful directions for further research. First, the study assumes that genuine PISA data—that is, statistically significant information from which one can seemingly generalize—can be taken from a certain population and applied to another population, specifically because that population lives and attends school in the same country or region. Regardless of any shared cultural norms, practices, or identities, differences in curriculum between countries, including issues of the order, speed of lessons, lesson design, pedagogic practices, and the timing and type of standardised testing were not considered, representing a further area of exploration.

Another area to consider might be the specific types of after-school programmes being examined: are they similar from country to country, and if so, how? Are they all taught by certified teachers, and do they include one-on-one instruction such as tutoring? If one-on-one instruction is not included, what do these programmes entail? This is another set of variables that might provide meaningful directions for future work. In fact, diving deeper into the data for each individual country or region (e.g., analyzing data from Hong Kong separately from that of Singapore) from the same kind of theoretical perspective might be useful in unearthing additional information about the differences uncovered here between (and among) different geographic areas and contexts.

In addition, the retention of knowledge, commodification of education, utilitarian learning orientations, levels of student anxiety and stress resulting from educational intensity within examination-oriented systems, the ways in which societies transform their education systems, and further analyses surrounding the role of socio-cultural and contextual determinants in specific societies are all important considerations for educators and policymakers. Is student data accumulated over the course of their lifespans to determine the effectiveness and sustainability of out-of-school-time lessons regarding the knowledge and tools they acquired? Are students in countries with rigorous, high performing education systems likely to experience more anxiety and stress? As noted by Winne and Nesbit (2010), learners are certainly considered agents in the educational process, choosing whether or not and exactly how they will engage in the learning process. However, they are not fully autocratic, as there are external and cognitive factors shaping the process. For example, a highly controlled and reflective metacognitive learner might address a problem and identify it as solvable, but memory activation might yield an understanding of the problem as being difficult, prompting anxiety in the learner.

It was only a few generations ago when South Korea's economic output was equivalent to that of Afghanistan and ranked 23rd in terms of educational output among OECD countries (OECD, 2010b). Today, it is a top performer, but how exactly did this happen? It has been suggested that a student's background as an immigrant can pose academic challenges (OECD, 2011a), but is it not important to look more closely at the exact demographics and experiences of immigrants in a particular location given they are not heterogeneous? In Hong Kong, for example, immigrant students tend to study at lower-grade levels, appearing to have weaker performance when compared to native peers studying at higher grade levels; however, after grade level is controlled, it seems that immigrant students actually benefit from this (Lam & Lau, 2014). The family structure must also be critically assessed to understand the types of assistive roles played by students' parents and siblings. In Hong Kong it has been found that many parental factors do not have a significant impact on achievement after student attitudes are considered (Lam & Lau, 2014), but what about the other countries? In their efforts to institutionalize a sustainable and effective curriculum which addresses systemic inequities, educators and policymakers alike must become cognizant of and responsive to these queries.

Socio-economic variables also need further investigation. Various studies (e.g., OECD, 2010b; Avvisati, 2020) suggest that a student's socio-economic background is a more significant consideration than individual school characteristics, especially because some students lack many basic necessities and privileges, including adequate housing, nutrition, and medical care. This information is relevant for the present study because PISA utilizes the index of economic, social, and cultural status (ESCS) as a control variable in regression analysis to measure the influence of socio-economic status. Nonetheless, Avvisati (2020) notes that the cross-sectional nature of PISA data poses challenges for the interpretation of analyses that relate ESCS to outcomes, as measures of family background and socio-economic status can account for possible factors that may suggest inaccurate relationships between academic outcomes and the types of out-of-school experiences students are exposed to. Thus, the direct relationship between the role of a student's socio-economic status and educational outcomes is not fully understood, but worth evaluating in future discussions surrounding equity in education.

Next steps might also include action research comparing currently active after-school programmes to determine best practices that might be generalizable across geographic areas and student populations. These practices could be grounded in the same theoretical concepts as the approach to the current study. Specifically, they might focus on the development of student self-efficacy, since data shows that its relationship to test-score improvement is poorly understood, but that its relationship to individuals' goals to advance in science and maths careers is significant. Self-concept is also worth exploring, considering that students in many high-performing Asian countries/regions tend to have low scores in self-concept (Lam & Lau, 2014). Finally, more can be done to understand the factors impeding educational outcomes in certain countries. For example, what is known about the effectiveness of online out-of-school learning that has intensified around the World because of the Covid-19 pandemic? Likewise, is out-of-school remediation an opportunity to help students that may have fallen behind due to Covid-19? Moreover, which countries are more successful at moving students into a space where they can perform tasks independently and what are their processes? Ultimately, various environmental and contextual factors are believed to help students with the creation of meaning and with their broader academic success, but inconsistent academic outcomes necessitate further exploration surrounding the exact composition of out-of-school-time education.

CONCLUSION

In conclusion, the relationships between out-of-school-time lessons in mathematics and science and student performance in mathematics and science unquestionably vary from one education system to another, and the findings from this research are inconsistent and inconclusive. However, several insights can be drawn from the pattern of the general findings of this study. For example, in Hong Kong scientific literacy improves with out of school maths lessons given to students and by increasing learning time, In Singapore, learning time increase in science lessons helps improve mathematical literacy of students. Remedial science or maths lessons have been found to be generally unhelpful in all the countries studied here and enrichment lessons in science were helpful for students in Singapore and Hong Kong and enrichment lessons in maths resulted in performance improvement for students in Shanghai and Korea. The discrepant findings concerning the relationships between out-of-school-time lessons in mathematics and science and student performance in these subjects may be due to variability in the nature and characteristics of out-of-school-time programmes in Hong Kong, Korea, Shanghai-China, and Singapore. The nature and characteristics of out-of-school-time programmes may vary from country to country in terms of structural dimensions, process quality, and programme content (Vandell et al., 2004; Vandell et al., 2005). Moreover, variability in structural dimensions, process quality, and programme content may have a differential impact on student achievement outcomes (Mahoney, Parente, & Zigler, 2010). Hence, future research that considers the inherent nature and characteristics of out-of-school-time lessons in mathematics and science in these high-performing education systems may help educators and policymakers better understand the effects of such lessons on student performance and, in turn, restructure them as necessary to promote more equitable educational outcomes for students across cultural and national boundaries.

REFERENCES

Avvisati, F. (2020). Large scale assessments in education. *IEA ETS Research Institute Journal, 8*. Advance online publication. doi:10.118640536-020-00086-x

Black, A. R., Doolittle, F., Zhu, P., Unterman, R., & Grossman, J. B. (2008). The evaluation of enhanced academic instruction in after-school programs: Findings after the first year of implementation (NCEE 2008-4021). National Center for Education Evaluation and Regional Assistance, Institute of Education Sciences, U.S. Department of Education.

Boudett, K. P., City, E. A., & Murname, R. J. (2013). *Data Wise: A Step-by-Step Guide to Using Assessment Results to Improve Teaching and Learning*. Harvard Education Press.

Branch, R. M., & Kopcha, T. J. (2014). Instructional design models. In J. Spector, M. Merrill, J. Elen, & M. Bishop (Eds.), *Handbook of research on educational communications and technology* (pp. 77–87). Springer. doi:10.1007/978-1-4614-3185-5_7

Cosden, M., Morrison, G., Gutierrez, L., & Brown, M. (2004). The effects of homework programs and after-school activities on school success. *Theory into Practice, 43*(3), 220–226. doi:10.120715430421tip4303_8

Dettmers, S., Trautwein, U., & Lüdtke, O. (2009). The relationship between homework time and achievement is not universal: Evidence from multilevel analyses in 40 countries. *School Effectiveness and School Improvement, 20*(4), 375–405. doi:10.1080/09243450902904601

Dick, W., Carey, L., & Carey, J. O. (2005). *The systematic design of instruction*. Pearson Merrill.

Driscoll, M., & Carliner, S. (2005). *Advanced web-based Training: Adapting real world strategies in your online learning*. Pfeiffer.

Durlak, J. A., Weissberg, R. P., & Pachan, M. (2010). A meta-analysis of after-school programs that seek to promote personal and social skills in children and adolescents. *American Journal of Community Psychology, 45*(3-4), 294–309. doi:10.100710464-010-9300-6 PMID:20300825

Gustafson, K., & Branch, R. (2002). *What is instructional design? Trends and issues in instructional design and technology*. Merrill.

Hamilton, L., Halverson, R., Jackson, S. S., Mandinach, E., Supovitz, J. A., & Wayman, J. C. (2009). *Using student achievement data to support instructional decision making*. https://files.eric.ed.gov/fulltext/ED506645.pdf

Harvard Family Research Project. (2003). *A review of out-of-school-time program quasi-experimental and experimental evaluation results*. Author.

Heinze, A., Reiss, K., & Franziska, R. (2005). Mathematics achievement and interest in mathematics from a differential perspective. *ZDM, 37*, 212–219.

IEA. 2009. IEA international database analyzer for PISA (version 2.0) [Computer software and manual]. Hamburg, Germany: IEA Data Processing and Research Centre.

Jensen, B. (2012). *Catching up: Learning from the best school systems in East Asia*. Grattan Institute. http://www.grattan.edu.au/publications/130_report_learning_from_the_best_detail. pdf

Köller, O., Baumert, J., & Schnabel, K. (2001). Does interest matter? The relationship between academic interest and achievement in mathematics. *Journal for Research in Mathematics Education*, *32*(5), 448–470. doi:10.2307/749801

Lam, T. Y. P., & Lau, K. C. (2014). Examining factors affecting science achievement of Hong Kong in PISA 2006 using hierarchical linear modeling. *International Journal of Science Education*, *36*(15), 2463–2480. doi:10.1080/09500693.2013.879223

Lauer, P. A., Akiba, M., Wilkerson, S. B., Apthorp, H. S., Snow, D., & Martin-Glenn, M. L. (2006). Out-of-school-time programs: A meta-analysis of effects for at-risk students. *Review of Educational Research*, *76*(2), 275–313. doi:10.3102/00346543076002275

Lauver, S. (2002). *Assessing the benefits of an after-school program for urban youth: Results of an experimental design and process evaluation* [Unpublished PhD diss.]. University of Pennsylvania.

Lee, J. (2007). Two worlds of private tutoring: The prevalence and causes of after-school mathematics tutoring in Korea and the United States. *Teachers College Record*, *109*(5), 1207–1234. doi:10.1177/016146810710900507

Mahoney, J. L., Parente, M. E., & Zigler, E. F. (2010). After-school program participation and children's development. In J. L. Meece & J. S. Eccles (Eds.), *Handbook of research on schools, schooling, and human development* (pp. 379–397). Routledge.

Merrill, M. D., Drake, L., Lacy, M. J., & Pratt, J. (1996). Reclaiming instructional design. *Educational Technology*, *36*(5), 5–7.

Mokhtari, K., Rosemary, C. A., & Edwards, P. A. (2007). Making instructional decisions based on data: What, how, and why. *The Reading Teacher*, *61*(4), 354–359. doi:10.1598/RT.61.4.10

National Center on Intensive Intervention. (n.d.). *What is data-based individuation?* American Institutes for Research. https://intensiveintervention.org/data-based-individualization

Organization for Economic Cooperation and Development. (2010a). *Participating countries/economies*. https://www.oecd.org/pages/0,3417,en_32252351_32236225_1_1_1_1_1,00.html

Organization for Economic Cooperation and Development. (2010b). *Strong performers and successful reformers in Education: Lessons from PISA for the United States*. OECD Publishing. https://www.oecd.org/dataoecd/32/50/46623978.pdf

Organization for Economic Cooperation and Development. (2010c). *PISA 2009 results: What students know and can do: Student performance in reading, mathematics, and science (Volume 1)*. OECD Publishing. https://www.oecd.org/dataoecd/10/61/48852548.pdf

Organization for Economic Cooperation and Development. (2010d). *PISA 2012 mathematics framework*. OECD Publishing. https://www.oecd.org/dataoecd/8/38/46961598.pdf

Organization for Economic Cooperation and Development. (2011a). *Quality time for students: learning in and out of school*. OECD Publishing. https://www.oecd-ilibrary.org/docserver/9789264087057-en.pdf?expires=1576462357&id=id&accname=guest&checksum=B1535560A911E8359B1EE95DFF221A2B

Organization for Economic Cooperation and Development. (2011b). *Education at a Glance 2011: OECD indicators*. OECD Publishing. https://www.oecd.org/dataoecd/61/2/48631582.pdf

Organization for Economic Cooperation and Development. (2018). *PISA 2018: Insights and interpretations*. OECD Publishing. https://www.oecd.org/pisa/PISA%202018%20Insights%20and%20Interpretations%20FINAL%20PDF.pdf

Pallegedara, A., & Mottaleb, K. A. (2018). Patterns and determinants of private tutoring: The case of Bangladesh households. *International Journal of Educational Development*, *59*, 43–50. doi:10.1016/j.ijedudev.2017.10.004

Prenovost, J. K. E. (2001). *A first-year evaluation of after-school learning programs in four urban middle schools in the Santa Ana unified school district*. Author.

Reigeluth, C. M. (1999). What is instructional design theory and how is it changing? In C. M. Reigeluth (Ed.), *Instructional-design theories and models: A new paradigm of instructional theory* (Vol. 2, pp. 5–29). Routledge.

Schwartz, S. E., & Noam, G. G. (2007). *Informal science learning in afterschool settings: A natural fit?* University of Massachusetts.

Smith, P. L., & Ragan, T. J. (2004). *Instructional design* (3rd ed.). John Wiley & Sons.

Stylianides, A. J., & Stylianides, G. J. (2014). Impacting positively on students' mathematical problem-solving beliefs: An instructional intervention of short duration. *The Journal of Mathematical Behavior*, *33*, 8–29. doi:10.1016/j.jmathb.2013.08.005

Suter, L. E. (2016). Outside school time: An examination of science achievement and non-cognitive characteristics of 15-year-olds in several countries. *International Journal of Science Education*, *38*(4), 663–687. doi:10.1080/09500693.2016.1147661

Tennyson, R., Dijkstra, S., Schott, F., & Seel, N. (1997). *Instructional design: International perspectives, theory, research, and models* (Vol. 1). Lawrence Erlbaum Associates, Inc.

Vandell, D. L., Reisner, E. R., Brown, B. B., Dadisman, K., Pierce, K. M., Lee, D., & Pechman, E. M. (2005). *The study of promising after-school programs: Examination of intermediate outcomes in year 2. University of Wisconsin*. Wisconsin Center for Education Research., http://childcare.wceruw.org/pdf/pp/year2_executive_summary_and_brief_report.pdf

Vandell, D. L., Reisner, E. R., Brown, B. B., Pierce, K. M., Dadisman, K., & Pechman, E. M. (2004). *The study of promising after-school programs: Descriptive report of the promising programs. University of Wisconsin*. Wisconsin Center for Education Research., http://childcare.wceruw.org/pdf/pp/study_of_after_school_activities_descriptive_report_year1.pdf

Vandell, D. L., Reisner, E. R., & Pierce, K. M. (2007). *Outcomes linked to high-quality afterschool programs: Longitudinal findings from the study of promising practices*. Policy Study Associates. https://files.eric.ed.gov/fulltext/ED499113.pdf

Walker, M. (2011). *PISA 2009 plus results: Performance of 15-year-olds in reading, mathematics, and science for 10 additional participants*. Acer Press. https://research.acer.edu.au/pisa/1/

Wang, J. (2005). Relationship between mathematics and science achievement at the 8th grade. *International Journal of Science and Mathematics Education*, *5*, 1–17.

Winne, P. H., & Nesbit, J. C. (2010). The psychology of academic achievement. *Annual Review of Psychology*, *61*(1), 653–678. doi:10.1146/annurev.psych.093008.100348 PMID:19575616

Yung, K. W. H. (2020). Comparing the effectiveness of cram school tutors and schoolteachers: A critical analysis of students' perceptions. *International Journal of Educational Development*, *72*, 102141. doi:10.1016/j.ijedudev.2019.102141

Zehr, M. A. (2009). Study finds mixed success for 'enhanced' after-school lessons. *Education Week*, *29*(6), 5–10.

Chapter 3
An Assessment of Self-Service Business Intelligence Tools for Students:
The Impact of Cognitive Needs and Innovative Cognitive Styles

Mohammad K. Daradkeh
University of Dubai, UAE & Yarmouk University, Jordan

ABSTRACT

While previous research has mainly focused on improving the technical capabilities of self-service business intelligence (SSBI) tools, very little is known about how students evaluate different self-service BI tools, especially if they have different levels of experience. The goal of this chapter is to understand how students' characteristics influence their evaluation of different self-service BI tools. In this chapter, the authors focus specifically on two important student characteristics: need for cognition (NFC) and innovative cognitive style (ICS). These end-user characteristics were incorporated into a research model developed based on the elaboration likelihood model (ELM). To test the model, a laboratory experiment was conducted with undergraduate students for data analysis and reporting tasks, and the resulting data were analyzed using the partial least squares (PLS) approach. The results showed that the effect of NFC and ICS on the evaluation of SSBI tools varied depending on students' experience and familiarity with the tool.

INTRODUCTION

Self-service has recently become a defining feature of modern business intelligence (BI) tools (Daradkeh & Al-Dwairi, 2017; Tavera Romero, Ortiz, Khalaf, & Ríos Prado, 2021). This wave of disruption has led to shifting the market and new buying trends away from IT-centric to business-centric BI platforms with self-service reporting and analytics capabilities (Alpar & Schulz, 2016). The goal of self-service

DOI: 10.4018/978-1-7998-9644-9.ch003

BI is to empower business users to analyze, visualize, and glean insights from corporate data without the intervention of IT department (Imhoff & White, 2011). Self-service BI tools are characterized by intuitive and easy-to-use interfaces that support a full range of BI and analytics capabilities such as visualization, dashboards, OLAP multidimensional analysis, predictive analysis and statistical modeling (Daradkeh & Al-Dwairi, 2017). These capabilities focus on four main objectives: 1) providing easy access to source data for reporting and analysis; 2) building easy-to-use BI applications and improved support for data analysis; 3) providing fast-to-deploy data warehouse options such as cloud or mobile environments; and 4) designing intuitive, customizable and collaborative end-user interfaces (Imhoff & White, 2011; Salisu, Bin Mohd Sappri, & Bin Omar, 2021).

As BI and analytics vendors such as Tableau, Microsoft, MicroStrategy, Sisense, and QlikView are promoting different self-service BI tools in the market, they are interested in how to attract more consumers and organizations to adopt and buy their products (Gartner, 2019). Often, end users need to carefully evaluate different self-service BI tools before making adoption decisions (Daradkeh & Al-Dwairi, 2017). Since these tools often have similar features and can support the same reporting and analytical tasks, end users often face a major challenge in choosing a tool that best meets their business needs. Previous research has made a great contribution towards maturing and advancing technical capabilities of self-service BI tools (Abelló et al., 2013; Acito & Khatri, 2014; Alpar & Schulz, 2016; Bani-Hani, Pareigis, Tona, & Carlsson, 2018; Eckerson, 2014; Schlesinger & Rahman, 2016). However, there is limited understanding of how students evaluate different self-service BI tools before making a decision about their use, and how they determine which BI tool is appropriate for learning data analytics and business intelligence skills from an end-user perspective.

The main purpose of this chapter is to understand how student characteristics influence the evaluation of different self-service BI tools. Among the many student characteristics that can have a significant impact on the evaluation of self-service BI tools, this study focuses on two important characteristics: need for cognition (NFC) (Cacioppo & Petty, 1982) and innovative cognitive style (ICS) (Bagozzi & Foxall, 1996; Stum, 2009). NFC refers to the level of students' elaboration and measures the cognitive effort that they are willing to exert in working on solving a problem or completing a task (Bhattacherjee & Sanford, 2006). Students with higher level of NFC are more inclined and motivated to exert greater effort to engage with technology evaluation (Xuequn & Yanjun, 2015). Therefore, NFC could have a significant impact on the evaluation of self-service BI tools. ICS, on the other hand, has been recognized as an important personality trait that can play a key role in the evaluation and adoption of new technologies (Xuequn & Yanjun, 2015). students with higher innovativeness are more flexible in trying new and different technologies. They also are more willing to break conventional paradigms of solving problems and more adaptable to the changes in the environment. Consequently, students with a higher innovativeness may learn creative features and innovative ways to perform a specific task; leading to a positive evaluation of self-service BI tools.

To assess the effect of NFC and ICS on the evaluation of self-service BI tools, this study proposes a research model based on the elaboration likelihood model (Bhattacherjee & Sanford, 2006). the ELM is chosen as a theoretical basis for this study because it classifies information processing mechanisms of students into two different routes– central and peripheral – and explains contexts where students are more likely to use one route rather than another (Bhattacherjee & Sanford, 2006). Therefore, the ELM seems appropriate for understanding different mechanisms that students employ for evaluating different self-service BI tools. To test the research model and hypotheses proposed in this study, a laboratory experiment was conducted, and the resulting data were analyzed using partial least square (PLS) approach

(Hair, Hult, Ringle, & Sarstedt, 2017). The results revealed that the effect of NFC and ICS on the evaluation of self-service BI tools varies according to the experience and familiarity of students with the tool. These results provide useful theoretical and practical implications and thus should help in understanding different mechanisms through which students evaluate self-service BI tools before actual adoption.

The reminder of this chapter is structured as follows. The following section discusses the theoretical background and presents the hypotheses and research model of this study. The next section presents the research methodology and the procedure of data collection and analysis. Then, the findings from the analysis are presented, followed by a discussion of the theoretical and practical implications as well as limitations of this study. Lastly, conclusion and future works are outlined in the last section.

THEORETICAL BACKGROUND

Self-Service Business Intelligence (SSBI)

According to Schuff, Corral, St. Louis, and Schymik (2018), SSBI is a facility within the BI environment that enables business users to analyze data, visualize insights, and capture and disseminate information in the form of dashboards and reports without the need to engage IT staff for support. Bani-Hani, Pareigis, et al. (2018) argued that SSBI is more than a function within BI; rather, it reflects a new paradigm of BI that aims to increase the level of co-production while reducing the dependency of individuals as users work with a wide range of applications and tools that are comprehensively embedded in the solution of an analytical task. They confirmed that SSBI enables business users, especially those with limited analytical skills, to be more independent and less dependent on IT experts and power BI users.

The promise of self-service business intelligence (SSBI) is to improve the ability of business users such as managers, executives, knowledge workers, and analysts to generate reports based on their needs to support their decisions and actions for business success (Salisu et al., 2021). Daradkeh (2019b) stated that the core idea of SSBI is to provide an environment where business users can access, analyze, and derive actionable insights from business data without direct intervention from IT. Such an environment can extend the reach and scope of reporting and analytics applications to address a broader range of business problems and opportunities. This expansion supports business users' needs for personalized and collaborative decision-making and information-sharing processes (Arnaboldi, Robbiani, & Carlucci, 2021; Bani-Hani, Tona, & Carlsson, 2018). SSBI could also enable organizations to adopt an analytics-focused culture, which would give them a competitive advantage over their peers (Daradkeh, 2019c). It can help business users manage their reporting and analytics needs without the help of technical IT teams, allowing IT staff to focus on other strategic business activities (Sharda, Delen, & Turban, 2021). In addition, SSBI is expected to fundamentally change every business activity and bring benefits to enterprises, such as improved customer service, optimized production levels, better capacity planning, reduced repair and maintenance costs, and improved working capital utilization (Daradkeh, 2019a, 2021).

Despite the promised benefits of SSBI technology, the development of innovative and sophisticated SSBI tools is not the end of the story. To fully realize the benefits of SSBI tools, further steps need to be taken to ensure that the tool can be used effectively and efficiently by business users to meet their reporting and analysis needs ((Daradkeh & Al-Dwairi, 2018). In fact, there is a lack of studies that have paid sufficient attention to the adoption of SSBI tools regardless of their great importance. Previous work on SSBI adoption has shown that the use of SSBI tools in organizations still has several drawbacks and does not fully meet the requirements for their adoption. Recent industry surveys report several barriers to SSBI adoption in organizations (Arnaboldi et al., 2021). For example, in a study by Daradkeh (2019b), lack of IT department or management support, limited budget, and data security and management were identified as the major barriers to the success of SSA adoption in organizations. Also, Bani-Hani, Tona, et al. (2018) identified the analytical skills of business users, lack of data quality and control, and lack of user training as the main barriers to the adoption of SSBI in enterprises. This indicates that making the SSBI tool as simple as possible and enabling it for the end user is the only way for enterprises to foster an analytics-driven culture and enable business users to develop analytical skills.

Organizations building an analytics-based culture must also consider the unique needs and requirements of different groups of business users when implementing SSBI tools. Executives, managers and other casual users of business analytics may simply want interactive reports and dashboards that they can drill through if they want to further analyze some of the data presented to them. Advanced users, on the other hand, are likely to acquire a high level of query and analysis skills (Daradkeh, 2020). Daradkeh (2022) stated that from a practical perspective, SSBI is recognized as a technological innovation that is primarily characterized by its advanced business intelligence and analytics (BI&A) capabilities. SSBI can add business value through its unique analytical, predictive, and decision support capabilities, enabling business users to gain knowledge and actionable insights from enterprise data that could not be obtained using traditional data analytics approaches (Clarke, Tyrrell, & Nagle, 2016; Tavera Romero et al., 2021).

For an SSBI tool to successfully support end users, it should be tailored to their reporting and analysis tasks as well as their decision-making style. Therefore, the tool should be flexible and adaptable to different users. If an SSBI tool is to support different styles, skills, and knowledge, it should not try to force a particular process. Rather, it should help end users use and develop their own styles, skills, and knowledge. Users will be more likely to adopt an SSBI tool if that tool is compatible with their analysis and decision-making processes within the organization (Passlick, Guhr, Lebek, & Breitner, 2020). Thus, the process of adopting and deciding on SSBI technologies is closely related not only to their unique ability to solve complicated data analysis problems, but also to individuals' idiosyncrasies of thinking about and dealing with original ideas, as well as to individuals' behaviors of seeking strategic opportunities and striving to explore new things and accomplish tasks (Salisu et al., 2021).

Elaboration Likelihood Model (ELM)

The role of individual tendency to break existing paradigms through deviant thinking and behavior has been explored through Elaboration Likelihood Model (ELM) [ref]. ELM is a dual process theory that attempts to explain the processes by which both the system and the information contained in the system are evaluated and used by students (Bhattacherjee & Sanford, 2006; Petty & Cacioppo, 1986). The basic premise of the ELM is that students process information through two routes; the central route based on detailed information contained in the system or peripheral route based on various cues such as visual and aesthetic design of the system (Bhattacherjee & Sanford, 2006). The extent to which students choose to exploit a route or another is based on their state of "elaboration likelihood." When students use the central route, they are expected to exert considerable cognitive effort to process and elaborate on the information, evaluate its content, and consider other arguments relevant to the information. On the other hand, the peripheral route requires less cognitive effort and elaboration than that required by the central route. Instead of engaging in scrutiny or thoughtful process of information, the peripheral route is based on processing various heuristics, cues, and attractiveness associated the source of information (Cyr,

Head, Lim, & Stibe, 2018; Kitchen, Kerr, Schultz, McColl, & Pals, 2014). In relation to the evaluation of self-service BI tools, students using the central route are more likely to scrutinize detailed functionality and features of the tool, while those using the peripheral route are inclined to rely on various cues rather than active, effortful evaluation of the tool.

The elaboration likelihood model (ELM) has been adapted in a variety of contexts, such as consumer behavior (James A. Eckert & Goldsby, 2018), internet marketing (Kitchen et al., 2014), and technology evaluation (Xuequn & Yanjun, 2015). According to Bhattacherjee and Sanford (2006), the ELM is not an student characteristic or habitual way of processing information. Rather, it is a temporal state that may fluctuate with the situation and time, even for the same student. In the context of self-service BI, for example, one student may be familiar with a particular tool but knows little about another. Therefore, the experience and familiarity of students with the self-service BI tool will influence the route that they would follow for evaluating that tool. When evaluating a relatively familiar tool, students are more likely to have the necessary motivation and ability to process information contained in the tool. In this situation, they are more likely to employ the central route, which devotes considerable effort and engage deep, systematic consideration of task-relevant issues. In contrast, students are expected to use the peripheral route when evaluating a relatively unfamiliar tool.

Need for Cognition (NFC)

The need for cognition (NFC) is a personality trait that describes the student's inclination to engage in cognitively effortful tasks (Cacioppo, Petty, Kao, & Rodriguez, 1986). If an student is more engaged in effortful tasks, this should lead to thoughtful evaluation of self-service BI tools. A study by Daradkeh and Al-Dwairi (2017) reported that the more amount of cognitive effort students are willing to exert on fulfilling a task, the more learning effort they are willing to take to learn a self-service BI tool, even if they have not used that tool before. However, students with a higher level of NFC may not always devote much effort; it depends on the specific route they use for processing information to complete the task. When evaluating a familiar self-service BI tool, students tend to evaluate that tool using the central route. The central route supports student with higher NFC to exert much effort to evaluate different capabilities and features of the self-service BI tool; leading to positive evaluation.

On the other hand, when evaluating an unfamiliar self-service BI tool, students may not be able to process the core functions and features of the tool, and in this situation, they might use the peripheral route that relies on various cues and heuristics such as the design aesthetic and user interface of the tool (Daradkeh & Al-Dwairi, 2017). even if students have a higher level of NFC, they still cannot devote much effort to evaluate the self-service BI tool; because they lack the necessary elaboration and motivation to do so. Therefore, students' NFC level may not have any influence on the evaluation of unfamiliar self-service BI tools. To summarize, this study posits that:

H1: students' familiarity with the self-service BI tool will interact with NFC such that:

(a) NFC will have a positive impact on students' evaluation of self-service BI tool when they evaluate a relatively familiar platform.
(b) NFC will not have any impact on students' evaluation of self-service BI tool when they evaluate a relatively unfamiliar platform.

Innovative Cognitive Style (ICS)

In addition to need for cognition, innovative cognitive style has been argued as another critical personal trait affecting individual ways of thinking about and dealing with original ideas. Innovativeness is a cognitive style that describes the inclination of students to embrace novelty and be more willing to break conventional ways of completing a task or activity (Daradkeh, 2019b). As suggested by Kirton's adaption-innovation theory (Kirton, 1976, 2003), the cognitive style of students ranges from highly adaptive to highly innovative. While highly adaptive students are unwilling to change their routines until they are convinced that a new technology can offer them benefits, highly innovative students are more likely to switch to a new technology when this technology is available to them (Chilton, Hardgrave, & Armstrong, 2005; Xuequn & Yanjun, 2015). In the context of self-service BI, when evaluating a new self-service BI tool, students probably employ the peripheral route and focus on various cues of that tool. In this situation, various cues of the new tool can show students innovative ways to finish certain tasks, even though they may not be the best solutions. Therefore, when evaluating a new self-service BI tool, students with a higher level of ICS may learn creative features and innovative ways to complete a specific task, leading to a positive evaluation.

On the other hand, when evaluating a familiar self-service BI tool, students are most likely to use the central route to process the core features of the tool and exert much effort during evaluation. Since students are familiar with the tool, they may find that these core functions cannot help in generating innovative solutions and are less likely to use them in the subsequent tasks, leading to a negative evaluation. Thus, this study posits that:

H2: students' familiarity with the self-service BI tool will interact with ICS such that:

(a) ICS will have a negative impact on students' evaluation of self-service BI tool when they evaluate a relatively familiar tool.
(b) ICS will have a positive impact on students' evaluation of self-service BI tool when they evaluate a relatively unfamiliar tool.

Figure 1 shows the research model used in this study.

RESEARCH METHOD

To assess the effect of NFC and ICS on the evaluation of self-service BI tools, this study designed and conducted an experiment based on the research model and hypotheses presented in the previous section. This section discusses the experimental tasks and procedures, measures development, and data analysis using PLS.

Experimental Tasks and Procedure

The experimental study was setup in a lab-based environment. A total of 120 undergraduate students from a business intelligence and analytics class were participated in this study. The average age of participants was 20.04 (SD 2.12), with the range from 18 to 23 years old. The percentage of female participants was 73.80%. The participants in this study were given a task of analyzing data and creating a dashboard

Figure 1. Research model

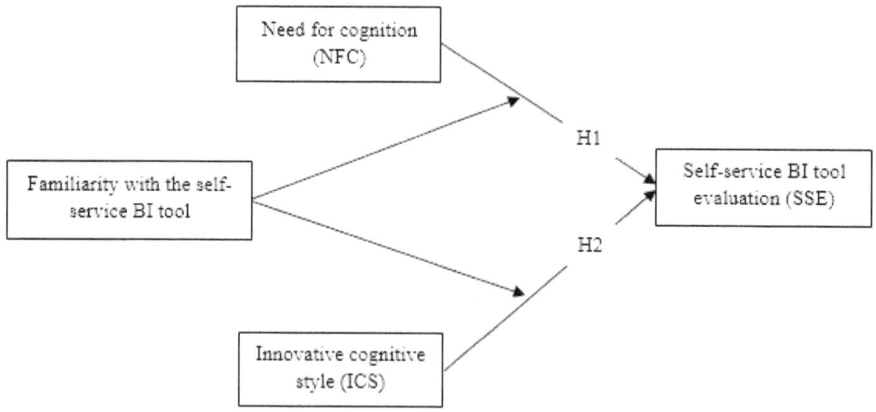

Table 1. Descriptive data of participants

	Group one (Microsoft Power BI)	Group two (Tableau Desktop)
No. of participants	60	60
Age	20.07 (SD 2.55)	20.00 (SD 2.40)
% Females	75.15%	72.44%

for an organization with multiple departments (e.g., marketing, customer service, finance, and HR) to monitor and manage their performance. The latest version of Microsoft Power BI and Tableau Desktop were used as self-service BI tools in this study. Although a broad range of self-service BI tools exists, these two tools were chosen as they are from among the most popular tools in the market according to Magic Quadrant for BI and Analytics platforms released by Gartner (2019). Both tools characterized by visual aesthetic design and easy-to-use interfaces and support a full range of BI and analytics capabilities such as visualization, dashboards, OLAP multidimensional analysis, predictive analysis and statistical modeling (Daradkeh & Al-Dwairi, 2017). However, students have different levels of experience with these two tools. Students were asked how good the tool was to complete the task.

After arriving at the lab where the experimental study was administrated, participants were briefly introduced to the study and then directed to fill in a short survey on their student characteristics (i.e., task experience, tool experience, NFC, and ICS). Then, the participants were randomly divided into two groups of 60 students each. Group one was presented with a video tutorial of Microsoft Power BI, followed by the evaluation survey. Group two was presented with a video tutorial of Tableau Desktop, followed by the evaluation survey as well. The descriptive data for the two groups is presented in Table 1. A One-way ANOVA was conducted, and results showed that there was no significant difference between the two groups in terms of gender and age.

Measures

To ensure content validity, the measurement items were mainly derived from prior research studies with minor modifications in wording to be appropriate for self-service BI tools (refer to the Appendix).

Items for task and tool experience were adapted from those developed and used by Goodhue, Klein, and March (2000); items for NFC were adapted from Cacioppo and Petty (1982); items for innovative cognitive style (ICS) were adapted from Kirton (1976); and items for user evaluation of self-service BI tools (SSE) were adapted from Dishaw and Strong (1999). A five-point Likert scale, ranging from 1 'strongly disagree' to 5 'strongly agree' was used to rate the measurement items.

Data Analysis

To validate the hypotheses, this study utilized partial least squares (PLS) for data analysis (Hair et al., 2017). PLS is a variance/component-based structural equation modeling method, which is designed to examine the significance of relationships and explain variance among measures; hence, it is appropriate for predictive modelling and theory building (Hair et al., 2017). SmartPLS version 3.0 was used for the analysis, and the bootstrap re-sampling method (using 5000 samples) was used to determine the significance of the paths in the structural model. Unlike the covariance-based packages, (e.g. AMOS or LISREL) that employs $\chi 2$ statistics, PLS uses R^2 statistics and does not place strict demands on sample size and data normality (Hair et al., 2017). In this study, the sample size for each group was 60, which was not appropriate to use covariance-based structural equation modelling. Further, PLS is better suited for predicting the validity of models than covariance-based structural equation modelling, which focuses instead on model fit (Chin, 2010). Two assessments are supported by PLS: the measurement model assessment – here item reliability, convergent and discriminant validities of the measurement scales are examined; and the structural model assessment – this aspect presents information related to the strength of paths in models. The path significance levels using t-values are estimated by the bootstrap method (Hair et al., 2017).

RESULTS

Manipulation Check

The average of task experience was 2.74 (SD 1.44), indicating that participants had a reasonable level of experience with the BI and analytic task given to them. Further, the average of tool experience for Microsoft Power BI was 3.87 (SD 0.76), which is significantly larger than that for Tableau Desktop (mean = 1.24, SD = 1.19) ($t(118)=21.57, p<0.001$). Further, the average of tool experience for Microsoft Power BI was significantly larger than 3.00, which is the midpoint of the scale ($t(59)=21.61, p<0.001$), while the average of tool experience for Tableau Desktop was significantly less than 3.00 ($t(59)= -12.41, p<0.001$). According to these statistics, participants from group one will be evaluating a relatively familiar self-service BI tool, whereas participants from group two will be evaluating a relatively unfamiliar tool.

Analysis of Group One

After testing the mean difference among the two groups in terms of tool experience, this study started by analyzing the data for group one. In the first stage, convergent and discriminant validity was established through meeting the following criteria. First, all factor loadings for items corresponding to the same construct were statistically significant and none of the factor loadings were found to be below the cut-off value of 0.60 as recommended by (Hair et al., 2017). Second, the composite reliability (CR) of all constructs were above 0.70. Finally, the average variance extracted (AVE) of all constructs were higher than the threshold value of 0.50. Table 2 summarizes the item loadings, AVE, CR, and Cronbach's α of constructs for group one. Discriminant validity was established by examining that the correlations between constructs were below 0.85 and that the square root of AVE for each construct exceeded all correlations between that construct and any other constructs (Fornell & Larcker, 1981). Overall, measures used in this study demonstrated good psychometric properties in group one, as shown in Table 3.

Table 2. Descriptive statistics, item loadings, and AVE and CR of constructs (Group one)

Scale item	Item mean	Item SD	Item loading	AVE	CR	Cronbach's α
NFC1	2.91	1.17	0.80	0.73	0.89	0.88
NFC2	2.76	1.21	0.83			0.72
NFC3	2.80	1.07	0.84			0.78
ICS1	3.39	1.20	0.70	0.65	0.85	0.90
ICS2	2.91	1.06	0.81			0.91
ICS3	3.27	1.06	0.82			0.76
SSE1	3.10	1.04	0.83	0.77	0.86	0.75
SSE2	2.91	1.13	0.82			0.81
SSE3	2.76	1.21	0.83			0.82

Table 3. Correlation between constructs and square root of AVEs (Group one)

Construct	NFC	ICS	SSE
NFC	0.85		
ICS	0.43	0.81	
SSE	0.10	0.29	0.82

After assessing and confirming the convergent and discriminant validity, this study examines the results of the structural model assessment for group one. H1a hypothesizes that NFC will have a positive effect on students' evaluation of self-service BI tools when they evaluate a relatively familiar tool. This hypothesis is supported with (β=0.313, t=2.111, $p<0.05$). H2a posits that ICS will have a negative effect on students' evaluation of self-service BI tools when they evaluate a relatively familiar tool. This hypothesis is not supported (β= -0.023, t=0.274, $p>0.05$). These results are presented in Figure 2.

Analysis of Group Two

The same procedure from group one was followed, and the results of the measurement model assessment are given in Table 4 and Table 5. Accordingly, the measures had also demonstrated good psychometric properties in group two.

Figure 2. Research results

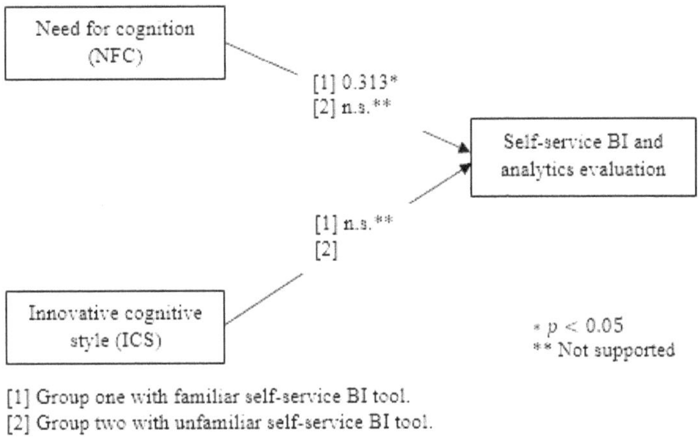

Table 4. Descriptive statistics, item loadings, and AVE and CR of constructs (Group two)

Scale item	Item mean	Item SD	Item loading	AVE	CR	Cronbach's α
NFC1	2.59	1.36	0.86	0.66	0.85	0.81
NFC2	2.81	1.35	0.82			0.84
NFC3	2.46	1.42	0.69			0.72
ICS1	3.24	1.10	0.83	0.68	0.86	0.82
ICS2	2.63	0.79	0.81			0.84
ICS3	3.00	1.02	0.67			0.74
SSE1	3.80	0.91	0.81	0.77	0.81	0.83
SSE2	3.59	1.08	0.84			0.78
SSE3	2.59	1.36	0.78			0.76

Table 5. Correlation between constructs, and square root of AVEs (Group two)

Construct	NFC	ICS	SSE
NFC	0.81		
ICS	0.50	0.83	
SSE	0.31	0.19	0.81

After assessing and confirming the convergent and discriminant validity, this study examines the results of the structural model assessment for group two. H1b states that NFC will not have any effect on students' evaluation of self-service BI tool when they evaluate a relatively unfamiliar tool. This hypothesis is supported (β= -0.054, t=0.442, p>0.05). H2b posits that ICS will have a positive effect on students' evaluation of self-service BI tools when they evaluate a relatively unfamiliar tool. This hypothesis is also supported (β=0.281, t=2.017, p<0.05). These results are presented in Figure 2.

Post-Hoc Analysis

To understand the results of students' evaluation of the two self-service BI tools, the average score of tool evaluation of each participant was calculated and the difference between the two groups was compared. The results of an independent sample t-test showed that tool evaluation of Microsoft Power BI (Mean = 3.62; SD = 0.87) from group one was not significantly different from that of Tableau Desktop from group two (Mean = 3.46; SD = 0.86) ($t(118)=1.11$, $p<0.05$).

DISCUSSION

Recent research goes some way to adding to the body of knowledge on commercial BI Tools. However, there is still a dearth of literature in the area of student perspectives of specific BI systems. This chapter provides an understanding of how students evaluate different self-service BI tools. Based on the ELM, this study developed a theoretical model to examine how two important characteristics of students' evaluation of self-service BI tools: NFC and ICS, influence students' evaluation of self-service BI tools. The results of this study show that NFC has a positive effect on students' evaluation of self-service BI tools when they evaluate a familiar tool. Conversely, ICS has a positive effect on students' evaluation of self-service BI tools when they evaluate a new and unfamiliar tool. The post hoc analysis shows that there is no significant difference between Microsoft Power BI and Tableau Desktop in the evaluation of the tools. This result is consistent with previous ELM research indicating that students can reach the same conclusion (e.g., to accept a particular tool) even if that decision is reached through different routes (central route or peripheral route) (Bhattacherjee & Sanford, 2006; Cyr et al., 2018; Xuequn & Yanjun, 2015).

Implications for Research

The main theoretical contribution of this study is that students evaluate different self-service BI tools with various mechanisms. Specifically, when evaluating a familiar tool, NFC has a positive effect on their evaluation. This study confirmed that when dealing with familiar self-service BI tools, students are more likely to process detained information and technical features of the tool and exert more effort during evaluation. The higher level of effort that students are willing to exert during evaluation, the more likely that they will evaluate the tool thoroughly, resulting in a positive evaluation. On the other hand, when students deal with a new and unfamiliar self-service BI tool, ICS has a positive impact on the tool evaluation. This study demonstrated that when dealing with unfamiliar self-service BI tool, students are more likely to evaluate the tool based on various cues (e.g., interactive and aesthetic features). Here, the level of NFC does not affect the tool evaluation. Instead, students with higher level of ICS are more likely to accept new, innovative tools, resulting in a positive evaluation.

From the perspective of a university instructor, this chapter outlines the needs of data analytics students. The chapter provides valuable information about the skills students need to acquire in order to pursue a graduate degree in data analytics. This chapter examines the specific tools that BI students are taught and need to master. This research provides a detailed assessment of Tableau and Power BI, as well as students' opinions of these tools. In addition, this chapter discusses the need to develop data analytics and business intelligence courses in college curricula. This chapter raises important questions for instructors and students about what instructors should teach. Tableau and Power BI are examples of BI tools covered in this chapter. These issues are discussed in detail and compared to the two BI tools covered in this chapter. Our user study clearly shows that the user characteristics we consider influence the effectiveness of the SSBI tools used in this research. We envision two possible forms of customization: first, selecting different SSBI tools for different users, and second, providing additional support only to some users who are likely to find it beneficial to look at a particular SSBI tool.

Implications for Practice

This chapter has also important practical implications. From the perspective of BI and analytics vendors, it is crucial to highlight and promote the core features of self-service BI tools that are being introduced in the market to improve their evaluation by potential end users. Since potential end users already have some knowledge about their reporting and analytics needs in organizations, they are more likely to focus on the core features of the self-service BI tool that satisfy their specific needs, especially for those with higher NFC and elaboration. On the other hand, when introducing a new self-service BI tool to compete with similar tools from other vendors, it should be expected that potential consumers will have little experience with the new tool. Therefore, vendors should highlight various cues of the tool (visual, aesthetic, social) to enhance perceptions regarding these features and receive positive evaluation from potential end users.

While this chapter focuses on the human element in terms of effective end-user training, the main purpose was to identify what elements influence and could influence business intelligence and analytics training for end users. Passlick et al. (2020) provide valuable insights into the effectiveness of business user training programs. In this case, the business users are students of BI tools, which include Qlik, Power BI, and Tableau. This chapter provides great value with their analysis of the data analytics skills needed in education and how higher education professionals are responding to those needs using disruption theory. The authors assert that higher education educators need to understand the relationship between "... Course content, students' analytic skills, and an emerging and disruptive technological world driven by increasingly powerful software that can support or even replace parts of human knowledge." (Passlick et al., 2020).

This chapter provides a detailed analysis of the skills required for data analysis and the curricula for data analysis. In particular, we note that SSBI tools cause two types of disruption. The first is when the performance of BI tools exceeds the ability of analysts to use the tools themselves. The second is when analysts demand more performance from BI tools than they are capable of delivering. The main conclusion of this chapter is that there is still much debate about what topics should be included in college curricula for business intelligence and analytics.

LIMITATIONS AND FUTURE RESEARCH

This study has several limitations, which suggest avenues for future research. First, this study used Microsoft Power BI and Tableau Desktop as self-service BI tools to examine how students evaluate different tools. The results of this study can be affected by the tools chosen. Future studies could examine the evaluation mechanisms with other popular self-service BI tools (e.g. QlikView and TIBCO Spotfire) (Gartner, 2019). Second, this study used a laboratory experiment with student participants. While students are familiar with the context and purpose of this study and therefore should be appropriate for this study, the results should be cautiously generalized to a more heterogeneous subject pool or beyond a laboratory setting. Future study might employ working professionals of different positions and industry sectors. Third, this study focuses on two important student characteristics – NFC and ICS. Other student characteristics might be examined in future studies (e.g., other cognitive styles, personality types, and decision-making styles).

CONCLUSION

Today, the market has proliferated with various self-service BI tools and solutions that promise to amplify the intelligence and analytics capabilities of students, especially those with limited analytic skills (Daradkeh & Al-Dwairi, 2017). While previous studies have been devoted towards advancing technical capabilities of self-service BI tools, limited research has examined how students evaluate different self-service BI tools. This study provides a useful theoretical foundation to understand different mechanisms through which students evaluate various self-service BI tools. The results from a laboratory experiment show that students indeed evaluate different self-service BI tools with different mechanisms, which may help researchers and practitioners alike to understand how to promote and enhance perception toward new self-service BI and analytics technologies.

Although the research objective was achieved based on the data collected and the comparative analysis of the research conducted, the research can be considered exploratory and it is suggested that this topic could be expanded in future research, specifically:

- Interviewing a large sample of students to further validate the results.
- Adding new criteria related to ease of use, cost, and available training and support for SSBI tools.
- Survey additional user groups for their opinions on the best type of SSBI systems.
- Further research on the functionality of SSBI tools, such as predictive analytics, including machine learning, artificial neural networks, and support vector machines.
- Further research on the database functionality of SSBI tools.

ACKNOWLEDGMENT

The authors of this study would like to thank all the participating students, without whom this study would not have been possible.

REFERENCES

Abelló, A., Darmont, J., Etcheverry, L., Golfarelli, M., Mazón, J., Naumann, F., Pedersen, T., Rizzi, S. B., Trujillo, J., Vassiliadis, P., & Vossen, G. (2013). Fusion Cubes: Towards Self-Service Business Intelligence. *International Journal of Data Warehousing and Mining*, *9*(2), 66–88. doi:10.4018/jdwm.2013040104

Acito, F., & Khatri, V. (2014). Business analytics: Why now and what next? *Business Horizons*, *57*(5), 565–570. doi:10.1016/j.bushor.2014.06.001

Alpar, P., & Schulz, M. (2016). Self-Service Business Intelligence. *Business & Information Systems Engineering*, *58*(2), 151–155. doi:10.100712599-016-0424-6

Arnaboldi, M., Robbiani, A., & Carlucci, P. (2021). On the relevance of self-service business intelligence to university management. *Journal of Accounting & Organizational Change*, *17*(1), 5–22. doi:10.1108/JAOC-09-2020-0131

Bagozzi, R. P., & Foxall, G. R. (1996). Construct validation of a measure of adaptive-innovative cognitive styles in consumption. *International Journal of Research in Marketing*, *13*(3), 201–213. doi:10.1016/0167-8116(96)00010-9

Bani-Hani, I., Pareigis, J., Tona, O., & Carlsson, S. (2018). A holistic view of value generation process in a SSBI environment: a service dominant logic perspective. *Journal of Decision Systems, 27*(sup1), 46-55. doi:10.1080/12460125.2018.1468155

Bani-Hani, I., Tona, O., & Carlsson, S. (2018). From an information consumer to an information author: A new approach to business intelligence. *Journal of Organizational Computing and Electronic Commerce*, *28*(2), 157–171. doi:10.1080/10919392.2018.1444358

Bhattacherjee, A., & Sanford, C. (2006). Influence processes for information technology acceptance: An elaboration likelihood model. *Management Information Systems Quarterly*, *30*(4), 805–825. doi:10.2307/25148755

Cacioppo, J. T., & Petty, R. E. (1982). The Need for Cognition. *Journal of Personality and Social Psychology*, *42*(1), 116–131. doi:10.1037/0022-3514.42.1.116

Cacioppo, J. T., Petty, R. E., Kao, C. F., & Rodriguez, R. (1986). Central and peripheral routes to persuasion: An individual difference perspective. *Journal of Personality and Social Psychology*, *51*(5), 1032–1043. doi:10.1037/0022-3514.51.5.1032

Chilton, M. A., Hardgrave, B. C., & Armstrong, D. J. (2005). Person-job cognitive style fit for software developers: The effect on strain and performance. *Journal of Management Information Systems*, *22*(2), 193–226. doi:10.1080/07421222.2005.11045849

Chin, W. W. (2010). *How to write up and report PLS analyses*. Springer Verlag. doi:10.1007/978-3-540-32827-8_29

Clarke, P., Tyrrell, G., & Nagle, T. (2016). Governing self service analytics. *Journal of Decision Systems, 25*(sup1), 145-159. doi:10.1080/12460125.2016.1187385

Cyr, D., Head, M., Lim, E., & Stibe, A. (2018). Using the elaboration likelihood model to examine online persuasion through website design. *Information & Management*, *55*(7), 807–821. doi:10.1016/j.im.2018.03.009

Daradkeh, M. (2019a). Critical Success Factors of Enterprise Data Analytics and Visualization Ecosystem: An Interview Study. *International Journal of Information Technology Project Management*, *10*(3), 34–55. doi:10.4018/IJITPM.2019070103

Daradkeh, M. (2019b). Determinants of Self-Service Analytics Adoption Intention: The Effect of Task-Technology Fit, Compatibility, and User Empowerment. *Journal of Organizational and End User Computing*, *31*(4), 19–45. doi:10.4018/JOEUC.2019100102

Daradkeh, M. (2019c). Determinants of visual analytics adoption in organizations: Knowledge discovery through content analysis of online evaluation reviews. *Information Technology &amp. People*, *32*(3), 668–695. doi:10.1108/ITP-10-2017-0359

Daradkeh, M. (2020). Driving Business Innovation and Sustainability through Internet of Things and Data Analytics: An Innovation Stage Model. *International Journal of Innovation, Creativity and Change*, *14*(9), 149–179.

Daradkeh, M. (2021). An Empirical Examination of the Relationship Between Data Storytelling Competency and Business Performance: The Mediating Role of Decision-Making Quality. *Journal of Organizational and End User Computing*, *33*(5), 42–73. doi:10.4018/JOEUC.20210901.oa3

Daradkeh, M. (2022). The Relationship Between Persuasion Cues and Idea Adoption in Virtual Crowdsourcing Communities: Evidence From a Business Analytics Community. *International Journal of Knowledge Management*, *18*(1), 1–34. doi:10.4018/IJKM.291708

Daradkeh, M., & Al-Dwairi, R. (2017). Self-Service Business Intelligence Adoption in Business Enterprises: The Effects of Information Quality, System Quality, and Analysis Quality. *International Journal of Enterprise Information Systems*, *13*(3), 65–85. doi:10.4018/IJEIS.2017070105

Daradkeh, M., & Al-Dwairi, R. (2018). Self-Service Business Intelligence Adoption in Business Enterprises: The Effects of Information Quality, System Quality, and Analysis Quality. In Operations and Service Management: Concepts, Methodologies, Tools, and Applications (pp. 1096-1118). Hershey, PA: IGI Global.

Dishaw, M. T., & Strong, D. M. (1999). Extending the technology acceptance model with task-technology fit constructs. *Information & Management*, *36*(1), 9–21. doi:10.1016/S0378-7206(98)00101-3

Eckerson, W. (2014). *Five steps for delivering self-service business intelligence to everyone*. Retrieved 10 March 2017, from: https://www.informationbuilders.com/about_us/analyst_reports/17340

Fornell, C., & Larcker, D. (1981). Evaluating structural equation models with unobservable and measurement error. *JMR, Journal of Marketing Research*, *18*(1), 39–50. doi:10.1177/002224378101800104

Gartner. (2019). *Magic Quadrant for Analytics and Business Intelligence Platforms*. Retrieved on 6 March 2018 from https://www.gartner.com/doc/3900992/magic-quadrant-analytics-business-intelligence

Goodhue, D., Klein, B., & March, S. (2000). User evaluations of IS as surrogates for objective performance. *Information & Management*, *38*(2), 87–101.

Hair, J. F., Hult, G., Ringle, C. M., & Sarstedt, M. (2017). A Primer on Partial Least Squares Structural Equation Modeling (PLS-SEM) (2nd ed.). Thousand Oaks, CA: SAGE Publications, Inc.

Imhoff, C., & White, C. (2011). *Self-Service Business Intelligence - Empowering Users to Generate Insights*. TDWI best practices report. Retrieved January 25, 2017, from https://tdwi.org/research/list/tdwi-best-practices-reports.aspx

James, A. (2018). Using the elaboration likelihood model to guide customer service-based segmentation. *International Journal of Physical Distribution & Logistics Management*, *27*(9/10), 600–615. doi:10.1108/09600039710188657

Kirton, M. (1976). Adaptors and innovators: A description and measure. *The Journal of Applied Psychology*, *61*(5), 622–629. doi:10.1037/0021-9010.61.5.622

Kirton, M. (2003). *Adaption-innovation: In the context of diversity and change*. Routledge.

Kitchen, P. J., Kerr, G., Schultz, D. E., McColl, R., & Pals, H. (2014). The elaboration likelihood model: Review, critique and research agenda. *European Journal of Marketing*, *48*(11/12), 2033–2050. doi:10.1108/EJM-12-2011-0776

Passlick, J., Guhr, N., Lebek, B., & Breitner, M. H. (2020). Encouraging the use of self-service business intelligence – an examination of employee-related influencing factors. *Journal of Decision Systems*, *29*(1), 1–26. doi:10.1080/12460125.2020.1739884

Petty, R. E., & Cacioppo, J. T. (1986). *Communication and Persuasion: Central and Peripheral Routes to Attitude Change*. Springer-Verlag. doi:10.1007/978-1-4612-4964-1

Salisu, I., Bin Mohd Sappri, M., & Bin Omar, M. F. (2021). The adoption of business intelligence systems in small and medium enterprises in the healthcare sector: A systematic literature review. *Cogent Business & Management*, *8*(1), 1935663. doi:10.1080/23311975.2021.1935663

Schlesinger, P., & Rahman, N. (2016). Self-Service Business Intelligence Resulting in Disruptive Technology. *Journal of Computer Information Systems*, *56*(1), 11–21. doi:10.1080/08874417.2015.11645796

Schuff, D., Corral, K., St. Louis, R. D., & Schymik, G. (2018). Enabling self-service BI: A methodology and a case study for a model management warehouse. *Information Systems Frontiers*, *20*(2), 275–288. doi:10.100710796-016-9722-2

Sharda, R., Delen, D., & Turban, E. (2021). *Analytics, Data Science, & Artificial Intelligence: Systems for Decision Support* (11th ed.). Pearson. doi:10.1201/9781003140351

Stum, J. (2009). Kirton's Adaption-Innovation Theory: Managing Cognitive Styles in Times of Diversity and Change. *Emerging Leadership Journeys*, *2*(1), 66–78.

Tavera Romero, C. A., Ortiz, J. H., Khalaf, O. I., & Ríos Prado, A. (2021). Business Intelligence: Business Evolution after Industry 4.0. *Sustainability*, *13*(18), 10026. doi:10.3390u131810026

Xuequn, W., & Yanjun, Y. (2015). How individual characteristics influence people's evaluation towards information technology in different contexts. *Behaviour & Information Technology*, *34*(3), 286–293. doi:10.1080/0144929X.2014.895045

Section 2
Applications

Chapter 4
Univariate and Multivariate Filtering Techniques for Feature Selection and Their Applications in Field of Machine Learning

Dharmendra Trikamlal Patel
https://orcid.org/0000-0002-4769-1289
Smt .Chandaben Mohanbhai Patel Institute of Computer Applications, CHARUSAT, India

Nirali Honest
Smt .Chandaben Mohanbhai Patel Institute of Computer Applications, CHARUSAT, India

Pranav Vyas
https://orcid.org/0000-0002-2669-6742
Smt .Chandaben Mohanbhai Patel Institute of Computer Applications, CHARUSAT, India

Atul Patel
Smt .Chandaben Mohanbhai Patel Institute of Computer Applications, CHARUSAT, India

ABSTRACT

Machine learning's feature selection technique aids in the selection of a subset of original features in order to decrease high-dimensional data space. As per the literature, there are two basic strategies for feature selection: supervised and unsupervised. This chapter will focus on supervised filtering approaches only. Filter, intrinsic, and wrapper are the three types of supervised filtering algorithms. Filtering strategies are the subject of this chapter. The chapter covers the most popular univariate filtering algorithms with examples, advantages and downsides, and R implementation. The chapter compares univariate filtering techniques with number of parameters. The chapter also depicts two popular multivariate filtering techniques: minimum redundancy and maximum relevance (mRMR) and correlation-based feature selection (CFS) using appropriate example and implementation with R programming. Finally, the chapter deals with prominent applications of filtering techniques in context to machine learning.

DOI: 10.4018/978-1-7998-9644-9.ch004

INTRODUCTION

High-dimensional data processing is a big issue for engineers and academics in the field of Machine Learning (ML). A large number of variables can be found in high-dimensional data. In nature, certain variables are redundant and irrelevant. By removing duplicate and irrelevant data, feature selection provides a simple yet efficient solution to this problem. Removing extraneous data increases learning accuracy, decreases computation time, and makes the learning model or data easier to grasp. In practice, not all of the variables in a dataset are valuable when building a machine learning model. The addition of redundant variables reduces the model's generalization competence and may also reduce a classifier's overall precision. Furthermore, adding more variables to a model leads to the development of a complicated model.

Definition 1.1: Feature Selection: Feature selection is the process of selecting a subset of relevant features FS= {Rf1, Rf2, Rf3,...Rfm} from n (where n > m) predictors that are most significant and appropriate for any type of predictive modelling issue in Machine Learning.

The goal of feature selection is to achieve a number of things.

1. It filters out irrelevant and noisy features, leaving just those with the least amount of redundancy and the greatest relevance to the target variable.
2. It cuts down on the amount of time and effort required to train and test a classifier, resulting in more cost-effective models.
3. It increases the effectiveness of learning algorithms, prevents overfitting, and aids in the creation of more general models.

The following are the several types of feature selection strategies used in Machine Learning:

- **Supervised methods**: These approaches are utilized for labelled data and to categories relevant features in supervised models like classification and regression.
- **Unsupervised methods**: These approaches are used for data that has not been labelled.

This chapter is only concerned with supervised approaches. Different forms of supervised feature selection algorithms are depicted in Figure 1.

Filter Techniques, Intrinsic Methods, and Wrapper Techniques are the three types of supervised feature selection techniques.

Filter approaches are scalable (up to very high-dimensional data) and perform quick feature selection before classification, ensuring that the learning algorithm's bias does not interact with the feature selection algorithm's bias.

They primarily serve as rankers, arranging features in order of best to worst.

The order in which characteristics are ranked is determined by the intrinsic properties of the data, such as variance, consistency, distance, information, correlation, and so on.

There are numerous filter methods available, and new ones are produced on a regular basis; each utilizes a different criterion to determine the data's relevancy.

Wrapper approaches rely on the classifier since they use a machine learning algorithm as a black box evaluator to discover the optimal subsets of features.

As a wrapper, you can use any combination of the search strategy and modelling algorithm.

Figure 1. Supervised Feature Selection

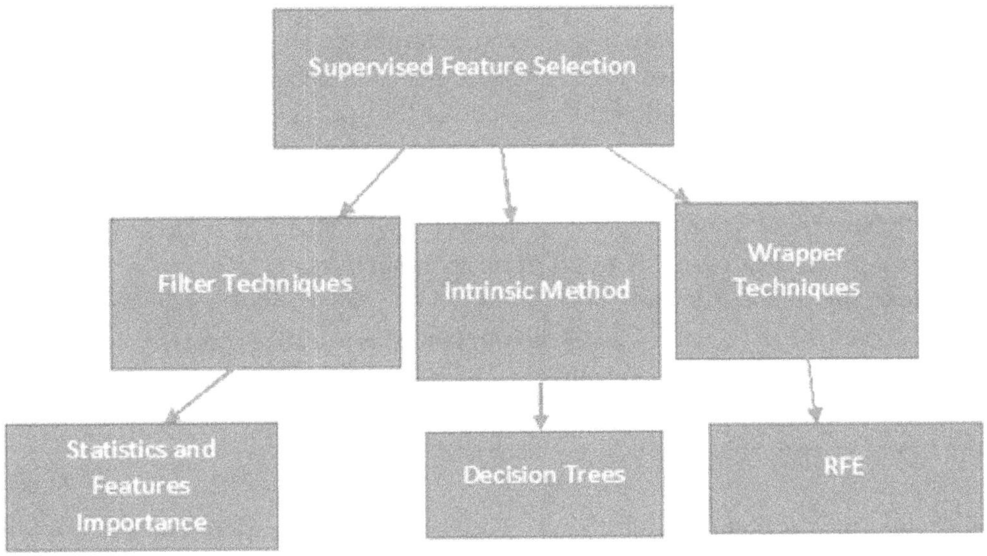

When a wrapper is used on a dataset with a lot of features, it uses a lot of computational resources and takes a long time to run.

Finally, these methods are straightforward to use and can be used to represent feature dependencies.

Intrinsic methods bridge the gap between filters and wrappers.

To begin, they employ a filter to combine measurable and statistical criteria to select some features, and then they apply a machine learning method to select the subset with the greatest classification performance.

They can describe feature relationships and lower the computational burden of wrappers without re-classifying the subsets in each iteration. They don't go through iterations.

Because feature selection is done during the learning phase, these approaches can fit models and select features at the same time. Their reliance on the classifier is one problem.

Wrapper approaches evaluate the "utility" of features based on the performance of the classifier. The filter approaches, on the other hand, measure the intrinsic qualities of the features (i.e., their "relevance") using univariate statistics rather than cross-validation performance. Wrapper methods essentially solve the "real" problem (improving classifier performance), but because of the repetitive learning processes and cross-validation, they are computationally more expensive than filter approaches. Intrinsic methods, the third class, are similar to wrapper methods in that they are likewise employed to improve the objective function or performance of a learning algorithm or model.

The focus of this chapter is on filtering strategies. Statistics for filter-based selection is vital and it's depends on variable's data type. The chapter discusses the statistics for filter-based feature selection in details. The chapter mainly focuses on popular univariate and multivariate techniques. The chapter deals with Pearson Correlation, Mutual information and maximal information coefficient (MIC) and Distance Correlation univariate techniques. The chapter compares of all univariate techniques with important parameters. Chapter also discusses multivariate filtering techniques with their pros and cons. Finally, the chapter discusses challenges of feature selection and particularly filer based selection methods.

STATISTICS FOR FILTER-BASED FEATURE SELECTION METHODS

The type of variable data has a big impact on the statistical measures you use. Numerical and categorical data types are both common, however each can be further classified into integer and floating point for numerical variables and boolean, ordinal, or nominal for categorical variables.

Variable data types that are commonly used as input variables include:

Variables with Numerical Values
Integer Variables are a type of variable that is made up of numbers.
Variables with a Floating Point Value.
Categorical Variables are Variables that Fall into One of Several Categories
Variables with Boolean Values (dichotomous).
Ordinal Variables are a type of variable.
Nominal Variables are variables that have no numerical value.

The more information about a variable's data type, the easier it is to select a statistical measure using a filter-based feature selection approach. The variables that are provided as input to a model are known as input variables. This is the group of variables that we want to shrink in size during feature selection. The output variables, also known as the response variables, are the ones that a model is supposed to predict.

The type of response variable used in predictive modelling usually indicates the sort of problem being solved. A numerical output variable, for example, signifies a regression predictive modelling challenge, whereas a categorical output variable signifies a classification predictive modelling problem.

In most cases, the statistical measures employed in filter-based feature selection are computed one input variable at a time with the target variable. As a result, they're called univariate statistical measures. This could imply that the filtering process ignores any interaction between input variables.

UNIVARIATE FILTERING METHODS

Univariate filtering methods rank and evaluate a single feature based on a set of criteria. They treat each feature as a separate entity from the feature space. In practice, it works like this: It ranks features based on a set of criteria, then chooses the highest-ranking features based on those criteria. There are numerous options for univariate selection.

Pearson Correlation

It is the simplest method to measure the linear correlation between two sets of the data (Shieh, 2010) (Bishara, 2012). It is applicable for population as well as sample data. Pearson Correlation Coefficient for population data is expressed as equation-1.

$$\rho_{i,j} = (E\ (i\text{-}\mu j)\ (j\text{-}\mu j))\ /\ (\sigma i.\sigma j) \tag{1}$$

Where E is the expected value

μ is Population Mean
σi is the standard deviation of i
σj is the standard deviation of j

If the data reveals uncentered moments than the formula is rewritten as equation-2.

$$\rho_{i,j} = (E|i.j| - E|i|.E|j|) / (\sqrt{E}\,|i^2| - (E|i|)^2).\,(\sqrt{E}\,|j^2| - (E|j|)^2 \quad (2)$$

The equation-3 depicts the Pearson 's correlation coefficient, when applied to a sample.

$$r_{ij} = \left(\sum_{p=1}^{n}(ip - \bar{i}).(jp - \bar{i})\right) / \left(\sqrt{\sum_{p=1}^{n}(ip - \bar{i})^{2}}\right).\left(\sqrt{\sum_{p=1}^{n}(jp - \bar{j})^{2}}\right) \quad (3)$$

Where n is the sample size

ip and jp are sample points indexed by p
σi is the standard deviation of i
$\bar{i}$ and $\bar{j}$ are sample mean

The correlation coefficient might be anywhere between -1 and 1. A linear equation with an absolute value of exactly 1 perfectly represents the relationship between two variables i and j, with all data points resting on a line. The regression slope determines the sign of the correlation: a value of +1 indicates that all data points sit on a line where j rises as i increases, and vice versa for a value of -1. A value of 0 indicates that the variables are not linearly related.

The Pearson correlation coefficient can be applied to any situation in which one variable is associated with multiple independent variables. The Pearson correlation coefficient determines how closely two variables are related. Consider a dataset that includes variables such as ID, Name, Attendance, Practical Skills, CGPA from all previous semesters, Sessional Performance, Case Study Performance, Unit Test Performance, Annual Family Income, Medium Language, Mind Mapping Score, and Final CGPA. The CGPA Dataset sample set is described in Table-1.

In order to determine the degree of correlation between two variables, the Pearson correlation coefficient requires numerical data. Because the second variable, "name," has categorical values, it is eliminated during the experiment. R programming is selected for the experimentation as it is best for statistical analysis and comprises of several statistical packages. R is accessible as free software under the GNU General Public License. It is compatible with all modern operating systems such as Linux, Windows, Mac OS and FreeBSD. Large numbers of individuals have contributed in development of R language; however, it was initiated by Ross Ihaka and Robert Gentleman at the Department of Statistics of the University of Auckland, New Zealand. **R language** supports very powerful functionalities such as:

- Structured programming features such as input/output, conditional statements, loop statements etc.
- Object Oriented Programming features

Table 1(a). Sample Dataset

ID	Name	Attendance	Practical Skills	First_CGPA	Second_CGPA	Third_CGPA	Sessional
1	KETULKUMAR	76	1	6	6.5	6.7	62
2	MEET PATEL	70	3	5.5	5.8	5.9	55
3	RAJ DAVE	80	4	4.9	5	4.6	47
4	DHARTI GOSWAMI	59	5	7.5	7	7.2	75
5	MOHAMMAD ABUBAK	61	2	8	8	8.3	85

- Distributed Computing features
- Data Mining and Machine Learning features
- Static and Dynamic Graphics Visualizations capabilities
- Basic Mathematics features
- Basic Statistics capability
- Big data Analytics
- Optimization Programming
- Signal Processing
- Statistical Modeling
- Simulations and random number generation etc.

The dataset, after removing second column, consists of 12 variables and 50 observations. The correlation using Pearson correlation is determined of all 11 variables with last Final_CGPA variable.

```
> cor(data[,1],data[,12], method = "pearson")
[1] -0.217527
> cor(data[,2],data[,12], method = "pearson")
[1] 0.02929361
> cor(data[,3],data[,12], method = "pearson")
[1] 0.9687768
```

Table 1(b). Sample Dataset

ID	Name	Case Study	Unit Test	Annual Income	Language of Medium	Mind Mapping Score	Final_ CGPA
1	KETULKUMAR	65	60	534847	1	22	6.9
2	MEET PATEL	60	57	504438	1	21	5.4
3	RAJ DAVE	53	43	815104	1	43	5
4	DHARTI GOSWAMI	78	70	675998	1	25	8
5	MOHAMMAD ABUBAK	87	81	540060	1	33	7.8

```
> cor(data[,4],data[,12], method = "pearson")
[1] 0.9648851
> cor(data[,5],data[,12], method = "pearson")
[1] 0.9674798
> cor(data[,6],data[,12], method = "pearson")
[1] 0.9468056
> cor(data[,7],data[,12], method = "pearson")
[1] 0.9368141
> cor(data[,8],data[,12], method = "pearson")
[1] 0.9337548
> cor(data[,9],data[,12], method = "pearson")
[1] -0.1117492
> cor(data[,10],data[,12], method = "pearson")
[1] -0.02136158
> cor(data[,11],data[,12], method = "pearson")
[1] 0.3270477
```

Based on the preceding findings, variables 3 to 8 are substantially associated to Final CGPA, implying that only those characteristics are important in predicting students' final CGPA. The results showed that Attendance,Practical Skills, CGPA of previous semesters and sessional exam result parameters are prominent for predicting students' performance. The results of all these parameters are nearer to 1 so highly correlated with final CGPA.

For feature selection, the Pearson correlation coefficient technique has a number of advantages:

- It is simple and effective technique in feature selection.
- This method not only identifies the presence or lack of correlation between any two variables, but also determines the exact extent, or degree, to which they are associated.
- We may also determine the direction of the correlation using this method, that is, whether the correlation between the two variables is positive or negative.

Despite its advantages, this approach has the following drawbacks:

- It is fairly difficult to compute since it requires sophisticated algebraic methods of calculation.
- It is heavily influenced by the values of outlier.
- It is dependent on a number of assumptions, such as linear relationships, cause-and-effect relationships, and so on, which may or may not be true.
- It's quite likely to be misconstrued, especially if the data is homogeneous.
- It takes a long time to get the results as compared to other techniques.

Mutual Information and Maximal Information Coefficient (MIC)

The maximal information coefficient (MIC) is significant in the research of correlation analysis due to the good possessions of generalization and equitability (Liu F. S., 2021) (Yuan Chen, 2016) (Yi Zhang1, 2014). It is introduced by Reshef et.al. (D. Reshef, 2011). The maximal information coefficient (MIC) is a statistic that measures the strength of a linear or nonlinear relationship between two variables X1 and X2. Binning is used by the maximal information coefficient to apply mutual information to continuous random variables. The logic is that the bins for both variables should be picked in such a way that the mutual information between the variables be utmost. When the mutual information is utmost over a binning of the data, we should assume that the following two stuffs hold:

(i) The bins would have roughly the identical size.
(ii) Each bin of *X1* will roughly relate to a bin in *Y1*.

The mutual information between two random variables X1 and X2 is defined in terms of their joint probability distribution p(X1,X2) as

$$\mathrm{I}\left|\mathrm{X1;X2}\right| = \int dX1.dX2.p\left(X1,X2\right)log2\frac{p\left(X1,X2\right)}{p\left(X1\right).p\left(X2\right)} \tag{4}$$

The value of I|X1;X2| is either zero or positive. When *p*(*X*1,*X*2) equals to *p*(*X*1).*p*(*X*2), the value of I|X1;X2| becomes zero. When X1 and X2 have any reciprocal dependency, mutual information will be greater than zero, regardless of how nonlinear that reliance is. Furthermore, the bigger the value of I | X1;X2|, the stronger the mutual reliance.

The same dataset, used in previous section, is used for the experimentation of Mutual information and maximal information coefficient (MIC). The correlation using MIC is determined of all 11 variables with last Final_CGPA variable.

```
install.packages("minerva")
library(minerva)
> mine(data[,1],data[,12])
$MIC
[1] 0.2645997
> mine(data[,2],data[,12])
$MIC
[1] 0.2242436
> mine(data[,3],data[,12])
$MIC
[1] 0.9167558
> mine(data[,4],data[,12])
$MIC
[1] 0.8876548
> mine(data[,5],data[,12])
$MIC
[1] 0.8267464
> mine(data[,6],data[,12])
$MIC
```

```
[1] 0.7651829
> mine(data[,7],data[,12])
$MIC
[1] 0.8876548
> mine(data[,8],data[,12])
$MIC
[1] 0.808226
> mine(data[,9],data[,12])
$MIC
[1] 0.3576122
> mine(data[,10],data[,12])
$MIC
[1] 0.2353784
> mine(data[,11],data[,12])
$MIC
[1] 0.3918752
```

The result shows that variables 3 to 8 are highly correlated with Final_CGPA. The results are identical with Pearson correlation coefficient. The results showed that like person correlation coefficient; Attendance,Practical Skills, CGPA of previous semesters and sessional exam result parameters are prominent for predicting students' performance. The results of all these parameters are nearer to 1 so highly correlated with final CGPA.

The pros and cons of MIC as follows:

Pros of MIC:

- Its mutual information base makes it resistant to outliers.
- The comparison and interpretation is simple as coefficient spans from [0,1].
- It can capture a wide range of linear and non-linear relationships.
- It is symmetric as based on mutual exclusion.
- No assumptions are made regarding the distribution of the variables.

Cons of MIC:

- It is computationally expensive.
- Direction and type of relationship cannot be determined.
- MIC has less statistical power in comparison of Pearson Correlation technique.

Distance Correlation

Another widely, robust and competing technique used for univariate filtering is distance correlation (Szekely, 2007). It is a correlation metric between two random vectors. The vector's dimensions may or may not be the same. It is the contrast to Pearson's correlation technique. It measures both linear and nonlinear correlation between two random variables.

Distance correlation between random vectors X1 and X2 can be defined with functions fX1(v1) and fX2(v2) as equation-5.

$$V^2(X1, X2) = [\ f_{(X1,X2)}(v1,v2) - f_{x1}\left(v1\right) f_{x2}\left(v2\right)]^2 \tag{5}$$

The function $f_{(X1,X2)}$ is a joint characteristic function of X1 and X2.

The distance correlation between X1 and X2 is defined with finite first moments M(X1, X2) by equation-6.

$$M^2(X1,X2) = (V^2\ (X1, X2)) / \ (\sqrt{V^2}\ (X1).V^2(X2)) > 0, \text{ otherwise}=0 \tag{6}$$

The distance correlation allows you to generalize the correlation between variables (X1 and X2) by M, which is specified on any dimension M 0 regardless of X1 or Y1. The distance correlation has a range of 0 M 1. M can be defined as a function of the Pearson correlation coefficient, with M(X1, X2) |(X1,X2)| equal to 1.

As per our previous example, the correlation using Distance Correlation with all 11 variables with last Final_CGPA variable is determined.

```
install.packages("energy")
library(energy)
> dcor(data[,1],data[,12])
[1] 0.2683121
> dcor(data[,2],data[,12])
[1] 0.1750382
> dcor(data[,3],data[,12])
[1] 0.9577139
> dcor(data[,4],data[,12])
[1] 0.9535812
> dcor(data[,5],data[,12])
[1] 0.9566595
> dcor(data[,6],data[,12])
[1] 0.9380037
> dcor(data[,7],data[,12])
[1] 0.9231567
> dcor(data[,8],data[,12])
[1] 0.9166817
> dcor(data[,9],data[,12])
[1] 0.2333345
> dcor(data[,10],data[,12])
[1] 0.1990728
> dcor(data[,11],data[,12])
[1] 0.338525
```

The results show that variables 3 to 8 are highly correlated with Final_CGPA variable. In this technique also it is revealed that Attendance,Practical Skills, CGPA of previous semesters and sessional exam result parameters are prominent. The advantages of distance correlation technique are:

- It is applicable to random variables of any dimensions. It is not limited to only two dimensions.
- It is able to detect linear as well as nonlinear associations among data.
- Distance correlation coefficient becomes zero only when variables are independent.
- It reveals more information than Pearson coefficient.

However, it suffers from following drawbacks:

- It shows only positive correlation among variables as distance are positive.
- The computation using Distance correlation is expensive in comparison of Pearson Correlation.
- It takes more time to generate results in comparison of Pearson Correlation.

COMPARISON OF UNIVARIATE FILTERING METHODS

The chapter dealt with three popular univariate filtering techniques: Pearson Correlation Coefficient, Mutual information and maximal information coefficient (MIC) and Distance correlation. All the techniques have experimented with one common dataset using R programming language. The results show that all are capable for determining highly correlated independent variables in context to dependent variable. The Figure-2 describes the comparison of results of univariate filtering techniques.

The results revealed that the Pearson and Distance correlation techniques are highly similar. Mutual information and maximal information coefficient (MIC) technique identified correlation effectively but correlation values are less in comparison of Pearson and Distance correlation techniques.

The table-2 describes the theoretical comparison of all three techniques based on several important parameters.

Based on comparison, it is revealed that Pearson Correlation is simple and effective technique to determine correlation among various features. However, it is applicable for only linear kind of relationship and highly influenced by outliers. The best thing is direction of relationship can be determined effectively using this technique. Mutual information and maximal information coefficient (MIC) and Distance Correlation are best suited for linear and nonlinear kind of relationship and treat outliers in effective way. However, both techniques are very complex and expensive in comparison of Pearson Correlation.

MULTIVARIATE FILTERING METHODS

High-dimensional data are increasingly being used in diverse predictive models across all fields. Predictive models face inherent obstacles when extracting knowledge from high-dimensional data with a large number of attributes and a short sample size. To build optimum predictive models, multivariate filtering methods can be used to analyze combinations of features.

The mRMR (Minimum Redundancy and Maximum Relevance) feature selection (Z. Zhao, 2019) (Sahin, 2014) (H. Peng, 2005) (N. D. Thang, 2010) (S. Ram´ırez-Gallego, 2017) is very popular mul-

Figure 2. Comparison of Results of Univariate Filtering Methods

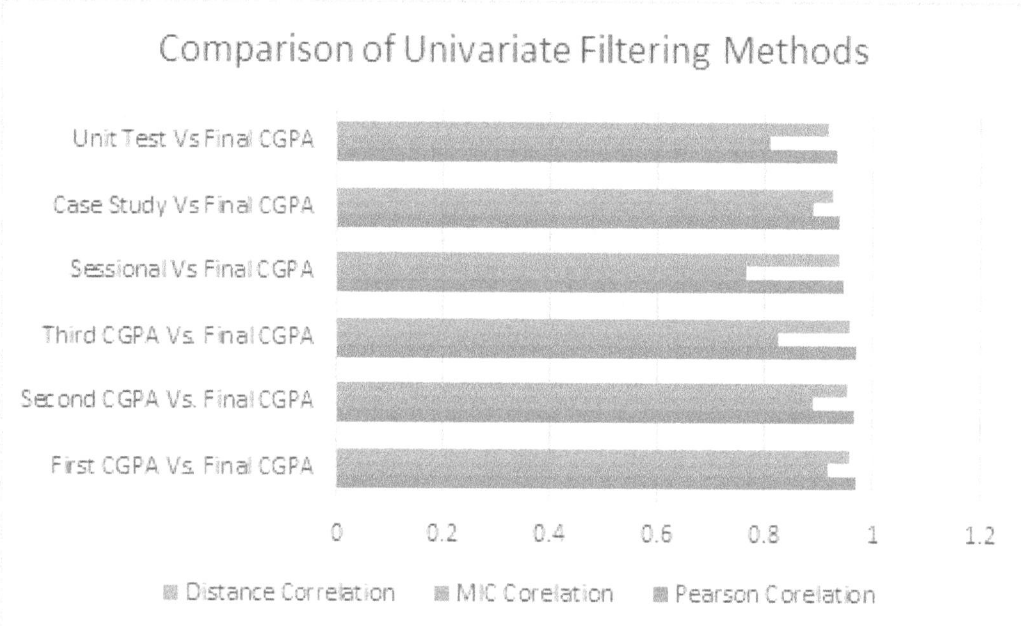

tivariate filtering method which solves the problem of NP-Complete problem by selecting the relevant features from high dimensional space while controlling for the redundancy with the selected features. Assume that there are m features fmi= {f1, f2,….fm}. The Minimum Redundancy and Maximum Relevance(mRMR) can be expressed as equation-7 (H. Peng, 2005).

$$F\left(fmi\right) = I\left(T, fmi\right) - \left(\frac{1}{|S|}\right)\sum_{fms\in S} I\left(fms, fmi\right) \tag{7}$$

Where T is the target variable, S is the set of selected features, and I is mutual information. The feature with the highest feature relevance score will be added to the selected feature set S at each step of the mRMR feature selection procedure.

Table 2. Theoretical Comparison of Univariate filtering methods

Parameter	Pearson Correlation	Mutual information and maximal information coefficient (MIC)	Distance Correlation
Implementation	Simple	Complex than Pearson and Distance Correlation	Complex than Pearson
Relationship	Only Linear	Linear and Nonlinear	Linear and Nonlinear
Outlier Handling	Influenced by Outliers	Treat Outliers effectively	Treat Outliers effectively
Direction of Relationship	Determine Direction of Relationship	Direction cannot be determined	Direction cannot be determined
Computation	Cheaper	Expensive	Expensive

Minimum Redundancy and Maximum Relevance algorithm can be applied to the situation where dataset consists of numerous variables and to select prominent features to predict target variable is vital. In this chapter, one dataset related to education domain is selected for the experimentation. The dataset comprises of 107 variables. The variable list is depicted as follows:

[1] "Sr.No" "Roll.No" "Temp.Student.ID"
[4] "Student.Name" "First.Name" "Middle.Name"
[7] "Last.Name" "Institute" "Degree"
[10] "Admission.Year" "Admission.Semester" "Admission.Term"
[13] "Current.Semester" "Semester" "Admission.Date"
[16] "Registration.Date" "Is.D2D" "Previous.Roll.No"
[19] "Gender" "Birth.Date" "Admission.Cast.Category"
[22] "Actual.Cast.Category" "ACPC.Rank" "GUJCAT.No"
[25] "MotherName" "Birth.Place" "Sub.Cast"
[28] "Religion" "Mother.Tongue" "Nationality"
[31] "Local.Address" "Local.City" "Local.Pincode"
[34] "Local.District" "Local.Taluka" "Local.State"
[37] "Local.Country" "University.Email" "Permanent.Address"
[40] "Permanent.City" "Permanent.Pincode" "Permanent.District"
[43] "Permanent.Taluka" "Permanent.State" "Permanent.Country"
[46] "Home.Phone.No" "Mobile.No" "Phone.No"
[49] "Emergency.No" "Email" "Guardian.Name"
[52] "Guardian.Address" "Guardian.City" "Guardian.PinCode"
[55] "Guardian.Mobile" "Guardian.Phone" "Guardian.Email"
[58] "Guardian.AnualIncome" "Guardian.Occupation" "Guardian.SectorType"
[61] "Guardian.IndustryType" "Guardian.Designation" "Blood.Group"
[64] "Marital.Status" "Student.Status" "Is.Handicapped"
[67] "Disablity" "Photo.Uploaded" "Belongs.to.Samaj"
[70] "Samaj.Village" "Is.Approved" "FeesPending.Y.N"
[73] "Total.Fees" "Received.Fees" "Pending.Fees"
[76] "Use.Hostel" "Detained" "Reshuffle.Date"
[79] "Reshuffle.Phase" "Last.Exam" "Seat.No"
[82] "Last.Exam.Percentage" "Last.Exam.Percentile" "Last.Exam.Passing"
[85] "Last.Exam.Board.Uni." "Last.Exam.Institute.Name" "Last.Exam.Institute.City"
[88] "Last.Exam.Institute.State" "Last.Exam.Institute.Country" "Aadhaar.Number"
[91] "Course.Reg..Status" "Counsellor" "ACPC.Merit.Marks"
[94] "Freeship.Card.Holder" "Existing.Ref..StudentID" "Attendance"
[97] "Practical.Skills" "First_CGPA" "Second_CGPA"
[100] "Third_CGPA" "Sessional" "Case.Study"
[103] "Unit.Test" "Annual.Income" "Language.of.Medium"
[106] "Mind.Mapping.Score" "Final_CGPA"

In order to predict Final_CGPA from numerous parameters suggested earlier is most tedious and complex task. Minimum Redundancy and Maximum Relevance algorithm does selection of prominent features from high dimensional data set with ease. The following is R programming code, in order to determine prominent features from the dataset:

```
d<-read.csv(file.choose(),header = TRUE) // Read the CSV file
df<-lapply(d,as.numeric) // Convert data as numeric
library(mRMRe) // Load the library
f_data <- mRMR.data(data = data.frame(df)) //Data conversion to mRMR
featureData(f_data)  //Retrieve features data in mRMR format
mRMR.ensemble(data = f_data, target_indices = 107, //Prominent features selec-
tion
+feature_count = 10, solution_count = 1) // based on Final_CGPA var
Formal class 'mRMRe.Filter' [package "mRMRe"] with 8 slots
  ..@ filters      :List of 1
  .. ..$ 107: int [1:10, 1] 60 80 101 54 102 99 103 100 96 98//Prominent fea-
tures
  ..@ scores       :List of 1
  .. ..$ 107: num [1:10, 1] 0.0105 0.0136 0.0944 0.0117 0.0953 ...
  ..@ mi_matrix    : num [1:107, 1:107] NA NA NA NA NA NA NA NA NA NA ...
  .. ..- attr(*, "dimnames")=List of 2
  .. .. ..$: chr [1:107] "Sr.No" "Roll.No" "Temp.Student.ID" "Student.Name"
...
  .. .. ..$: chr [1:107] "Sr.No" "Roll.No" "Temp.Student.ID" "Student.Name"
...
  ..@ causality_list:List of 1
  .. ..$ 107: num [1:107] NaN NaN NaN NaN NaN NaN NaN NaN NaN NaN ...
  ..@ sample_names : chr [1:50] "1" "2" "3" "4" ...
  ..@ feature_names: chr [1:107] "Sr.No" "Roll.No" "Temp.Student.ID" "Student.
Name" ...
  ..@ target_indices: int 107
  ..@ levels       : int [1:10] 1 1 1 1 1 1 1 1 1 1
```

The output of the code retrieves the features numbers 60 80 101 54 102 99 103 100 96 98 as 10 most prominent features from the dataset. According to the results Guardian.PinCode, Guardian.SectorType, Last. Exam, Attendance, First_CGPA,Second_CGPA, Third_CGPA, Sessional Case.Study, Unit.Test parameters are vital in order to determine Final CGPA of students. However, in reality, Guardian information is not important for predicting CGPA of students so you can remove those features for better prediction.

The technique has several advantages such as:

- It is a successful dimensionality reduction technology that is appropriate for high-dimensional data seen in two or more separate groups.
- It determines the greatest relevance for a classification task while controlling for redundancy of the selected set of variables, making it straightforward and effective to select significant characteristics from a huge number of variables.

However, traditional relevance and redundancy criteria have the drawbacks of being very sensitive to outlying observations and/or ineffective.

Correlation based feature selection(CFS) is another powerful feature selection technique developed by Hall and Smith (Hall & Smith, 1999). The CFS assigns a grade to each feature subgroup based on their association, which is determined by a heuristic evaluation of the function. CFS creates the class-feature correlation matrix (Gupta & Nagar, 2004) and the feature-feature correlation on the training, and then searches the subset of feature space using best-first search (Xie & Holte, 2014) (Kishimoto, Fukunaga, & Botea, 2009). CFS's feature subset evaluation equation is depicted in equation-8.

$$H_M = \frac{m\overline{rcf}}{\sqrt{m + m\left(m-1\right)\overline{rff}}} \tag{8}$$

Where H_M is the heuristic merit.

m is number of features
$\overline{rcf}$ is the mean feature-class correlation
$\overline{rff}$ is the mean feature-feature interrelation

The following is R programming code, in order to determine prominent features from the dataset:

```
library(caret)
d <- read.csv(file.choose(),header = TRUE)
d1 <- as.matrix(d)
findCorrelation(d1)
```

According to the results Last. Exam, Attendance, First_CGPA,Second_CGPA, Third_CGPA, Sessional Case.Study, Unit.Test parameters are vital in order to determine Final CGPA of students.

This method has following main advantages: (i) It has less computational complexity (ii) Less prone to overfitting and (iii) Easily scale to high dimensional dataset. However, it ignores the communication with the classifier.

APPLICATIONS AREAS OF FILTERING METHODS

Filtering methods can be applicable to number of application areas in order to select relevant features. This chapter deals with some prominent application areas where filtering methods play a vital role.

- **Text Mining**: Text mining (Feldman & James, 2007) (Berry, 2004) (Hotho, Nürnberger, & Paaß, 2005) is the conversion of unstructured text into structured data with the purpose of extracting relevant information. Because the quantity of documents in digital format is continually rising, automatic text classification is a critical application in the machine learning field. In order to identify meaningful features from high-dimensional data, text classification relies heavily on filtering algorithms (Forman, 2003) (Liu, Liu, Chen, & Ma, 2003). Feature selection aids in improving classifier performance, reducing overfitting to speed up the creation and testing of classification models, and making models more understandable.

There are two main subfields of Text Mining where feature selection plays an important role. Text classification and Text Clustering are two prominent subfields of this domain. In order to do the research, various datasets are available based on both subfields. Reauters, TREC, Web directory, Newsgroups are popular datasets of these categories. Various features selection methods are used by researchers for these categories. Bi-normal separation, chi-square document frequency, F1-measure, information gain, term strength, entropy based ranking, iterative feature selection are few popular feature selection methods for Text Classification and Clustering. The results of these techniques are evaluated with several evaluation techniques such as Accuracy, F-Measure, Precision, Recall etc.

- **Image Processing:** Image processing involves steps like image capture, enhancement, segmentation and feature extraction (Pitas, 2000) (Ekstrom, 2012) (Burger, Burge, Burge, & Burge, 2009). Feature extraction and representation is a crucial step for image processing. For useful and effective feature extractions, univariate and multivariate filtering approaches are essential. Filtering strategies aid in the efficient handling of image analysis. These methods not only reduce the input dimensionality, but they also reduce the computing load associated with extracting information from images (Barbu, She, Ding, & Gramajo, 2016) (Datta, Joshi, Li, & Wang, 2008).

Image classification is prominent subfield of this domain. Researchers have used numerous datasets for experimentation. Few popular datasets of this category is Mini-MIAS, KBD-FER, The Digits Data etc. Some popular techniques are K-means, Best fit with forward, backward and bi-directional search, KNN and Naïve Bayes Classifiers, Sequential floating backward selection etc. Entropy, Precision and MSE are important evaluation metrics of this category.

- **Natural Language Processing(NLP)**: Natural language processing (NLP) is a branch of Artificial Intelligence (AI) concerned with the elucidation and understanding of free text by machine (Yim, Yetisgen, Harris, & Kwan, 2016) (Hirschberg & Manning, 2015). Feature extraction techniques play a vital role in Natural Language Processing(NLP) to convert text into a matrix of features. In (Sammons, et al., 2016) author described a java based tool for feature extraction based on a set of generic NLP data structures. The tool comprises of filtering techniques for feature extraction for various NLP related tasks.

Sentiment analysis is prominent subfield of NLP. Class term frequency is the powerful technique of feature selections in NLP kind of applications. Stanford Twitter Sentiment test dataset is available for research in this field.

- **Bioinformatics:** Many bioinformatics applications have identified the need for feature selection strategies. Filter approaches evaluate the significance of features by focusing solely on the data's intrinsic attributes. A feature relevance score is determined in most circumstances, and low-scoring features are deleted. After that, the classification algorithm receives this selection of features as input. Filter approaches have the advantages of being able to scale to very large datasets, being computationally simple and fast, and being independent of the classification algorithm. As a result, feature selection only needs to be done once, and different classifiers may then be compared (Al-Shahib, Breitling, & Gilbert, 2005) (Bø & Jonassen, 2002) (Chuzhanova, Jones, & Margetts, 1998).

Biomarker discovery and Microarray gene expression data classification are two important subfields of this domain. Freije,Philips, DNA microarray datasets are available for the research in this field.Chi-square, Information gain,OneR,ReliefF,SVM are prominent techniques in this field. As far as evaluation is concerned, accuracy is the prominent measure.

CHALLENGES OF FEATURES SELECTION

With data collected from millions of IoT devices and sensors, today's datasets are extremely rich in information. This increases the data's dimensionality, and it's not uncommon to find datasets with hundreds of characteristics, if not tens of thousands. A Data Scientist's workflow is incomplete without feature selection. Models typically choke when faced with data with a large dimensionality since training time grows exponentially with the number of features. With an increasing amount of features, models run the risk of overfitting. Feature selection will solve these issues but to identify appropriate techniques which reduce dimensions without much loss of total information is most challenging task.

The development of high-dimensional data across a wide range of areas has presented academics with an unprecedented challenge. This problem can be solved in two ways: (a) with a large number of samples, or (b) with a large number of characteristics. In the first situation, the issue is that learning algorithms' performance is likely to degrade, but in the second case, the issue is that a large number of features reduces the interpretability of a learning model, as well as its computing efficiency. For all these reasons, scaling up learning algorithms is a challenging task.

Digital information is increasing exponentially in the high-speed era, which is useful in the business, institute, scientific, engineering, and technology, and other areas for making precise decisions and predictions. Because data mining approaches are incapable of handling such large amounts of data, big data analytics play a significant role. Big data is a research area these days since it has huge, complex, and fast features. For enormous volumes of data with high dimensions, new or updated feature selection approaches are required.

In modern era, data is collected from heterogeneous sources so there is a possibility that all features are not located at centralized space. When features are distributed across a number of locations, traditional feature selection will fail.

Every day, organizations across a wide range of industries generate a large volume of heterogeneous data. Such information may be analyzed in real time to help these businesses make better judgments. However, storing and analyzing massive, diverse information (also known as big data) in real time is difficult. Streaming feature selection has long been thought to be a superior strategy for picking relevant subset features from highly dimensional data and thereby lowering learning complexity in machine learning.

For data analysis, traditional statistical models have been the basis. However, as dataset sizes have grown in terms of sample size (n) and feature dimension (p), classic statistical data analysis methodologies have faced considerable obstacles. Identifying the significant features from the input feature space for performing final statistical analysis has been utilized as a typical strategy to address the high dimensionality difficulty. However, appropriate feature selection from high dimensional data is complex and time consuming process.

Due to the need to deal with a large number of features during data processing, high-dimensional data has made feature selection challenging, posing many hurdles in terms of efficiency and quality. These difficulties can be used to learn and research new clever ways for generating a concise set of useful features.

Filter methods of features selections also facing several challenges. One of the most evident issues in filter approaches is that various results can be achieved from the same dataset when multiple methods are used.

Another problem with filtering technique is with features ranking. The process of picking n" number of features based on their computed weights/scores is referred to as feature ranking. The weights are usually calculated depending on the relevance of a feature to the class variable. All Flter-based feature selection approaches employ a "Ranker" to score the features using statistics, information theory, or some functions of the classifier's output. Domain experts employ feature ranking as a basic approach of selecting the best feature subsets; however, Ranker search methods do not specify the amount of features to be selected, leaving the decision to the domain expert. The majority of existing ranking search algorithms use a simple strategy to display features alongside their ranking. More crucially, they delegate the decision of which features to select to the users' expertise and experience, necessitating time, attention, and precision. As a result, a new intelligent Ranker search strategy is required, one that expressly specifies which traits should be chosen and which should be ignored. The new Ranker should serve as a suggestion to the feature selection process, be completely independent, and not be dependent on the Filter-based technique. This allows the Ranker to be used with any Filter method without requiring any dependencies or data sensitivity, effectively making it a general search technique.

Another important aspect of feature selection is determining the best threshold between useful and worthless features. The majority of existing filter methods do not distinguish between cut-off values, which could allow these methods supply a small subset of characteristics instead of relying on the domain expert. Because of the various nature of datasets, their qualities, and the mathematical metrics employed by Filter techniques to determine weights for each feature, distinguishing between features is a tough undertaking. This challenging activity necessitates additional time, effort, and resources because it is dependent on the domain expert's knowledge. More research and development is needed to develop an automated feature selection technique with an inbuilt metric for determining the best threshold between informative and uninformative features without relying on a domain expert, dataset characteristics, or mathematical equations, as the Filter method does.

When identifying the best subsets during feature analysis, most feature selection-based Filter approaches ignore feature-to-feature association. It is critical to value this since it aids in the reduction of the number of characteristics available, resulting in a set that does not overlap in data instances and is distinct from one another while being connected with the class.

Class imbalance is a significant problem that arises in datasets with significantly diverse class distributions, which is frequently encountered in classification tasks and can lead to results that favor the dominant class in the dataset. When the majority of categorization examples belong to one class and only a few instances belong to a minority class, the data is said to be imbalanced. Machine learning algorithms are susceptible to data with skewed class labels because they build classifiers that favor the majority class while ignoring the minority class. This is due to the fact that data examples put into the learning algorithm tend to assume unavailable points in order to create predictions by generalizing accessible points to the full population.

A high level of noise is a major issue that makes data management difficult, and this noise is frequently caused by the technology used to collect data or the data source itself. Filter-based feature selection, which reduces dimensionality, is a frequent technique for resolving this issue. Filter approaches, on the other hand, have practical issues that have been infrequently addressed in recent research in the era of big data, where we have multiple feature kinds, sparse data, and unstructured data, among other things.

CONCLUSION

The chapter covered popular Supervised category univariate and multivariate filtering algorithms. Three typical univariate filtering strategies were reviewed, with examples and R programming language implementations. The chapter concluded that the Pearson Correlation approach is straightforward, easy to use in R programming, and determines the exact extent, or degree, to which attributes are connected. In compared to Pearson Correlation, the Mutual information and maximal information coefficient (MIC) technique is more complicated and does not indicate the direction of the relationship, but it successfully treats outliers. The Distance Correlation shares many of the same features as the MIC. Another benefit of Mutual Information, Maximal Information Coefficient, and Distance Correlation is that they can handle both linear and nonlinear relationships. The chapter covered two popular multivariate filtering techniques: Minimum Redundancy and Maximum Relevance (mRMR) and feature selection based on correlation (CFS). According to the chapter, the Minimum Redundancy and Maximum Relevance (mRMR) technique determines the most relevance for a classification job while controlling for redundancy of the specified set of variables. Correlation-based feature selection (CFS), on the other hand, has a lower computational complexity, is less prone to overfitting, and can easily scale to large datasets. The chapter also dealt with challenges of features selection methods in terms of high dimensional data and filter based techniques. Finally, the chapter finished with a discussion of how filtering techniques might be used in conjunction with Machine Learning.

REFERENCES

Al-Shahib, A., Breitling, R., & Gilbert, D. (2005). Feature selection and the class imbalance problem in predicting protein function from sequence. *Applied Bioinformatics*, *4*(3), 195–203. doi:10.2165/00822942-200504030-00004 PMID:16231961

Barbu, A., She, Y., Ding, L., & Gramajo, G. (2016). Feature selection with annealing for computer vision and big data learning. *IEEE Transactions on Pattern Analysis and Machine Intelligence*, *39*(2), 272–286. doi:10.1109/TPAMI.2016.2544315 PMID:27019473

Berry, M. W. (2004). *Survey of text mining* (Vol. 45). Springer. doi:10.1007/978-1-4757-4305-0

Bishara, A. J., & Hittner, J. B. (2012). Testing the significance of a correlation with nonnormal data: Comparison of Pearson, Spearman, transformation, and resampling approaches. *Psychological Methods*, *17*(3), 399–417. doi:10.1037/a0028087 PMID:22563845

Bø, T. H., & Jonassen, I. (2002). New feature subset selection procedures for classification of expression profiles. *Genome Biology*, *3*(4), 1–11. doi:10.1186/gb-2002-3-4-research0017 PMID:11983058

Burger, W., Burge, M. J., Burge, M. J., & Burge, M. J. (2009). *Principles of digital image processing*. Springer.

Chuzhanova, N. A., Jones, A. J., & Margetts, S. (1998). Feature selection for genetic sequence classification. *Bioinformatics (Oxford, England)*, *14*(2), 139–143. doi:10.1093/bioinformatics/14.2.139 PMID:9545445

Datta, R., Joshi, D., Li, J., & Wang, J. Z. (2008). Image retrieval: Ideas, influences, and trends of the new age. *ACM Computing Surveys*, *40*(2), 1–60. doi:10.1145/1348246.1348248

Ekstrom, M. P. (2012). *Digital image processing techniques*. Academic Press.

Feldman, R., & James, S. (2007). *The text mining handbook: advanced approaches in analyzing unstructured data*. Cambridge University Press.

Forman, G. (2003). An extensive empirical study of feature selection metrics for text classification. *Journal of Machine Learning Research*, *3*, 1289–1305.

Gupta, A. K., & Nagar, D. K. (2004). Distribution of the Determinant of the Sample Correlation Matrix from a Mixture Normal Model. *Random Operators and Stochastic Equations, 12*, 193-199.

Hall, M. A., & Smith, L. A. (1999). Feature Selection for Machine Learning: Comparing a Correlation-based Filter Approach to the. In *Proceedings of the Twelfth International FLAIRS Conference*. FLAIRS.

Hirschberg, J., & Manning, C. D. (2015). Advances in natural language processing. *Science*, *349*(6245), 261–266. doi:10.1126cience.aaa8685 PMID:26185244

Hotho, A., Nürnberger, A., & Paaß, G. (2005). A brief survey of text mining. *GLDV Journal for Computational Linguistics and Language Technology, 20*(1), 19-62.

Kishimoto, A., Fukunaga, A., & Botea, A. (2009). Scalable, Parallel Best-First Search for Optimal Sequential Planning. *Proceedings of the International Conference on Automated Planning and Scheduling*.

Liu, F. S. (2021). The Theoretical and Experimental Analysis of the Maximal Information Coefficient Approximate Algorithm. *Journal of Systems Science and Information*, *9*(1), 95–104. doi:10.21078/JSSI-2021-095-10

Liu, T., Liu, S., Chen, Z., & Ma, W.-Y. (2003). An evaluation on feature selection for text clustering. *Proceedings of the 20th international conference on machine learning (ICML-03)*.

Peng, F. L. (2005). Feature selection based on mutual information: criteria of max-dependency, max-relevance, and minredundancy. *IEEE Transactions on Pattern Analysis & Machine Intelligence, 8*, 1226–1238.

Pitas, I. (2000). *Digital image processing algorithms and applications*. John Wiley & Sons.

Ram'ırez-Gallego, S., Lastra, I., Martínez-Rego, D., Bolón-Canedo, V., Benítez, J. M., Herrera, F., & Alonso-Betanzos, A. (2017). Fast-mrmr:Fast minimum redundancy maximum relevance algorithm for high dimensional big data. *International Journal of Intelligent Systems*, *32*(2), 134–152. doi:10.1002/int.21833

Reshef, D., Reshef, Y. A., Finucane, H. K., Grossman, S. R., McVean, G., Turnbaugh, P. J., Lander, E. S., Mitzenmacher, M., & Sabeti, P. C. (2011). Detecting novel associations in large. *Science*, *6062*(334), 1518–1524. doi:10.1126cience.1205438 PMID:22174245

Sahin, G. C. (2014). A survey on feature selection methods. *Computers & Electrical Engineering*, *40*(1), 16–28. doi:10.1016/j.compeleceng.2013.11.024

Sammons, M., Christodoulopoulos, C., Kordjamshidi, P., Khashabi, D., Srikumar, V., & Roth, D. (2016). Edison: Feature extraction for nlp, simplified. *Proceedings of the Tenth International Conference on Language Resources and Evaluation (LREC'16).*

Shieh, G. (2010). Estimation of the simple correlation coefficient. *Behavior Research Methods, 42*, 906–917.

Szekely, G. J., Rizzo, M. L., & Bakirov, N. K. (2007). Measuring and testing dependence by Correlation of distances. *Annals of Statistics*, *35*(6), 2769–2794. doi:10.1214/009053607000000505

Tang, J. S. A. (2014). Feature Selection for Classification: A Review. CRC Press.

Thang, N. D. Y.-K. L. (2010). An improved maximum relevance and minimum redundancy feature selection algorithm based on normalized mutual information. *2010 10th IEEE/IPSJ International Symposium on Applications and the Internet*.

Xie, F. M., & Holte, R. (2014). Adding Local Exploration to Greedy Best-First Search in Satisficing Planning. *Twenty-Eighth AAAI Conference on Artificial Intelligence*.

Yi Zhang, S. J. (2014). A Novel Algorithm for the Precise Calculation of the Maximal Information Coefficient. *Scientific Reports, 4*(6662), 1-5.

Yim, W., Yetisgen, M., Harris, W. P., & Kwan, S. W. (2016). Natural language processing in oncology: A review. *JAMA Oncology*, *2*(6), 797–804. doi:10.1001/jamaoncol.2016.0213 PMID:27124593

Yuan Chen, Y. Z. (2016). A New Algorithm to Optimize Maximal Information Coefficient. *PLoS One*, 1–13. PMID:27333001

Zhao, Z., R. A. (2019). Maximum Relevance and Minimum Redundancy Feature Selection Methods for a Marketing Machine Learning Platform. *2019 IEEE International Conference on Data Science and Advanced Analytics (DSAA)*. 10.1109/DSAA.2019.00059

Chapter 5
Scalable Personalization for Student Success:
A Framework for Using Machine Learning Methods in Self-Directed Online Courses

Thomas Wagner
Western Governors University, USA

Morgan Diederich
Western Governors University, USA

ABSTRACT

Most online courses are self-directed, "navigate anywhere" in their design. Personalization in those courses involve drawing students' attention to the modules where they need additional study time. Using an example from an online, competency-based institution, the authors explore the steps necessary to use machine-learning-directed personalization in a way that can scale to hundreds of courses. This process is broken down into eight steps: feature selection, clustering, identification of targeted behaviors, identifying the most important modules, determining the student's location in the course, assessing what the student understands at a point in time, understanding where they are in their assessment cycle, and then using all that information to create business rules that can be coded into software to produce recommendations.

INTRODUCTION

Learning analytics sits at the intersection of big data in education, combining learning sciences, data science, and human-centered design (Society for Learning Analytics, n.d.). Computational methods continue to evolve, and exceptional levels of data are being collected in the education sphere. There is great opportunity to improve our students' experiences and learning, and to augment teacher and curricular designers' abilities to track and encourage behavior changes in curriculum and summative assessments (Dietz-Huler & Hurn, 2013; Ifenthaler, 2017). With increased computational power and data, personalized education is possible (Garcia-Penalvo et al., 2011; Tempelaar et al., 2015). Furthermore, insights

DOI: 10.4018/978-1-7998-9644-9.ch005

driven by underlying analytics need to be scalable to many courses while retaining a requisite level of quality (Liu et al., 2017). This chapter will cover a framework for a scalable, personalized feedback and recommendation engine in an open, self-directed learning environment. We call this the Content Recommendation Engine (CRE).

The CRE is built on a foundation of prior work completed by researchers across decades and disciplines. From Skinners "Teaching Machine" to computationally heavy machine learning based recommendation systems and intelligent tutoring systems, researchers are focused on improving self-directed learning through technology (Skinner, 1958; Khanal et al., 2020; Graesser et al., 2012). It is deeply rooted in self-directed learning (SDL) theory which is based on the principle that students are the drivers in their own learning (Song & Hill, 2007). Such learning environments and traits thrive on built-in scaffolding and feedback. Because of the self-directed nature in an open learning environment, direct interactions between faculty and student might only exist for those struggling the most, such as those with multiple failed assessment attempts, for those already predisposed to respond to faculty outreach, or for the proactive students who reach out to faculty themselves. Not only do we need tools to augment and assist in focusing instructor outreach, but curriculum designers also need to understand better how students are interacting with the content and assessments.

Intelligent Tutoring Systems (ITS) strive to be an adaptive, personalized tool. The main purpose of an ITS is offering suggestions, feedback, or individualized paths to view a course's curriculum or perform knowledge tasks (Larkin & Chabay, 1992). Such feedback helps students to focus their efforts, set clear goals, self-identify errors in their work, and self-regulate their own learning (Hattie and Timperley, 2007; Bimba et al., 2017). This involves feedback to review content, practice related questions, etc., prior to taking the summative assessment. Useful feedback should be task related, immediate, and intervene when there is potential misunderstanding (Van der Kleij et al., 2015). Adaptive feedback in computer-based environments can provide similar benefits to having a one-on-one tutor by leveraging computer technology (Van der Kleij et al, 2015). Intelligent tutoring systems (ITS) allow for feedback that incorporates and responds to a student's knowledge, skill, learning strategy, motivation, or emotions to meet the goals and learning outcomes throughout the educational process (Graesser et al., 2012; Erümit & Çetin, 2020).

Feedback may also come in the form of recommendations. Recommendation systems have become pervasive in the way we consume information. The term recommendation algorithms conjure up thoughts of eCommerce applications where the system identifies "people who buy A also buy B." From online shopping to video streaming services, recommendation systems consider past behavior, peers' similar patterns of behavior, and user ratings (Recker et al., 2003). Many different forms of recommendation systems exist in higher education, ranging from suggesting additional courses, recommending peers with similar interests to connect with, and pathways to progress through the content based on peers, prior behavior, and expressed interests (Manouselis et al., 2011). Personalization for online learning is a much more complex problem. Standard recommendation algorithms such as collaborative filtering are not applicable in this use case. For instance, being able to say "students who don't do practice problems in module 3 also do not complete the practice problems in module 4" is clearly not helpful advice. The Course Recommendation Engine (CRE) framework answers the problem at hand which is: given behavior of prior successful students, what kind of effort in which modules is most likely to drive improvement in a particular student success outcome. Phrased another way, the CRE builds recommendations focusing on content and actionable behaviors that a student can improve in to drive student success based on historic data and institutional knowledge.

As noted in Dietz-Uhler and Hurn's work, many institutions have worked on creating methods and software for tracking progress, sending alerts for intervention, enhancing knowledge, and more (2013). For automated personalized learning recommendations to be scalable to hundreds of courses, several quantitative methods are needed to group students into relevant learner profiles (i.e., clusters) that differentiate low- and higher-performing students with different behavior patterns, identify the course material most important to course completion (where does a difference in module engagement or performance makes a difference in outcomes), and determine student knowledge of the material. In order to be scalable, the data captured, and analyses performed need to reduce the need for people-intensive domain-specific knowledge (e.g., let the analyses determine the most important modules for predicting course completion, rather than have that be an expert-directed a-priori determination). Similarly, in the review work by Khanal et al., main attributes of successful recommendation systems include student profile data, student classifications, analyzing data, and leveraging such analysis through concepts such as content selection or generating a prediction rating (2020). Evaluating students' digital behaviors and comparing that to student like them who completed the course in prior terms allows course instructors to identify holes in students' curriculum focus in areas where additional reading or practice is recommended, and places where excessive engagement is a sign of student struggle and one-on-one instructor interaction is therefore recommended. This allows instructors to identify what may need to be taught differently, when to provide additional resources or work on study skills, or otherwise intervene on the self-directed learning path. This framework covers the Western Governors University (WGU) process for creating the CRE, key considerations, and potential alternatives to implementation.

CONTENT RECOMMENDATION ENGINE

Creating a Framework

The primary goal for the course recommendation engine (CRE) is to support instructor and student interactions by providing an in depth look at the student's behavior within the learning resources and highlight areas of potential concern. By drawing the instructor's attention to these areas, instructors may be empowered to encourage additional areas to review prior to taking their first summative assessment, or be alerted when students are making great effort, without making progress. For example, a student may be reviewing a chapter many times, but are not improving formative assessment scores. Armed with this information, the instructor may be able to provide additional resources, address misunderstandings, and continue to help students be successful in the areas that are most needed, and most indicative of success in the course. Not only does the CRE highlight where a student may be stuck on or skipping key material, but this framework also addresses how a student is doing compared to prior students with similar learner profiles on targeted behaviors. These steps may be adjusted as needed to fit the institution applying them. The following sections will describe each step-in detail, provide ideas for tailoring to the institution, as well as discuss a WGU course example.

The WGU Context

Western Governors University (WGU) offers over 500 courses and has an enrollment of 130,000. Almost all coursework is online and self-paced except for field experience courses. Students may complete the course at any time by passing the summative assessment (grading is Pass / Not Pass), and students rarely proceed through the course in a purely linear fashion. As self-directed learners, there is potential to feel overwhelmed or to lack a clear goal or path to success, reinforcing the critical need for focusing a student's attention on the content and learning activities in which they are underperforming or under-engaging. While a rather unique educational context, the framework built can be tailored to other institutions, learning contexts, and delivery methods. To develop a robust, accurate, quantitative recommendation engine, we have identified seven primary steps: (1) feature selection, (2) clustering, (3) identify targeted behaviors, (4) most important modules, (5) location in the course, (6) stage in the assessment cycle, and (7) creating business rules. We note that some of these steps may not apply to all institutions and contexts. As such, institutions should use what data they have readily available in early iterations.

DEVELOPING A COURSE RECOMMENDATION SYSTEM

Step 1 – Feature Selection

One of the key elements of the CRE is the ability to compare a student to other similar students. In order to build these learner profiles, one must first define success. This may include outcomes such as passing/failing a course, resilience, passing a final exam, or other metric that is important to the institution. As a competency-based institution, WGU students must complete the final summative assessments at or above the required cut score in order to complete the course. Therefore, the success metric often used at WGU is course completion, a binary outcome.

Once the success metric is defined, it is time to identify key student features that predict the defined success metric. For instance, one may use sequences of behavior (e.g., Kolekar et al., 2016) or student declared goals and prior education (Lazarinis et al., 2010). Feature availability will vary institution to institution, as a reflection of the different data collection and retention policies found at each institution. Once data sources are identified, the analytics team may run a variety of different models to assess the impact each feature has on the model predicting the success measure. In particular, features to initially consider include measures such as incoming GPA, course completion in prior terms, scores on other tools such as our Personal Learning Guide (a third-party tool which evaluates reading, writing and math readiness; technology competency, life factors including support from friends and family, and individual attributes such as procrastination or help-seeking behavior), and early-in-term engagement metrics such as the number of days engaged with course materials during the first week of the term. We have found that the Personal Learning Guide (PLG) is just as predictive of course completion as a collection of traditional demographics such as ethnicity, income, and gender. Furthermore, the PLG measures things for which we can provide supplemental materials and/or coaching.

Further, we recommend considering what the students know prior to the start of the course. A critical component of personalized learning is understanding that students do not enter the course with the same level of knowledge. This is especially true for institutions who have a large population of non-traditional students with significant work histories and life experience. Therefore, prior knowledge should be considered in order to evaluate what they know so we can provide appropriate recommendations. For instance, prior to starting the course, WGU students complete Course Planning Tool (CPLT) which includes a knowledge section comprised of a limited number of items drawn from the summative assessment item bank. The CPLT is an assessment taken at the beginning of the course that measures the student's knowledge based on a small set of items taken from the summative assessment item bank, confidence, and prior experience with the subject of the course. While this is a standardized tool used across our institution (see Gyll & Hayes, 2021 for additional details), an institution may also use any form of pre-assessment issued prior to curriculum exposure or other similar data they may have access to. This provides the institution with a very general estimate of pre-course competence and may be suited for clustering efforts.

If this course is taken in a student's first term at WGU, we have a somewhat limited set of academic performance data about them, such as prior institution GPA, transcript details, and their performance on the CPLT for that course. In addition, if the student has already completed a term with WGU, we can see their prior term's course completion percent, including in courses within the same academic domain (e.g., Math, Sciences), the number of credits earned at WGU, whether they achieved On-Time Progress in those prior terms (a WGU metric similar to satisfactory academic progress) and other metrics to gauge general and domain-specific demonstrated academic ability.

With the developed list of features to test, the analytics team should create a model that has good predictive power for the success metric and provide feature impacts. As course completion is a binary outcome, a variety of predictive modeling methods can be used. Particularly, we have found good success using a Generalized Additive Model (GAM), which is similar to a Logistic Regression model. GAM is advantageous in that is not limited to linear coefficients that create log-odds outcomes, but rather can choose a different type of function for each variable (e.g., variable A might have a linear relationship, variable B might be exponential, and variable C might be logarithmic) (Hastie & Tibshirani, 2017). It has the added benefit of creating student-level partial feature importances, meaning that it not only can identify the most valuable features for the model as a whole, but can also calculates partial feature importance values for each individual student (e.g., two students may have the same probability of completing the course, but for Student A it's mainly because of Features 1 and 2, but for Student B it's mainly because of Features 3 and 4). These student level feature importance values can be utilized later in clustering to create the better discrimination with respect to course completion.

Other advanced machine learning techniques have also been tested, which have included neural networks, boosted decision trees, and others. Generally, the predictive accuracy for many of these models is about the same – for example, across dozens of model types we might find Area Under the Curve (AUC) measurements of between 0.80 and 0.85. General model interpretability can be more important than maximizing the accuracy measure. Modeling should result in a handful of features that will help distinguish learners in the next step of clustering.

Example in a WGU Course

In our WGU example, we used a Generalized Additive Model (GAM) to model a wide variety of potential predictor variables to predict the binary outcome of Course Completion (yes/no). GAM creates a line graph that shows the Relative Entropy associated with individual features, and pairs of features. In the example graph below, the strongest feature in this model for predicting completion of this course is the student's CCR or "Course Completion Rate" (the number of courses completed in a term, divided by the number of courses assigned to that student) in prior terms. This is not surprising – past success in other courses is predictive of success in this course. The next best feature is Average Prior OTP, where OTP (On Time Progress) is a binary measure somewhat similar to satisfactory academic progress – it is the student's number of units earned this term on-pace with what they would need to graduate in

Figure 1. Relative (Entropy Kullback-Leibler Divergence) of Features

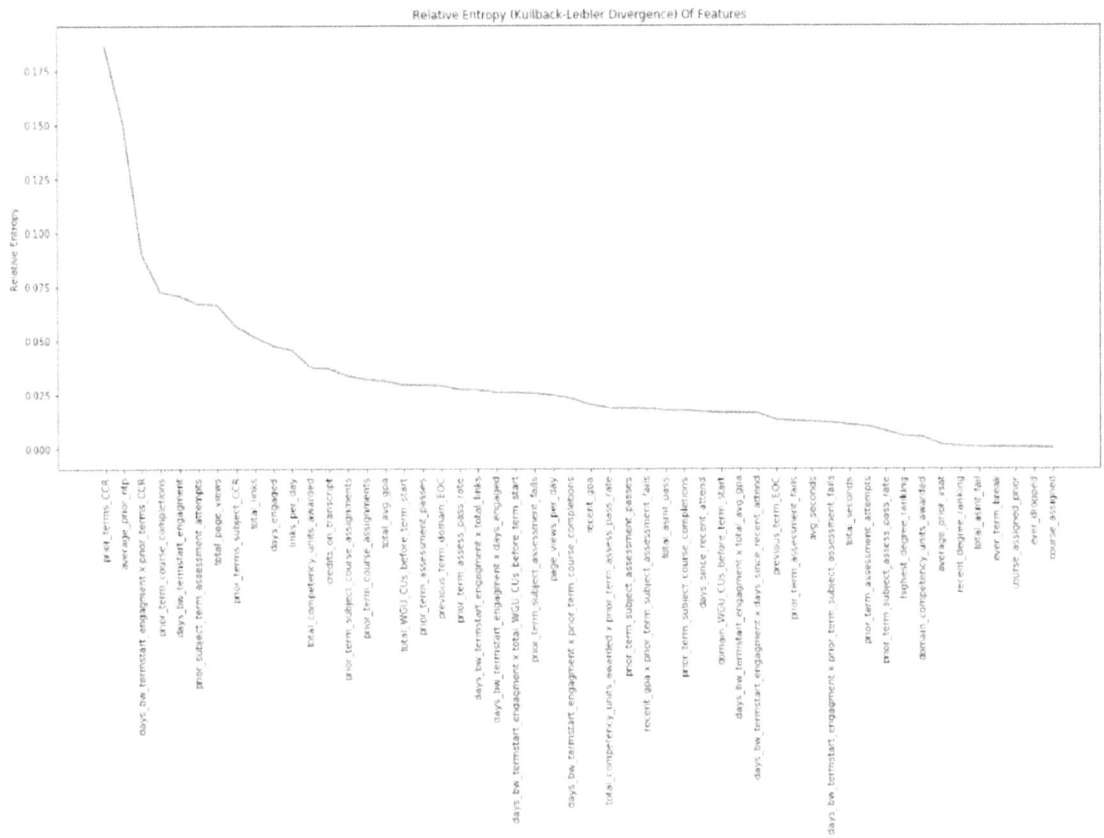

four years for an undergraduate degree, or in two years for a graduate degree. Again, this feature makes sense. The next feature is an interaction variable between prior terms CCR and "Days between term start and engagement" which is the number of days between the start of the student's term and the day they hit the "Start course" button for this particular course (which then gives them access to all the course materials and assessments).

We use this graphic (see Figure 1) to select which features to include in our clustering. We start with the features on the far left and work our way to the right. How far to the right we go is somewhat subjective, but the fundamental idea is to stop including features at a point where the entropy curve starts to flatten out. The purpose of this feature selection is to create clusters in the next step, and we want the clusters to comprehensible by the course instructors. If we include too many variables in the clustering, it can be hard for faculty to wrap their minds around the kind of student we are describing with each cluster, so we generally include four to six features in the clustering.

Step 2 – Clustering

Based on the previously selected features, clusters are created that place each student in a category with similar peers. These clusters then serve as the "students like you" benchmarks against which a given student's engagement or formative success is compared. Clusters should differentiate with respect to the data elements that comprise them (which is something the clustering algorithms inherently address), and with respect to the success metric. This creates a challenge of using an unsupervised method where clusters are created to minimize intra-cluster variation, as opposed to maximizing inter-cluster variation. In order to achieve both intra- and inter-cluster variation, supervised clustering methods are useful. Initial cluster assignment should occur as soon as possible after starting the course. The timing of this may differ from institution to institution. Within WGU, students are encouraged to take one course at a time and often finish a course in 30 days or less. For the WGU case, waiting two or three weeks into the course would be problematic as many students would be at least halfway through the course by that time. By selecting a combination of variables available on the first day of the term - or "Day Zero" - plus some very early in the term behavior such as number of link clicks, number of days with at least one click, and early attempts on pre-assessments or summative assessments during the first seven days of the term across all their courses, a comprehensive view of the student can be built early on. While some of this urgency is specific to the WGU delivery model, the use Day Zero variables are still encouraged for all institutions. Then, institutions should work to identify the earliest cutoff date that still shows strong predictive power and aligns with business rules. For instance, even though there may be more predictive power at day 14 or 21, we found engagement measures at day 7 provided strong predictive power as well. The earlier you can cluster students, the better.

Next, student-level partial feature importances are generated from the selected features. By clustering using these student-level partial feature importances rather than the nominal values, such as GPA or PLG scores, we create a form of supervised clustering. For example, students whose early-in-term learning resource engagement level as measured by the number of link clicks, has a strongly positive impact on their course completion probability. High engagement students tend to be grouped together. This can be completed across the other variables. By leveraging the feature importances, clustering outputs tend to maximize the difference in course completion percentage between high- and low-performing clusters.

When developing the actual clusters, a variety of methods are available. We have found the most success using either K-means clustering, or agglomerative hierarchical clustering (which tends to create more evenly sized clusters). Various metrics can be used to evaluate the optimal number of clusters, including Silhouette, Davies-Bouldin, and Calinski-Harabasz methods. However, these metrics often offer conflicting advice, and sometimes notably unhelpful advice, such as recommending only two clusters as the optimal number. Our experience is that the process of selecting the optimal number of clusters is more art than science. Typically, we look at the center points of the resulting clusters and keep adding to the number of clusters until we start to see two clusters that are largely the same (subjectively speaking) across the various features that define them, and stop at that point. We recommend a number somewhere between 5 and 15, so that we have enough detail to be useful in creating targeted recommendations, but not so many that faculty would have difficulty understanding the differences between them.

Example in a WGU Course

In the example below we used k-means; however sometimes we have found k-means will create unevenly sized clusters, where a single cluster may contain 50%+ of all students, and others may only contain 1-3% of all students. In those cases, we have found agglomerative hierarchical clustering provides more evenly-sized clusters – for example in a scheme with 8 clusters, we might see membership of between 10% and 20% of students in each cluster. We generally like to have at least 200 students in each cluster if possible, so having these equal cluster sizes is helpful.

Table 1. Defined Clusters and their Associated Metrics

Top Features(T1)-NEW	1	2	3	4	5	6	7
Days between term start and engagement	71.25	37.43	100.53	11.28	7.02	60.15	137.31
credits on transcript	80.5	84.8	69.97	80.9	86.36	76.23	81.33
total avg gpa	3.39	3.3	3.05	2.61	3.37	2.66	3.01
total seconds	571.75	651.69	580.42	812.54	760.3	620.28	559.08
N	1735	2433	2216	1502	1875	1411	1431
CCR	90%	88%	77%	74%	86%	79%	58%
Top Features(T2+)	8	9	10	11	12	13	14
Days between term start and engagement	120.35	26.18	121.33	21.07	17.85	37.01	19.85
Prior Term CCR	0.77	0.88	0.55	0.58	0.76	0.89	0.58
Avg prior otp	0.53	0.89	0.02	0.03	0.46	0.99	0.05
Days Engaged	3.12	6.2	2.95	2.05	2.9	2.68	5.14
Total links	2.5	10.41	2.43	1.06	1.93	2.46	5.87
N	354	325	772	1262	966	437	883
CCR	30%	75%	20%	31%	44%	65%	42%

In creating clusters, we need to have a value for each variable for each student (no missing values). Sometimes we find features that have strong predictive value, but we may not have data for all students. In some cases, there are ways to segment the students before running the clustering model to eliminate this problem. As an example, Prior Term CCR is a valuable feature in our GAM model, but obviously does not exist for a student who is in their first term at WGU. To address that, we do a separate clustering run for our Term 1 students vs. our Term 2-and-beyond students. As a result, the features used may differ, as you can see in the example below where Term 1 students occupy clusters #1 through #7, and Term 2+ students are in clusters #8 through #14. You will see the features used in the two groupings of clusters vary somewhat.

Because we created the clusters using features that are predictive of Course Completion, the resulting clusters as seen in Table 1 do a good job of differentiating between higher-performing and lower-performing students with respect to CCR: you will notice cluster #1 has 90% CCR, while at the low-end cluster #10 has only 20% CCR. You will also notice as you look across each row/feature, that the clusters differ with respect to that feature, such as cluster #1 showing a 3.39 entering GPA while #4 has only 2.61.

While we have found that clustering based on student-level partial feature importances creates even greater differentiation in CCR between the clusters (than does using the nominal values) we have not yet implemented that process. Doing so would require running each new student in the course through the GAM model in order to calculate their feature importances; however, this enhancement is planned for the coming year.

Step 3 – Targeted Behaviors

Targeted behaviors are the behaviors we want to provide recommendations about (things the student should do more of, like reading or practice questions). Ideally, these behaviors should be selected based on availability of data, their predictive power, and interventions that can be created around the behaviors.

For example, a student is completing a large number of formative assessment items could be guessing and not learning the material, a student with low page views may have skipped the material, or a student watching a video repeatedly may be missing a critical piece of information needed to help them progress in the material.

Such behaviors are included at the nominal value, and may be aggregated as necessary at the page, module/chapter, or unit level as determined by the analytics team and stakeholders. Then, these behaviors for the individual student are compared to the median of similar students in the assigned students-like-me cluster. The interpretation of such comparisons is "The student has completed a certain number of practice questions less than successful students like them." From an intervention standpoint, an instructor may see this data and – after talking with the student - recommend the student revisit the module and complete additional practice problems. The data collected for the targeted behavior and the comparisons with the cluster will then be displayed in the final dashboard. This data is also used to understand which modules are most predictive of the success metric (see Step 4 – Most Important Modules).

Further, by incorporating formative items, some additional information is provided about what the student does and does not know about the content of that module, even though these formative items are not primarily designed to assess material competency.

Once they are active in the course, we also have the formative assessment percent correct as a measure, although the usefulness of this data can be limited by certain student behaviors, such as completing many attempts until they determine the correct answers, or by the very nature of formative items which is not to assess competency but to prompt learning and discovery (Black & Wiliam, 2009). Then subsequently when they take the pre-assessment, we now have results from a psychometrically valid instrument that demonstrates overall competency at the course level and provides some information about competency at the individual competency level.

Example: in a WGU Course

In this example we have access to "event level" data that shows the date and time of each individual page that loads, and each formative item that is answered. In addition to the page number and timestamp, we know the student ID, module number, unit number, and competency (a typical course contains 2 to 5 competencies) related to that page (and therefore to the formative items on that page).

Prior to taking the Pre-assessment, we have so far evaluated what students know based on their performance on formative assessment items within each module. Generally speaking, there are two types of formative items: (1) knowledge checks which are often fairly straightforward items designed to ensure the student is engaged with the material and (2) module and unit quizzes are designed to help learners both develop competence and measure their progress toward the goal of competence. Instructors can filter to include only Module/Unit quizzes, or to include all formative items. Because we have a date/timestamp on each pageview and formative item response, we have another filter to include only items that occurred prior to (or after) the date of their first Summative Assessment attempt. If a student fails their first attempt, we can see how well they've done on the formative items since that failed first attempt.

Step 4 – Most Important Modules

Not only is this framework concerned with student behavior, but it seeks to place its recommendations in context. By identifying the most important modules for predicting success measures, students' behavior is compared to the benchmarks for each module or even down to the lesson level. Multiple lessons on a topic make up a module, and multiple modules create a unit. A course has multiple units. A predictive model can identify which modules, and which metrics within those modules (e.g., total number of pageviews vs. number of formative items attempted) are most valuable in discriminating between completers and non-completers. Extra emphasis is then given to these modules and metrics in the subsequent recommendations. For example, we often find – not surprisingly - that differences in performance on introductory modules are less predictive of course completion than success on more substantive, complex material.

To identify the most important modules, aggregation of target behaviors is done at the module level at various stages of course completion (e.g., before and after their first summative attempt). These individual student values are then compared to those of their successful peers within their cluster. Each behavior counts within a module, such as number of pageviews, and each like-you calculated value become a feature in a new predictive model that the success metric. Features are therefore comprised of both a module and a behavior/ metric (e.g., most predictive might be percent correct in module 3, or pageviews relative to students like you in module 5). This data is then fed through a wide variety of modeling techniques, including logistic regression, decision trees, boosted trees, neural networks, and generalized additive models. Each model type creates its own set of feature importances (that is, which features are most predictive (DataRobot, n.d). If multiple modeling methods identify a feature as a top performer (e.g., percent correct in module 3), then we tag that in the CRE user interface as a "most important module" and give it extra weight in the recommendations created by CRE.

The direction of the effect of these features should be considered through a partial dependency plot, or through point-biserial correlations with the success metric. For example, we often find that more questions attempted is correlated with a higher expected course completion percentage, while a large number of pageviews is often correlated with a lower course completion percentage (as this may be a sign the student is not understanding the material). Whether "more is better" or more is a "sign of struggle" is indicated in the faculty user interface and incorporated into the recommendations (see Step 7 - Business Rules below).

Implicit in many adaptive Intelligent Tutoring Systems is the assumption that formative items are measures of competency. Once a student has completed the formative items in a module with a particular score, they are now competent in that material and qualified to move on to subsequent material (including skipping some material). This is not necessarily the case with our university's courses. The formative items themselves are not psychometrically equivalent to the summative forms, so skipping material based on formative item success may not be advisable.

Example in a WGU Course

In this example, we had 224 features (23 modules, times 7 engagement and success measures for each). We ran 14 different model types, and with variations in hyperparameter and pre-processing steps, there were 56 different models run. We chose 5 top performing models which had an Area Under the Curve (AUC) of between 0.8617 and 0.8766 on the cross validation set (see Table 2 for model fit measurements). These top models were: Generalized Additive Model, eXtreme Gradient Boosted Trees classifier with Early Stopping, Regularized Logistic Regression with L2 regularization, Keras Slim Residual Neural Network Classifier using Training Schedule, and an entropy based random forest classifier.

From these analyses, outputs seen below in Figure 3 and Figure 4 are generated based on the top 5 performing models, creating a grid of 50 features (across the 5 models). We look for modules that ap-

Table 2. Predictive model – Area Under the Curve (AUC) performance

Model Features	Model Type	Sample Size	AUC
Constant Splines, Regularized Logistic Regression (L2)	Regularized Logistic Regression (L2)	8172	0.87767
Numeric Data Cleansing, Smooth Ridit Transform, Keras Slim Residual Neural Network Classifier using Training Schedule (1 Layer: 64 Units)	Keras Slim Residual Neural Network Classifier using Training Schedule (1 Layer: 64 Units)	8172	0.87701
Tree-based Algorithm Preprocessing v20	eXtreme Gradient Boosted Trees Classifier with Early Stopping	8172	0.87642
Numeric Data Cleansing, Standardize, Elastic-Net Classifier (L2 / Binomial Deviance), Light Gradient Boosting on ElasticNet Predictions	Light Gradient Boosting on ElasticNet Predictions	4086	0.87629
Numeric Data Cleansing, Standardize, Elastic-Net Classifier (L2 / Binomial Deviance), Light Gradient Boosting on ElasticNet Predictions	Light Gradient Boosting on ElasticNet Predictions	8172	0.87488
Tree-based Algorithm Preprocessing v22 with Unsupervised Learning Features	eXtreme Gradient Boosted Trees Classifier with Early Stopping and Unsupervised Learning Features	8172	0.87403
Tree-based Algorithm Preprocessing v1	Light Gradient Boosted Trees Classifier with Early Stopping	8172	0.87383
Missing Values Imputed, Generalized Additive2 Model, Text fit on Residuals (L2 / Binomial Deviance)	Generalized Additive2 Model	8172	0.87321
Missing Values Imputed, Generalized Additive2 Model, Text fit on Residuals (L2 / Binomial Deviance)	Generalized Additive2 Model	4086	0.87313
Tree-based Algorithm Preprocessing v1	eXtreme Gradient Boosted Trees Classifier with Early Stopping	8172	0.8723
Tree-based Algorithm Preprocessing v22 with Unsupervised Learning Features	eXtreme Gradient Boosted Trees Classifier with Early Stopping and Unsupervised Learning Features	4086	0.87185
Tree-based Algorithm Preprocessing v1	eXtreme Gradient Boosted Trees Classifier with Early Stopping	2043	0.86963
Tree-based Algorithm Preprocessing v20	eXtreme Gradient Boosted Trees Classifier with Early Stopping	4086	0.86845
Tree-based Algorithm Preprocessing v1	eXtreme Gradient Boosted Trees Classifier with Early Stopping	4086	0.86825
Constant Splines, Regularized Logistic Regression (L2)	Regularized Logistic Regression (L2)	4086	0.86779
Numeric Data Cleansing, Elastic-Net Classifier (L2 / Binomial Deviance) with Binned numeric features	Elastic-Net Classifier (L2 / Binomial Deviance) with Binned numeric features	4086	0.86494
Missing Values Imputed, Generalized Additive2 Model, Text fit on Residuals (L2 / Binomial Deviance)	Generalized Additive2 Model	2043	0.86484
Tree-based Algorithm Preprocessing v1	Light Gradient Boosted Trees Classifier with Early Stopping	4086	0.86427
Numeric Data Cleansing, Smooth Ridit Transform, Keras Slim Residual Neural Network Classifier using Training Schedule (1 Layer: 64 Units)	Keras Slim Residual Neural Network Classifier using Training Schedule (1 Layer: 64 Units)	4086	0.86369
Tree-based Algorithm Preprocessing v1	Light Gradient Boosted Trees Classifier with Early Stopping	2043	0.86321
Constant Splines, Regularized Logistic Regression (L2)	Regularized Logistic Regression (L2)	2043	0.86298
Numeric Data Cleansing, Smooth Ridit Transform, Keras Slim Residual Neural Network Classifier using Training Schedule (1 Layer: 64 Units)	Keras Slim Residual Neural Network Classifier using Training Schedule (1 Layer: 64 Units)	2043	0.86235
Tree-based Algorithm Preprocessing v1	Gradient Boosted Trees Classifier with Early Stopping	4086	0.86191
Numeric Data Cleansing, Elastic-Net Classifier (L2 / Binomial Deviance) with Binned numeric features	Elastic-Net Classifier (L2 / Binomial Deviance) with Binned numeric features	2043	0.86143
Numeric Data Cleansing, Standardize, Elastic-Net Classifier (L2 / Binomial Deviance), Light Gradient Boosting on ElasticNet Predictions	Light Gradient Boosting on ElasticNet Predictions	2043	0.86137
Tree-based Algorithm Preprocessing v2	RandomForest Classifier (Entropy)	4086	0.8603
Tree-based Algorithm Preprocessing v2	RandomForest Classifier (Entropy)	2043	0.85911
Missing Values Imputed, RandomForest Classifier (Gini)	RandomForest Classifier (Gini)	4086	0.85804
Regularized Linear Model Preprocessing v20	Nystroem Kernel SVM Classifier	4086	0.8573
Tree-based Algorithm Preprocessing v1	RandomForest Classifier (Gini)	4086	0.85725
Regularized Linear Model Preprocessing v2	Regularized Logistic Regression (L2)	4086	0.85676
Tree-based Algorithm Preprocessing v1	Gradient Boosted Trees Classifier with Early Stopping	2043	0.85651
Regularized Linear Model Preprocessing v19	Elastic-Net Classifier (L2 / Binomial Deviance)	4086	0.85625
Tree-based Algorithm Preprocessing v1	RandomForest Classifier (Gini)	2043	0.85495
Missing Values Imputed, RandomForest Classifier (Gini)	RandomForest Classifier (Gini)	2043	0.85396
Tree-based Algorithm Preprocessing v20	eXtreme Gradient Boosted Trees Classifier with Early Stopping	2043	0.85308
Regularized Linear Model Preprocessing v20	Nystroem Kernel SVM Classifier	2043	0.85247
Tree-based Algorithm Preprocessing v22 with Unsupervised Learning Features	eXtreme Gradient Boosted Trees Classifier with Early Stopping and Unsupervised Learning Features	2043	0.85092
Regularized Linear Model Preprocessing v2	Regularized Logistic Regression (L2)	2043	0.85034
Missing Values Imputed, RuleFit Classifier	RuleFit Classifier	2043	0.85031
Regularized Linear Model Preprocessing v19	Elastic-Net Classifier (L2 / Binomial Deviance)	2043	0.85023
Tree-based Algorithm Preprocessing v17	ExtraTrees Classifier (Gini)	2043	0.84602
Missing Values Imputed, Gradient Boosted Trees Classifier	Gradient Boosted Trees Classifier	2043	0.84502
Tree-based Algorithm Preprocessing v15	Gradient Boosted Greedy Trees Classifier with Early Stopping	2043	0.84458
Missing Values Imputed, Standardize, Regularized Logistic Regression (L2)	Regularized Logistic Regression (L2)	2043	0.83296
Numeric Data Cleansing, Standardize, Elastic-Net Classifier (mixing alpha=0.5 / Binomial Deviance)	Elastic-Net Classifier (mixing alpha=0.5 / Binomial Deviance)	2043	0.82866
Regularized Linear Model Preprocessing v22 with Unsupervised Features	Elastic-Net Classifier (mixing alpha=0.5 / Binomial Deviance)	2043	0.82864
Missing Values Imputed, Standardize, Elastic-Net Classifier (mixing alpha=0.5 / Binomial Deviance)	Elastic-Net Classifier (mixing alpha=0.5 / Binomial Deviance)	2043	0.8286
Missing Values Imputed, Standardize, Logistic Regression	Logistic Regression	2043	0.82099
Regularized Linear Model Preprocessing v5	Auto-tuned K-Nearest Neighbors Classifier (Euclidean Distance)	2043	0.81889
Missing Values Imputed, Eureqa Generalized Additive Model Classifier (1061 Generations)	Eureqa Generalized Additive Model Classifier (1061 Generations)	2043	0.81097
Missing Values Imputed, Standardize, Auto-tuned K-Nearest Neighbors Classifier (Euclidean Distance)	Auto-tuned K-Nearest Neighbors Classifier (Euclidean Distance)	2043	0.80272
Missing Values Imputed, Feature Selection for dimensionality reduction, Eureqa Classifier (Quick Search: 250 Generations)	Eureqa Classifier (Quick Search: 250 Generations)	2043	0.79406
Missing Values Imputed, Decision Tree Classifier (Gini)	Decision Tree Classifier (Gini)	2043	0.78433
Missing Values Imputed, Gaussian Naive Bayes classifier (scikit-learn), Naive Bayes combiner classifier, Calibrate predictions	Naive Bayes combiner classifier	2043	0.7619
Majority Class Classifier	Majority Class Classifier	2043	0.5

Figure 2. Course "A" most important modules

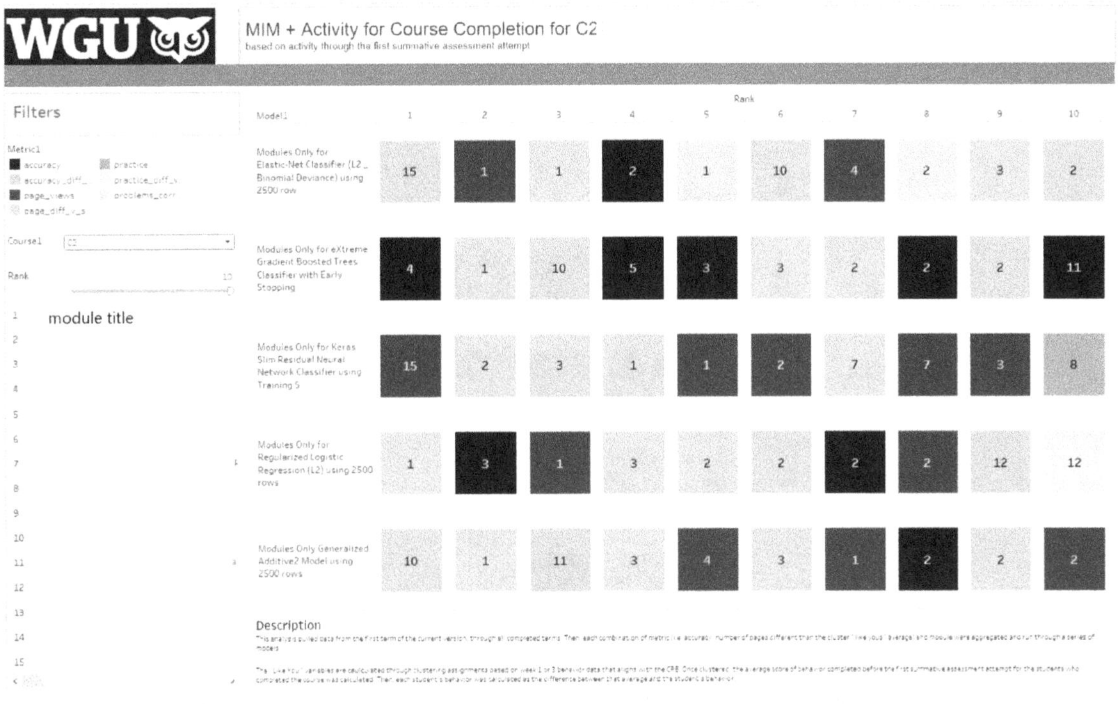

pears frequently, and metrics (e.g., pageviews, formative question count, and formative % correct) that appear frequently among those 50 features. The numbers in the boxes represent the Module number; the color of the box represents the type of metric (see legend in the upper left of the Figures). For the example analysis of two different courses, Course A modules 15,1 and 4 seem to be particularly important, especially with accuracy like you and page views like you, where Course B values include more accuracy like you on the unit quizzes, practice problems completed, as well as the nominal page values.

Step 5 – Location in the Course

Recommendations should be made that are relevant to where the student is in the course (e.g., are they early in the course in module 3 vs. later in the course in module 9). By understanding where a student is within the course, we are able to flag relevant data. Despite designed to be completed in a linear fashion, few students go through the course content in module order. Most will either "peek ahead" to later content even while they are still primarily engaged in earlier content, while others will skip entire modules and loop back to them later. Therefore, there is a need to identify their general location in the course to provide the appropriate recommendations.

As an initial rule-of-thumb, we estimate the student's location as being at their 90th percentile pageview. This is calculated by counting each pageview the student has had and sorting the pageviews in the associated page number order. Then after calculating the 90th percentile pageview, we identify the page number that corresponds to the 90th percentile pageview. For example, if a student has 200 pageviews, the 90th percentile pageview would be page 180. If page 180 is in Module 7 we assume that

Figure 3. Course "B" most important modules

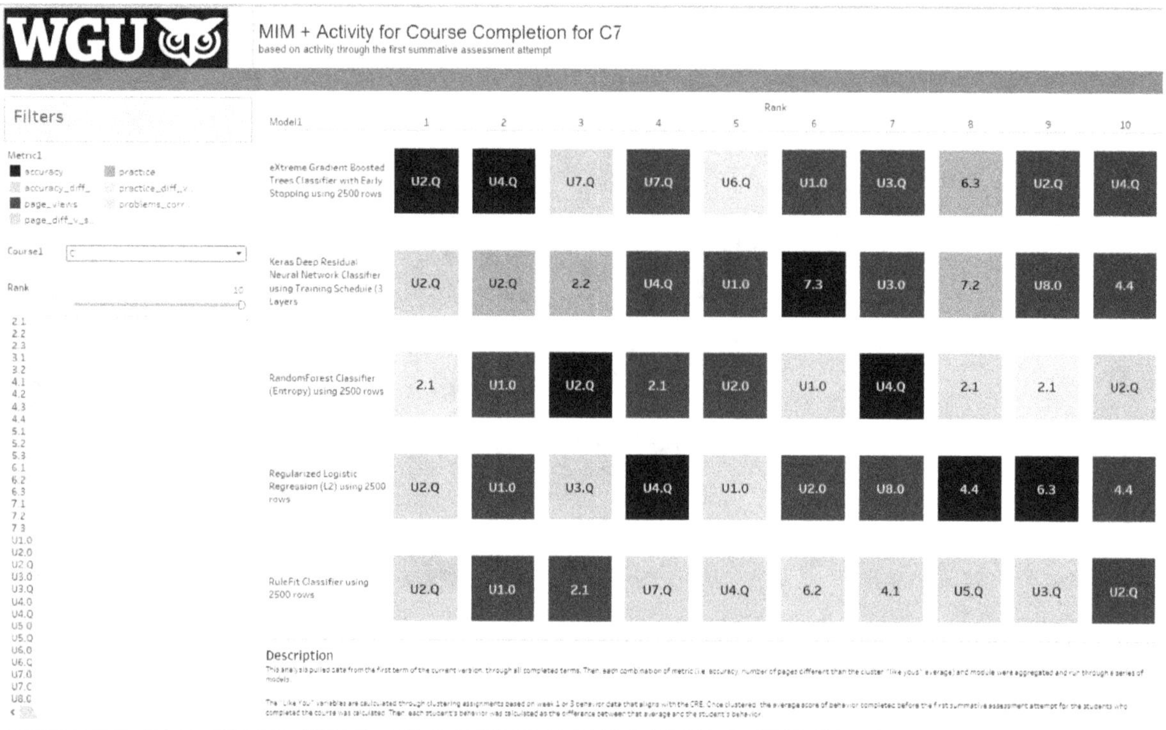

is the location of the student. We then offer recommendations for this module, and prior modules no more than five modules back (the count of modules here includes modules and the Unit Introductions and Unit Summaries). This current method may become more nuanced in the future as additional data is incorporated on the most recent pages visited. As with all steps, how the location for a student is defined will be dependent on the course that the CRE is being developed for, and the availability of data from the institution, LMS, or educational learning resource provider.

Step 6 – Stage in the Assessment Cycle

Prior to taking the pre-assessment, our understanding of what a student knows is limited to prior-term work, the CPLT, and their performance on formative items. However, the location in the assessment cycle enables us to modify recommendations in light of their performance on the pre-assessment or summative assessments. For example, based on formative item success, if the student appears to be under-engaging or under-performing in units or competencies #2 and #3, but if they subsequently take the pre-assessment and perform well on competency #2 but poorly on competency #3, a recommendation will be made to focus their attention on #3. Prior to taking the pre-assessment, our understanding of what they know is limited to the CPLT and their performance on formative items. Students are encouraged to take a pre-assessment prior to attempting the summative assessment. The pre-assessment is psychometrically equivalent to the summative assessment, meaning the pre-assessment scores evaluate which of the three to five competencies typically included in a WGU course may require more effort by the student to reach competency and therefore indicate where a student should improve their knowledge before attempting

Figure 4. A Flow of Business Rules to Generate a Recommendation

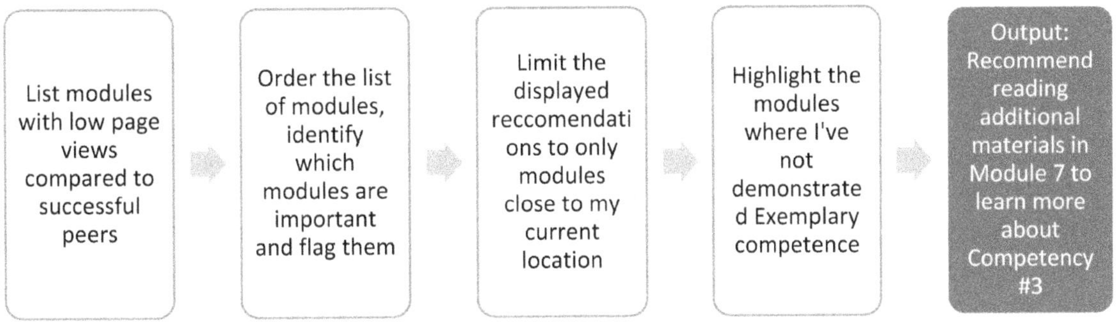

the final, summative assessment. A summative assessment attempt can provide even further evidence as to which competencies or units need more attention before attempting the summative assessment again.

Both in terms of measuring the student's activity and success in the learning resource, and in creating the "like you" benchmarks, we take into account where the student is in their assessment cycle in the course (e.g., before or after first pre-assessment, before or after first summative attempt), and the recommendations reflect this data. If a student is low on formative assessment success for a particular module but showed as competent for the corresponding unit on the pre-assessment, that shortfall in formative assessment achievement would be given less weight when determining where the student should spend more time.

Example in a WGU Course

After student completes the PreAssessment attempt or Summative Assessment attempt occurs, they receive a Coaching Report which shows them – by competency – how they performed (Unsatisfactory, Approaching Competency, Competent, Exemplary). If we see a module where their formative performance is below the median for students-like-me, but they performed at an Exemplary level in the Competency associated with that Unit, we do not recommend further study in those areas. Instead, we look for opportunities in modules that are part of Units where the student performed less well.

Step 7 – Business Rules

Lastly, business rules are created. Like all recommendations systems, once algorithmically established, one should consider the practices of the institution and recommend relevant, prescriptive actions. All the information from the prior steps needs to be combined through a set of business rules into that recommendation. An example of a business rule might be "recommend more reading in the module that shows the greatest shortfall in pageviews relative to the students-like-you benchmark, which is within five modules of the current location and is in a module where at least some pageviews have been recorded, and where the student scored below competent on the pre-assessment." Logically, this might look like Figure 4.

A set of business rules determine which modules are recommended for additional focus. There are four types of recommendations in the CRE – below we describe how our business rules for CRE were constructed (your rules may vary):

- Read more – determined by the module with the greatest pageview shortfall (vs. successful peers) that is within five modules of the current module. If this is evaluated after the first pre-assessment attempt, any units (and corresponding modules) where the student has scored "competent" or "very competent" are excluded from the recommendation list.
- Practice more – determined by the module with the greatest formative assessment percent correct shortfall that is within five modules of the current module. A similar filter as above is applied after the Pre-assessment results are available.
- Instructor intervention – this identifies any module (could be one or could be many) where there is a shortfall in the student's percent correct for any module where both pageviews and number of questions attempted exceed that of successful peers. In other words, these are cases where engagement with the learning resource is high, but formative results are not as high as we would like, so a conversation with the instructor may be warranted.
- Signs of struggle – for modules and metrics where "more is a sign of struggle" (e.g., more pageviews is associated with lower course completion %), modules with a positive variance (meaning more pageviews than successful peers) that exceeds 25% of the successful peer benchmark are displayed here

While the specific methods used in each step may vary among institutions, and adaptions will need to be made. These include feature selection based on what data is available, and in terms of stage in the assessment cycle (based on the institution's delivery model); however, the basic elements of the framework will persist. Some modifications that may be needed include:

- Ways of accounting for successful completion in situations where graded assignments are included in the final grade, in addition to the final summative assessment
- Circumstances where letter grades are awarded, and not just Pass/NotPass
- Situations where a substantial amount of faculty/student interaction and learning resource interactions by students are not done in an electronic medium where activity can be tracked.

Finally, these data, considerations, and business rules are constructed into a final view for the instructor.

Example in a WGU Course

This is where all the information we have collected are put through a set of rules in the software that determine what recommendation is made. These rules will likely evolve over time as we get further feedback from faculty. All of the rules together create the recommendation:

- Read more
  - The largest difference in pageviews vs. students-like-you who passed the course in prior terms (one module is recommended)
  - Where the absolute value of that difference is more than 25% of the students-like-you baseline (e.g., if the baseline pageview count is 10, only differences of more than 3, or less than -3 would be considered for a recommendation)
  - For a module that is within five modules of your current location (for this rule we count a Unit Introduction as a module, and Unit Summary as a module).

    - Where the module is part of a Unit where you have not yet demonstrated Exemplary performance
    - With optional filters for:
        - Only take into account activity after date of first attempt
- Practice more
    - Similar to the rules above, except based on the percent correct you've achieved vs. students like you (one module is recommended)
    - With an additional filter for:
        - Only looking at Module/Unit Quizzes (rather than "all formative items", which would include knowledge checks)
- Instructor intervention
    - Any module (more than one module may be recommended) where:
        - Pageviews and the number of formative items attempted are both higher than students-like-you
        - But percent correct on formative items is below students-like-you.
        - Filters can include "since date of first attempt" and "Module/Unit quizzes only"
- Highlighting on the detail table
    - Beneath the three groups of recommendations is a detailed table showing each module and unit, and the student's values for the three metrics (pageviews, number of question, and percent correct), and the difference between the student's value and the like-you benchmark (e.g., if I have 11 pageviews, and the benchmark is 15, the 12 would appear, and a difference of -4). Certain values are highlighted on this table:
        - If there is a difference is more than 1 standard deviation worse than the benchmark (for some metrics, a higher number is worse, and for others a lower number is worse).

Deployment

In our initial deployment, the analytics team created a Tableau dashboard to surface student-level and faculty caseload-level insights about students. Leveraging Tableau as an initial environment for the user interface layer for faculty is sufficient for the current CRE pilot needs. However, this analytics process was designed with a "web service deployment" in mind, where a variety of software applications including faculty facing as well as student facing could provide the content recommendation engine based on a student ID and a course number. Future development of the web service would return a list of recommended modules and the size of the percent correct shortfall.

This information could be displayed in a variety of contexts, including as a part of other applications where the data is retrieved in real time about a specific student by the faculty member or student (e.g., as part of a more comprehensive "learner care dashboard" that faculty use each day), to create summary reports across a faculty member's caseload such as identifying the modules where the most students are struggling, or in "push" models where – for example - all the students who are struggling in a particular module could be invited via email or text to a live event on that topic. Analytics teams should work closely with their stakeholders to develop a meaningful interface in a platform that works for the targeted users. Further, conducting pilots of the CRE will allow for additional insight, what information is useful, not used, and what may be missing to make the final tool even more powerful. Specifically, we encourage user tests and focus groups with a small group of instructors who are excited about analytics and tools like this, and maybe a few that are less interested, to get critical feedback that can be used in subsequent iterations.

Scaling

This framework can be used to tailor a CRE for any course at an institution. However, given the broader steps, there are several steps an institution may take to streamline efforts. We encourage analytics teams to develop code that can be automated and have a need for minimal interaction outside of decisions to be made.

CONCLUSION

The purpose of this framework is to identify the steps required so that institutions can build a "good enough" version of each of the seven steps, implement their system, and begin the process of faculty feedback and iterative improvement. For example, for version 1 perhaps a single variable like "prior GPA" is used to cluster students to create the like-you benchmarks, rather than going through advanced feature selection and clustering. As faculty use the system, they may help identify other variables that would be valuable for identifying different student types, and those variables can be used for a version 2 that incorporates feature selection and clustering. The key is to develop recommendations that will actually be used by and be valuable for faculty and students, and that almost certainly will be an iterative development process.

As more institutions adapt online, self-directed learning practices, analytics teams will need to continue to develop tools to aid and support their instructors and students. Further, the context of such education provides a wealth of data that can be leveraged, and such analytics can provide value to the institution at multiple levels. The Course Recommendation Engine framework is a compilation of steps an educational analytics team may take to develop a personalized, scalable content recommendation engine that facilitates instructors' ability to monitor a student's progress towards success in an online, self-directed learning environment. Information such as targeted behaviors, prior knowledge, and benchmarking against successful students provide insight to areas where students may wish to focus their efforts, where instructors can provide additional support, and what modules are important to the ultimate success of the student.

REFERENCES

Bimba, A. T., Idris, N., Al-Hunaiyyan, A., Mahmud, R. B., & Shuib, N. L. B. M. (2017). Adaptive feedback in computer-based learning environments: A review. *Adaptive Behavior*, *25*(5), 217–234. doi:10.1177/1059712317727590

Black, P., & Wiliam, D. (2009). Developing the theory of formative assessment. *Educational Assessment, Evaluation and Accountability, 21*(1), 5. doi:10.1007/s11092-008-9068-5

DataRobot. (n.d.). Feature Impact. *DataRobot | AI Cloud*. Retrieved November 15, 2021, from https://www.datarobot.com/wiki/feature-impact/

Dietz-Uhler, B., & Hurn, J. E. (2013). Using Learning Analytics to Predict (and Improve) Student Success: A Faculty Perspective. *Journal of Interactive Online Learning*, *12*(1), 10.

Erümit, A. K., & Çetin, İ. (2020). Design framework of adaptive intelligent tutoring systems. *Education and Information Technologies*, *25*(5), 4477–4500. doi:10.100710639-020-10182-8

García-Peñalvo. (n.d.). *Opening Learning Management Systems to Personal Le.pdf*. Retrieved November 15, 2021, from https://www.jucs.org/jucs_17_9/opening_learning_management_systems/jucs_17_09_1222_1240_garcia.pdf

Graesser, A. C., Conley, M. W., & Olney, A. (n.d.). Intelligent tutoring systems. In APA educational psychology handbook, Vol 3: Application to learning and teaching. APA.

Gyll, S. P., & Hayes, H. (2021). Learning and individual differences in skilled competency-based performance: Using a course planning and learning tool as an indicator for student success. *The Journal of Competency-Based Education*, *6*(3), e1259. doi:10.1002/cbe2.1259

Hastie, T. J., & Tibshirani, R. J. (2017). *Generalized Additive Models*. Routledge. doi:10.1201/9780203753781

Hattie, J., & Timperley, H. (2007). The Power of Feedback. *Review of Educational Research*, *77*(1), 81–112. doi:10.3102/003465430298487

Ifenthaler, D. (2017). Are Higher Education Institutions Prepared for Learning Analytics? *TechTrends*, *61*(4), 366–371. doi:10.100711528-016-0154-0

Khanal, S. S., Prasad, P. W. C., Alsadoon, A., & Maag, A. (2020). A systematic review: Machine learning based recommendation systems for e-learning. *Education and Information Technologies*, *25*(4), 2635–2664. doi:10.100710639-019-10063-9

Larkin, J. H., & Chabay, R. W. (2021). *Computer Assisted Instruction and Intelligent Tutoring Systems: Shared Goals and Complementary Approaches*. Routledge. doi:10.4324/9781315044361

Liu, D. Y.-T., Bartimote-Aufflick, K., Pardo, A., & Bridgeman, A. J. (2017). Data-Driven Personalization of Student Learning Support in Higher Education. In A. Peña-Ayala (Ed.), *Learning Analytics: Fundaments, Applications, and Trends: A View of the Current State of the Art to Enhance e-Learning* (pp. 143–169). Springer International Publishing. doi:10.1007/978-3-319-52977-6_5

Manouselis, N., Drachsler, H., Vuorikari, R., Hummel, H., & Koper, R. (2011). Recommender Systems in Technology Enhanced Learning. In F. Ricci, L. Rokach, B. Shapira, & P. B. Kantor (Eds.), *Recommender Systems Handbook* (pp. 387–415). Springer US. doi:10.1007/978-0-387-85820-3_12

Molenaar, I., & Knoop-van Campen, C. (2017). Teacher Dashboards in Practice: Usage and Impact. In É. Lavoué, H. Drachsler, K. Verbert, J. Broisin, & M. Pérez-Sanagustín (Eds.), *Data Driven Approaches in Digital Education* (pp. 125–138). Springer International Publishing. doi:10.1007/978-3-319-66610-5_10

Recker, M. M., Walker, A., & Lawless, K. (2003). *What do you recommend? Implementation and analyses of collaborative information filtering of web resources for education*. Academic Press.

Skinner, B. F. (1958). Teaching Machines. *Science*, *128*(3330), 969–977. doi:10.1126cience.128.3330.969 PMID:13592277

Society for Learning Analytics. (n.d.). *What Is Learning Analytics?* Retrieved December 6, 2021, from https://www.solaresearch.org/about/what-is-learning-analytics/

Song, L., & Hill, J. R. (2007). A Conceptual Model for Understanding Self-Directed Learning in Online Environments. *Journal of Interactive Online Learning*, *6*(1), 27–42.

Tempelaar, D. T., Rienties, B., & Giesbers, B. (2015). In search for the most informative data for feedback generation: Learning analytics in a data-rich context. *Computers in Human Behavior*, *47*, 157–167. doi:10.1016/j.chb.2014.05.038

Van der Kleij, F. M., Feskens, R. C. W., & Eggen, T. J. H. M. (2015). Effects of Feedback in a Computer-Based Learning Environment on Students' Learning Outcomes: A Meta-Analysis. *Review of Educational Research*, *85*(4), 475–511. doi:10.3102/0034654314564881

Chapter 6
User Sentiment Analysis and Review Rating Prediction for the Blended Learning Platform App

Md Shamim Hossain
https://orcid.org/0000-0003-1645-7470
Hajee Mohammad Danesh Science and Technology University, Bangladesh

Md. Kutub Uddin
https://orcid.org/0000-0001-8495-3789
Hajee Mohammad Danesh Science and Technology University, Bangladesh

Md. Kamal Hossain
Széchenyi István University, Hungary

Mst Farjana Rahman
Hajee Mohammad Danesh Science and Technology University, Bangladesh

ABSTRACT

Understanding how to assess the learners' evaluation has become an essential topic for both academics and practitioners as blended mobile learning applications have proliferated. This study examines users' sentiment and predicts the review rating of the blended learning platform app using machine learning (ML) techniques. The data for this study came from Google Play Store reviews of the Google Classroom app. The VADER and AFINN sentiment algorithms were used to determine if the filtered summary sentences were positive, neutral, or negative. In addition, five supervised machine learning algorithms were used to differentiate user evaluations of the Google Classroom app into three sentiment categories in the current study. According to the results of this investigation, the majority of reviews for this app were negative. While all five machine learning algorithms are capable of correctly categorizing review text into sentiment ratings, the random logistic regression outperforms in terms of accuracy.

DOI: 10.4018/978-1-7998-9644-9.ch006

INTRODUCTION

In today's fast-paced world, information moves digitally between users, potentially influencing how other users interpret an event (Hossain et al., 2021). As a result, understanding public opinion is crucial (Daudert, 2021). Because Web 2.0 has given rise to blogs, forums, and online social networks, users may now discuss and share their opinions on any topic. They could, for example, express their unhappiness with a product they bought, talk about current events, or express their political views. Many applications (such as recommender systems), as well as corporate survey analysis and political campaign planning, rely on this type of user data (Dang et al., 2020). To put it another way, data is critical to the operation of every organization. In order to stay competitive or fall farther behind, data-driven decisions are becoming increasingly vital. In today's world, massive amounts of information may be acquired. However, manually acquiring and assessing data is extremely challenging (Aslam et al., 2020), necessitating the use of artificial intelligence (AI) to efficiently acquire and analyze large amounts of data. for example, 1,85,407 users' data will be acquired and reviewed in the present project, utilizing ML programming, which is a subset of AI.

A review is a piece of feedback given by a person who has either bought and utilized the product or service, or has had some other engagement with it. Customer feedback that is found on the internet is known as user reviews (Hossain and Rahman, 2022). Electronic user reviews are peer-generated product assessments and judgements published on a company's or third-party website such as the Google Play Store. User reviews lend weight to a decision and increase confidence in the person making it (Dwidienawati et al., 2020). In addition, Wang et al. (2021) suggested that increasing the quantity and quality of assessments increased a company's profitability. Online evaluations by customers have a significant impact on product and service income, according to Chevalier and Mayzlin (2006).

Smartphone applications have grown in popularity over the previous few years (Hassan et al., 2017). Mobile applications have tended to enhance people's capacities to execute daily chores and activities. The number of applications downloaded from app stores rises in lockstep with the number of smartphones in use throughout the world (Triantafyllou et al., 2020).

App platforms like the Google Play Store and others provide app developers with a one-of-a-kind user feedback mechanism in the form of app reviews. The Google Play Store is a digital distribution platform run by Google. In addition to apps, it sells other digital items such as e-books, movies, and music. Users may discover both paid and free programs in app stores. Paid apps must be purchased before they can be used, whereas free apps can be downloaded without charge. The Google Play store allows you to download and update apps manually or automatically (McIlroy et al., 2015). Aslam et al. (2020) also discussed how developers can keep track of their apps by using ratings and reviews. App evaluations include information about the user's experience, information about issues, suggestions for additional features, and a word rating of the app.

Manually classifying app reviews is time-consuming and important for developers. Automatic categorisation of app reviews may be beneficial to developers, especially when it comes to promptly addressing mistakes. Additionally, much as they do with other online retailers, customers usually read reviews before installing an app. Ratings and reviews are linked to sales and download rankings, according to study (Finkelstein et al. 2017). Stable multiple ratings are linked to more downloads and sales (Martens and Maalej, 2019). Nonetheless, categorizing app user reviews for the purpose of obtaining helpful data for app software development is a difficult and diverse problem. It takes a complicated combination of text pre-processing, feature extraction, and machine learning approaches to categorize app assessments into specific subjects. Manually reading each review individually was previously not a practical technique (Maalej et al., 2016; Aslam et al., 2020). That is, when an app becomes more popular, it receives more reviews, making it more difficult to evaluate them. Several earlier researches have developed automated feature engineering schemas capable of categorizing reviews based on ratings or general subjects (Triantafyllou et al., 2020; Maalej et al., 2016; Aslam et al., 2020).

Because app reviews are so important in making decisions, both other users and developers may benefit from them. There haven't been any published research on evaluations of blended learning platform apps as far as we know. As a consequence, we looked at how users felt while writing and reading blended learning platform app ratings in order to forecast how they would rank the app in the present research. For this study, we used the Google Classroom app, which is a blended learning platform.

LITERATURE REVIEW

M-Learning and Apps

The incorporation of developing mobile technologies into the education area is becoming more common (Tu et al., 2020). The widespread availability of a variety of low-cost and powerful mobile devices has opened up new possibilities for moving the educational process away from traditional classrooms and toward personalized learning settings of "virtual location" and "negotiated time" (Zou et al., 2018). Smartphone applications (sometimes known as mobile apps or just apps) have been gaining traction as educational tools to supplement traditional teaching and extend learning beyond the classroom (Tu and Hwang, 2018). It is hoped that by using mobile apps, the difficulty of traditional classrooms can be greatly reduced (Tu et al., 2020). According to RnRMarketResearch.com (April 2015), the global market for mobile learning applications (apps) would rise from US$7.98 billion in 2015 to US$325 billion by 2025, with a compound annual growth rate (CAGR) of more than 7%. The largest growth rates are expected in North America, Europe, and the Asia-Pacific area throughout this time period. Furthermore, nearly 47% of corporations throughout the world are currently employing mobile devices for online training.

Mobile computing devices help to personalize M-learning (Wang et al., 2019; Herrington & Herrington, 2007; Gikas & Grant, 2013; Valk et al., 2010). A mobile learner (m-learner) can gain information at any time and from anywhere by using wirelessly linked mobile computing equipment. M-learning has become commonplace due to the rapid growth and market penetration of mobile computers (Motiwalla, 2007). Mobile content production, E-books, portable learning management systems (LMS), video-based courseware, and a variety of m-learning apps created specifically for mobile devices are all examples of m-learning (e.g. dictionaries, language learning, image editing, and math games) (Wang et al., 2019).

The sector of m-learning apps is very competitive due to its enormous development potential. M-learners already have access to a vast array of providers and learning alternatives, many of which are free. Effective and profitable m-learning applications must take use of the benefits of mobile technology while also employing the most appropriate and effective pedagogies (Wang et al., 2019). However, nothing is known about how learners feel about m-learning apps. As a result, the purpose of this study was to look at the learners' feelings and how to predict review ratings for an m-learning app.

How we educate in the classroom is continually changing and evolving as a result of technological advancements. Millennials and digital natives are today's students, who seem to incorporate technology into every area of their life. They are, nevertheless, digital immigrants with varying levels of technology proficiency (Kumar & Bervell, 2019). According to Margaryan et al. (2011), millennials do not adapt as quickly to new technologies in the classroom as we might expect. As a result, how they adopt these tools has a direct impact on their behavioral intent and the learning process' success (Esteban-Millat et al. 2018). The Learning Management System (LMS) software, which is believed to be the most extensively used educational technology tool in higher education, is one such disruptive instrument (Abazi-bexheti et al. 2018). Moodle, Blackboard, Edmodo, Schoology, Sakai, and Google Classroom are examples of LMS. Among them, Google Classroom has recently grown in popularity, relevance, and adoption as the most widely used tool in higher education (Jakkaew and Hemrungrote 2017; Kumar & Bervell, 2019). It is a free web-based learning management platform that lets anybody with a Google account to create and administer classes online. Gmail, Google Drive, Google Docs, Google Calendar, and Google Hangout are all part of the G Suite for Education, which hosts and allows parallel use of its other web-based applications such as Gmail, Google Drive, Google Docs, Google Calendar, and Google Hangout for collaborative learning across devices, primarily mobile. As a result, it is extremely convenient and suitable for mobile learning (Kumar & Bervell, 2019). Additionally, the purpose of Google Classroom is to eliminate paper work, exchange materials, increase teacher-student communication, and successfully manage classrooms with a large number of students (Jakkaew and Hemrungrote 2017). Also, Google Classroom is more useful than other LMS since it is available as a free mobile app, is simple to use, trustworthy, and provides a platform for network community with a user experience that resembles that of Facebook (Kumar & Bervell, 2019). As a result, in this study, we chose the Google Classroom app to analyze user sentiment and predict review rating.

Sentiment Analysis

User reviews are the most well-known and widely-used application of sentiment analysis. Many sorts of machine learning algorithms are utilized to analyze the feedback or reviews (Nasreen Taj & Girisha, 2021). Sentiment analysis has been used to analyze educational data (Ali et al., 2020), drug-related data (Basiri et al., 2020), and transportation-related data (Ali et al., 2020).

Sentiment analysis is a fast-emerging study topic as a result of the massive increase of digital information (Hossain and Rahman, 2022). In today's artificial intelligence era, sentiment analysis is one of the most essential methods for collecting emotion data from enormous volumes of data (Kumar et al., 2020). Sentiment analysis is a type of natural language processing (NLP) that uses machine learning techniques to evaluate text (Feizollah et al., 2019; Hossain and Rahman, 2022). Sentiment analysis seeks to understand how emotions are conveyed in texts. Sentiment analysis (SA) is a technique for determining whether emotions expressed in texts are positive, neutral, or negative toward a topic (Daudert, 2021). In essence, SA is a natural language processing-based strategy for understanding and comprehending human emotions (Yue et al., 2019; Pak & Paroubek, 2010). Sentiment analysis has grown into a powerful method for learning about people's views, with a variety of uses (Dang et al., 2020).

Nasukawa and Yi (2003) created the phrase "sentiment analysis" to define the process of determining the subjective polarity (negative or positive) and polarity strength (slightly positive, highly positive, weakly positive, etc.) of a consumer's review text, or determining the writer's attitude. The method of extracting emotions, ideas, and feelings from text is called sentiment analysis (Ravi & Ravi, 2015). From consumer happiness to political ideals (Ravi & Ravi, 2015; Borg and Boldt, 2020; Mäntylä et al., 2018), the field has applications.

The term "sentiment analysis" is a broad term that covers a wide range of issues. Sentiment analysis, for example, can encompass sentiment classification, subjectivity classification, and opinion spam identification, among other things. Other components of sentiment categorization, such as polarity determination, ambiguity resolution, and others, are also covered (Ravi & Ravi, 2015). The introduction of a massive supply of opinionated data via the internet, as well as its wide range of applications in many parts of life, has resulted in a recent explosion in popularity for sentiment analysis (Garay et al., 2019). Sentiment analysis is a branch of NLP that categorizes the polarity of a text's conveyed attitude (for example, positive, negative, or neutral) (Amin et al., 2019). The assessment theory is a psychological theory that explains why individuals express themselves in the manner they do.

Based on Systemic Functional Linguistics (SFL), Appraisal Theory focuses on how language transmits positive or negative assessments as well as how attitudes and emotions define interpersonal offers and propositions (Barcena et al., 2020; Martin and White, 2005). Furthermore, appraisal theory is a theoretical framework utilized in SFL to distinguish between various forms of evaluative statements (Martin and White, 2005). It sees meaning as a collection of decisions made by the speaker or writer, and it shows how these decisions are represented in the SFL lexicon and syntactic structure of evaluative writing (Halliday and Matthiessen, 2004). According to appraisal theory, emotions are produced by our judgments (appraisals or estimations) of experiences that provoke various reactions in different people. To put it another way, our evaluation of a situation triggers an emotional, or affective, reaction (Scherer et al., 2001). Syntactic structure, despite its complexity, may be investigated via the lens of a local grammar since it is affected by a variety of unique overlapping issues outside the scope of evaluation theory. Local grammars explain the patterns that emerge when linguistic events occur at random in a text and are articulated with a variety of linguistic resources. Appraisal theory and local grammar specify the functions of an assessment statement. Appraisal theory describes how languages interact with one another by informing the reader how they feel (or think) about things and people. It is an interpersonal meaning notion used to mediate interpersonal connections by telling the reader how they feel (or think) about things and people (Widyaningrum et al., 2019; Read and Carroll, 2012). Although Appraisal Theory has been used to examine reviewer sentiment, it has not been utilized to assess the sentiment of blended learning platform app users, especially how they feel when writing reviews.

The majority of sentiment analysis (SA) research analyzes subjective data from internet reviews. These surveys provide a quick snapshot of public sentiment about a certain institution or product, such as a hotel. For example, Kanna and Pandiaraja (2019) studied consumer sentiment in product reviews, whereas Al Ajrawi et al. (2021) studied customer review star ratings sentiment analysis. Instead of reviewing reviews manually, SA analyzes them and provides timely information using machine learning (ML) technology. In recent years, a slew of machine learning-based sentiment analysis techniques have been introduced. The most commonly used technique for sentiment analysis is polarity detection (Han et al., 2018). Supervised learning techniques and lexicon-based learning methods (unsupervised learning methods) are the two types of learning methods available (Saif et al., 2016; Jurek et al., 2015). Consumer reviews have been employed in a number of recent studies to gauge customer attitudes (Feizollah et al., 2019; Luo and Xu, 2021; Mostafa, 2020; Mostafa, 2019; Mostafa, 2018), but reviews of blended learning platform apps have yet to be explored. Thus, we employed two lexicon-based unsupervised learning approaches to evaluate the sentiment of users of a blended learning platform app and five supervised learning methods to predict review rating in the current study.

Research Questions

A few questions about user reviews of the blended learning platform app have yet to be answered. Although such inquiries are required for a blended learning platform app to learn about its users' viewpoints, in these proposals, we're particularly interested in finding answers to the four research questions listed below.

Lexicon-based Sentiment Analysis Approaches

The two primary methods for conducting sentiment analysis with text mining tools are lexicon-based and corpus-based sentiment analysis (Hossain and Rahman, 2022; Miao et al., 2010). In contrast, the corpus-based approach for determining sentiment orientation is rarely used in research. In both circumstances, whether the two approaches outlined above are based on a pre-defined expert vocabulary or a corpus of subjective phrases, the sentiment score is generated by comparing the phrase supplied against an expert-defined dictionary entry. Various lexicons are available for sentiment analysis (Hossain and Rahman, 2022; Preethi et al., 2015); lexicon-based techniques are straightforward to implement, and they have been used in several recent and comparable investigations (Hossain and Rahman, 2022; Machová et al., 2020; Yang et al., 2020). Using lexicon-based methodologies to analyze emotions has a number of advantages, which embrace the following: (i) lexicon-based approach is cross-domain well-matched and ideal for social media material; (ii) it entails no training instances; and (iii) it can read the sentiment of a text containing emoticons, slang, capital letters, conjunctions, punctuation, and other quirks. As a result, Afinn and VADER sentiment algorithms, both lexicon-based machine learning techniques, were employed in this investigation.

Finn Rup Nielsen designed Afinn, a simple yet widely used sentiment analysis vocabulary. Afinn uses a wordlist technique to analyze sentiment, which comprises around 3300 words, each with a polarity score ranging from -5 (the highest total for negative emotion) to 5 (the highest total for positive emotion) (the highest score for positive sentiment). The AFINN object's Score () function accepts a sentence and returns a score. which may be received a positive, neutral, or negative score.

The AFINN lexicon, which is unquestionably one of the most fundamental and extensively used lexicons for sentiment analysis, has been utilized in previous studies (Tan and Guan, 2021; Vashishtha & Susan, 2020; Kim and Chung, 2020). After examining the results of the fuzzy technique on three benchmark datasets: the hotel reviews dataset, the polarity movie dataset by Pang and Lee (2008), and the IMDB dataset, Vashishtha and Susan (2020) determined that the AFINN lexicon has the highest accuracy. Furthermore, one of the objectives of the study is to categorize consumers' emotions into three groups: good, negative, and neutral. Another aim is to figure out which customers have the most positive opinions and which have the most negative opinions. As a result, the AFINN lexicon was employed in this inquiry.

On the other hand, VADER is a reviewer sentiment analysis tool that has been fine-tuned to recognize emotions on social networking sites using language and parsimonious criteria. Popular social media terms, acronyms, slang, gestures, and emojis are all understood by the VADER emotion lexicon (Pano and Kashef, 2020). The frameworks outperformed human raters on Twitter data. In addition, VADER sentiment fared similarly well or better than seven other sentiment analysis lexicons (Hutto and Gilbert, 2014). It's frequently faster than supervised machine learning algorithms since it doesn't require any training. VADER sentiment creates an emotion score vector for each sentence that contains negative, neutral, positive, and compound polarities for each sentence. As a result, in our inquiry, we used the VADER vocabulary.

Users' tweets about online learning (Mujahid et al., 2021), tweets (Bhaumik and Yadav, 2021), news (Nemes & Kiss, 2021), and stock market (Oliveira et al., 2016) were among the sectors where lexicon-based techniques were used to extract a score from textual data and identify the most positive and negative sentences, but not in blended learning platform app reviews. As a consequence, we employed two lexicon-based algorithms to determine sentiment ratings and the top positive and negative reviews in the current study.

We'd want to use our research to find answers to the following research questions:

(a) How do lexical tools rate in the Google Classroom app reviews?
(b) How could we discover the most vehemently negative and positive evaluations of Google Classroom?

Length and Rating of the Review

According to Zeelenberg and Pieters (2004), when people are consuming with others, they are more likely to show negative feelings (such as unhappiness or rage). Unhappy customers are more inclined to share their unhappiness with others by submitting a negative review. Bad is more potent than good when it comes to grabbing attention (Fors Brandebo et al., 2016). Negative experiences, sentiments, and facts carry more weight and have a higher impact than good information, emotions, or similar situations in general (Baumeister et al., 2001). Additionally, significantly unfavorable feedback has a higher influence on brand impressions than slightly negative or exceptionally positive product reviews. These events are referred to as the "negativity effect" or "negativity bias" (Lee et al., 2009). According to Rodrguez-Hidalgo et al. (2015), negative feelings exceed pleasant feelings in web posts.

According to this argument, negative emotions are more likely to develop longer written connections in online evaluations, similar to how negative emotions speed up spoken exchanges in face-to-face conversations (i.e., resulting in longer and more extensive verbal exchanges). As a result, if someone is unhappy with a product or a brand, they are more inclined to tell others about it (Ghasemaghaei et al., 2018). Consumers who have had a negative experience with a product or service are more willing to share their thoughts and feelings with others. Hence, negative feedback in the form of online user evaluations is more likely to be lengthier than positive input (Jiménez-Zafra et al., 2017).

From January 2012 to December 2015, Ghasemaghaei et al. (2018) used database scraping technologies to evaluate a panel dataset of learner evaluations for house, auto, and life insurance, finding that lengthier review content was related to lower review ratings. In this study, we also want to see if there's a relationship between review duration and emotion classifications. With the results of our study, we'd want to answer the following research question:

(c) Does the length of a review of the Google Classroom app influence its rating?

Performance of Machine Learning Models

Furthermore, the support vector machine (SVM) shows remarkable efficiency and precision in the majority of supervised learning-based research. Gul (2021) claimed that SVM had the highest classification accuracy when it came to determining the kind of spillway. Mullen and Collier (2004) introduced a sentiment classification method based on SVMs that allocated values to phrases and words before merging them to construct a text classification model. The efficacy of supervised machine learning algorithms for sentiment categorization in the movie domain was investigated by Pang et al. (2019), who discovered that the SVM technique beats the Naive Bayes method.

According to Ye et al. (2009), who used a controlled tool to discover sentiment learner ratings on traveler review websites, the SVM beat the Nave Bayes technique. An SVM-based sentiment analysis prediction was created by Preethi et al. (2015). They claim that SVM has the following benefits: (a) It is resistant to overfitting, (b) it can handle large feature regions, and (c) it is very good at extracting attitudes and even predicting knowledge from large social media datasets.As a result, in this study, we use five machine learning approaches to predict Google Classroom app users' attitudes (SVC, logistic regression, k-neighbors classifier, random forest classifier, and decision tree classifier), and we want to see how well each model works in the context of the Google Classroom app.

To acquire an answer to the following research question, we'd want to create a new query:

(d) Which machine learning models are more accurate in predicting user ratings for Google Classroom apps?

METHOD

Google Play, formerly known as the Android Market and now known as the Google Play Store, is a Google-owned and operated digital distribution platform. It serves as the official app store for certified Android and Android-based devices as well as Chrome OS, allowing users to browse and download apps built using Google's Android software development kit (SDK). Customer purchase decisions are heavily influenced by online reviews (von Helversen et al., 2018). Users may leave a review and a star rating on any app in the Google Play store (https://play.google.com/store/apps) to share their personal experience with it (low to high satisfaction). In the app stores, each app has its own page. The app's title, developer, star rating, description, comparable applications, upload date, user reviews, thumbnails, video previews, and a download link are all included on the page (McIlroy et al., 2015). We chose Google Classroom (id = com.google.android.apps.classroom) as the most popular blended learning platform app in this survey. This is a free service available to schools, non-profits, and anybody with a Google account. The classroom makes it simple for students and teachers to communicate both within and outside of the classroom. The Classroom helps you establish courses, distribute assignments, communicate, and stay organized while saving time and paper. In this study, the Google-play-scraper module in Python was used to collect all reviews, as well as the name of the reviewer, the date, and the number of likes for each review. As a consequence, the TF-IDF (Term Frequency Inverse Document Frequency) vectorizer was used to convert text into an acceptable numerical representation after eliminating punctuations, stopwords, and missing values from user evaluations. After the data was sanitized, the feelings of consumers were analyzed using AFINN Sentiment and VADER (Valence Aware Dictionary for sEntiment Reasoning), two lexicon-based intrinsic Python programming tools.

The emotions of the users were assessed based on the rating stars they gave when submitting their review message. Assuming the reviewers gave negative sentiments 1 and 2 stars, happy feelings 5 and 4 stars, and neutral feelings 3 stars, we generated a score of -1 for negative sentiment (1 and 2 stars), 0 for neutral sentiment (3 stars), and 1 for positive sentiment (5 and 4 stars).

Finally, five machine learning models were used to predict users' sentiments regarding the Google Classroom app: SVC, logistic regression, k-neighbors classifier, random forest classifier, and decision tree classifier. In addition, accuracy, precision, recall, R squared, and F1-Score were used to evaluate the research models' performance. To evaluate the research findings, Python scripts must be run in a Jupyter notebook after importing the necessary machine learning packages such as pandas, seaborn, wordcloud, Afinn, and vaderSentiment.

RESULTS AND DISCUSSION

Table 1 shows the number of app reviews in proportion to the number of stars. Positive reviews received four and five stars, neutral reviews received three stars, and negative reviews received one and two stars. According to our analysis of 185,407 Google Classroom app reviews, 51 percent of reviewers have a bad impression of the app, 44.56 percent have a favorable opinion, and just 4.43 percent have a neutral opinion (shown in Table 2).

Table 1. Number of google classroom app reviews against review star

Score	Number of reviews
1	88170
2	6391
3	8220
4	11331
5	71295

Table 2. The number and percentage of Google Classroom App Reviews in relation to various types of sentiments

Sentiment	Reviews	%
Negative	94561	51.00
Positive	82626	44.56
Neutral	8220	4.43
Total	185407	100.00

Using the def word count (text string) function, we calculated the average number of words in the review text for each emotion type, finding that negative sentiment has 8.904 words, neutral sentiment has 16.17 words, and positive sentiment only has 7.16 words (presented in Table 3). As a consequence, we've determined that longer review material correlates with neutral sentiments. This shows that neutral app users are more inclined to share their ideas with others and write more words in their Google Classroom app evaluations than both pleased and dissatisfied app users.

Table 3. In relation to various types of sentiments, the average word count, Afinn score, and Vader score

sentiment	word_count	afinn_score	vader_neg	vader_neu	vader_pos	vader_compound
Negative	8.904199	-1.07454	0.3001	0.63482	0.065081	-0.22269
Neutral	16.16971	1.409002	0.064837	0.669527	0.265635	0.197927
Positive	7.158037	2.547358	0.018878	0.477998	0.503124	0.42976

Table 4. AFINN score statistics in relation to various types of sentiments

sentiment	count	mean	std	min	25%	50%	75%	max
-1	94561.0	-1.074544	2.357611	-48.0	-3.0	0.0	0.0	42.0
0	8220.0	1.409002	2.602818	-28.0	0.0	1.0	3.0	21.0
1	82626.0	2.547358	2.310335	-69.0	1.0	3.0	3.0	64.0

In this study, the polarity scores for 1,85,407 instances were calculated. The polarity ratings in the AFINN Sentiment Lexicon varied from -48 to 42 (as shown in Table 4) for negative sentiments, with a mean value of -1.07, and from -28 to 21 for neutral feelings, with a mean value of 1.41. Positive feelings range from -69 to 64, with a mean score of 2.54. Tables 5 and 6 show the top ten positive and negative review messages, respectively. Although a machine learning system might show the complete review text, we simply presented one line of each text from the entire review.

Table 5. Top 10 google classroom negative reviews based on afinn score

	content	afinn_score
181779	I hate it I hate it I hate it I hate it I hate it I hate it I hate it I hate it I hate it I hate...	-48
109365	Bad bad bad bad bad bad bad bad bad bad bad this is the app that gave me depression and suicidal...	-35
141274	worst worst worst appp in the world so bad bad bad bad .Does not uploads assingment files.I got ...	-30
103067	Terrible, putrid, awful, detrimental, horrid, infuriating, substandard, inept, unpleasant, abomi...	-30
133502	Thank you for your time and lack of water and sewer line and we will be in a bad to redirect htt...	-28
167578	Bad bad bad bad bad bad bad bad bad	-27
98465	Very bad app, worst, bad bad bad bad bad bad, ekdomm faltu, ke banay eto baaler jinish, saala Co...	-24
8494	It's totally not worth it, racist, classist, sexist, homophobic, transphobic, islamophobic, disg...	-24
163453	Bad bad bad bad bad bad bad when I want to remove something it say something went wrong try agai...	-22
154197	BAD BAD BAD BAD BAD BAD DO NOT PUT ON YOUR PHONE IT GIVES IT A VIRUS IM HAVING TO GET A NEW PHON...	-21

According to Table 7, the mean polarity score for unfavorable emotions for VADER positive was 0.065, -0.3 for VADAR negative, 0.635 for VADAR neutral, and -0.223 for VADER compound. The mean polarity score for neutral emotions was 0.266 for VADAR positive, 0.064 for VADAR negative,

Table 6. Top 10 google classroom positive reviews based on afinn score

	content	afinn_score
41209	I am very intelligent but in Corona I stayed at home but this app is very helpful to me thanks t...	64
93564	So nice app I never like this app super super super super super super super super super super su...	50
99654	Uh oh stinky poop hahahahaha poopies funny poopies alalalahahaha funny poop poop funny weeeeeee ...	42
120490	TO ALL STUDENTS: Please. Realize how fortunate you are to have the chance to acquire knowledge w...	34
104141	Very nice teaching super perfect all is very good that only I will tell ok a is very very super ...	32
147059	This is amazing super very good very good very good very good very good very good all of you dow...	32
24348	Yes mam is a good friend of the family and she has a very strong family pack and I am sure that ...	31
19318	Great experience I have about this is amazing app I may like to use this app further and I will ...	31
41432	The ek h, and the rest is the most important part in a couple more information about your busine...	29
169113	This app is the best of them all what I like about it most is that you can keep in touch with yo...	29

0.67 for VADAR neutral, and 0.2 for VADAR compound, whereas the mean polarity score for positive emotions was 0.503 for VADER positive, 0.02 for VADAR negative, 0.478 for VADAR neutral, and 0.43 for VADER compound.

Table 7. AFINN and VADER scores statistics in relation to various types of sentiments

sentiment	afinn_score	vader_neg	vader_neu	vader_pos	vader_compound
-1	-1.07454	0.3001	0.63482	0.065081	-0.22269
0	1.409002	0.064837	0.669527	0.265635	0.197927
1	2.547358	0.018878	0.477998	0.503124	0.42976

Finally, Table 8 shows the performance ratings of several models. SVC, logistic regression, k-neighbors classifier, random forest classifier, and decision tree classifier accuracy scores were 83.80, 84.099, 76.917, 83.605, and 80.022, respectively. Based on the data, all of the models successfully detect users' review texts; nevertheless, logistic regression produces the best result. Furthermore, the ratio of true positives to all positives for the SVC, logistic regression, k-neighbors classifier, random forest classifier, and decision tree classifier was 0.816, 0.822, 0.748, 0.811, and 0.791, respectively, for the SVC, logistic regression, k-neighbors classifier, random forest classifier, and decision tree classifier. SVC, logistic regression, k-neighbors classifier, random forest classifier, and decision tree classifier all have recall scores of 0.838, 0.841, 0.769, 0.836, and 0.818, respectively. Furthermore, our research discovered that, when compared to other approaches, logistic regression provides the greatest validity and completeness of data in terms of accuracy and recall values. The F1 scores for the SVC, logistic regression, k-neighbors classifier, random forest classifier, and decision tree classifier models were 0.821, 0.826, 0.754, 0.818, and 0.795, respectively, indicating that logistic regression was more effective than the others. Also, with the lowest mean squared error value of 0.498, the logistic regression indicated stronger influence efficacy than the

Table 8. Performance of machine learning models

Model	accuracy	precision	recall	f1_score	mean_squared_error
SVC	83.80	0.816	0.838	0.821	0.513
Logistic Regression	84.099	0.822	0.841	0.826	0.498
KNeighborsClassifier	76.917	0.748	0.769	0.754	0.782
RandomForestClassifier	83.605	0.811	0.836	0.818	0.519
DecisionTreeClassifier	80.022	0.791	0.800	0.795	0.607

others. The results show that logistic regression is the most efficient machine learning model for classifying user evaluations of the Google Classroom app.

APPLICATIONS

Learning app creators, in particular, must be conscious of their customers' emotions. Because there is so much user-generated material, precise approaches for evaluating and distinguishing viewpoints are required. App developers may leverage users' psychological perspectives to improve their programs, and users can make rapid judgments about whether or not to install apps based on this knowledge. By providing a foundation of information on the sentiment of learning app evaluations, our research will assist both creators and consumers of learning applications. Furthermore, professionals will benefit greatly from this research. It's difficult to overlook the commercial applications of sentiment analysis. Sentiment analysis in the workplace has the potential to transform how companies function. The capacity to extract significant insights from unstructured data is critical for a data-driven organization to prosper. In today's internet era, when businesses are suffering from data overload, companies may have a significant amount of client comments collected (which does not always equal better or deeper insights). People are still finding it challenging to manually review it without making mistakes or being biased. As a result, our findings may be applicable to a wide range of apps, not only learning apps.

Users who are neutral or dissatisfied also leave lower review scores and write lengthier reviews, indicating that they are more inclined to inform others about their emotions of neutrality or dissatisfaction. As a consequence, when confronted with a large number of complaints to examine and reply to, app developers may opt to focus on the longer reviews in order to figure out why customers are dissatisfied with their services. They'd be able to respond to unfavorable input faster, reducing the harm they could do to their organization.

Finally, logistic regression provides the greatest accuracy score for estimating user sentiment of blended learning apps, according to our research. As a result, learning app developers may be able to use logistic regression to acquire the best outcomes when assessing user behavior toward their products and services. Understanding consumer behavior may be a critical success factor in today's competitive business environment. This will assist companies in developing new strategies while operating in a fast-paced environment. The findings of the study, which can be tweaked and applied to a variety of problems, might help merchants as well as service industries like banking and healthcare.

CONCLUSION AND LIMITATIONS

App evaluations might be a valuable, one-of-a-kind source of data for software engineering teams, expressing genuine users' perspectives and needs. Potential customers read reviews before downloading an app, much like they do when buying other goods on the Internet.However, classifying app user evaluations in order to acquire useful data for app software development is a challenging and varied challenge. To classify app ratings into particular subjects, a complex mix of text pre-processing, feature extraction, and machine learning algorithms is necessary. Previously, manually reading each review was not a viable option. That is, when an app's popularity grows, it receives more reviews, making it more difficult to assess it. Machine learning approaches capable of classifying reviews and predicting user ratings in a short amount of time are examples of automated feature engineering schemas.

We used different machine learning algorithms to examine reviewers' attitudes for the Google Classroom app in the current study because of the relevance of app reviews. Initially, we analyzed sentiment using lexicon-based techniques such as AFINN Sentiment and VADER Sentiment, and our findings revealed that the majority of shopping app evaluations were unfavorable. We were able to identify the top ten negative and positive reviews, as well as the link between review text length, review rating, and emotion, using lexicon-based approaches. In this study, we discovered that longer review content is associated with neutral feelings. This demonstrates that neutral app users are more likely than both delighted and unsatisfied app users to share their opinions with others and write more words in their Google Classroom app ratings. According to our statistics, 51% of reviewers have a negative opinion about Google Classroom applications, 44.56 percent have a good attitude, and only 4.43 percent have a neutral attitude. Finally, we discovered that all five machine learning algorithms (SVC, logistic regression, k-neighbors classifier, random forest classifier, and decision tree classifier) can reliably predict user review scores, with logistic regression outperforming the others.

There are several flaws in our investigation. Because the dataset employed in this study is limited, the results have suffered. To determine the findings' generalizability, more research is needed across a variety of sites, including the Apple App Store, the Galaxy Store, and others. Future research on the Google Classroom app might collect and compare data from a variety of sources.

Furthermore, our findings suggest that reviews may be classified using both supervised and unsupervised machine learning techniques. However, temporal and location-based features have yet to be examined, meaning that attitudes may be influenced by assessments from diverse geographical regions and cultures. It may be a study issue to investigate in the future in order to enhance the review classification findings. It could also be interesting to test the linked approaches with a larger sample from other countries.

Finally, an illicit market for false app reviews has emerged, with the goal of assisting app creators in improving their ratings and standings in app stores. In our study, we did not utilize any phony app reviews to exclude them, but future researchers should do so in order to obtain more credible results.

REFERENCES

Ali, S., Wang, G., & Riaz, S. (2020). Aspect based sentiment analysis of ridesharing platform reviews for kansei engineering. *IEEE Access: Practical Innovations, Open Solutions*, *8*, 173186–173196. doi:10.1109/ACCESS.2020.3025823

Amin, A., Hossain, I., Akther, A., & Alam, K. M. (2019). Bengali VADER: A Sentiment Analysis Approach Using Modified VADER. *2019 International Conference on Electrical, Computer and Communication Engineering (ECCE)*. 10.1109/ECACE.2019.8679144

Aslam, N., Ramay, W. Y., Kewen, X., & Sarwar, N. (2020). Convolutional Neural Network Based Classification of App Reviews. *IEEE Access: Practical Innovations, Open Solutions*, *8*, 1–1. doi:10.1109/ACCESS.2020.3029634

Barcena, E., Read, T., & Sedano, B. (2020). An Approximation to Inclusive Language in LMOOCs Based on Appraisal Theory. *Open Linguistics*, *6*(1), 38–67. doi:10.1515/opli-2020-0003

Basiri, M. E., Abdar, M., Cifci, M. A., Nemati, S., & Acharya, U. R. (2020). A novel method for sentiment classification of drug reviews using fusion of deep and machine learning techniques. *Knowledge-Based Systems*, *198*, 105949. Advance online publication. doi:10.1016/j.knosys.2020.105949

Bhaumik, U., & Yadav, D. K. (2021). Sentiment Analysis Using Twitter. In J. K. Mandal, I. Mukherjee, S. Bakshi, S. Chatterji, & P. K. Sa (Eds.), *Computational Intelligence and Machine Learning. Advances in Intelligent Systems and Computing* (Vol. 1276). Springer. doi:10.1007/978-981-15-8610-1_7

Borg, A., & Boldt, M. (2020). Using VADER Sentiment and SVM for Predicting Customer Response Sentiment. *Expert Systems with Applications*, *162*, 113746. Advance online publication. doi:10.1016/j.eswa.2020.113746

Chevalier, J. A., & Mayzlin, D. (2006). The Effect of Word of Mouth on Sales: Online Book Reviews. *JMR, Journal of Marketing Research*, *43*(3), 345–354. doi:10.1509/jmkr.43.3.345

Dang, N. C., Moreno-García, M. N., & De la Prieta, F. (2020). Sentiment analysis based on deep learning: A comparative study. *Electronics (Switzerland)*, *9*(3), 483. Advance online publication. doi:10.3390/electronics9030483

Daudert, T. (2021). Exploiting textual and relationship information for fine-grained financial sentiment analysis. *Knowledge-Based Systems*, *230*, 107389. Advance online publication. doi:10.1016/j.knosys.2021.107389

Dwidienawati, D., Tjahjana, D., Abdinagoro, S. B., Gandasari, D., & Munawaroh. (2020). Customer review or influencer endorsement: Which one influences purchase intention more? *Heliyon*, *6*(11), e05543. Advance online publication. doi:10.1016/j.heliyon.2020.e05543 PMID:33294687

Finkelstein, A., Harman, M., Jia, Y., Martin, W., Sarro, F., & Zhang, Y. (2017). Investigating the relationship between price, rating, and popularity in the Blackberry World App Store. *Information and Software Technology*, *87*, 119–139. doi:10.1016/j.infsof.2017.03.002

Fors Brandebo, M., Nilsson, S., & Larsson, G. (2016). Leadership: Is bad stronger than good? *Leadership and Organization Development Journal*, *37*(6), 690–710. doi:10.1108/LODJ-09-2014-0191

Garay, J., Yap, R., & Sabellano, M. J. (2019). An analysis on the insights of the anti-vaccine movement from social media posts using k-means clustering algorithm and VADER sentiment analyzer. *IOP Conference Series. Materials Science and Engineering*, *482*, 012043. doi:10.1088/1757-899X/482/1/012043

Ghasemaghaei, M., Eslami, S. P., Deal, K., & Hassanein, K. (2018). Reviews' length and sentiment as correlates of online reviews' ratings. *Internet Research*, *28*(3), 544–563. doi:10.1108/IntR-12-2016-0394

Gikas, J., & Grant, M. M. (2013). Mobile computing devices in higher education: Student perspectives on learning with cellphones, smartphones & social media. *Internet and Higher Education*, *19*, 18–26. doi:10.1016/j.iheduc.2013.06.002

Gul, E., Alpaslan, N., & Emiroglu, M. E. (2021). Robust optimization of SVM hyper-parameters for spillway type selection. *Ain Shams Engineering Journal*, *12*(3), 2413–2423. Advance online publication. doi:10.1016/j.asej.2020.10.022

Halliday, M. A. K., & Matthiessen, C. M. I. M. (2004). *An Introduction to Functional Grammar* (3rd ed.). Edward Arnold.

Han, H., Zhang, Y., Zhang, J., Yang, J., & Zou, X. (2018). Improving the performance of lexicon-based review sentiment analysis method by reducing additional introduced sentiment bias. *PLoS One*, *13*(8), e0202523. Advance online publication. doi:10.1371/journal.pone.0202523 PMID:30142154

Hassan, S., Tantithamthavorn, C., Bezemer, C.-P., & Hassan, A. E. (2017). Studying the dialogue between users and developers of free apps in the Google Play Store. *Empirical Software Engineering*, *23*(3), 1275–1312. doi:10.100710664-017-9538-9

Herrington, A., & Herrington, J. (2007, November). *Authentic mobile learning in higher education.* Paper presented at Australian Association for Research in Education, Fremantle, Australia.

Hossain, M. S., & Rahman, M. F. (2022). Detection of potential customers' empathy behavior towards customers' reviews. *Journal of Retailing and Consumer Services*, *65*, 102881. doi:10.1016/j.jretconser.2021.102881

Hossain, M. S., Rahman, M. F., & Zhou, X. (2021). Impact of customers' interpersonal interactions in social commerce on customer relationship management performance. *Journal of Contemporary Marketing Science*, *4*(1), 161–181. doi:10.1108/JCMARS-12-2020-0050

Jakkaew, P., & Hemrungrote, S. (2017). The use of UTAUT2 model for understanding student perceptions using Google Classroom: A case study of Introduction to Information Technology course. In *2nd Joint International Conference on Digital Arts, Media and Technology 2017: Digital Economy for Sustainable Growth, ICDAMT 2017* (pp. 205–209). Institute of Electrical and Electronics Engineers Inc. 10.1109/ICDAMT.2017.7904962

Jurek, A., Mulvenna, M. D., & Bi, Y. (2015). Improved lexicon-based sentiment analysis for social media analytics. *Security Informatics*, *4*(1), 9. Advance online publication. doi:10.118613388-015-0024-x

Kanna, P. R., & Pandiaraja, P. (2019). An Efficient Sentiment Analysis Approach for Product Review using Turney Algorithm. In *Procedia Computer Science* (Vol. 165, pp. 356–362). Elsevier B.V. doi:10.1016/j.procs.2020.01.038

Kastrati, Z., Imran, A. S., & Kurti, A. (2020). Weakly Supervised Framework for Aspect-Based Sentiment Analysis on Students' Reviews of MOOCs. *IEEE Access: Practical Innovations, Open Solutions*, *8*, 106799–106810. doi:10.1109/ACCESS.2020.3000739

Kim, J. C., & Chung, K. Y. (2020). Knowledge expansion of metadata using script mining analysis in multimedia recommendation. *Multimedia Tools and Applications*. Advance online publication. doi:10.100711042-020-08774-0

Kumar, J. A., & Bervell, B. (2019). Google Classroom for mobile learning in higher education: Modelling the initial perceptions of students. *Education and Information Technologies*, *24*(2), 1793–1817. Advance online publication. doi:10.100710639-018-09858-z

Lee, M., Rodgers, S., & Kim, M. (2009). Effects of valence and extremity of eWOM on attitude toward the brand and website. *Journal of Current Issues and Research in Advertising*, *31*(2), 1–11. doi:10.1080/10641734.2009.10505262

Luo, Y., & Xu, X. (2021). Comparative study of deep learning models for analyzing online restaurant reviews in the era of the COVID-19 pandemic. *International Journal of Hospitality Management*, *94*, 102849. Advance online publication. doi:10.1016/j.ijhm.2020.102849 PMID:34785843

Maalej, W., Kurtanović, Z., Nabil, H., & Stanik, C. (2016). On the automatic classification of app reviews. *Requirements Engineering*, *21*(3), 311–331. doi:10.100700766-016-0251-9

Machová, K., Mikula, M., Gao, X., & Mach, M. (2020). Lexicon-based sentiment analysis using particle swarm optimization. *Electronics (Switzerland)*, *9*(8), 1–22. doi:10.3390/electronics9081317

Mäntylä, M. V., Graziotin, D., & Kuutila, M. (2018). The evolution of sentiment analysis—A review of research topics, venues, and top cited papers. *Computer Science Review*, *27*, 16–32. doi:10.1016/j.cosrev.2017.10.002

Margaryan, A., Littlejohn, A., & Vojt, G. (2011). Are digital natives a myth or reality? University students' use of digital technologies. *Computers & Education*, *56*(2), 429–440. doi:10.1016/j.compedu.2010.09.004

Martens, D., & Maalej, W. (2019). Towards understanding and detecting fake reviews in app stores. *Empirical Software Engineering*, *24*(6), 3316–3355. doi:10.100710664-019-09706-9

Martin, J. R., & White, P. R. R. (2005). *The Language of Evaluation: Appraisal in English. The Language of Evaluation: Appraisal in English*. Palgrave Macmillan. doi:10.1057/9780230511910

McIlroy, S., Ali, N., & Hassan, A. E. (2015). Fresh apps: An empirical study of frequently-updated mobile apps in the Google play store. *Empirical Software Engineering*, *21*(3), 1346–1370. doi:10.100710664-015-9388-2

Miao, Q., Li, Q., & Zeng, D. (2010). Fine-grained opinion mining by integrating multiple review sources. *Journal of the American Society for Information Science and Technology*, *61*(11), 2288–2299. doi:10.1002/asi.21400

Mostafa, M. M. (2018). Mining and mapping halal food consumers: A geo-located Twitter opinion polarity analysis. *Journal of Food Products Marketing*, *24*(7), 858–879. doi:10.1080/10454446.2017.1418695

Mostafa, M. M. (2019). Clustering halal food consumers: A Twitter sentiment analysis. *International Journal of Market Research*, *61*(3), 320–337. doi:10.1177/1470785318771451

Mostafa, M. M. (2020). Global halal food discourse on social media: A text mining approach. *Journal of International Communication*, *26*(2), 211–237. doi:10.1080/13216597.2020.1795702

Motiwalla, L. F. (2007). Mobile learning: A framework and evaluation. *Computers & Education*, *49*(3), 581–596. doi:10.1016/j.compedu.2005.10.011

Mujahid, M., Lee, E., Rustam, F., Washington, P. B., Ullah, S., Reshi, A. A., & Ashraf, I. (2021). Sentiment analysis and topic modeling on tweets about online education during covid-19. *Applied Sciences (Switzerland)*, *11*(18), 8438. Advance online publication. doi:10.3390/app11188438

Mullen, T., & Collier, N. (2004). Sentiment Analysis using Support Vector Machines with Diverse Information Sources. In D. Lin & D. Wu (Eds.), *Proceedings of EMNLP 2004* (pp. 412–418). Association for Computational Linguistics. Retrieved from http://research.nii.ac.jp/~collier/papers/emnlp2004.pdf

Nasreen Taj, M. B., & Girisha, G. S. (2021). Insights of strength and weakness of evolving methodologies of sentiment analysis. *Global Transitions Proceedings*, *2*(2), 157–162. doi:10.1016/j.gltp.2021.08.059

Nasukawa, T., & Yi, J. (2003). Sentiment analysis: Capturing favorability using natural language processing. In *Proceedings of the 2nd International Conference on Knowledge Capture, K-CAP 2003* (pp. 70–77). Association for Computing Machinery, Inc. 10.1145/945645.945658

Nemes, L., & Kiss, A. (2021). Prediction of stock values changes using sentiment analysis of stock news headlines. *Journal of Information and Telecommunication*, *5*(3), 375–394. doi:10.1080/24751839.2021.1874252

Oliveira, N., Cortez, P., & Areal, N. (2016). Stock market sentiment lexicon acquisition using microblogging data and statistical measures. *Decision Support Systems*, *85*, 62–73. doi:10.1016/j.dss.2016.02.013

Pak, A., & Paroubek, P. (2010). Twitter as a corpus for sentiment analysis and opinion mining. In *Proceedings of the 7th International Conference on Language Resources and Evaluation, LREC 2010* (pp. 1320–1326). European Language Resources Association (ELRA). 10.17148/IJARCCE.2016.51274

Pang, B., & Lee, L. (2008). Opinion mining and sentiment analysis. *Foundations and Trends in Information Retrieval*, *2*(1–2), 1–135. doi:10.1561/1500000011

Pano, T., & Kashef, R. (2020). A Complete VADER-Based Sentiment Analysis of Bitcoin (BTC) Tweets during the Era of COVID-19. *Big Data and Cognitive Computing*, *4*(4), 33. Advance online publication. doi:10.3390/bdcc4040033

Preethi, P. G., Uma, V., & Kumar, A. (2015). Temporal sentiment analysis and causal rules extraction from tweets for event prediction. In *Procedia Computer Science* (Vol. 48, pp. 84–89). Elsevier B.V. doi:10.1016/j.procs.2015.04.154

Ravi, K., & Ravi, V. (2015). A survey on opinion mining and sentiment analysis: Tasks, approaches and applications. *Knowledge-Based Systems*, *89*, 14–46. doi:10.1016/j.knosys.2015.06.015

Rodríguez-Hidalgo, C. T., Tan, E. S. H., & Verlegh, P. W. J. (2015). The social sharing of emotion (SSE) in online social networks: A case study in Live Journal. *Computers in Human Behavior*, *52*, 364–372. doi:10.1016/j.chb.2015.05.009

Saif, H., He, Y., Fernandez, M., & Alani, H. (2016). Contextual semantics for sentiment analysis of Twitter. *Information Processing & Management*, *52*(1), 5–19. doi:10.1016/j.ipm.2015.01.005

Scherer, K. R., Schorr, A., & Johnstone, T. (Eds.). (2001). *Appraisal processes in emotion: Theory, methods, research*. Oxford University Press.

Sigirci, I. O., Ozgur, H., Oluk, A., Uz, H., Cetiner, E., Oktay, H. U., & Erdemir, K. (2020). Sentiment Analysis of Turkish Reviews on Google Play Store. *2020 5th International Conference on Computer Science and Engineering (UBMK)*. doi:10.1109/ubmk50275.2020.921

Tan, M. J., & Guan, C. H. (2021). Are people happier in locations of high property value? Spatial temporal analytics of activity frequency, public sentiment and housing price using twitter data. *Applied Geography (Sevenoaks, England)*, *132*, 102474. Advance online publication. doi:10.1016/j.apgeog.2021.102474

Triantafyllou, I., Drivas, I. C., & Giannakopoulos, G. (2020). How to utilize my app reviews? A novel topics extraction machine learning schema for strategic business purposes. *Entropy (Basel, Switzerland)*, *22*(11), 1–21. doi:10.3390/e22111310 PMID:33287075

Tu, Y., Zou, D., & Zhang, R. (2020). A comprehensive framework for designing and evaluating vocabulary learning apps from multiple perspectives. *International Journal of Mobile Learning and Organisation*, *14*(3), 370–397. doi:10.1504/IJMLO.2020.108199

Tu, Y. F., & Hwang, G. J. (2018). The roles of sensing technologies and learning strategies in library-associated mobile learning: A review of 2007–2016 journal publications. *International Journal of Mobile Learning and Organisation*, *12*(1), 42–54. doi:10.1504/IJMLO.2018.089233

Valk, J.-H., Rashid, A. T., & Elder, L. (2010). Using mobile phones to improve educational outcomes: An analysis of evidence from Asia. *International Review of Research in Open and Distance Learning*, *11*(1), 117–140. doi:10.19173/irrodl.v11i1.794

Vashishtha, S., & Susan, S. (2020). Fuzzy Interpretation of Word Polarity Scores for Unsupervised Sentiment Analysis. In *2020 11th International Conference on Computing, Communication and Networking Technologies, ICCCNT 2020*. Institute of Electrical and Electronics Engineers Inc. 10.1109/ICCCNT49239.2020.9225646

Wang, Y., Kim, J., & Kim, J. (2021). The financial impact of online customer reviews in the restaurant industry: A moderating effect of brand equity. *International Journal of Hospitality Management*, *95*, 102895. Advance online publication. doi:10.1016/j.ijhm.2021.102895

Wang, Y. Y., Wang, Y. S., Lin, H. H., & Tsai, T. H. (2019). Developing and validating a model for assessing paid mobile learning app success. *Interactive Learning Environments*, *27*(4), 458–477. doi:10.1080/10494820.2018.1484773

Widyaningrum, P., Ruldeviyani, Y., & Dharayani, R. (2019). Sentiment analysis to assess the community's enthusiasm towards the development chatbot using an appraisal theory. *Procedia Computer Science, 161, 723–730*. doi:10.1016/j.procs.2019.11.176

Yang, L., Li, Y., Wang, J., & Sherratt, R. S. (2020). Sentiment Analysis for E-Commerce Product Reviews in Chinese Based on Sentiment Lexicon and Deep Learning. *IEEE Access: Practical Innovations, Open Solutions*, *8*, 23522–23530. doi:10.1109/ACCESS.2020.2969854

Yue, L., Chen, W., Li, X., Zuo, W., & Yin, M. (2019). A survey of sentiment analysis in social media. *Knowledge and Information Systems*, *60*(2), 617–663. doi:10.100710115-018-1236-4

Zeelenberg, M., & Pieters, R. (2004). Beyond valence in learner dissatisfaction: A review and new findings on behavioral responses to regret and disappointment in failed services. *Journal of Business Research*, *57*(4), 445–455. doi:10.1016/S0148-2963(02)00278-3

Zou, D., Xie, H., & Wang, F. L. (2018). Future trends and research issues of technology-enhanced language learning: A technological perspective. *Knowledge Management and E-Learning*, *10*(4), 426–440. doi:10.34105/j.kmel.2018.10.026

ADDITIONAL READING

Fiok, K., Karwowski, W., Gutierrez, E., & Wilamowski, M. (2021). Analysis of sentiment in tweets addressed to a single domain-specific Twitter account: Comparison of model performance and explainability of predictions. *Expert Systems with Applications*, *186*, 115771. Advance online publication. doi:10.1016/j.eswa.2021.115771

Hossain, M. S., & Rahman, M. F. (2022). Detection of potential customers' empathy behavior towards customers' reviews. *Journal of Retailing and Consumer Services*, *65*, 102881. doi:10.1016/j.jretconser.2021.102881

Keramatfar, A., & Amirkhani, H. (2019). Bibliometrics of sentiment analysis literature. *Journal of Information Science*, *45*(1), 3–15. doi:10.1177/0165551518761013

Li, H., Chen, Q., Zhong, Z., Gong, R., & Han, G. (2022). E-word of mouth sentiment analysis for user behavior studies. *Information Processing & Management*, *59*(1), 102784. Advance online publication. doi:10.1016/j.ipm.2021.102784 PMID:34580562

Ligthart, A., Catal, C., & Tekinerdogan, B. (2021). Systematic reviews in sentiment analysis: A tertiary study. *Artificial Intelligence Review*, *54*(7), 4997–5053. doi:10.100710462-021-09973-3

Nasreen Taj, M. B., & Girisha, G. S. (2021). Insights of strength and weakness of evolving methodologies of sentiment analysis. *Global Transitions Proceedings*, *2*(2), 157–162. doi:10.1016/j.gltp.2021.08.059

Taboada, M., Brooke, J., Tofiloski, M., Voll, K., & Stede, M. (2011). Lexicon-basedmethods for sentiment analysis. *Computational Linguistics*, *37*(2), 267–307. doi:10.1162/COLI_a_00049

Yang, L., Li, Y., Wang, J., & Sherratt, R. S. (2020). Sentiment Analysis for E-Commerce Product Reviews in Chinese Based on Sentiment Lexicon and Deep Learning. *IEEE Access: Practical Innovations, Open Solutions*, *8*, 23522–23530. doi:10.1109/ACCESS.2020.2969854

KEY TERMS AND DEFINITIONS

App: A mobile application, often known as a mobile app or just an app, is a computer program or software application that runs on a mobile device such a tablet, phone, or watch.

Blended Learning Platform: Is a set of hardware, software, scheduling, and logistics that make up a learning program that includes online training or technology-assisted teaching.

Emotion Analysis: Also known as sentiment analysis is a method of analyzing people's feelings. Natural language processing (NLP), biometrics, text analysis, and computational linguistics are used to identify, quantify, extract, and investigate emotional states and subjective data.

Lexicon-Based Sentiment Analysis: A method of evaluating a document by aggregating the sentiment scores of all the words in the text, which is done using a sentiment lexicon that has already been produced.

M-Learning: Also known as mobile learning, is a type of distance education that allows students to study in numerous situations through social and content exchanges on personal electronic devices such as smartphones.

Machine Learning: Is a sort of data analysis that uses artificial intelligence to automate the process of developing analytical models. It's a branch of AI based on the premise that robots can learn from data, discover patterns, and make judgments with little or no human involvement.

Review: A comment made by a customer who has bought and utilized the goods or service, or has had contact with it. User reviews are a type of user feedback seen on the internet.

Chapter 7

Analyzing and Predicting Learner Sentiment Toward Specialty Schools Using Machine Learning Techniques

Md Shamim Hossain
https://orcid.org/0000-0003-1645-7470
Hajee Mohammad Danesh Science and Technology University, Bangladesh

Mst Farjana Rahman
Hajee Mohammad Danesh Science and Technology University, Bangladesh

Md. Kutub Uddin
https://orcid.org/0000-0001-8495-3789
Hajee Mohammad Danesh Science and Technology University, Bangladesh

ABSTRACT

The objective of the research is to use machine learning techniques to evaluate and predict learners' sentiment toward specialty school. The current study used the Yelp website's reviews to obtain data on specialty schools after filtering. Following cleaning, the filtered summary sentences were rated as positive, neutral, or negative sentiments using the AFINN and VADER sentiment algorithms. In addition, to split learner ratings of specialty schools into three sentiment categories, the current study also used four supervised machine learning techniques. The majority of ratings for specialty schools were favorable, according to the findings of the present study. Furthermore, while all of the techniques (decision tree, K-neighbors classifier, logistic regression, and SVM) can accurately classify review text into sentiment class, and SVM outperforms in terms of high accuracy. Specialty educational institutes will be able to better understand learners' psychological sentiments based on the findings of the study, allowing them to improve and adjust their services.

DOI: 10.4018/978-1-7998-9644-9.ch007

INTRODUCTION

Specialty schools differ from regular schools in that they provide more in-depth coverage of the disciplines in which they concentrate (Prieto et al., 2019). Secondary schools with expanded coverage of particular topics that make up the school's specialty are known as specialized schools (Walls & Kemper, 2018). They should not be confused with vocational schools, which aim to provide skills for a specific career. Learning should be promoted early and regularly, and specialized technical or vocational skills are important to labor market success, according to international consensus (Akhter et al., 2021; World Bank Group, 2011). Specialized schools were established in England to enhance choice and encourage diversity, and they are a popular choice for parents due to their specialist status (West & Noden, 2000). Indeed, specialty schools now account for 88 percent of state-funded secondary schools in England (DfES, 2005; Prieto et al., 2019).

Students' self-expression in activities that are relevant to them is facilitated by the diversified approach to the creation of the contingent of specialist schools (Lazarev, 1992). The area of specialty schools give education in the labor process, as well as in the interaction between students and scientists that is developed via academics and extracurricular activities, as well as during periods of individual and group initiatives. Many nations have begun educational reforms in recent decades with the goal of increasing educational access, promoting equity, and boosting educational efficiency and effectiveness. The World Bank's "Learning for All" Education Sector 2020 Strategy was created with the objective of "ensuring that all children not only attend school, but also learn" (World Bank Group, 2011). One of the objectives is to foster educational equity, ensuring that all students, not only the most advantaged, gain the information and skills necessary for success in life (Prieto et al., 2019; Akhter et al., 2021).

Educational psychology, as an area of study and a focus of psychological research, is a relatively new phenomenon that is expanding and being actively contested across the world due to its potential contributions to the educational environment (Ferreira et al., 2016). The field of psychology dealing with the scientific study of human learning is known as educational psychology. Individual variations in intellect, cognitive development, emotions, motivation, self-regulation, and self-concept, as well as their function in learning, may all be understood via the study of learning processes from both cognitive and behavioral perspectives. Most educational psychologists regard their field as a scientific study concerned with understanding and improving how people learn a wide range of talents via formal classroom instruction (Snowman, 1997; Jones et al., 2019). Physiological arousal, psychological evaluation, and subjective experiences combine to create our emotional states. The components of emotion are all of these things put together. By analyzing user sentiment the emotional psychology of learners can be deduced from the supplied reviews (Geng et al., 2020). Which analysis is a form of text mining that extracts certain emotional expressions from text in order to predict the human mind, especially a person's emotional condition (Geng et al., 2020; Pang & Lee, 2008).

Due to various stakeholders in education and data availability, present research on sentiment analysis techniques in educational contexts is significantly lagging behind in comparison to other sectors (e.g., business, social networks). Sentiment analysis is becoming increasingly popular as a subfield of natural language processing. In the context of teaching assessment, sentiment analysis may assist educators in quickly discovering students' real sentiments about a course and accurately and timely adjusting the teaching plan to improve the quality of education and teaching (Zhai et al., 2020). The appraisal theory may be used to describe the psychology underlying users' sentiments.

In Systemic Functional Linguistics (SFL), appraisal theory is a theoretical framework for recognizing distinct forms of evaluative expression (Moors et al., 2021; Martin and White, 2005). It views meaning as a series of choices made by the speaker or writer, and it describes how these choices are represented in the SFL tradition's lexicon and syntactic structure of evaluative writing (Halliday and Matthiessen, 2004). According to appraisal theory, emotions are derived from our judgements (appraisals or estimates) of events that elicit various reactions in different persons. In essence, our evaluation of a situation causes an emotional, or affective, reaction that is based on that evaluation (Grundlingh, 2018; Scherer et al., 2001). Although syntactic structure is complex, it may be seen via the lens of a local grammar since it is influenced by a variety of other overlapping concerns beyond the scope of evaluation theory. Local grammars explain the patterns that linguistic occurrences use when they arise at random within a text and are articulated using a range of linguistic resources. To specify how an assessment statement acts, appraisal theory and local grammars operate together. Appraisal theory essentially describes how a language communicates with one another (Moors et al., 2021; Read and Carroll, 2012; Widyaningrum et al., 2019; Appraisal theory is a concept of interpersonal meaning that is used to mediate interpersonal connections by telling the reader how they feel about things and people (Grundlingh, 2018; Widyaningrum et al., 2019).

Sentiment analysis is a fast-growing research topic as a result of the huge rise of digital data in order to understand the psychological emotions of learners toward businesses and their products and services (Geng et al., 2020). One of the most significant methods for collecting emotion information from vast volumes of data in today's artificial intelligence age is sentiment analysis (Hossain and Rahman, 2022; Kumar et al., 2020). During the last two decades, sentiment analysis, also known as opinion mining, has gained prominence as a sub-field of text analytics that deals with the computer processing of subjectivity and opinion in texts (Jena, 2020; Yadav et al, 2020). Sentiment analysis has become an important technique for monitoring and understanding reviewer sentiment as learners express their thoughts and feelings more freely on review sites than ever before. Sentiment analysis is a technique for determining if a text has positive, neutral, or negative feelings (Geng et al., 2020). Businesses frequently use it to assess brand reputation, analyze sentiment in social data, and learn more about their consumers. Sentiment analysis is a technique for determining people's feelings on a topic.

A review is a piece of feedback given by a consumer who has purchased and used the product or service or has made contact with it. On the internet, user reviews are a form of learner feedback. Electronic user reviews are peer-generated product ratings and assessments placed on the organization's or third party's websites. Learner reviews give extra support for a decision and increase confidence in the decision maker (Dwidienawati et al., 2020; Geng et al., 2020). Furthermore, Wang et al., (2021) stated that the volume and rating of reviews improved organizational profitability. According to Chevalier and Mayzlin (2006), learners' online reviews have a significant impact on product and service earnings.

People who have recently purchased items or services from Yelp-listed businesses may write a review and award a star rating from 1 to 5 stars (low to high pleasure) on the Yelp platform (yelp.com). In Yelp, there are also several educational institutions, including specialist schools, where users may write and/or rate reviews. A potential customer (the reviewee) would then go to the yelp page, read the review, and rate both the informational (e.g., star rating) and normative (e.g., star rating) elements of the review (e.g., statement quality, recommendation framing) (Meek et al., 2021; Eslami et al., 2018). This twofold processing of the learner review affects the readers' impression of the review's value and their subsequent action, which might range from liking the review (clicking "Like") to opting to buy the items and services. As a result, the essential characteristics of online reviews that impact a learner's feeling of usefulness play an important role in influencing consumer behavior (Ghosh, 2018; Meek et al., 2021). Learners read reviews and evaluate other learners' star ratings while deciding whether or not to buy.

Furthermore, Yelp does not provide ratings based on products or services; rather, it gives reviews based on categories, which include a few organizational tags like "education" and "specialty schools." In the Yelp database, there are several sorts of specialty schools. These include art schools, CPR classes, bartending schools, cheerleading, cooking schools, childbirth education, cosmetology schools, vocational & technical Schools, DUI schools, dance schools, drama schools, traffic schools, swimming lessons/ schools, driving schools, firearm training, surf schools, first aid classes, speech training, ski schools, flight instruction, food safety training, language schools, pole dancing classes, massage schools, nursing schools, parenting classes, and photography classes (blog.yelp.com). To satisfy the study's aims, we employed a few techniques (explained in the method section) to filter specialty schools-related reviews altogether from the original dataset and analyzed the filtered dataset using machine learning techniques in the current analysis. Our study's goals are to (a) investigate specialty school reviewers' sentiments, (b) use lexicon tools to rate review texts for specialty schools, (c) calculate the average number of words in reviews for negative, neutral, and positive sentiments, (d) use the lexical-based technique to find the association between length of review text and review rating, and (e) predict the feelings of reviewers using machine learning approaches.

LITERATURE REVIEW

Learners' Sentiment

The views of others are quite important while making decisions (Eachempati et al., 2022). The web has grown into a great resource for user viewpoints across a wide range of issues as a result of increased Internet use. However, the growing volume of opinionated content, along with the complexities generated by variations in people's viewpoints, makes reading all of these evaluations and making an informed selection nearly difficult (Derakhshan and Beigy, 2019). As a result, businesses must assess learner perceptions of items in order to assess their real performance (Geng et al., 2020). Sentiment analysis or opinion mining is a way of computationally classifying and categorizing views conveyed in a piece of text to determine whether the writer's attitude toward a certain subject, product, or other object is positive, negative, or neutral (Wang et al., 2022). Sentimental analysis, often referred to as opinion mining, is the study of people's feelings, sentiments, evaluations, perceptions, and emotions about various institutions such as commodities, programs, organizations, people, issues, events, and subjects (Preethi et al., 2015).

In recent years, a lot of research has been done on sentiment analysis to develop more effective and accurate algorithms. Sentiment analysis' main objective is to automatically detect biased content in documents (Wang et al., 2022; Geng et al., 2020; Rout et al., 2017). Luo and Huang (2011) compare positive and negative phrases, collecting data from the internet and manually marking sentiment, which requires a lot of time and work. For sentiment analysis of Chinese texts, Liu et al., (2010) developed a rule-based technique based on BaseLine and Support-vector machine (SVM), in which a sentiment word dictionary captures the overall document polarity of particular words and modifies it according to background detail. In this study, we analyzed reviewers' attitudes about specialty schools using two lexicon-based methods. As a result, it's critical to comprehend how people react to specialist schools. Despite this, there has never been a research that examines and predicts consumers' attitudes about specialist schools. To fill the gap, we use AFINN and VADAR lexical tools to assess learner attitudes toward specialist schools and machine learning approaches to forecast sentiments.

Lexicon Based Sentiment Analysis

In our research, we employed AFINN and VADER sentiment, two prominent lexicon-based sentiment analyzers to analyze the review sentiment of specialty schools. Lexical tools are highly popular in the field of Sentiment Analysis because they provide a resource that clearly contains emotional data. Sentiment lexica are commonly used to estimate polarity by comparing the sentiment polarities of terms in a text to their lexicon sentiment polarities (Hossain and Rahman, 2022). Given the subjective nature of sentiment analysis, sentiment words are a key predictor of sentiment polarity. Positive adjectives like good, lovely, and brilliant may be used to express positive attitudes, whereas negative words like bad, worst, and disastrous can be used to express negative attitudes. As a result, academics frequently utilize sentiment lexicons, which gather sentiment words (Araque et al., 2019; Ravi and Ravi, 2015). Borg and Boldt (2020) utilized VADER sentiment and a Swedish sentiment vocabulary to incorporate the first marking of the e-mails. Two SVM models for extracting and categorizing e-mail sentiment are then trained using the e-mail content and sentiment labels. A semantic similarity measure between text terms and lexica vocabulary is computed by Araque et al. (2019).

Review Prediction

In this work, we used four machine learning algorithms to predict users' review ratings: decision tree classifier, SVM, logistic regression, and K neighbors classifier.

Decision Tree Classifier

The Decision Tree algorithm is a machine learning technique that is supervised. Unlike most other supervised learning algorithms, the decision tree approach may also be utilized to handle classification and regression issues (Burke et al., 2020). It trains a decision tree classifier using an unseen instance. A decision tree has the benefit of using less data to train and giving the best outcomes in terms of assessment (Panhalkar and Doye, 2021). The decision tree-building algorithms utilize a divide-and-conquer strategy to generate a tree. Decision tree models have been used to tackle a variety of real-world issues. The training data-derived information is organized in a hierarchical structure with implications and nodes.

This method is straightforward to comprehend due to the way the tree's production is understood. Categorical, numerical, or all sorts of inputs may be accommodated by decision trees (Al-Mashraie et al., 2020).

Support-Vector Machine (SVM)

A supervised machine learning model known as a support-vector machine (also known as a support-vector network) examines data for classification and regression analysis in machine learning (Boser et al., 1992). SVM utilizes learning techniques to discover patterns and understand data in the context of regression and classification, with kernel functions employed to increase the classifier's accuracy (Zhang et al., 2021). SVM's ability to map inputs using linear and nonlinear classification effectively employing kernel functions such as linear, longitudinal, logarithmic, and sigmoid parameters is one of its most important characteristics (Ganaie et al., 2021).

Logistic Regression

A mathematical approach for determining the relationship between input and output variables is logistic regression in regression analysis. It's a statistical model that predicts the interaction between one or more independent factors and a dependent variable. According to the range of possible values for the dependent variable, logistic regression models can be binary or multinomial. The dependent variables' values are usually expressed as zeros and ones to reflect the two probable outcomes in binary logistic regression models (Al-Mashraie et al., 2020). In the field of social science, logistic regression is a well-known approach of independent prediction (De Caigny et al., 2018).

K-Neighbors Classifier

Cover and Hart introduced the K-nearest Neighbors (KNN) classifier in 1967 as a statistical-based machine learning approach. The main principle behind the KNN classifier is that a distance formula is used to find the k nearest samples of a test sample, and then the test sample belongs to the category with the greatest number in the k nearby samples. Varied k values provide different classification results; the KNN classifier's performance is best when k is set to an acceptable value (Liu et al., 2019). The KNN classifier has been widely utilized in classification and regression issues, and has shown significant promise in predicting different protein characteristics such as subcellular localization and protein structure categorization (Qiao et al., 2018).

Research Questions

Few inquiries about consumer reviews of specialist schools have yet to be explained. Although such inquiries are crucial for specialist schools to learn about learner perspectives. In these propositions, we're primarily searching for solutions to the four research questions described below.

Sentiment Analysis Using Lexicon Based Approaches

The two major methods for conducting sentiment analysis with text mining tools are lexicon-based and corpus-based (Miao et al., 2010). On the other hand, the corpus-based method for assessing sentiment orientation is rarely used in the literature. In all instances, whether the two approaches mentioned above are based on a pre-defined expert dictionary or a corpus of subjective words, the sentiment score is calculated by comparing the phrase supplied against an expert-defined dictionary entry. Several lexicons are available for sentiment analysis (Preethi et al., 2015); lexicon-based techniques are straightforward to implement, and lexicon-based approaches have been used in a number of recent and comparable research (Machová et al., 2020; Yang et al., 2020). As a result, we utilized two lexicon-based methods to discover sentiment scores and top favorable and negative reviews in the current study. More specifically, we wish to use our inquiry to find answers to the following research questions:

(a) How do lexicon tools rate review texts?

(b) How can we identify the most prominently negative and positive review texts?

Length of a Review and its Rating

According to Zeelenberg and Pieters (2004), consumers are more prone to show negative emotions (such as despair or rage) while consuming alongside others. A dissatisfied user is more likely to inform someone about it by writing a negative review. Bad is more potent than good when it comes to grabbing concentration (Fors Brandebo, Nilsson, and Larsson, 2016). In general, negative experiences, sentiments, and facts carry more weight and have a bigger influence than good information, emotions, or occurrences of the same type (Baumeister et al.,2001). Additionally, severely negative feedback has a bigger influence on brand impression than slightly unfavorable or exceptionally positive product reviews. This phenomenon has been referred to as the "negativity effect" or "negativity bias" (Lee et al., 2009). Negative emotions exceed good emotions in web posts, according to Rodrguez-Hidalgo et al. (2015). These results supported the likely link between bigger review length and reduced review ratings, because negative feelings that are more likely to experience lower review ratings are also more likely to generate longer written connections in online reviews, similar to how negative emotions accelerate verbal exchanges in face-to-face interactions, according to this concept (i.e., resulting in longer and more extensive verbal exchanges). As a result, if a person is unsatisfied with an item or brand, they are more quick to refer someone about it (Ghasemaghaei et al., 2018). Bad feedback in the form of online user evaluations is more likely to be lengthier than positive feedback, as consumers who have had a negative experience with a product/service are more willing to share their opinions and experience with others (Jiménez-Zafra et al., 2017).

From January 2012 to December 2015, Ghasemaghaei et al. (2018) used a database scraping tool to analyze a panel dataset of learner reviews for house, car, and life insurance and discovered that lengthier review content was related with lower review rating. We also want to see if there's a relationship between the length of a review and its emotion classifications in this study. We'd want to utilize the results of our research to answer the following research question:

(c) Is there a link between the length of a review and its rating?

Performance of Machine Learning Models

Furthermore, support vector machine (SVM) exhibits great efficiency and precision in the majority of supervised learning-based research. Gul (2021) claimed that SVM had the highest classification accuracy when it came to determining the kind of spillway. Mullen and Collier (2004) introduced an SVM-based sentiment classification system that gave values to selected phrases and words and merged them to create a text classification model. In the movie domain, Pang et al. (2019) investigated the efficiency of supervised machine learning approaches for sentiment classification (Nave Bayes, maximum entropy classification, and support vector machine), indicating that the SVM method performed best while the Naive Bayes method performed worst. Ye et al. (2009) used a controlled tool to find sentiment learner ratings on traveler review websites and showed that the SVM outperformed the Nave Bayes technique. SVM-based sentiment analysis prediction was created by Preethi et al. (2015). They claim that SVM has the following benefits. (a) it has a high level of overfitting resistance, (b) large feature areas can be accommodated. (c) It excels at extracting sentiments from large social media datasets and can even predict knowledge. As a result, in this work, we employ four machine learning techniques to predict learner

Table 1. Our extracted dataset's statistics

Total reviews	34765
Number of 5 star review	20297
Number of 4 star review	5094
Number of 3 star review	2013
Number of 2 star review	1939
Number of 1 star review	5422

attitude toward speciality schools: decision tree classifier, SVM, logistic regression, and K neighbors classifier, and we want to see how well each model performs in the context of the halal restaurant dataset. We want to utilize another investigation to obtain an answer to the following study question:

(d) When it comes to categorizing user emotions about specialist schools, which machine learning models perform better?

METHOD

Data

We used yelp.com (https://www.yelp.com/dataset/download) to get our study data, which was updated on July 17, 2021. Yelp.com is a crowd-sourced small business review site with a social networking component (O'Brien, 2007), where users may score items and services on a one to five-star scale (Chafkin, 2010), and everyone can download data files for research and educational purposes. A Jupyter notebook was used to implement all machine-learning Python scripts in this study. We used two level strings from the tags of categories to identify the data we needed for this investigation after downloading the Yelp dataset. "Education" was the first layer string, and "Specialty Schools" was the second layer string, suggesting that all of the data was for Specialty Schools alone. As a result, we saved the dataset as a filtered dataset, which was used in this research, after removing punctuation, stopwords, and missing values from user reviews. The statistics of our extracted dataset are shown in Table 1. In addition, we introduced support for huge, multi-dimensional arrays and matrices to the Python programming language by importing a wide number of high-level kernel equations to work on these arrays, including pandas, seaborn, matplotlib, numpy, string, sklearn, nltk, and others.

We assessed the users' sentiment based on the review star they gave while submitting their review message. We assumed that the reviewers assigned 5 and 4 stars to positive feelings, 3 stars to neutral sentiments, and 1 and 2 stars to negative feelings. As a consequence, we assigned +1 for positive sentiment, 0 score for neutral sentiment and -1 score for negative sentiment. Table 2 showed percentages and numbers of users' emotional states, as well as the average amount of words in review text for negative, neutral, and positive sentiments (shown in Figure 1).

Figure 1. Histogram of reviewers' sentiment statistics of our dataset (1 for positive, -1 for negative, and 0 for neutral)

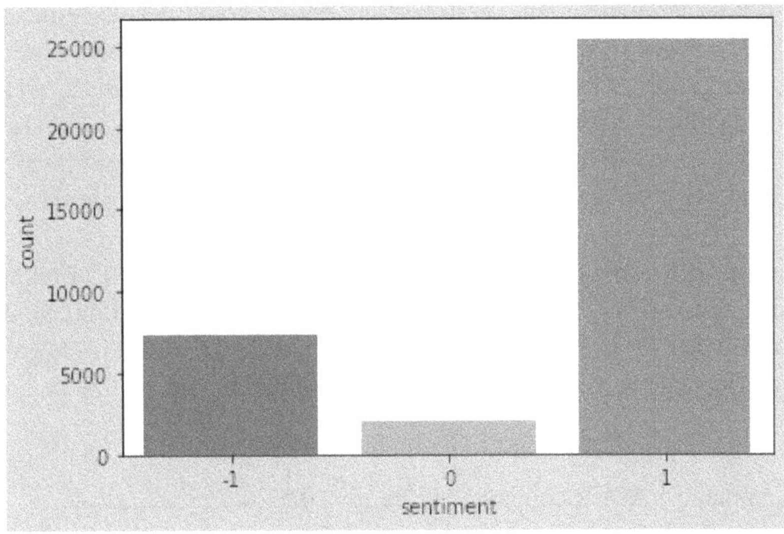

Learner Sentiment Analysis

AFINN Sentiment and VADER (Valence Aware Dictionary for sEntiment Reasoning), two Unsupervised Learning (UL) methods integrated packages, were used to assess the users' review sentiment in this study. Using a lexicon-based technique to assess feelings has a number of advantages, including: (i) It does not require any training data; (ii) it can understand the sentiment of a text that contains emoticons, slangs, conjunctions, capital words, punctuation, and much more; (iii) it can understand the sentiment of a text that contains emoticons, slangs, conjunctions, capital words, punctuation, and much more.

(iv) It is ideal for social media text and is cross-domain compatible.

Finn Rup Nielsen designed Afinn, a basic yet widely used vocabulary for sentiment analysis. Afinn uses a wordlist technique to evaluate sentiment and has approximately 3300 words, each with a polarity score ranging from -5 (highest score for negative emotion) to 5 (highest score for positive sentiment) (highest score for positive sentiment). The AFINN object's Score () method accepts a sentence as input and returns a score as output. A positive, neutral, or negative score can be obtained. The AFINN lexicon, which is probably one of the most fundamental and commonly used lexicons for sentiment analysis, has been utilized in previous research (Vashishtha & Susan, 2020; Tan and Guan, 2021; Kim and Chung, 2020). After examining the outcomes of the fuzzy approach on three benchmark datasets: hotel reviews dataset, polarity movie dataset by Pang and Lee (2008), and IMDB dataset, Vashishtha and Susan (2020) found that the AFINN lexicon has the highest accuracy. Furthermore, one of the study's objectives is to categorize consumers' emotions into three categories: good, negative, and neutral. Another objective is to figure out which consumer attitudes are the most favorable and negative. The AFINN lexicon was chosen in this study.

In contrast, VADER is a vocabulary and Parsimonious rule-based reviewer sentiment analysis tool that has been fine-tuned to recognize emotions on social networking sites. VADER sentiment lexicon can comprehend words, acronyms, slang, gestures, and emojis commonly used in social media (Pano and Kashef, 2020). The frameworks performed just as well as human raters on Twitter data. In addition, when compared to seven sentiment analysis lexicons, VADER sentiment fared as well as or better than the others (Hutto and Gilbert, 2014). It is generally considerably faster than supervised machine learning algorithms since it does not require training. VADER sentiment creates an emotion score vector with negative, neutral, positive, and compound polarities for each text. Thus in this study we also used VADER lexicon.

The compound VADER score equals positive, neutral, and negative lexical ratings that have been averaged between -1 (highest negative value) and +1 (highest positive value) (Liu, 2010). Compound VADER ratings of less than or equal to -.05, more than -.05 but less than 0.05, and greater than or equal to 0.05, respectively, indicate negative learner sentiment, neutral learner sentiment, and positive learner sentiment.

User's negative sentiment: VADER compound score <= -0.5
Users' positive sentiment: VADER compound score >= 0.5
User's neutral sentiment: 0.05> VADER compound score> -0.5

In this investigation, we scored learner feelings from review texts of specialty schools indexed in the Yelp dataset using the AFINN and VADER Sentiment lexicons.

Sentiment Prediction

After removing punctuations, stopwords, and missing values from learner reviews, we utilized the TF-IDF (Term Frequency Inverse Document Frequency) vectorizer to convert the text into a consistent numerical representation, which was then used to train a machine learning algorithm. The TF-IDF is a statistical test that determines if a word is relevant to a text in a collection of documents. This is achieved by multiplying two metrics: the number of times a word appears in a text and the reciprocal reference frequency of that term across a group of documents. It has a number of uses, including automatic text interpretation and term ranking in Natural Language Processing (NLP) machine learning algorithms. The bag-of-words concept argues that a text is essentially a list of words that may be vectorized by measuring the relative value of each word, i.e., taking into account the word's occurrence in the document and importance in the corpus (Kim et al., 2019). We utilized five classifiers to estimate consumer attitude about insurance products: decision tree classifier, K neighbors classifier, SVM, and logistic regression. All models are constructed with 75% of the filtered dataset, with the remaining 25% utilized to ensure that our research models are accurate. The study's findings are summarized in Table 7.

Performance Measures

Developing an optimum model or classifier that can properly categorize each occurrence in a test series is nearly impossible. Using the following performance criteria, we computed the number of TP (true positive), TN (true negative), FP (false positive), and FN (false negative) in our study models. where TP + FN = P and TN + FP =N.

a) a) **Accuracy**: is the percentage of users' reviews that are accurately classified as positive, negative, or neutral. It can be calculated using the formula below:

$$ccuracy\left(MA\right) = \frac{TP + TN}{P + N}$$

b) b) **Precision and Recall: Precision**: The percentage of genuine positives to all positives is described as precision, and the proportion of true positives to related components is defined as recall. Furthermore, recall relates to the correctness of the results, whereas accuracy refers to the completeness of the data. The positive recall is the percentage of real positive cases that are assessed as such.

$$Recall\left(MR\right) = \frac{TP}{TP + FN} = \frac{TP}{P}$$

$$Precision\left(MP\right) = \frac{TN}{TN + FP} = \frac{TN}{N}$$

c) **Cohen's kappa statistics**: Cohen's kappa statistics can be used to determine interrater reliability. The classifier would be ineffective if the kappa statistic value was 0 or below. The most important consequence of Cohen's kappa is to understand and detect the degree of right variable demonstration for the training model. Cohen's kappa values over 1 suggest a good variable demonstration in the training model, whereas values approaching 0 indicate that the model is unknown.

d) **F1-score**: The F1-score is a complete assessment metric based on recall and precision; the higher the F1 value, the better the classification results.

e) **MCC:** The Matthews correlation coefficient (MCC), sometimes known as the phi coefficient, is a machine learning statistic used to assess the consistency of binary classifications. MCC values of -1 and +1, respectively, represent total disagreement and perfect prediction between prediction and observation.

f) f) **R squared:** The ratio of the dependent variable's variance that the independent variable can estimate is called R squared. R-squared (R2) is a statistical metric that reflects how much variance is explained by an independent variable or variables in a regression model with a dependent variable. R-squared determines how often one variable's variance explains the variance of the other, whereas correlation determines how closely an independent and dependent variable are related. As a result, a model's inputs will account for approximately half of the observed variation if its R2 is 0.50. The coefficient of determination is also called R-squared (R2).

$$R^2 = 1 - \frac{\text{Unexplained Variation}\left(\text{UV}\right)}{Total\,\text{Variation}\left(\text{TV}\right)}$$

Table 2. Number of sentiments with percentages for each category

Sentiment	Number	Percentage
-1	7361	21.17
0	2013	5.79
1	25391	73.04
Total	34765	100.00

g) **MSE, MSLE, and RMSE:** The mean squared error (MSE) is a measure used to evaluate the accuracy of an estimate. MSE levels around 0 are higher, and it never goes negative. A popular measure for measuring the discrepancies between anticipated and actual values in a model is the root-mean-square error (RMSE). The value of RMSE is positive, and the closer it is to zero, the better. The mean squared log error, on the other hand, shows the degree of regression loss (MSLE). The difference between actual and predicted values is calculated here.

RESULT AND DISCUSSION

On Yelp, 73.04 percent of reviewers have a good attitude towards specialty schools, 21.17 percent have a negative attitude, and just 5.79 percent have a neutral attitude, according to our data (shown in Table 2). The bulk of the analysis text indicated positive sentiments regarding specialty schools as a consequence of our investigation. Using the def word count (text string) function, we calculated the average number of words in the review text for each sentiment type, finding that negative sentiment has 186.06 words, neutral sentiment has 176.85 words, and positive sentiment has 122.13 words (presented in Figure 4). As a consequence, we see a link between lengthier review content and unfavorable emotions. This indicates that dissatisfied learners are more inclined than delighted learners to convey their views to others and write more words in their reports on web pages (Ghasemaghaei et al., 2018).

In this study, the polarity scores were calculated for 34,765 instances. According to Table 3, the AFINN Sentiment Lexicon's polarity ratings varied from -80 to 72.7, with a mean value of -0.52 for negative feelings, -22.22 to 80, with a mean value of 7.13 for neutral sentiments, and -46 to 172.22, with a mean value of 16.60 for positive sentiments. The top ten unfavorable and positive review messages are shown in Tables 5 and 6, respectively (we only showed one line of each text from the entire text). The complete review texts can also be shown using the iloc [] machine learning function. We examined the complete text of iloc [7741] and iloc [5145] (provided in appendix-1 and 2) to see the full learner review texts of a minimum AFINN negative score and a maximum AFINN positive score, respectively.

In addition, the mean polarity score for negative feelings was 0.095 for VADAR negative, 0.82 for VADAR neutral, 0.08 for VADER positive, and -0.06 for VADER compound, according to table-6. While the mean polarity score for neutral sentiments was 0.02 for VADAR negative, 0.75 for VADAR neutral, 0.22 for VADAR positive, and 0.90 for VADAR compound, the mean polarity score for positive emotions was 0.02 for VADAR negative, 0.81 for VADAR neutral, 0.13 for VADER positive, and 0.63 for VADER compound. Figure 2 shows the histogram of vadar compound score, whereas Figure 3 shows the positive and negative VADAR scores.

Table 3. AFINN score (descriptive statistics) for each sentiment class

sentiment	count	mean	std	min	25%	50%	75%	Max
-1	7361	-0.5233	7.81562	-80	-4.0609	0	3.4965	72.7273
0	2013	7.12791	7.6832	-22.222	2.52101	6.19469	10.4895	80
1	25391	16.6048	12.2949	-46.154	8.69565	14.0777	21.5054	172.222

Figure 2. Histogram of VADAR compound score

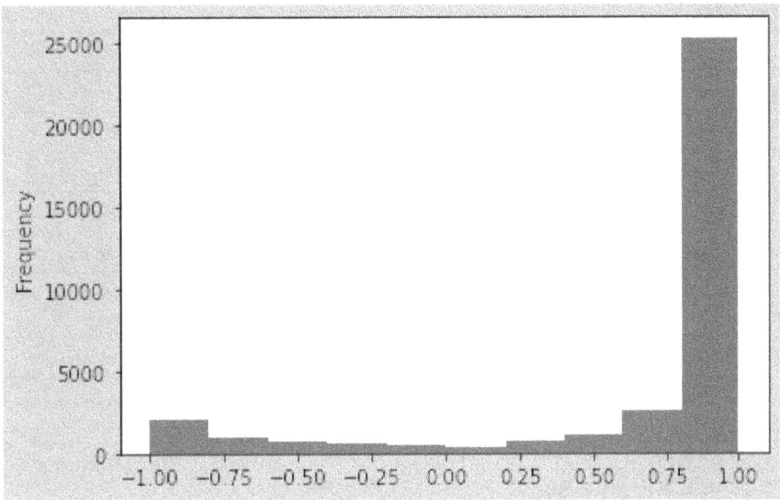

Figure 3. Histogram of positive and negative VADAR scores

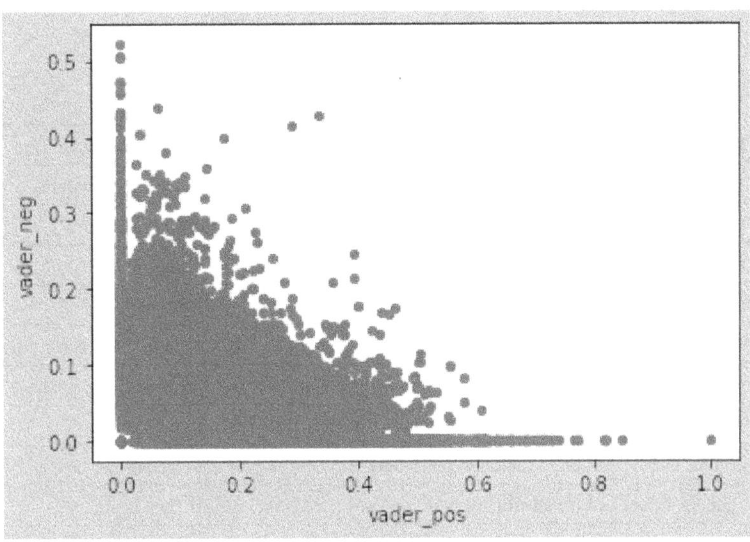

Table 4. Average number of words, average afinn and vader polarity score for each sentiment class

sentiment	word_count (Average)	afinn_score (Average)	vader_neg (Average)	vader_neu (Average)	vader_pos (Average)	vader_compound (Average)
-1	186.0561	0.23217	0.095662	0.82317	0.081165	-0.06266
0	176.8455	10.00397	0.054531	0.810482	0.134981	0.626432
1	122.1304	15.09425	0.024722	0.753711	0.221566	0.895938

Table 5. AFINN score of the top ten unfavorable reviews

	text	afinn_score
7741	This is the most dishonest, disorganized and unprofessional “college” out there. Needless to sa...	-67.0
7760	I attended this school just over two years ago as a student. I was originally a learner twice t...	-65.0
6485	First off, I want to start by saying I found this guy through yelp. I needed a rear sight install...	-59.0
7009	Y’all if I could give no stars I would, I’ve been going here for years on top of that it’s alway...	-55.0
33536	I don’t have words strong enough to adequately warn you off of this place, this approach, and th...	-52.0
3163	FUTURE COSMETOLOGY STUDENT? LOVER OF AVEDA PRODUCTS? \n\nAs far as I can see, there is only one...	-52.0
10888	Subject: Complaint about rude bad learner services at Beaverton campus\n\nHello,\nOn my appoint...	-51.0
24322	HOPEFUL FUTURE COSMETOLOGY STUDENT? LOVER OF AVEDA PRODUCTS? \n\nAs far as I can see, there is ...	-50.0
21628	WARNING!!!! SCAM SCAM SCAM\nDO NOT DO A DRIVING COURSE WITH AMERICAN SAFETY COUNCIL YOU WILL RE...	-49.0
7737	I HAD THE ABSOLUTELY MOST UNACCEPTABLY APPALLING INTERACTIONS AS A DISABLED VETERAN ATTENDING TH...	-49.0

Table 6. AFINN score of the top ten positive reviews

	text	afinn_score
28925	Things are hopping at the downtown Y. It is a VERY busy place, but happy. Everyone seems to be...	94.0
24094	Hello All,\nI know some of you are going to see 5 stars and just pass this buy as some guy who i...	95.0
30115	I may add or change the stars as time goes on. I wish I could give it a 4.5 for most things gym/...	98.0
31074	Brass Ovaries is the studio where you will get THE best pole instruction experience in Texas. I’...	101.0
19564	All my wife wanted for her birthday was a big party she didn’t have to plan. Fortunately, she di...	104.0
30407	TONI&GUY (aka home) is the best hair school you can ever attend to I mean compared to other cosm...	120.0
5505	I’m am very seriously considering attending. I live in So OR, and made the four hour trek up-sta...	124.0
34164	Pros: Great food, beautiful, lots to do, nice people, great light rail, laid back, other things\...	126.0
19519	This place is quite simply amazing. I took my fiance here for our five-year anniversary because ...	127.0
5145	Okay, y’all, pull up a chair...I have a feeling this is gonna be a long one!\n\nBut then again, ...	127.0

Table 7. Performance of ML models

Model	accuracy	Precision	Recall	f1_ score	mean_squared_ error	RMSE	r2_ score	cohen_kappa_ score	matthews_ corrcoef	mean_squared_ log_error
Decision Tree	77.07	0.767	0.771	0.769	0.627	0.791	0.067	0.449	0.449	0.186
SVC	89.99	0.88	0.9	0.886	0.218	0.467	0.679	0.747	0.751	0.065
LogisticRegression	89.945	0.881	0.899	0.881	0.223	0.473	0.669	0.742	0.749	0.065
K-Nearest Neighbor	79.199	0.754	0.792	0.767	0.644	0.802	0.038	0.434	0.445	0.192

Table 7 shows the performance metrics of several models. The decision tree classifier, SVM, logistic regression, and K neighbors classifier all had accuracy ratings of 77.07, 89.99, 89.95, and 79.20, respectively. Based on the accuracy of the findings, all of the models accurately identify learners' review texts, but SVC produces the best results. Furthermore, the ratio of true positives to all positives, which indicates the degree of validity of the results, was 0.767, 0.880, 0.881, and 0.754 for the decision tree classifier, SVM, logistic regression, and K neighbors classifier, respectively. The decision tree classifier, SVM, logistic regression, and K neighbors classifier all have recall scores of 0.771, 0.9, 0.899, and 0.792, respectively. Based on accuracy and recall values, our research revealed that SVC delivers the highest validity and completeness of results when compared to other techniques. As a result, the F1 scores for the decision tree classifier, SVM, logistic regression, and K neighbors classifier models were 0.769, 0.886, 0.881, and 0.767, respectively, indicating that SVC had a higher influential efficacy than the others, and the r2 scores were 0.067, 0.679, 0.669, and 0.038, respectively, indicating that SVC had a higher influential efficacy than the others. Similarly, for the training model, we observed that SVC has the greatest quality of binary classifications (Matthew's corrcoef) and degree of correct variable demonstration, as well as reduced mean squared error, RMSE, and mean squared log error.

APPLICATIONS

Professionals will benefit greatly from this research. The commercial applications of sentiment analysis are difficult to overlook. Sentiment analysis in the workplace has the potential to revolutionize organizational development. The ability to get meaningful insights from unstructured data is critical for running a data-driven firm. In today's internet era, when businesses are suffering from data overload, companies may have a high volume of consumer feedback collected (which does not always equal better or deeper insights). Manually evaluating it without mistake or prejudice is still challenging for humans. As a result, our study may benefit a wide range of businesses, not only specialty schools.

In addition, better learner ratings help firms fine-tune their marketing tactics and improve their services by giving them with relevant data. Poorly rated businesses could be missing out on a potential expansion opportunity. The outcomes of this study will help companies better understand how machine learning techniques may be utilized to predict learner rating intentions toward enterprises. We also showed that Lexicon-based methods may be used to grade the review texts. Employing such systems to automatically determine the score of learner review data can benefit businesses.

Furthermore, our research looked at learners' psychological reactions to specialty schools as expressed on social media. Based on the findings of our study, specialty educational institutes will be able to assess learners' psychological feelings, allowing them to enhance and adapt their services. Families face significant obstacles while selecting a specialty school. Our research will assist parents and students in understanding the general attitude of learners toward specialist schools. This will assist them in making better decisions. Although the majority of users reported favorable sentiment, businesses should not dismiss negative feedback since negative feedback spreads faster than positive feedback. Therefore, they should closely monitor all forms of consumer sentiment. People make more fast judgements, according to the cognitive load theory. As a result, online consumers make their judgments quickly and rely on the advice of others to do so. Our findings will help both specialty and conventional schools anticipate the pace at which future purchasing choices will be made. Because more positive ratings encourage people to purchase more, while negative ones encourage them to refrain from purchasing.

Furthermore, classifying positive, negative, and neutral evaluations is one of the most common uses of sentiment analysis in business. Using sentiment analysis tools, businesses can discern between positive and negative feedback. Organizations will learn how to utilize the AFINN and VADER sentiment algorithms to detect positive, neutral, and negative sentiment based on the findings of this study.

Additionally, learners that are dissatisfied give lower review ratings and write lengthier evaluations, indicating that they are more inclined to share their dissatisfaction with others. As a result, when confronted with a large number of complaints to analyze and reply to, specialty schools may focus on the longer reviews to figure out why consumers are dissatisfied with their services. They'd be able to respond to unfavorable criticism faster, reducing the damage they might cause to their organization.

Furthermore, the current study uncovered the most positive and negative learner feedback. As a consequence of the approach utilized in this study to discover the top positive and negative reviews, specialty educational institutes will be able to understand how to acquire top positive and negative reviews using machine learning techniques. Top favorable and negative evaluations may help specialty educational institutes take the necessary measures, such as modifying and delivering learner-oriented courses and training, more quickly.

Besides, SVM has the greatest accuracy score for forecasting learner sentiment of specialty educational institutes, according to our research. As a result, specialty educational institutes may be able to use SVM to get the finest results when analyzing consumer behavior toward their products and services. Understanding consumer behavior may be a critical success driver in today's competitive business environment. This will assist organizations in developing new strategies while operating in a fast-paced environment. The findings of the study, which may be modified and applied to a variety of issues, might benefit specialty educational establishments as well as service industries such as banking and healthcare.

CONCLUSION AND LIMITATIONS

Knowing the emotions of learners is crucial for educational institutions. Because of the large volume of user-generated material, precise methods for evaluating and defining viewpoints are required. Learners' psychological perspectives are a valuable source of data that educational institutions may utilize to improve learning procedures and training activities. Institutes can discover appropriate teaching techniques to encourage student interest and contribute to constructive monitoring of learning progress throughout the course or improve future courses by collecting learners' review data linked to their learning. The content created by the learners, as well as their evaluations and comments, give information about the educational institutions they attended and the training activities they took part in. Opinion mining techniques in educational systems must be able to collect comments from students and automatically describe their thoughts and attitudes regarding the courses and learning activities that are available to them.

We used several machine learning approaches to assess reviewers' sentiment toward specialty schools in this study. Initially, we assessed sentiment using lexicon-based methods such as AFINN Sentiment and VADER Sentiment, and our findings revealed that the majority of evaluations of specialty schools were favorable. We were able to discover the top ten negative and positive reviews using lexicon-based techniques, as well as the link between review text length and review rating and emotion. Finally, we discovered that all four machine learning algorithms (decision tree, K Neighbors Classifier, logistic regression, and SVM) can correctly predict learners' review ratings, with SVC showing the best results.

There are several shortcomings in our research. Because the dataset utilized in this study is limited, the output is degraded. To determine the findings' generalizability, more research across additional sites is necessary. Future research may gather data on specialist schools from a variety of sources and compare the results. The hybrid and noun-verb methods presented in this research may be used to construct a real-time model that predicts reviewer ratings based on sentiment toward specialist schools. Additionally, employing the aspect level of sentiment analysis will enhance efficiency for future study on our filtered dataset, and we will be able to understand precisely what individuals liked or disliked. For example, the sorts of courses and training offered, the organizations that give services, and any pre-existing problems, among other things, which is a fine-grained strategy that yields consistent results. Furthermore, the current study has certain additional limitations, such as the research corpus's limited scope due to the lack of specialized school datasets. More experiments with big datasets are needed to prove the efficacy of the suggested models.

REFERENCES

Akhter, Z., Malik, G., & Plummer, V. (2021). Nurse educator knowledge, attitude and skills towards using high-fidelity simulation: A study in the vocational education sector. *Nurse Education in Practice*, *53*, 103048. Advance online publication. doi:10.1016/j.nepr.2021.103048 PMID:33857911

Al-Mashraie, M., Chung, S. H., & Jeon, H. W. (2020). Learner switching behavior analysis in the telecommunication industry via push-pull-mooring framework: A machine learning approach. *Computers & Industrial Engineering*, *106476*. Advance online publication. doi:10.1016/j.cie.2020.106476

Araque, O., Zhu, G., & Iglesias, C. A. (2019). A semantic similarity-based perspective of affect lexicons for sentiment analysis. *Knowledge-Based Systems*, *165*, 346–359. doi:10.1016/j.knosys.2018.12.005

Baumeister, R. F., Bratslavsky, E., Finkenauer, C., & Vohs, K. D. (2001). Bad is stronger than good. *Review of General Psychology*, *5*(4), 323–370. doi:10.1037/1089-2680.5.4.323

Borg, A., & Boldt, M. (2020). Using VADER Sentiment and SVM for Predicting Learner Response Sentiment. *Expert Systems with Applications*, *113746*. Advance online publication. doi:10.1016/j.eswa.2020.113746

Boser, B. E., Vapnik, V. N., & Guyon, I. M. (1992). Training Algorithm Margin for Optimal Classifiers. *Perception*, 144–152.

Burke, T. A., Jacobucci, R., Ammerman, B. A., Alloy, L. B., & Diamond, G. (2020). Using machine learning to classify suicide attempt history among youth in medical care settings. *Journal of Affective Disorders*, *268*, 206–214. doi:10.1016/j.jad.2020.02.048 PMID:32174479

Chevalier, J. A., & Mayzlin, D. (2006). The Effect of Word of Mouth on Sales: Online Book Reviews. *JMR, Journal of Marketing Research*, *43*(3), 345–354. doi:10.1509/jmkr.43.3.345

De Caigny, A., Coussement, K., & De Bock, K. W. (2018). A new hybrid classification algorithm for learner churn prediction based on logistic regression and decision trees. *European Journal of Operational Research*, *269*(2), 760–772. doi:10.1016/j.ejor.2018.02.009

Derakhshan, A., & Beigy, H. (2019). Sentiment analysis on stock social media for stock price movement prediction. *Engineering Applications of Artificial Intelligence*, *85*, 569–578. doi:10.1016/j.engappai.2019.07.002

DfES. (2005). *Education and skills Hispanic paper*. London, UK: Author. Retrieved from http://www.educationengland.org.uk/documents/pdfs/2005-white-paper-14-19-education-and-skills.pdf

Dwidienawati, D., Tjahjana, D., Abdinagoro, S. B., Gandasari, D., & Munawaroh. (2020). Learner review or influencer endorsement: Which one influences purchase intention more? *Heliyon*, *6*(11), e05543. Advance online publication. doi:10.1016/j.heliyon.2020.e05543 PMID:33294687

Eachempati, P., Srivastava, P. R., Kumar, A., Prat, J. M., & Delen, D. (2022). Can customer sentiment impact firm value? An integrated text mining approach. *Technological Forecasting and Social Change*, *174*, 121265. doi:10.1016/j.techfore.2021.121265

Eslami, S. P., Ghasemaghaei, M., & Hassanein, K. (2018). Which online reviews do consumers find most helpful? A multi-method investigation. *Decision Support Systems*, *113*, 32–42. doi:10.1016/j.dss.2018.06.012

Ferreira, J. M., Amorim, K. de S., Mäkinen, M., & Moura, G. G. (2016). The Network of Meanings and Educational Psychology: Theoretical and Practical Possibilities. *Procedia: Social and Behavioral Sciences*, *217*, 501–511. doi:10.1016/j.sbspro.2016.02.027

Fors Brandebo, M., Nilsson, S., & Larsson, G. (2016). Leadership: Is bad stronger than good? *Leadership and Organization Development Journal*, *37*(6), 690–710. doi:10.1108/LODJ-09-2014-0191

Ganaie, M. A., & Tanveer, M. (2021). Fuzzy least squares projection twin support vector machines for class imbalance learning. *Applied Soft Computing*, *113*, 107933. doi:10.1016/j.asoc.2021.107933

Geng, S., Niu, B., Feng, Y., & Huang, M. (2020). Understanding the focal points and sentiment of learners in MOOC reviews: A machine learning and SC-LIWC-based approach. *British Journal of Educational Technology*, *51*(5), 1785–1803. Advance online publication. doi:10.1111/bjet.12999

Ghasemaghaei, M., Eslami, S. P., Deal, K., & Hassanein, K. (2018). Reviews' length and sentiment as correlates of online reviews' ratings. *Internet Research*, *28*(3), 544–563. doi:10.1108/IntR-12-2016-0394

Ghosh, T. (2018). Predicting hotel book intention: The influential role of helpfulness and advocacy of online reviews. *Journal of Hospitality Marketing & Management*, *27*(3), 299–322. doi:10.1080/19368623.2017.1364198

Grundlingh, L. (2018). Exploring the possibility of using appraisal theory to determine the legitimacy of suicide notes. *Lingua*, *214*, 1–10. doi:10.1016/j.lingua.2018.07.004

Gul, E., Alpaslan, N., & Emiroglu, M. E. (2021). Robust optimization of SVM hyper-parameters for spillway type selection. *Ain Shams Engineering Journal*, *12*(3), 2413–2423. Advance online publication. doi:10.1016/j.asej.2020.10.022

Halliday, M. A. K., & Matthiessen, C. M. I. M. (2004). *An Introduction to Functional Grammar* (3rd ed.). Edward Arnold.

Hossain, M. S., & Rahman, M. F. (2022). Detection of potential customers' empathy behavior towards customers' reviews. *Journal of Retailing and Consumer Services*, *65*, 102881. doi:10.1016/j.jretconser.2021.102881

Hossain, M. S., Rahman, M. F., & Zhou, X. (2021). Impact of learners' interpersonal interactions in social commerce on learner relationship management performance. *Journal of Contemporary Marketing Science*, *4*(1), 161–181. Advance online publication. doi:10.1108/JCMARS-12-2020-0050

Hutto, C. J., & Gilbert, E. (2014). VADER: A parsimonious rule-based model for sentiment analysis of social media text. In *Proceedings of the 8th International Conference on Weblogs and Social Media, ICWSM 2014* (pp. 216–225). The AAAI Press.

Jena, R. (2020). An empirical case study on Indian consumers' sentiment towards electric vehicles: A big data analytics approach. *Industrial Marketing Management*, *90*, 605–616. Advance online publication. doi:10.1016/j.indmarman.2019.12.012

Jiménez-Zafra, S. M., Martín-Valdivia, M. T., Maks, I., & Izquierdo, R. (2017, March 1). Analysis of patient satisfaction in Dutch and Spanish online reviews. In *Procesamiento de Lenguaje Natural*. Sociedad Espanola para el Procesamiento del Lenguaje Natural.

Jones, M. H., Hackel, T. S., Hershberger, M., & Goodrich, K. M. (2019). Queer Youth in Educational Psychology Research. *Journal of Homosexuality*, *66*(13), 1797–1816. doi:10.1080/00918369.2018.1510262 PMID:30247992

Kim, D., Seo, D., Cho, S., & Kang, P. (2019). Multi-co-training for document classification using various document representations: TF–IDF, LDA, and Doc2Vec. *Information Sciences*, *477*, 15–29. doi:10.1016/j.ins.2018.10.006

Kim, J. C., & Chung, K. Y. (2020). Knowledge expansion of metadata using script mining analysis in multimedia recommendation. *Multimedia Tools and Applications*. Advance online publication. doi:10.100711042-020-08774-0

Kumar, S., Gahalawat, M., Roy, P. P., Dogra, D. P., & Kim, B. G. (2020). Exploring impact of age and gender on sentiment analysis using machine learning. *Electronics (Basel)*, *9*(2), 374. Advance online publication. doi:10.3390/electronics9020374

Lazarev, V. A. (1992). Specialty Schools. *Russian Education & Society*, *34*(1), 23–31. doi:10.2753/RES1060-9393340123

Lee, M., Rodgers, S., & Kim, M. (2009). Effects of valence and extremity of eWOM on attitude toward the brand and website. *Journal of Current Issues and Research in Advertising, 31*(2), 1–11. doi:10.1080/10641734.2009.10505262

Liu, L., Hu, X., Feng, Z., Zhang, X., Wang, S., Xu, S., & Sun, K. (2019). Prediction of acid radical ion binding residues by K-nearest neighbors classifier. *BMC Molecular and Cell Biology, 20*(S3), 52. Advance online publication. doi:10.118612860-019-0238-8 PMID:31823720

Liu, R., Xiong, R., & Song, L. (2010). A sentiment classification method for chinese document. In *ICCSE 2010 - 5th International Conference on Computer Science and Education, Final Program and Book of Abstracts* (pp. 918–922). 10.1109/ICCSE.2010.5593462

Luo, Y., & Huang, W. (2011). Product review information extraction based on adjective opinion words. In *Proceedings - 4th International Joint Conference on Computational Sciences and Optimization, CSO 2011* (pp. 1309–1313). 10.1109/CSO.2011.209

Machová, K., Mikula, M., Gao, X., & Mach, M. (2020). Lexicon-based sentiment analysis using particle swarm optimization. *Electronics (Switzerland), 9*(8), 1–22. doi:10.3390/electronics9081317

Martin, J. R., & White, P. R. R. (2005). *The Language of Evaluation: Appraisal in English*. Palgrave. doi:10.1057/9780230511910

Meek, S., Wilk, V., & Lambert, C. (2021). A big data exploration of the informational and normative influences on the helpfulness of online restaurant reviews. *Journal of Business Research, 125*, 354–367. doi:10.1016/j.jbusres.2020.12.001

Miao, Q., Li, Q., & Zeng, D. (2010). Fine-grained opinion mining by integrating multiple review sources. *Journal of the American Society for Information Science and Technology, 61*(11), 2288–2299. doi:10.1002/asi.21400

Moors, A., Van de Cruys, S., & Pourtois, G. (2021). Comparison of the determinants for positive and negative affect proposed by appraisal theories, goal-directed theories, and predictive processing theories. *Current Opinion in Behavioral Sciences, 39*, 147–152. doi:10.1016/j.cobeha.2021.03.015

Mullen, T., & Collier, N. (2004). Sentiment Analysis using Support Vector Machines with Diverse Information Sources. In D. Lin & D. Wu (Eds.), *Proceedings of EMNLP 2004* (pp. 412–418). Association for Computational Linguistics. Retrieved from http://research.nii.ac.jp/~collier/papers/emnlp2004.pdf

Pang, B., & Lee, L. (2008). Opinion mining and sentiment analysis. *Foundations and Trends in Information Retrieval, 2*(1–2), 1–135. doi:10.1561/1500000011

Panhalkar, A. R., & Doye, D. D. (2021). Optimization of decision trees using modified African buffalo algorithm. *Journal of King Saud University - Computer and Information Sciences*. doi:10.1016/j.jksuci.2021.01.011

Pano, T., & Kashef, R. (2020). A Complete VADER-Based Sentiment Analysis of Bitcoin (BTC) Tweets during the Era of COVID-19. *Big Data and Cognitive Computing, 4*(4), 33. Advance online publication. doi:10.3390/bdcc4040033

Preethi, P. G., Uma, V., & Kumar, A. (2015). Temporal sentiment analysis and causal rules extraction from tweets for event prediction. In *Procedia Computer Science* (Vol. 48, pp. 84–89). Elsevier B.V. doi:10.1016/j.procs.2015.04.154

Prieto, L. M., Aguero-Valverde, J., Zarrate-Cardenas, G., & Van Maarseveen, M. (2019). Parental preferences in the choice for a specialty school. *Journal of School Choice*, *13*(2), 198–227. doi:10.1080/15582159.2018.1442087

Qiao, S., Yan, B., & Li, J. (2018). Ensemble learning for protein multiplex subcellular localization prediction based on weighted KNN with different features. *Applied Intelligence*, *48*(7), 1813–1824. doi:10.100710489-017-1029-6

Ravi, K., & Ravi, V. (2015). A survey on opinion mining and sentiment analysis: Tasks, approaches and applications. *Knowledge-Based Systems*, *89*, 14–46. doi:10.1016/j.knosys.2015.06.015

Read, J., & Carroll, J. (2012). Annotating expressions of Appraisal in English. *Language Resources and Evaluation*, *46*(3), 421–447. doi:10.100710579-010-9135-7

Rodríguez-Hidalgo, C. T., Tan, E. S. H., & Verlegh, P. W. J. (2015). The social sharing of emotion (SSE) in online social networks: A case study in Live Journal. *Computers in Human Behavior*, *52*, 364–372. doi:10.1016/j.chb.2015.05.009

Rout, J. K., Choo, K.-K. R., Dash, A. K., Bakshi, S., Jena, S. K., & Williams, K. L. (2017). A model for sentiment and emotion analysis of unstructured social media text. *Electronic Commerce Research*, *18*(1), 181–199. doi:10.100710660-017-9257-8

Scherer, K. R., Schorr, A., & Johnstone, T. (Eds.). (2001). *Appraisal processes in emotion: Theory, methods, research*. Oxford University Press.

Snowman, J. (1997). Educational Psychology: What Do We Teach, What Should We Teach? *Educational Psychology Review*, *9*(2), 151–170. doi:10.1023/A:1024740512959

Tan, M. J., & Guan, C. H. (2021). Are people happier in locations of high property value? Spatial temporal analytics of activity frequency, public sentiment and housing price using twitter data. *Applied Geography (Sevenoaks, England)*, *132*, 102474. Advance online publication. doi:10.1016/j.apgeog.2021.102474

Vashishtha, S., & Susan, S. (2020). Fuzzy Interpretation of Word Polarity Scores for Unsupervised Sentiment Analysis. In *2020 11th International Conference on Computing, Communication and Networking Technologies, ICCCNT 2020*. Institute of Electrical and Electronics Engineers Inc. 10.1109/ICCCNT49239.2020.9225646

Walls, J., & Kemper, S. (2018). Fitting In to Stand Out: How Teachers at Small, Urban "Specialty Schools" Experience Extra-Organizational Influence. *Leadership and Policy in Schools*, 1–27. doi:10.1080/15700763.2018.1453936

Wang, W., Guo, L., & Wu, Y. J. (2022). The merits of a sentiment analysis of antecedent comments for the prediction of online fundraising outcomes. *Technological Forecasting and Social Change*, *174*, 121070. doi:10.1016/j.techfore.2021.121070

Wang, Y., Kim, J., & Kim, J. (2021). The financial impact of online learner reviews in the restaurant industry: A moderating effect of brand equity. *International Journal of Hospitality Management, 95*, 102895. Advance online publication. doi:10.1016/j.ijhm.2021.102895

West, A., & Noden, P. (2000). *School reform in England: Increasing choice and diversity through specialist schools?* Paper presented at the Annual Meeting of the American Educational Research Association, New Orleans, LA. Retrieved from https://files.eric.ed.gov/fulltext/ED445417.pdf

Widyaningrum, P., Ruldeviyani, Y., & Dharayani, R. (2019). Sentiment analysis to assess the community's enthusiasm towards the development chatbot using an appraisal theory. *Procedia Computer Science, 161, 723–730.* doi:10.1016/j.procs.2019.11.176

World Bank Group. (2011). *Learning for all: Investing in people's knowledge and skills to promote development.* World Bank Group Education Strategy 2020.

Yadav, A., Jha, C. K., Sharan, A., & Vaish, V. (2020). Sentiment analysis of financial news using unsupervised approach. In *Procedia Computer Science* (Vol. 167, pp. 589–598). Elsevier B.V. doi:10.1016/j.procs.2020.03.325

Yang, L., Li, Y., Wang, J., & Sherratt, R. S. (2020). Sentiment Analysis for E-Commerce Product Reviews in Chinese Based on Sentiment Lexicon and Deep Learning. *IEEE Access: Practical Innovations, Open Solutions*, *8*, 23522–23530. doi:10.1109/ACCESS.2020.2969854

Zeelenberg, M., & Pieters, R. (2004). Beyond valence in learner dissatisfaction: A review and new findings on behavioral responses to regret and disappointment in failed services. *Journal of Business Research*, *57*(4), 445–455. doi:10.1016/S0148-2963(02)00278-3

Zhai, G., Yang, Y., Wang, H., & Du, S. (2020). Multi-attention fusion modeling for sentiment analysis of educational big data. *Big Data Mining and Analytics*, *3*(4), 311–319. doi:10.26599/BDMA.2020.9020024

Zhang, Y., Yu, J., Dong, X., & Zhong, P. (2021). Multi-task support vector machine with pinball loss. *Engineering Applications of Artificial Intelligence*, *106*, 104458. Advance online publication. doi:10.1016/j.engappai.2021.104458

ADDITIONAL READING

Fiok, K., Karwowski, W., Gutierrez, E., & Wilamowski, M. (2021). Analysis of sentiment in tweets addressed to a single domain-specific Twitter account: Comparison of model performance and explainability of predictions. *Expert Systems with Applications*, *186*, 115771. Advance online publication. doi:10.1016/j.eswa.2021.115771

Hossain, M. S., & Rahman, M. F. (2022). Detection of potential customers' empathy behavior towards customers' reviews. *Journal of Retailing and Consumer Services*, *65*, 102881. doi:10.1016/j.jretconser.2021.102881

Keramatfar, A., & Amirkhani, H. (2019). Bibliometrics of sentiment analysis literature. *Journal of Information Science*, *45*(1), 3–15. doi:10.1177/0165551518761013

Li, H., Chen, Q., Zhong, Z., Gong, R., & Han, G. (2022). E-word of mouth sentiment analysis for user behavior studies. *Information Processing & Management*, *59*(1), 102784. Advance online publication. doi:10.1016/j.ipm.2021.102784 PMID:34580562

Ligthart, A., Catal, C., & Tekinerdogan, B. (2021). Systematic reviews in sentiment analysis: A tertiary study. *Artificial Intelligence Review*, *54*(7), 4997–5053. doi:10.100710462-021-09973-3

Nasreen Taj, M. B., & Girisha, G. S. (2021). Insights of strength and weakness of evolving methodologies of sentiment analysis. *Global Transitions Proceedings*, *2*(2), 157–162. doi:10.1016/j.gltp.2021.08.059

Taboada, M., Brooke, J., Tofiloski, M., Voll, K., & Stede, M. (2011). Lexicon-basedmethods for sentiment analysis. *Computational Linguistics*, *37*(2), 267–307. doi:10.1162/COLI_a_00049

Yang, L., Li, Y., Wang, J., & Sherratt, R. S. (2020). Sentiment Analysis for E-Commerce Product Reviews in Chinese Based on Sentiment Lexicon and Deep Learning. *IEEE Access: Practical Innovations, Open Solutions*, *8*, 23522–23530. doi:10.1109/ACCESS.2020.2969854

KEY TERMS AND DEFINITIONS

Lexicon-Based Sentiment Analysis: A technique to assess a document by combining the sentiment scores of all the words in the text, which is done using a pre-prepared sentiment lexicon.

Machine Learning: A type of data analysis that automates the process of creating analytical models. It's a branch of artificial intelligence (AI) based on the idea that machines can learn from data, detect patterns, and make decisions with little or no human input.

Review: A piece of feedback given by a consumer who has purchased and used the product or service or has made contact with it. On the internet, user reviews are a form of user's feedback.

Sentiment Analysis: Also known as emotion AI or opinion mining is the systematic identification, quantification, extraction, and study of emotional states and subjective information using natural language processing (NLP), biometrics, text analysis, and computational linguistics.

Specialty Schools: Secondary schools that provide more in-depth coverage of specific disciplines.

APPENDIX 1: SAMPLE = DF.ILOC[7741]['TEXT']:TOP NEGATIVE REVIEW

This is the most dishonest, disorganized and unprofessional "college" out there. Needless to say, my experience with CHCP has turned out to be a miserable one. So please, take my advice and RUN FAST. I attended the ultrasound program and experienced problem after problem.

First off, I was lied to by my admission's rep. I was told that clinical sites would be "no more than 2 hours away", however, the students from my class who are still attending are currently traveling weekly to clinical sites in DALLAS and HOUSTON. The director of education (who recently went MIA), would continuously barge into our classroom barking and complaining that the school was "losing clinical sites". They sure have lost numerous sites due to this school being a serious JOKE in the healthcare community. The students who still attend CHCP are often laughed at and ridiculed during clinicals by other healthcare professionals solely for being a CHCP student. After much research, CHCP has had a horrible rep for some time. They should be ashamed of themselves and cleaning up their act-but they are NOT.

If you attend CHCP, you will not be taught by certified teachers or professors. They will have you reading out of textbooks as opposed to proper lectures and demonstrations that real colleges provide. The ultrasound teacher in particular, is simply an ultrasound tech from out of state. She does not even have a teaching license nor a bachelor's degree. She came in as a new teacher and developed a big head causing her to relentlessly degrade and talk down to the students often forcing them to leave class in tears. During exams she would bully myself and other students insulting our skills and threatening to fail us. She followed through with her threats and failed a couple of students. After complaints to the director of education and even the campus president, nothing was ever done about this teacher because they keep losing teachers. A teacher who no longer teaches at this school said there were so many "shady" things going on behind the scenes.

After passing all prerequisite courses and hours, students are supposed to go into the clinical portion of the program. All except me, that is. Somehow I became the exception and was told that the teachers did not feel that I was "ready" to go into clinicals, mind you I had passed all classes. They had a "plan" set aside for me to "practice scanning" for a few months, ultimately pushing my graduation date out. They said they would send me to clinicals whenever they felt I was ready. Appalled, I spoke to higher ups and eventually the campus president. I expected her to be on my side after this obvious abuse, but she was not. She agreed with the staff and assured me that this sort of situation happens to other students all the time. So, instead of being honest with you, they will lie and try to buy time with their plans of "extra scanning time". Pathetic. The new director of the ultrasound program suggested that I could volunteer or shadow during their little break period for me, she also suggested that I could scan animals at a vet clinic lol. Really?

Also, this school has been through 3, THREE, ultrasound tech program directors within 6 months- if that tells you anything at all.

I have consulted with a lawyer and will not back down until I am refunded the $20k+ that this school has charged me as well as wasting my time/stress. The school is currently refusing to refund me. This is holding me back financially from being able to attend a REAL school. Did I mention that their credits will not transfer any where else? Most people are forced to stay and carry out their phony degree plan solely because of this.

What this college has done to me and numerous other students is completely illegal and a breach of contract on their end. CHCP is known as a dishonest school full of ruthless, money hungry goons. Don't be their next victim.

** Current students have not been able to pass the SPI exam which is required in order to take the ARDMS exam. Without having ARDMS registry it is nearly impossible for an ultrasound tech to find a job.

APPENDIX 2: SAMPLE = DF.ILOC[5145]['TEXT']:TOP POSITIVE REVIEW

Okay, y'all, pull up a chair...I have a feeling this is gonna be a long one!
But then again, it's your FACE, so you should be wiling to do your homework in deciding who you will let do semi-permanent stuff to your FACE. Right?
SO.... (go ahead and make yourself a cup of tea-- I'll wait...)
Laura is that rare, rare person, that rare combination of truly kind, truly thoughtful, and truly and completely and dazzlingly gifted in her chosen field. Exponentially! I am a writer by trade and can't think of enough superlatives to describe how truly tremendously fantastic she is. If you are considering having eyebrow work done, consider yourself lucky to have found Laura (I know I am!).
(I am a new learner of hers and already know I will be a forever learner!)
I first had permanent makeup done on my eyebrows in 2000, when it was still pretty new. I had bald patches in spots from overtweezing, and also my eyebrows kind of drooped at the tail and I thought could use some reshaping. Well, because I didn't do MY homework (my bad!), and b/c I just trusted a friend was taking me to someone who knew what she was doing, I got a job that maybe wasn't so great in terms of color (though, thank goodness, the shape was good). The color faded weird right away, and despite many new permanent jobs over that original since then, they all fade into that original really unappealing color, and quite quickly. But, even if the color were good, they're just solid (no hairstrokes), so they wouldn't look all that natural.
I decided to just give up and just powder over the color, but upon moving to the Austin area, I thought I'd check to see if there were any professionals out here I was moved to try. After looking at some professionals' pics of their work I didn't like, I found Laura's portfolio pics online, and Holy Noteworthy Artistry, Batman! I was impressed right away. Her work is SO natural-looking, and so flattering. And it's clear she doesn't do cookie-cutter work on faces, but treats faces like the individual beauties they are. I knew right away she was the one.
I was further impressed when I called to consult with her, to tell her about my history, to ask questions. It was immediately clear that she is EXTREMELY patient, kind, thorough, smart, and considerate (even before I was a learner). She educated me as to the difference between the permanent kind I'd had several times, and the microblading. And she answered my gazillion questions, and she asked me thoughtful questions about me. I felt heard and understood and taken care of. And I hadn't even met her!
She sent me great pre-procedure instructions (as a former teacher, I love stuff like that). When I met her, yet again, I was even more impressed with her. I know she must do a bunch of these (she is just so so good, incredibly talented, that I know she must do a lot of them to be that great!), but she makes you

feel like you are her sole priority for the time you're there; she makes you feel like she is literally there just to make you beautiful. That is a rare feeling in our busy world!
She explained everything to me very clearly, gave me clear after-instructions to take home, and she went to work. Again, she is so thoughtful, making sure I understood everything and liked everything she was going to do. Because I wanted an old tattoo covered up, she was more limited than if I hadn't had anything to cover, but, and here's the most important part, SHE TRANSFORMED ME, TRANSFORMED MY WHOLE FACE with her careful artistry (and make no mistake, she's an artist, and that's who you want working on your FACE, an artist). I can't believe how amazing my brows look. Unbelievable! I couldn't be happier! Microblading is the way to go, so natural, but you have to have the right artist wielding the tool. And for me, that artist will always be Laura!
I am so grateful to her and grateful that she's decided to share her consummate skill with the world and to help women who might be self-conscious feel better about themselves. That's such important work. Although I was already a fan of hers from looking at her portfolio, seeing the results on my own face has me over the moon happy.
Thank you, thank you, Laura-- for your kindness, your amazing talent, your graciousness, and your remarkable investment in how I look and feel. I feel super-lucky to be part of your learner "family"!

Section 3
Advancing the Profession

Chapter 8
Working Towards a Data Science Associates Degree Program:
Impacts, Challenges, and Future Directions

Wendy Chin
Community College of Baltimore County, USA

James Braman
https://orcid.org/0000-0001-6080-3903
Community College of Baltimore County, USA

Hanks Melissa
Community College of Baltimore County, USA

Paulette Comet
Community College of Baltimore County, USA

ABSTRACT

As data science continues to grow and become intertwined into many domains, its application becomes increasingly relevant. Data science is becoming a part of an interdisciplinary web of methodologies that can be used to extract essential insights from many types of data and are used in numerous occupations. Due to the rising importance of this emerging field, additional educational opportunities to learn data science will be beneficial in the future. In this chapter, the authors discuss the development of an associate's degree program in data science that provides students with specific coursework required to transfer to other institutions that offer bachelor's degrees in data science. Alternatively, students could also use this program to learn new skills in data science to change career paths or to continue their education. First, the general development of the data science program is discussed, followed by development challenges and opportunities, specific courses, and future directions.

DOI: 10.4018/978-1-7998-9644-9.ch008

INTRODUCTION

The mission of the Community College of Baltimore County (CCBC) aims to "[transform] lives by providing an accessible, affordable, and high-quality education that prepares students for transfer and career success, strengthens the regional workforce, and enriches our community" (CCBC, 2021). The College strives for excellence, innovative and timely programs relevant to today's ever-changing society and the needs of the students as they are preparing for their careers, transfer opportunities, and personal advancement. One recent and significant initiative aimed at this mission is the development of a Data Science Associates degree program. This program has been the culmination of many months of research, meetings, and collaborations both within the College and with many outside organizations. At the time of this writing, the degree program is pending approval and under review by the Maryland Higher Education Commission (MHEC). The goal is to start offering this major in late 2022 or sometime in 2023. This chapter presents the overall development of the data science program, including details of classes, challenges and opportunities, and future directions of the program.

The proposed Associates of Science degree program in Data Science emphasizes a robust curriculum that will prepare students to succeed in their careers as well as assist with their transfer. We envision that many students will transfer to a related 4-year program. In addition, many students transfer into other degree programs to complete their bachelor's degree to ultimately pave the way for career success in this emerging discipline. Some students at the College already have a bachelor's or master's degree but are looking to expand their knowledge or change fields and require additional coursework. Students who are successful in this degree program will have a broad spectrum of transfer options with multiple career tracks, such as those pursuing Computer Science, Data Science, Data Analytics, Accounting, Business, and more. The program builds on many existing courses and degree programs and requires the creation of several new courses specific to the field of data science. Development of the Data Science degree aligns with CCBC's "Rethinking what's Possible" Transformational Academics strategic priority by ensuring seamless transfer opportunities for students through expanded partnerships with local and regional four-year institutions. At the same time, it supports Transformational Academics by providing a high-quality program that will promote market viability and respond to the needs of the student, community, and workforce.

To provide some context, CCBC is a public community college located in Maryland, USA, and is an important part of Baltimore County. Baltimore County is the third most populated county in Maryland. CCBC collaborates with the government, businesses, and many local organizations for various initiatives and educational activities. Based on 2017 data, the college-educated 61,191 students, including 29,115 credit students and 33,247 non-credit students (CCBC, 2020). Through the operation of three main campuses (Catonsville, Essex, and Dundalk) and three extension centers, CCBC serves a diverse population of Maryland residents and is well known locally. The computer science/information technology department (CSIT) offers associate degrees in Information Technology, Computer Science, and Computer Science with a concentration in Information Systems Management as well as five credit-based certificates. The certificates include a Database certificate, Information Management certificate, Mobile Development certificate, Programming certificate, and an Office Specialist certificate. Many courses are offered in various modalities and time frames to better serve the needs of the students. These modalities include face-to-face courses, online, blended (a hybrid mixture of face-to-face and online), and remote (which are live instructor-led online courses conducted through video conferencing technology). Online courses are highly assessed and evaluated. To ensure quality and consistency for all CSIT class sections, specific guidelines are in place for developing and maintaining online and blended courses (Paniagua, 2019). Instructors teaching online must go through training to teach online or blended sections. Online courses must also pass evaluation through internal review mechanisms in combination with Quality Matters (QM) review and rubric.

During the fall 2020 academic semester, one of the CSIT department's goals included making substantial improvements and revisions to current course offerings. Data science was discussed many times as a possible new degree program based on feedback from faculty, the CSIT department's industry advisory board, and administrators within the College. Both data science and data analytics programs were initially planned, but the two programs were merged, and data science was ultimately selected. A committee was formed, including several CSIT faculty members and faculty from other departments such as Mathematics and Business. The committee met numerous times for several months, building the program requirements, discussing key topics, examining resources and different needs. This was in collaboration with the Dean and other faculty and using feedback from the CSIT industry advisory board. The advisory board serves a key role in providing insights on current business needs and industry trends. The remaining chapter discusses the development of the data science program. First, the authors provide additional background describing the rationale of the program development, followed by development challenges and opportunities, specific courses, future directions, and then the conclusion.

BACKGROUND

Over the past several years, the field of data science has been growing exponentially. Couple this growth with its ever-expanding overlap into other areas such as computer science, analytics, artificial intelligence, information technology, and more, there is great potential and impact. Data science is undoubtedly a field that intersects many other disciplines with far-reaching impacts. Those learning to become data scientists need broad skills that draw upon many disciplines but need to have both deep domain knowledge and analytical skills (Waller & Fawcett, 2013). This can be challenging to include all of these areas into one academic program (especially at an associate's level), however key courses and topic areas can be prioritized. As noted by Izizarry (2020), there are benefits from an educational standpoint to focus on teaching relevant software applications, essential programming skills, and providing real-world examples or experiences as part of a data science program. Strong skills in mathematics are also necessary for this domain.

Data Scientists are analytical data experts who have the technical skills to solve complex problems (Sas, 2022). Data scientists must be part mathematicians and part computer scientists to navigate the world of big data, databases, and other informatics. To assess and interpret data sets, data scientists must implement advanced analytics programs, statistical methods, and machine learning in predictive modeling. To that end, our data science program aims at combining courses that tap into these areas to provide students with a strong foundation in many of these skills. This includes requiring several math courses, including statistics, several programming courses (in Java and Python), and a machine learning course as well as several core data science courses. These are all designed in such a way to be flexible as technologies change and the field advances. Data scientists must solve business-related problems using data-driven techniques, have a solid grasp of statistics, and stay on top of analytical techniques such as machine learning, deep learning, and text analytics. Data scientists must be able to navigate between

Table 1. Maryland Occupational Projections 2018-2028 for Data Science (Maryland Department of Labor, 2021)

SOC	Occupation Title	Employment			Openings	
		2016	2026	Change	Growth Openings	Total
15-2041	Statisticians	3,449	4,350	901	2,996	3,897
15-0000	Computer and Mathematical Occupations	113,209	130,011	16,802	88,553	105,355
15-2000	Mathematical Science Occupations	8,740	11,032	2,292	6,894	9,186

information technology and business effectively. They look for order and patterns in data and help a business's bottom line.

The data in Table 1 below highlights several fields associated with data science that have a ten-year job growth potential of ten percent. These career fields include but are not limited to those related to business, government, sciences, education, engineering, and data science specialists. At the time of this writing, the median salary for data scientists is $98,000 (U.S. Bureau of Labor Statistics, 2020). The job outlook is growing much faster than the average for all related occupations. In particular, the Baltimore-Washington area has one of the highest employment levels in the United States for technology-related occupations. In addition, Maryland has a high concentration of data science-related positions with high-paying salaries (U.S. Bureau of Labor Statistics, 2020). These are all very positive indicators for the outlook for a new data science program and show the need for this career path.

Table 1 also illustrates Maryland's potential demand for graduates in the Data Science degree program over the next several years. The evidence provided is based upon the program's proposed Classification of Program (CIP) code of 15-2098 and cross-referenced with the Bureau of Labor Statistics Standard Occupational Classifications (SOC) that classify and indicate the professions and occupations of graduates of programs with this CIP code are likely to pursue. This data provides evidence to support the potential for 118,438 new and additional positions in professions that prepare graduates over ten years, or 1,184 positions per year (Maryland Department of Labor, 2021).

A strategy of the Maryland State Plan for Postsecondary Education (Strategy 8) is "to develop new partnerships between colleges and businesses to support workforce development and improve workforce

Table 2. States with the highest concentration of jobs and location quotients in Data Scientists and Mathematical Science Occupations (U.S. Bureau of Labor Statistics, 2020)

State	Employment	Employment per thousand jobs	Location quotient	Hourly mean wage	Annual mean wage
District of Columbia	590	0.86	2.00	$ 51.06	$ 106,210
Washington	2,610	0.82	1.90	$ 56.88	$ 118,320
Maryland	1,890	0.75	1.74	$ 52.39	$ 108,960
Virginia	2,450	0.66	1.54	$ 47.92	$ 99,670
Illinois	3,290	0.58	1.36	$ 48.33	$ 100,520

Table 3. Percentile wage estimates for Data Scientists and Mathematical Science Occupations: (U.S. Bureau of Labor Statistics, 2020)

Percentile	10%	25%	50% (Median)	75%	90%
Hourly Wage	$ 25.46	$ 34.51	$ 47.23	$ 62.68	$ 79.44
Annual Wage	$ 52,950	$ 71,790	$ 98,230	$ 130,370	$ 165,230

readiness" (MHEC, 2017, p. 3). The field of Data Science is clearly in high demand. However, in both the United States and worldwide, the industry is experiencing a shortage of skilled Data Scientists. As such, the proposed program will ensure that CCBC is able to help educate students to meet the needs of regional and state-wide industry need for the advancement of current data science-related skill sets. Even the cover of the Maryland State Plan for Postsecondary Education has the slogan "Increasing Student Success with Less Debt" (MHEC, 2017, p. 1). With this in mind, offering the Data Science A.S. degree as a two-year program will assist students in reaching their educational goals at a much lower cost. Financially, the cost for a student to come to CCBC full time is $4,992 annually (tuition and fees) as of the time of this writing. This is a savings of almost half when compared to similar programs at four-year institutions. Therefore, a student attending CCBC could reduce expenses substantially by earning an Associate's degree prior to transfer.

DEVELOPMENT

The following section discusses the strengths, challenges, and other considerations for developing the data science program. Starting a data science program is a significant endeavor that we are excited about the opportunities and benefits to the students. As we continue to build the program and launch new related projects, we foresee many new opportunities for students and faculty of the College and new ways to leverage other courses. In addition, the proposed degree program is designed to prepare students for transfer to obtain later a bachelor's, master's degree or both and ultimately fill the workforce demand for this new, high-demand skillset. In the next section, we discuss several elements of the development of the degree, which include consideration of student skills, transfer considerations, textbook resources as part of the First Day program, technology resources, and diversity. The discussion is then followed by a listing of the current course requirements and descriptions.

Student Skill

Within the community college environment, some courses, especially technical courses, can be challenging due to the diverse set of student skill levels, varied technology literacy, and course workload balance. Some of these issues can also be impacted by differences in enrollment statuses compared to students enrolled in more traditional four-year institutions (Cohen & Brawer, 2003). The courses offered in the CSIT department go through many types of evaluation in order to examine the course design to not only best reach and engage with students but also build students' skills. Many of the topics and core competencies are scaffolded to link to next-level courses or materials. There are many challenges that faculty are faced with when dealing with underprepared learners (Gabriel & Flake, 2008) or at-risk learners (Zheng, Warschauer, Hwang, & Collins, 2014). These are all elements that are considered.

For the data science courses, instructors need to be resourceful and open to change as new challenges arise in this discipline. This also applies to the need to be innovative and knowledgeable with and about technology and potential limitations. One challenge in course design is to be mindful of specific technological needs of the courses, but at the same time consider limitations of skill level and technology access of the students. For example, we do not want to require an expensive option for data visualization or analysis software applications if there are similar open-source options. This would require even online students to have to travel to campus. Currently, a virtual desktop infrastructure is used in regard to expensive specialized hardware where possible.

Transfer Considerations

Another consideration is how the program, as a completed degree and that of individual courses, may transfer to other institutions. For example, some students in the program will have a degree and are taking a single class to learn a new skill or working towards a new degree in a new field. Others will be taking individual courses for personal, educational enrichment. Therefore, working towards sustainable transfer agreements with 4-year institutions with similar degree programs will be essential.

Another hurdle is many other data science programs are at the bachelor's degree level or higher. This issue poses many challenges in terms of transferability. At the associate's degree level, the highest level of course type is the 200 level. At the same time, those graduating from the program need to have a significant level of knowledge and a breadth of expertise in data science. Transferring to a 4-year institution will allow students to further their knowledge and provide depth, therefore, expanding and strengthening their understanding. We are actively working with academic partners to ensure best options for students to transfer courses.

To assist students in completing their degree, CCBC has in place Academic Pathways (CCBC Academic Pathways, 2022). Pathways are a way to group students by degree program, certificate, training or area of interest. The following areas are the current academic Pathways: Arts, Business, Criminal Justice and Law, Education, Health Professions, Humanities, Social Sciences, Mathematics and Science, and Technology and Engineering. There is significant support for students in each Pathway to ensure that students are aware of the related programs, courses or training, and opportunities at the College. Course sequence lists are available to help keep student on their path to graduate. Each semester there are numerous events and other outreach initiatives to make sure students have the opportunity to ask questions and learn more about their Pathway and career path. Internships are also a possibility for some students. There are guest speakers from industry graduates, academic and business partners that provide insights to students. Numerous academic support services, campus activity resources and transfer information is provided to students.

First Day Program

As of the fall 2019 semester, the Computer Science and Information Technology department started to use a new textbook access program and has continued to be very successful (Clements & Braman, 2021). This was in collaboration with the college bookstore, Barnes and Nobel (CCBC Bookstore, 2022). This inclusive access program is referred to as "First Day" or the "First Day Program". There were several motivations for adopting an inclusive access program. One major element is the significant cost savings for students and the convenience of having inclusive access to the course textbook embedded into the course. Through this program, students have access to an eBook version of the traditional physical book as an embedded link in the LMS. Students do still have the option to opt out of the program and purchase a printed version of the textbook (Clements & Braman, 2021). Students through the First Day program have access to the textbook on the very first day of class allowing faculty to start teaching content right away. This eliminates delay in purchasing books at the beginning of the semester and allows for access during the semester.

The initial rollout was in several highly enrolled general education courses within the department (Clements & Braman, 2021). After receiving very positive initial feedback from both students and faculty, the program was expanded to other courses by the spring 2020 semester, including CSIT 210 - Introduction to Programing, CSIT 211 – Advanced programing, CSIT 214 - C+ + Programming, and CSIT 216 - Python Programming. These additional courses represent most of our programming courses and are typically taken by those majoring in Computer Science, Information Technology, Management Information Systems, or other related majors. Use during the fall 2019 semester resulted in an estimated cost savings of more than $78,000 (Clements & Braman, 2021). The First Day program was expanded to include four upper-level programming courses during the spring 2020 semester, with the total cost savings for students throughout 2020 estimated to be more than $249,000 (Clements & Braman, 2021). In terms of the data science program, we intend to continue this approach as a way to provide students with the convenience of having the textbook "on the go" while at the same time providing cost savings. In addition, it is estimated that some of the data science courses will need more than one-course textbook due to their complex nature. Having these cost savings will help reduce extra costs.

Technology Considerations

A complex and dynamic challenge is the technological needs of the program. Existing programs' established courses are already fully designed with their specific needs known and established. This is especially true for programming courses, as mainly all required is IDE updates or the installation of new or specific libraries (or updates to those libraries). Current security settings in computer labs do not allow for updating or changing software and are managed exclusively by CCBC's Information Technology department. We see software updates as being a challenge for the data science courses, as there may be more updates needed in a more frequent time frame. At this time, class projects require multiple complex library installations, which will need monitoring; otherwise, proposed assignments may not function correctly.

A significant concern is a need for large amounts of storage and computational capabilities for the machine learning course and those courses where projects may involve the topic of Big Data and those requiring extensive analysis. Based on feedback from faculty and the advisory board, it was suggested that several cloud-based services be examined for course activities. This would eliminate the need for extensive hardware and storage requirements. Additionally, updates would be handled by the service providers. The drawback to this approach would be the potential cost for numerous student accounts.

Internal Approval Processes

All new program proposals at CCBC are reviewed and approved according to the process developed through college governance, which includes approval by the Curriculum and Instruction Committee (CIC) and the full College Senate. The data science degree program was carefully reviewed by the College President and her Senior Staff prior to submission to the CCBC Board of Trustees for their endorsement. The President has affirmed that the program can be implemented within existing institutional resources. Professor Wendy Chin (CSIT Department chair) will serve as the coordinator of Data Science and oversee the program. As the Data Science degree program has been approved by the College Senate, President, and Board of Trustees, adequate funding will be in place for at least the first five years of program implementation.

Online Learning

CCBC's strategic plan places an increased emphasis on online learning (distance education). Sustaining and growing online learning is interwoven into the academic schools' programs as well as the Department of Online Learning's (DOL) goals and objectives. CSIT, in particular, has a robust set of courses that are offered each semester, including various programming courses and general education courses. Courses are routinely reviewed and revised. Outcomes of course content are also assessed. In addition, the instructional technology budget supports technologies related to online learning and other curriculum needs. The DOL also has a budget, which provides resources for faculty training, technology and the promotion of a quality assurance process.

CCBC has a dedicated, public-facing webpage for online learning, which displays programs offered in an online format. It also provides potential and current students with links to all of the services they might need to be successful. Potential students are provided with a questionnaire to help determine if online learning is proper for them. Students also have access to technical requirements for online coursework and online class policies, which they may need to know before admission. The COVID-19 pandemic has opened many new opportunities for students to take online or remote courses and has allowed faculty to experiment with new methods of student engagement. Many students that would have otherwise stayed away from online classes have signed up for online and remote modalities. Academic requirements for online programs do not differ from traditional face-to-face programs. Potential and current students have access to all relevant student services, such as disability support services, financial aid, etc. In addition, each online course identifies links to these same services for students.

CCBC is a Quality Matters (QM) institution and uses the QM rubric as its basis for design, faculty training, and quality assurance of all online course offerings. Faculty serve as subject matter experts are the principal course developers, while instructional designers in DOL oversee the overall process. Additionally, DOL provides the faculty with mandatory training for course facilitation and course development. Online course development incorporates sound online learning pedagogy to provide students with the most appropriate experiences in the discipline. CCBC has developed its own internal quality assurance process using the Quality Matters rubric as its backbone. This process leverages the content knowledge as well as the course design knowledge of the faculty, providing a high-quality, fiscally responsible manner to increase the quality of the College's online learning courses.

Many of online learning policies have been vetted and approved by the CCBC College Senate. DOL is responsible for the implementation of those policies. Additionally, shared governance is an integral part of the College's formal curriculum approval and review process for all its courses, regardless of the mode of delivery. Curricular expectations of online courses do not differ from those in the traditional format. CCBC faculty and staff understand the challenges that online learning students face. Online course class sizes maximums are limited to 25. CCBC tracks the success rates of online classes and compares that data to its face-to-face counterpart. Online courses are also subject to the College's standard evaluations, with the Common Course Outline (CCO) reviewed on a regular basis. CCOs serve as a standard course outline that all sections of a course must include, no matter the faculty teaching a class and no matter the course modality. The institution also assesses general education outcomes for all General Education (Core) coursework on a three-year cycle, and course-level objectives are assessed through learning outcomes assessment projects.

Student Diversity

To promote minority student success, one of the hallmarks of CCBC's strategic plan is the value of inclusiveness. We honor the diversity of people, cultures, ideas, and viewpoints. To help faculty appreciate and to maximize the potential of a diverse student population, CCBC has a Culturally Responsive Teaching and Learning (CRT-L) training program. The CRT-L program is a multi-faceted initiative that engages faculty, staff, administrators, and students in the recursive process of self-reflection, dialogue, change, and growth regarding cultural understanding and cooperation. Since its inception in 2004, the CRT-L Program has led 500+ faculty and staff and thousands of students to actively address individual and collective self-awareness, attitudes and beliefs, knowledge of others, and the skills needed to implement new understandings through best practices of cultural competence. The CSIT department is excited for a diverse set of students to enroll in the program to add to the rich experiences and perspectives of the courses.

CURRENT PROGRAM AND COURSE DESCRIPTIONS

In addition to the general education requirements and degree requirements, this degree program prepares students to excel at a transfer to other institutions where students can continue in the field of data science. As noted by Salloum *et al.*, many data science programs are master-level programs and lack appropriate preparation in computer science, math, or statistics (2021). The goal of our associate's data science program is to provide a strong foundation to key topic areas so that students have choices to continue their education at the bachelor's level, master's level (assuming they may have a degree in another field), or to meet other educational goals. The current program goals of the Data Science program are listed as follows:

Upon successful completion of the Data Science degree program, students will be able to:

1. Transfer to a four-year institution for a degree in Data Science or a related field.
2. Develop and design well-written code to manipulate data for analysis.
3. Design and implement solutions in the context of the discipline.
4. Apply fundamental data science concepts and algorithms to perform modeling and exploratory data analysis.
5. Explain the Data Analytics Life Cycle in the development of computer programs.

Table 4. Data Science Curriculum Outline

Course	Credits
General Education	
CSIT 111 - Logic and OO Design	3
ENGL 101 -College Composition	3
CMNS 101- Fundamentals of Communication	3
BIOL 110 - Biology I: Molecules and Cells	4
MATH 153 Introduction to Statistical Methods	4
PSYC 105 - Multicultural Psychology *	3
ENVS 101 & 102 Introduction to Environmental Science or CHEM 107 & 108 - Fundamentals of Chemistry	4
SOCL 101 - Introduction to Sociology	3
PHIL 101- Introduction to Philosophy	3
Program Requirements	
MNGT 136 - Business Analytics	3
MATH 163 - Pre Calculus 1	3
CSIT 142 - Introduction to MIS	3
CSIT 210 - Introduction to Programming	4
CSIT 211 - Advanced Programming	4
CSIT 251 - Data Visualization	3
CSIT 154 - Database Concepts	4
CSIT 255 - Fundamentals of Data Science	4
CSIT 260 - Introduction to Machine Learning	3
Total	**60**

6. Demonstrate the ability to critically examine, interpret, organize, and describe multiple forms of data.
7. Demonstrate appropriate ethical and professional conduct related to technology and data science practices.
8. Demonstrate statistical reasoning in everyday life using real-world data.
9. Construct a solution to real-world problems using problem-solving methods.

Table 4 below illustrates the required courses in the data science degree program (subject to change). The first set of courses are the required general education courses and highlight a sample set of courses that students can take. Some classes like English 101 and CSIT 111 would be specifically required, whereas courses in some of the other general education course categories allow for some flexibility. For instance, a student could take another four-credit science course other than Biology 110. It is often recommended that students to check carefully with their potential transfer school for specific class recommendations for that program. In the second part of Table 4, the specific core courses of the program is shown.

The following section lists all of the course descriptions in the program, including the course name, number, credit hours, and class prerequisites. It is possible that some of these courses may be changed or replaced as the program grows. A potential option for a capstone course is discussed in the next section. New courses have established common course outlines and have been approved by CIC. Several courses already exist and are used in other majors and are generally well established.

MNGT 136 - Business Analytics

3 Credits

MNGT 136 – Business Analytics: introduces the concept of business analytics and provides students with a sound conceptual understanding of the role that business analytics plays in the decision-making process. Data-driven decision making and the use of analytical approaches in the decision-making process are explored. Various tools will be used to create, manipulate, and report data. Statistical theories and models will be integrated into objective decision-making.

Prerequisites: MATH 153

MATH 163 - Pre-Calculus I

3 Credits

Explores the nature and scope of college mathematics through the study of functions. Topics include the study of polynomial, rational, radical, piece-wise defined, and absolute value functions and their graphs and applications as well as modeling with these functions. Additional topics include complex numbers, the binomial theorem, inverse functions, operations with functions, and exponential and logarithmic functions and their graphs and applications. Note: 3 credits awarded for MATH 163 for a CLEP Precalculus Exam score of 50 or higher. NOTE: Course offered fall, spring, and may be offered during additional sessions.

Prerequisite(s): ESOL 052 and ESOL 054 or ACLT 052 or ACLT 053; and Algebra I and II in high school and a satisfactory score on the placement exam; or MATH 083

CSIT 142 – Introduction to MIS

3 Credits

Introduces students to Management Information Systems (MIS) from the business professional's perspective. Students learn how MIS supports organizational strategy, collaboration, competitive advantage, decision making, and global commerce. Other topics discussed are systems development, systems management, outsourcing, security, and ethical issues. NOTE: Course offered fall, spring, and may be offered during additional sessions.

Prerequisite(s): CSIT 101 or OFAD 114

CSIT 210 - Introduction to Programming

4 Credits

Provides an introduction to computer science through the development of problem-solving skills using accepted programming practices. An overview of algorithm design, data structures, and fundamental syntax of an object-oriented language is provided. Topics include data types, control structures, file

I/O, classes, objects, methods, and arrays. NOTE: Course offered every fall, spring, and may be offered during additional sessions.

Corequisite(s): CSIT 111 or permission of program director.

CSIT 211 - Advanced Programming

4 Credits

Provides skills for solving complex problems and working with advanced topics using object-oriented programming. Topics include data structures (such as lists, stacks, queues, trees, and graphs), recursion, graphical user interfaces, simple database connectivity, sorting, and searching. NOTE: Course offered every fall, spring and may be offered during additional sessions.

Prerequisite(s): A letter grade of "B" or higher in CSIT 210 (was CINS 236 or CMSC 201) or permission of program director.

CSIT 251 - Data Visualization

3 Credits

Provides an introduction to the fundamentals of data visualization by examining best practices for data exploration, modeling, management, collection, and organization as well as various visualization tools and techniques. Topics include summarizing and presenting data using various tools, data cleansing, and working with diverse sources and types of data.

Prerequisites: CSIT 210 and Math 153 or permission of the program director

CSIT 154 - Database Concepts

4 Credits

Database concepts provide in-depth coverage of the content of database management systems (DBMS) and their capabilities and limitations, and it covers both physical and logical data structure with an emphasis on meaningful data relationships, the role of the database administrator, and the data dictionary. NOTE: Course offered fall, spring, and may be offered during additional sessions.

Prerequisite(s): ENGL 101 and CSIT 101 or the consent of the Program Director.

CSIT 255 - Fundamentals of Data Science

4 Credits

Provides students with an overview of the fundamentals of data science using practical techniques, tools, and programming to analyze and manipulate data to solve problems. Students work with data using the programming languages of Python and R to analyze, visualize, model, acquire and interpret data in various formats.

Prerequisites: CSIT 210, CSIT 154, and MATH 153 or permission of the program director

CSIT 260 - Introduction to Machine Learning

3 Credits

Allows students to explore current trends and techniques related to machine learning (ML), blending theoretical concepts with applied projects in artificial intelligence. Topics include machine learning methodologies, classification algorithms, evolutionary computation, neural networks, deep learning, reasoning, modeling, and examination of emerging trends in the field.

Prerequisites: CSIT 210 and Math 153 or permission of the program director

INCLUDING A CAPSTONE COURSE

When developing the data science program, there was much discussion about the need and possibility of allowing students the option to take a project-based capstone course. The rationale for this course was to provide the option for students to work on real-life projects, conduct research, and gain additional skills. The department is currently in the process of expanding capabilities, increasing department-led projects, and creating a student research lab to be used for artificial intelligence and data science-related initiatives. To this end, in 2019, several faculty members started working towards implementing big data projects into several courses in order to enhance the database curriculum (Tavegia, Braman, Vincenti, & Yancy, 2019). Several projects are underway where students can capture data to create large datasets as part of the EDNA project (Extraction of Diverse Datasets and Analysis). Although the EDNA project is aimed at students working with and creating large datasets, this can easily be intertwined into the data science program as a rich source of projects.

For example, a group of students has been working on creating a small sensor network to collect temperature, air pressure, and air quality data (Richard, Braman, Colclough, & Bishwakarma, 2020). This data is being measured over various time intervals and sent to an external web server. Not only are students learning how to use the Python programming language working on this project, but they are also working with neural networks and creating this large data set of real-world data that other students can then analyze and work with for other projects. Currently, this data is being used by students to test a machine learning algorithm and a web-based affective computing-based display. Another example from using student and faculty projects is through the use of public social media and search engine data to contribute to the datasets. For text analysis purposes students can make use of data collected from the web crawling component of PAsSIVE (Personalized Assisted Search in a Virtual Environment) as it crawls web content for a fixed depth (Braman & Dierbach, 2015). Although the interface of PAsSIVE resides in a 3D format, the content extracted from this program can be used for an array of text-mining projects and applications. Additional content can also be obtained through public social media posts by the use of the SADD Agent (Social Media Agent for the Detection of the Deceased) where text content from posts, time stamps, related posts, and more can be evaluated (Braman, Dudley, & Vincenti, 2018). Content generated by SADD has generally been complex, providing difficult problems for students for several semesters to work on. This data will be particularly useful for students wanting to learn more about conducting sentiment analysis on text-based content.

The following is the course description for the new project course. At this time, the course is not a required course in the program but an optional course that a student can take if desired. We are currently evaluating ways to incorporate this course into the computer science and information technology program as well as for data science.

CSIT 265 – CSIT Capstone: is an applied project-based course in Computer Science and Information Technology. Students demonstrate technology proficiency related to their degree program using research methodologies and design principles by conducting original research or project implementation while working on real-world projects. Topics relate to Artificial Intelligence, Data Science, data analytics, or other computer-related domains.

FUTURE WORK

There is a multitude of initiatives that are planned for the data science program. Student enrollment must be a main priority for the program initially as well as continued feedback and assessment about courses, course design and topics. As part of student recruitment, there are several ongoing efforts in place to grow articulation agreements and collaborations with other institutions. Prior to this initiative, work was underway to share course content as it relates to the database courses, included the creation and collaboration with large datasets to be used to enhance the curriculum. Collaborations with the University of Baltimore and Project Red would provide interesting data to provide real world problem sets (Tavegia, et al., 2019). Similar to projects discussed as part of the capstone course above, the list below illustrates some sample projects under development as part EDNA that can be infused into the program (Tavegia, et al., 2019):

- Project 1 — Students will be given access to a raw data dump of simulated or donated telephone records. They will need to ascertain which information is relevant for a given scenario and consider how additional information can be derived.
- Project 2 — Students will use graphic files to demonstrate how information can be requested by characteristics other than file name or structure. Students can learn other categorization techniques.
- Project 3 — Students will utilize social media imports from public posts to examine connections between accounts and other attributes.
- Project 4 — Students will analyze simulated logs, network traffic and server files to identify anomalous activity.

Additional faculty are actively working on adding to their skillset to better prepare for more projects and data science courses. There has been training provided to faculty to strengthen their programming skills, Python programming skills and on using several external libraries that could be used in data science. Some faculty members are working on adding to their professional training through degree programs, certificates, and additional workshops. As we prepare for the program, efforts are being put in place for potential collaboration for including access to students in continuing education programs. As additional requirements are discovered, faculty are working on securing additional grant funding for equipment for students, to expand on the curriculum and to support students. CSIT already has a well utilized student homework lab and study space available at all three main campuses, but the creation of a dedicated project lab in underway. There is much room to grow the data science program and we look forward to the upcoming opportunities.

CONCLUSION

Data science is an important field that requires innovative and interdisciplinary elements to educate and prepare the next set of skilled professionals entering this career. Other employment options may require similar skillsets as data scientists but may be classified or labeled differently. As stated previously focusing on teaching relevant software applications, programming skills, and providing real-world examples are essential for data science programs as well as mathematics and having various domain knowledge. Our data science program aims at combining courses that tap into core areas to provide students with a strong foundation needed to succeed and for the possibility to continue their education.

In this chapter, we have discussed the CSIT department's latest initiative (one of many) in creating and developing a new Data Science associates degree program. Based on feedback from numerous meetings with faculty and industry partners in the field, the program requirements, key topics, resource and other needs to launch the program were discussed. At the time of this writing, the degree program is pending approval and under review by the Maryland Higher Education Commission (MHEC). As noted, the goal is to start offering this major in late 2022 or sometime in 2023. This chapter presented the overall development of the data science program, including details of classes, challenges and opportunities, and future directions of the program. Once the program is underway, we will be eager to share our lessons learned and additional detail from this exciting endeavor.

REFERENCES

Braman, J., & Dierbach, C. (2015). Utilizing Virtual Worlds for Personalized Search: Developing the PAsSIVE Framework. In Social Computing and Social Media (pp. 3-11). Springer International Publishing.

Braman, J., Dudley, A., & Vincenti, G. (2018). Designing SADD: A Social Media Agent for the Detection of the Deceased. *Proceedings of the 20th HCI International Conference on Online Communities and Social Computing*. 10.1007/978-3-319-91485-5_26

CCBC. (2020). *Mission and Values*. Retrieved from https://www.ccbcmd.edu/About-CCBC/Mission-and-Values.aspx

CCBC Academic Pathways. (2022). https://www.ccbcmd.edu/Programs-and-Courses/Degrees-and-Certificates/Pathways.aspx

CCBC Bookstore. (2022). https://www.ccbcmd.edu/Resources-for-Students/Bookstore.aspx

CCBC Office of Planning, Research, and Evaluation. (2021). *CCBC Fact Book*. http://www.ccbcmd.edu/~/media/CCBC/About%20CCBC/Administrative%20Offices/PRE/ccbc_factbook.ashx

Clements, M., & Braman, J. (2021). Exploring Factors of an Inclusive Textbook Access Program in Computer Technology Courses. In G. Meiselwitz (Ed.), Lecture Notes in Computer Science: Vol. 12775. *Social Computing and Social Media: Applications in Marketing, Learning, and Health. HCII 2021*. Springer. doi:10.1007/978-3-030-77685-5_15

Cohen, A., & Brawer, F. (2003). *The American community college* (4th ed.). Jossey-Bass Publishing.

Gabriel, K., & Flake, S. (2008). *Teaching unprepared students: strategies for promoting success and retention in higher education*. Stylus Publishing.

Irizarry, R. A. (2020). The role of academia in data science education. *The Role of Academia in Data Science Education, 2*(1).

Maryland Department of Labor. (2021). *Maryland Occupational Projections 2018 - 2021 Workforce Information and Performance*. https://www.dllr.state.md.us/lmi/iandoproj/maryland.shtml

Maryland Higher Education Commission (MHEC). (2017). *2017 – 2021 Maryland State Plan for Post-secondary Education*. https://mhec.maryland.gov/About/Pages/2017StatePlanforPostsecondaryEducation.aspx

Paniagua, F. G. (2019). Quality Assurance in Online Education: A Development Process to Design High-Quality Courses. In *International Conference on Human-Computer Interaction* (pp. 182-194). Springer. 10.1007/978-3-030-21905-5_14

Richard, J., Braman, J., Colclough, M., & Bishwakarma, S. (2020). A Neural Affective Approach to an Intelligent Weather Sensor System. In C. Stephanidis, M. Antona, & S. Ntoa (Eds.), *HCI International 2020 Late-Breaking Posters. HCII 2020. Communications in Computer and Information Science* (Vol. 1293). Springer. doi:10.1007/978-3-030-60700-5_46

Salloum, M., Jeske, D., Ma, W., Papalexakis, V., Shelton, C., Tsotras, V., & Zhou, S. (2021). Developing an interdisciplinary data science program. In *Proceedings of the 52nd ACM Technical Symposium on Computer Science Education* (pp. 509-515). 10.1145/3408877.3432454

Sas. (2022). *What is a Data Scientist? Who they are, what they do and why you want to be one*. https://www.sas.com/en_us/insights/analytics/what-is-a-data-scientist.html

Tavegia, S., Braman, J., Vincenti, G., & Yancy, B. (2019). Enhancing Database Courses through the EDNA Project: A Preliminary Framework for the Extraction of Diverse Datasets and Analysis. *Proceedings of the 21th HCI International Conference on Online Communities and Social Computing*. 10.1007/978-3-030-21905-5_18

U.S. Bureau of Labor Statistics. (2020). *Data Scientists and Mathematical Science Occupations*. https://www.bls.gov/oes/current/oes152098.htm#nat

U.S. Bureau of Labor Statistics. (2021). *Occupational Employment and Wage Statistics*. https://www.bls.gov/oes/tables.htm#nat

Waller, M. A., & Fawcett, S. E. (2013). Data science, predictive analytics, and big data: A revolution that will transform supply chain design and management. *Journal of Business Logistics*, *34*(2), 77–84. doi:10.1111/jbl.12010

Zheng, B., Warschauer, M., Hwang, J. K., & Collins, P. (2014). Laptop use, interactive science software, and science learning among at-Risk students. *Journal of Science Education and Technology*, *1*(5), 591–603. doi:10.100710956-014-9489-5

Chapter 9
A Storied Approach to Learning Data Analytics in a Graduate Data Analytics Program

Brandon Vaughn
Western Governors University, USA

ABSTRACT

This study considers the construction and application of a storied approach to teaching graduate level data analytics. Although some research stresses replacing traditional lectures with more active learning methods, the approach of this study is to construct an entire data analytics program around a "story" idea of active learning and projects. The results of this study indicate that such a storied approach to learning not only improves student cognition of course material, but student morale as well. An instructional approach that combines active-learning activities in a progressive, storied approach appears to be a better approach than traditional lecturing alone for teaching graduate-level students.

PURPOSE

If you think back to when you learned how to ride a bike, you probably didn't master this skill by listening to a series of riveting lectures on bike riding. Rather, you tried it out for yourself, made mistakes, fell down a few times, picked yourself back up, and tried again. When mastering an activity, there's no substitute for active learning - the interaction and feedback that comes from practice.

Would we see the same level of mastery if classroom learning was a little more active? Would university instruction be more effective if students spent some of their class time on active forms of learning like activities, discussions, or group work, instead of spending all of their class time listening? And would this even be possible with a completely online program? What would be the effect if an entire program was built around this idea instead of isolated courses?

Theresa is typical of most online graduate students I meet in the first statistical course of their program. Sounding uneasy as we make phone introductions, Theresa starts out with basic information about

DOI: 10.4018/978-1-7998-9644-9.ch009

herself, and then exclaims "To be honest, I have tried avoiding this class for as long I could! I'm scared to death of statistics!" She isn't alone.

Students often consider statistics as the "worst" course they take while in college (Hogg, 1991). For instructors, there is often a struggle with how best to reach students, to help them learn statistics, and to help them become practical consumers of the knowledge – especially when students enter statistics courses with negative self-images. As some of this negative imagery comes from the massive amounts of formulas students can face while in the course, one solution is to structure an introductory statistics course (possibly all statistical courses) around data analysis versus mathematical technique. Another solution is found in innovative instructional paradigms in which the traditional lecture, with students passively listening, is replaced with more hands-on activities.

Yet in graduate statistical education, the actual implementation of these different approaches into a classroom setting can be quite challenging and confusing. This is amplified when it comes to online learning. Many of these approaches involve unique learning opportunities which have not customarily been incorporated in traditional graduate-level statistics classes. Moreover, because most research has been conducted on undergraduate statistics classes (see next section), one might ask "Would the same techniques of active or cooperative learning actually work in a graduate introductory statistics class? Or possibly in more advanced classes?"

The purpose of this research is to consider alternative instructional methods in the teaching of an online graduate-level data analytics program. Based upon personal informal surveying of graduate instructors, many have only seen graduate programs where courses might be prerequisites for others, yet the courses feel very independent of each other. Indeed, for many graduate instructors I have interviewed, an integrated storied program is an idea never considered. Thus, I created a graduate-level data analytics program around projects where the students become part of the "story."

The "storied" approach to teaching (with both projects and active learning) of interest in this study would allow many graduate programs the opportunity to explore the advantages of active learning in a manner that is both fun to the student and also progressive in learning concepts. Thus, the purpose of this research is to explore an instructional model that involves projects and active/cooperative learning in a graduate statistics program. Comparisons were made with previous terms in which these approaches were not undertaken. Specifically, this study attempted to answer the following research questions:

1. Can active or cooperative learning be successfully implemented and accepted in a graduate-level data analytics program? Can these strategies be combined with a story to create a cohesive instructional approach?
2. Does more active student involvement help graduate students learn complex statistics?
3. What benefit in affective and cognitive measures is seen by introducing active or cooperative learning throughout a graduate statistics program? As males and females may gravitate toward different teaching approaches, do these benefits differ by gender?
4. Does a particular story work better than others with graduate students?

THEORETICAL FRAMEWORK

The question of how a student best learns statistics has been much considered in articles on statistics teaching (e.g., Chance, 2005; Gal & Garfield, 1997; Garfield, 1995; Lovett & Greenhouse, 2000), and has mainly focused on instructional content or methods. In terms of instructional content, many statisticians, including Bradstreet (1996) and Cobb (1991), are convinced that an introductory statistics course should emphasize data analysis over mathematical technique and concepts over formulas. Hogg (1991) stressed that statistics should not be presented as a mathematics course at all. Rather, the andragogy should emphasize statistical reasoning and thinking rather than algebraic precision.

Hogg (1991) further describes the problem of traditional instruction of statistics in terms of instructional design: Students are passive learners and do not directly come into contact with the many issues that occur in data collection and analysis. He suggests students would be better off generating their own data rather than utilizing a data set from a textbook or instructor. By working with projects involving their own data, students have opportunities to define problems, formulate hypotheses, design experiments, and have genuine data to analyze and summarize. In support of Hogg, Snee (1993) emphasized that because collecting data is the nucleus of statistical analysis, learning that centers on the analysis of real data that students collect connects them to the practicality of statistical thinking. Singer and Willett (1990) argued that real data should be the nucleus of all statistical education, although their emphasis was more on using available datasets and not on students collecting their own data.

Emphasizing this statistical content also leads to a more active involvement of students in the course, and the traditional lecture approach in teaching statistics has had much criticism in the last two decades of research (e.g., Delucchi, 2006; Garfield, 1993; Giraud, 1997; Moore, 1997). Garfield (1995) suggests that students learn best by constructing knowledge and becoming active participants in the learning process. Smith (1998) indicated that

One way to help students develop their statistical reasoning is to incorporate active learning strategies that allow students to supplement what they have heard and read about statistics by actually doing statistics -- designing studies, collecting data, analyzing their results, preparing written reports, and giving oral presentations. (¶ 3.7)

Steinhorst and Keeler (1995) is another great resource in this matter. In support of an active-learning approach, Bradstreet (1996) writes that "Learning is situated in activity. Students who use the tools of their education actively rather than just acquire them build an increasingly rich implicit understanding of the world in which they use the tools and of the tools themselves" (pp. 73-74). Thus in this study, "active learning" refers to any activities in which the student participates and learns in a non-passive way (e.g., simply answering questions from the teacher would not be considered "active learning" in this study).

There are a variety of ways in which to incorporate active learning and projects into instruction, in particular, personal collection of data. These might include some of the following: computer simulations (Garfield & delMas, 1991); laboratory-based courses (Bradstreet, 1996); in-class activities (Dietz, 1993; Gnanadesikan, Scheaffer, Watkins, & Witmer, 1997); a single three-week project (Hunter, 1977); or a course-long project (Chance, 1997; Fillebrown, 1994; Ledolter, 1995; Mackisack, 1994).

In regard to cooperative learning, many researchers have reported significant accomplishments from introducing cooperative learning experiences in introductory statistics classes (Dietz, 1993; Jones, 1991; Keeler & Steinhorst, 1995; Shaughnessy, 1977). Teams help encourage cooperative learning, develop team-working skills, and usually build substantial friendships (Smith, 1998). However, some of this research tends to limit such activities to external learning situations such as homework or studying. Although much research exists indicating the effectiveness of alternative teaching techniques, how a teacher should implement such teaching strategies is not always clear and should be a point of more research

(Garfield, 1995). Johnson and Dasgupta (2006) found that undergraduate students predominately prefer non-traditional instructional styles. Yet, exactly how a class should be structured and which techniques work best with each other was not considered in this research and would seem to be of importance to instructors wishing to incorporate such styles. Jordan (2007) stressed that the implementation of such instructional styles is open to much interpretation. In fact, some research has indicated that the implementation of these techniques does not always happen. Cobb (1993) investigated the results of various NSF grants whose purpose was to significantly improve statistical instruction, and discovered that none of the grants involved team projects, nor cooperative learning situations. Bryce (2005) indicated that few textbooks have embraced these new ideas in statistical education.

Furthermore, it is not clear which methods work better for different students. Students have differing learning styles. Ford and Chen (2002) showed that males and females performed differently under various teaching styles. Kolb (1984) provided a model of learning styles: concrete–abstract and reflective–active. The combinations of these styles indicate learners that are labeled as accommodators (concrete, active), divergers (concrete, reflective), assimilators (abstract, reflective), and convergers (abstract, active). Grasha (1996) suggested bipolar characteristics of learning styles: competitive vs. collaborative, dependent vs. independent, and participant vs. avoidant. Regardless of the label, research has shown that students vary in how they best learn. Thus, a class structure that only emphasizes one learning style (e.g., lecture or active learning) might in fact disadvantage some students in the attempt to reach others. In terms of classroom dynamics and pedagogical styles, Grasha identified five teacher styles: expert, formal authority, personal model, delegator, and facilitator. One can see in these labels the full spectrum of classroom dynamics from pure lecture (expert) to pure active/collaborative learning (facilitator). Instruction that flows in and out of these different dynamics would in essence touch on the diversity of learning styles of students.

Lovett (2001) said that "a successful route to improving students transfer of statistical reasoning skill may rely heavily on integrating instructional and cognitive theory, while maintaining a link to the realities of the classroom" (p. 348). Some research has considered the effect of combining different instructional techniques to create an amalgamated approach in teaching statistics. Ward (2004) created an amalgamated class consisting of online and face-to-face classes and found little difference in student performance. Keeler and Steinhorst (1995) created an amalgamated class consisting of collaborative groups and mini-lectures. They showed an improvement in students' attitudes and grades when incorporating more active student involvement with lectures. Their research focused on undergraduate, introductory-level statistics classes. No research has been found that applies such techniques to graduate-level statistics classes.

In fact lecture-based approaches appear to still dominate graduate-level statistics classes. A preliminary study by this researcher which interviewed 14 graduate instructors from colleges and departments of Education, Business, and Statistics at four major universities in the United States found this tendency, and when asked about the possibility of utilizing different learning strategies in their higher-level statistics classes, the response is typically expressed somewhat like "Yes, that may work for an undergraduate statistics class, but it would never work in this class. This class is too high level and demands a lecture format be predominant or even exclusive." Although these instructors are familiar with the vast research on innovative learning strategies in statistical education, there appears to be a huge gap between knowledge and practice. For these instructors, whether the same results shown in undergraduate statistics education would apply to graduate students has been minimally investigated.

Bligh (2000) suggests that lectures do have their place in education, yet the problem lies with instructional strategies that have unrealistic expectations. For example, Bligh indicates that whereas lectures are

Figure 1. An example of a Traditional vs Corequisite Approach to Education

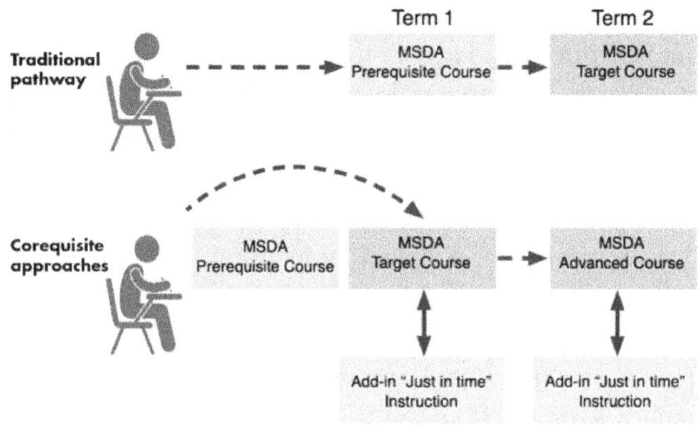

good at imparting ideas, they are not as good at motivating students: "Use lectures to teach information. Do not rely on them to promote thought, change attitudes, or develop behavioral skills if you can help it" (p. 20). For Bligh, many critics of lecture-based approaches in instruction almost de-emphasize the role of lectures completely. Yet, the complexity of graduate-level statistics classes suggests that some form of lecture might be beneficial. It has been this researcher's own observation that a statistics class that revolves around total active learning does not provide students with enough security in statistical methodology, especially for more advanced statistics classes. Often students need to see things demonstrated before they can apply those techniques to real life. However, this does not exclude the possibility of incorporating many of the proven techniques that have been shown to make a difference in undergraduate education.

Of interest in this study is allowing students to choose from a dataset that they carry throughout the entire program analyzing. The datasets would be in various fields such as manufacturing, health care, finance, and so on. Skills will be dispersed across different courses, resulting in atomic, just-in-time corequisite instruction (Garvin, 2010; Herman & Webb, 2007). The uniqueness of this approach is shown in Figure 1. In the figure below, the Master's of Science in Data Analytics is abbreviated as MSDA.

The courses will implement the project-based learning (PBL) paradigm that covers the material with the end in mind. For each topic area, the learner will engage with an essential step of the DPLC. This approach will provide the learner with the opportunity to practice the skills they will need to master to successfully complete the performance assessment for the course. After the activity, learners will be directed to resources such as text and video(s) to help them explore more deeply and gain insights into unanswered questions. Students will be exploring and engaging with resources on concepts and topics that they've previously experienced. Research suggests they will be more likely to make sense of what they are reading or watching (Azer, 2017). This course construction approach is more in line with design efforts around the learning experience and more recently, Beautiful Learning (Gallagher, 2017).

Experts suggest that more can be learned in less time and at higher levels of learning if program courses are connected and concepts integrated (Drake and Reid, 2010). When integration is used as a venue for developing complex-cognitive and career-related soft skills, the graduate has a documented advantage in the workforce (Torres, 2017). Integration results in teaching depth versus breadth, encourages multiple intelligences, and allows for the infusion of literacy and/or thinking skills (Hartzler, 2000; Drake, 2007). The inclusion of higher-order cognitive processing leads to longer-lasting achievement regardless of socioeconomic status by embedding skills, expanding content knowledge, and increasing understanding (Bransford, 2002). This approach has also been shown to improve student motivation, individualized learning opportunities, and long-term skill application with different populations of students (Hartzler, 2000). The approaches documented above have been shown to have positive effects in these underserved populations (Logue, 2018). Many underserved students hope to obtain work experience in addition to a high-quality education or university degree, and they are often frustrated by the constraints imposed by traditional education models (Farnsworth, 2018; Torres, 2017). Institutions can manage student expectations more effectively if they begin the discussion of work options before applicants leave their program of study. Another option is to help students become more attractive candidates for work experience through summer internships, part-time work on campus, or full-time work following graduation. With online instruction, this becomes complex. This proposed model seeks to simulate this type of experience without the complexity.

Freeman et al (2014) found more specifics of how active learning compares to lecture-based learning. They found in their experiment that students in a traditional lecture course were 1.5 times more likely to fail, compared to students in courses with active learning. The authors found that 34% of students failed their course under traditional lecturing, compared to 22% of students under active learning. This suggests that, just in the studies that they analyzed, 3,500 more students would have passed their courses if taught with active learning. By conservative estimates, this would have saved the students about 3.5 million dollars in tuition. They also found that students in active learning classes outperformed those in traditional lectures on identical exams. On average, students taught with active learning outperformed those taught by lectures by 6 percentage points on their exam. The authors describe this as picturing a student in a traditional lecture class who scored higher than 50% of the students on the exam. If the same student were taught with active learning instead, they would score higher than 68% of the students in this lecture class.

The blending of integrated learning and corequisite structure has been shown in research to produce significant impact on students' social-emotional skills and effective communication and leadership skills (Cardichon & Darling-Hammond, 2017). In order to maximize this result, these studies have stressed the need for consistent exposure to these skills. By developing the MSDA with an integrated curriculum, students will continually be utilizing knowledge and tools learned, in addition to communicating results, throughout the entirety of the program (instead of just one course).

PROGRAM DESIGN

Design of the Program

The program was designed for a graduate program (MSDA) at Western Governor's University (WGU) in 2020. The program first launched in November 2021. The bulk of the design originated with the author of the chapter as well as Goran Trajkovski.

The first part of the design was to take a "typical day" or analysis from an analyst and divide it up into courses. So, typically, an analyst is given a problem in which they would need to define the research questions and stakeholders (Course 1). They would then turn to pull data for the project, usually using SQL (Course 2). Once the data is pulled, the person would need to clean the data and prep it for analysis

Figure 2. The storied-journey developed for MSDA

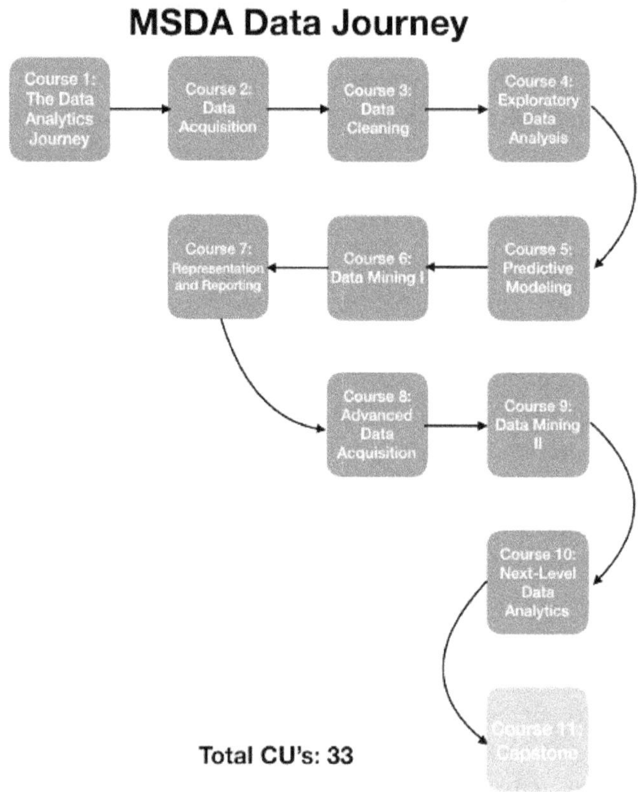

(Course 3). The initial analysis would be more exploratory in nature, covering many of the same topics found in an introductory statistics class (Course 4).

This pattern continues throughout the journey of the program until the final course on advanced machine learning models. Each course is progressive and builds upon the previous work. There is a natural progression of difficulty as well. An illustration of this design is shown below in Figure 2:

An example of the main topics covered in each course is diagramed in the Figure 3 below.

An illustration of how the story might work out for a military student is shown in Figure 4 below.

There are two unique callouts of this design. At the time of writing, both Python and R were industry standards for analytic languages. In most programs, there is a course (usually one) dedicated to each. Developing mastery of these languages in a single course is almost impossible. Mastery takes both time and repeated exposure/use. In this design, Python and R are equally taught in every course with "just in time learning". That is, every nuance of Python and R are not taught at a single moment. Rather, only what the student needs is shown to them at that point. For example, a student would not need to know how to construct classification trees until Course 6, so these commands/libraries are not covered until then. Teaching Python and R in this way provides a sequential two-year exposure to each language. Students end up learning both Python/R in a depth not found in other programs.

Another unique callout of this design is the re-introduction of SQL in Course 8. There are several reasons for this. First, if all SQL is covered early, then the student will not have worked with it in a year and a half beyond graduation. We wanted students who had good SQL skills upon graduation. Second,

Figure 3. Examples of some of the main topics in each course

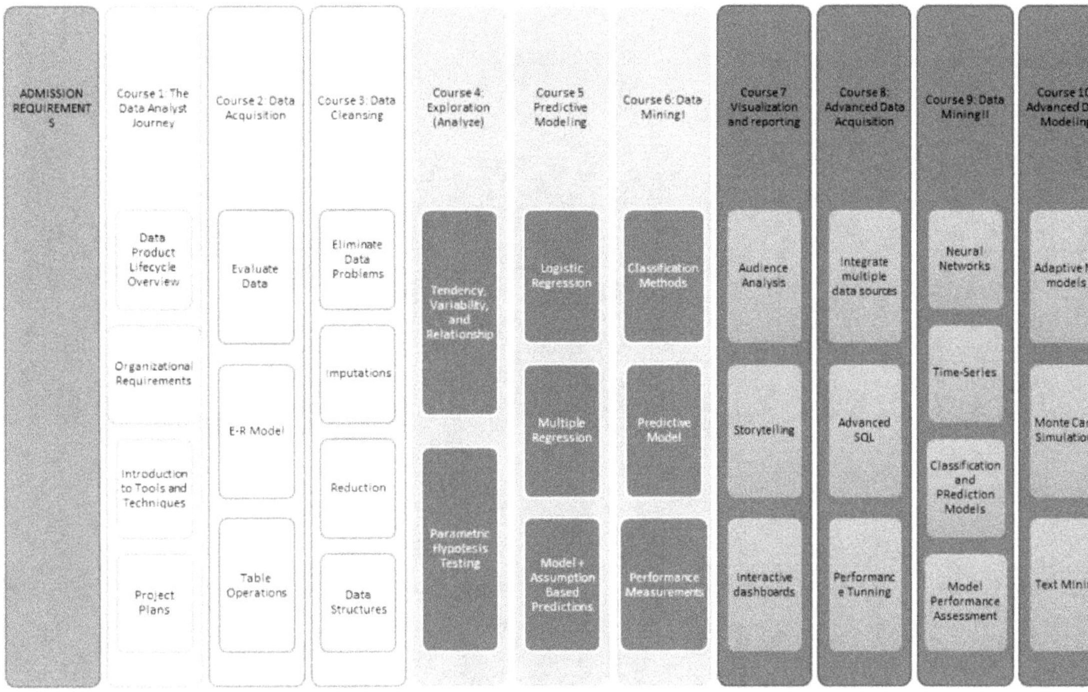

the use of SQL later makes sense with the story. In this story, in order for the student to progress toward more sophisticated modeling, they will need additional data they do not currently have. For example, time-series analysis is covered in Course 10. Up to that point in time, the student had no need of repeated measures so that data is kept from them. At this point, they will need to pull that data using more advanced knowledge of SQL.

Datasets

The question of how to create a variety of stories was a big challenge to overcome. The idea would be to allow students to choose a "story" of their choice. The biggest problem in using existing datasets is that eventually answers will leak out and there will be a need to find another equivalent dataset to replace it. The other problem is that differing datasets would also have differing psychometric properties such as difficulty and discrimination. Thus, one dataset could be easier to clean than another because the proportion of missing data or outliers is greatly different.

This problem was overcome by simulating the data. By simulating the datasets, a variety of issues could be controlled and made uniform between the datasets: number of records, proportion of missing data, proportion of outliers, number of variables, presence of particular outcome variables (e.g., binary outcomes to enable logistic regression), and so on. Even demographic data (e.g., job, state, number of kids, etc) were simulated. All of the simulation was done in R.

Various themes in industries were chosen for the first datasets. The program started with a telecommunications churn dataset as well as a medical readmission dataset. Various variables were modeled after real data so that the simulated data behaves like actual data.

Figure 4. An example of a storied-journey for a military student in MSDA

Assessments

All assessment apart from the first class were project based. For every project, students not only analyzed the data, but the students had to construct a write-up and video presentation of the analysis results. More detail on the artifacts developed are shown in Figure 5 below.

INITIAL RESULTS

The program effectiveness will be studied in another year after a full 2-years of data is provided. To fully know how well the program has performed, a 2-year window would enable the first cohort to enter the program enough time to finish the program.

However, there have been two aspects where improvements have already been seen. First of all, there is indication that KPI's have improved. The previous program had quite a bit of student dissatisfaction

Figure 5. Sample artifacts in the storied-program

on satisfaction surveys. The launch of the new program has shown a 20% reduction in DSAT, while overall VSAT has increased by 5%. Other metrics such as increased course completion and lower drop rates has been noted.

Secondly, the student sentiment for students has greatly improved. This has been seen especially among students who were in the previous program and moved to the new design. As one example, a program mentor told us for one of their students:

She said that the course material has made an immediate impact on her job and she sees significant opportunities to leverage course material to add value to her work product for her employer. She also asked if she would have access to the course material after graduation. She believes that the course material will be a valuable resource in the future even after course and degree completion.

Another student expressed the following:

It is building my confidence, and I am liking the new program 100% better. I've been really enjoying them. The content is way more interesting/relevant/current, and the videos are FANTASTIC. That is huge for me.

We have seen both positive feedback from males and especially females which we were hoping that the new design would encourage longevity in the program.

SUMMARY

This research attempted to answer a central question: Does a structure incorporating more active student involvement help graduate students learn statistics? The answer based on this study does appear to be "yes." Still, the question of what combinations of instructional design to use remains unanswered. Though incorporating both active learning and storied projects with lectures showed positive effects there is still need to fully investigate its effectiveness after 2-years. Furthermore, from this instructor's experience, student attitudes are often better when the instructor was more in control of the active component. Perhaps the inclusion of team projects shifts the locus of control too far for graduate students? Such consideration is worthy of future study. Regardless, this study suggests that any active component in a graduate-level statistics class makes it better, both affectively and cognitively.

Implementation Strategies

My own experience with incorporating active learning in teaching has always been successful. When I incorporated the active component into the class, I could see an immediate effect upon students. In previous terms, I had tried a more constructivist approach to teaching and felt that the class was not successful. Based on that experience, the inclusion of some form of lecture component seemed necessary. This amalgamated approach took away many of the fears I had in incorporating the ideas. By having small active-learning components in a storied-program approach, I could see whether students really understood what I had just shown them. Also, this builds confidence in students.

Theresa, the student mentioned earlier, was one such of this confidence. By the end of the second course, she expressed to me how she was really enjoying the class and how it was not nearly as bad as she had originally thought. She expressed great joy in that for the first time she understood how data analytics applied to real life situations and could already apply this knowledge to her current job.

I cannot imagine teaching without some form of active learning now. I have applied this same teaching paradigm to more advanced statistical classes with similar results of improved morale, attention, and assimilation of information. In this design, team projects were not considered. The inclusion of team projects posed mixed results in previous research. First, there was more of a struggle with how to allocate class time for such matters. Although including active learning would seem to present the same challenge, team projects always presented the major challenge in time. For me, team dynamics was a factor that grew tiring to oversee. I still see the benefits in team projects, yet it seems that I see little difference in performance by leaving it out and using active components in class (which still involve working with data). This is a matter of further investigation for me. Of particular interest would be studying the different outlooks and motivations for undergraduate versus graduate students in regard to team projects and team learning.

To successfully implement such a change in a college program requires a radical shift in perspective for most instructors and developers. Thus, I offer the following suggestions that I have learned over the past 20 years of trying to incorporate such designs in my own classes:

1. Review learning and cognition materials – Although direct research (like this study) is obviously important to consider, I have found that there is a wealth of information about such matters in the learning and cognition domain. One would also greatly benefit by finding someone who specializes in this field and discussing matters with them. Though I have not always incorporated their ideas or techniques, I have often come away from such conversations with clarity of thought and purpose. The statistical education domain would greatly benefit if there were more collaborations in research with learning/cognition researchers, not to mention how beneficial textbooks might be if such collaborations extended into authorship. As mentioned previously, most current graduate statistical textbooks ignore these new teaching methods altogether.
2. Study effective teaching models – There is a wealth of ideas often right on our own campuses about effective teaching models. I occasionally ask other faculty members to let me sit in on their class for my own personal benefit. In my younger years, I would too often want to emulate the habits and mannerisms of those I admired or respected. I remember the first time I saw Jaime Escalante in the Stand and Deliver famed movie. After seeing him in action, I wondered if I should dress up in costumes and use props in my classes, or have my classes do chants in the classroom. Yet, in time, I have seen that I need to become a unique expression of these effective techniques I have learned. I believe this is important because at times I have rejected whole approaches in teaching because I could not see myself implementing them in the same manner. For example, I have seen instructors using a "game" for an in-class activity, and had inner struggles with incorporating this particular expression: "That may work for an undergraduate class, but this is a graduate class on Bayesian analysis! Won't this seem 'childish' to the students? Even if I were to try it, how can I come up with a game in this class?" What I have learned is that I may not always prefer or use a particular expression, but I can still strive to incorporate the spirit of the expression (e.g., in this case by creating active components that are interesting and fun to students).
3. Start small – If you are new to active-based learning (whether in-class activities or team projects), it might be beneficial to incorporate this new learning style in small ways until you are comfortable with the approach. While the strength of this current study was providing an integrated story throughout an entire program of study, if this is new to you then you might consider starting smaller. One suggested approach for a traditional class is to design such a storied worksheet for a particular class lecture, and have students work on it for a few minutes in the middle or end of class. The key to incorporating such active-based learning is to keep the activities short (average of 5-10 minutes). Some activities may require longer periods of time to complete, possibly up to 30 minutes. But those activities should be the exception, not the rule. Take one lecture and add one active component to it. Do this over a period of time and increase the amount that you use until you feel you have reached a balance that works for you and your teaching style. Then consider trying this for an entire course, and then possibly an entire program of study.

4. Plan and delegate – One concern in using active learning along with lecture is anxiety about covering the breadth of material that is covered in a lecture-only format. Though this concern might have some degree of merit, I have found in my own experience that this is not the case. However, successful implementation does require some degree of thought and preparation. I have personally found that I save time while lecturing by not spending as much time working through an example in class. Before, I would spend a lot of time in order to make sure students understood every facet. Now, I realize that any part they don't understand will be magnified in the active component which follows my example. Also, there are often concepts that can be learned in the active component rather than taught in lecture. This provides a unique form of constructivist learning and is easy to implement within such a structure. Whereas there is much discussion of the fatigue that faces students in a long lecture, I think a neglected area of research is the fatigue that occurs with an instructor. I find by using mini-lectures that I stay focused on my teaching and can cover the same material in less time. For WGU based courses, instructors serve more as mentors and coaches. Thus, students must often self-learn and the storied approach works very well to give context and meaning to what the student is learning.
5. Be active yourself – If you are in traditional courses, while students are working on an activity, consider walking among them and observe their progress. This can be beneficial for many reasons including making sure students are working on the task you have asked them to work on. Also, some students may not volunteer problems they are having in front of the entire class and this provides you with an opportunity to see particular problems they may be having. Obviously with moderate (as in the case of this study) to large classes, it might be impossible to go to each person or group in the allotted time for the activity. In this situation, if you have more than one activity for that day, consider randomly moving around during each activity. In my case, I will mentally cluster students in various parts of the room and randomly choose clusters to visit during an activity. I strive to visit each cluster at least once during a class. For online instructors, you will find it important to do the project yourself so you understand the unique challenges that students will face with the project.
6. Don't confuse noise for control (or lack of) – Students in my traditional classes are often quiet during the first few weeks of active components, perhaps because it seems such a foreign approach for a mathematically-based class. Students in the WGU program can also be quiet in that they might not always reach out for help if they are struggling with the storied project. Yet over time, they usually embrace it heartedly to the point that the students are eagerly engaging with instructors for feedback and guidance. For someone coming from a lecture-only format, this can seem threatening, as if you have lost control of the class or your students. Always keep in mind that you are actively engaging your students and helping them master the material. Some of my classes have been so engaged that it has taken me quite a few seconds to regain their attention. At WGU, students can often go way beyond what is required of them and do additional aspects that severely impact their timely completion of the course. At first this would bother me greatly to the point of questioning my new approach. Now, I can usually regain control of student progress by simply talking to them while looking over their work and simply saying, "OK, let's talk about something that I see you are having a problem with." For traditional course instructors, you may wish to utilize visible clues to re-center your class (e.g., turning the lights on and off a few times). If you are new to this teaching style, do not let such matters deter you from exploring this "brave new world."

FUTURE RESEARCH

One possible extension of this study is to adjust the way in which student projects are done. Some students wished for more freedom in the choice of their projects. A future study could consider this effect. Another consideration is the use of team projects compared to single student projects. Smaller group sizes should also be considered as this may reduce some of the tensions in groups found in this study. Also, an approach in which the instructor supervises the teams more vigorously might prove valuable and eliminate the slightly diminishing results from team projects. The approach taken in this study was not as rigorous because the instructor assumed that graduate students would not need as much oversight. This study considered an entire program for graduate students to serve as a bridge with similar research in undergraduate studies. Further studies to look at the unique advantages to advanced courses (e.g., regression, multi-level models, structural equation modeling) should be investigated. Tying together affective and cognitive measures in a unified statistical analysis, as well as tracking changes or growth over time in longitudinal studies, would also be beneficial.

REFERENCES

Aliaga, M., & Gunderson, B. (2003). *Interactive statistics*. Prentice Hall.

Bligh, D. A. (2000). *What's the use of lectures?* Jossey-Bass.

Azer, S. A. (2017, April). Top-Cited Articles in Problem-Based Learning: A Bibliometric Analysis and Quality of Evidence Assessment. *Journal of Dental Education*, *81*(4), 458–478. doi:10.21815/JDE.016.011 PMID:28365611

Bradstreet, T. E. (1996). Teaching introductory statistics courses so that nonstatisticians experience statistical reasoning. *The American Statistician*, *50*, 69–78.

Committee on Learning Research and Educational Practice. (2014). *How People Learn: Brain, Mind, Experience, and School: Expanded Edition*. National Academy Press.

Bryce, G. R. (2005). Developing tomorrow's statisticians. *Journal of Statistics Education: An International Journal on the Teaching and Learning of Statistics*, *13*(1).

Cardichon, J., & Darling-Hammond, L. (2017). *Advancing educational equity for underserved youth: How new state accountability systems can support school inclusion and student success*. Learning Policy Institute.

Chance, B. L. (1997). Experiences with authentic assessment techniques in an introductory statistics course. *Journal of Statistics Education: An International Journal on the Teaching and Learning of Statistics*, *5*(3).

Chance, B. L. (2005). Integrating pedagogies to teach statistics. In J. Garfield (Ed.), *Innovations in Teaching Statistics. MAA Notes* (Vol. 65, pp. 101–112). Mathematical Association of America.

Cho, S. W., Kopko, E., Jenkins, D., & Jaggars, S. S. (2012). *New Evidence of Success of Community College Remedial English Students: Tracking the Outcomes of Students in the Accelerated Learning Program (ALP)*. CCRC Working Paper No. 53. New York: Columbia University, Teachers College, Community College Research Center.

Cobb, G. W. (1991). Teaching statistics: More data, less lecturing. *Amstat News, 182*.

Cobb, G. W. (1993). Reconsidering statistics education: A National Science Foundation conference. *Journal of Statistics Education: An International Journal on the Teaching and Learning of Statistics*, *1*(1).

Delucchi, M. (2006). The efficacy of collaborative learning groups in an undergraduate statistics course. *College Teaching*, *54*(2), 244–248. doi:10.3200/CTCH.54.2.244-248

Dietz, E. J. (1993). A cooperative learning activity on methods of selecting a sample. *The American Statistician*, *47*, 104–108.

Drake, S. M. (2007). *Creating standards-based integrated curriculum: Aligning content, standards, instructional strategies and assessment* (2nd ed.). Corwin.

Drake, S. M., & Reid, J. (2010). Research Monograph #28: Integrated Curriculum-Increasing Relevance While Maintaining Accountability. The Literacy and Numeracy Secretariat & the Ontario Association of Deans of Education.

Farnsworth, B. (2018). *Enhancing the Quality of the International Student Experience. Beyond the Margins: Meeting the Needs of Underserved Students*. Retrieved from: https://www.higheredtoday.org/2018/07/02/enhancing-quality-international-student-experience/

Fillebrown, S. (1994). Using projects in an elementary statistics course for non-science majors. *Journal of Statistics Education: An International Journal on the Teaching and Learning of Statistics*, *2*(2).

Freeman, S., Eddy, S. L., McDonough, M., Smith, M. K., Okoroafor, N., Jordt, H., & Wenderoth, M. P. (2014). Active learning boosts performance in STEM courses. *Proceedings of the National Academy of Sciences*. 10.1073/pnas.1319030111

Ford, N., & Chen, S. Y. (2002). Matching/mismatching revisited: An empirical study of learning and teaching styles. *British Journal of Educational Technology*, *32*(1), 5–22. doi:10.1111/1467-8535.00173

Gagné, R. M., Briggs, L. J., & Wager, W. W. (1992). *Principles of instructional design* (4th ed.). Harcourt Brace Jovanovich College Publishers.

Gal, I., & Garfield, J. B. (Eds.). (1997). *The assessment challenge in statistics education*. IOS Press/International Statistical Institute.

Gallagher, K. (2017, July 31). *Beautiful Learning* [Blog Post]. Retrieved from: www.kerryhawk02.com/2017/07/beautiful-learning.html

Garfield, J. (1993). Teaching statistics using small-group cooperative learning. *Journal of Statistics Education: An International Journal on the Teaching and Learning of Statistics*, *1*(1).

Garfield, J. (1995). How students learn statistics. *International Statistical Review*, *63*(1), 35–48. doi:10.2307/1403775

Garfield, J., & delMas, R. (1991). Students' conceptions of probability. In D. Vere-Jones (Ed.), *Proceedings of the Third International Conference on Teaching Statistics*, Volume 1 (pp. 340-349). Voorburg, The Netherlands: International Statistical Institute.

Gavrin, A. (2010). Using Just-in-Time Teaching in the Physical Sciences. In Just-in-Time Teaching: Across the Disciplines, Across the Academy. Sterling, VA: Stylus Publishing.

Giraud, G. (1997). Cooperative learning and statistics instruction. *Journal of Statistics Education: An International Journal on the Teaching and Learning of Statistics*, *5*(3).

Gnanadesikan, M., Scheaffer, R. L., Watkins, A. E., & Witmer, J. A. (1997). An activitybased statistics course. *Journal of Statistics Education: An International Journal on the Teaching and Learning of Statistics*, *5*(2).

Grasha, A. F. (1996). *Teaching with style*. Alliance Press.

Hartzler, D. S. (2000). *A Meta-analysis of Studies Conducted on Integrated Curriculum Programs and Their Effects on Student Achievement* [Dissertation]. School of Education, Indiana University.

Hogg, R. V. (1991). Statistical education: Improvements are badly deeded. *The American Statistician*, *45*, 342–343.

Hunter, W. G. (1977). Some ideas about teaching design of experiments, with 25 examples of experiments conducted by students. *The American Statistician*, *31*, 12–17.

Herman, J. L., & Webb, N. M. (2007). Alignment Methodologies. *Applied Measurement in Education*, *20*(1), 1–5.

Johnson, H. D., & Dasgupta, N. (2005). Traditional versus non-traditional teaching: Perspectives of students in introductory statistics classes. *Journal of Statistics Education: An International Journal on the Teaching and Learning of Statistics*, *13*(2).

Jones, L. (1991). *Using cooperative learning to teach statistics*. Research Report Number 91-2, The L. L. Thurstone Psychometric Laboratory, University of North Carolina.

Jordan, J. (2007). The application of statistics education research in my classroom. *Journal of Statistics Education: An International Journal on the Teaching and Learning of Statistics*, *15*(2).

Keeler, C. M., & Steinhorst, R. K. (1995). Using small groups to promote active learning in the introductory statistics course: A report from the field. *Journal of Statistics Education: An International Journal on the Teaching and Learning of Statistics*, *3*(2).

Kolb, D. A. (1984). *Experiential learning: Experience as the source of learning and development*. Prentice Hall.

Ledolter, J. (1995). Projects in introductory statistics courses. *The American Statistician*, *49*, 364–367.

Logue, A. W. (2018, July 17). *The Extensive Evidence of Co-Requisite Remediation's Effectiveness*. Retrieved from Inside Higher Ed: https://www.insidehighered.com/views/2018/07/17/data-already-tell-us-how-effective-co-requisite-education-opinion

Lovett, M. C. (2001). A collaborative convergence on studying reasoning processes: A case study in statistics. In S. M. Carver & D. Klahr (Eds.), *Cognition and instruction: Twenty-five years of progress* (pp. 347–384). Erlbaum.

Lovett, M. C., & Greenhouse, J. B. (2000). Applying cognitive theory to statistics instruction. *The American Statistician, 54*(3), 196–206.

Mackisack, M. (1994). What is the use of experiments conducted by statistics students? *Journal of Statistics Education: An International Journal on the Teaching and Learning of Statistics, 2*(1).

Moore, D. S. (1997). New pedagogy and new content: The case of statistics. *International Statistical Review, 65*(2), 123–137. doi:10.1111/j.1751-5823.1997.tb00390.x

Neter, J., Kutner, M. H., Nachtsheim, C. J., & Wasserman, W. (1996). *Applied linear statistical models* (4th ed.). McGraw-Hill.

Shadish, W. R., Cook, T. D., & Campbell, D. T. (2002). *Experimental and quasiexperimental designs for generalized causal inference*. Houghton Mifflin Company.

Shaughnessy, J. M. (1977). Misconceptions of probability: An experiment with a smallgroup activity-based model building approach to introductory probability at the college level. *Educational Studies in Mathematics, 8*(3), 285–315. doi:10.1007/BF00385927

Singer, J. D., & Willett, J. B. (1990). Improving the teaching of applied statistics: Putting the data back into data analysis. *The American Statistician, 44*, 223–230.

Smith, G. (1998). Learning statistics by doing statistics. *Journal of Statistics Education: An International Journal on the Teaching and Learning of Statistics, 6*(3).

Snee, R. D. (1993). What's missing in statistical education? *The American Statistician, 47*, 149–154.

Steinhorst, R., & Keeler, C. (1995). Developing material for introductory statistics courses from a conceptual, active learning viewpoint. *Journal of Statistics Education: An International Journal on the Teaching and Learning of Statistics, 3*(3).

Torres, M. A. (2017, November 6). *This is What Powerful Learning Looks Like: Students Share Their Stories* [Blog Post]. Retrieved from: www.digitalpromise.org/2017/11/06/powerful-learning-looks-like-students-share-stories/

Ward, B. (2004). The best of both worlds: A hybrid statistics class. *Journal of Statistics Education: An International Journal on the Teaching and Learning of Statistics, 12*(3).

Chapter 10
Identifying Structure in Program-Level Competencies and Skills:
Dimensionality Analysis of Performance Assessment Scores From Multiple Courses in an IT Program

Heather Hayes
Western Governors University, USA

Goran Trajkovski
https://orcid.org/0000-0002-3745-3009
Western Governors University, USA

ABSTRACT

Programs in an online competency-based higher education (OCBHE) institute will focus on a set of skills and competencies that form a theme throughout multiple courses, where one course builds upon another in terms of increasing the strength or depth of competency. Thus, for students within a given program or major, it is ideal for scores from course assessments with overlapping content to correlate and indicate higher-order skills or competencies. The purpose of this study was to use factor analysis to test the internal and structural validity of course-level performance assessment scores for a group of courses taken as part of a data analytics program in an OCBHE institution. Moreover, the presence of program-level competencies was investigated using hierarchical factor analysis for two groups: a faster, shorter course track and a slow, longer course track. Results supported validity at the course level as well as the presence of a higher-order factor (program-level competency) for the fast course track but not the slow track.

DOI: 10.4018/978-1-7998-9644-9.ch010

An important concern in assessment of any construct is the validity of assessment outcomes (e.g., AERA, APA, & NCME, 2014; Kane, 2016; Messick, 1989; 1995). In the case of competency-based education, validity addresses the question, "Is the assessment score indicative of one's achievement or mastery of a competency?" In other words, do assessment scores accurately reflect whether or not one has successfully demonstrated knowledge gained in course content and are ready to move forward in their program? Students in an online competency-based higher education institute (OCBHE) must pass one, summative, high-stakes assessment in order to demonstrate that they have achieved competencies central to the course and thus complete the course. Given the high-stakes nature of these assessments, evidence of validity is crucial to maintaining quality assessments and fairness to the students in terms of appropriate material for the assessment. Once the assessments are built and have collected data, one method of examining validity of assessment outcomes is Exploratory Factor Analysis (EFA). It is one of the most commonly-used statistical techniques in the social and behavioral sciences (e.g., Osborne, Costello, & Kellow, 2008) and a crucial step in testing the internal validity or structure of the assessment scores and comparing them to expectations or a latent trait theory (e.g., Knetkta, Runyon, & Eddy, 2019). It is a dimension reduction technique wherein patterns of covariance among a potentially large number of variables (i.e., item scores) can be used to group items into a smaller number of factors. It is important to distinguish EFA, also referred to as Principal Axis Factoring (PAF), from Principal Components Analysis (PCA) in order to understand when it is appropriate to use one or the other (Bartholomew, Steele, Moustaki, & Galbraith, 2002; Jensen, 1998). In PAF, factors are interpreted as latent constructs which cause or predict covariance among item scores. The goal in PAF is to establish a testable measurement model in which total variance in item scores is separated into common and unique (plus error) variance and only the former is considered when extracting factors. PCA, on the other hand, is more descriptive in nature and does not support measurement theory due to the use of total variance (common plus unique) among item scores. Therefore, PAF is preferable to PCA when analyzing assessment data, where there is theory surrounding the source of item scores (i.e., latent traits or factors).

Much of early social science research using factor analysis revolved around intelligence testing and attempts to determine how many types, forms, or manifestations of intelligence are measurable from the scores on several different cognitive ability tests (e.g., reading comprehension; verbal reasoning; quantitative reasoning; spatial ability; analytical reasoning). For example, two predominant theories of intelligence emerged early in the 20th century and were based on the dominant patterns of results from factor analytic studies. Spearman (Spearman, 1904) posited that there is one, unitary general intelligence (g) and used factor analysis to support his theory. Specifically, studies revealed that one factor accounts for a large proportion of variance in scores from multiple cognitive ability tests (Spearman, 1927; Beaujean & Benson, 2019). Other researchers argued that the g factor did not account for a sufficient amount of variance in test scores to validate its existence and superiority over the alternate theory that there are multiple factors (forms) of intelligence (e.g., Bartholomew et al., 2002; Beaujean & Benson, 2019; Carroll, 1993; Thurstone, 1932). Nevertheless, the support for g grew over time as it was discovered that the factor structure uncovered in many data sets involving scores from a variety of cognitive ability tests was hierarchical in nature, with multiple "primary factors" (intelligences) that covary to produce a higher-order factor, g. Thus, there is support for both theories (Gottfredson, 1998). For example, the Weschler Adult Intelligence Scale (WAIS) has items representing Arithmetical Reasoning, Memory Span, Picture Completion, Object Assembly, and Vocabulary. A factor analytic study revealed that it had multiple factors, one of which was identified and described as g (Bartholomew et al., 2002). Indeed, g has been uncovered in a wide variety of educational tests as well (Jensen, 1998).

For online competency-based education (OCBHE) institutes such as Western Governor's University, the quality of assessments depends upon multiple evidences of validity including but not limited to the results of factor analytic studies. Validation of assessment outcomes typically occurs at the course level where an assessment score is often intended to represent multiple competencies and sub-skills. For example, if a course is meant to teach students competence in, say, regression analysis using R, then scores on that course assessment should reflect whether or not a student has achieved competency in performing regression analysis in R. On the other hand, scores may represent multiple skills within that competency such as a) ability to program in R and b) understanding of regression analysis. The summative assessments that students must pass in order to complete the course should produce scores that tap into the competencies that are the focus of said courses. Thus, dimensionality of assessment scores should reflect the dominant competencies that are of deemed by experts to be of high importance (and priority) to learning and mastering course material. However, these course-specific competencies are further driven by a higher-level analysis of persistent and dominant skills and competencies associated with an entire program or major of study.

Specifically, an important step in designing and developing a program of study is to carefully and expertly identify a large set of competencies and skills that form a skills architecture unique to that program (DeMark & Kozyrev, 2020). Skills-competency mapping or tagging is conducted to more fully define the nature of the competencies and, thus, more effectively guide course learning and assessment designs. These competencies and skills form a common theme within a program, typically linked to job and industry-relevant skills which are heavily researched and confirmed by subject matter experts. For example, oral and written communication as well as critical thinking skills (Cecil & Krohn, 2012) are often emphasized in all courses because they are skills deemed highly desirable assets to potential employers (Kleckner & Butz, 2021).

These competencies and skills are designed to recur, develop, or build across courses within a track for a program or major of study. Thus, in addition to exploring validity of assessment outcomes for each of multiple courses for the purpose of course-level assessment score validation studies), the larger perspective such as the longitudinal educational experiences of students necessitates exploring the convergence in factor scores from multiple, related courses in demonstrating achievement or mastery of program-level skills and competencies (that form a theme across courses in a series or track). In other words, we're now asking the question, "To what extent does performance across course assessments reflect overarching or dominant skills and competencies required to complete a particular program?"

An important factor in an educational program is the design and development of course sequences that are appropriate for accumulating skills and competencies. However, majors may allow for flexibility in the course sequence as is the case at OCBHE institutes such as WGU. For example, students may take some of the same courses (required by all students in a program or major) but be allowed to choose from a selection of courses that cover the same material (emphasize the same skills and competencies). In other words, there may be multiple prescribed tracks that can be taken to achieve the same set of competencies. Specifically, course material related to program-level competencies and skills, and thus courses and course scope, can be structured differently – e.g., multiple competencies covered simultaneously in one, larger course versus split up into multiple, smaller courses taken at different time periods. And thus, the question becomes, which course track is associated with greater evidence of assessment score and program-level factor score validity? Are higher-order skills more evident from multiple assessment scores with large or small chunking of course material?

The purpose of this chapter is to test and recommend an approach to simultaneously assessing internal, structural validity of assessment scores at the course level and the program-level for a series of courses that students must complete as part of the Information Technology Data Analytics program at an OCBHE institute, WGU. First, EFAs can be conducted at the course level to determine the dominant competencies and skills underlying course assessment scores and compare these findings to expectations (i.e., content specifications and competency structure for course assessments). In other words, do course assessment scores reflect the competencies and skills intended when the course was designed? For example, if an assessment score is intended to measure only one competency or skill, then only one factor should emerge in the EFA. Second, an EFA will be performed on item scores from multiple course assessments for two separate tracks: a fast track in which skills and competencies are covered in fewer courses taken closer together in time, and a slow track in which the same skills and competencies are covered across a larger number of smaller courses that are taken in separate terms. Finally, for each track, a further EFA will be performed on the factor scores to determine if there is a higher order factor. In other words, does a higher-order factor emerge for a set of courses that taken in larger versus smaller chunks? Is there less evidence of cohesion among competencies when courses are taken in smaller chunks over a longer period of time?

METHOD

Sample and Courses of Study

The current study included a sample of n=922 students. All students completed one of two possible course tracks for the data analytics concentration of the data analytics program in the College of Information Technology. Data covers a 1-year period and thus includes 2 terms for each student. All courses are online as part of a competency-based higher education institute, Western Governors University. Thus, all summative assessments are completed online and can be completed at any time in the course (once the student has exhausted and/or mastered application of the skills and competencies inherent in the content, which is done on their own time and at their own pace).

The assessments are also performance-based (PAs). PAs are graded individually by human raters and based on a rubric rather than a cut score. All PAs in this course series have just one task but with multiple criteria or "aspects" which correspond with specific skills associated with the overall competency as reflected in the rubric (Baryla, Shelley, & Trainor, 2012). For example, in the case of data analytics, one aspect may correspond with the ability to clean and organize data, another refers to the subsequent analysis performed, and others focus on proficient use of the software used to perform data collection, cleaning, and analysis. It is also worth noting that every PA task has a written communications aspect (e.g., interpretation of findings to a certain audience) due to its importance in the program. Therefore, task aspects serve as items in the current analysis. Task aspects are scored based on a rubric where 0 = non-competent, 1 = approaching competence, and 2 = competent. Thus, there is a possibility of 0-2 points per task aspect. More detailed information on each course assessment, including the rubric, is located in the Appendix A.

There are two course tracks that run in parallel in terms of competencies and skills covered by course material and the summative assessment. The first, short track (C740, C742) included 246 students. The second, long track (C740, C996 and C997) included 426 students. The first course, C740: Fundamentals of Data Analytics, is an introductory course that emphasizes proficient use of excel, particularly for data cleaning, organization, and statistical analyses such as regression. All students in the data analytic program take this course. The second course is either C742: Data Science Techniques, which covers both Python programming to collect data from websites and use of R for regression analysis of collected data (and is taken in the same term as C740), or two courses that cover Python programming (C996: Programming in Python) and Regression in R (C997: R for Data Analysis) separately and respectively. Moreover, C996 and C997 are taken in separate terms. All four courses emphasize one or more of the following steps in data manipulation and analysis: use and application of a computer software program to collect, organize, and analyze data using multiple regression, and subsequently interpret the results (as well as explain the rationale behind code). Thus, certain university-level skills such as verbal communication and critical thinking are measured in all assessment scores.

Analysis

The first step of the analysis for testing multi-level validity in course assessments involved the use of principle axis factoring (PAF) to determine the underlying structure of scores for each assessment and compare it to the assessment specifications as well as the intended focus of the course (which is aligned to the assessment). The number of factors associated with each assessment score can determined by examining one or more of a variety of criteria. For the current study, a number of criteria were used to determine the optimal number of factors to extract, all of which utilized the scree plot (which plot the eigenvalues of, or variance explained by, each factor). First, iis there a point at which the eigenvalue associated with the extraction of an additional factor does not significantly contribute to the amount of common variance explained by previous factors. The point in the scree plot in which the drop in eigenvalue is most dramatic ("the elbow") is considered the optimal cut-off for the optimal number of factors necessary to account for an acceptable amount of common variance among assessment items (Cattell, 1963). However, it's also important to extract enough factors to account for a sizeable portion of the item score covariance, which should be at least 50%, preferably higher. Thus, a balance of criteria were used in our determination.

In order to more easily interpret the nature of factors based on an examination of the patterns of factor loadings, an oblique rotation, promax, was conducted to achieve simple structure in factor loading patterns. Simple structure is attained when each item loads predominantly onto only one factor and the identity of factors is easily identified based on the content of the items that most strongly load onto each factor. An oblique rotation was used because it is expected that the factors that emerge in each course assessment are correlated due to use and interpretation of a single data set and overlap in nature of the tasks performed on the data sets (e.g., all involve software programming, explanation of steps taken to manipulate or analyze data, and interpretation of results of analysis). Finally, factor scores were obtained using regression, as is recommended for increasing validity estimates (e.g., correlations between factor scores and other variables) and for oblique solutions (cite). Once the dominant factors were identified in each course assessment, results and interpretation of factors were compared to expectation – namely, whether or not there is support for the primary competencies that the assessment score is supposed to capture.

Next, two additional PAFs were conducted for items from multiple courses in each of the two tracks. The first PAF only took into account assessment items from C740 and C742 for those who took the short track. The second PAF was conducted for all items from C740, C996, and C997 for those who took the long track. The presence of higher-order factors will be tested by submitting factor scores to further analysis. This step was also performed separately for each track in order to compare the converge in performance on multiple factors or course-specific competencies (i.e., dominant skills taught in the course series) between the two tracks. Again, the distinction between the two tracks is that in the short track, half of the skills (particularly Python programming and performing regression in R) are taught in the same course, whereas in the long track, this content is split into two separate courses that are taken in different terms (i.e., more compartmentalized and separated by time).

RESULTS

Course-Level Analysis

The results of all factor analyses are located in Appendix B, beginning with validation at the course and assessment level. For C740: Fundamentals of Data Analytics, a two-factor solution provided the best fit to the assessment data based on eigenvalue size (e.g., above 1), an examination of the scree plot (e.g., number of factors preceding the "elbow" or largest drop in common variance explained), and total variance explained by dominant factors, which is 69% (see Table 1). These same criteria were used in all PAFs performed in this study. After rotation to simple structure, aspects A through D loaded most strongly onto the first factor, and aspects E through K loaded most strongly onto the second factor (Table 2). The first factor is best described as the initial steps preceding an inferential statistical analysis, specifically, regression analysis – i.e., data cleaning, variable computations, organization, and summary statistics in excel ("Data Preparation in Excel"), whereas the second factor represents steps of the actual regression analysis (also in performed in excel) and interpretation of these results ("Regression in Excel"). In other words, interpretation of results, or written-communication aspects, did not form a separate factor in the analysis but were part of whichever part of the task to which the written communication was referring (in this case, regression analysis). The correlation between these two factors is .56. These findings partially support the content specifications and competency structure intended for the course and its summative assessment. Namely, "Data Preparation in Excel" matches the "Introduction to Data Analytics" as well as "Data Analytics Activities," and "Regression in Excel" matches "Data Models and Making Predictions" and "Data Analytic Activities." In other words, the Data Analytic Activities competency is found in nearly every item score. "Ethical Principles and Data Analytics" appears to be subsumed in the "Regression in Excel" factor.

For C742: Data Science Techniques, a two-factor solution was the optimal selection. The amount of common variance explained by these two factors was 64.9% (Table 3). After rotation (Table 4), it appears that aspects A through H, which focus on Python programming (scraping websites for data, organizing data into a csv file), load onto the first factor ("Python programming"). The second factor is best represented by aspects I through L, which focus on regression analysis in R ("Regression in R"). Aspects M and N, which focus on organization and clarity of the PA task submission as well as the inclusion of citations in the results, load equally on both factors. This finding supports the equal importance of adequately explaining the steps taken in both Python programming and regression analysis in R. The two factors had a correlation of .35. These findings are largely consistent with the content specifications and competency structure intended for the course and its summative assessment. Specifically, "Python programming" matches "Data Wrangling" while "Regression in R" most closely matches "Data Analysis." The first competency, "Database Management System" is present in nearly every item score and thus, spread out among the various aspects.

For C996: Programming in Python, one factor accounted for the majority of common variance in item scores; however, it was relatively low (54.3%; see Table 5). All aspects pertained specifically to Python programming – the same web-scraping and data file storage process covered in the first part of the PA for C742 (Table 6). Similar results were found for C997: R for Data Analysis, one factor accounted for the majority of common variance in item scores; however, it was relatively low (44.1%) (Table 7). All aspects focused on the ability to use R to perform a multiple regression – the same process covered in the second part of the PA for C742 (Table 8). These results support evidence for alignment between the content specifications and competency structure intended for the course and interpretation of scores from its summative assessment. Specifically, each course assessment is defined by three competencies; however, all three competencies are best represented by one factor per course.

Program-Level Analysis

For the students who completed the short track (2 courses: C740 and C742), four factors emerged. Namely, the largest drop in eigenvalues occurred after extraction of the fourth factor, resulting in 67.8% common variance explained by four correlated factors (Table 9). However, it could also be interpreted as a one-factor model given the large difference between eigenvalues for first and second factors; hence, the impetus to test for hierarchical structure. Interpretation of individual factors extracted is as follows (see Table 10). Factor 1 in this multi-course analysis corresponds predominantly with aspects related to the factor "Python programming" for C742, factor 2 corresponds with "Regression in R" C742, factor 3 corresponds with "Data prep Excel" in C740, and factor 4 corresponds with "Regression in Excel" in C740. A factor analysis of the four factor scores (Tables 11 and 12), revealed a predominant factor or "g" likely reflecting "competency in data analytics, the theme of the program. However, this general factor only accounted for approximately 30% of the variance in primary factor scores.

For students in the long track (3 courses: C740, C996, and C997), four factors emerged. Namely, the largest drop in eigenvalues occurred after extraction of the fourth factor, resulting in 54.8% common variance explained by four correlated factors (Table 13). Factors are interpreted based on their loadings, as follows. Factor 1 in this multi-course analysis corresponds with "Python programming" for C996, factor 2 corresponds with "Preparing data in Excel" C740, factor 3 corresponds with "Regression in Excel" in C740, and factor 4 corresponds with "Regression in R" in C997 (see Table 14). Thus, factors are almost identical to what was found for individual course assessments. A higher-order factor analysis of the four factor scores indicates that there is no general factor but, rather, two (see Table 15). The interpretation of factor structure based on the pattern of loadings indicates that the first factor pertains to C740, and the second to C742 (Table 16). This could be due differences in the specifics of the task (e.g., data, variables, type of regression) or differences between the programs used to conduct regression analysis. Correlation between factors is .211.

DISCUSSION

In OCBHE institutions, summative assessment scores are high-stakes because they are used to determine whether or not students pass a course. Therefore, it is crucial to ensure that assessments outcomes accurately indicate whether or not a student has achieved versus not achieved the competencies and skills associated with the course. One way to test validity of assessment scores is to evaluate the internal structure of scores and determine whether or not the latent structure underlying scores is appropriate given the learning goals of the course – namely, what are the underlying competencies and skills that the assessment scores are intended to measure? Moreover, there may be higher-order competencies associated with a group of course assessments for a program or major of study, which reflect the theme of the program. However, the factor structure may vary between multiple course tracks which vary by how the material is organized or "chunked" (i.e., one, larger course versus two, smaller courses taken in different terms). Therefore, we conducted a multi-level validity study using EFA and PAF for a series of course assessments completed by the students for a degree in data analytics. EFA was chosen over confirmatory factor analysis (CFA) because the course assessments are relatively new and have not yet undergone extensive validity testing. Thus, further studies are required, using CFA, to confirm the present findings.

Results of PAFs indicate that only one to two factors explain a majority of the covariance in item scores in each course-level assessment, which is consistent with expectations for each course. The factor structure is nearly identical for the two tracks, and factors are modestly correlated for both tracks as well. Thus, there is support for consistency between the competency structure underlying PA scores and content specifications as well as consistency in performance on dimensions or competencies that are covered in multiple courses (i.e., "program theme"). However, support for a higher-order, general factor is only found for assessments in the fast track. Thus, It appears that when a certain set of skills are separated into multiple courses that occur over a more extended period of time (e.g., one year), rather than one in the same six month period as the preceding required course (C740), there is less cohesion in performance among dominant competencies, skills, or factors. Thus, there is partial evidence of program-level validity based on specific findings that provide stronger justification for combining multi-dimensional content into one assessment rather than dividing it between two separate courses. The lack of a higher-order factor for the slow track may be due to a difference in the complexity and nature of the programs used in C740 versus C996 and C997 or greater separation in time between course assessments (and thus variance in performance).

One implication for course design is that larger "chunking" of course material into fewer, larger courses taken closer together in time results in greater evidence of internal validity of multiple course assessments in a program. What remains to be seen is if larger chunking of course material results in higher program-level success rate. In other words, research on criterion-related validity as well as other forms of validity is warranted in order to determine not only whether or not assessment scores are predictive of academic success such as completing the program but whether evidence supporting course-level and program-level validity differ between multiple course tracks. For example, the impact of program content chunking in courses on the success rates for completing the program may vary among students. For some students, larger chunking of program content may be more beneficial, whereas the opposite may be true for other students. Moreover, only a small snapshot of courses taken within a program were evaluated in the current study. Future research should incorporate more courses within the program in order to identify more higher-order, program-level competencies.

In summary, this paper contributes to the literature on assessment score validity in OCBHE institutions by employing factor analysis to the test the internal structure of course PA scores as well as higher-order factors that identify program-level competencies that are best represented in PA scores across multiple courses in the program. Although one might recommend, based on these findings, that it is ideal to chunk course material into larger courses taken within a shorter amount of time in order to adhere to validated internal structure of PA scores. However, this may not be the best course of action with respect to program-level success. More research is warranted, in the form of criterion-related validity.

REFERENCES

American Educational Research Association, American Psychological Association, & National Council for Measurement in Education. (2014). Standards for educational and psychological testing. Author.

Bartholomew, D. J., & Knott, M. (1999). *Latent Variable Models and Factor Analysis* (2nd ed.). Arnold.

Bartholomew, D. J., Steele, F., Moustaki, I., & Galbraith, J. I. (2002). *The Analysis and Interpretation of Multivariate Data for Social Scientists*. Chapman and Hall/CRC.

Baryla, E., Shelley, G., & Trainor, W. (2012). Transforming rubrics using factor analysis. *Practical Assessment, Research & Evaluation*, *17*, 4. Advance online publication. doi:10.7275/5nt2-g458

Beaujean, A. A., & Benson, N. F. (2019). The one and the many: Enduring legacies of Spearman and Thurstone on Intelligence Test Score Interpretation. *Applied Measurement in Education*, *32*(3), 198–215. doi:10.1080/08957347.2019.1619560

Carroll, J. B. (1993). *Human cognitive abilities: A survey of factor-analytic studies*. Cambridge University Press. doi:10.1017/CBO9780511571312

Cattell, R. B., Radcliffe, J. A., & Sweney, A. B. (1963). The nature and measurement of components of motivation. *Genetic Psychology Monographs*, *68*(1), 49–211.

Cecil, A., & Krohn, B. D. (2012). The process of developing a competency-based academic curriculum in tourism management. *Journal of Teaching in Travel & Tourism*, *12*(2), 129–145. doi:10.1080/15313220.2011.624417

DeMark, S. & Kozyrev, J. (2020). Enabling pathways to opportunity through a skills-based architecture. *Journal of Competency-Based Education*. . doi:10.1002/cbe2.1241

Gottfredson, L. S. (1998). *The General Intelligence Factor*. https://www.hucama.com/wp-

Jensen, A. R. (1998). The g factor and the design of education. In R. J. Sternberg & W. M. Williams (Eds.), Intelligence, Instruction, and Assessment: Theory Into Practice (pp. 111–131). Academic Press.

Kane, M. T. (2016). Explicating validity. *Assessment in Education: Principles, Policy & Practice*, *23*(2), 198–211.

Kleckner, M. J., & Butz, N. (2021). Addressing undergraduate skill gaps in higher education: Revisiting communication in the major course outcomes. *Journal of Education for Business*, *97*(7), 411–423.

Knekta, Runyon, & Eddy. (2019). One size doesn't fit all: Using factor analysis to gather validity evidence when using surveys in your research. *CBE Life Sciences Education, 18*, 1. doi:10.1187/cbe.18-04-0064

Messick, S. (1989). Validity. In R. L. Linn (Ed.), Educational measurement (pp. 13-103). Macmillan Publishing Col, Inc.

Messick, S. (1995). Validity of psychological assessment- Validation of inferences from person's responses and performances as scientific inquiry into score meaning. *The American Psychologist*, *50*(9), 741–749.

Osborne, J. W., Costello, A. B., & Kellow, J. T. (2008). Best Practices in Exploratory Factor Analysis. In J. W. Osborne (Ed.), *Best Practices in Quantitative Methods* (pp. 205–213). Sage Publishing.

Spearman, C. (1904). General intelligence objectively determined and measured. *The American Journal of Psychology*, *15*, 201–293.

Spearman, C. (1927). *The abilities of man: Their nature and measurement*. Macmillan.

Thurstone, L. L. (1932). *The Theory of Multiple Factors*. Edwards Brothers.

APPENDIX A: RUBRIC ASPECTS BY COURSE

C740 Fundamentals of Data Analytics

Figure 1. Task directions for the C740 performance assessment

COMPETENCIES

4030.1.10 : Introduction to Data Analytics and Data Visualization
The graduate uses descriptive statistics and data visualization to summarize data.

4030.1.11 : Data Models and Making Predictions
The graduate applies statistical models to make predictions in real-world situations.

4030.1.12 : Data Mining Activities
The graduate analyzes data mining activities including data preparation, data summary, and modeling.

4030.1.13 : Introduction to Data Simulations
The graduate analyzes simulation modeling and simulation outputs.

4030.1.14 : Ethical Principles and Data Analytics
The graduate summarizes ethical principles specific to data analytics.

INTRODUCTION

As a data analyst you will be asked to create visually present data in a variety of formats to make it easier for others to understand. You will also be asked to aggregate data and use it to make predictions, solve problems, and determine trends. This information will be used to support business initiatives and inform fiscal decisions.

In this task, you will use the raw data found in the attached "Raw Data and Linear Regression" to analyze the logs from emergency 911 calls for the local police department in the provided scenario. Then you will provide a written brief with visual representations. You will need to clean the data, aggregate the data to create a visualization, and interpret the provided linear regression.

You will then use the aggregated data to determine if the local police department qualifies for additional government funding, using a Monte Carlo method. You will need to include screenshots for each step of the solver you use, including your selected parameters, in your submission.

Two files should be submitted for this assessment. The first file should be a spreadsheet file (.xls or .xlsx) that contains multiple pages, representing the work done with the raw data and cleaned data in part one, as well as your Monte Carlo simulation and screenshots. The second file should be a word document (.doc or .docx) with your written summaries or responses.

SCENARIO

The governor has offered a funding incentive for police departments that are able to meet a minimum standard of having at least 2.5 officers per incident. Each police department must apply for this funding and provide data to prove eligibility.

You are a data analyst that has been recruited to do consulting work for your local police department. The police chief has asked you to analyze the logs from emergency 911 calls in the city and then provide a summary of that data, including graphic representations. He has also tasked you with using this data to determine if the department qualifies for the governor's funding incentive.

REQUIREMENTS

Your submission must be your original work. No more than a combined total of 30% of the submission and no more than a 10% match to any one individual source can be directly quoted or closely paraphrased from sources, even if cited correctly. An originality report is provided when you submit your task that can be used as a guide.

You must use the rubric to direct the creation of your submission because it provides detailed criteria that will be used to evaluate your work. Each requirement below may be evaluated by more than one rubric aspect. The rubric aspect titles may contain hyperlinks to relevant portions of the course.

Part 1: Data Analysis

Prepare the data provided in the attached, "Raw Data and Linear Regression." Remove any potential errors or outliers, duplicate records, or data that are not necessary to address the problem or scenario.

A. Explain why you removed each column or row from the raw data file or why you imputed data in the empty fields as you prepared the data for analysis. Include a clean data set with your submission.

B. Create data sheets using the cleaned data. Provide the following tables with accurate counts, and vertical or horizontal bar graphs to represent the requested aggregated data. Be sure all tables are appropriately labeled.

- Table: date and number of events
- Bar graph: date and number of events
- Table: number of incident occurrences by event type
- Bar graph: number of incident occurrences by event type
- Table: sectors and total number of events
- Bar graph: sectors and total number of events

C. Describe the fit of the linear regression line to the data, using the linear regression model that is provided in the attachment. Provide graphical representations or tables as evidence to support your description.

D. Describe the impact of the outliers on the data, using the linear regression model that is provided in the attachment. Provide graphical representations or tables as evidence to support your description.

E. Provide a residual plot and explain how to improve the linear regression model based on your interpretation of the plot.

Part 2: Simulation and Recommendation

Run a simulation (Monte Carlo) based on a normally distributed random variable of the same mean and standard deviation as the variable "Number of officers at the scene" in the clean data set.

F. Determine if the police department currently qualifies for the funding. Provide your simulation results as evidence to support your findings.

G. Calculate the probability that the department will or will not qualify for the funding in the future. Provide evidence to support your findings.

H. Describe the precautions or behaviors that should be exercised when working with and communicating about the sensitive data in this scenario.

I. Acknowledge sources, using in-text citations and references, for content that is quoted, paraphrased, or summarized.

Figure 2. The scoring rubric for the C740 performance assessment

RUBRIC

Criterion	Not Evident	Approaching Competence	Competent
A:DATA PREPARATION	An explanation is not provided or a clean data set is not included.	The submission explains why columns or rows were removed or empty fields were imputed but does not include justification for the interventions made to the data. Or the clean data does not match the justification.	The submission explains why columns or rows were removed or empty fields were imputed and includes justification for the interventions made to the data. A clean data set, that matches the justification, is provided.
B:DATA SHEETS	Created data sheets are not provided or all tables and bar graphs are not included.	The submission includes created data sheets but the tables and bar graphs are inaccurate or do not include all necessary labels.	The submission includes created data sheets with accurate tables and bar graphs that include all necessary labels.
C:LINEAR REGRESSION	A description of the fit of the linear regression line to the data is not provided.	The submission describes the fit of the linear regression line to the data, but does not use accurate graphical representations or tables as evidence to support the description.	The submission describes the fit of the linear regression line to the data and uses accurate graphical representations or tables as evidence to support the description.
D:OUTLIERS	A description is not provided or the submission does not include graphical representations or tables.	The submission inaccurately describes the impact of the outliers on the data. Or the graphical representations or tables do not support the description.	The submission uses the linear regression model to accurately describe the impact of the outilers on the data and provides graphical representations or tables as evidence to support the description.
E:RESIDUAL PLOT	A residual plot is not provided or the submission does not include an explanation.	The submission provides a residual plot, but the explanation does not match the plot or will not improve the linear regression model.	The submission provides a residual plot and a matching explanation that will improve the linear regression model.
F:CURRENT QUALIFICATION	A determination of the department's current qualification for the funding is not provided, or the submission does not include simulation results.	The submission incorrectly determines if the department currently qualifies for the funding or includes simulation results that do not support the findings.	The submission correctly determines if the department currently qualifies for the funding and includes simulation results that support the findings.
G:FUTURE QUALIFICATION	A calculation of probability is not provided or the submission does not include evidence.	The submission inaccurately calculates the probability that the department will or will not qualify for the funding in the future or provides evidence that does not support the findings.	The submission accurately calculates the probability that the department will or will not qualify for the funding in the future and provides evidence to support the findings.
H:ETHICS	A description is not provided.	The submission describes precautions or behaviors to be exercised when working with or communicating about sensitive data, but not both. Or the precautions or behaviors are not specific to the scenario.	The submission describes the necessary precautions or behaviors to be exercised when working with and communicating about the sensitive data in the scenario.
I:SOURCES	The submission does not include both in-text citations and a reference list for sources that are quoted, paraphrased, or summarized.	The submission includes in-text citations for sources that are quoted, paraphrased, or summarized, and a reference list; however, the citations and/or reference list is incomplete or inaccurate.	The submission includes in-text citations for sources that are properly quoted, paraphrased, or summarized and a reference list that accurately identifies the author, date, title, and source location as available.
PROFESSIONAL COMMUNICATION:	Content is unstructured, is disjointed, or contains pervasive errors in mechanics, usage, or grammar. Vocabulary or tone is unprofessional or distracts from the topic.	Content is poorly organized, is difficult to follow, or contains errors in mechanics, usage, or grammar that cause confusion. Terminology is misused or ineffective.	Content reflects attention to detail, is organized, and focuses on the main ideas as prescribed in the task or chosen by the candidate. Terminology is pertinent, is used correctly, and effectively conveys the intended meaning. Mechanics, usage, and grammar promote accurate interpretation and understanding.

C742 Data Science Tools and Techniques

Figure 3. Task directions for the C742 assessment

COMPETENCIES

4032.1.1 : Database Management System
The graduate performs data analysis using database systems and query language.

4032.1.2 : Data Wrangling
The graduate manages data using wrangling tools, techniques, and methods.

4032.1.3 : Data Analysis
The graduate performs data analysis using software tools and techniques.

INTRODUCTION

The United States collects and analyzes demographic data from the U.S. population. The U.S. Census Bureau provides annual estimates of the population size of each U.S. state and region. Many important decisions are made using the estimated population dynamics, including the investments in new infrastructure, such as schools and hospitals; establishing new job training centers; opening or closing schools and senior centers; and adjusting the emergency services to the size and characteristics of the demographics of metropolitan and other areas, states, or the country as a whole. The census data and estimates are publicly available on the U.S. census website.

As a professional in the data analytics industry, you should know how to use tools that support the different stages and methods of analyzing data. These tools include environments that support performing data scraping, wrangling data, or applying various analyses.

For this project, you will use Python to scrape the web links from the HTML code of the U.S. Census Bureau's Population Estimates web page, use SQL to spot differences in the population size, and use linear regression in R to predict the size of the population of your state in 2020.

The goal is to demonstrate your skill sets with Python, SQL, and R to support various data analytics processes.

You will use versions of Python, SQL, and R of your choosing that you will indicate in the attached "Student Submission Form." You will also include the names of the files that house your responses to the task prompts, the code used, and all input and output files you used in your analyses.

REQUIREMENTS

Your submission must be your original work. No more than a combined total of 30% of the submission and no more than a 10% match to any one individual source can be directly quoted or closely paraphrased from sources, even if cited correctly. An originality report is provided when you submit your task that can be used as a guide.

You must use the rubric to direct the creation of your submission because it provides detailed criteria that will be used to evaluate your work. Each requirement below may be evaluated by more than one rubric aspect. The rubric aspect titles may contain hyperlinks to relevant portions of the course.

Submit a completed copy of the attached "*Student Submission Form*" that includes the following elements:

1. versions of the programming environments for Python, SQL, and R used for the task
2. an inventory of the code, input, and output files used in each part

Submit one zipped folder with three subfolders that include the code, input, and output files from each part of the task. Place the completed "Student Submission Form" in the main folder. Place the responses to the task prompts from each part in one PDF file for each part, and include these PDF files in the respective subfolders.

Part I: Python
Develop a web links scraper program in Python that extracts *all* of the unique web links that point out to other web pages from the HTML code of the "Current Estimates" web link and that populates them in a comma-separated values (CSV) file as absolute uniform resource indicators (URIs).

A. Explain how the Python program extracts the web links from the HTML code of the "Current Estimates" web link.

B. Explain the criteria you used to determine if a link is a locator to another HTML page. Specify the code segment that executes this action as part of your explanation.

C. Explain how the program ensures that relative links are saved as absolute URIs in the output file. Specify the code segment that executes this action as part of your explanation.

D. Explain how the program ensures that there are no duplicated links in the output file. Specify the code that executes this action as part of your explanation.

E. Provide the Python code you wrote to extract *all* the unique web links from the HTML code of the "Current Estimates" web link that point out to other HTML pages.

F. Provide the HTML code of the "Current Estimates" web page.

G. Provide the CSV file that your script created.

H. Test your script and provide a screenshot of the successfully executed results.

Part II: SQL
I. Calculate the mathematical difference in the population size estimates for each U.S. state the Census Bureau provided in two consecutive years using the most current data and the latest historical datasets for the national total population. Provide the SQL code and resulting table in your submission.

J. Write a code to join the two tables on the year and state fields into one SQL table that identifies the absolute differences (in whole rounded hundreds) in the estimates of 10,000 individuals or more between the two datasets. If the earlier estimates are larger than 10,000, the cells should indicate a negative value. Provide a screenshot of your tested code showing successful execution.

K. Explain how you prepared the data and how the datasets were imported into two SQL tables. Provide a screenshot of the successfully executed SQL code.

L. Export the data from the SQL table into a CSV file, with rows representing the states and columns representing the years that both datasets estimate, that only shows the differences between the datasets (in whole rounded tens of thousands) that exceed 10,000 individuals.

Part III: R
M. Create a linear regression analysis with R to predict the size of the population for the state you live in for 2020 based on the Current Estimates Data dataset.

N. Explain how you prepared the data and how the dataset was imported into R, including a screenshot of your results.

O. Using the estimates for the most recent year in the dataset, create an R script to display a histogram (using one million as the interval size) of the current estimated population size of your state. Provide a screenshot of your results.

P. Create an R script that will tabulate a statistical description of the estimated 2020 data. Provide a screenshot of your results.

Q. Predict the population size of your state using a linear regression. Provide a screenshot of your results.

R. Acknowledge sources, using in-text citations and references, for content that is quoted, paraphrased, or summarized.

Figure 4. C742 Rubric (part 1)

RUBRIC

Criterion	Not Evident	Approaching Competence	Competent
A:PYTHON: HOW THE PROGRAM EXTRACTS LINKS	The explanation does not address how the Python program extracts the web links from the HTML code of the "Current Estimates" web link.	The explanation addresses how the Python program extracts the web links from the HTML code of the "Current Estimates" web link but contains inaccuracies.	The explanation accurately explains how the Python program extracts the web links from the HTML code of the "Current Estimates" web link.
B:PYTHON: CRITERIA USED	The criteria used to determine if a link is a locator to another HTML page is not explained.	The submission explains the criteria used to determine if a link is a locator to another HTML page, but either the explanation contains inaccuracies, or it does not specify the correct code segment that executes this action.	The submission explains the criteria used to determine if a link is a locator to another HTML page, specifying the code segment that executes this action.
C:PYTHON: RELATIVE LINKS	The criteria in the program that translates and ensures that relative links are saved as absolute URIs in the output file is not explained.	The submission explains the criteria in the program that translates and ensures that relative links are saved as absolute URIs in the output file, but either the explanation contains inaccuracies, or it does not specify the correct code segment that executes this action.	The submission explains the criteria in the program that translates and ensures that relative links are saved as absolute URIs in the output file, specifying the code segment that executes this action.
D:PYTHON: DUPLICATED LINKS	The submission does not explain how the program ensures that there are no duplicated links in the output file.	The submission explains how the program ensures that there are no duplicated links in the output file, but it does not specify the code segment that executes this action. The explanation contains inaccuracies.	The submission explains how the program ensures that there are no duplicated links in the output file, specifying the code segment that executes this action.
E:PYTHON: FUNCTIONING PYTHON CODE	The submission does not provide a Python code.	The submission provides a functioning Python code but the code does not extract all the unique web links from the HTML code of the "Current Estimates" web link that point out to other HTML pages.	The submission provides the functioning Python code written to extract all the unique web links from the HTML code of the "Current Estimates" web link that point out to other HTML pages.
F:PYTHON: HTML CODE	The submission does not provide a HTML code of the "Current Estimates" web page.	The submission provides an HTML code but it is not for "Current Estimates" web page.	The submission provides the HTML code of the "Current Estimates" web page.
G:PYTHON: CSV FILE	The CSV file is not provided.	Not applicable.	The CSV file that the script created is provided.
H:PYTHON: SCREENSHOT OF RESULTS	A screenshot of the successfully executed results is not provided.	Not applicable.	A screenshot of the successfully executed results from the written script is provided.

Figure 5. C742 Rubric (part 2)

Criterion	Not Evident	Approaching Competence	Competent
I:SQL: DIFFERENCES IN POPULATION SIZE ESTIMATES	The submission does not identify the differences in population size.	The submission calculates the difference in population size and provides SQL code, but either the differences identified or the SQL code provided contains inaccuracies, or the code provided does not match the given data outcome.	The submission calculate the difference in population size and provides accurate and logical SQL code that created the new data table.
J:SQL: JOINING TABLES	The submission does not provide SQL code that joins the two tables.	Not applicable.	The submission provides SQL code that joins the two tables and provides a screenshot to show successful execution of the code.
K:SQL: HOW DATA WAS PREPARED	The submission does not explain how the data was prepared and how the datasets were imported into the SQL tables.	The submission explains how the data was prepared and how the datasets were imported into the SQL tables, but either the explanation contains inaccuracies, or a screenshot of the successfully executed SQL code was not provided.	The submission explains how the data was prepared and how the datasets were imported into the SQL tables. The submission includes a screenshot of the successfully executed SQL code.
L:SQL: CSV FILE	The data from the SQL table is not exported into a CSV file.	The data from the SQL table is exported into a CSV file, but it does not show the differences between the datasets computed, or data set contains errors.	The data from the SQL table is correctly exported into a CSV file that shows that the differences between the datasets are accurately computed.
M:R: LINEAR REGRESSION ANALYSIS	A linear regression analysis with R is not created.	A linear regression analysis is created with R to predict the size of the population for the state selected for the year 2020 based on the Current Estimates Data dataset, but the regression contains errors.	A linear regression analysis is created with R for use in predicting the size of the population for the state selected for the year 2020 based on the Current Estimates Data dataset.
N:R: HOW DATA WAS PREPARED	The submission does not explain how the data was prepared and imported into R.	The submission explains how the data was prepared and imported into R, but it does not include a screenshot of the results, or the explanation contains inaccuracies.	The submission explains how the data was prepared and imported into R and includes a screenshot of the results.
O:R: HISTOGRAM	An R script using the estimates for the most recent year in the dataset is not created.	An R script is created using the estimates for the most recent year in the dataset, but it does not display a histogram (using one million as the interval size) of the current latest estimated population size of the selected state, or the submission does not include a screenshot of the results.	An R script is accurately created, using the estimates for the most recent year in the dataset, to display a histogram (using one million as the interval size) of the current latest estimated population size of the selected state. The submission includes a screenshot of the results.
P:R: STATISTICAL DESCRIPTION	An R script that will tabulate a statistical description of the estimated 2020 data using the summary method in R is not created.	An R script is created that will tabulate a statistical description of the estimated 2020 data, but either it did not use the summary method in R, or the submission does not provide a screenshot of accurate results.	An R script is accurately created that will tabulate a statistical description of the estimated 2020 data using the summary method in R. The submission includes a screenshot of accurate results.
Q:R: POPULATION SIZE OF STATE	The submission does not predict the population size of the selected state.	The submission proposes a prediction of the population size of the selected state but does not use data to support the prediction or does not provide a screenshot of the results.	The submission proposes a data-supported prediction of the population size of the selected state based on the data points for each year from the most current data dataset for the year 2020 using linear regression. The submission includes a screenshot of the results.
R:SOURCES	The submission does not include both in-text citations and a reference list for sources that are quoted, paraphrased, or summarized.	The submission includes in-text citations for sources that are quoted, paraphrased, or summarized, and a reference list; however, the citations and/or reference list is incomplete or inaccurate.	The submission includes in-text citations for sources that are properly quoted, paraphrased, or summarized and a reference list that accurately identifies the author, date, title, and source location as available.
PROFESSIONAL COMMUNICATION:	Content is unstructured, is disjointed, or contains pervasive errors in mechanics, usage, or grammar. Vocabulary or tone is unprofessional or distracts from the topic.	Content is poorly organized, is difficult to follow, or contains errors in mechanics, usage, or grammar that cause confusion. Terminology is misused or ineffective.	Content reflects attention to detail, is organized, and focuses on the main ideas as prescribed in the task or chosen by the student. Terminology is pertinent, is used correctly, and effectively conveys the intended meaning. Mechanics, usage, and grammar promote accurate interpretation and understanding.

C996 Programming in Python

Figure 6. C996 task directions

COMPETENCIES

4064.1.1 : Python as a Programming Language
The graduate integrates Python elements to create programming solutions.

4064.1.2 : Python for Data Wrangling
The graduate integrates Python elements to create scripts that support data wrangling activities.

4064.1.3 : Tools for Data Collection, Exploration and Preparation
The graduate performs data collection, exploration, and preparation activities.

INTRODUCTION

Data analysts frequently need to extract large amounts of data from websites and save them to local files for use in the analysis of a phenomenon that is under investigation. That often includes creating a copy of all web links in a page later processing or automating maintenance tasks on a web site, such as checking links or validating HTML code.

For this project, you will use the Python programming language to scrape the web links from the HTML code of the "U.S. Census Bureau's Population Estimates."

REQUIREMENTS

Your submission must be your original work. No more than a combined total of 30% of a submission can be directly quoted or closely paraphrased from sources, even if cited correctly. Use the report provided when submitting your task as a guide.

You must use the rubric to direct the creation of your submission because it provides detailed criteria that will be used to evaluate your work. Each requirement below may be evaluated by more than one rubric aspect. The rubric aspect titles may contain hyperlinks to relevant portions of the course.

Submit **one** zipped folder that includes the code, input, and output files from the task. Place the responses to the task prompts in **one** PDF file.

> *Note: This assessment requires you to submit pictures, graphics, and/or diagrams. Each file must be an attachment no larger than 30 MB in size. Diagrams must be original and may be hand-drawn or drawn using a graphics program. Do not use CAD programs because attachments will be too large.*

Develop a web links scraper program in Python that extracts *all* of the unique web links that point out to other web pages from the HTML code of the "Current Estimates" web link, *both* from the "US Census Bureau" website (see web link below) and outside that domain, and that populates them in a comma-separated values (CSV) file as absolute uniform resource indicators (URIs).

A. Explain how the Python program extracts the web links from the HTML code of the "Current Estimates," found in web links section.

B. Explain the criteria you used to determine if a link is a locator to another HTML page. Identify the code segment that executes this action as part of your explanation.

C. Explain how the program ensures that relative links are saved as absolute URIs in the output file. Identify the code segment that executes this action as part of your explanation.

D. Explain how the program ensures that there are no duplicated links in the output file. Identify the code that executes this action as part of your explanation.

> *Note: Please consider weblinks that point to the same web pages as identical* (e.g., www.commerce.gov and www.commerce.gov/).

E. Provide the Python code you wrote to extract *all* the unique web links from the HTML code of the "Current Estimates" (in the web links section), that point out to other HTML pages.

F. Provide the HTML code of the "Current Estimates" web page scrapped at the time when the scraper was run and the CSV file was generated.

G. Provide the CSV file that your script created.

H. Run your script and provide a screenshot of the successfully executed results.

I. Acknowledge sources, using in-text citations and references, for content that is quoted, paraphrased, or summarized.

J. Demonstrate professional communication in the content and presentation of your submission.

Figure 7. C996 rubric

RUBRIC

A:HOW THE PROGRAM EXTRACTS LINKS

Not Evident	Approaching Competence	Competent
The explanation does not address how the Python program extracts the web links from the HTML code of the "Current Estimates" web link.	The explanation addresses how the Python program extracts the web links from the HTML code of the "Current Estimates" web link but contains inaccuracies.	The explanation accurately explains how the Python program extracts the web links from the HTML code of the "Current Estimates" web link.

B:CRITERIA USED

Not Evident	Approaching Competence	Competent
The criteria used to determine if a link is a locator to another HTML page is not explained.	The submission explains the criteria used to determine if a link is a locator to another HTML page, but either the explanation contains inaccuracies, or it does not specify the correct code segment that executes this action.	The submission explains the criteria used to determine if a link is a locator to another HTML page, specifying the code segment that executes this action.

C:RELATIVE LINKS

Not Evident	Approaching Competence	Competent
The criteria in the program that translates and ensures that relative links are saved as absolute URIs in the output file is not explained.	The submission explains the criteria in the program that translates and ensures that relative links are saved as absolute URIs in the output file, but either the explanation contains inaccuracies, or it does not specify the correct code segment that executes this action.	The submission explains the criteria in the program that translates and ensures that relative links are saved as absolute URIs in the output file, specifying the code segment that executes this action.

D:DUPLICATED LINKS

Not Evident	Approaching Competence	Competent
The submission does not explain how the program ensures that there are no duplicated links in the output file.	The submission explains how the program ensures that there are no duplicated links in the output file, but it does not specify the code segment that executes this action. The explanation contains inaccuracies.	The submission explains how the program ensures that there are no duplicated links in the output file, specifying the code segment that executes this action.

E:FUNCTIONING PYTHON CODE

Not Evident	Approaching Competence	Competent
The submission does not provide a Python code.	The submission provides a functioning Python code but the code does not extract all the unique web links from the HTML code of the "Current Estimates" web link that point out to other HTML pages.	The submission provides the functioning Python code written to extract all the unique web links from the HTML code of the "Current Estimates" web link that point out to other HTML pages.

F:HTML CODE

Not Evident	Approaching Competence	Competent
The submission does not provide a HTML code of the "Current Estimates" web page.	The submission provides an HTML code but it is not for "Current Estimates" web page.	The submission provides the HTML code of the "Current Estimates" web page.

G:CSV FILE

Not Evident	Approaching Competence	Competent
The CSV file is not provided.	The CSV file that the script created is provided, but incomplete.	The complete CSV file that the script created is provided.

H:SCREENSHOT OF RESULTS

Not Evident	Approaching Competence	Competent
A screenshot is not provided.	A screenshot is provided, but does not confirm the successfully executed results from the written script.	A screenshot confirming the successfully executed results from the written script is provided.

I:SOURCES

Not Evident	Approaching Competence	Competent
The submission does not include both in-text citations and a reference list for sources that are quoted, paraphrased, or summarized.	The submission includes in-text citations for sources that are quoted, paraphrased, or summarized and a reference list; however, the citations or reference list is incomplete or inaccurate.	The submission includes in-text citations for sources that are properly quoted, paraphrased, or summarized and a reference list that accurately identifies the author, date, title, and source location as available.

J:PROFESSIONAL COMMUNICATION

Not Evident	Approaching Competence	Competent
Content is unstructured, is disjointed, or contains pervasive errors in mechanics, usage, or grammar. Vocabulary or tone is unprofessional or distracts from the topic.	Content is poorly organized, is difficult to follow, or contains errors in mechanics, usage, or grammar that cause confusion. Terminology is misused or ineffective.	Content reflects attention to detail, is organized, and focuses on the main ideas as prescribed in the task or chosen by the candidate. Terminology is pertinent, is used correctly, and effectively conveys the intended meaning. Mechanics, usage, and grammar promote accurate interpretation and understanding.

C997 Data Analytics with R

Figure 8. C997 task prompts

COMPETENCIES

4065.1.1: R as a Programming Language
The graduate integrates R elements to create programming solutions.

4065.1.2: Data Analysis with R
The graduate manages data analysis using the R programming language.

4065.1.3: Tools for Data Preparation
The graduate performs activities to support data analysis.

INTRODUCTION

The United States collects and analyzes demographic data from the U.S. population. The U.S. Census Bureau provides annual estimates of the population size of each U.S. state and region. Many important decisions are made using the estimated population dynamics, including the investments in new infrastructure, such as schools and hospitals; establishing new job training centers; opening or closing schools and senior centers; and adjusting the emergency services to the size and characteristics of the demographics of metropolitan and other areas, states, or the country as a whole. The census data and estimates are publicly available on the U.S. census website. Data analysts use a variety of tools to create models for predictions, including models of population dynamics of a state of a region.

For this project, you will use R to create a linear regression model of the population dynamics of your state and predict the size of its population.

The goal is to demonstrate your skill sets with R to support the various stages of the data analytics process.

REQUIREMENTS

Your submission must be your original work. No more than a combined total of 30% of the submission and no more than a 10% match to any one individual source can be directly quoted or closely paraphrased from sources, even if cited correctly. An originality report is provided when you submit your task that can be used as a guide.

You must use the rubric to direct the creation of your submission because it provides detailed criteria that will be used to evaluate your work. Each requirement below may be evaluated by more than one rubric aspect. The rubric aspect titles may contain hyperlinks to relevant portions of the course.

Submit **one** zipped folder that includes the code, input, and output files from *each* part of the task. Place the responses to the task prompts **one** PDF file, and include the PDF file.

Note: This assessment requires you to submit pictures, graphics, and/or diagrams. Each file must be an attachment no larger than 30 MB in size. Diagrams must be original and may be hand-drawn or drawn using a graphics program. Do not use CAD programs because attachments will be too large.

A. Create a linear regression analysis with R to predict the size of the population for the state you live in based on the "Current Estimates Data" dataset (see weblink below). Provide a screenshot of your results.

B. Explain how you prepared the data from part A and how the dataset was imported into R, including screenshots of your results.

C. Create an R script that will tabulate a statistical description of the model using R's summary() function and provide a screenshot of your results.

D. Predict the population size of your state in five years using a linear regression from part A and provide a screenshot of your results.

E. Acknowledge sources, using in-text citations and references, for content that is quoted, paraphrased, or summarized.

F. Demonstrate professional communication in the content and presentation of your submission.

Figure 9. C997 rubric

RUBRIC

Criterion	Not Evident	Approaching Competence	Competent
A:LINEAR REGRESSION ANALYSIS	A linear regression analysis with R is not created.	A linear regression analysis is created with R to predict the size of the population for the state selected, based on the Current Estimates Data dataset, but the regression contains errors.	A linear regression analysis is created with R for use in predicting the size of the population for the state selected, based on the Current Estimates Data dataset.
B:HOW DATA WAS PREPARED	The submission does not explain how the data was prepared and imported into R.	The submission explains how the data was prepared and imported into R, but it does not include a screenshot of the results, or the explanation contains inaccuracies.	The submission explains how the data was prepared and imported into R and includes a screenshot of the results.
C:STATISTICAL DESCRIPTION	An R script that will tabulate a statistical description of the model using the summary method in R is not created.	An R script is created that will tabulate a statistical description of the model, but either it did not use the summary method in R, or the submission does not provide a screenshot of accurate results.	An R script is accurately created that will tabulate a statistical description of the model using the summary method in R. The submission includes a screenshot of accurate results.
D:POPULATION SIZE OF STATE	The submission does not predict the population size of the selected state	The submission predicts the population size of the selected state in 5 years but does not use the linear regression model from part I to support the prediction. A screenshot of the results is not provided.	The submission predicts the population size of the selected state in 5 years, based on the data points for each year from the most current data dataset using the linear regression model from part D. A screenshot of the results is provided.
E:SOURCES	The submission does not include both in-text citations and a reference list for sources that are quoted, paraphrased, or summarized.	The submission includes in-text citations for sources that are quoted, paraphrased, or summarized and a reference list; however, the citations or reference list is incomplete or inaccurate.	The submission includes in-text citations for sources that are properly quoted, paraphrased, or summarized and a reference list that accurately identifies the author, date, title, and source location as available.
F:PROFESSIONAL COMMUNICATION	Content is unstructured, is disjointed, or contains pervasive errors in mechanics, usage, or grammar. Vocabulary or tone is unprofessional or distracts from the topic.	Content is poorly organized, is difficult to follow, or contains errors in mechanics, usage, or grammar that cause confusion. Terminology is misused or ineffective.	Content reflects attention to detail, is organized, and focuses on the main ideas as prescribed in the task or chosen by the candidate. Terminology is pertinent, is used correctly, and effectively conveys the intended meaning. Mechanics, usage, and grammar promote accurate interpretation and understanding.

APPENDIX B: RESULTS OF PAFS

C740: Fundamentals of Data Analytics

Table 1. Extraction Sums of Squared Loadings

Extraction Sums of Squared Loadings			
Factor	**Eigenvalues**	**% Common Variance Explained**	**Cumulative % Variance Explained**
1	6.04	54.88	54.88
2	1.58	14.39	69.27

Table 2. Rotated Factor Pattern Matrix

Aspect	Factor	
	1	2
A: Provide clean data set	-.03	.92
B: Provide justifications for modifications made to data	.09	.87
C: Provided completed data sheets with tables and bars graphs	-.08	.96
D: Provide summary of observations	.06	.85
E: Describe fit of linear regression line to data using graphics	.85	-.09
F: Describe impact of outliers on regression results	.90	-.09
G: Provide residual plot with explanation of how model can be improved	.71	.02
H: Interpretation of results	.76	.01
I: Describe precautions for communicating results of sensitive data	.72	.06
J: Inclusion of in-text citations and reference list	.66	.06
K: Organization, grammar, vocabulary of overall submission	.73	.19

C742: Data Science Techniques

Table 3. Extraction Sums of Squared Loadings

Extraction Sums of Squared Loadings			
Factor	Eigenvalues	% Common Variance Explained	Cumulative % Variance Explained
1	6.26	44.69	44.69
2	2.82	20.16	64.85

*Note: a third factor only accounted for an additional 5.90% of variance and therefore was not included in subsequent analysis

Table 4. Rotated Factor Pattern Matrix

Aspect	Factor	
	1	2
A: Explain how Python program extracts web links from HTML code	.54	.21
B: Describe criteria used to determine if link is locator to another HTML page	.78	.28
C: Explain how program ensures links are saved as URIs	.69	.28
D: Explain how program ensures no duplicate links in output file	.79	.20
E: Provide working Python code for web link extraction	.86	.15
F: Provide correct HTML code for web link scraped	.44	.30
G: Provide CSV file of all web links	.89	.28
H: Provide screenshot of successful execution of code	.88	.33
I: Linear regression analysis in R for Python-extracted data	.21	.95
J: Explain how data was prepared and imported into R	.28	.95
K: Provide R script for summary results of analysis	.24	.90
L: Interpretation of effects with screen shot	.32	.79
M: Inclusion of in-text citations and reference list	.56	.63
N: Organization, grammar, vocabulary of overall submission	.67	.74

C996: Programming in Python

Table 5. Extraction Sums of Squared Loadings

Extraction Sums of Squared Loadings			
Factor	**Eigenvalues**	**% Common Variance Explained**	**Cumulative % Variance Explained**
1	5.44	54.35	54.35

Table 6. Rotated Factor Pattern Matrix

Aspect	Factor
	1
A: Explain how Python program extracts web links from HTML code	.28
B: Describe criteria used to determine if link is locator to another HTML page	.73
C: Explain how program ensures links are saved as URIs	.83
D: Explain how program ensures no duplicate links in output file	.89
E: Provide working Python code for web link extraction	.90
F: Provide correct HTML code for web link scraped	.37
G: Provide CSV file of all web links	.86
H: Provide screenshot of successful execution of code	.92
I: Inclusion of in-text citations and reference list	.53
J: Organization, grammar, vocabulary of overall submission	.74

C997: R for Data Analysis

Table 7. Extraction Sums of Squared Loadings

Extraction Sums of Squared Loadings			
Factor	**Eigenvalues**	**% Common Variance Explained**	**Cumulative % Variance Explained**
1	2.65	44.1	44.1

Table 8. Rotated Factor Pattern Matrix

Aspect	Factor
	1
A: Linear regression analysis in R for Python-extracted data	.68
B: Explain how data was prepared and imported into R	.79
C: Provide R script for summary results of analysis	.44
D: Interpretation of effects with screen shot	.55
E: Inclusion of in-text citations and reference list	.34
F: Organization, grammar, vocabulary of overall submission	.97

Hierarchical Factor Analysis: FastTrack

Table 9. Extraction Sums of Squared Loadings- Level 1

Extraction Sums of Squared Loadings			
Factor	**Eigenvalues**	**% Common Variance Explained**	**Cumulative % Variance Explained**
1	8.745	34.98	34.98
2	3.833	15.33	50.31
3	2.689	10.755	61.067
4	**1.686**	**6.742**	**67.809**
5	.841	3.365	71.174

Table 10. Rotated Factor Pattern Matrix

Course Assessment: Aspect	Factor			
	1	2	3	4
C740				
A: Provide clean data set	.16	.26	.92	.45
B: Provide justifications for modifications made to data	.21	.28	.98	.51
C: Provided completed data sheets with tables and bars graphs	.20	.28	.94	.48
D: Provide summary of observations	.28	.31	.90	.53
E: Describe fit of linear regression line to data using graphics	.19	.04	.19	.61
F: Describe impact of outliers on regression results	.28	.21	.35	.79
G: Provide residual plot with explanation of how model can be improved	.31	.15	.42	.67
H: Interpretation of results	.18	.35	.32	.70
I: Describe precautions for communicating results of sensitive data	.19	.32	.54	.71
J: Inclusion of in-text citations and reference list	.22	.28	.54	.69
K: Organization, grammar, vocabulary of overall submission	.28	.35	.56	.82
C742				
A: Explain how Python program extracts web links from HTML code	.57	.26	.30	.32
B: Describe criteria used to determine if link is locator to another HTML page	.72	.32	.16	.34
C: Explain how program ensures links are saved as URIs	.73	.23	.16	.22
D: Explain how program ensures no duplicate links in output file	.78	.30	.18	.23
E: Provide working Python code for web link extraction	.84	.12	.05	.12
F: Provide correct HTML code for web link scraped	.49	.38	.25	.27
G: Provide CSV file of all web links	.90	.33	.19	.30
H: Provide screenshot of successful execution of code	.89	.38	.19	.25
I: Linear regression analysis in R for Python-extracted data	.25	.95	.23	.21
J: Explain how data was prepared and imported into R	.32	.95	.25	.33
K: Provide R script for summary results of analysis	.31	.89	.28	.24
L: Interpretation of effects with screen shot	.40	.81	.28	.29
M: Inclusion of in-text citations and reference list	.62	.65	.29	.31
N: Organization, grammar, vocabulary of overall submission	.75	.76	.32	.34

Table 11. Higher-order Factor Extraction Sums of Squared Loadings

Extraction Sums of Squared Loadings			
Higher-order Factor	**Eigenvalues**	**% Common Variance Explained**	**Cumulative % Variance Explained**
1	1.205	30.13	30.13

Table 12. Higher-order Factor Pattern Matrix

Factor	Higher-order Factor
	1
Regression in Excel (C740)	.682
Data prep in Excel (C740)	.636
Python programming (C996)	.381
Regression in R (C997)	.437

*Note: correlation between factors is $r = .211$

Hierarchical Factor Analysis: Slow Track

Table 13. Extraction Sums of Squared Loadings- Level 1

Extraction Sums of Squared Loadings			
Factor	**Eigenvalues**	**% Common Variance Explained**	**Cumulative % Variance Explained**
1	5.66	20.95	20.95
2	4.56	16.87	37.82
3	2.94	10.90	48.72
4	**1.71**	**6.35**	**55.06**
5	.743	2.75	57.81
6	.537	1.99	59.80

Table 14. Rotated Factor Pattern Matrix

Course Assessment: Aspect	Factor			
	1	2	3	4
C740				
A: Provide clean data set	.05	.94	.44	.03
B: Provide justifications for modifications made to data	.01	.90	.42	.002
C: Provided completed data sheets with tables and bars graphs	.001	.96	.38	.05
D: Provide summary of observations	.01	.89	.40	.09
E: Describe fit of linear regression line to data using graphics	-.06	.25	.68	.13
F: Describe impact of outliers on regression results	.03	.27	.78	.10
G: Provide residual plot with explanation of how model can be improved	.08	.25	.53	.07
H: Interpretation of results	.08	.19	.46	-.06
I: Describe precautions for communicating results of sensitive data	.09	.32	.59	.01
J: Inclusion of in-text citations and reference list	.11	.22	.56	-.05
K: Organization, grammar, vocabulary of overall submission	.09	.54	.76	.07
C996				
A: Explain how Python program extracts web links from HTML code	.29	.02	.06	.10
B: Describe criteria used to determine if link is locator to another HTML page	.75	-.01	.02	.11
C: Explain how program ensures links are saved as URIs	.82	-.03	.03	.04
D: Explain how program ensures no duplicate links in output file	.87	-.04	.03	.04
E: Provide working Python code for web link extraction	.93	.04	.09	.15
F: Provide correct HTML code for web link scraped	.34	.05	.07	.24
G: Provide CSV file of all web links	.86	.06	.07	.16
H: Provide screenshot of successful execution of code	.92	.03	.03	.08
I: Inclusion of in-text citations and reference list	.51	.09	.10	-.06
J: Organization, grammar, vocabulary of overall submission	.73	.01	.13	-.10
C997				
A: Linear regression analysis in R for Python-extracted data	.13	.08	.10	.77
B: Explain how data was prepared and imported into R	.01	.01	-.01	.77
C: Provide R script for summary results of analysis	.08	.03	.04	.50
D: Interpretation of effects with screen shot	.09	.03	.11	.56
E: Inclusion of in-text citations and reference list	-.01	.01	.01	.35
F: Organization, grammar, vocabulary of overall submission	.08	.02	-.01	.94

Table 15. Extraction Sums of Squared Loadings

Extraction Sums of Squared Loadings			
Higher-order Factor	**Eigenvalues**	**% Common Variance Explained**	**Cumulative % Variance Explained**
1	.736	18.4	18.4
2	.271	6.79	25.19

Table 16. Rotated Factor Pattern Matrix

Factor	**Higher-order Factor**	
	1	**2**
Regression in Excel (C740)	.601	.174
Data prep in Excel (C740)	.594	.079
Python programming (C996)	.050	.381
Regression in R (C997)	.108	.377

*Note: correlation between factors is $r = .211$

Section 4
Considerations

Chapter 11
Don't @ Me:
A Study of the Perception of Twitter Users of Educational Offerings

Goran Trajkovski
https://orcid.org/0000-0002-3745-3009
Western Governors University, USA

Eduard Fabregat
Universitat Abat Oliba, Spain

ABSTRACT

With the changes in societies and economies, new formats and packaging of educational products have been emerging as alternatives to the traditional degrees and certificates. Most of these offerings emerge outside higher education institutions and aim to alleviate the gap between the supply of skills and the needs of industries which had a big impact on the educational space. The authors studied approximately four hundred thousand tweets discussing educational offerings. They used a combination of topic modeling and network analysis to group topics into wider themes over the topic network. They also used word embeddings to measure semantic similarity of words related to specific educational packagings and further understand the discussion carried out on Twitter. The results of this study show how public opinion on Twitter discussed formal and non-formal educational offerings in ways that stress economic and professional advancement. Finally, the results from the word embeddings analysis revealed a need for common and clear taxonomy that differentiates between educational formats.

INTRODUCTION

The last several decades have experienced an increased volume of experimentations and changes triggered by the changing needs of societies and industries. These changes have involved national restructuring of educational offerings at the formal level, where universities have incorporated aspects that traditionally belonged to vocational programs and professional schools such as teaching or nursing (Kyvik, 2004), as

DOI: 10.4018/978-1-7998-9644-9.ch011

well as global common frames of education and the explosion of the knowledge society which contribute to the reorganization of economies (Schofer, Ramirez & Meyer, 2021).

At the same time, with the advent of the internet, students have found alternatives to formal education for professional advancement and upskilling in Massive Open Online Courses (MOOC) through different platforms (Wang; Sun; Qu & Xu, 2021). These alternatives include university sanctioned platforms like Coursera or EdX (Mikheieva, et al., 2021), which provide access to short courses and certificates offered by universities, social media platforms like Youtube with audio-visual educational content (Rahmatirrizki & Sukmayadi, 2020), or educational platforms outside of the formal education field like Udemy (Szabo, 2021). These platforms, educational offerings, and MOOCs have garnered great attention and extremely high numbers of students. For example, Andrew Ng's Machine Learning course on Coursera (Ng, n.d.) has been taken by more than four million people.

Realizing that educational institutions do not always produce graduates with needed skills, some organizations have been creating and operating in-house training for skilling, upskilling, and reskilling their workforce (Trajkovski, Killian, & Cohen, 2021). Some of those training solutions have become available to the public at large and provide opportunities to earn credentials. Publicly facing credential offerings are abundant and include notable examples such as Google Career Certificates (Pichai, 2021), the IBM badging program (IBM, n.d.), and Hubspot's certificates (HubSpot, n.d.), some of which are now already integrated in many higher education curricula. Some perceive these activities as an initiation of a parallel higher education system that was started with the emergence of Information Technology certificates by Microsoft, Cisco, Novell, and others in the 1990s (Gallagher & Zanville, 2021).

Given the massive impact on the educational space that these new educational offerings have had, it is important to understand not only how people perceive them, but also whether these offerings are able to distinguish themselves from one another. We studied approximately four hundred thousand tweets discussing educational offerings. Twitter offers the possibility to study public opinion because of its conversational capabilities (Honeycutt & Herring, 2009). Twitter facilitates the expression of opinions and the following of low media-coverage topics (Zhao, et al., 2011), even if, as the influx of information increases, the topics for discussion are adopted and discarded at a higher speed (Lorez-Spreen, et al., 2019). To study these tweets, we used a combination of topic modeling and network analysis (Walter & Ophir, 2019). Topic modeling is an unsupervised machine-learning technique for content analysis. The algorithm extracts topics by assigning each word a probability of being found in each topic in a model where a group of documents contains a mixture of topics (Blei, et al., 2003). This method allows the researcher to quickly identify thematic structures in large amounts of data, using an inductive method with quantitative measurements, hence helping reduce researcher bias (Maier, et al., 2018). Community detection was used to group topics into themes over the topic network (Blondel et al., 2008). We also used Word2Vec's word embeddings (Goldberg & Levy, 2014) to measure semantic similarity of specific words and further understand the discussion carried out on twitter.

The results from this study help educational institutions, both formal and non-formal, understand the way people discuss traditional and new educational packages. Accompanying these insights, we also provide evidence of a necessity for creating a shared vocabulary that allows educational packages to clearly differentiate from one another so as to help the students and users understand what each package offers.

Skill Acquisition

Learners are looking for alternative, quicker, just-in-time opportunities to demonstrate competencies and readily applicable skills. Skills have become labor market currency, and job seekers, employers, and learners need better, faster, more efficient ways to develop skills to use as currency (Pulsipher, 2020).

Learner-workers need opportunities to demonstrate and receive credit for their skills, no matter where they gained them. They seek educational programming options and the ability to identify potential career pathways based on their goals and current skill set. These learner-workers want access to educational options that match their goals and allow for the ability to skill and reskill to stay ahead of the obsolescence curve. Learner-workers want to tell a compelling story about the skills they have gained throughout a lifetime of work and learning.

While learner-workers are looking to skill up to be employable, employers want value and efficiency in options for skilling, upskilling, and reskilling their employees. Employers want to hire individuals who have the knowledge, skills, abilities, and any additional credentials to do the job well. One of the biggest challenges the United States faces today is ensuring that the workers are adequately skilled to support the demand for future work. Skills of job seekers often do not match the experience required for specialized jobs. Job applicants are faced with a highly competitive job market in which their qualifications might not be enough to secure the kind of work they desire (Puckett et al., 2020).

The difference between the skills needed by employers and the skills of candidates defines a widening skills gap. The skills gap is expected to increase in severity (IBM Institute for Business Value, n.d.). The labor market is tightening as unemployment rates generally continue to decline. The gap in this complex ecosystem is rooted in various factors, including a changing population demographics profile; however, the bulk of the skills gap is attributed to an educational system that has not been synchronized with the evolving economy (The Conference Board, n.d.).

As organizations have been trying various approaches to develop their workforce to align with current and future needs, higher education has been exploring ways to align better with industry. Higher education is recognizing that the learner profiles, behaviors, and needs have been changing as the distinction between traditional and non- or post-traditional learners is disappearing. Learners expect a return on the investment in their education with a stable financial future rather than becoming more well-rounded individuals. Pressures for graduation rates to rise and for the time to degree to accelerate come from accreditors, regulators, and the learners themselves. Teaching, in many cases, remains insufficiently informed by the science of learning. Too many learners that start a degree never complete it, and many of those that complete a degree reside inside the job market underemployed.

In addition to its many roles, such as driving innovation, higher education aims to focus on creating a quality workforce, increasing the employability of the consumer of educational products, and upskill existing workforces. The higher education sector is perceived as one of the key drivers of growth, performance, prosperity, and competitiveness of an economy (Digital Marketing Institute, 2018). To bridge the skill gap between the skills of job seekers and the skills employers are seeking, higher education can prepare individuals with the skills they need to be successful in the workplace. For higher education institutions to effectively teach learner-workers the skills industry seeks, they need to know what skills are in demand in the industry, understand the obsolescence curve of some skills, and be proactive in pre-skilling learners.

Learner-workers need opportunities to demonstrate and receive credit for their skills, no matter where they gained them. Learners seek educational programming options and the ability to identify potential career pathways based on their goals and current skill set. These learner-workers want access to educational options that match their goals and allow for the ability to skill and reskill to stay ahead of the obsolescence curve. They want to tell a compelling story about the skills they have gained throughout a lifetime of work and learning.

It is notable that multiple resources provided by job seeker portals, higher-education institutions career centers' websites, and other relevant resources offer guidance on compositing skills-based resumes. However, the general guidance is that these are mostly a fit for job applicants that are recent graduates, have little experience in the field into which they desire to move, or cannot make a case of a succession of positions with increased responsibility (Indeed, 2021).

Job-application portals are frequently able to use data from professional social networks, such as Linkedin, to populate applications. Some of those networks are able to populate data on skills and accomplishments directly into the applications. The entity receiving the application may or may not capture all of the available data and evidence of skills, depending on technology solutions used, interoperability between systems, and level of interest of the receiving entity for that data.

While some employers provide tuition assistance programs to send employees to higher education for upskilling and right-skilling, others have been creating and operating in-house training. Some of those training solutions are available to the public at large, usually providing opportunities to earn credentials. Publicly facing credential offerings are abundant and include notable examples such as Google Career Certificates (Pichai, 2021), the IBM badging program (IBM, n.d.), and Hubspot's certificates (HubSpot, n.d.), which are already integrated into many higher education curricula. Some perceive these activities as an initiation of a parallel higher education system that was started with the emergence of Information Technology certificates by Microsoft, Cisco, Novell, and others in the 1990s (Gallagher & Zanville, 2021).

A common perception of the distinction between higher education and employee training is that higher education focuses on foundational concepts and training on practical experiences (Rutherford, 2021). Higher education focuses (perceptually) on operating products comprised of course groupings, assuming that learning is a dominant learner's dominant priority. Employee training, often in the form of microlearning, focuses on just-in-time training to acquire a critical skill. While this distinction is disappearing, challenges in reconciling the legacies in approaches in product design, development processes, form and format of product, assessment paradigms used, measurement of impact, and the architectures and standards of delivery infrastructures.

Massive Open Online Courses (MOOCs) emerged in the 2010s as an experimental response to a real opportunity in the training realm to offer lifelong learners opportunities for just-in-time learning. Technology, the primary enabler for mass instruction, has been providing sound information infrastructures for operating product en masse and has allowed the focus of higher education to shift to investigating adequate product design and assessment of learners' competence. 'Newer-age' academia can now focus on instructional design and assessment for learning construction without insurmountable technology challenges. "In reality, there has not been a radical movement in concepts or theories of learning in a long time. They appear new as technology has finally risen to the occasion and provided tools to enable the exploration of and the realization – the embodiment – of these old concepts" (Berzinski & Trajkovski, 2018).

Higher education institutions have started adopting approaches that have been piloted at a scale in companies offering career training, not degrees. In providing video-based training and human-scored performance assessments, Udacity's nanodegree in Data Analytics, for example, exhibits sound implementations of skills-oriented product design and assessment (Udacity, n.d.). A nanodegree is a certified online educational program that helps students develop specialized skills that target professionals who want to learn new advanced skills or develop their current abilities, which will allow them to work with the latest technological developments.

Given the importance of the current changes in education, it is crucial to understand and study the perception of the offerings from the student/learner perspective. The internet provides researchers with the means to listen in on conversations and study public discourse without the need for polls and surveys. Social media offers spaces where people can discuss and interact with one another in public, leaving a record of the conversation to be studied by researchers and social scientists. Twitter is a very important social media platform, one that is especially suited for online discussion because its interactional model is asymmetrical (Hong & Nadler, 2011). This asymmetrical interaction model makes all tweets public and accessible to followers and non-followers by default, allowing users to interact and discuss with virtually anyone in the platform (Bruns, 2018). Replies and hashtags are innovations that enhance these conversational possibilities (Cabiddu et al., 2014). At the same time, by the nature of the platform itself, Twitter facilitates the discussion and following of low media-coverage topics (Zhao et al., 2011). For this reason, we decided to access Twitter data to understand the way the public discusses educational offerings and answer our first research question.

RQ1: How are educational offerings discussed on Twitter?

Frameworks and Changes in Higher Education Offerings

Various efforts both in higher education and across industries have resulted in a wide range of products and product packaging. Some products result in a degree or certificate, others in badges or certificates of completion. The same terms are being used in different contexts. While some more traditional terms used for educational packaging might be somewhat clearly recognized in society, others are just emerging as results from various efforts.

Ryan (2019), for example, used badges, micro-credentials, nanodegrees, certificates, and degrees as the nomenclature in explaining the progressing through credentials. His learning ladder includes a credit model where smaller modules, such as badges, would have a credit equivalency that could be collected and leveraged as a micro-credential that could be added to a nano degree. From here, a working learner could apply those nano degrees to certificate programs and ultimately complete a degree.

Post-secondary education has traditionally been dominated by a long-form learning model, comprising of carefully curated, sequenced and selected curriculum aggregated to form a body of knowledge considered appropriate for one's future role or profession. The size of standard qualifications is typically constructed by calculating the 'hours of learner effort' and organized into smaller modules. These smaller modules (subjects, units, courses, classes) have not been credentialed/recognized independently from their whole (beyond 'credits').

New, alternative forms of learning and verification are gaining credibility. In an environment where the rising cost of degrees and formal education outstrips government and individuals' ability to pay, a plethora of pathways, alternatives and substitutes have arisen over the past 5-10 years, alongside the speed of change in skill requirements. However, it remains a messy and complex landscape of providers, options and models. Different stakeholders bring very different perspectives, and this segmentation is by no means exhaustive. Formal degrees are by far the largest component of the overall post-secondary education market, with a total spend of $2.2T in 2019 (pre-COVID). Although growing fast, the global alternative and micro-credential market still only accounted for $10B in 2019. 2020 initiated explosive growth, and a key question for the future is to what extent the traditional in-person degree market will be supported by, transformed into, or replaced by, online degrees or alternative and micro-credentials (HolonIQ, 2021).

Degrees could be considered as "bundles" of a carefully selected sequenced and integrated curriculum (HolonIQ, 2021). Associate degrees typically include 60-65 credit hours equivalent of work or approximately 20 courses. Bachelor's degrees take approximately 4,000-5,000 hours (125 eight-hour days per year). Master's degrees include 30-60 credit hours of courseware. These terms are used as a standard in academic discussions and university offerings. Accreditation/regulatory guidelines and expectations almost consistently use these terms in outlining the expectations from academic institutions, as well as measures when imposing expectations of quality. Credential Engine (n.d.) provides a list of definitions of educational products packages (Figure 1).

The 2019 Credential Engine Data are the basis for the illustration of the credentialing landscape in the United States. Educational products are discerned by complexity and time to complete, and include visualizations from the number of credentials awarded by academic and other institutions in 2019. The term NDO (non-Degree offering) denotes credentialing solutions that do not result in a traditional university degree (associate, baccalaureate, master's, or doctoral). Figures 2 and 3 are visualizations of the data supporting the thesis of the discussion in this writing.

The larger the hexagons, the larger is the number of credentials awarded. The closer a packaging is to the centre of the image, the more relevant it is to the development of the person and to concepts, whereas the far regions of the circles denote trainings solutions more closely aligned with the specific skilling needs of organizations.

There are three prominent approaching to generating non-degree offerings in academic institutions in efforts to mimic market developments (Figures 4-6).

Hence, based on the situation just described, we attempt to understand whether the educational offerings are clearly understood and differentiated from one another. We then pose the following two research questions:

RQ2: How successful have educational product packages been in informing the public of what they are?
RQ3: What do the results tell us about how people understand the formal/non-formal educational products?

Method and Data

The data were retrieved using Twitter's public API by searching for keywords that were deemed relevant based on our theoretical frame. The words can be found in Table 1. Our corpus contains 377,175 tweets that used one or more of the keywords we identified between May 17 and May 25, 2021.

In order to answer research question one (How are educational offerings discussed on Twitter?) and study the conversations on Twitter, we used topic modeling, an unsupervised machine-learning method for content analysis. With this method the researcher can reduce bias since the document classification is done by the algorithm.

We removed duplicate tweets, setting the threshold similarity at .95 degrees to remove tweets that might have slight differences, and tweets shorter than five characters as they do not add any useful information. This removed 37,331, leaving 339,844 tweets in the final sample. The pre-processing followed the guidelines established by Maier and colleagues (2018). The stop words were removed, all letters were

Figure 1. Credential Engine's definitions of educational product packaging

A **degree** is a type of award conferred by a college, university, or other postsecondary educational institution as official recognition for the successful completion of a program of study. Primary degree levels include associate's, bachelor's, master's, doctoral, and specific professional degrees (such as M.D. [doctor of medicine] and J.D. [Juris doctor of law]).

A **certificate** is a type of award conferred by a college, university, or other postsecondary educational institution certifying the satisfactory completion of a non-degree program of study. Typically, the course requirements for earning a certificate are less than those for earning a degree. Most certificates can be completed with one year of full-time academic effort. A certificate may be for-credit (academic certificate) or non-credit (continuing education certificate). This credential category counts both academic and continuing education certificates in Title IV institutions. Students taking continuing education programs at Title IV institutions are not eligible to receive federal financial aid to pay for program tuition.

A **micro-credential** is defined as an online educational credential that covers more than a single course but is less than a full degree.

MOOC providers offer opportunities to earn an academic degree (primarily bachelor's or master's) online from a **university outside the US**. The majority of these degree programs are sponsored by universities in Australia, the United Kingdom, and France and so are not included in IPEDS.

Non-academic organizations. Each state requires persons practicing specific professions and vocations to first obtain an occupational license from a state licensing board. According to the National Conference of State Legislatures (NCSL), "When implemented properly, occupational licensing can help protect the health and safety of consumers by requiring practitioners to undergo a designated amount of training and education in their field.

An **industry-recognized certification** is a time-limited, renewable credential awarded by an authoritative body—such as an industry or professional association—to an individual who demonstrates designated knowledge, skills, and abilities in a particular occupation. An individual takes courses to prepare for a competency examination. The organizations providing the courses, administering the tests, and designing the courses and tests are not always the same organizations sponsoring the certification.

Military certifications: Each branch of the U.S. Military (Air Force, Army, Marine Corps, Navy, and Coast Guard) offers service personnel opportunities to obtain certifications of achievement of specific competencies.

Registered apprenticeships: An apprenticeship is a program for training practitioners of a trade or profession with a combination of on-the-job training and classroom instruction. The Office of Apprenticeship (OA) in the U.S. Department of Labor (DOL) manages a registered apprenticeship system, as authorized by the National Apprenticeship Act

Unregistered apprenticeships: While the registered apprenticeship system operated by the U.S. Department of Labor (DOL) is the primary mechanism for organizing the nation's apprenticeship programs, a number of organizations sponsor apprenticeship programs outside that system. In particular, a number of firms headquartered in Germany and Switzerland (nations with strong apprenticeship systems) offer unregistered apprenticeship programs in the U.S.

Coding bootcamps are a new type of training organization. The first coding bootcamp was founded in 2012, according to Course Report, the primary information source for the industry. Their intent is to improve markets for coders by reducing the length and cost of training compared to universities, to agilely adjust curricula in light of constant technological changes and employer demand, and to better meet employer needs for skilled coders.

Online course completion certificate: In addition to MOOC providers, a number of other web-based organizations offered a wide array of online courses. Courses vary greatly in length and depth, with many able to be completed in a few hours. The largest of these include Udemy, Lynda.com, SkillSuccess, and Skillshare. While MOOC providers are intermediaries that offer a web platform for course delivery and multi-course credential programs by academic institutions and businesses, online course providers do not serve large education and training organizations, and do not offer microcredentials or degrees.

Digital badges: Open badges are verifiable, portable digital badges with embedded metadata about skills and achievements. They comply with the Open Badges Specification and are shareable across the web. Each open badge is associated with an image and information about the badge, its recipient, the issuer, and any supporting evidence. All this information may be packaged within a badge image file that can be displayed via online CVs and social networks. Thousands of organizations across the world issue badges in accordance with the Open Badges Specification, from nonprofits to major employers to educational institutions at all levels. Because the system is based on an open standard, recipients can combine multiple badges from different issuers to tell the complete story of their verifiable achievements— both online and off. Open badges can be displayed wherever recipients want them on the web, including on social media profiles and through services that store and display badges. Badges can be shared for employment, education, or lifelong learning. Anyone can issue a badge, receive one, verify that a badge is real, or inspect the metadata and any associated evidence. Badge issuers can certify that their badges are technically compliant with the specification, and therefore can be readily moved among issuers and display sites. Badges can be used to set goals, motivate behaviors, connect learning environments, and communicate achievements across many contexts.

converted to lowercase, punctuation and numbers were removed, as well as all the words that appeared in more than 95%, and in fewer than 0.5% of the documents.

To establish the appropriate number of topics we used a 5-fold cross-validation, which tested the perplexity of different models in skips of 5 between 10 and 100 topics (see Wang & Blei, 2009). The test established the correct number of topics at 40. Both authors then read the documents, along with the frequent words, for each topic and applied a label based on the content of said documents. To carry out the frame analysis we followed the method ANTMN (Analysis of Topic Models Network) developed by Walter and Ophir (2019). ANTMNT has been used successfully in different contexts (i.e. Fabregat & Kperogi, 2021; Ophir, et al, 2021). First, the removed tweets were reintroduced to calculate the correct

Figure 2. Complexities and volumes of credentials awarded in the United States in 2019 (Credential Engine data)

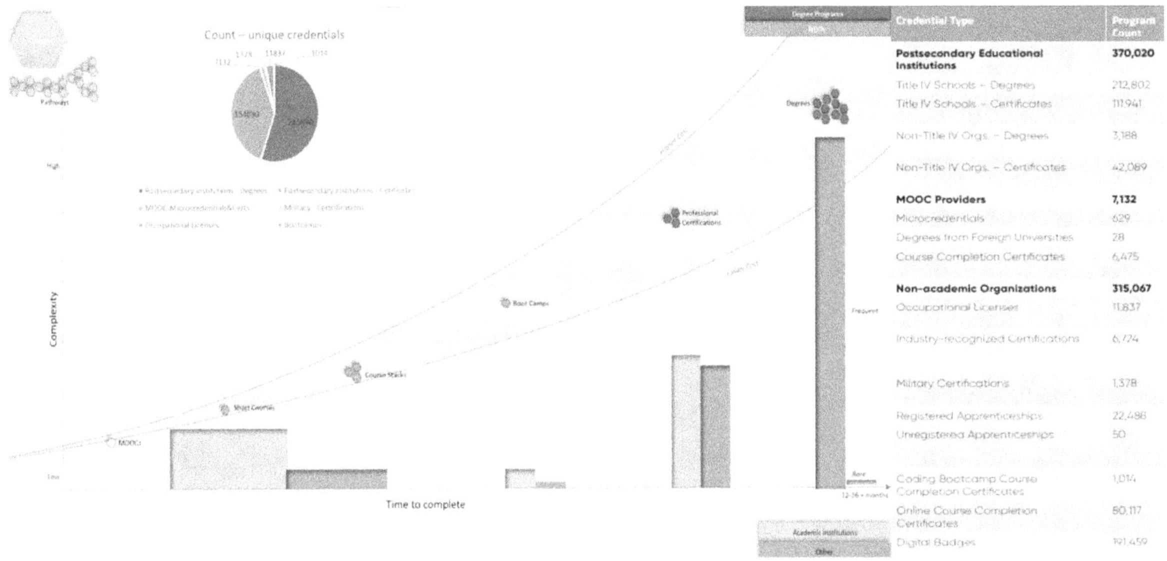

size and proportion of each topic. Then, we established the cosine similarity between the topics using the theta matrix resulting from the topic modeling. That allowed us to create a fully connected, undirected, network where the topics were the nodes, and the similarities between the topics were the edges. After removing the boilerplate topics, topics with no substantive meaning as a result of the statistical distribution of words, leaving the final number at 32, we applied the Louvain clustering algorithm (Blondel, et al., 2008) in order to establish communities of topics that, according to the ANTMN method, will be considered frames. The analysis and coding of the topics supplied the external validation for the appropriate number and distribution of clusters, which has to necessarily be based on the corpus and the specific research needs (Fortunato & Hric, 2016).

We also used word embeddings to further understand the discussions on Twitter and answer research questions two (How successful have educational product packages been in informing the public of what they are?) and three (What do the results tell us about how people understand the formal/non-formal educational products?). Word embeddings have the capacity to capture and retain a much deeper level of semantic information that other methods (Mikolov, et al., 2013a). In this method the words are used for predicting the next word given a window of surrounding words where the words in the corpus are projected into a matrix with n numerical dimensions (Mikolov, et al., 2013b). Because each word is given these numerical dimensions, one can ultimately find the similarity between the words and understand their usage within the same corpus. Ultimately, the algorithm assigns each word a value. This value is assigned based on the usage of word within the corpus, and places the word in a multidimensional space. Words that have similar meanings end up in close proximity to one another, indicating that those words were used in similar contexts. Word embeddings, with the Word2Vec algorithm, allowed us to identify words that have similar meanings. In this case the algorithm was trained with our corpus of tweets so as to find the representation of meaning of the words in our data at the unigram and bigram level. We then used Principal Component Analysis to reduce the number of dimensions to two and be able to visualize the results, Figure 8. We also present the results in table form in Table 3.

Figure 3. Depiction of various educational packaging by format and providers (academia, workplace, other training organizations)

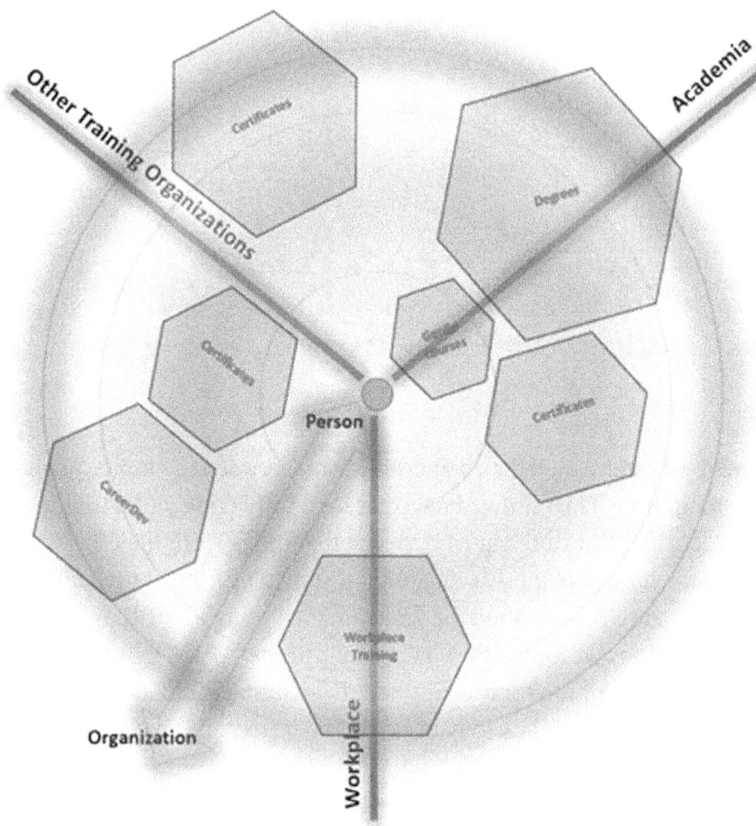

Credential Type	Program Count
Postsecondary Educational Institutions	**370,020**
Title IV Schools - Degrees	212,802
Title IV Schools - Certificates	111,941
Non-Title IV Orgs. - Degrees	3,188
Non-Title IV Orgs. - Certificates	42,089
MOOC Providers	**7,132**
Microcredentials	629
Degrees from Foreign Universities	28
Course Completion Certificates	6,475
Non-academic Organizations	**315,067**
Occupational Licenses	11,837
Industry-recognized Certifications	6,724
Military Certifications	1,378
Registered Apprenticeships	22,488
Unregistered Apprenticeships	50
Coding Bootcamp Course Completion Certificates	1,014
Online Course Completion Certificates	80,117
Digital Badges	191,459

Figure 4. Model A. The academic institution offers degree products and academic certificates only

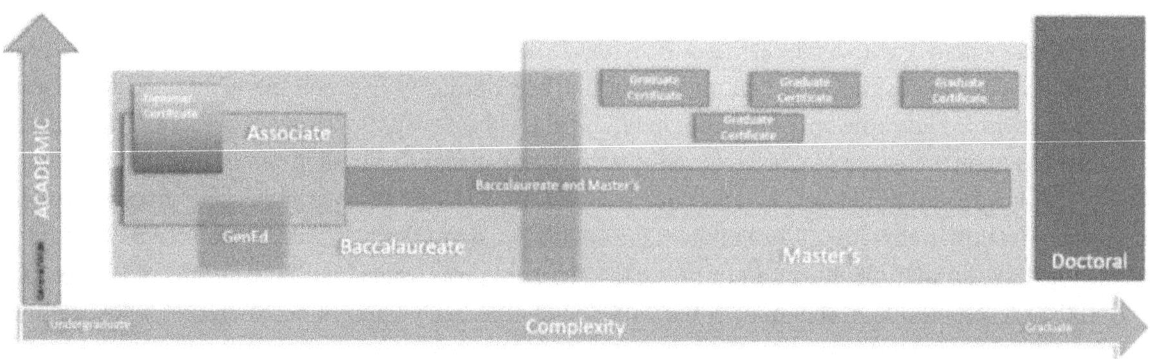

Figure 5. Model B. Academic instantiations continue to delineate between core academic product and continuing education (PRO-Professional) activities

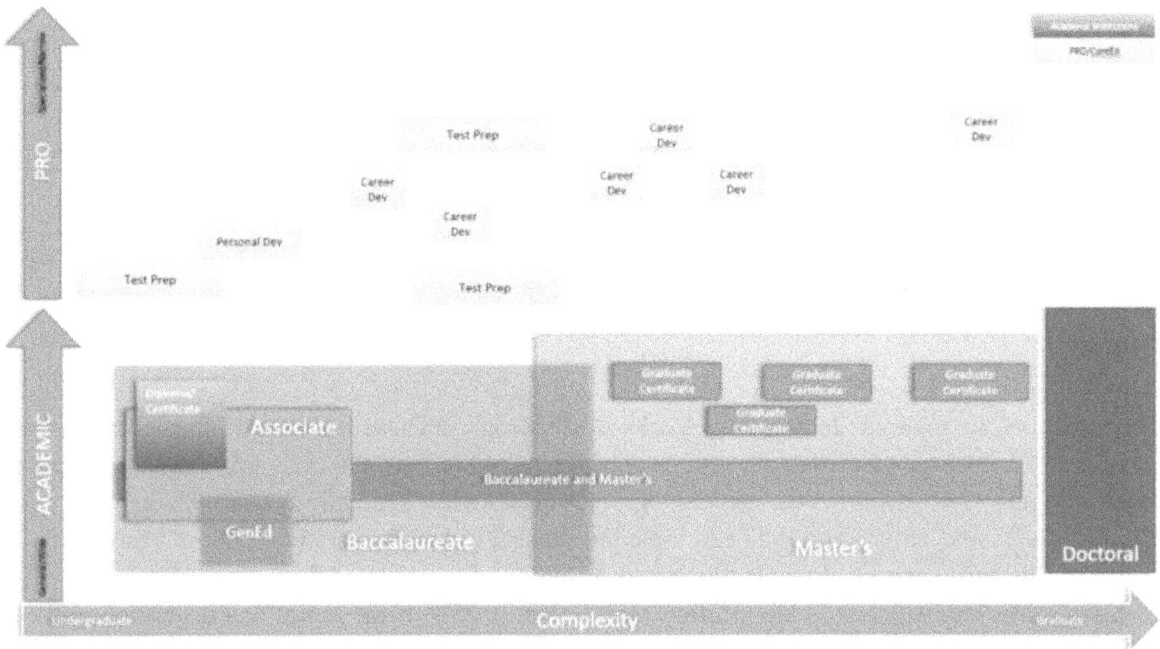

Figure 6. Model C. The PRO segment of the academic institution uses elements from existing academic and continuing education products to offer new product formats

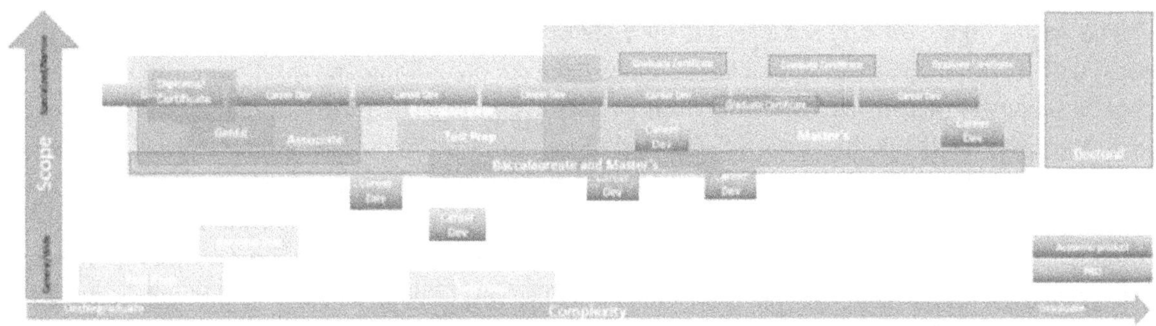

Table 1. Keywords

Keywords
skills, degree, work, learning, credentials,resume, learning and employment record employers,job seekers, talent, learning outcomes, assessmentware, learning resources, inquiry-based, problem-based, certificate, skills-oriented, courseware, microcredential, industry-recognized certifications,military certification, apprenticeship, bootcamp,digital badge

Table 2. Topics by Theme

Theme	Topics
Effort	Pay for Homework, Help with Homework, Sun Halo/Art Degree, Hard Work, Work, Language Learning, Talent, Art Skills, Tests and Certificates, Learning
Discussions	Discussions, Labor Shortage Debate, Mental Health, Discussions on Skills and People's Work, Work, Law
Resources	Online Learning, Educational Resources, Online Courses, Machine Learning, Resources for Schools and Formal Education, Online Professional Certificates
Advancement	Tests and Problems, Importance of Developing New Skills, Degrees as Expertise, Job Vacancies and Apprenticeships, Resume Building, University Degrees, Advertising and Offerings, Ads About Marketing Courses, Comprehension Skills and Critical Thinking, Job Fairs and Resume Building

Results

The results of the topic modelling provided 32 distinct topics. These topics were further aggregated using network analysis clustering algorithms, which resulted in four main themes. The themes can be found in figure 1, which shows the network of topics clustered by semantic similarity, where the color indicates the theme and the size indicates topic prevalence, or how important the topic was within our corpus. Table 2 also presents in table form the distribution of topics by theme.

The first theme, which we termed Effort, represents 31.25% of the topics and discusses time and effort put into work and degrees. This theme is located at the top of the network with purple nodes. Topics like Hard Work, Work, Learning, Tests and Certificates, and Language Learning, discuss the strive for achieving a goal, in this case, a goal related to education. On the other hand, Talent, Art Skills and Sun Halo/Art Degree discuss the importance of working hard to maximize the talent someone might have. Interestingly, two of the topics found in this theme discuss paying people to do homework (Pay for Homework, Help with Homework). These two topics are found in this theme because the time and effort required in doing homework is the justification for paying someone to do it for you.

The orange nodes, directly below and to the right of the previous theme, belong to the theme Discussions, with 18.75% of all the topics. These topics have people talking and discussing different issues, from the labor shortage to mental health. These are all topics related to the workforce and career advancement; however, the theme focuses on discussing those issues from a social perspective rather than the practical perspective of upskilling. What is interesting about this theme is that all the topics have users giving arguments in favor or against, and providing personal anecdotes about, the issue at hand. For example, Mental Health discusses situations where employees have suffered a deterioration of mental health and the strategies they used to overcome the issue. Discussions on Skills and People's Work has people talking about how their skills were acquired and how they applied to their jobs. Law, on the other hand, discusses labor issues and how the credentials of the employees put them in a stronger or weaker position towards their employers.

The blue theme, termed Resources, talked about educational resources that students, or people looking to further their career or gain skills, can utilize, and had 18.75% of the topics. These resources, as the topics show, can be online educational offerings -- like Online Courses, Online Learning, and Online Professional Certificates -- but also strategies to fund formal education (Educational Resources), opportunities for directly funding schools (Resources for Schools and Formal Education) and specific courses

Figure 7. Network graph of the themes identified on Twitter by the users discussing educational offerings and professional advancement. The nodes represent topics, the edges represent the co-occurrences of topics in different documents, and the size is established by the importance of the topics. The image was created in Gephi 0.9.2 using the Force Atlas 2 layout algorithm

for learning machine learning (Machine Learning). Ultimately, this theme has people discussing, giving advice, and listing educational resources people can use.

Finally, the green theme, Advancement, at the bottom of the network and with 31.25% of the topics, discusses the importance of developing new skills (Importance of Developing New Skills), the importance of degrees (University Degrees) and how they confer expertise (Degrees as Expertise), as well as presents job openings and offers internship opportunities (Job Vacancies and Apprenticeships). Other interesting and important issues discussed are the importance of critical thinking (Comprehension Skills and Critical Thinking), ways to make resumes more successful (Resume Building) and exercises to show and demonstrate one's skills (Tests and Problems). Importantly, this theme discussing how to advance professionally by developing new skills and making use of opportunities, contains the most prevalent topic, Degrees as Expertise.

Table 3. Top 10 most similar words

bootcamp	badge	degree	microcredential	nanodegree	certification
'coding_bootcamp', 0.59	'digitally', 0.51)	'master_degree', 0.72	'edtechchat', 0.51	'bootstrap4', 0.55	'certify', 0.62
'boot_camp', 0.53	'bronze', 0.48	'undergraduate_ degree', 0.68	'course', 0.50	'css3', 0.51	'pentest', 0.56
'developer_ bootcamp', 0.42	'digital', 0.46	'bachelor_degree', 0.63	'highered', 0.49	'vuejs', 0.50	'redteam', 0.54
'caitlin', 0.41	'fcl', 0.46	'degree_holder', 0.50	'lifelonglearner', 0.49	'redux', 0.50	'4-week', 0.53
'12-week', 0.39	'keychain', 0.45	'college_degree', 0.50	'elearning', 0.49	'nodejs', 0.49	'pentester', 0.53
'certificate_ completion', 0.38	'digital_badge', 0.45	'medical_degree', 0.49	'partnership', 0.49	('udemycoupon', 0.49	'appsec', 0.52
'masterclass', 0.38	'charm', 0.44	'doctorate_degree', 0.48	'program', 0.49	'django', 0.49	'activedirectory', 0.51
'coder', 0.38	'millie', 0.43	'finish_degree', 0.44	'offering', 0.48	'laravel', 0.49	'certified', 0.50
'beginner', 0.36	'custom', 0.43	'bachelor', 0.41	'pathway', 0.48	'mongodb', 0.47	'military', 0.50
'apprenticeship_ program', 0.36	'dofe', 0.4360498)	'uni', 0.40	'udl', 0.48	'onlinetutorial', 0.46	'nationally', 0.50

The results from the word embeddings provided a measure of word similarity that allowed us to understand what words were associated with specific educational offerings and packages. Table 3 shows the top 10 most similar words, using the cosine similarity as the similarity measure, to words that represent an educational packaging. Each cell contains the most similar words in descending order and the cosine similarity. The main words the other words compare to were decided based on the theoretical frame and the list of educational offerings exposed there (Ryan, 2019).

Showing the top 10 most similar words helps understand how each educational packaging was discussed. However, Table 3 does not help easily understand the relationship between the words. To further understand the relationship between the words we decided to plot their similarity in a 2D space, which shows, in a graphical way, the relationship and interaction between words from different educational offerings. Thus, if we can find clearly differentiated clusters of words, the educational packaging has found a way to identify itself from the other educational packages. If, on the other hand, the clusters overlap, the educational packages share semantic similarity and there is no clear disambiguation of terms. Figure 8 shows the distribution of the most similar words and how they cluster based on the results of the word embeddings. The input words are shown in black. Ultimately, Figure 8 allows us to see which of these educational packages have achieved a higher level of differentiation by understanding the degree of overlapping or separation of the clusters of words used in the discussions of those packaging on Twitter.

The results show a clear cluster of words related to the educational offering *degree* on the top right corner in green. This cluster presents the most differentiated groups of words. The educational packaging *nanodegree* also shows a clear separation with the other clusters of words. This cluster is found on the top to mid left side of the plot in yellow. Finally, the last cluster with a clear separation is the educational packaging *microcredential.* This cluster is found in the bottom center portion of the plot in purple. On the other hand, the educational packages *certification, badge* and *bootcamp* show clear overlaps in their clusters, indicating a lack of a distinct disambiguation in the terms used in the discussions of their offerings. These three clusters are found in the center of the plot with the packaging *certification* in light blue, *badge* in red and *bootcamp* in dark blue.

Out of the 6 educational packages we studied here, three show high levels of differentiation, *degree, nanodegree,* and *microcredential.* The other three, however, have a high degree of overlap in the words used in the discussion of the educational offerings, which might hinder their recognition by possible users and students.

CONCLUSION AND DISCUSSION

Our results show, to answer research question 1 (How are educational offerings discussed on Twitter?), evidence that formal and non-formal educational offerings are discussed on Twitter in similar ways, indicating that non-formal educational packages are considered by users and students valid possibilities for professional advancement. The results from the theme analysis using machine learning and network analysis methods provided evidence of four main themes that guided the discussions of educational packages. In these themes, the users considered educational packages from different perspectives: 1) from the perspective of the effort and time that working and finishing an education take, 2) resources that students and users can use to gain skills or further their careers, 3) the importance of degrees, expertise and learning new skills, and 4) relevant discussions of current events like labor shortage or mental health.

In these four themes we can see a relevant and pertinent discussion of the different opportunities and possibilities afforded by different educational offerings. Unsurprisingly, traditional formal educational packages, like university degrees, are widely discussed. These are talked about in the four themes, generally linked to possible future employment opportunities and advancement that degrees help create, the skills gained in the process of finishing a degree or the effort put into finishing said degree. However, non-formal educational offerings are also widely discussed in three of the four themes we identified. In this case, non-formal educational packages are talked about in terms of a means for professional advancement in the form certificates and online courses, found in the themes *resources* and *advancement,* as well as in the theme *effort.* The importance of these results lie in the fact that we have found evidence that non-formal educational packages are discussed in similar ways to formal educational packages, which have traditionally been associated with economic and professional advancement. Although there are specific ways through which formal educational offerings are discussed, like for example in terms of the expertise degrees confer to degree holders, the discussions of professional advancement that degrees provide overlapped with discussions of professional advancement provided by non-formal educational packages.

The results from the word embeddings and similarity measure help us answer research question 2 (How successful have educational product packages been in informing the public of what they are?). The analysis from the Twitter discussions showed how three educational packages were talked about in a clear and defined way. Figure 8 shows three clusters, *degree, nanodegree,* and *microcredential,* with a substantial separation with the other clusters. As we discussed in the results section, that indicates a high level of recognition and disambiguation. The fact that *degree* is clearly understood by users and students is not surprising. Formal educational offerings have been, for decades, the standard through which the acquisition of knowledge and skills happened. Interestingly, microcredentials seem to still be somewhat associated with formal educational institutions. This can be seen in Table 3, where the top

Figure 8. 2D representation of the most similar words for the words used in Table 3. The positioning of each word is the result of the word embeddings and PCA algorithm

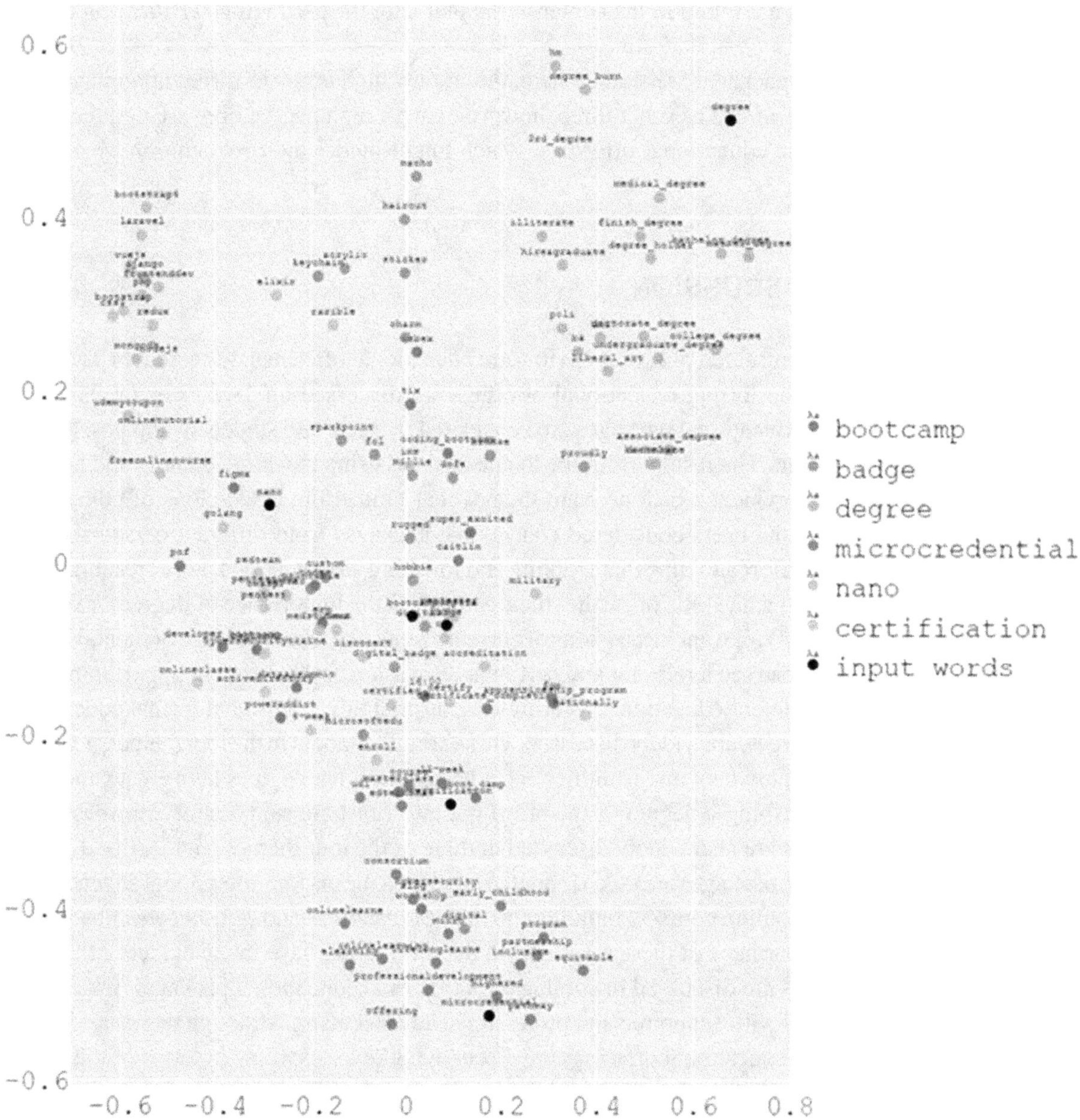

words semantically associated with microcredentials are associated with formal highered learning. Some of these words are course, highered, or program. At the same time, nanogrees have the word degree in the name, creating the possible link with the educational offerings found in formal education. Of course, nanodegrees can also be offered by non-formal educational institutions, we mentioned data science nanodgrees offered by Udacity, but these educational packaging are presented as a shorter version of what formal educational institutions offer. It is also important to mention that Table 3 shows how the most semantically similar words to nanodegree in our corpus are highly specialized in the programming and technology field with words like redux, css3, django or mongodb.

On the other hand, the other three clusters (*certification, badge* and *bootcamp*) show high levels of overlap, which indicates a low degree of disambiguation, and ultimately suggests that people discussing certifications badges and bootcamps could not define them in clear and exclusive ways. As an example, one of the most semantically similar terms to bootcamp is certificate completion, and both certifications and bootcamp share references to the time it took people to complete both programs (12-weeks for bootcamps and 4-weeks for certifications). The results provide empiric knowledge of a need for finding ways to present each educational packaging in clear and distinct ways. Each of these educational packaging offer different situations and contexts through which the acquisition of skills happen differently, that is, these are at a theoretical level different steps in a possible educational path (Ryan, 2019). The fact that some of these are not distinctly and clearly discussed hinders the understanding of each educational packaging as a separate step and prevents users and students from using these opportunities for professional advancement and skills acquisition to the full extent. Hence, to answer research question 3 (What do the results tell us about how people understand the formal/non-formal educational products?), Twitter users discussing educational packages seem to lack a clear understanding of certain offerings, which provides opportunities for educating the public in what the educational packages are and how they can contribute to their educational path.

Our contribution to the understanding of the perception of educational offerings and packages seem to clearly point towards a strong need to create a common and clear taxonomy that differentiates between educational formats, that is, a shared vocabulary that clearly distinguishes between the different steps and stages of the educational path and that helps students and users fully understand what each step can provide to them and what type of skills they will be able to acquire. The importance of skills a knowledge acquisition in a labor context where skills can be used as currency (Pulsipher, 2020) demands a taxonomy that helps users and students understand the differences between the educational packages, especially in markets like the tech labor market where constant change and learning are not only a necessity but a requirement.

REFERENCES

Berzinski, P. A., & Trajkovski, G. (2018). Future Trends in Global Online Learning. In H. Takooshian, U. P. Gielen, F. L. Denmark, & A. M. O'Roark (Eds.), *Visions and resources for international psychology: 75 years of the International Council of Psychologists* (pp. 232–241). Global Scholarly Publications.

Blei, D. M., Ng, A. Y., & Jordan, M. I. (2003). Latent dirichlet allocation. *Journal of Machine Learning Research*, *3*, 993–1022.

Blondel, V. D., Guillaume, J.-L., Lambiotte, R., & Lefebvre, E. (2008). Fast unfolding of communities in large networks. *Journal of Statistical Mechanics*, *10*(10), 1–12. doi:10.1088/1742-5468/2008/10/P10008

Blondel, V. D., Guillaume, J.-L., Lambiotte, R., & Lefebvre, E. (2008). Fast unfolding of communities in large networks. *Journal of Statistical Mechanics*, *10*(10), 1–12. doi:10.1088/1742-5468/2008/10/P10008

Bruns, A. (2018). Digital public spheres in Australia. In J. K. Schapals, A. Bruns, & B. McNair (Eds.), *Digitizing Democracy*. Routledge. doi:10.4324/9781351054867-14

Cabiddu, F., De Carlo, M., & Piccoli, G. (2014). Social media affordances: Enabling customer engagement. *Annals of Tourism Research, 48*, 175–192. doi:10.1016/j.annals.2014.06.003

Credential Engine. (n.d.). *Making ALL Credentials Transparent & Revealing the Marketplace of Credentials.* Retrieved from Credential Engine: https://credentialengine.org/

Digital Marketing Institute. (2018, December 6). *What's the Importance of Higher Education on the Economy?* https://digitalmarketinginstitute.com/blog/what-is-the-importance-of-higher-education-on-the-economy

Fabregat, E., & Kperogi, F. A. (2021). The "other" in the bowels of the hegemon: U.S. media portrayals of Guam during the U.S.-North Korea tension. *International Journal of Media and Cultural Politics, 17*(2), 119–137. doi:10.1386/macp_00043_1

Fortunato, S., & Hric, D. (2016). Community detection in networks: A user guide. *Physics Reports, 659*, 1-44.

Gallagher, S., & Zanville, H. (2021, March 25). *More employers are awarding credentials. Is a parallel higher education system emerging?* https://www.edsurge.com/news/2021-03-25-more-employers-are-awarding-credentials-is-a-parallel-higher-education-system-emerging

Goldberg, Y. & Levy, O. (2014). *Word2vec Explained: Deriving Mikolov et al.'s negative-sampling word-embedding method.* Academic Press.

Greene, D. (2021). *Diversity, equity, and inclusion in the workplace — Trends for 2021.* https://www.adp.com/spark/articles/2020/12/diversity-equity-and-inclusion-in-the-workplace-trends-for-2021.aspx

Holon, I. Q. (2021, February 18). *Micro & Alternative Credentials. Size, Shape and Scenarios - Part 1.* Retrieved from HolonIQ: https://www.holoniq.com/notes/micro-and-alternative-credentials.-size-shape-and-scenarios-part-1/

Honeycutt, C., & Herring, S. C. (2009). Beyond Microblogging: Conversation and Collaboration via Twitter. *42nd Hawaii International Conference on System Sciences.* 10.1109/HICSS.2009.89

Hong, S., & Nadler, D. (2011). Does the early bird move the polls? The use of the social media tool 'Twitter' by U.S. politicians and its impact on public opinion. *dg.o '11 Proceedings of the 12th Annual International Digital Government Research Conference: Digital Government Innovation in Challenging*, 182-186. 10.1145/2037556.2037583

HubSpot. (n.d.). *HubSpot Academy.* https://academy.hubspot.com/certification-overview

IBM Institute for Business Value. (n.d.). *The enterprise guide to closing the skills gap.* https://www.ibm.com/downloads/cas/EPYMNBJA

IBM. (n.d.). *IBM Credentials: Badges and Certifications.* https://www.ibm.com/training/credentials

Indeed. (2021, February 22). *How to Write a Skills Based Resume: Template and Examples.* https://www.indeed.com/career-advice/resumes-cover-letters/skills-based-resume-template

Kyvik, S. (2004). Structural changes in higher education systems in Western Europe. *Higher Education in Europe, 24*(3), 393–408. doi:10.1080/0379772042000331679

Lorenz-Spreen, P., Mønsted, B. M., Hövel, P., & Lehmann, S. (2019). Accelerating dynamics of collective attention. *Nature Communications*, *10*(1), 1759. Advance online publication. doi:10.103841467-019-09311-w PMID:30988286

Maier, D., Waldherr, A., Miltner, P., Wiedemann, G., Niekler, A., Keinert, A., Pfetsch, B., Heyer, G., Reber, U., Häussler, T., Schmid-Petri, H., & Adam, S. (2018). Applying LDA topic modeling in communication research: Toward a valid and reliable methodology. *Communication Methods and Measures*, *12*(2-3), 93–118. doi:10.1080/19312458.2018.1430754

Maier, D., Waldherr, A., Miltner, P., Wiedemann, G., Niekler, A., Keinert, A., Pfetsch, B., Heyer, G., Reber, U., Häussler, T., Schmid-Petri, H., & Adam, S. (2018). Applying LDA topic modeling in communication research: Toward a valid and reliable methodology. *Communication Methods and Measures*, *12*(2-3), 93–118. doi:10.1080/19312458.2018.1430754

Mikheieva, O., Otroshko, T., Sydorenko, T., Kvotun, A., & Sviderska, O. (2021). New technologies and pedagogical profession: analysis of best practices (on the example of a group of universities). *Laplage em Revista (International), 7*(B), 135-147.

Mikolov, K., Chen, G., & Corrado, J. (2013). *Efficient Estimation of Word Representations in Vector Space*. arXiv Preprint. arXiv:1301.3781v3

Mikolov, W. T., Yih, G., & Zweig. (2013). Linguistic Regularities in Continuous Space Word Representations. *Proceedings of NAACL-HLT 2013*, 746–751.

Ng, A. (n.d.). *Machine Learning*. Retrieved from Coursera: https://www.coursera.org/learn/machine-learning

Ophir, Y., Walter, D., Arnon, D., Lokmanoglu, A., Tizzoni, M., Carota, J., D'Antiga, L., & Nicastro, E. (2021, March 4). The Framing of COVID-19 in Italian media and its relationship with community mobility: A mixed-method approach. *Journal of Health Communication*, *26*(3), 161–173. Advance online publication. doi:10.1080/10810730.2021.1899344 PMID:33787462

Pichai, S. (2021, March 11). *Career certificates and more ways we're helping job seekers*. https://blog.google/outreach-initiatives/grow-with-google/career-certificates

Puckett, J., Boutenko, V., Hoteit, L., Polunin, K., Perapechka, S., & Stepanenko, A. (2020, January 15). *Fixing the Global Skills Mismatch*. https://www.bcg.com/publications/2020/fixing-global-skills-mismatch

Pulsipher, S. (2020, June 26). *Forget Bitcoin—Skills Are the Currency of The Future*. https://www.forbes.com/sites/scottpulsipher/2020/06/26/forget-bitcoin-skills-are-the-currency-of-the-future/?sh=518823d274e7

Rahmaturrizki, M. I., & Skumayadi, Y. (2020). Youtube as audio visual media learning in music education. *Advances in Social Science, Education and Humanities Research*, *519*, 297–303.

Rutherford, T. (2021, April 7). *At a Crossroad: The Intersection of Higher Education and Corporate Training*. https://www.chieflearningofficer.com/2021/04/07/at-a-crossroads-the-intersection-of-higher-education-and-corporate-training/

Ryan, W. (2019, January 29). *Microcredentials Forge the Links Between Businesses, the Community and their College.* Academic Press.

Schofer, E., Ramirez, F. O., & Meyer, J. W. (2021). The societal consequences of higher education. *Sociology of Education*, *94*(1), 1–19. doi:10.1177/0038040720942912

Szabo, E. (2021). Online platform courses between educational and business. Annals of the "Constantin Brâncusi" University of Târgu Jiu. *Economy Series*, *1*, 197–204.

The Conference Board. (n.d.). *US Labor Shortages: Challenges and Solutions*. https://conference-board.org/pdfdownload.cfm?masterProductID=20471

Trajkovski, G., Killian, R., & Cohen, S. (2021). Bridging the Gaps between Higher Education, Industry, and the Learner: The Skills First Approach. In S. Ramlall, T. Cross, & M. Love (Eds.), *Handbook of Research on Future of Work and Education: Implications for Curriculum Delivery and Work Design*. IGI Global.

Udacity. (n.d.). *Become a Data Analyst*. https://www.udacity.com/course/data-analyst-nanodegree--nd002

Walter, D., & Ophir, Y. (2019). News Frame Analysis: An Inductive Mixed-Method Computational Approach. *Communication Methods and Measures*, *13*(4), 248–266. Advance online publication. doi: 10.1080/19312458.2019.1639145

Wang, C., & Blei, D. M. (2009). Decoupling sparsity and smoothness in the discrete hierarchical Dirichlet process. *Neural Information Processing Systems*, *22*, 1982–1989.

Wang, S., Sun, T., Qu, X., & Xu, W. (2021). Online education of atomic physics based on MOOC platform. *Journal of Physics: Conference Series*, *1881*(3), 1–5. doi:10.1088/1742-6596/1881/3/032009

Zhao, W. X., Jiang, J., Weng, J., & Lim, E. P. (2011). Comparing Twitter and traditional media using topic models. In *Advances in Information Retrieval: 33rd European Conference on IR Research, ECIR 2011, Dublin, Ireland, April 18-21, 2011. Proceedings*. Berlin: Springer Verlag.

Chapter 12
The Secret Lives of ePortfolios:
Text Network Analysis and the Future of Algorithmic Hiring

Samuel Collins
Towson University, USA

ABSTRACT

This chapter looks at student ePortfolios as a potential resource for graduate careers through text network analysis. The chapter begins with a critical examination of the current state of applicant tracking systems (ATS) and the way they utilize ranking algorithms to reduce graduates to a bundle of fungible skills. As a complementary corrective to these systems, the essay suggests text network analysis of ePortfolios, arguing that this would be one way to hire graduates for the future by opening the possibility for latent networked skills and meanings to re-define jobs. Network applications allow for prospective employers to quickly analyze ePortfolio content and see potential connections and innovations. Moreover, a text network analysis would be one way to develop more team-based approaches that would focus less on the individual than on the way that graduates might combine with each other in innovative teams. ePortfolios emerge here as a way of bringing back complexity into what is fast becoming an entirely automated hiring process.

INTRODUCTION

University departments and programs have been requiring portfolios of one kind or another from students for decades. Portfolios (whether physical or digital) are a collection of artifacts: class assignments, papers, graphics, programs, achievements and narratives. Initially, these were print, and, typically, were utilized in program assessment. Circulated within universities, early portfolios were ideal data on which to evaluate curricular effectiveness. For example, programs at the author's university have long required students to compile portfolios for the university-wide assessment, conceived of as an iterative, evidence-based process. Were students learning what educators wanted them to learn? And how would the university know? Many publications from that period concentrated their attention on the assessment

DOI: 10.4018/978-1-7998-9644-9.ch012

Figure 1. ePortfolio using Wix, a free web-hosting service and webpage editor

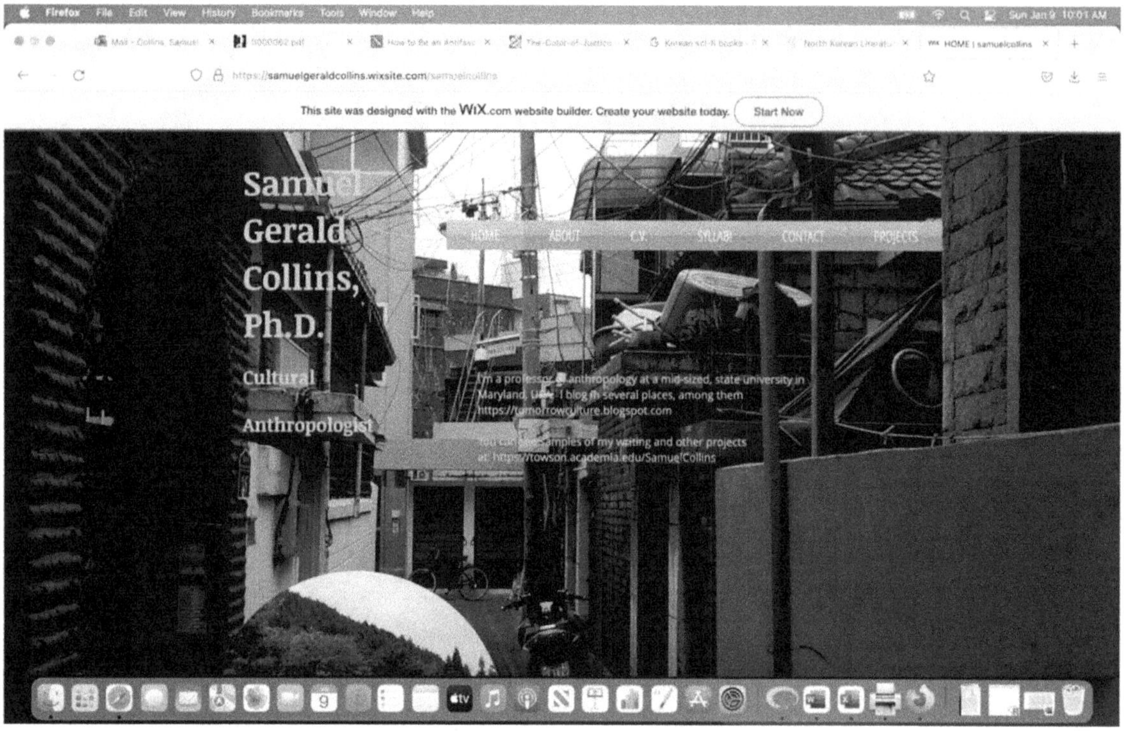

process itself, and the way that faculty can "score" or "read" portfolios in order to transform largely textual evidence into quantifiable data of student success. As portfolios shifted to online "ePortfolios," though, the possibilities for these expanded to include multimodal artifacts chronicling student achievement, and the audience for portfolios expanded to include recruiters and prospective employers. The "ePortfolio," when utilized like this, offers students a chance to consciously shape their education and to communicate their aspirations to future employers (Cordie et al 2019). Now, many programs require students to produce ePortfolios during their undergraduate careers, and some even have courses devoted to portfolio development.

As students are encouraged to think of ePortfolios as chronicling their professional development as lifelong learners, third-party platforms have emerged that allow people to keep and maintain portfolios for free or for a low cost. For the most part, the cost of these platforms tracks with the multimedia requirements of the portfolio. Artists and videographers, for example, might utilize something like SquareSpace, while coders might use GitHub pages to build a portfolio of their work and skills. People with more text- and resume-based portfolio needs can look to a variety of free hosting services with templates, such as Wix (see below), WordPress or LinkedIn, which allows users to upload content or links to the its profile interface. Finally, all of these platforms can also host the digital badges and certifications that come with lifelong learning beyond the undergraduate degree.

At this point, then, ePortfolios move from their initial roles as instruments of student achievement and program assessment to "career ePortfolios," "a specific type of portfolio that is created by a student to showcase their best academic work and unique attributes that may not be demonstrated on a traditional resume or during an interview" (Bonsignore 2013). Liberated from their "in-house" use, ePortfoloios are being utilized to help students to network with prospective employers. Recruiters might either chance upon artifacts in the student's portfolio or follow a link to the portfolio through a submitted resume or application. This has a big advantage over the limitations of a cover letter and resume: prospective employees can showcase their professional development and, through the addition of narratives or through the careful curation of artifacts, can utilize ePortfolios to tell their story and narrate the arc of their training. The problem: scholarly work on the utility of ePortfolios has largely been on the value of these sites to students and to institutions. The assumption is that employers will find them important as well and, more importantly, that they will find them important in the same ways.

In the abstract, surveyed employers prefer ePortfolios to transcripts, but the question is: do they read them, and how do they read them? What are the reading practices associated with ePortfolios? There are conflicting reports on this. On the one hand, many employers express interest in ePortfolios and claim to value them over, say, college transcripts (Ward and Moser 2008). On the other hand, in a recent survey, most employers said that they were not familiar with ePortfolios—despite the widespread usage of eProfolios by a larger percentage of the workforce over the last ten years. As Holtzman et al (2021) conclude, "Employers' enthusiasm for ePortfolios was tempered by the lack of familiarity with them and suggest that these digital platforms continue to supplement, rather than replace, more traditional hiring tools."

While there seems to be wide interest in ePortfolios, analyzing their contents takes significant time, and the companies and HR departments surveyed suggest that employers are unlikely to examine ePortfolios until the final stages of a hire—in order, for example, to decide between 2-3 equally qualified candidates on a short list (Holtzman et al 2021). In other words, ePortfolios would come after checking social media, which a majority of employers have reported checking (Marcus 2020). By the time employers get to this stage in the hiring process, their sense of a candidate may be already formed. In any case, the prospective employee has lost the ability to shape the narrative in any meaningful way: ePortfolios become another way of confirming qualifications. This raises questions about the efficacy of the ePortfolio. Given the time it takes to set up an ePortfolio and update it on a regular basis to reflect current skills and projects, is it really worthwhile to do one—outside of art and design fields where portfolios are a necessity? Still, surveys of employers over the last two decades suggest growing interest in ePortfolios as part of the hiring process (Finley 2021). Yet this interest is concurrent with trends towards algorithmic hiring which would tend to eliminate reading practices altogether.

BACKGROUND

For nearly three decades, institutions have been utilizing Applicant Tracking Systems (ATS) or Automated Hiring Platforms (AHP) in their efforts to recruit employees. Now almost entirely web-based, these systems allow employers a number of affordances, among them uniformity of applications, timesaving through automation, and tracking systems that enable employers to log and document each stage of hiring, training, performance and tenure. They also typically include capabilities for algorithm-driven candidate ranking. These have rapidly evolved over the past decades, and are now used nearly universally by almost every sector of employment in the United States and Europe, including higher education (Fuller et al 2021).

ATS are adopted for a variety of reasons—the primary of which is to save money. But the hope had also been that the technology would also have benefits beyond cost, namely the reduction of bias in the hiring process. For decades, researchers have noted that efforts to diversify the workforce have been hampered by a generalized homophily at every stage; people tend to hire others they feel resemble themselves. In a race- and gender stratified society, this means, generally, white, cisgender men hiring other white, cisgender men. But by applying algorithmic ranking systems, bias is said to be eliminated. That said, it is difficult to assess the claims of algorithm providers, given that much of the hiring information from private corporations is proprietary. Moreover, it's unclear what "nonbiased" means in a particular context; depending on the organization, this may diverge considerably from ideas of social equity (Raghavan et al 2020). It's worth asking: can bias be "eliminated" without addressing the underlying structural inequalities which (over)determines it?

In addition, like other algorithmic tools, ATS may contain biases themselves (Noble 2018). First, they can reproduce the biases that led to the stratified workforce in the first place. For example, "supervised learning"-based algorithms rely on historical datasets of applicants in order to build predictive models of future applicant success (Eastwood 2020). Thus, paradoxically, algorithms designed to reduce human bias end up strengthening that bias by "blackboxing" biased decision-making behind a proprietary, algorithmic wall (Benjamin 2019; McKenzie 2018). Second, the algorithmic ranking ignores context, and in the process might disqualify pools of otherwise promising hires. A typical example: people who have had to take time off of work to care for a child or a loved one will show a gap in their resume, and algorithms might rank such an applicant near the bottom for the "inconsistencies" in their employment records (Fuller et al 2021). In an era of COVID, this is especially troubling. Not only have jobseekers' needs changed towards jobs with more flexibility and more options for remote work, job experiences have changed during the pandemic. Early on the pandemic, many workers found themselves unemployed and, even after employers began re-hiring, many people found themselves unable to return to the labor force because of illness or caregiving responsibilities that had taken precedence amongst widespread school closure.

The following essay suggests ways of building context back into the ATS process through text network analysis of ePortfolios. In the interest of opening up post-pandemic employment in the context of post-pandemic education, ePortfolios add nuance and fill "holes" that might otherwise disqualify applications. By suggesting ways of automating the process of ePortfolio assessment, the following proposes ePortfolios as a corrective to the algorithmic reductions of applicants to de-contextualized bundles of skills and certifications. Rather than an alternative to what has become a dominant platform in almost all sectors of employment, text network analysis here is imagined as a supplement to ATS by working on networked associations that may lie to the outside of the discursive frames built into the hiring platform.

Types of ATS

ATS generally features ranking algorithms of some sort. These rely on a variety of data, and include, for example, resumes, audio analysis from interviews, biometrics, social media postings, online games and other sources of information about a candidate (Holm 2020). These have not been without controversy. Not just in terms of surveillance, but in terms of its secrecy. Typically, the proprietary algorithm doesn't allow for people to, say, find out which part of their interview were scored lower - or which f their social media posts led to a lowered ranking.

In addition, most ATS systems feature "resume parsing," Hrala estimates that 75% percent of applicants are rejected from a search based on ATS algorithms, which include online keyword searching and other criteria (time between employment, type of degree, etc.) (Hrala 2021; Weber 2012). Those remaining resumes may be subjected to additional tests (e.g., automated interviews) which can then be parsed with algorithmic tools. For some sectors of employment, only a very small number of resumes will be examined by a human and, overall, there has been a marked decrease in human involvement in the hiring process.

Backwards and Forwards

The reliance on hiring algorithms tends to produce a predictable reaction against automation in general, leading to, for example, predictions of humanity working on behalf of robots (Collins 2018). On the other hand, humans may reject applicants for all kinds of reasons, and it is incorrect that human review of applicant materials is inherently more "fair" than algorithmic review (Lee 2018). The biggest obstacles to ATS, though, is its reliance on the past.

In "training" the algorithm, the criteria thought to be predictive of applicant success are based on the resumes and employment records of past employees. Of course, if past employees skewed white, cisgender and male, then those databases will be biased towards people with similar experiences and life courses. Even if, for example, race, gender and sexuality are unmarked in the application materials, differences derived from the impacts of social oppression mean that inequalities can be reinscribed on the applicant. In academics, for example, graduate students may lack both the social and monetary capital necessary to attend graduate programs far from their homes, particularly if they must contribute to the well-being of their families. The programs they ultimately graduate from may not be the "best" in the sense of global rankings, yet the applicants themselves may be more talented than their counterparts at top graduate programs. And while there are many promising techniques for the correction of bias in datasets based on past employees, using, for example, deep neural networks, the core problem remains: algorithms proceed from historical data to an anticipated future (Li and Vasconcelos 2019). In a static world, this would be a simple, Newtonian matter: people resembling earlier employees will tend to do as well as their predecessors. But what about when the challenges are unknown? And when the hope that the future contributions of employees are both unexpected but revolutionary—i.e., that they re-define both the position and what counts as "success" in that position?

In a sense, much of hiring and recruitment--even when not automated--is similarly backwards-facing. Human resources departments, after all, are trying to "fill a position"--by definition, a pre-determined slot in an organizational structure. This introduces inertia from the outset. What these hiring algorithms accomplish is forcing people to comply with the algorithm. And while this may be a measure of an applicant's desire to join the company, it is a poor proxy for someone's potential. Yet there are other ways to assess applicants. But probably the most obvious insight is that there is no, one technological fix that can repair centuries of structural bias. Moreover, algorithms are a reduction of the human, unlikely to represent or to predict human potential.

On the other hand, ePortfoilios allow people to assemble documentary evidence of learning and achievements over the course of training and previous employment. While there is evidence that employers generally do not consider them in employment applications, they are a rich source of text that can be form the basis for more nuanced assessments of applicant fit and futures. But how might this be accomplished?

RQ1: How Can the analysis of ePortfolios be Automated in order to Preserve their Richness and Complexity?

The chief impediment to utilizing ePortfolios in the hiring process is time. As Mitchell et al (2021) report: "The primary perceived disadvantage was the time for candidates to develop ePortfolios and for recruiters to review them" (95). For the former, there are many programs (chiefly in business) that require students to assemble ePortfolios as a record of their learning (Okoro 2011). For the latter, there are many tools based in semantic networks and text networks that allow analysts to visualize the relationships between terms and concepts in any text corpora.

If the length and complexity of ePortfolios are the chief obstacle in their utilization, what about tools (algorithmic or not) that might help in this process? Semantic networks are utilized in a variety of ranking algorithms, especially when combined with other tools such as convolutional neural networks (CNN) and various forms of natural language processing to analyze a variety of application materials (Maheswary and Misra 2018; Thun 2020).

Text Networks

Text network analysis describes a variety of techniques for reducing complex texts to an adjacency matrix, where terms the co-occur in a sentence or locutions are represented as nodes (or dots) linked together by edges (or lines) (Miranda 2019). These sociographs can help analysts identify key terms and their relationship to each other through different measures (e.g., centrality). While "degree centrality" (or word frequency) identifies the number of times a term appears in a text corpora, the true power of the approach is in measures of what is called "betweenness centrality", which is a "measure of how often a given vertex lies on the shortest path between two other vertices. This can be thought of as a kind of "bridge" score, a measure of how much removing a person would disrupt the connections between other people in the network" (Hansen et al 2020: 41).

Thinking of nodes according to this measure of centrality means that we can begin to identify not only the associations of words with each other, but the ways in which certain concepts are used to think others–the ways, in other words, that concepts are used as "gateways" onto other concepts. In other words, text networks divulge complex associations of words, the ways in which they are grouped with others and, in general, a cognitive mapping of human thinking.

Like other forms of language processing, text networks are achieved through a series of reductions, beginning in the elimination of "stop words," which include articles, propositions, many verbs and other words that are thought to be extraneous to the networked concepts at the core of the corpora. From there, analysis follows the "natural language processing pipelines," which includes the reduction of text through "tokenization," "lemmatization," or the conversion of different, grammatical permutations of a term or concept (e.g., verb tense) into a "lemma," or a "standard" or "dictionary" form. Finally, the lemmas can be related to each other by the co-occurrence in a sentence, their adjacency to each other, or their structural homologies (e.g., though grammar) (Arnold and Tilton 2015).

There are many advantages to text networks, but probably one of the most compelling is the accessibility of the approach. There are many free and open source applications for text analysis, including several R packages and projects archives on GitHub and elsewhere, in addition to many free dictionaries for natural language processing, available in most languages. In addition, the sociographs that can be one product of text network analysis support both mathematical measures of importance and highly intuitive understandings based on the size and position of nodes; in other words, the data are more accessible to people without technical backgrounds.

Infranodus

The graphs in this essay have been produced using "Infranodus, "a web-based, text analysis application that uses word co-occurrence to construct a network. Nodes are key terms, and the edges (or lines) between them show words (actually lemmas) separated by 1 word or words separated by two words" (Paranyushkin 2019). The network visualizations show betweenness centrality through the size of the node, and also suggest topics through the identification of clusters. Finally, a variety of different tools and analytics are available through the application, including word frequencies and measures of centrality.

In order to explore the relevance of text network analysis for hiring platforms, this essay utilizes several texts to measure the "fit" of a hypothetical applicant to a hypothetical job inquiry. The job ad–for a User Experience (UX) researcher—is actually an amalgam of multiple job postings from different IT corporations, while the job "applicant" is the author. Instead of an ePortfolio, however, this simplified demonstration utilizes a CV as a proxy in order to keep the network graph more legible without having to excessively filter data. In addition, as a proxy for hiring by teams, the essay includes a CV from one of this volume's editors. In the actual analysis of ePortfolios, the greater size of text corpora would make network visualizations considerably more dense, although scaling to several thousand lemmas would make no substantial difference in the kinds of analyses that could be used on these data.

Measuring Fit

Infranodus allows not only the analysis and graphing of a text, but the comparison of that graph with others in order to identify both absence and overlap. This capacity to help users visualize the difference between texts as well as their similarities is one of key features of this platform. For assessing applicants, it allows not only an immediate sense of applicant "fit," but allows more subtle insights on the basis of network association.

In the first graph, the job posting itself has been visualized. By the node size, we can identify terms by their betweenness centrality. This is a measure of their importance to the job, since the terms literally serve as "gatekeepers" onto other terms. The chart below shows two measures of centrality in networks: degree centrality and betweenness centrality. "Degree centrality" measures the number of connections—i.e., the number of the co-occurrences of the lemma with other lemmas in the graph. But betweenness suggests more of a mental map—how do some concepts lead to other concepts? Ultimately, it is betweenness centrality that generates meaning and, as the essay suggests below, the potential for innovation.

The terms with the highest betweenness centrality ("Research," "Product," "People," "Experience," "Team") suggest terms common to, perhaps, any knowledge-intensive job description—the applicant will join a team to research the user experiences of people in order to share the development of an undefined product. The second tier (in terms of nodes size) provides a little more clarity: "Partner," "Design," "User," "Method," and "Science." Here, the description includes utilizes user experience as a scientific method in order to impact design. The other terms stipulate some of the desired characteristics of the successful applicant.

How might an applicant measure up? The following shows a hypothetical applicant for the hypothetical job description using the author's CV as a proxy for a more expansive ePortfolio. This graph shows terms in the original job posting that are not in the applicant materials—in other words, the terms missing from the applicant CV.

Table 1. Lemmas with the highest betweenness centrality measure

node name	degree	betweenness
research	90	0.41553
product	66	0.300679
experience	49	0.243571
people	56	0.166548
team	46	0.150536
design	35	0.08658
user	32	0.086234
partner	33	0.081321
science	39	0.071121
method	36	0.066602

At first glance, the applicant does not appear like a close fit for the job posting. Many of the key terms are missing from the CV, notably "product," "people," "experience," "user," "design" "team" and "partner." Out of the terms with the highest betweenness centrality in the job posting, only "research" appears in the CV—clearly the resume of an academic! But a network is not simply a list of keywords; those terms are linked together through their associations in a sentence. Moreover, terms are not only related to each other through co-occurrence, but through geodesic distance. For example, if we merge the text networks, and highlight the term "product" again, the results show a more complex picture:

Now, we see that "product," although absent in the CV, is linked to terms from the CV. Through "research," we can see "product" as involved with the ideas and the study of culture, perhaps suggesting a role for an anthropologist after all. Finally, we can travel from "Research" to many other terms:

Now, at a geodesic distance of 2 (i.e., two "hops" from "product"), an entire universe of possibilities opens up, terms and concepts that are separated, but still tenuously linked, to "product." More than just establishing a connection, this has the ultimate effect of re-defining what "product" might mean by introducing novel connections (or co-occurrences) at a geodesic distance of 2. From the perspective of an employer, these connections interject novel potentialities for future projects that could develop over time, in the same way that "weak ties" offer people and communities new information and novel ideas (Keuchenius et al 2018).

Hiring Teams

Teams and team-based projects are the foundation of work in a knowledge economy. So while there is a broad and robust literature on hiring teams, including designing algorithms for maximum team impact (Golshan et al 2014) and for maximizing skills while minimizing overlap (Selvarajah 2020). There is also a considerable literature on bias in team or cluster hiring, one that is often thought amenable to changes in algorithm programming. Yet, much of the hiring process is still premised on the individual applicant. This, after all, is the neoliberal model: job applicants are forced to compete against each other for positions that they all might qualify for (Gershon 2017). And yet, despite the fetishization of

Figure 2. Job description

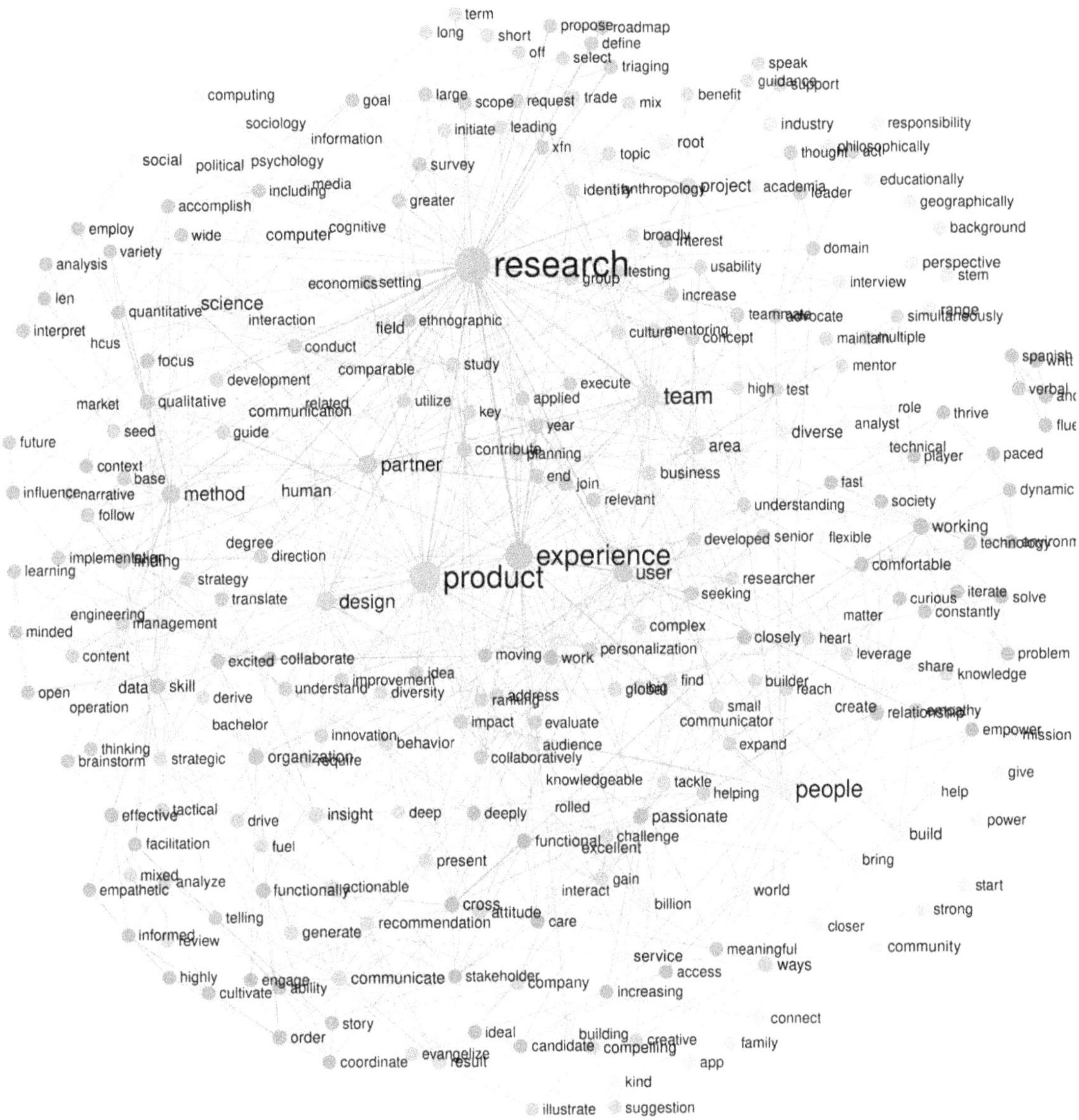

hypercompetitive individualism in the neoliberal job market, employers of all kinds have gone to great lengths to build productive teams—a tension that has not gone unremarked (Boreham 2004).

If we go back to Figure 1 (above), we can see that the applicant's CV, while not a particularly strong fit, nevertheless adds interesting nuance to the job posting. What if another applicant is added to the "team"? In the example below, the CV for one of the editors of this volume (Goran Trajkovski) has been added to the initial applicant, and then the whole compared to the original job posting. The resulting sociograph shows the terms in the original job posting missing from the combined CVs of the team members.

What is immediately evident is the much larger coverage from tie two, combined CVs. Most the terms absent from Figure 1 (above) are now present in Figure 5. The second applicant has more experience

Figure 3. Terms in Figure 1 (above) that are missing from the author's CV

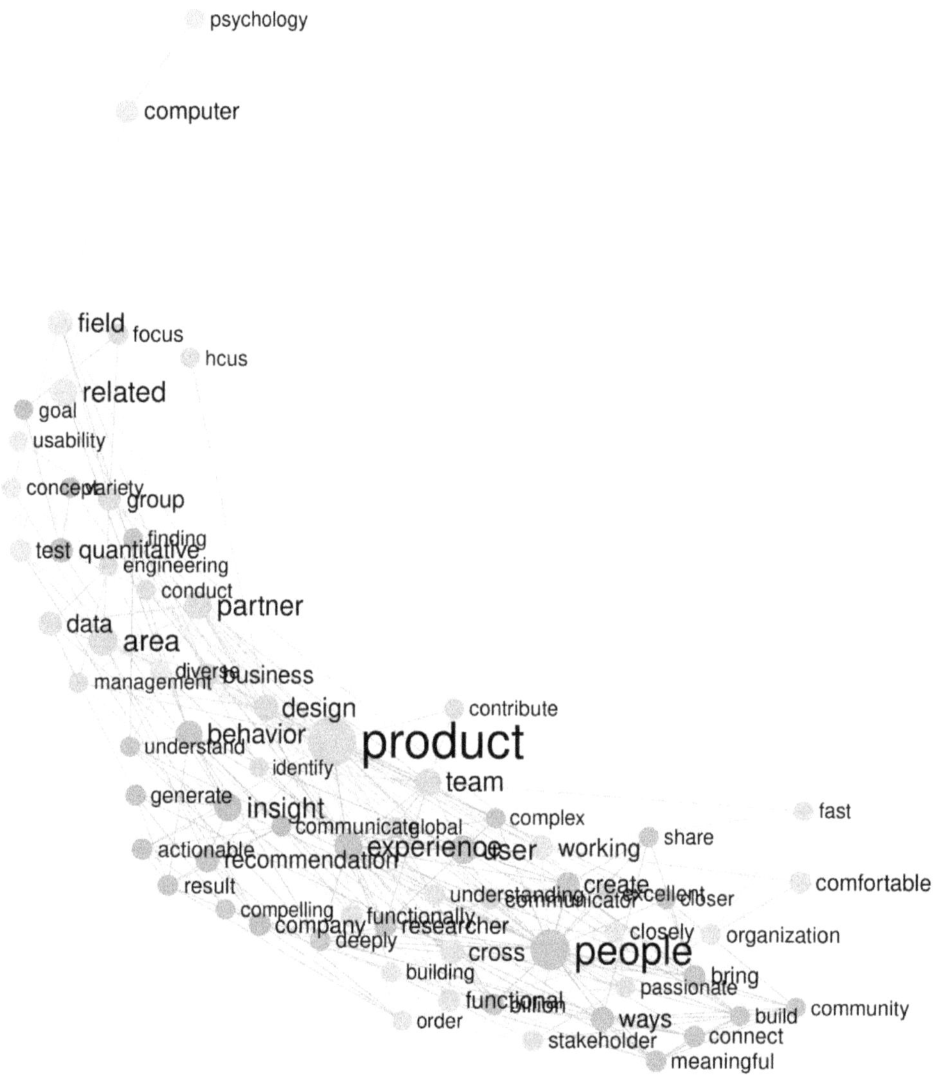

in project design and management, and this comes through in the combined graph. Interestingly (but perhaps, not surprisingly) "product" is still missing from the combined graph, and this, perhaps, might prove pivotal in the rejection of this hypothetical team for a user experience research group.

On the other hand, adding another team member adds more nuance to the original, and multiplies the meanings that "product" and other keywords might have and (eventually) come to include.

The resulting graph covers a lot of semantic territory—academics, business, government, management, community. When "product" and "research" are highlighted in the graph, a large number of additional connections become visible:

Some of the new connections include "robotics," "computational," "education" and "institutional"—again adding novelty to networks composed of "product" and "research." With the addition of each,

Figure 4. Combining the job posting with the sample CV

networked concept, new possibilities emerge that both re-define the original job posting while at the same time gesturing to a future horizon.

In the end, the graphs challenge what is meant by "presence" and "absence." If the word "product" does not appear in applicant materials, that does not mean that applicant materials cannot suggest new meanings and nuances for the lemma "product." At its core, networked meanings exist as latencies for the future, gesturing to the possibilities for futures that exist in the grey interstices of applicant materials and the job application process.

This works in the opposite direction as well, with the identification of structural holes. Nodes that command the space within structural holes in a graph command the flow of ideas in a text network.

Figure 5. Terms at a geodesic distance of 2 from "product"

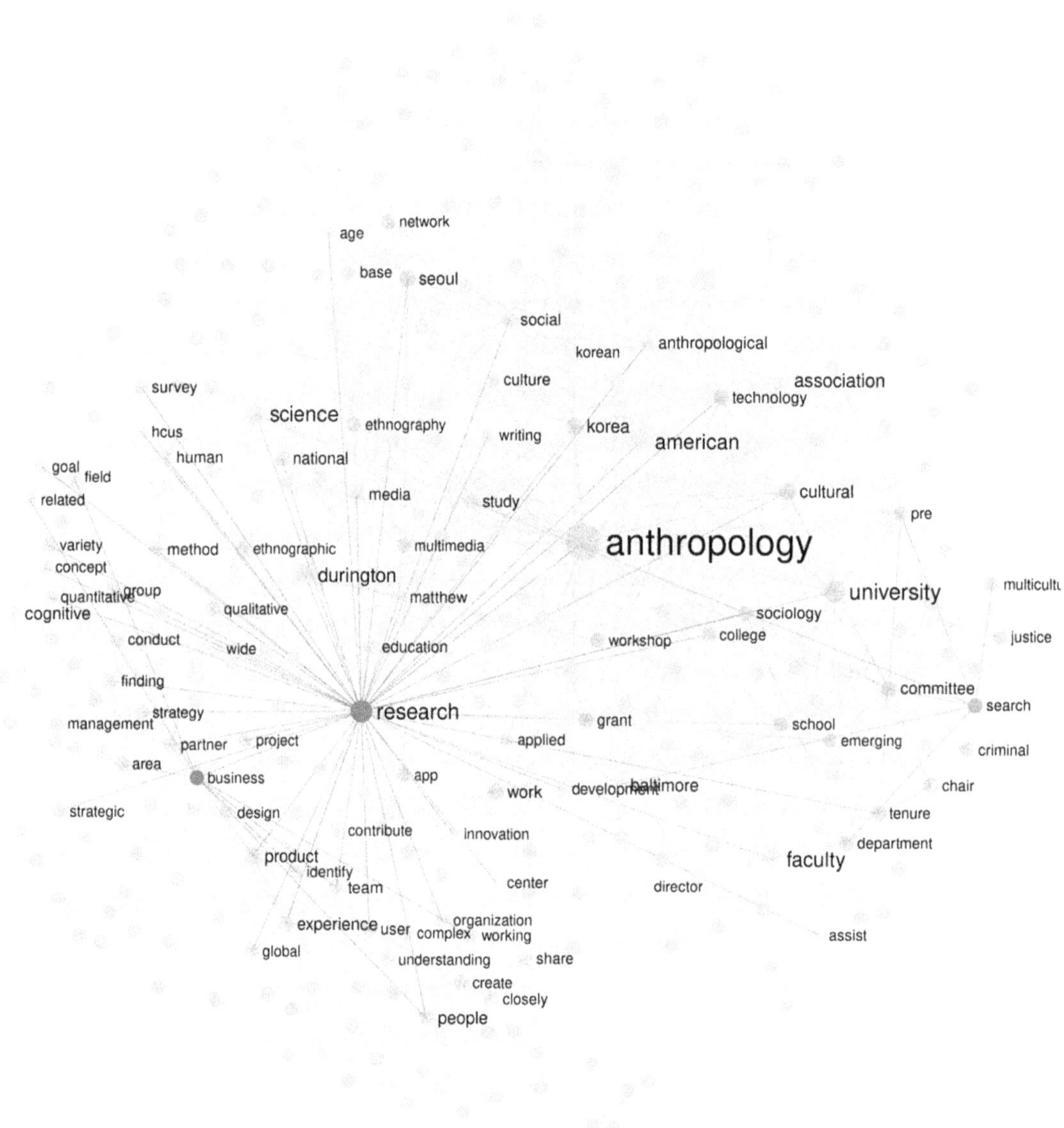

They describe terms and concepts that are literally used to think other terms and concepts (Burt 2004). Attending to those concepts "can be used to identify those gaps and to propose new connections between different ideas, topics and topical clusters" (Paranyushkin 2019: 2). In the network above, "culture" seems to fill that structural hole, and opens up a number potentially creative connections and associations.

Diversity and Uncertainty

With the widespread adoption of Applicant Tracking and Automated Hiring Systems, a fundamental contradiction is introduced into hiring practices. On the one hand, AHS are said to grant HR depart-

Figure 6. Terms in the job posting that do not appear in the combined graph of the two applicants

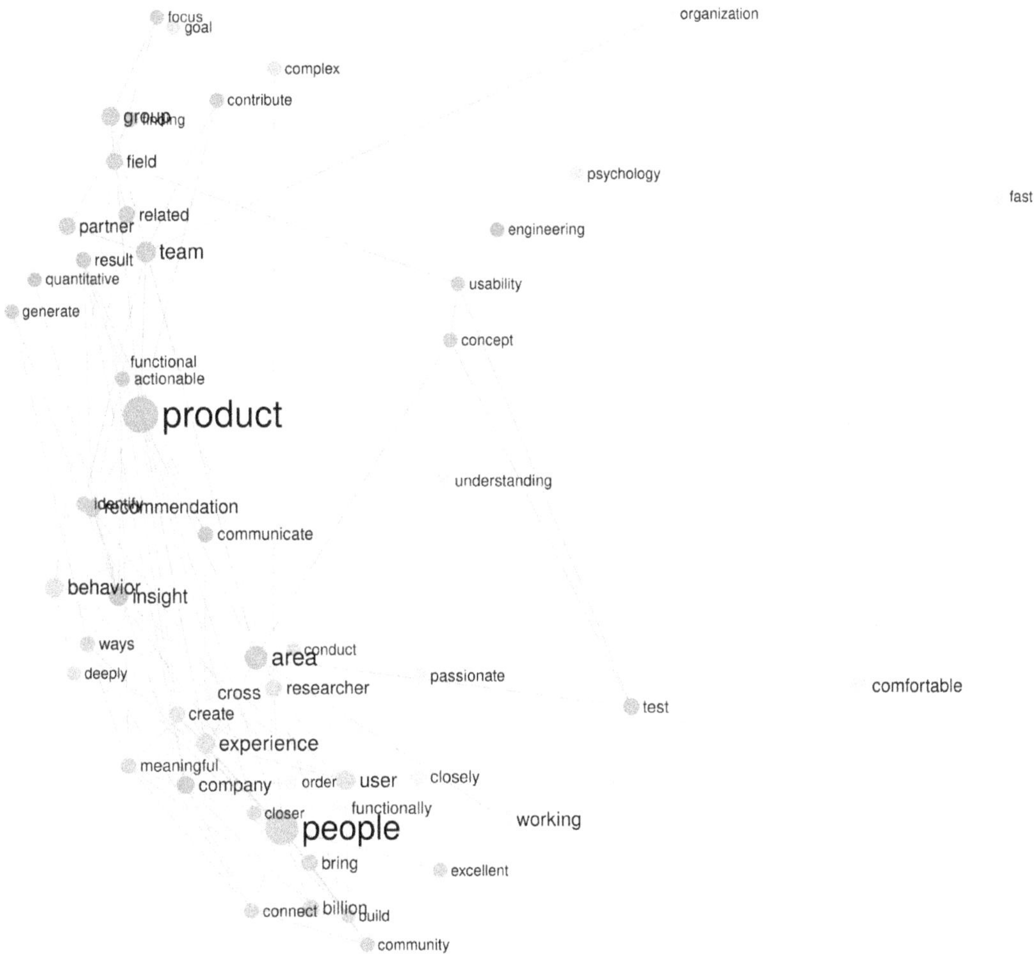

ments unparalleled accuracy in identifying prospective employees with particular skill sets that match predictive models of success at their organization. On the other hand, innovation and creativity have emerged as highly desirable traits, implying, at some level, a departure from the expected. This has led to a demand for a basket of "soft skills" from universities, particularly in providing students with a broad education that might add creative value to their employers. After all, as Hunter et al (2012: 307) point out, "Although it is intuitively clear that high levels of domain-specific knowledge (i.e., expertise) are necessary for innovation, it also appears useful for individuals to have broader forms of knowledge as well." This tension is reproduced in ePortfolios as well, which are asked, on the one hand, to display exact skills and competencies that have been identified as essential for a particular position, while at the same time valuing the innovative and the (by definition) unexcepted.

Over the past 40 years, strong evidence in small group dynamics suggests that more diverse groups are more creative and productive (McLeod et al 1996). What is called the "business case for diversity" affirms "that organizations with more diverse workforces outperform organizations with less diversity

Figure 7. The job posting combined with the two applicants

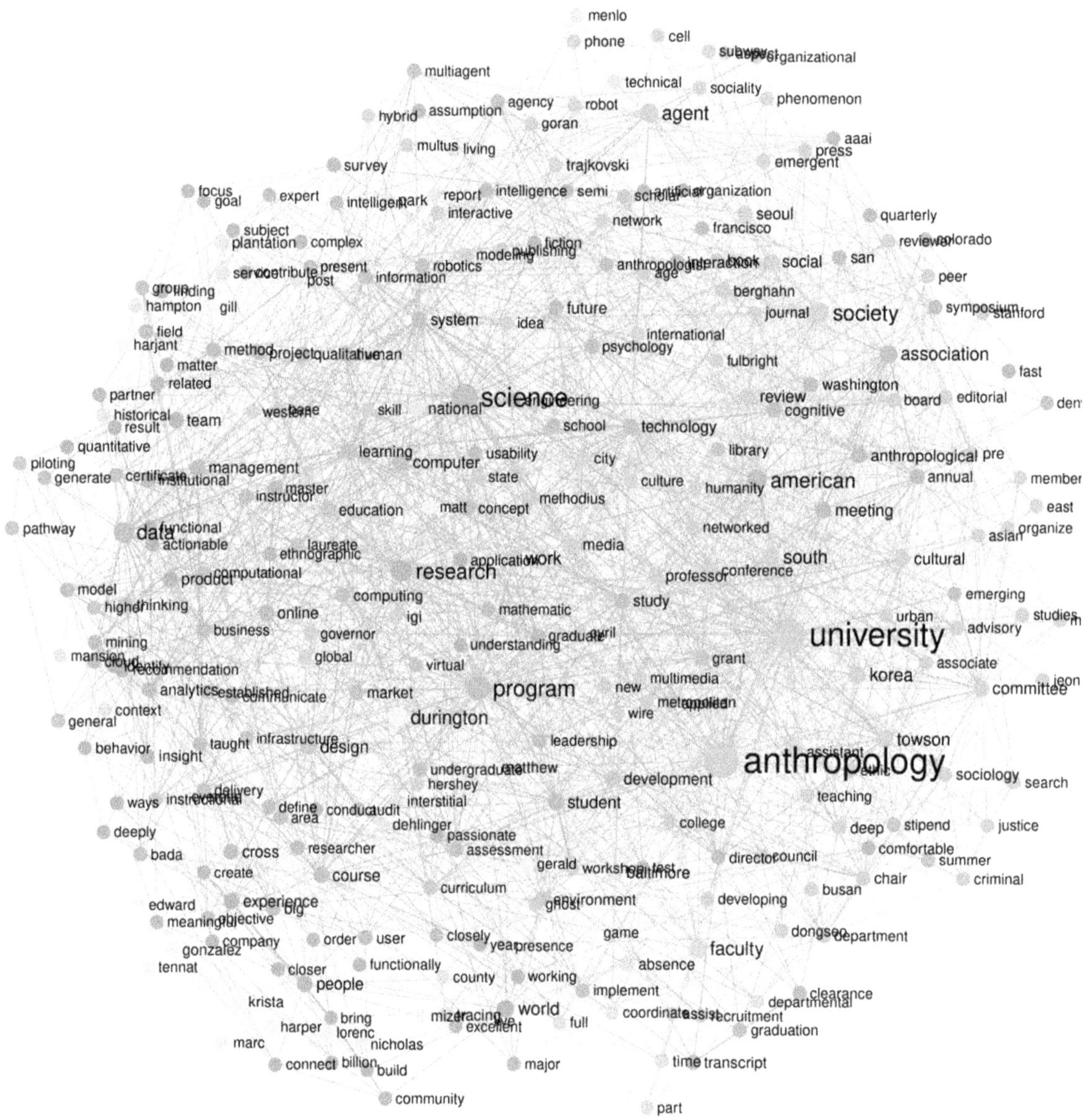

among their employees" (van Knippenberg et al 2020: 75). Hiring that diversity has become a major goal in human resources, and managing that diversity an important element of scholarship in business and management.

Yet there is also a sense of a backwardness about popular discussions of diversity, as if the goal of DEI initiatives was simply to "collect" underrepresented populations into the organization. Of course, these are just stereotypes; actual DEI initiatives are more complex, more nuanced and, ultimately, bound up with the moral desiderata of social justice. Ironically, these more reductive approaches are inherent in hiring algorithms. After all, analysis involves a series of reductions of context to signifiers of applicant potential for success. The candidate is reduced to a series of ranked classifications of merit and

Figure 8. Nodes related to "product" through "research" on the combined graph

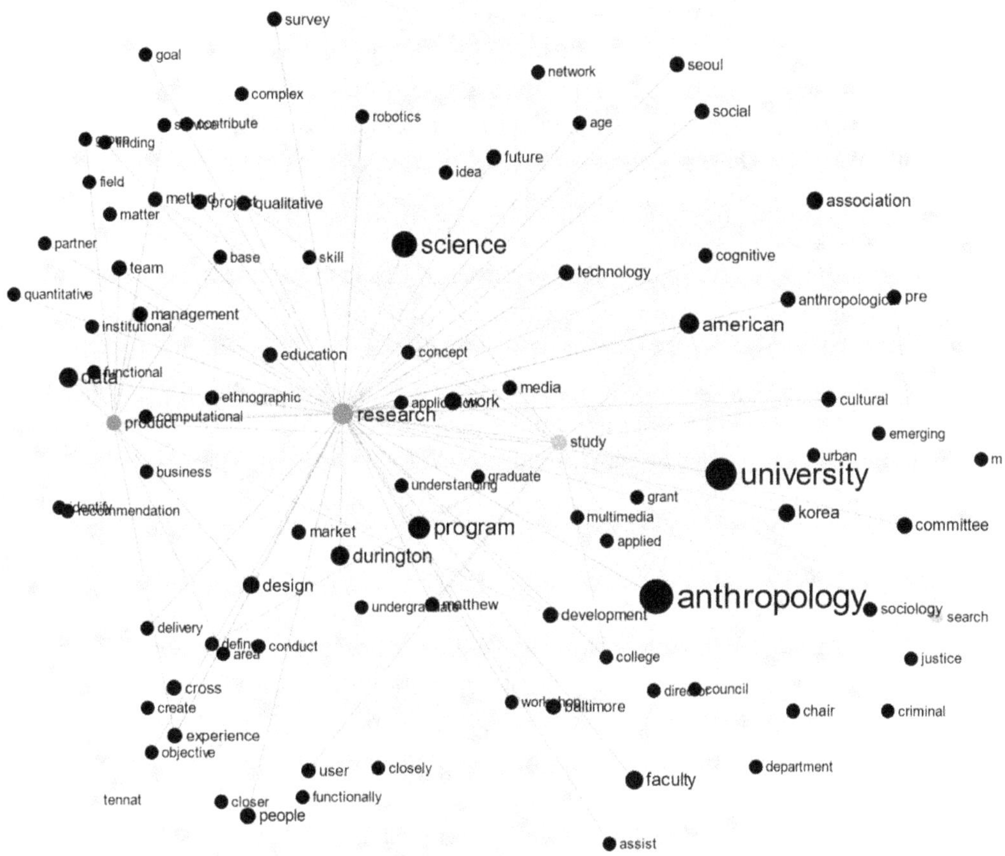

potential. And while this may be a "perception problem," with algorithms in general, it would be hard to argue that the "value-added" of hiring algorithms do not hinge on exactly these kinds of reductions (Newman et al 2020).

What this essay suggests is another element of diversity, on that readily complements social equity goals: the promise of uncertainty. Margaret Mead, writing in the wake of her involvement with the Josiah Macy, Jr. Conferences on Cybernetics (where she had worked with Kurt Lewin), suggests that the emergent properties of the group are the most important factor in small group dynamics. For Mead, the most important tasks were to assemble the group and set up conditions for them to prosper. She was less certain that there was any one "method" for the formation of productive groups. "For such an emergent cluster no precise formula can be written. The only possible formulation is a delimitation of the conditions under which clusters of this kind can come into being" (Mead 1964: 301). In fact, her uncertainty was to be one of the bases for what later was termed "second-order cybernetics" (Collins 2010).

The hope, really, is that diversity brings new ideas, yet these new ideas themselves cannot be predicted in advance—they are an emergent property of the small group. As many studies have pointed out, hiring homogenous groups creates a redundant "echo chamber" of ideas. In contrast, having different people work together is supposed to generate new ideas. And there are data supporting this, but the mechanism of diversity and creativity is the black box of social psychology. Effort like Google's "Project Aristotle" revealed that there was no "perfect" mix of talent, individuality and leadership that would predict the success of one team over another. Instead, one of the project leaders on the Google study suggested that "psychological safety" is a better predictor: "a climate in which people feel safe to speak up and take interpersonal risks" (King 2021: 220-21). In other words, pace Mead, the innovative team is contingent upon creating the conditions for human striving. And one component of this might be the realization that skills and competencies are not "present" or "absent." Instead, these describe networked phenomena that shift in meaning as they flow through networked structures. Here, innovation through diversity become a "networked effect"—the effect of weak ties—but one that is dependent upon the capacity of an individual to transform new knowledge and ideas flowing through weak ties into innovation. As Kim et al suggest, this is highly dependent upon the individual themselves, and seems to be at least partly due to a combination of specific expertise and broad knowledge (Kim et al 2016).

CONCLUSION

The rapid growth of hiring algorithms is consistent with a desire to take advantage of IT and social media affordances for recruitment. But the biggest attraction of algorithmic hiring comes from the reduction in cost and in time. From an HR perspective, it is vastly cheaper to have algorithms rank candidates–pushing the work onto the algorithm and, ultimately, to the job applicants themselves who needs to "game" the algorithm, prepare for the surreal strangeness of the algorithm-driven interview and, in general, attempt to accommodate themselves to a complex, multiagent system composed of both human- and non-human agencies. Whether ranking resumes or quantifying facial expressions, algorithmic systems beget algorithmic behaviors; in turn, applicants must become more algorithmic in their approach in order to accommodate the will of the algorithm.

The result is certainly cost-saving, but it is also highly reductionist. "The master themes of the reduction of *friction* in the labor market, by *fragmenting* workers into discrete skills and dispositions" (Ajunwa and Green 2019: 78). But the trade-off for these efficiencies is steep: not only much of the complexity of applicant, but much of the promise of the applicant, including the potential to combine dynamically in innovative teams, falls away from the applicant.

While bias may be one of the most pressing problems of algorithm approaches, the purpose of the tool is literally to reduce–reduce time, reduce cost, and, ultimately, reduce the labor force into fungible skills. Yet it would be a mistake to return to earlier, human-led practices of applicant ranking. These were, after all, at the core of employment bias, structural and pervasive practices that resulted not only in a terrible human cost, but in the failure to utilize an enormous reservoir of human talent.

Yet there is another side to digital tools in the hiring process. This essay has traced the application of text network analysis as one way of opening the possibility for *anticipatory* hiring—that is to say, hiring people (singly or in teams) with the expectation that they will redefine the tasks for which they were initially hired. In other words, hiring for emergent employment and future success, not for iterations of a (putatively) successful past.

The idea of "weak ties" suggests that new opportunities and new ideas come from sources outside the relatively tight clusters that make up everyday life. But like innovation in teams, it is difficult to predict exactly what will come of the weak ties that enable these latent sources of value. "The randomness of weak ties is where their value lies but is also exactly what makes them difficult to purposefully mobilize" (King 2021: 44). This essay has argued for an approach that involves less the "mobilization" of weak ties than the creation of conditions where weak ties might generate novelty. That is, by hiring people who are semantically linked to desired traits—even if those traits themselves seem absent—employers set into motion a transformative process.

The Future of e-Portfolios

There is little doubt that ePortfolios will continue in one way or another in colleges and universities in their role as data for assessment and for student achievement. Reading, interpreting and analyzing those artifacts will continue to be an issue for higher education (Yancey et al 2013). But as the role of ePortfolios continues to expand beyond undergraduate education into professional life and lifelong learning, the possibility grows for the increasing relevance in recruitment, hiring and promotion. Yet the availability of more data does not mean that it will be utilized more effectively or more equitably. More accurately, "data" already implies a transformation, a "datafication" of diverse multimedia: "the conversion of qualitative aspects of life into quantified data" (Ruckenstein and Schull 2017: 261). Indeed, there are many examples of datafication that work against diversity, creativity and innovation. When HR departments turn, for example, to algorithms that analyze social media accounts, much of what is flagged as "problematic" may disproportionately impact candidates of color and people who fall outside of cisgender categories. "Let's say you and 99 other people all applied for the same job, but because you are a person of color and tend to like posts by and about people of color, the algorithms (created by programmers who are 71% White, 20% Asian, and only 5% Black) deem your posts politically extreme or obscene" (Marcus 2021). In other words, people negotiating or reflecting on marginalized or oppressed identities would be "flagged" by the algorithm—the very people that might diversify a labor force.

This essay has explored one way ePortfolios might be used by prospective employers, one that places a premium on the creativity implied in novel word associations. By allowing employers to automate the process of ePortfolio review, the hope is that portfolios can become part of the initial stages of review, rather than a very last step undertaken only with the final candidates in the job search. Of course, this process might also be subject to abuse. As Les Perelman's "Babel" generator has shown, it's entirely possible to compose a nonsense essay made of up keywords and complex phrases and receive the maximum possible score from automated essay scoring (AES) (Perelman 2020). Like any qualitative work, it seems unlikely that any algorithmic technique will prevent "gaming" the system. And, indeed, the early stages of the job search seem to require strategies for ensuring that one's resume passes the initial stages of screening. Even in a pre-digitized stage, applicants were advised to include certain keywords, to avoid certain phrases, to "clean up" their resume. Like these, HR departments will have to resort to human screening in the final stages of their decision-making process. But considering ePortfolios mean that students and graduates will have an opportunity to bring the complexity of their education into the employment process in a way that was only possible in an extremely attenuated way—through, for example, the display of badges and certifications.

For this to be an effective tool, students will need to curate the artifacts in their portfolios to reflect their best and most original work. Moreover, they will need to carefully narrate their projects, framing each for prospective employers. More than this, though, students should take into account the vicissitudes of text-based analysis. Portfolios can contain any media—from essays to computer code to photographs. Without textual framing, much of this would be meaningless to a text network analysis, so students and graduates should concentrate on adding text alternatives (alt-text) to all media, together with framing narratives that explain their relevance. Other factors improving performance in text analysis would include many of the same traits that signal effective communication skills: a large, descriptive vocabulary and a thoughtful contextualization of varied experiences that emphasizes their common links.

Finally, students should utilize the analytics available through their platforms to gauge interest in their work. For example, most basic analytics on sites (e.g., WordPress) allow site owners to track page views over time, see search terms that brought visitors and even look at time spent on a page. All of these are useful in changing a portfolio over time as a student's professional goals and experiences change. This includes text network analysis itself. Although this essay has explored the usefulness of this techniques to employers, students can mine their own ePortfolios for insights into their own work and for some clues of areas they might explore next in their quest for lifelong learning. By examining their ePortfolios for connections they might make to new projects, new training and new disciplines, students can generate creativity and innovation in their own careers (Metz and Albernhe-Giordan 2010).

REFERENCES

Acquisti, A., & Fong, C. (2020). An Experiment in Hiring Discrimination Via Online Social Networks. *Management Science*, *66*(3), 1005–1024. doi:10.1287/mnsc.2018.3269

Ajunwa, I., & Green, D. (2019). Platforms at Work. *Research in the Sociology of Work*, *33*, 61–91. doi:10.1108/S0277-283320190000033005

Arnold, T., & Tilton, L. (2015). *Humanities Data in R*. Springer. doi:10.1007/978-3-319-20702-5

Barnabo, G., Leonardi, S., Fazzone, A., & Schwiegelsohn, C. (2019). Algorithms for Fair Team Formation in Online Labour Marketplaces. *WWW '19 Companion*.

Behzad, G., Lappas, T., & Terzi, E. (2014). Profit-maximizing Cluster Hires. *KDD'14*.

Benjamin, R. (2019). *Race After Technology*. Polity Press.

Bonsignore, K. (2013). Career ePortfolios. In K. Wills & R. Rice (Eds.), *ePortfolio Performance Support Systems*. The WAC Clearinghouse.

Boreham, N. (2004). A Theory of Collective Competence. *British Journal of Educational Studies*, *52*(1), 5–17. doi:10.1111/j.1467-8527.2004.00251.x

Burt, R. S. (2004). Structural Holes for Ideas. *American Journal of Sociology*, *110*(2), 349–399. doi:10.1086/421787

Collins, S. G. (2010). An Electronic Buzzer is Laughing. *Cybernetics & Human Knowing*, *17*(3), 45–64.

Collins, S. G. (2018). Working for the Robocracy. *Anthropology of Work Review*, *39*(1), 5–9. doi:10.1111/awr.12131

Daugherty, P.R., Wilson, J, & Chowdury, R. (2018). Using Artificial Intelligence to Promote Diversity. *MIT Sloan Management Review*. mitsmr.com/2DQz2XT

Eastwood, B. (n.d.). *Exploration-based algorithms can improve hiring quality and diversity*. https://mitsloan.mit.edu/ideas-made-to-matter/exploration-based-algorithms-can-improve-hiring-quality-and-diversity

Finley, A. (2021). *How college contributes to workforce success*. https://d1y8sb8igg2f8e.cloudfront.net/AACUEmployerReport2021.pdf

Fuller, J., Raman, M., Sage-Gavin, E., & Hines, K. (2021). *Hidden Workers: Untapped Talent*. Harvard Business School Project on Managing the Future of Work and Accenture.

Gershon, I. (2017). *Down and Out in the New Economy*. University of Chicago Press. doi:10.7208/chicago/9780226452289.001.0001

Hansen, D. L., Schneiderman, B., Smith, M. A., & Himelboim, I. (2020). *Analyzing Social Media networks with NodeXL*. Morgan Kaufmann.

Holm, A. (2020). *Applicant Tracking Systems. Encyclopedia of Electronic HRM*. De Gruyter Oldenbourg.

Holtzman, D. M., Kraft, E. M., & Small, E. (2021). Use of ePortfolios for making hiring decisions. *Journal of Work-Applied Management*. Advance online publication. doi:10.1108/JWAM-01-2021-0001

Hrala, J. (2021). *Defeating Robots: 75 Percent of Resumes are Never Read by a Human*. https://blog.careerminds.com/75-percent-of-resumes-are-never-read

Hunter, S., Cushenbery, L., & Friedrich, T. (2012). Hiring an innovative workforce. *Human Resource Management Review*, *22*(4), 303–322. doi:10.1016/j.hrmr.2012.01.001

Keuchenius, A., Tornberg, P. & Uitermark, J. (2018). *How Communities Mediate the Diffusion of New Ideas*. University of Amsterdam Odycceus.

Kim, K. S., Shin, S. J., Shin, J., & Miller, D. R. (2016). Social Networks and Individual Creativity. *The Journal of Creative Behavior*, *52*(4), 285–296. doi:10.1002/jocb.153

Kim, P., & Bodie, M.T. (2021). Artificial Intelligence and the Challenges of Workplace Discrimination and Privacy. *ABA Journal of Labor & Employment Law*, *289*.

King, M. (2021). *Social Chemistry*. Dutton.

Lee, M. K. (2018). Understanding perception of algorithmic fairness. *Big Data & Society*, (January-June), 1–16.

Li, Y., & Vansconcelos, N. (2019). *REPAIR: Removing Representation Bias by Dataset Resampling*. Computer Vision Foundation.

Maheshwary, S., & Misra, H. (2018). Matching Resumes to Jobs via Deep Siamese Network. *WWW 2019*.

Marcus, A. (2020). The Dark Side of Social Media Screening Technology. *Medium*. https://medium.com/digital-diplomacy/the-dark-side-of-social-media-screening-technology-bd6f70da1d0b

McKenzie, R. (2018). Bots, Bias and Big Data: Artificial Intelligence, Algorithmic Bias and Disparate Impact Liability in Hiring Practices. *Arkansas Law Review*, *71*(2). https://scholarworks.uark.edu/alr/vol71/iss2/7

Metz, S., & Albernhe-Giordan, H. (2010). E-portfolio: A pedagogical tool to enhance creativity in student's project design. *Procedia: Social and Behavioral Sciences*, *2*(2), 3563–3567. doi:10.1016/j.sbspro.2010.03.552

Miranda, S. (2019). *Social Analytics*. Prospect Press.

Mitchell, L., Campbell, C., Somerville, M., Cardell, E., & Williams, L. (2021). Enhancing graduate employability through targeting ePortfolios to employers' expectations. *The Journal of Teaching and Learning for Graduate Employability*, *12*(2), 82–98. doi:10.21153/jtlge2021vol12no2art1003

Newman, D. T., Fast, N. J., & Harmon, D. J. (2020). When eliminating bias isn't fair: Algorithmic reductionism and procedural justice in human resource decisions. *Organizational Behavior and Human Decision Processes*, *160*, 149–167. doi:10.1016/j.obhdp.2020.03.008

Noble, S. U. (2018). *Algorithms of Oppression*. NYU Press. doi:10.2307/j.ctt1pwt9w5

Okoro, E. A., Washington, M. C., & Cardon, P. W. (2011). Eportfolios in Business Communication Courses as Tools for Employment. *Business Communication Quarterly*, *74*(3), 347–351. doi:10.1177/1080569911414554

Paranyushkin, D. (2019). Infranodus. *Proceedings of WWW '19: The Web Conference*. 10.1145/3308558.3314123

Perelman, L. (2020). The BABEL Generator and E-Rater. *Journal of Writing Assessment*, *13*(1). http://journalofwritingassessment.org

Raghavan, M., Barocas, S., Kelinberg, J., & Levy, K. (2020). Mitigating Bias in Algorithmic Hiring: Evaluating Claims and Practices. *Conference on Fairness, Accountability, and Transparency*. 10.1145/3351095.3372828

Reagans, R., & Zuckerman, E. W. (2001). Networks, Diversity, and Productivity. *Organization Science*, *12*(4), 502–517. doi:10.1287/orsc.12.4.502.10637

Rosenblat, A., Kneese, T., & boyd, d. (2014). Networked Employment Discrimination. *Data&Society*. https://www.datasociety.net/pubs/fow/EmploymentDiscrimination.pdf

Selvarajah, K., Kobti, Z., & Kargar, M. (2020). Cultural Algorithms for Cluster Hiring. *The 11th International Conference on Ambient Systems, Networks and Technologies (ANT)*.

Smith-Doerr, L., Alegria, S., & Sacco, T. (2017). How Diversity matters in the US Sicence and Engineering Workforce. *Engaging Science, Technology, and Society*, *3*, 139–153. doi:10.17351/ests2017.142

Suhr, T., Hilgard, S., & Lakkaraju, H. (2021). Does Fair Ranking Improve Minority Outcomes? *AIES '21*.

Taskin, Y., Hecking, T., & Hopope, H. U. ESA-T2N: A Novel Approach to Network-Text Analysis. In H. Cherifi, J. Mendes, L. Rocha, S. Gaito, & E. Moro (Eds.), *Complex Networks and Their Applications VIII* (Vol. 2, pp. 129–139). Springer. doi:10.1007/978-3-030-36683-4_11

Thun, A. (2020). *Matching Job Applicants to Free Text Job Ads Using Semantic Networks and natural Language Inference* [Unpublished MA thesis]. KTH Royal Institute of Technology, Stockholm, Sweden.

van Knippenberg, D., Nishii, L. H., & Dwertmann, D. J. G. (2020). Synergy from diversity: Managing team diversity to enhance performance. *Behavioral Science & Policy*, *6*(1), 75–92. doi:10.1353/bsp.2020.0007

Weber, L. (2012). Your Résumé vs. Oblivion, Inundated Companies Resort to Software to Sift Job Applications for Right Skills. *The Wallstreet Journal*. http://online.wsj.com/news/articles/SB1000142405 2970204624204577178941034941330

Yancey, K. B., McElroy, S., & Powers, E. (2013). Composing, Networks, and Electronic Portfolios. In H. McKee & D. DeVoss (Eds.), *Digital writing assessment & evaluation*. Computers and Composition Digital Press/Utah State University Press. https://ccdigitalpress.org/dwae

Chapter 13
Do We Need a Digital Data Exorcism?
End of Life Considerations of Data Mining Educational Content

James Braman
https://orcid.org/0000-0001-6080-3903
Community College of Baltimore County, USA

Alfreda Dudley
Towson University, USA

ABSTRACT

Considering the many interactions we have with technology over our lifetime, many data points, records, files, and other content are recorded in many digital forms. We inevitably construct a narrative of various life events in a digital format that often lasts well beyond the expiration date of our physical form. This construction of a digital narrative is especially true regarding education records and their use for data mining as our files can be used for analysis. In this chapter, the authors discuss the idea of a digital data exorcism as the potential ability to purge educational records if it is the desire of the individual. A data exorcism can be seen as the needed process for removing or expelling data, done so to protect those from which it was derived. Many forms of data will be discussed in this chapter; however, the focus will be on educational records related to end-of-life considerations. The main theme of this chapter is that facet that we have the right to be forgotten. The right to be deleted or, in other words, "exorcised" from the various systems in which our data resides.

INTRODUCTION

The concept of an "exorcism" often involves the expulsion or removal of a spirit, demon, or other entity that is inhabiting a body, object, or additional physical space where it does not belong or is otherwise unwelcome. The removal can be conducted through the use of special talismans, prayers, or rituals aimed

DOI: 10.4018/978-1-7998-9644-9.ch013

at removing the unwanted element. Other invocations can be used to protect and repel negative forces through directed intent (Miller, 2006). Usually, this would invoke a state of peace and harmony within the original space, object, or body that was affected. How then does all this talk of exorcisms relate to data? More precisely, what do we mean by a "digital data exorcism"? Indeed, the aim is to examine digital artifacts and the potential for the immediate removal of content (otherwise referred to as a "digital exorcism"). Like an exorcism whose aim is to remove an unwanted negative spirit, a digital exorcism aims to remove the potential harm caused by unwanted data. The goal here is still to invoke peace and harmony as part of the final wishes of the user who generated the data or is described by such data. Consider that email, chat logs, social media posts, and other technological interactions inevitably construct a narrative of our life events (Mitra, 2010), particularly if such use is over prolonged periods of our life. When we die, this content is what is left behind representing many aspects of our life. Just on Facebook alone, some projections estimate 4.9 billion users or more will die by the year of 2100 (assuming a continued rate of growth) which would leave an enormous amount of data behind by deceased users (Öhman & Watson, 2019). This is also true for technologies users interact with while in an educational setting, where massive data sets would include information about the deceased.

All these interactions with technology leave a digital trail and become (intentionally or unintentionally) part of the online legacy one leaves behind when one dies. It is not a matter of if a person dies, but a matter of when a person dies. The Latin phrase *Memento Mori* comes to mind as we must all "remember" death and that one day we all will die. However, it is a bit more complicated when it comes to our data, as much of the information continues to exist as extensions of ourselves long after we are gone. It is a topic that most people want to forget about and not tackle in an effort of avoidance. There are long-term implications of our data as there is a significant amount of it that we leave behind when we die and continue on afterward as part of our digital afterlife (Wright, 2014, Braman, Dudley, Vincenti, 2011). A data exorcism can be seen as the needed process for removing or expelling data. Instead of the traditional sense of an exorcism, we envision the need for the forcible expulsion of data (conducted purposefully) to protect those from which it was derived. Many forms of data will be discussed in this chapter; however, the focus will be on educational records related to end-of-life considerations. The central theme of this chapter is that facet that *we have the right to be forgotten*. Therefore, we have the right to be *deleted* or, in other words, "exorcised" from the various systems in which our data resides.

The massive amount of data available today has opened an unprecedented opportunity for analysis and interpretation to improve our understanding of students, faculty, and school performance in the realm of higher education. Some of this recorded data is essential for regular record-keeping purposes (such as grades, transcripts, courses histories, and more), but other data is useful for pedagogical improvements. Other data is helpful for administrative purposes in predictive models and classification of possible student outcomes (Kumar & Vijayalakshmi, 2012). Analysis of student data can also be valuable to improve student success metrics when used to make improvements to courses or assignments. As more students, faculty, and administrators interact with school-related programs and learning management systems, increasing volumes of data can be collected and retained on a growing subset of the general population.

Consider the many years that a student is engaged within the educational system. In the United States, students would typically spend twelve years in the educational system following kindergarten. This time period would include attending the first grade until graduation in grade twelve. This number can be extended if one counts kindergarten or if a student is compelled to repeat a grade. In some states, a student can legally "drop out" of school at the age of sixteen, thus reducing the amount of time in the school system. According to a 2019 report, 28.1% of the population in the United States noted that a High

School diploma (or equivalent) was the highest level of educational attainment (U.S. Census Bureau, 2020). Suppose we include those that attempted some college courses (but never graduated) and those that continue their education to earn an associate degree, certificates, credentialing, or higher. In that case, the number of years spent in education is much higher.

Another aspect is the records themselves that these many years spent interacting with the educational systems create. It is not simply academic records that are stored, but financial information, disciplinary notes, interactions with parents, emails, paperwork for registration, and much more. Assignments submitted electronically in an LMS (or those on paper) could be stored for quite some time without the student's knowledge. Consider times when you may have been searching online for a topic and stumbled across a website project or hosted report uploaded by a high school or college student that was indexed by a search engine? With any type of record, there must be some discussion regarding its storage, how it may be used to make other decisions (as being part of some data analysis or comparison), the privacy and protection of the content, and consideration of ownership and use after the user has died. In this chapter, we discuss these aspects in relation to educational-related content.

Examining Educational Records

There are many factors that must be considered when it comes to student records. An educational record can contain a student ID, grades, rosters, disciplinary information, financial, and other information that is maintained in some format (electronic or otherwise) by a school system. In the United States, these types of documents would be protected under The Family Educational Rights and Privacy Act (FERPA). A discussion of the protections of such data will be addressed later. Records can be considered as any documentary materials, be in any format, transferred or received, those systematically preserved, whether it be administrative or academic in nature (Onwudebelu, Fasola, Williams, 2013). Duranti (2009) notes that a digital record must have the following characteristics: 1) an identifiable context; 2) an originator; 3) an action, in which the record participates or which the record supports either procedurally or as part of the decision-making process; 4) explicit linkages to other records within or outside the digital system 5) a fixed form; and 6) stable content.

For this chapter, we expand this definition to consider any record that is generated by the student, about the student, or aggregate data that the student may be part of the originating record. We also see these records as those maintained on paper, electronically, image or voice. As an example, consider an LMS that records the length of time, IP address, click-through data as students browse course content as they are studying and completing assignments. We would view this data as part of a student's education record. Although some of the derived content would not be protected under FERPA, it still has importance for the purposes of this chapter. For example, Koffi identified several key components of transcript records in French-speaking universities, including course listing, grade point average (GPA), the grade scale, official logo or motto, official university seal, and signature of a university official (Koffi, 2006). Although this specific format may not fit all academic institutions, it highlights several key components that are universally similar across institutions and potential differences in record formats. Records can also document contractual relationships between students and the institution (like financial information, including awards, academic progress, or documentation of services provided to students such as accommodations, counseling services, library support, career services, medical information, and more (Azameti & Adjei, 2014).

Consider records when students transfer from one academic institution to the next. This transfer could be due to various reasons such as a move to a new location, change of major, change in a degree program, or other causes. When a student changes regions and moves to a new country and attempts to transfer their transcript to an institution that uses a different system or one that is in another language, challenges arise. Translating records from one language to another brings about challenges such as dealing with other formats, untranslatable elements, grade computation, academic distinctions, degree equivalencies, and professional ethics (Koffi, 2006). These changes and conversions from one system to another may cause duplication of records. How are these shard accounts maintained if a student does transfer to another system? Hopefully, the system allows for specific content to be flagged or noted.

In other cases, students may have additional information stored across various databases where data may not be collected by the academic institution but still related and tied to the student and their academic performance, such as the NCAA Clearinghouse as an example. The aim here is to determine the eligibility of students to compete in collegiate sports. A high school student would need to submit content to this clearinghouse, including specific test scores and transcripts (Perry, 2005). As institutions develop more interactive content, more information can therefore be saved. These can include test scores and interactions used to assess student engagement and to make improvements. Online educational tools can be used to analyze student learning and behaviors better and to make recommendations. As more institutions explore ebook systems in courses (Clements & Braman, 2021), even more systems can retain potential student information such as books read, used, notes, and bookmarks.

In general, records should exhibit the following characteristics: complete if they are kept regularly, accurate, retrievable, usable, and supported by original documentation (Onwudebelu *et al.*, 2013). Despite the many benefits that technology has made in terms of record-keeping, including preservation, transport, communication, and storage, there is an increased potential for loss of privacy. Maintenance of student records are essential to (Azameti & Adjei, 2014):

- Manage relationships between the institution and the student;
- Provide support and other services and facilities to the student;
- Controlling student academic progress and measuring achievement, both at the institution and subsequently;
- Provide support to the student after they leave the institution

Keeping and preservation of records will become easier as technology drives innovation. With the increased number of documents and their diversity in formats, the complexity of maintenance will become both more difficult and essential. The preservation and storage of these records and their security will need to be prioritized. Keeping these characteristics in mind for the long-term storage of these records will ensure that they can be maintained in a way that they are used properly and potentially able to be marked for destruction.

As the idea of a "digital data exorcism" is based on the theme of having the right to be forgotten, data retention policies need to be examined when it comes to educational records. What are the data retention policies for academic institutions, vendors, faculty, and electronic systems? The educational sector produces an enormous amount of data in numerous formats. This data can consist of information not only about students, but faculty, administration, school performance, and other metrics. In the next section, we discuss how educational content stored in these records can be used by institutions for the purposes of data mining.

Data Mining of Educational Content

Data mining involves the indirect gathering of personal information through an analysis of implicit patterns discoverable in data. Data mining activities can generate new and sometimes non-obvious classifications or categories (Tavani, 2020). In an education context, this can be very useful in determining patterns in a student's data in determining success, strengths and weakness, aptitude, academic level, and more. Through the use of data mining algorithms and techniques, data can be explored that reveal factors that influence students' performance. Saa, Al-Emran, and Shaalan (2018) examined several such factors through an in-depth literature review that explored items such as demographics, e-learning activity within the LMS, instructor attributes, access, school, chat, course style, course assessments, schedules, time, clicks, and much more. Multiple data points can be used to examine trends, make predictions, and analyze student achievement. Student data can also be combined with feedback from surveys and other metrics to gauge how attitudes and behaviors impact student learning (Akey, 2006).

Using past student records for decision-making processes is not new. Research from Boli *et al.* noted several years ago that there were cases where Universities used data from students to make informed choices rather than going by the conventional wisdom of the faculty or informed guesses (Boli, Katchadourian & Mahoney, 1988). This included majors, course selection, classroom performance, class sizes, and many other trends. As record-keeping has become more digital in nature, more detail can be obtained, analyzed, and stored. With all of these digital options, there is great potential for data mining as well as other considerations. The use of analytics and data mining continues to be an emerging and evolving area leading to many improvements. Studies that show how educational and institutional data mining and analysis can be used to support decision making related to student performance and making informed managerial decisions based on the discoveries in order to make improvements (Durairaj & Vijitha, 2014; Daud, Aljohani, Abbasi, Lytras, Abbas, Alowibdi, 2017, Shahiri & Husain, 2015).

Pros of data mining:

1. The majority of personal data collection and usage from data mining is considered to be public data.
2. Patterns from data mining can point to 'new' facts, relationships, or associations about students.

Cons of data mining:

1. Current privacy laws offer individuals no protection regarding information about them that is acquired through data-mining activities and is subsequently used.
2. Important decisions can be made about those individuals based on the patterns found in the mined personal data.

In addition, data mining techniques can be very helpful in keeping educational records updated. Automated processes can be in place to flag records or relationships between records to be verified after a prescribed time period has passed. Another area where data mining is helpful is the identification of students whose records are no longer viable in the system. Missing data in the records can be problematic. Not only can this lead to fragmentation or lost information, but errors or bias can occur in any derived data. It would seem normal that paper records would degrade over time. Problems could also occur in older digital records if the content is not backed up, destroyed, corrupted, or saved in an incompatible format. There has been research related to missing data for educational records using various algorithms for data imputation (Jove et al., 2020). This is based on Markov chain methods and other hybrid techniques.

As data storage and backup become less expensive, it is becoming easier to retain large data sets and more tempting to retain this material as it may later become useful in some form. Once the data is destroyed, then there would be no way to know if it would have been useful to retain it. Institutions may lean towards keeping as much information as possible just in case it is needed in the future. However, the long-term consideration of educational-related data needs to be considered, particularly if it is of a sensitive nature. Policies need to strengthen the security of the records but also limit access. Policies should be in place to that ensure that records are used and handled consistently (Azameti & Adjei, 2014):

- Records relating to an individual student are complete, accurate, and up to date;
- Duplication of student data is deliberate rather than uncontrolled and kept to the minimum needed to support effective administration;
- Records are held and stored securely to prevent unauthorized access;
- Records related to the academic aspect of the student are segregated from other aspects such as financial, disciplinary, social, support, etc.

Some additional questions which are related to student records include 1) How long should this data be kept? 2) How long will this data be relevant or potentially useful? 3) Who owns it? And 4) Should this data be purged after a period of time? Indeed, some data will always need to be kept, such as who graduated and when, but other data should be destroyed and purged when possible since it is unknown how long student records may be used for data mining purposes. Should an institution have the right to use such data for many years in an effort to predict trends, examine test scores, create predictive models, or more? This ability would be extremely valuable to an institution as they would have more data as it is recorded over time.

Privacy and Security of Educational Data Records

The privacy and security of educational data are a major cause of concern today. The University of California Global Information Industry defines "information" as any flow of data delivered to people. This data can be in any form. An organization must find ways to protect its data. It must ensure that data can be used for operational reasons (Grama, 2015). This definition of information adequately applies to educational institutions and organizations, considering how this data is used, stored, and transported. Educational institutions and organizations have the same responsibilities and accountability for their data collection, storage, retrieval, and management processes. Educational institutions have long been required to protect the privacy and security of their students. Online data and information regarding privacy and security issues are further complicated when questions arise regarding the personal data of the deceased.

Understanding Privacy Laws

The concept of privacy is vague in its definition and understanding when it comes to online information and data. In American culture, the practice and interpretation of privacy is seen as an individual's right. Often this right to privacy is assumed for all types of educational content, but this is not always the case.

Table 1. Amendments and Privacy

Amendment I	Privacy of Beliefs
Amendment III	Privacy of the Home
Amendment IV	Privacy of Person and Possessions
Amendment IX	More General Protection of Privacy?
Amendment XIV	Liberty Clause

The right to privacy is not mentioned in the Constitution per se. However, the Supreme Court has used several amendments to support the basis of privacy. The Fourth Amendment is used extensively in online privacy cases: *...the right of the people to be secure in their persons, houses, papers, and effects, against unreasonable searches and seizures, shall not be violated, and no Warrants shall issue, but upon probable cause, supported by Oath or affirmation.*

The following amendments also have been used regarding 'privacy' issues (Linder, 2021):

An important privacy law regarding educational institutions is The Family Educational Rights and Privacy Act (FERPA). This act was passed by Congress in 1974. The focus of FERPA is the privacy protection of students' educational records. Parents of students can review the records until the student reaches the age of consent (age 18). When the student reaches the age of 18, the right to access and consent will be turned over to the student. *"FERPA has four main requirements: Annual notification, access to education records, amendment of education records and disclosure of education records"* (Grama, p. 137, 2015).

Privacy can also be viewed as the antithesis of security. One view is that to have security (or protection), the violation of some privacy rights is secondary and warranted. Another view is that privacy and security complement each other. *In contrast, privacy encompasses people's right to have control of their personal data. Privacy means that a person has the right to specify how that data is collected, used, and shared. Information security practices are used to make sure that a person's privacy decisions are respected (Grama, p. 88, 2015).*

After reviewing the general view and focus of 'privacy' in our laws, there are no specifics as to the rights of the deceased individual privacy rights. This leaves a vacuum in policies regarding information and data belonging to the dead.

What are the Security Responsibilities of Educational Institutions?

To protect children's access and exposure to certain online content, there are current laws in place. The following chart indicates some of these laws:

Educational institutions are mandated by the federal government to provide security measures, oversight, and reporting of their data and records. Congress created the Federal Information Security Management Act (FISMA) to protect federal data and IT resources. All U.S. federal agencies must comply with this law. FISMA ensures that all federal institutions are maintaining security protocols of their data, records, and information. Security measures include the protection of the confidentiality, integrity, and availability (often referred to as the C-I-A triad) of that data. Confidentiality protection ensures that only persons with the proper credentials can obtain access to the IT system. Integrity is the oversight of the accuracy of the data and the IT system. Availability is the oversight of the proper functioning of the

Table 2. Listing of Some Laws Protecting Children

The Children's Online Privacy Protection Act (COPPA)	**Regulates how children's information is collected and used on library and school computers;**
The Children's Internet Protection Act (CIPA)	**Protects children from obscene, extreme violent, etc. online content;**
The Family Educational and Privacy Act (FERPA)	**Oversees the privacy rights of students and their educational data and records;**

IT system. Basic security concepts include vulnerabilities, threats, and risks. Educational institutions must report annually to FISMA regarding the security protocols of the storage, management, access, and processes of the data and information.

To make sure that all security protocols are being met and to report any failures, an IT systems auditor is crucial. The system auditor's role includes, but not limited, to the following activities/actions:

To make sure there is compliance with laws, regulations, and standards.
To make sure there is the availability of information and data on a continuous basis.
To make sure of the integrity and confidentiality of information and sensitive data while stored in transit.
To establish security awareness programs: Important for an IS auditor to evaluate the effectiveness of various security programs. Interaction and interviews with employees will help to evaluate the state of awareness of information security requirements. (Kim & Solomon, 2012)

Records After End of Life

Building on the numerous topics discussed in this chapter, it begs the question as to why we should care about all these educational records and data in terms of a student's final wishes? However, the final wishes are an important factor to consider in determining what to do with a user's data. A significant yet often overlooked element is the human element of death and loss of the user or originator of the data. In the context of educational content, one needs to consider data retention policies that have prescribed time limits or limited use in the event of a student's death. These could be records of students that have been stored in the system after many years (and therefore may be stale), or these records could be of a current student that has died suddenly. There is a sufficient need for death management to be included as a design factor in information systems as more and more data is stored and recorded. COVID-19, for instance, has certainly made this apparent as many people have died since 2020 from the virus and its complications that otherwise would still be alive and interacting with these systems. A recent example of the importance of keeping the information of deceased students updated and secured was reported in a news segment. In this news report, a former high school principal stated that in 2016 she reported, during an audit, that there were enrollment issues, which included five dead students that were currently enrolled on the school's roster (Papst, 2021).

Although not student records, but still educational related, records that include faculty notes and research data that is unpublished or unknown to others or where the final wishes are unknown. Without knowing the owner's final wishes, this data may go unnoticed, be inaccessible, or perhaps should be marked for destruction. We should be asking several questions in terms of records after the end of a user's life such as:

- What are the specific final wishes of the user regarding educational records?
- What are the implications related to the end of life of students?
- How does recently deceased students vs. former student that die years later after graduation factor in?
- Should students and parents have more control of their data and privacy?

As data breaches are becoming common for many types of records and accounts, security is an increasing concern. Many accounts involve a wealth of information, in which the deceased are still susceptible, particularly for identity theft. This is also true in the realm of education. Consider that when dealing with social media, email or other online accounts, companies often notify current users of compromised accounts or other security concerns and send notifications to reset passwords. However, the accounts of the deceased cannot act on these notifications. Family and friends of the deceased most likely will not receive these notifications on their behalf or even realize what accounts the deceased had active before their death. What data then was compromised and what steps could be made to protect this information? It is also possible that the data contained in the breach could impact the living in unknown ways. These accounts are still technically active and compromised, and the deceased user cannot monitor or take corrective security actions to repair the issue. There may be other information that would be useful to hackers such as data stored in the cloud, particularly in accounts that remain active and unmonitored. Similar to information that can be reconstructed from obtaining data printed on documents through "dumpster diving," discarded electronic devices of the deceased should also be presumed to contain sensitive data. What data could be gained from discarded wearable devices, cell phones, tablets, cameras and more? Family members or those dealing with the person's estate that are managing the items may not realize its importance and discard potentially sensitive items that contain information of concern. Were there passwords for sensitive accounts saved on a spreadsheet that was discarded? There is a growing importance of considering some type of death management as part of computer services. Particularly useful would be a systematic "dead man's switch" that automatically flags and deactivates all accounts and profiles associated with the deceased.

Similarly, having the ability to quickly flag the accounts of students to mark them as deceased would be beneficial, even if the person has graduated some time ago. Of course, a currently enrolled student would need to be flagged as soon as possible. Increasingly as part of a will, information about a person's final wishes is being recorded. One major reason that denoting a record as being representative of a deceased user is due to security and privacy concerns of the content. More specifically concerning is the time between the person's death and public knowledge or official notification that the person has died. We refer to this transitional time and the related security concerns as Transitional Weakness. Our previous work described four states of being related to death, as viewed in Figure 1 below (Braman, Dudley, Vincenti, 2011). This figure not only describes various states of a person and the state of their content but highlights issues for the transition time between one type to the next. In Figure 1, "virtual life" is representative of computer-created content, virtual spaces, and online environments related to records and various accounts.

Type A represents users who are physically alive and maintain an active presence in an online platform or environment. Type B represents users who are alive, but who do not have a presence in an online platform. Type C users are those who have physically died but have an "active" virtual memorial, social networking site, or record that still makes them appear as being alive. Type D users represent those that have died and have no online presence or active records. The online persona of a Type D user

Figure 1. Four States of Being

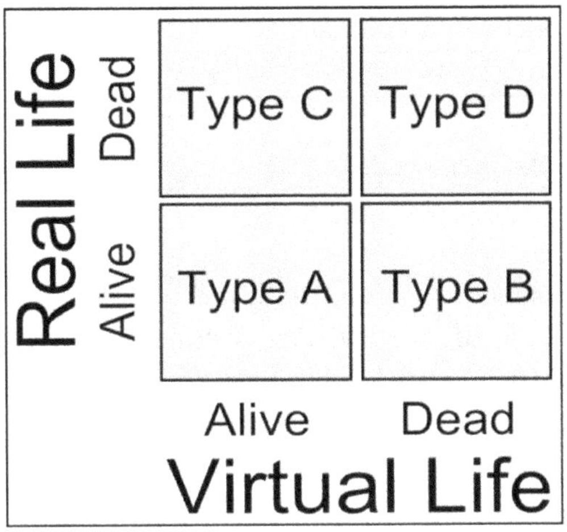

could have been erased after their death (based on their final wishes). There is a time period where the deceased's data is more vulnerable. This temporal transition period in the states of being can be problematic. Essentially this attack window comprises the time period in which it is not known that the user is deceased, opening several vulnerabilities. For instance, the accounts of the deceased are still active with an expectation that there will still be activity. Therefore, unauthorized access and use of the account might not be detected for some time. This attack window also includes the time when family and friends know that the person is deceased, but due to their grief, may not be actively monitoring certain account information. Although for some, these accounts may be visited much more often during this time. It may take a significant amount of time to identify what accounts and information the now deceased stored online or kept in some digital format.

Consider the scenario using social media where a distant friend might not know that their friend has died. Perhaps their death was only a day or so ago (or even longer in some cases), and news of the death is not well known. Perhaps the friend lives far away and has limited contact with others that are close to the deceased. If the deceased's profile becomes compromised by an attacker, they could then send messages to everyone connected to the user asking for information or financial "assistance" relying on the relationship between the friend and the deceased. The friend may have no reason to question the request. Until the death is known and the deceased's profile transitions from Type A to Type C for instance, there are vulnerabilities. More research is needed regarding these transitions, timing, and ways to protect content in these situations.

Feedback on Deleted Content

In several previous studies, we asked groups of students questions related to death, grief, and social networks. As part of the research, several questions were related to seeking specific feedback on their final wishes related to their digital content. The majority of the participants in all the studies had not thought about or considered their digital content if they were to die. Although many of the questions were aimed at gaining feedback on social networks, many of the questions are helpful for the discussion in this chapter. In this section, we present the feedback from a few selected questions from 140 participants from

Table 3. Summary of Final Wishes

Option Choices for Content	Frequency (n=140)
A. Deleted	51 (36.4%)
B. Preserved with Restrictions	67 (47.9%)
C. Remain the Same (where anything could happen with access)	22 (15.7%)

previous research (Braman, Thomas, Vincenti, Dudley, & Rodgers, 2013; Braman, Vincenti, Dudley, Wang, Rodgers, & Thomas, 2013; Braman, Dudley, & Vincenti, 2017; Braman, Dudley, & Vincenti, 2018). This is the first time any of the data has been reported in aggregate.

The surveys used were deployed in various courses at a large metropolitan university and at a community college over the years 2013 - 2014 and 2017 - 2018. Combining the information from the four surveys, there were a total of 140 participants. The average age for all the respondents was 21.5 years old. There was a wide range of declared majors which included Computer Science, Information Technology, Engineering, Biology, Physics, Chemistry, Business, English, Exercise Science, Deaf Studies, Sports Management, Psychology, Pre-nursing, and Electronic Media and Film, or General Studies. Several participants noted that their major was currently unknown or undeclared. In the questionnaire, we asked, "After your death would you want your digital content to be deleted, preserved with some restrictions, or remain the same (where anything could happen in terms of access or preservation)?" The results from this question are summarized in Table 3 below.

In three of the surveys, we asked, "Are there files or content that you would want erased so no one would know about them?" (This could be content on a social networking site, platform, or other computer device).

Table 4. Content to be erased

Choice	Frequency (n=112)
A. Yes	39 (34.8%)
B. No	73 (65.2%)

We also asked participants to generalize what type of content that they would want to be erased when they died. This is assuming that there was some automated way to do this, or if they had given the rights to someone to carry this out and had made their final wishes known. The following content is what was noted by the participants:

- chat logs
- messages
- personal information
- internet history
- credit card information
- emails

- address information
- pictures
- social media data/posts
- tax information
- status updates

Also, worth mentioning here are a few comments from the participants. Here they were allowed to make any additional final comments about the survey. These comments included:

- "I think that it is important to protect one's virtual information after death and more information should be available on this topic."
- "Very interesting, never really thought about it until now!"
- "It's in one's own interest that should decide what happens to their online accounts and information after death."
- "I think it's more important for financial information to be protected online after one's death."
- "I think that this topic will be increasingly relevant throughout the next decade."

In previous research, we have proposed several key questions that one can use to assess content as they are posting or storing content online which include: 1) Is this content something I'm alright with if it becomes part of my digital legacy? 2) Is this content something that should be protected if something were to happen to me? and 3) If this content should be protected, how can it be protected? (Braman, Thomas, Vincenti, Dudley, Rodgers, 2013). Some information, and some social media posts, can have negative effects causing feelings of regret after certain content has been posted, particularly if the content is very personal. This could be particularly troublesome if content becomes part of someone's digital legacy and content is taken out of context. Also, one should consider posts that may be viewed by unintended audiences (Wang, Norcie, Komanduri, Acquisti, Leon, Cranor, 2011). All this data has the potential to be analyzed and used in various ways.

CONCLUSION AND FUTURE WORK

As mentioned earlier, the Latin phrase *Memento Mori* serves as a reminder of death and that one day we all will die. Although this phrase pops up in art and literature in various forms or as a label to describe a symbol of death, this ideology should carry over into our digital lives. We can say that the field of thanatechnology is any technology that "Include[s] all types of communication technology that can be used in the provision of death education, grief counseling, and thanatology research" (Solfka, 2012, p. 33). Technology has influenced how we deal with and interact with death in many new and profound ways. It is our desire that thanatechnology and various aspects of the potential of death be considered in the design of computer technology. There is a great amount of research that is still needed in this field as new issues and problems are arising. This will be certainly true as educational institutions continue to collect data and analyze its contents.

As the wealth, depth and invasiveness of educational records continue to grow, so too does the need to protect such content. If it is the final wish of a student (user) to have their educational records purged or removed upon their death, there should exist the ability to do so. At the very least, the data should be able to be made disaggregated. Educational institutions have this wealth of valuable hidden data (Baradwaj & Pal, 2012). This wealth of data needs to be better addressed in terms of the ability to have the data removed. Although there are some technologies that could potentially address and deal with these issues, there is a lot of research that is needed. An interesting development in terms of record-keeping is use of blockchain technology. Using the blockchain, certain types of data can be kept and maintained in a way that ensures its integrity and availability for future use. Life-long documentation of learning activities and achievements can be stored securely as immutable and verifiable records as part of the blockchain (Gräthe, Kolvenbach, Ruland, Schütte, Torres, & Wendland, 2018; Ocheja, Flanagan, Ueda & Ogata, 2019). Although some content would become public, there are certainly some tradeoffs in doing so. The blockchain would allow the maintainability of records in a decentralized way but would allow data related to the accounts of the deceased to be flagged very quickly and across all systems. Using blockchain technology would allow for the ability to opt-out of learning activity tracking and allow parents of underage students or the learners themselves the right to manage aspects of their record (Ocheja, Flanagan, Ueda & Ogata, 2019). Ocheja et. Al., propose as an example, a specific blockchain in their research titled blockchain of learning logs (BOLL) that would allow records to be connected across various institutions mainly addressing the problem of interoperability and transfer. As part of our future work, we intend to investigate this technology in the context of death and the execution of wills and protection or deletion of records of the deceased.

The information presented in this chapter is an extension of the authors' previous works in the area of thanatechnology. We aim to expand our investigations into the digital data of the deceased users pertaining to educational records and in other areas as well. Studies that focus on the information on the death of the user (online and offline) are still limited because of the lack of research in this area. As more institutions and businesses start to experience an increase in deceased users listed in their systems, the number of these records will continue to grow. It is vital that the educational sector look closely at ways to integrate the ability to delete data at the user's request, or at the least disaggregate information if it is still needed an analysis. It is our hope that there are many more options in the future and this problem is better understood and considered.

In conclusion, we have discussed the concept of a digital data "exorcism where the aim is to remove unwanted data in an effort of privacy and in executing a person's final wishes when it comes to managing their digital content. Just as in a spiritual exorcism where a negative spirit is removed, a digital exorcism is aimed at removing the potential harm caused by unwanted data. Considering all of the many interactions we have with technology over our lifetime where various data points are saved and maintained, we inevitably construct a narrative of our life events. In this chapter, we have focused on educational records and the need for the ability to be to delete content if that is the final wishes of a deceased individual. Just as more awareness has been made in designing systems for the inevitable death of users, so too does this consideration need to be made to protect education records from long-term storage and datamining of the content for ongoing research or usage by the managing institution. The main theme of this chapter is that facet that *we have the right to be forgotten*. The right to be *deleted* or, in other words, "exorcised" from the systems in which our data resides if that is our final wish.

REFERENCES

Akey, T. M. (2006). *School Context, Student Attitudes and Behavior, and Academic Achievement: An Exploratory Analysis*. MDRC.

Azameti, M. S., & Adjei, E. (2014). *A Conceptual Framework Explaining the Impacts of misconducts Associated with Academic Records Creation and Management Practices in Tertiary Institutions*. Academic Press.

Baradwaj, B. K., & Pal, S. (2012). *Mining educational data to analyze students' performance*. arXiv preprint arXiv:1201.3417

Boli, J., Katchadourian, H., & Mahoney, S. (1988). Analyzing academic records for informed administration: The Stanford curriculum study. *The Journal of Higher Education*, *59*(1), 54–68. doi:10.1080/00221546.1988.11778304

Braman, J., Dudley, A., & Vincenti, G. (2018). Designing SADD: A Social Media Agent for the Detection of the Deceased. *Proceedings of the 20th HCI International Conference on Online Communities and Social Computing*. 10.1007/978-3-319-91485-5_26

Braman, J., Dudley, A., & Vincenti, G. (2017). Memorializing the Deceased using Virtual Worlds: A Preliminary Study. *Proceedings of the 19th HCI International Conference on Online Communities and Social Computing*. 10.1007/978-3-319-58562-8_5

Braman, J., Dudley, A., & Vincenti, G. (2011). Death, Social Networks and Virtual Worlds: A Look into the Digital Afterlife. *Proceedings of the 9th International Conference on Software Engineering Research, Management and Applications (SERA 2011)*. 10.1109/SERA.2011.35

Braman, J., Thomas, U., Vincenti, G., Dudley, A., & Rodgers, K. (2013). Preparing your Digital Legacy: Assessing Awareness of Digital Natives. In G. Mallia (Ed.), The Social Classroom: Integrating Social Network Use in Education. Academic Press.

Braman, J., Vincenti, G., Dudley, A., Wang, Y., Rodgers, K., & Thomas, U. (2013). Teaching about the Impacts of Social Networks: An End of Life Perspective. *Proceedings of the 15th HCI International Conference on Online Communities and Social Computing*. 10.1007/978-3-642-39371-6_28

Clements, M., & Braman, J. (2021). Exploring Factors of an Inclusive Textbook Access Program in Computer Technology Courses. In G. Meiselwitz (Ed.), Lecture Notes in Computer Science: Vol. 12775. *Social Computing and Social Media: Applications in Marketing, Learning, and Health. HCII 2021*. Springer. doi:10.1007/978-3-030-77685-5_15

Daud, A., Aljohani, N. R., Abbasi, R. A., Lytras, M. D., Abbas, F., & Alowibdi, J. S. (2017, April). Predicting student performance using advanced learning analytics. In *Proceedings of the 26th international conference on world wide web companion* (pp. 415-421). 10.1145/3041021.3054164

Duranti, L. (2009). From digital diplomatics to digital records forensics. *Archivaria*, 39–66.

Durairaj, M., & Vijitha, C. (2014). Educational data mining for prediction of student performance using clustering algorithms. *International Journal of Computer Science and Information Technologies*, *5*(4), 5987–5991.

Grama, J. L. (2015). *Legal Issues in Information Security*. Jones & Bartlett.

Gräther, W., Kolvenbach, S., Ruland, R., Schütte, J., Torres, C., & Wendland, F. (2018). Blockchain for education: lifelong learning passport. *Proceedings of 1st ERCIM Blockchain workshop 2018. European Society for Socially Embedded Technologies (EUSSET)*.

Jove, E., Blanco-Rodríguez, P., Casteleiro-Roca, J. L., Quintián, H., Moreno Arboleda, F. J., LóPez-Vázquez, J. A., Rodríguez-Gómez, B. A., Meizoso-López, M. D. C., Piñón-Pazos, A., De Cos Juez, F. J., Cho, S.-B., & Calvo-Rolle, J. L. (2020). Missing data imputation over academic records of electrical engineering students. *Logic Journal of the IGPL*, *28*(4), 487–501. doi:10.1093/jigpal/jzz056

Kim, D., & Solomon, M. G. (2012). *Fundamentals of Information Security: Information Systems Security & Assurance Series*. Jones & Bartlett.

Koffi, E. (2006). *The challenges of translation academic records*. The ATA Chronicle.

Kumar, S., & Vijayalakshmi, M. (2012). Mining of student academic evaluation records in higher education. *International Conference on Recent Advances in Computing and Software Systems*, 67-70. 10.1109/RACSS.2012.6212699

Linder, D. (2021). *The right of privacy*. Retrieved from: http://law2.umkc.edu/faculty/projects/ftrials/conlaw/rightofprivacy.html

Miller, J. (2006). *Protection Reversal Magick: A Witch's Defense Manual*. New Page Books.

Mitra, A. (2010). Creating a Presence on Social Networks via Narbs. *Global Media Journal*, (9), 16.

Ocheja, P., Flanagan, B., Ueda, H., & Ogata, H. (2019). Managing lifelong learning records through blockchain. *Research and Practice in Technology Enhanced Learning*, *14*(1), 1–19. doi:10.118641039-019-0097-0

Öhman, C. J., & Watson, D. (2019). Are the dead taking over Facebook? A Big Data approach to the future of death online. *Big Data & Society*, *6*(1). doi:10.1177/2053951719842540

Onwudebelu, U., Fasola, S., & Williams, E. O. (2013). Creating Pathway for Enhancing Student Collection of Academic Records in Nigeria-a New Direction. *Computer Science and Information Technology*, *1*(1), 65–71. doi:10.13189/csit.2013.010108

Papst, C. (2021). *Bombshell allegations at another Ciry school – Dead students enrolled, Classes didn't exist*. Fox 45 News. https://foxbaltimore.com/news/project-baltimore/dead-students-enrolled-classes-didnt-exist-baltimore-school

Perry, J. (2005). *Privacy and Student Records An Analysis of the NCAA Clearinghouse in Relation to FERPA*. Retrieved from: http://www.c3schools.org/CourseInfo/educ473/james_educ_final_698v.pdf

Saa, A. A., Al-Emran, M., & Shaalan, K. (2019, March). Mining student information system records to predict students' academic performance. In *International conference on advanced machine learning technologies and applications* (pp. 229-239). Springer.

Shahiri, A. M., Husain, W., & Rashid, N. A. (2015). A review on predicting student's performance using data mining techniques. *Procedia Computer Science*, *72*, 414–422. doi:10.1016/j.procs.2015.12.157

Sofka, C., Cupit, I., & Gilbert, K. (2012). *Dying, death, and grief in an online universe: For counselors and educators*. Springer Publishing Company.

Tavani, H. (2020). *Ethics and Technology: Controversies, Questions, and Strategies for Ethical Computing*. John Wiley & Sons.

U.S. Census Bureau. (2020). *U.S. Census Bureau Releases New Educational Attainment Data*. U.S. Census Bureau Releases New Educational Attainment Data.

Wang, Y., Norcie, G., Komanduri, S., Acquisti, A., Leon, P. G., & Cranor, L. F. (2011). I regretted the minute I pressed share: A qualitative study of regrets on Facebook. In *Proceedings of the Seventh Symposium on Usable Privacy and Security* (p. 10). ACM. 10.1145/2078827.2078841

Wright, N. (2014). Death and the Internet: The implications of the digital afterlife. *First Monday*. Advance online publication. doi:10.5210/fm.v19i6.4998

Compilation of References

Abelló, A., Darmont, J., Etcheverry, L., Golfarelli, M., Mazón, J., Naumann, F., Pedersen, T., Rizzi, S. B., Trujillo, J., Vassiliadis, P., & Vossen, G. (2013). Fusion Cubes: Towards Self-Service Business Intelligence. *International Journal of Data Warehousing and Mining*, *9*(2), 66–88. doi:10.4018/jdwm.2013040104

Acito, F., & Khatri, V. (2014). Business analytics: Why now and what next? *Business Horizons*, *57*(5), 565–570. doi:10.1016/j.bushor.2014.06.001

Acquisti, A., & Fong, C. (2020). An Experiment in Hiring Discrimination Via Online Social Networks. *Management Science*, *66*(3), 1005–1024. doi:10.1287/mnsc.2018.3269

Ajunwa, I., & Green, D. (2019). Platforms at Work. *Research in the Sociology of Work*, *33*, 61–91. doi:10.1108/S0277-283320190000033005

Akey, T. M. (2006). *School Context, Student Attitudes and Behavior, and Academic Achievement: An Exploratory Analysis*. MDRC.

Akhter, Z., Malik, G., & Plummer, V. (2021). Nurse educator knowledge, attitude and skills towards using high-fidelity simulation: A study in the vocational education sector. *Nurse Education in Practice*, *53*, 103048. Advance online publication. doi:10.1016/j.nepr.2021.103048 PMID:33857911

Aliaga, M., & Gunderson, B. (2003). *Interactive statistics*. Prentice Hall.

Ali, S., Wang, G., & Riaz, S. (2020). Aspect based sentiment analysis of ridesharing platform reviews for kansei engineering. *IEEE Access: Practical Innovations, Open Solutions*, *8*, 173186–173196. doi:10.1109/ACCESS.2020.3025823

Al-Mashraie, M., Chung, S. H., & Jeon, H. W. (2020). Learner switching behavior analysis in the telecommunication industry via push-pull-mooring framework: A machine learning approach. *Computers & Industrial Engineering*, *106476*. Advance online publication. doi:10.1016/j.cie.2020.106476

Alpar, P., & Schulz, M. (2016). Self-Service Business Intelligence. *Business & Information Systems Engineering*, *58*(2), 151–155. doi:10.100712599-016-0424-6

Al-Shahib, A., Breitling, R., & Gilbert, D. (2005). Feature selection and the class imbalance problem in predicting protein function from sequence. *Applied Bioinformatics*, *4*(3), 195–203. doi:10.2165/00822942-200504030-00004 PMID:16231961

American Educational Research Association, American Psychological Association, & National Council for Measurement in Education. (2014). Standards for educational and psychological testing. Author.

Amin, A., Hossain, I., Akther, A., & Alam, K. M. (2019). Bengali VADER: A Sentiment Analysis Approach Using Modified VADER. *2019 International Conference on Electrical, Computer and Communication Engineering (ECCE)*. 10.1109/ECACE.2019.8679144

Araque, O., Zhu, G., & Iglesias, C. A. (2019). A semantic similarity-based perspective of affect lexicons for sentiment analysis. *Knowledge-Based Systems*, *165*, 346–359. doi:10.1016/j.knosys.2018.12.005

Arnaboldi, M., Robbiani, A., & Carlucci, P. (2021). On the relevance of self-service business intelligence to university management. *Journal of Accounting & Organizational Change*, *17*(1), 5–22. doi:10.1108/JAOC-09-2020-0131

Arnold, T., & Tilton, L. (2015). *Humanities Data in R*. Springer. doi:10.1007/978-3-319-20702-5

Aslam, N., Ramay, W. Y., Kewen, X., & Sarwar, N. (2020). Convolutional Neural Network Based Classification of App Reviews. *IEEE Access: Practical Innovations, Open Solutions*, *8*, 1–1. doi:10.1109/ACCESS.2020.3029634

Avvisati, F. (2020). Large scale assessments in education. *IEA ETS Research Institute Journal*, *8*. Advance online publication. doi:10.118640536-020-00086-x

Azameti, M. S., & Adjei, E. (2014). *A Conceptual Framework Explaining the Impacts of misconducts Associated with Academic Records Creation and Management Practices in Tertiary Institutions*. Academic Press.

Azer, S. A. (2017, April). Top-Cited Articles in Problem-Based Learning: A Bibliometric Analysis and Quality of Evidence Assessment. *Journal of Dental Education*, *81*(4), 458–478. doi:10.21815/JDE.016.011 PMID:28365611

Bagozzi, R. P., & Foxall, G. R. (1996). Construct validation of a measure of adaptive-innovative cognitive styles in consumption. *International Journal of Research in Marketing*, *13*(3), 201–213. doi:10.1016/0167-8116(96)00010-9

Baker, R., Ocumpaugh, J., & Andres, A. (2018). BROMP Quantitative Field Observations: A Review. In R. Feldman (Ed.), Learning Science: Theory, Research, and Practice. Academic Press.

Bani-Hani, I., Pareigis, J., Tona, O., & Carlsson, S. (2018). A holistic view of value generation process in a SSBI environment: a service dominant logic perspective. *Journal of Decision Systems, 27*(sup1), 46-55. doi:10.1080/12460125.2018.1468155

Bani-Hani, I., Tona, O., & Carlsson, S. (2018). From an information consumer to an information author: A new approach to business intelligence. *Journal of Organizational Computing and Electronic Commerce*, *28*(2), 157–171. doi:10.1080/10919392.2018.1444358

Baradwaj, B. K., & Pal, S. (2012). *Mining educational data to analyze students' performance.* arXiv preprint arXiv:1201.3417

Barbu, A., She, Y., Ding, L., & Gramajo, G. (2016). Feature selection with annealing for computer vision and big data learning. *IEEE Transactions on Pattern Analysis and Machine Intelligence*, *39*(2), 272–286. doi:10.1109/TPAMI.2016.2544315 PMID:27019473

Barcena, E., Read, T., & Sedano, B. (2020). An Approximation to Inclusive Language in LMOOCs Based on Appraisal Theory. *Open Linguistics*, *6*(1), 38–67. doi:10.1515/opli-2020-0003

Barnabo, G., Leonardi, S., Fazzone, A., & Schwiegelsohn, C. (2019). Algorithms for Fair Team Formation in Online Labour Marketplaces. *WWW '19 Companion.*

Bartholomew, D. J., & Knott, M. (1999). *Latent Variable Models and Factor Analysis* (2nd ed.). Arnold.

Bartholomew, D. J., Steele, F., Moustaki, I., & Galbraith, J. I. (2002). *The Analysis and Interpretation of Multivariate Data for Social Scientists.* Chapman and Hall/CRC.

Baryla, E., Shelley, G., & Trainor, W. (2012). Transforming rubrics using factor analysis. *Practical Assessment, Research & Evaluation*, *17*, 4. Advance online publication. doi:10.7275/5nt2-g458

Basiri, M. E., Abdar, M., Cifci, M. A., Nemati, S., & Acharya, U. R. (2020). A novel method for sentiment classification of drug reviews using fusion of deep and machine learning techniques. *Knowledge-Based Systems, 198*, 105949. Advance online publication. doi:10.1016/j.knosys.2020.105949

Baumeister, R. F., Bratslavsky, E., Finkenauer, C., & Vohs, K. D. (2001). Bad is stronger than good. *Review of General Psychology, 5*(4), 323–370. doi:10.1037/1089-2680.5.4.323

Beaujean, A. A., & Benson, N. F. (2019). The one and the many: Enduring legacies of Spearman and Thurstone on Intelligence Test Score Interpretation. *Applied Measurement in Education, 32*(3), 198–215. doi:10.1080/08957347.2019.1619560

Behzad, G., Lappas, T., & Terzi, E. (2014). Profit-maximizing Cluster Hires. *KDD'14.*

Benjamin, R. (2019). *Race After Technology.* Polity Press.

Berry, M. W. (2004). *Survey of text mining* (Vol. 45). Springer. doi:10.1007/978-1-4757-4305-0

Berti, A., van Zelst, S. J., & van der Aalst, W. (2019). *Process mining for python (PM4Py): bridging the gap between process and data science.* arXiv preprint arXiv:1905.06169.

Berzinski, P. A., & Trajkovski, G. (2018). Future Trends in Global Online Learning. In H. Takooshian, U. P. Gielen, F. L. Denmark, & A. M. O'Roark (Eds.), *Visions and resources for international psychology: 75 years of the International Council of Psychologists* (pp. 232–241). Global Scholarly Publications.

Bhattacherjee, A., & Sanford, C. (2006). Influence processes for information technology acceptance: An elaboration likelihood model. *Management Information Systems Quarterly, 30*(4), 805–825. doi:10.2307/25148755

Bhaumik, U., & Yadav, D. K. (2021). Sentiment Analysis Using Twitter. In J. K. Mandal, I. Mukherjee, S. Bakshi, S. Chatterji, & P. K. Sa (Eds.), *Computational Intelligence and Machine Learning. Advances in Intelligent Systems and Computing* (Vol. 1276). Springer. doi:10.1007/978-981-15-8610-1_7

Bimba, A. T., Idris, N., Al-Hunaiyyan, A., Mahmud, R. B., & Shuib, N. L. B. M. (2017). Adaptive feedback in computer-based learning environments: A review. *Adaptive Behavior, 25*(5), 217–234. doi:10.1177/1059712317727590

Bishara, A. J., & Hittner, J. B. (2012). Testing the significance of a correlation with nonnormal data: Comparison of Pearson, Spearman, transformation, and resampling approaches. *Psychological Methods, 17*(3), 399–417. doi:10.1037/a0028087 PMID:22563845

Black, A. R., Doolittle, F., Zhu, P., Unterman, R., & Grossman, J. B. (2008). The evaluation of enhanced academic instruction in after-school programs: Findings after the first year of implementation (NCEE 2008-4021). National Center for Education Evaluation and Regional Assistance, Institute of Education Sciences, U.S. Department of Education.

Black, P., & Wiliam, D. (2009). Developing the theory of formative assessment. *Educational Assessment, Evaluation and Accountability, 21*(1), 5. doi:10.1007/s11092-008-9068-5

Blei, D. M., Ng, A. Y., & Jordan, M. I. (2003). Latent dirichlet allocation. *Journal of Machine Learning Research, 3*, 993–1022.

Bligh, D. A. (2000). *What's the use of lectures?* Jossey-Bass.

Blondel, V. D., Guillaume, J.-L., Lambiotte, R., & Lefebvre, E. (2008). Fast unfolding of communities in large networks. *Journal of Statistical Mechanics, 10*(10), 1–12. doi:10.1088/1742-5468/2008/10/P10008

Boli, J., Katchadourian, H., & Mahoney, S. (1988). Analyzing academic records for informed administration: The Stanford curriculum study. *The Journal of Higher Education, 59*(1), 54–68. doi:10.1080/00221546.1988.11778304

Bonsignore, K. (2013). Career ePortfolios. In K. Wills & R. Rice (Eds.), *ePortfolio Performance Support Systems*. The WAC Clearinghouse.

Boreham, N. (2004). A Theory of Collective Competence. *British Journal of Educational Studies*, *52*(1), 5–17. doi:10.1111/j.1467-8527.2004.00251.x

Borg, A., & Boldt, M. (2020). Using VADER Sentiment and SVM for Predicting Customer Response Sentiment. *Expert Systems with Applications*, *162*, 113746. Advance online publication. doi:10.1016/j.eswa.2020.113746

Boser, B. E., Vapnik, V. N., & Guyon, I. M. (1992). Training Algorithm Margin for Optimal Classifiers. *Perception*, 144–152.

Bø, T. H., & Jonassen, I. (2002). New feature subset selection procedures for classification of expression profiles. *Genome Biology*, *3*(4), 1–11. doi:10.1186/gb-2002-3-4-research0017 PMID:11983058

Boudett, K. P., City, E. A., & Murname, R. J. (2013). *Data Wise: A Step-by-Step Guide to Using Assessment Results to Improve Teaching and Learning*. Harvard Education Press.

Boulton, C. A., Kent, C., & Williams, H. T. (2018). Virtual learning environment engagement and learning outcomes at a 'bricks-and-mortar' university. *Computers & Education*, *126*, 129–142. doi:10.1016/j.compedu.2018.06.031

Bradstreet, T. E. (1996). Teaching introductory statistics courses so that nonstatisticians experience statistical reasoning. *The American Statistician*, *50*, 69–78.

Braman, J., & Dierbach, C. (2015). Utilizing Virtual Worlds for Personalized Search: Developing the PAsSIVE Framework. In Social Computing and Social Media (pp. 3-11). Springer International Publishing.

Braman, J., Thomas, U., Vincenti, G., Dudley, A., & Rodgers, K. (2013). Preparing your Digital Legacy: Assessing Awareness of Digital Natives. In G. Mallia (Ed.), The Social Classroom: Integrating Social Network Use in Education. Academic Press.

Braman, J., Dudley, A., & Vincenti, G. (2011). Death, Social Networks and Virtual Worlds: A Look into the Digital Afterlife. *Proceedings of the 9th International Conference on Software Engineering Research, Management and Applications (SERA 2011)*. 10.1109/SERA.2011.35

Braman, J., Dudley, A., & Vincenti, G. (2017). Memorializing the Deceased using Virtual Worlds: A Preliminary Study. *Proceedings of the 19th HCI International Conference on Online Communities and Social Computing*. 10.1007/978-3-319-58562-8_5

Braman, J., Dudley, A., & Vincenti, G. (2018). Designing SADD: A Social Media Agent for the Detection of the Deceased. *Proceedings of the 20th HCI International Conference on Online Communities and Social Computing*. 10.1007/978-3-319-91485-5_26

Braman, J., Vincenti, G., Dudley, A., Wang, Y., Rodgers, K., & Thomas, U. (2013). Teaching about the Impacts of Social Networks: An End of Life Perspective. *Proceedings of the 15th HCI International Conference on Online Communities and Social Computing*. 10.1007/978-3-642-39371-6_28

Branch, R. M., & Kopcha, T. J. (2014). Instructional design models. In J. Spector, M. Merrill, J. Elen, & M. Bishop (Eds.), *Handbook of research on educational communications and technology* (pp. 77–87). Springer. doi:10.1007/978-1-4614-3185-5_7

Bruns, A. (2018). Digital public spheres in Australia. In J. K. Schapals, A. Bruns, & B. McNair (Eds.), *Digitizing Democracy*. Routledge. doi:10.4324/9781351054867-14

Bryce, G. R. (2005). Developing tomorrow's statisticians. *Journal of Statistics Education: An International Journal on the Teaching and Learning of Statistics, 13*(1).

Burger, W., Burge, M. J., Burge, M. J., & Burge, M. J. (2009). *Principles of digital image processing*. Springer.

Burke, T. A., Jacobucci, R., Ammerman, B. A., Alloy, L. B., & Diamond, G. (2020). Using machine learning to classify suicide attempt history among youth in medical care settings. *Journal of Affective Disorders, 268*, 206–214. doi:10.1016/j.jad.2020.02.048 PMID:32174479

Burt, R. S. (2004). Structural Holes for Ideas. *American Journal of Sociology, 110*(2), 349–399. doi:10.1086/421787

Cabiddu, F., De Carlo, M., & Piccoli, G. (2014). Social media affordances: Enabling customer engagement. *Annals of Tourism Research, 48*, 175–192. doi:10.1016/j.annals.2014.06.003

Cacioppo, J. T., & Petty, R. E. (1982). The Need for Cognition. *Journal of Personality and Social Psychology, 42*(1), 116–131. doi:10.1037/0022-3514.42.1.116

Cacioppo, J. T., Petty, R. E., Kao, C. F., & Rodriguez, R. (1986). Central and peripheral routes to persuasion: An individual difference perspective. *Journal of Personality and Social Psychology, 51*(5), 1032–1043. doi:10.1037/0022-3514.51.5.1032

Cardichon, J., & Darling-Hammond, L. (2017). *Advancing educational equity for underserved youth: How new state accountability systems can support school inclusion and student success*. Learning Policy Institute.

Carroll, J. B. (1993). *Human cognitive abilities: A survey of factor-analytic studies*. Cambridge University Press. doi:10.1017/CBO9780511571312

Carver, C. S., & Scheier, M. F. (1981). A control-systems approach to behavioral self regulation. In L. Wheeler (Ed.), Vol. 2, pp. 107–140). Review of personality and social psychology. Sage.

Cattell, R. B. (1966). The scree test for the number of factors. *Multivariate Behavioral Research, 1*(2), 245–276. doi:10.120715327906mbr0102_10 PMID:26828106

Cattell, R. B., Radcliffe, J. A., & Sweney, A. B. (1963). The nature and measurement of components of motivation. *Genetic Psychology Monographs, 68*(1), 49–211.

CCBC Academic Pathways. (2022). https://www.ccbcmd.edu/Programs-and-Courses/Degrees-and-Certificates/Pathways.aspx

CCBC Bookstore. (2022). https://www.ccbcmd.edu/Resources-for-Students/Bookstore.aspx

CCBC Office of Planning, Research, and Evaluation. (2021). *CCBC Fact Book*. http://www.ccbcmd.edu/~/media/CCBC/About%20CCBC/Administrative%20Offices/PRE/ccbc_factbook.ashx

CCBC. (2020). *Mission and Values*. Retrieved from https://www.ccbcmd.edu/About-CCBC/Mission-and-Values.aspx

Cecil, A., & Krohn, B. D. (2012). The process of developing a competency-based academic curriculum in tourism management. *Journal of Teaching in Travel & Tourism, 12*(2), 129–145. doi:10.1080/15313220.2011.624417

Chance, B. L. (1997). Experiences with authentic assessment techniques in an introductory statistics course. *Journal of Statistics Education: An International Journal on the Teaching and Learning of Statistics, 5*(3).

Chance, B. L. (2005). Integrating pedagogies to teach statistics. In J. Garfield (Ed.), *Innovations in Teaching Statistics. MAA Notes* (Vol. 65, pp. 101–112). Mathematical Association of America.

Chevalier, J. A., & Mayzlin, D. (2006). The Effect of Word of Mouth on Sales: Online Book Reviews. *JMR, Journal of Marketing Research, 43*(3), 345–354. doi:10.1509/jmkr.43.3.345

Chilton, M. A., Hardgrave, B. C., & Armstrong, D. J. (2005). Person-job cognitive style fit for software developers: The effect on strain and performance. *Journal of Management Information Systems*, *22*(2), 193–226. doi:10.1080/07421222.2005.11045849

Chi, M. T. H., Bassok, M., Lewis, M. W., Reimann, P., & Glaser, R. (1989). Self-explanations: How students study and use examples in learning to solve problems. *Cognitive Science*, *13*(2), 145–182. doi:10.120715516709cog1302_1

Chin, W. W. (2010). *How to write up and report PLS analyses*. Springer Verlag. doi:10.1007/978-3-540-32827-8_29

Cho, S. W., Kopko, E., Jenkins, D., & Jaggars, S. S. (2012). *New Evidence of Success of Community College Remedial English Students: Tracking the Outcomes of Students in the Accelerated Learning Program (ALP)*. CCRC Working Paper No. 53. New York: Columbia University, Teachers College, Community College Research Center.

Chuzhanova, N. A., Jones, A. J., & Margetts, S. (1998). Feature selection for genetic sequence classification. *Bioinformatics (Oxford, England)*, *14*(2), 139–143. doi:10.1093/bioinformatics/14.2.139 PMID:9545445

Cicchinelli, A., Veas, E., Pardo, A., Pammer-Schindler, V., Fessl, A., Barreiros, C., & Lindstädt, S. (2018). Finding traces of self-regulated learning in activity streams. In *Proceedings of the 8th International conference on learning analytics and knowledge (LAK)* (pp. 191-200). 10.1145/3170358.3170381

Clarke, P., Tyrrell, G., & Nagle, T. (2016). Governing self service analytics. *Journal of Decision Systems, 25*(sup1), 145-159. doi:10.1080/12460125.2016.1187385

Clements, M., & Braman, J. (2021). Exploring Factors of an Inclusive Textbook Access Program in Computer Technology Courses. In G. Meiselwitz (Ed.), Lecture Notes in Computer Science: Vol. 12775. *Social Computing and Social Media: Applications in Marketing, Learning, and Health. HCII 2021*. Springer. doi:10.1007/978-3-030-77685-5_15

Cobb, G. W. (1991). Teaching statistics: More data, less lecturing. *Amstat News, 182*.

Cobb, G. W. (1993). Reconsidering statistics education: A National Science Foundation conference. *Journal of Statistics Education: An International Journal on the Teaching and Learning of Statistics*, *1*(1).

Cohen, A., & Brawer, F. (2003). *The American community college* (4th ed.). Jossey-Bass Publishing.

Collins, S. G. (2010). An Electronic Buzzer is Laughing. *Cybernetics & Human Knowing*, *17*(3), 45–64.

Collins, S. G. (2018). Working for the Robocracy. *Anthropology of Work Review*, *39*(1), 5–9. doi:10.1111/awr.12131

Committee on Learning Research and Educational Practice. (2014). *How People Learn: Brain, Mind, Experience, and School: Expanded Edition*. National Academy Press.

Corbin, J., & Strauss, A. (2014). *Basics of Qualitative Research*. Sage.

Cosden, M., Morrison, G., Gutierrez, L., & Brown, M. (2004). The effects of homework programs and after-school activities on school success. *Theory into Practice*, *43*(3), 220–226. doi:10.120715430421tip4303_8

Credential Engine. (n.d.). *Making ALL Credentials Transparent & Revealing the Marketplace of Credentials*. Retrieved from Credential Engine: https://credentialengine.org/

Cyr, D., Head, M., Lim, E., & Stibe, A. (2018). Using the elaboration likelihood model to examine online persuasion through website design. *Information & Management*, *55*(7), 807–821. doi:10.1016/j.im.2018.03.009

Dang, N. C., Moreno-García, M. N., & De la Prieta, F. (2020). Sentiment analysis based on deep learning: A comparative study. *Electronics (Switzerland)*, *9*(3), 483. Advance online publication. doi:10.3390/electronics9030483

Daradkeh, M., & Al-Dwairi, R. (2018). Self-Service Business Intelligence Adoption in Business Enterprises: The Effects of Information Quality, System Quality, and Analysis Quality. In Operations and Service Management: Concepts, Methodologies, Tools, and Applications (pp. 1096-1118). Hershey, PA: IGI Global.

Daradkeh, M. (2019a). Critical Success Factors of Enterprise Data Analytics and Visualization Ecosystem: An Interview Study. *International Journal of Information Technology Project Management*, *10*(3), 34–55. doi:10.4018/IJITPM.2019070103

Daradkeh, M. (2019b). Determinants of Self-Service Analytics Adoption Intention: The Effect of Task-Technology Fit, Compatibility, and User Empowerment. *Journal of Organizational and End User Computing*, *31*(4), 19–45. doi:10.4018/JOEUC.2019100102

Daradkeh, M. (2019c). Determinants of visual analytics adoption in organizations: Knowledge discovery through content analysis of online evaluation reviews. *Information Technology &amp. People*, *32*(3), 668–695. doi:10.1108/ITP-10-2017-0359

Daradkeh, M. (2020). Driving Business Innovation and Sustainability through Internet of Things and Data Analytics: An Innovation Stage Model. *International Journal of Innovation, Creativity and Change*, *14*(9), 149–179.

Daradkeh, M. (2021). An Empirical Examination of the Relationship Between Data Storytelling Competency and Business Performance: The Mediating Role of Decision-Making Quality. *Journal of Organizational and End User Computing*, *33*(5), 42–73. doi:10.4018/JOEUC.20210901.oa3

Daradkeh, M. (2022). The Relationship Between Persuasion Cues and Idea Adoption in Virtual Crowdsourcing Communities: Evidence From a Business Analytics Community. *International Journal of Knowledge Management*, *18*(1), 1–34. doi:10.4018/IJKM.291708

Daradkeh, M., & Al-Dwairi, R. (2017). Self-Service Business Intelligence Adoption in Business Enterprises: The Effects of Information Quality, System Quality, and Analysis Quality. *International Journal of Enterprise Information Systems*, *13*(3), 65–85. doi:10.4018/IJEIS.2017070105

DataRobot. (n.d.). Feature Impact. *DataRobot | AI Cloud*. Retrieved November 15, 2021, from https://www.datarobot.com/wiki/feature-impact/

Datta, R., Joshi, D., Li, J., & Wang, J. Z. (2008). Image retrieval: Ideas, influences, and trends of the new age. *ACM Computing Surveys*, *40*(2), 1–60. doi:10.1145/1348246.1348248

Daud, A., Aljohani, N. R., Abbasi, R. A., Lytras, M. D., Abbas, F., & Alowibdi, J. S. (2017, April). Predicting student performance using advanced learning analytics. In *Proceedings of the 26th international conference on world wide web companion* (pp. 415-421). 10.1145/3041021.3054164

Daudert, T. (2021). Exploiting textual and relationship information for fine-grained financial sentiment analysis. *Knowledge-Based Systems*, *230*, 107389. Advance online publication. doi:10.1016/j.knosys.2021.107389

Daugherty, P.R., Wilson, J, & Chowdury, R. (2018). Using Artificial Intelligence to Promote Diversity. *MIT Sloan Management Review*. mitsmr.com/2DQz2XT

De Caigny, A., Coussement, K., & De Bock, K. W. (2018). A new hybrid classification algorithm for learner churn prediction based on logistic regression and decision trees. *European Journal of Operational Research*, *269*(2), 760–772. doi:10.1016/j.ejor.2018.02.009

del Valle, R., & Duffy, T. M. (2007). Online learning: Learner characteristics and their approaches to managing learning. *Instructional Science*, *37*(2), 129–149. doi:10.100711251-007-9039-0

Delucchi, M. (2006). The efficacy of collaborative learning groups in an undergraduate statistics course. *College Teaching, 54*(2), 244–248. doi:10.3200/CTCH.54.2.244-248

DeMark, S. & Kozyrev, J. (2020). Enabling pathways to opportunity through a skills-based architecture. *Journal of Competency-Based Education*. . doi:10.1002/cbe2.1241

Derakhshan, A., & Beigy, H. (2019). Sentiment analysis on stock social media for stock price movement prediction. *Engineering Applications of Artificial Intelligence, 85*, 569–578. doi:10.1016/j.engappai.2019.07.002

Dettmers, S., Trautwein, U., & Lüdtke, O. (2009). The relationship between homework time and achievement is not universal: Evidence from multilevel analyses in 40 countries. *School Effectiveness and School Improvement, 20*(4), 375–405. doi:10.1080/09243450902904601

DfES. (2005). *Education and skills Hispanic paper*. London, UK: Author. Retrieved from http://www.educationengland.org.uk/documents/pdfs/2005-white-paper-14-19-education-and-skills.pdf

Dick, W., Carey, L., & Carey, J. O. (2005). *The systematic design of instruction*. Pearson Merrill.

Dietz, E. J. (1993). A cooperative learning activity on methods of selecting a sample. *The American Statistician, 47*, 104–108.

Dietz-Uhler, B., & Hurn, J. E. (2013). Using Learning Analytics to Predict (and Improve) Student Success: A Faculty Perspective. *Journal of Interactive Online Learning, 12*(1), 10.

Digital Marketing Institute. (2018, December 6). *What's the Importance of Higher Education on the Economy?* https://digitalmarketinginstitute.com/blog/what-is-the-importance-of-higher-education-on-the-economy

Dishaw, M. T., & Strong, D. M. (1999). Extending the technology acceptance model with task-technology fit constructs. *Information & Management, 36*(1), 9–21. doi:10.1016/S0378-7206(98)00101-3

Downer, J. T., Booren, L. M., Lima, O. K., Luckner, A. E., & Pianta, R. C. (2010). The Individualized Classroom Assessment Scoring System (inCLASS): Preliminary reliability and validity of a system for observing preschoolers' competence in classroom interactions. *Early Childhood Research Quarterly, 25*(1), 1–16. doi:10.1016/j.ecresq.2009.08.004 PMID:23175598

Drake, S. M., & Reid, J. (2010). Research Monograph #28: Integrated Curriculum-Increasing Relevance While Maintaining Accountability. The Literacy and Numeracy Secretariat & the Ontario Association of Deans of Education.

Drake, S. M. (2007). *Creating standards-based integrated curriculum: Aligning content, standards, instructional strategies and assessment* (2nd ed.). Corwin.

Driscoll, M., & Carliner, S. (2005). *Advanced web-based Training: Adapting real world strategies in your online learning*. Pfeiffer.

Durairaj, M., & Vijitha, C. (2014). Educational data mining for prediction of student performance using clustering algorithms. *International Journal of Computer Science and Information Technologies, 5*(4), 5987–5991.

Duranti, L. (2009). From digital diplomatics to digital records forensics. *Archivaria*, 39–66.

Durlak, J. A., Weissberg, R. P., & Pachan, M. (2010). A meta-analysis of after-school programs that seek to promote personal and social skills in children and adolescents. *American Journal of Community Psychology, 45*(3-4), 294–309. doi:10.100710464-010-9300-6 PMID:20300825

Dwidienawati, D., Tjahjana, D., Abdinagoro, S. B., Gandasari, D., & Munawaroh. (2020). Customer review or influencer endorsement: Which one influences purchase intention more? *Heliyon*, *6*(11), e05543. Advance online publication. doi:10.1016/j.heliyon.2020.e05543 PMID:33294687

Eachempati, P., Srivastava, P. R., Kumar, A., Prat, J. M., & Delen, D. (2022). Can customer sentiment impact firm value? An integrated text mining approach. *Technological Forecasting and Social Change*, *174*, 121265. doi:10.1016/j.techfore.2021.121265

Eastwood, B. (n.d.). *Exploration-based algorithms can improve hiring quality and diversity*. https://mitsloan.mit.edu/ideas-made-to-matter/exploration-based-algorithms-can-improve-hiring-quality-and-diversity

Eccles, J. S., & Wigfield, A. (2002). Motivational beliefs, values, and goals. *Annual Review of Psychology*, *53*(1), 109–132. doi:10.1146/annurev.psych.53.100901.135153 PMID:11752481

Eckerson, W. (2014). *Five steps for delivering self-service business intelligence to everyone*. Retrieved 10 March 2017, from: https://www.informationbuilders.com/about_us/analyst_reports/17340

Education Council. (2006) Recommendation of the European Parliament and the Council of 18 December 2006 on key competencies for lifelong learning. Official Journal of the European Union, 30.

Education Council. (2018). *Council Recommendation on key competences for lifelong learning*. ST/9009/2018/INIT, 1–13

Ekstrom, M. P. (2012). *Digital image processing techniques*. Academic Press.

Elliot, A. J., & McGregor, H. A. (2001). A 2 × 2 achievement goal framework. *Journal of Personality and Social Psychology*, *80*(3), 501–519. doi:10.1037/0022-3514.80.3.501 PMID:11300582

Erümit, A. K., & Çetin, İ. (2020). Design framework of adaptive intelligent tutoring systems. *Education and Information Technologies*, *25*(5), 4477–4500. doi:10.100710639-020-10182-8

Eslami, S. P., Ghasemaghaei, M., & Hassanein, K. (2018). Which online reviews do consumers find most helpful? A multi-method investigation. *Decision Support Systems*, *113*, 32–42. doi:10.1016/j.dss.2018.06.012

Fabregat, E., & Kperogi, F. A. (2021). The "other" in the bowels of the hegemon: U.S. media portrayals of Guam during the U.S.-North Korea tension. *International Journal of Media and Cultural Politics*, *17*(2), 119–137. doi:10.1386/macp_00043_1

Farnsworth, B. (2018). *Enhancing the Quality of the International Student Experience. Beyond the Margins: Meeting the Needs of Underserved Students*. Retrieved from: https://www.higheredtoday.org/2018/07/02/enhancing-quality-international-student-experience/

Feldman, R., & James, S. (2007). *The text mining handbook: advanced approaches in analyzing unstructured data*. Cambridge University Press.

Ferreira, J. M., Amorim, K. de S., Mäkinen, M., & Moura, G. G. (2016). The Network of Meanings and Educational Psychology: Theoretical and Practical Possibilities. *Procedia: Social and Behavioral Sciences*, *217*, 501–511. doi:10.1016/j.sbspro.2016.02.027

Fillebrown, S. (1994). Using projects in an elementary statistics course for non-science majors. *Journal of Statistics Education: An International Journal on the Teaching and Learning of Statistics*, *2*(2).

Finkelstein, A., Harman, M., Jia, Y., Martin, W., Sarro, F., & Zhang, Y. (2017). Investigating the relationship between price, rating, and popularity in the Blackberry World App Store. *Information and Software Technology*, *87*, 119–139. doi:10.1016/j.infsof.2017.03.002

Finley, A. (2021). *How college contributes to workforce success.* https://d1y8sb8igg2f8e.cloudfront.net/AACUEmployerReport2021.pdf

Ford, N., & Chen, S. Y. (2002). Matching/mismatching revisited: An empirical study of learning and teaching styles. *British Journal of Educational Technology, 32*(1), 5–22. doi:10.1111/1467-8535.00173

Forman, G. (2003). An extensive empirical study of feature selection metrics for text classification. *Journal of Machine Learning Research, 3*, 1289–1305.

Fornell, C., & Larcker, D. (1981). Evaluating structural equation models with unobservable and measurement error. *JMR, Journal of Marketing Research, 18*(1), 39–50. doi:10.1177/002224378101800104

Fors Brandebo, M., Nilsson, S., & Larsson, G. (2016). Leadership: Is bad stronger than good? *Leadership and Organization Development Journal, 37*(6), 690–710. doi:10.1108/LODJ-09-2014-0191

Fortunato, S., & Hric, D. (2016). Community detection in networks: A user guide. *Physics Reports, 659*, 1-44.

Freeman, S., Eddy, S. L., McDonough, M., Smith, M. K., Okoroafor, N., Jordt, H., & Wenderoth, M. P. (2014). Active learning boosts performance in STEM courses. *Proceedings of the National Academy of Sciences*. 10.1073/pnas.1319030111

Fuller, J., Raman, M., Sage-Gavin, E., & Hines, K. (2021). *Hidden Workers: Untapped Talent.* Harvard Business School Project on Managing the Future of Work and Accenture.

Gabriel, K., & Flake, S. (2008). *Teaching unprepared students: strategies for promoting success and retention in higher education.* Stylus Publishing.

Gagné, R. M., Briggs, L. J., & Wager, W. W. (1992). *Principles of instructional design* (4th ed.). Harcourt Brace Jovanovich College Publishers.

Gal, I., & Garfield, J. B. (Eds.). (1997). *The assessment challenge in statistics education.* IOS Press/International Statistical Institute.

Gallagher, K. (2017, July 31). *Beautiful Learning* [Blog Post]. Retrieved from: www.kerryhawk02.com/2017/07/beautiful-learning.html

Gallagher, S., & Zanville, H. (2021, March 25). *More employers are awarding credentials. Is a parallel higher education system emerging?* https://www.edsurge.com/news/2021-03-25-more-employers-are-awarding-credentials-is-a-parallel-higher-education-system-emerging

Ganaie, M. A., & Tanveer, M. (2021). Fuzzy least squares projection twin support vector machines for class imbalance learning. *Applied Soft Computing, 113*, 107933. doi:10.1016/j.asoc.2021.107933

Garay, J., Yap, R., & Sabellano, M. J. (2019). An analysis on the insights of the anti-vaccine movement from social media posts using k-means clustering algorithm and VADER sentiment analyzer. *IOP Conference Series. Materials Science and Engineering, 482*, 012043. doi:10.1088/1757-899X/482/1/012043

García-Peñalvo. (n.d.). *Opening Learning Management Systems to Personal Le.pdf.* Retrieved November 15, 2021, from https://www.jucs.org/jucs_17_9/opening_learning_management_systems/jucs_17_09_1222_1240_garcia.pdf

Garfield, J. (1993). Teaching statistics using small-group cooperative learning. *Journal of Statistics Education: An International Journal on the Teaching and Learning of Statistics, 1*(1).

Garfield, J. (1995). How students learn statistics. *International Statistical Review, 63*(1), 35–48. doi:10.2307/1403775

Garfield, J., & delMas, R. (1991). Students' conceptions of probability. In D. Vere-Jones (Ed.), *Proceedings of the Third International Conference on Teaching Statistics*, Volume 1 (pp. 340-349). Voorburg, The Netherlands: International Statistical Institute.

Gartner. (2019). *Magic Quadrant for Analytics and Business Intelligence Platforms*. Retrieved on 6 March 2018 from https://www.gartner.com/doc/3900992/magic-quadrant-analytics-business-intelligence

Gavrin, A. (2010). Using Just-in-Time Teaching in the Physical Sciences. In Just-in-Time Teaching: Across the Disciplines, Across the Academy. Sterling, VA: Stylus Publishing.

Geng, S., Niu, B., Feng, Y., & Huang, M. (2020). Understanding the focal points and sentiment of learners in MOOC reviews: A machine learning and SC-LIWC-based approach. *British Journal of Educational Technology*, *51*(5), 1785–1803. Advance online publication. doi:10.1111/bjet.12999

Gershon, I. (2017). *Down and Out in the New Economy*. University of Chicago Press. doi:10.7208/chicago/9780226452289.001.0001

Ghasemaghaei, M., Eslami, S. P., Deal, K., & Hassanein, K. (2018). Reviews' length and sentiment as correlates of online reviews' ratings. *Internet Research*, *28*(3), 544–563. doi:10.1108/IntR-12-2016-0394

Ghosh, T. (2018). Predicting hotel book intention: The influential role of helpfulness and advocacy of online reviews. *Journal of Hospitality Marketing & Management*, *27*(3), 299–322. doi:10.1080/19368623.2017.1364198

Gikas, J., & Grant, M. M. (2013). Mobile computing devices in higher education: Student perspectives on learning with cellphones, smartphones & social media. *Internet and Higher Education*, *19*, 18–26. doi:10.1016/j.iheduc.2013.06.002

Giraud, G. (1997). Cooperative learning and statistics instruction. *Journal of Statistics Education: An International Journal on the Teaching and Learning of Statistics*, *5*(3).

Gnanadesikan, M., Scheaffer, R. L., Watkins, A. E., & Witmer, J. A. (1997). An activitybased statistics course. *Journal of Statistics Education: An International Journal on the Teaching and Learning of Statistics*, *5*(2).

Goldberg, Y. & Levy, O. (2014). *Word2vec Explained: Deriving Mikolov et al.'s negative-sampling word-embedding method*. Academic Press.

Goodhue, D., Klein, B., & March, S. (2000). User evaluations of IS as surrogates for objective performance. *Information & Management*, *38*(2), 87–101.

Gottfredson, L. S. (1998). *The General Intelligence Factor*. https://www.hucama.com/wp-

Graesser, A. C., Conley, M. W., & Olney, A. (n.d.). Intelligent tutoring systems. In APA educational psychology handbook, Vol 3: Application to learning and teaching. APA.

Grama, J. L. (2015). *Legal Issues in Information Security*. Jones & Bartlett.

Grasha, A. F. (1996). *Teaching with style*. Alliance Press.

Gräther, W., Kolvenbach, S., Ruland, R., Schütte, J., Torres, C., & Wendland, F. (2018). Blockchain for education: lifelong learning passport. *Proceedings of 1st ERCIM Blockchain workshop 2018. European Society for Socially Embedded Technologies (EUSSET).*

Greene, D. (2021). *Diversity, equity, and inclusion in the workplace — Trends for 2021*. https://www.adp.com/spark/articles/2020/12/diversity-equity-and-inclusion-in-the-workplace-trends-for-2021.aspx

Grundlingh, L. (2018). Exploring the possibility of using appraisal theory to determine the legitimacy of suicide notes. *Lingua*, *214*, 1–10. doi:10.1016/j.lingua.2018.07.004

Gul, E., Alpaslan, N., & Emiroglu, M. E. (2021). Robust optimization of SVM hyper-parameters for spillway type selection. *Ain Shams Engineering Journal*, *12*(3), 2413–2423. Advance online publication. doi:10.1016/j.asej.2020.10.022

Gupta, A. K., & Nagar, D. K. (2004). Distribution of the Determinant of the Sample Correlation Matrix from a Mixture Normal Model. *Random Operators and Stochastic Equations*, *12*, 193-199.

Gustafson, K., & Branch, R. (2002). *What is instructional design? Trends and issues in instructional design and technology*. Merrill.

Gyll, S. P., & Hayes, H. (2021). Learning and individual differences in skilled competency-based performance: Using a course planning and learning tool as an indicator for student success. *The Journal of Competency-Based Education*, *6*(3), e1259. doi:10.1002/cbe2.1259

Hair, J. F., Hult, G., Ringle, C. M., & Sarstedt, M. (2017). A Primer on Partial Least Squares Structural Equation Modeling (PLS-SEM) (2nd ed.). Thousand Oaks, CA: SAGE Publications, Inc.

Hall, M. A., & Smith, L. A. (1999). Feature Selection for Machine Learning: Comparing a Correlation-based Filter Approach to the. In *Proceedings of the Twelfth International FLAIRS Conference*. FLAIRS.

Halliday, M. A. K., & Matthiessen, C. M. I. M. (2004). *An Introduction to Functional Grammar* (3rd ed.). Edward Arnold.

Halpern, D. F. (1998). Teaching Critical Thinking for Transfer Across Domains. *The American Psychologist*, *53*(4), 449–455. doi:10.1037/0003-066X.53.4.449 PMID:9572008

Hamilton, L., Halverson, R., Jackson, S. S., Mandinach, E., Supovitz, J. A., & Wayman, J. C. (2009). *Using student achievement data to support instructional decision making*. https://files.eric.ed.gov/fulltext/ED506645.pdf

Han, H., Zhang, Y., Zhang, J., Yang, J., & Zou, X. (2018). Improving the performance of lexicon-based review sentiment analysis method by reducing additional introduced sentiment bias. *PLoS One*, *13*(8), e0202523. Advance online publication. doi:10.1371/journal.pone.0202523 PMID:30142154

Hansen, D. L., Schneiderman, B., Smith, M. A., & Himelboim, I. (2020). *Analyzing Social Media networks with NodeXL*. Morgan Kaufmann.

Hartzler, D. S. (2000). *A Meta-analysis of Studies Conducted on Integrated Curriculum Programs and Their Effects on Student Achievement* [Dissertation]. School of Education, Indiana University.

Harvard Family Research Project. (2003). *A review of out-of-school-time program quasi-experimental and experimental evaluation results*. Author.

Hassan, S., Tantithamthavorn, C., Bezemer, C.-P., & Hassan, A. E. (2017). Studying the dialogue between users and developers of free apps in the Google Play Store. *Empirical Software Engineering*, *23*(3), 1275–1312. doi:10.100710664-017-9538-9

Hastie, T. J., & Tibshirani, R. J. (2017). *Generalized Additive Models*. Routledge. doi:10.1201/9780203753781

Hattie, J., & Timperley, H. (2007). The Power of Feedback. *Review of Educational Research*, *77*(1), 81–112. doi:10.3102/003465430298487

Hautamäki, J., Arinen, P., Eronen, S., Hautamäki, A., Kupiainen, S., Lindblom, B., Niemivirta, M., Pakaslahti, L., Rantanen, P., & Scheinin, P. (2002). *Assessing learning-to-learn: a framework*. National Board of Education.

Heinze, A., Reiss, K., & Franziska, R. (2005). Mathematics achievement and interest in mathematics from a differential perspective. *ZDM*, *37*, 212–219.

Henderson, S. A. (2018). Pedagogical contraband: A phenomenological approach to understanding student engagement during simulations. *Dissertations and Theses @ UNI*. 936. https://scholarworks.uni.edu/etd/936

Herman, J. L., & Webb, N. M. (2007). Alignment Methodologies. *Applied Measurement in Education*, *20*(1), 1–5.

Herrington, A., & Herrington, J. (2007, November). *Authentic mobile learning in higher education*. Paper presented at Australian Association for Research in Education, Fremantle, Australia.

Hirschberg, J., & Manning, C. D. (2015). Advances in natural language processing. *Science*, *349*(6245), 261–266. doi:10.1126cience.aaa8685 PMID:26185244

Hogg, R. V. (1991). Statistical education: Improvements are badly deeded. *The American Statistician*, *45*, 342–343.

Holm, A. (2020). *Applicant Tracking Systems. Encyclopedia of Electronic HRM*. De Gruyter Oldenbourg.

Holon, I. Q. (2021, February 18). *Micro & Alternative Credentials. Size, Shape and Scenarios - Part 1*. Retrieved from HolonIQ: https://www.holoniq.com/notes/micro-and-alternative-credentials.-size-shape-and-scenarios-part-1/

Holtzman, D. M., Kraft, E. M., & Small, E. (2021). Use of ePortfolios for making hiring decisions. *Journal of Work-Applied Management*. Advance online publication. doi:10.1108/JWAM-01-2021-0001

Honeycutt, C., & Herring, S. C. (2009). Beyond Microblogging: Conversation and Collaboration via Twitter. *42nd Hawaii International Conference on System Sciences*. 10.1109/HICSS.2009.89

Hong, S., & Nadler, D. (2011). Does the early bird move the polls? The use of the social media tool 'Twitter' by U.S. politicians and its impact on public opinion. *dg.o '11 Proceedings of the 12th Annual International Digital Government Research Conference: Digital Government Innovation in Challenging*, 182-186. 10.1145/2037556.2037583

Hossain, M. S., & Rahman, M. F. (2022). Detection of potential customers' empathy behavior towards customers' reviews. *Journal of Retailing and Consumer Services*, *65*, 102881. doi:10.1016/j.jretconser.2021.102881

Hossain, M. S., Rahman, M. F., & Zhou, X. (2021). Impact of customers' interpersonal interactions in social commerce on customer relationship management performance. *Journal of Contemporary Marketing Science*, *4*(1), 161–181. doi:10.1108/JCMARS-12-2020-0050

Hotho, A., Nürnberger, A., & Paaß, G. (2005). A brief survey of text mining. *GLDV Journal for Computational Linguistics and Language Technology, 20*(1), 19-62.

Hrala, J. (2021). *Defeating Robots: 75 Percent of Resumes are Never Read by a Human*. https://blog.careerminds.com/75-percent-of-resumes-are-never-read

HubSpot. (n.d.). *HubSpot Academy*. https://academy.hubspot.com/certification-overview

Hunter, S., Cushenbery, L., & Friedrich, T. (2012). Hiring an innovative workforce. *Human Resource Management Review*, *22*(4), 303–322. doi:10.1016/j.hrmr.2012.01.001

Hunter, W. G. (1977). Some ideas about teaching design of experiments, with 25 examples of experiments conducted by students. *The American Statistician*, *31*, 12–17.

Hutto, C. J., & Gilbert, E. (2014). VADER: A parsimonious rule-based model for sentiment analysis of social media text. In *Proceedings of the 8th International Conference on Weblogs and Social Media, ICWSM 2014* (pp. 216–225). The AAAI Press.

Hymavathy, C., Krishnamani, V., & Sumathi, C. P. (2014). Analyzing learner engagement to enhance the teaching-learning experience. In *Proceedings of the International Conference on MOOC, Innovation and Technology in Education (MITE)*. IEEE. 10.1109/MITE.2014.7020243

IBM Institute for Business Value. (n.d.). *The enterprise guide to closing the skills gap*. https://www.ibm.com/downloads/cas/EPYMNBJA

IBM. (n.d.). *IBM Credentials: Badges and Certifications*. https://www.ibm.com/training/credentials

IEA. 2009. IEA international database analyzer for PISA (version 2.0) [Computer software and manual]. Hamburg, Germany: IEA Data Processing and Research Centre.

Ifenthaler, D. (2017). Are Higher Education Institutions Prepared for Learning Analytics? *TechTrends*, *61*(4), 366–371. doi:10.100711528-016-0154-0

Imhoff, C., & White, C. (2011). *Self-Service Business Intelligence - Empowering Users to Generate Insights*. TDWI best practices report. Retrieved January 25, 2017, from https://tdwi.org/research/list/tdwi-best-practices-reports.aspx

Indeed. (2021, February 22). *How to Write a Skills Based Resume: Template and Examples*. https://www.indeed.com/career-advice/resumes-cover-letters/skills-based-resume-template

Irizarry, R. A. (2020). The role of academia in data science education. *The Role of Academia in Data Science Education, 2*(1).

Jakkaew, P., & Hemrungrote, S. (2017). The use of UTAUT2 model for understanding student perceptions using Google Classroom: A case study of Introduction to Information Technology course. In *2nd Joint International Conference on Digital Arts, Media and Technology 2017: Digital Economy for Sustainable Growth, ICDAMT 2017* (pp. 205–209). Institute of Electrical and Electronics Engineers Inc. 10.1109/ICDAMT.2017.7904962

James, A. (2018). Using the elaboration likelihood model to guide customer service-based segmentation. *International Journal of Physical Distribution & Logistics Management*, *27*(9/10), 600–615. doi:10.1108/09600039710188657

Jena, R. (2020). An empirical case study on Indian consumers' sentiment towards electric vehicles: A big data analytics approach. *Industrial Marketing Management*, *90*, 605–616. Advance online publication. doi:10.1016/j.indmarman.2019.12.012

Jensen, A. R. (1998). The g factor and the design of education. In R. J. Sternberg & W. M. Williams (Eds.), Intelligence, Instruction, and Assessment: Theory Into Practice (pp. 111–131). Academic Press.

Jensen, B. (2012). *Catching up: Learning from the best school systems in East Asia*. Grattan Institute. http://www.grattan.edu.au/publications/130_report_learning_from_the_best_detail. pdf

Jiménez-Zafra, S. M., Martín-Valdivia, M. T., Maks, I., & Izquierdo, R. (2017, March 1). Analysis of patient satisfaction in Dutch and Spanish online reviews. In *Procesamiento de Lenguaje Natural*. Sociedad Espanola para el Procesamiento del Lenguaje Natural.

Johnson, H. D., & Dasgupta, N. (2005). Traditional versus non-traditional teaching: Perspectives of students in introductory statistics classes. *Journal of Statistics Education: An International Journal on the Teaching and Learning of Statistics*, *13*(2).

Jones, L. (1991). *Using cooperative learning to teach statistics*. Research Report Number 91-2, The L. L. Thurstone Psychometric Laboratory, University of North Carolina.

Jones, M. H., Hackel, T. S., Hershberger, M., & Goodrich, K. M. (2019). Queer Youth in Educational Psychology Research. *Journal of Homosexuality*, *66*(13), 1797–1816. doi:10.1080/00918369.2018.1510262 PMID:30247992

Jordan, J. (2007). The application of statistics education research in my classroom. *Journal of Statistics Education: An International Journal on the Teaching and Learning of Statistics*, *15*(2).

Jove, E., Blanco-Rodríguez, P., Casteleiro-Roca, J. L., Quintián, H., Moreno Arboleda, F. J., LóPez-Vázquez, J. A., Rodríguez-Gómez, B. A., Meizoso-López, M. D. C., Piñón-Pazos, A., De Cos Juez, F. J., Cho, S.-B., & Calvo-Rolle, J. L. (2020). Missing data imputation over academic records of electrical engineering students. *Logic Journal of the IGPL*, *28*(4), 487–501. doi:10.1093/jigpal/jzz056

Jurek, A., Mulvenna, M. D., & Bi, Y. (2015). Improved lexicon-based sentiment analysis for social media analytics. *Security Informatics*, *4*(1), 9. Advance online publication. doi:10.118613388-015-0024-x

Kaiser, H. F. (1974). An index of factorial simplicity. *Psychometrika*, *39*(1), 31–36. doi:10.1007/BF02291575

Kane, M. T. (2016). Explicating validity. *Assessment in Education: Principles, Policy & Practice*, *23*(2), 198–211.

Kanna, P. R., & Pandiaraja, P. (2019). An Efficient Sentiment Analysis Approach for Product Review using Turney Algorithm. In *Procedia Computer Science* (Vol. 165, pp. 356–362). Elsevier B.V. doi:10.1016/j.procs.2020.01.038

Kastrati, Z., Imran, A. S., & Kurti, A. (2020). Weakly Supervised Framework for Aspect-Based Sentiment Analysis on Students' Reviews of MOOCs. *IEEE Access: Practical Innovations, Open Solutions*, *8*, 106799–106810. doi:10.1109/ACCESS.2020.3000739

Keeler, C. M., & Steinhorst, R. K. (1995). Using small groups to promote active learning in the introductory statistics course: A report from the field. *Journal of Statistics Education: An International Journal on the Teaching and Learning of Statistics*, *3*(2).

Kent, C., Laslo, E., & Rafaeli, S. (2016). Interactivity in online discussions and learning outcomes. *Computers & Education*, *97*, 116–128. doi:10.1016/j.compedu.2016.03.002

Keuchenius, A., Tornberg, P. & Uitermark, J. (2018). *How Communities Mediate the Diffusion of New Ideas*. University of Amsterdam Odycceus.

Khanal, S. S., Prasad, P. W. C., Alsadoon, A., & Maag, A. (2020). A systematic review: Machine learning based recommendation systems for e-learning. *Education and Information Technologies*, *25*(4), 2635–2664. doi:10.100710639-019-10063-9

Kim, P., & Bodie, M.T. (2021). Artificial Intelligence and the Challenges of Workplace Discrimination and Privacy. *ABA Journal of Labor & Employment Law, 289.*

Kim, D., Seo, D., Cho, S., & Kang, P. (2019). Multi-co-training for document classification using various document representations: TF–IDF, LDA, and Doc2Vec. *Information Sciences*, *477*, 15–29. doi:10.1016/j.ins.2018.10.006

Kim, D., & Solomon, M. G. (2012). *Fundamentals of Information Security: Information Systems Security & Assurance Series*. Jones & Bartlett.

Kim, J. C., & Chung, K. Y. (2020). Knowledge expansion of metadata using script mining analysis in multimedia recommendation. *Multimedia Tools and Applications*. Advance online publication. doi:10.100711042-020-08774-0

Kim, K. S., Shin, S. J., Shin, J., & Miller, D. R. (2016). Social Networks and Individual Creativity. *The Journal of Creative Behavior*, *52*(4), 285–296. doi:10.1002/jocb.153

King, M. (2021). *Social Chemistry*. Dutton.

Kirton, M. (1976). Adaptors and innovators: A description and measure. *The Journal of Applied Psychology*, *61*(5), 622–629. doi:10.1037/0021-9010.61.5.622

Kirton, M. (2003). *Adaption-innovation: In the context of diversity and change*. Routledge.

Kishimoto, A., Fukunaga, A., & Botea, A. (2009). Scalable, Parallel Best-First Search for Optimal Sequential Planning. *Proceedings of the International Conference on Automated Planning and Scheduling*.

Kitchen, P. J., Kerr, G., Schultz, D. E., McColl, R., & Pals, H. (2014). The elaboration likelihood model: Review, critique and research agenda. *European Journal of Marketing*, *48*(11/12), 2033–2050. doi:10.1108/EJM-12-2011-0776

Kleckner, M. J., & Butz, N. (2021). Addressing undergraduate skill gaps in higher education: Revisiting communication in the major course outcomes. *Journal of Education for Business*, *97*(7), 411–423.

Knekta, Runyon, & Eddy. (2019). One size doesn't fit all: Using factor analysis to gather validity evidence when using surveys in your research. *CBE Life Sciences Education, 18*, 1. doi:10.1187/cbe.18-04-0064

Koffi, E. (2006). *The challenges of translation academic records*. The ATA Chronicle.

Kolb, D. A. (1984). *Experiential learning: Experience as the source of learning and development*. Prentice Hall.

Köller, O., Baumert, J., & Schnabel, K. (2001). Does interest matter? The relationship between academic interest and achievement in mathematics. *Journal for Research in Mathematics Education*, *32*(5), 448–470. doi:10.2307/749801

Kumar, J. A., & Bervell, B. (2019). Google Classroom for mobile learning in higher education: Modelling the initial perceptions of students. *Education and Information Technologies*, *24*(2), 1793–1817. Advance online publication. doi:10.100710639-018-09858-z

Kumar, S., Gahalawat, M., Roy, P. P., Dogra, D. P., & Kim, B. G. (2020). Exploring impact of age and gender on sentiment analysis using machine learning. *Electronics (Basel)*, *9*(2), 374. Advance online publication. doi:10.3390/electronics9020374

Kumar, S., & Vijayalakshmi, M. (2012). Mining of student academic evaluation records in higher education. *International Conference on Recent Advances in Computing and Software Systems*, 67-70. 10.1109/RACSS.2012.6212699

Kyvik, S. (2004). Structural changes in higher education systems in Western Europe. *Higher Education in Europe*, *24*(3), 393–408. doi:10.1080/0379772042000331679

Lam, T. Y. P., & Lau, K. C. (2014). Examining factors affecting science achievement of Hong Kong in PISA 2006 using hierarchical linear modeling. *International Journal of Science Education*, *36*(15), 2463–2480. doi:10.1080/09500693.2013.879223

Larkin, J. H., & Chabay, R. W. (2021). *Computer Assisted Instruction and Intelligent Tutoring Systems: Shared Goals and Complementary Approaches*. Routledge. doi:10.4324/9781315044361

Lau, C., Sinclair, J., Taub, M., Azevedo, R., & Jang, E. E. (2017). Transitioning self-regulated learning profiles in hypermedia-learning environments. In *Proceedings of the 7th International Learning Analytics & Knowledge Conference (LAK)* (pp. 198-202). 10.1145/3027385.3027443

Lauer, P. A., Akiba, M., Wilkerson, S. B., Apthorp, H. S., Snow, D., & Martin-Glenn, M. L. (2006). Out-of-school-time programs: A meta-analysis of effects for at-risk students. *Review of Educational Research*, *76*(2), 275–313. doi:10.3102/00346543076002275

Lauver, S. (2002). *Assessing the benefits of an after-school program for urban youth: Results of an experimental design and process evaluation* [Unpublished PhD diss.]. University of Pennsylvania.

Lazarev, V. A. (1992). Specialty Schools. *Russian Education & Society*, *34*(1), 23–31. doi:10.2753/RES1060-9393340123

Ledolter, J. (1995). Projects in introductory statistics courses. *The American Statistician*, *49*, 364–367.

Lee, J. (2007). Two worlds of private tutoring: The prevalence and causes of after-school mathematics tutoring in Korea and the United States. *Teachers College Record*, *109*(5), 1207–1234. doi:10.1177/016146810710900507

Lee, M. K. (2018). Understanding perception of algorithmic fairness. *Big Data & Society*, (January-June), 1–16.

Lee, M., Rodgers, S., & Kim, M. (2009). Effects of valence and extremity of eWOM on attitude toward the brand and website. *Journal of Current Issues and Research in Advertising*, *31*(2), 1–11. doi:10.1080/10641734.2009.10505262

Linder, D. (2021). *The right of privacy*. Retrieved from: http://law2.umkc.edu/faculty/projects/ftrials/conlaw/rightofprivacy.html

Liu, R., Xiong, R., & Song, L. (2010). A sentiment classification method for chinese document. In *ICCSE 2010 - 5th International Conference on Computer Science and Education, Final Program and Book of Abstracts* (pp. 918–922). 10.1109/ICCSE.2010.5593462

Liu, D. Y.-T., Bartimote-Aufflick, K., Pardo, A., & Bridgeman, A. J. (2017). Data-Driven Personalization of Student Learning Support in Higher Education. In A. Peña-Ayala (Ed.), *Learning Analytics: Fundaments, Applications, and Trends: A View of the Current State of the Art to Enhance e-Learning* (pp. 143–169). Springer International Publishing. doi:10.1007/978-3-319-52977-6_5

Liu, F. S. (2021). The Theoretical and Experimental Analysis of the Maximal Information Coefficient Approximate Algorithm. *Journal of Systems Science and Information*, *9*(1), 95–104. doi:10.21078/JSSI-2021-095-10

Liu, L., Hu, X., Feng, Z., Zhang, X., Wang, S., Xu, S., & Sun, K. (2019). Prediction of acid radical ion binding residues by K-nearest neighbors classifier. *BMC Molecular and Cell Biology*, *20*(S3), 52. Advance online publication. doi:10.118612860-019-0238-8 PMID:31823720

Liu, T., Liu, S., Chen, Z., & Ma, W.-Y. (2003). An evaluation on feature selection for text clustering. *Proceedings of the 20th international conference on machine learning (ICML-03).*

Li, Y., & Vansconcelos, N. (2019). *REPAIR: Removing Representation Bias by Dataset Resampling*. Computer Vision Foundation.

Lloyd, S. (1982). Least squares quantization in PCM. *IEEE Transactions on Information Theory*, *28*(2), 129–137. doi:10.1109/TIT.1982.1056489

Logue, A. W. (2018, July 17). *The Extensive Evidence of Co-Requisite Remediation's Effectiveness*. Retrieved from Inside Higher Ed: https://www.insidehighered.com/views/2018/07/17/data-already-tell-us-how-effective-co-requisite-education-opinion

Lorenz-Spreen, P., Mønsted, B. M., Hövel, P., & Lehmann, S. (2019). Accelerating dynamics of collective attention. *Nature Communications*, *10*(1), 1759. Advance online publication. doi:10.103841467-019-09311-w PMID:30988286

Lovett, M. C. (2001). A collaborative convergence on studying reasoning processes: A case study in statistics. In S. M. Carver & D. Klahr (Eds.), *Cognition and instruction: Twenty-five years of progress* (pp. 347–384). Erlbaum.

Lovett, M. C., & Greenhouse, J. B. (2000). Applying cognitive theory to statistics instruction. *The American Statistician*, *54*(3), 196–206.

Luo, Y., & Huang, W. (2011). Product review information extraction based on adjective opinion words. In *Proceedings - 4th International Joint Conference on Computational Sciences and Optimization, CSO 2011* (pp. 1309–1313). 10.1109/CSO.2011.209

Luo, Y., & Xu, X. (2021). Comparative study of deep learning models for analyzing online restaurant reviews in the era of the COVID-19 pandemic. *International Journal of Hospitality Management, 94*, 102849. Advance online publication. doi:10.1016/j.ijhm.2020.102849 PMID:34785843

Maalej, W., Kurtanović, Z., Nabil, H., & Stanik, C. (2016). On the automatic classification of app reviews. *Requirements Engineering, 21*(3), 311–331. doi:10.100700766-016-0251-9

Machová, K., Mikula, M., Gao, X., & Mach, M. (2020). Lexicon-based sentiment analysis using particle swarm optimization. *Electronics (Switzerland), 9*(8), 1–22. doi:10.3390/electronics9081317

Mackisack, M. (1994). What is the use of experiments conducted by statistics students? *Journal of Statistics Education: An International Journal on the Teaching and Learning of Statistics, 2*(1).

Maheshwary, S., & Misra, H. (2018). Matching Resumes to Jobs via Deep Siamese Network. *WWW 2019.*

Mahoney, J. L., Parente, M. E., & Zigler, E. F. (2010). After-school program participation and children's development. In J. L. Meece & J. S. Eccles (Eds.), *Handbook of research on schools, schooling, and human development* (pp. 379–397). Routledge.

Maier, D., Waldherr, A., Miltner, P., Wiedemann, G., Niekler, A., Keinert, A., Pfetsch, B., Heyer, G., Reber, U., Häussler, T., Schmid-Petri, H., & Adam, S. (2018). Applying LDA topic modeling in communication research: Toward a valid and reliable methodology. *Communication Methods and Measures, 12*(2-3), 93–118. doi:10.1080/19312458.2018.1430754

Manouselis, N., Drachsler, H., Vuorikari, R., Hummel, H., & Koper, R. (2011). Recommender Systems in Technology Enhanced Learning. In F. Ricci, L. Rokach, B. Shapira, & P. B. Kantor (Eds.), *Recommender Systems Handbook* (pp. 387–415). Springer US. doi:10.1007/978-0-387-85820-3_12

Mäntylä, M. V., Graziotin, D., & Kuutila, M. (2018). The evolution of sentiment analysis—A review of research topics, venues, and top cited papers. *Computer Science Review, 27*, 16–32. doi:10.1016/j.cosrev.2017.10.002

Marcus, A. (2020). The Dark Side of Social Media Screening Technology. *Medium.* https://medium.com/digital-diplomacy/the-dark-side-of-social-media-screening-technology-bd6f70da1d0b

Margaryan, A., Littlejohn, A., & Vojt, G. (2011). Are digital natives a myth or reality? University students' use of digital technologies. *Computers & Education, 56*(2), 429–440. doi:10.1016/j.compedu.2010.09.004

Martens, D., & Maalej, W. (2019). Towards understanding and detecting fake reviews in app stores. *Empirical Software Engineering, 24*(6), 3316–3355. doi:10.100710664-019-09706-9

Martin, J. R., & White, P. R. R. (2005). *The Language of Evaluation: Appraisal in English. The Language of Evaluation: Appraisal in English.* Palgrave Macmillan. doi:10.1057/9780230511910

Maryland Department of Labor. (2021). *Maryland Occupational Projections 2018 - 2021 Workforce Information and Performance.* https://www.dllr.state.md.us/lmi/iandoproj/maryland.shtml

Maryland Higher Education Commission (MHEC). (2017). *2017 – 2021 Maryland State Plan for Postsecondary Education.* https://mhec.maryland.gov/About/Pages/2017StatePlanforPostsecondaryEducation.aspx

Matcha, W., Gašević, D., Uzir, N. A. A., Jovanović, J., & Pardo, A. (2019, March). Analytics of learning strategies: Associations with academic performance and feedback. In *Proceedings of the 9th International Conference on Learning Analytics & Knowledge* (pp. 461-470). 10.1145/3303772.3303787

Matrić, M. (2018). Self-regulatory systems: Self-regulation and learning. Journal of Process Management. *Nuclear Technology*, *6*(4), 79–84. doi:10.5937/jouproman6-19338

McIlroy, S., Ali, N., & Hassan, A. E. (2015). Fresh apps: An empirical study of frequently-updated mobile apps in the Google play store. *Empirical Software Engineering*, *21*(3), 1346–1370. doi:10.100710664-015-9388-2

McKenzie, R. (2018). Bots, Bias and Big Data: Artificial Intelligence, Algorithmic Bias and Disparate Impact Liability in Hiring Practices. *Arkansas Law Review*, *71*(2). https://scholarworks.uark.edu/alr/vol71/iss2/7

Meek, S., Wilk, V., & Lambert, C. (2021). A big data exploration of the informational and normative influences on the helpfulness of online restaurant reviews. *Journal of Business Research*, *125*, 354–367. doi:10.1016/j.jbusres.2020.12.001

Merrill, M. D., Drake, L., Lacy, M. J., & Pratt, J. (1996). Reclaiming instructional design. *Educational Technology*, *36*(5), 5–7.

Messick, S. (1989). Validity. In R. L. Linn (Ed.), Educational measurement (pp. 13-103). Macmillan Publishing Col, Inc.

Messick, S. (1995). Validity of psychological assessment- Validation of inferences from person's responses and performances as scientific inquiry into score meaning. *The American Psychologist*, *50*(9), 741–749.

Metz, S., & Albernhe-Giordan, H. (2010). E-portfolio: A pedagogical tool to enhance creativity in student's project design. *Procedia: Social and Behavioral Sciences*, *2*(2), 3563–3567. doi:10.1016/j.sbspro.2010.03.552

Miao, Q., Li, Q., & Zeng, D. (2010). Fine-grained opinion mining by integrating multiple review sources. *Journal of the American Society for Information Science and Technology*, *61*(11), 2288–2299. doi:10.1002/asi.21400

Mikheieva, O., Otroshko, T., Sydorenko, T., Kvotun, A., & Sviderska, O. (2021). New technologies and pedagogical profession: analysis of best practices (on the example of a group of universities). *Laplage em Revista (International)*, *7*(B), 135-147.

Mikolov, K., Chen, G., & Corrado, J. (2013). *Efficient Estimation of Word Representations in Vector Space*. arXiv Preprint. arXiv:1301.3781v3

Mikolov, W. T., Yih, G., & Zweig. (2013). Linguistic Regularities in Continuous Space Word Representations. *Proceedings of NAACL-HLT 2013*, 746–751.

Miller, J. (2006). *Protection Reversal Magick: A Witch's Defense Manual*. New Page Books.

Miranda, S. (2019). *Social Analytics*. Prospect Press.

Mitchell, L., Campbell, C., Somerville, M., Cardell, E., & Williams, L. (2021). Enhancing graduate employability through targeting ePortfolios to employers' expectations. *The Journal of Teaching and Learning for Graduate Employability*, *12*(2), 82–98. doi:10.21153/jtlge2021vol12no2art1003

Mitra, A. (2010). Creating a Presence on Social Networks via Narbs. *Global Media Journal*, (9), 16.

Mokhtari, K., Rosemary, C. A., & Edwards, P. A. (2007). Making instructional decisions based on data: What, how, and why. *The Reading Teacher*, *61*(4), 354–359. doi:10.1598/RT.61.4.10

Molenaar, I., Horvers, A., Dijkstra, R., & Baker, R. (2019). Designing Dashboards to support learners' Self-Regulated Learning. *Proceedings 9th International Conference on Learning Analytics & Knowledge*, 1-12.

Molenaar, I., & Knoop-van Campen, C. (2017). Teacher Dashboards in Practice: Usage and Impact. In É. Lavoué, H. Drachsler, K. Verbert, J. Broisin, & M. Pérez-Sanagustín (Eds.), *Data Driven Approaches in Digital Education* (pp. 125–138). Springer International Publishing. doi:10.1007/978-3-319-66610-5_10

Moore, D. S. (1997). New pedagogy and new content: The case of statistics. *International Statistical Review*, *65*(2), 123–137. doi:10.1111/j.1751-5823.1997.tb00390.x

Moors, A., Van de Cruys, S., & Pourtois, G. (2021). Comparison of the determinants for positive and negative affect proposed by appraisal theories, goal-directed theories, and predictive processing theories. *Current Opinion in Behavioral Sciences*, *39*, 147–152. doi:10.1016/j.cobeha.2021.03.015

Mostafa, M. M. (2018). Mining and mapping halal food consumers: A geo-located Twitter opinion polarity analysis. *Journal of Food Products Marketing*, *24*(7), 858–879. doi:10.1080/10454446.2017.1418695

Mostafa, M. M. (2019). Clustering halal food consumers: A Twitter sentiment analysis. *International Journal of Market Research*, *61*(3), 320–337. doi:10.1177/1470785318771451

Mostafa, M. M. (2020). Global halal food discourse on social media: A text mining approach. *Journal of International Communication*, *26*(2), 211–237. doi:10.1080/13216597.2020.1795702

Motiwalla, L. F. (2007). Mobile learning: A framework and evaluation. *Computers & Education*, *49*(3), 581–596. doi:10.1016/j.compedu.2005.10.011

Motz, B., Quick, J., Schroeder, N., Zook, J., & Gunkel, M. 2019. The validity and utility of activity logs as a measure of student engagement. In *Proceedings of the 9th International Conference on Learning Analytics & Knowledge (LAK)*. Association for Computing Machinery. 10.1145/3303772.3303789

Mujahid, M., Lee, E., Rustam, F., Washington, P. B., Ullah, S., Reshi, A. A., & Ashraf, I. (2021). Sentiment analysis and topic modeling on tweets about online education during covid-19. *Applied Sciences (Switzerland)*, *11*(18), 8438. Advance online publication. doi:10.3390/app11188438

Mullen, T., & Collier, N. (2004). Sentiment Analysis using Support Vector Machines with Diverse Information Sources. In D. Lin & D. Wu (Eds.), *Proceedings of EMNLP 2004* (pp. 412–418). Association for Computational Linguistics. Retrieved from http://research.nii.ac.jp/~collier/papers/emnlp2004.pdf

Nasreen Taj, M. B., & Girisha, G. S. (2021). Insights of strength and weakness of evolving methodologies of sentiment analysis. *Global Transitions Proceedings*, *2*(2), 157–162. doi:10.1016/j.gltp.2021.08.059

Nasukawa, T., & Yi, J. (2003). Sentiment analysis: Capturing favorability using natural language processing. In *Proceedings of the 2nd International Conference on Knowledge Capture, K-CAP 2003* (pp. 70–77). Association for Computing Machinery, Inc. 10.1145/945645.945658

National Center on Intensive Intervention. (n.d.). *What is data-based individuation?* American Institutes for Research. https://intensiveintervention.org/data-based-individualization

Nemes, L., & Kiss, A. (2021). Prediction of stock values changes using sentiment analysis of stock news headlines. *Journal of Information and Telecommunication*, *5*(3), 375–394. doi:10.1080/24751839.2021.1874252

Neter, J., Kutner, M. H., Nachtsheim, C. J., & Wasserman, W. (1996). *Applied linear statistical models* (4th ed.). McGraw-Hill.

Newman, D. T., Fast, N. J., & Harmon, D. J. (2020). When eliminating bias isn't fair: Algorithmic reductionism and procedural justice in human resource decisions. *Organizational Behavior and Human Decision Processes*, *160*, 149–167. doi:10.1016/j.obhdp.2020.03.008

Ng, A. (n.d.). *Machine Learning*. Retrieved from Coursera: https://www.coursera.org/learn/machine-learning

Noble, S. U. (2018). *Algorithms of Oppression*. NYU Press. doi:10.2307/j.ctt1pwt9w5

Ocheja, P., Flanagan, B., Ueda, H., & Ogata, H. (2019). Managing lifelong learning records through blockchain. *Research and Practice in Technology Enhanced Learning*, *14*(1), 1–19. doi:10.118641039-019-0097-0

Öhman, C. J., & Watson, D. (2019). Are the dead taking over Facebook? A Big Data approach to the future of death online. *Big Data & Society*, *6*(1). doi:10.1177/2053951719842540

Okoro, E. A., Washington, M. C., & Cardon, P. W. (2011). Eportfolios in Business Communication Courses as Tools for Employment. *Business Communication Quarterly*, *74*(3), 347–351. doi:10.1177/1080569911414554

Oliveira, N., Cortez, P., & Areal, N. (2016). Stock market sentiment lexicon acquisition using microblogging data and statistical measures. *Decision Support Systems*, *85*, 62–73. doi:10.1016/j.dss.2016.02.013

Onwudebelu, U., Fasola, S., & Williams, E. O. (2013). Creating Pathway for Enhancing Student Collection of Academic Records in Nigeria-a New Direction. *Computer Science and Information Technology*, *1*(1), 65–71. doi:10.13189/csit.2013.010108

Ophir, Y., Walter, D., Arnon, D., Lokmanoglu, A., Tizzoni, M., Carota, J., D'Antiga, L., & Nicastro, E. (2021, March 4). The Framing of COVID-19 in Italian media and its relationship with community mobility: A mixed-method approach. *Journal of Health Communication*, *26*(3), 161–173. Advance online publication. doi:10.1080/10810730.2021.1899344 PMID:33787462

Organization for Economic Cooperation and Development. (2010a). *Participating countries/economies*. https://www.oecd.org/pages/0,3417,en_32252351_32236225_1_1_1_1_1,00.html

Organization for Economic Cooperation and Development. (2010b). *Strong performers and successful reformers in Education: Lessons from PISA for the United States*. OECD Publishing. https://www.oecd.org/dataoecd/32/50/46623978.pdf

Organization for Economic Cooperation and Development. (2010c). *PISA 2009 results: What students know and can do: Student performance in reading, mathematics, and science (Volume 1)*. OECD Publishing. https://www.oecd.org/dataoecd/10/61/48852548.pdf

Organization for Economic Cooperation and Development. (2010d). *PISA 2012 mathematics framework*. OECD Publishing. https://www.oecd.org/dataoecd/8/38/46961598.pdf

Organization for Economic Cooperation and Development. (2011a). *Quality time for students: learning in and out of school*. OECD Publishing. https://www.oecd-ilibrary.org/docserver/9789264087057-en.pdf?expires=1576462357&id=id&accname=guest&checksum=B1535560A911E8359B1EE95DFF221A2B

Organization for Economic Cooperation and Development. (2011b). *Education at a Glance 2011: OECD indicators*. OECD Publishing. https://www.oecd.org/dataoecd/61/2/48631582.pdf

Organization for Economic Cooperation and Development. (2018). *PISA 2018: Insights and interpretations*. OECD Publishing. https://www.oecd.org/pisa/PISA%202018%20Insights%20and%20Interpretations%20FINAL%20PDF.pdf

Osborne, J. W., Costello, A. B., & Kellow, J. T. (2008). Best Practices in Exploratory Factor Analysis. In J. W. Osborne (Ed.), *Best Practices in Quantitative Methods* (pp. 205–213). Sage Publishing.

Pak, A., & Paroubek, P. (2010). Twitter as a corpus for sentiment analysis and opinion mining. In *Proceedings of the 7th International Conference on Language Resources and Evaluation, LREC 2010* (pp. 1320–1326). European Language Resources Association (ELRA). 10.17148/IJARCCE.2016.51274

Pallegedara, A., & Mottaleb, K. A. (2018). Patterns and determinants of private tutoring: The case of Bangladesh households. *International Journal of Educational Development, 59*, 43–50. doi:10.1016/j.ijedudev.2017.10.004

Pang, B., & Lee, L. (2008). Opinion mining and sentiment analysis. *Foundations and Trends in Information Retrieval, 2*(1–2), 1–135. doi:10.1561/1500000011

Panhalkar, A. R., & Doye, D. D. (2021). Optimization of decision trees using modified African buffalo algorithm. *Journal of King Saud University - Computer and Information Sciences*. doi:10.1016/j.jksuci.2021.01.011

Paniagua, F. G. (2019). Quality Assurance in Online Education: A Development Process to Design High-Quality Courses. In *International Conference on Human-Computer Interaction* (pp. 182-194). Springer. 10.1007/978-3-030-21905-5_14

Pano, T., & Kashef, R. (2020). A Complete VADER-Based Sentiment Analysis of Bitcoin (BTC) Tweets during the Era of COVID-19. *Big Data and Cognitive Computing, 4*(4), 33. Advance online publication. doi:10.3390/bdcc4040033

Papst, C. (2021). *Bombshell allegations at another Ciry school – Dead students enrolled, Classes didn't exist*. Fox 45 News. https://foxbaltimore.com/news/project-baltimore/dead-students-enrolled-classes-didnt-exist-baltimore-school

Paranyushkin, D. (2019). Infranodus. *Proceedings of WWW '19: The Web Conference*. 10.1145/3308558.3314123

Pardo, A., Han, F., & Ellis, R. A. (2016, April). Exploring the relation between self-regulation, online activities, and academic performance: A case study. In *Proceedings of the 6th International Conference on Learning Analytics & Knowledge (LAK)* (pp. 422-429). 10.1145/2883851.2883883

Passlick, J., Guhr, N., Lebek, B., & Breitner, M. H. (2020). Encouraging the use of self-service business intelligence – an examination of employee-related influencing factors. *Journal of Decision Systems, 29*(1), 1–26. doi:10.1080/12460125.2020.1739884

Peng, F. L. (2005). Feature selection based on mutual information: criteria of max-dependency, max-relevance, and minredundancy. *IEEE Transactions on Pattern Analysis & Machine Intelligence, 8*, 1226–1238.

Perelman, L. (2020). The BABEL Generator and E-Rater. *Journal of Writing Assessment, 13*(1). http://journalofwritingassessment.org

Perry, J. (2005). *Privacy and Student Records An Analysis of the NCAA Clearinghouse in Relation to FERPA*. Retrieved from: http://www.c3schools.org/CourseInfo/educ473/james_educ_final_698v.pdf

Petty, R. E., & Cacioppo, J. T. (1986). *Communication and Persuasion: Central and Peripheral Routes to Attitude Change*. Springer-Verlag. doi:10.1007/978-1-4612-4964-1

Pichai, S. (2021, March 11). *Career certificates and more ways we're helping job seekers*. https://blog.google/outreach-initiatives/grow-with-google/career-certificates

Pintrich, P., Smith, D., Garcia, T., & McKeachie, W. (1991). *A manual for the use of the motivated strategies for learning questionnaire (MSLQ)*. National Center for Research to Improve Postsecondary Teaching and Learning.

Pitas, I. (2000). *Digital image processing algorithms and applications*. John Wiley & Sons.

Poropat, A. E. (2009). A meta-analysis of the five-factor model of personality and academic performance. *Psychological Bulletin, 135*(2), 322–338. doi:10.1037/a0014996 PMID:19254083

Preethi, P. G., Uma, V., & Kumar, A. (2015). Temporal sentiment analysis and causal rules extraction from tweets for event prediction. In *Procedia Computer Science* (Vol. 48, pp. 84–89). Elsevier B.V. doi:10.1016/j.procs.2015.04.154

Prenovost, J. K. E. (2001). *A first-year evaluation of after-school learning programs in four urban middle schools in the Santa Ana unified school district*. Author.

Prieto, L. M., Aguero-Valverde, J., Zarrate-Cardenas, G., & Van Maarseveen, M. (2019). Parental preferences in the choice for a specialty school. *Journal of School Choice, 13*(2), 198–227. doi:10.1080/15582159.2018.1442087

Puckett, J., Boutenko, V., Hoteit, L., Polunin, K., Perapechka, S., & Stepanenko, A. (2020, January 15). *Fixing the Global Skills Mismatch*. https://www.bcg.com/publications/2020/fixing-global-skills-mismatch

Pulsipher, S. (2020, June 26). *Forget Bitcoin—Skills Are the Currency of The Future*. https://www.forbes.com/sites/scottpulsipher/2020/06/26/forget-bitcoin-skills-are-the-currency-of-the-future/?sh=518823d274e7

Qiao, S., Yan, B., & Li, J. (2018). Ensemble learning for protein multiplex subcellular localization prediction based on weighted KNN with different features. *Applied Intelligence, 48*(7), 1813–1824. doi:10.100710489-017-1029-6

Raghavan, M., Barocas, S., Kelinberg, J., & Levy, K. (2020). Mitigating Bias in Algorithmic Hiring: Evaluating Claims and Practices. *Conference on Fairness, Accountability, and Transparency*. 10.1145/3351095.3372828

Rahmaturrizki, M. I., & Skumayadi, Y. (2020). Youtube as audio visual media learning in music education. *Advances in Social Science, Education and Humanities Research, 519*, 297–303.

Ram'ırez-Gallego, S., Lastra, I., Martínez-Rego, D., Bolón-Canedo, V., Benítez, J. M., Herrera, F., & Alonso-Betanzos, A. (2017). Fast-mrmr:Fast minimum redundancy maximum relevance algorithm for high dimensional big data. *International Journal of Intelligent Systems, 32*(2), 134–152. doi:10.1002/int.21833

Ravi, K., & Ravi, V. (2015). A survey on opinion mining and sentiment analysis: Tasks, approaches and applications. *Knowledge-Based Systems, 89*, 14–46. doi:10.1016/j.knosys.2015.06.015

Read, J., & Carroll, J. (2012). Annotating expressions of Appraisal in English. *Language Resources and Evaluation, 46*(3), 421–447. doi:10.100710579-010-9135-7

Reagans, R., & Zuckerman, E. W. (2001). Networks, Diversity, and Productivity. *Organization Science, 12*(4), 502–517. doi:10.1287/orsc.12.4.502.10637

Recker, M. M., Walker, A., & Lawless, K. (2003). *What do you recommend? Implementation and analyses of collaborative information filtering of web resources for education*. Academic Press.

Reigeluth, C. M. (1999). What is instructional design theory and how is it changing? In C. M. Reigeluth (Ed.), *Instructional-design theories and models: A new paradigm of instructional theory* (Vol. 2, pp. 5–29). Routledge.

Reshef, D., Reshef, Y. A., Finucane, H. K., Grossman, S. R., McVean, G., Turnbaugh, P. J., Lander, E. S., Mitzenmacher, M., & Sabeti, P. C. (2011). Detecting novel associations in large. *Science, 6062*(334), 1518–1524. doi:10.1126cience.1205438 PMID:22174245

Richard, J., Braman, J., Colclough, M., & Bishwakarma, S. (2020). A Neural Affective Approach to an Intelligent Weather Sensor System. In C. Stephanidis, M. Antona, & S. Ntoa (Eds.), *HCI International 2020 Late-Breaking Posters. HCII 2020. Communications in Computer and Information Science* (Vol. 1293). Springer. doi:10.1007/978-3-030-60700-5_46

Richardson, M., Abraham, C., & Bond, R. (2012). Psychological correlates of university students' academic performance: A systematic review and meta-analysis. *Psychological Bulletin, 138*(2), 353–387. doi:10.1037/a0026838 PMID:22352812

Rodríguez-Hidalgo, C. T., Tan, E. S. H., & Verlegh, P. W. J. (2015). The social sharing of emotion (SSE) in online social networks: A case study in Live Journal. *Computers in Human Behavior, 52*, 364–372. doi:10.1016/j.chb.2015.05.009

Rosenblat, A., Kneese, T., & boyd, d. (2014). Networked Employment Discrimination. *Data&Society*. https://www.datasociety.net/pubs/fow/EmploymentDiscrimination.pdf

Rout, J. K., Choo, K.-K. R., Dash, A. K., Bakshi, S., Jena, S. K., & Williams, K. L. (2017). A model for sentiment and emotion analysis of unstructured social media text. *Electronic Commerce Research*, *18*(1), 181–199. doi:10.100710660-017-9257-8

Rutherford, T. (2021, April 7). *At a Crossroad: The Intersection of Higher Education and Corporate Training*. https://www.chieflearningofficer.com/2021/04/07/at-a-crossroads-the-intersection-of-higher-education-and-corporate-training/

Ryan, W. (2019, January 29). *Microcredentials Forge the Links Between Businesses, the Community and their College.* Academic Press.

Saa, A. A., Al-Emran, M., & Shaalan, K. (2019, March). Mining student information system records to predict students' academic performance. In *International conference on advanced machine learning technologies and applications* (pp. 229-239). Springer.

Sabou, M., Wroe, C., Goble, C., & Stuckenschmidt, H. (2005). Learning domain ontologies for semantic web service descriptions. *Journal of Web Semantics*, *3*(4), 340–365. doi:10.1016/j.websem.2005.09.008

Sahin, G. C. (2014). A survey on feature selection methods. *Computers & Electrical Engineering*, *40*(1), 16–28. doi:10.1016/j.compeleceng.2013.11.024

Saif, H., He, Y., Fernandez, M., & Alani, H. (2016). Contextual semantics for sentiment analysis of Twitter. *Information Processing & Management*, *52*(1), 5–19. doi:10.1016/j.ipm.2015.01.005

Saint, J., Fan, Y., Singh, S., Gasevic, D., & Pardo, A. (2021, April). Using process mining to analyze self-regulated learning: a systematic analysis of four algorithms. In *Proceedings of the 11th International Learning Analytics and Knowledge Conference (LAK)* (pp. 333-343). 10.1145/3448139.3448171

Salisu, I., Bin Mohd Sappri, M., & Bin Omar, M. F. (2021). The adoption of business intelligence systems in small and medium enterprises in the healthcare sector: A systematic literature review. *Cogent Business & Management*, *8*(1), 1935663. doi:10.1080/23311975.2021.1935663

Salloum, M., Jeske, D., Ma, W., Papalexakis, V., Shelton, C., Tsotras, V., & Zhou, S. (2021). Developing an interdisciplinary data science program. In *Proceedings of the 52nd ACM Technical Symposium on Computer Science Education* (pp. 509-515). 10.1145/3408877.3432454

Sammons, M., Christodoulopoulos, C., Kordjamshidi, P., Khashabi, D., Srikumar, V., & Roth, D. (2016). Edison: Feature extraction for nlp, simplified. *Proceedings of the Tenth International Conference on Language Resources and Evaluation (LREC'16).*

Sas. (2022). *What is a Data Scientist? Who they are, what they do and why you want to be one*. https://www.sas.com/en_us/insights/analytics/what-is-a-data-scientist.html

Scherer, K. R., Schorr, A., & Johnstone, T. (Eds.). (2001). *Appraisal processes in emotion: Theory, methods, research.* Oxford University Press.

Schlesinger, P., & Rahman, N. (2016). Self-Service Business Intelligence Resulting in Disruptive Technology. *Journal of Computer Information Systems*, *56*(1), 11–21. doi:10.1080/08874417.2015.11645796

Schofer, E., Ramirez, F. O., & Meyer, J. W. (2021). The societal consequences of higher education. *Sociology of Education*, *94*(1), 1–19. doi:10.1177/0038040720942912

Schuff, D., Corral, K., St. Louis, R. D., & Schymik, G. (2018). Enabling self-service BI: A methodology and a case study for a model management warehouse. *Information Systems Frontiers*, *20*(2), 275–288. doi:10.100710796-016-9722-2

Schunk, D. H. (2012). *Learning Theories–An Educational Perspective* (6th ed.). Pearson Education.

Schwartz, S. E., & Noam, G. G. (2007). *Informal science learning in afterschool settings: A natural fit?* University of Massachusetts.

Selvarajah, K., Kobti, Z., & Kargar, M. (2020). Cultural Algorithms for Cluster Hiring. *The 11th International Conference on Ambient Systems, Networks and Technologies (ANT)*.

Shadish, W. R., Cook, T. D., & Campbell, D. T. (2002). *Experimental and quasiexperimental designs for generalized causal inference*. Houghton Mifflin Company.

Shahiri, A. M., Husain, W., & Rashid, N. A. (2015). A review on predicting student's performance using data mining techniques. *Procedia Computer Science*, *72*, 414–422. doi:10.1016/j.procs.2015.12.157

Sharda, R., Delen, D., & Turban, E. (2021). *Analytics, Data Science, & Artificial Intelligence: Systems for Decision Support* (11th ed.). Pearson. doi:10.1201/9781003140351

Shaughnessy, J. M. (1977). Misconceptions of probability: An experiment with a smallgroup activity-based model building approach to introductory probability at the college level. *Educational Studies in Mathematics*, *8*(3), 285–315. doi:10.1007/BF00385927

Shieh, G. (2010). Estimation of the simple correlation coefficient. *Behavior Research Methods, 42*, 906–917.

Sigirci, I. O., Ozgur, H., Oluk, A., Uz, H., Cetiner, E., Oktay, H. U., & Erdemir, K. (2020). Sentiment Analysis of Turkish Reviews on Google Play Store. *2020 5th International Conference on Computer Science and Engineering (UBMK)*. doi:10.1109/ubmk50275.2020.921

Singer, J. D., & Willett, J. B. (1990). Improving the teaching of applied statistics: Putting the data back into data analysis. *The American Statistician*, *44*, 223–230.

Skinner, B. F. (1958). Teaching Machines. *Science*, *128*(3330), 969–977. doi:10.1126cience.128.3330.969 PMID:13592277

Smith-Doerr, L., Alegria, S., & Sacco, T. (2017). How Diversity matters in the US Sicence and Engineering Workforce. *Engaging Science, Technology, and Society*, *3*, 139–153. doi:10.17351/ests2017.142

Smith, G. (1998). Learning statistics by doing statistics. *Journal of Statistics Education: An International Journal on the Teaching and Learning of Statistics*, *6*(3).

Smith, P. L., & Ragan, T. J. (2004). *Instructional design* (3rd ed.). John Wiley & Sons.

Snee, R. D. (1993). What's missing in statistical education? *The American Statistician*, *47*, 149–154.

Snowman, J. (1997). Educational Psychology: What Do We Teach, What Should We Teach? *Educational Psychology Review*, *9*(2), 151–170. doi:10.1023/A:1024740512959

Society for Learning Analytics. (n.d.). *What Is Learning Analytics?* Retrieved December 6, 2021, from https://www.solaresearch.org/about/what-is-learning-analytics/

Sofka, C., Cupit, I., & Gilbert, K. (2012). *Dying, death, and grief in an online universe: For counselors and educators*. Springer Publishing Company.

Song, L., & Hill, J. R. (2007). A Conceptual Model for Understanding Self-Directed Learning in Online Environments. *Journal of Interactive Online Learning*, *6*(1), 27–42.

Spann, C. A., Schaeffer, J., & Siemens, G. (2017, March). Expanding the scope of learning analytics data: Preliminary findings on attention and self-regulation using wearable technology. In *Proceedings of the 7th international learning analytics & knowledge conference (LAK)* (pp. 203-207). 10.1145/3027385.3027427

Spearman, C. (1904). General intelligence objectively determined and measured. *The American Journal of Psychology*, *15*, 201–293.

Spearman, C. (1927). *The abilities of man: Their nature and measurement*. Macmillan.

Steinhorst, R., & Keeler, C. (1995). Developing material for introductory statistics courses from a conceptual, active learning viewpoint. *Journal of Statistics Education: An International Journal on the Teaching and Learning of Statistics*, *3*(3).

Stum, J. (2009). Kirton's Adaption-Innovation Theory: Managing Cognitive Styles in Times of Diversity and Change. *Emerging Leadership Journeys*, *2*(1), 66–78.

Stylianides, A. J., & Stylianides, G. J. (2014). Impacting positively on students' mathematical problem-solving beliefs: An instructional intervention of short duration. *The Journal of Mathematical Behavior*, *33*, 8–29. doi:10.1016/j.jmathb.2013.08.005

Suhr, T., Hilgard, S., & Lakkaraju, H. (2021). Does Fair Ranking Improve Minority Outcomes? *AIES '21*.

Suraworachet, W., Villa-Torrano, C., Zhou, Q., Asensio-Pérez, J. I., Dimitriadis, Y., & Cukurova, M. (2021). Examining the relationship between reflective writing behaviour and self-regulated learning competence: A time-series analysis. In *European Conference on Technology Enhanced Learning* (pp. 163-177). Springer. 10.1007/978-3-030-86436-1_13

Suter, L. E. (2016). Outside school time: An examination of science achievement and non-cognitive characteristics of 15-year-olds in several countries. *International Journal of Science Education*, *38*(4), 663–687. doi:10.1080/09500693.2016.1147661

Szabo, E. (2021). Online platform courses between educational and business. Annals of the "Constantin Brâncusi" University of Târgu Jiu. *Economy Series*, *1*, 197–204.

Szekely, G. J., Rizzo, M. L., & Bakirov, N. K. (2007). Measuring and testing dependence by Correlation of distances. *Annals of Statistics*, *35*(6), 2769–2794. doi:10.1214/009053607000000505

Tang, J. S. A. (2014). Feature Selection for Classification: A Review. CRC Press.

Tan, M. J., & Guan, C. H. (2021). Are people happier in locations of high property value? Spatial temporal analytics of activity frequency, public sentiment and housing price using twitter data. *Applied Geography (Sevenoaks, England)*, *132*, 102474. Advance online publication. doi:10.1016/j.apgeog.2021.102474

Taskin, Y., Hecking, T., & Hopope, H. U. ESA-T2N: A Novel Approach to Network-Text Analysis. In H. Cherifi, J. Mendes, L. Rocha, S. Gaito, & E. Moro (Eds.), *Complex Networks and Their Applications VIII* (Vol. 2, pp. 129–139). Springer. doi:10.1007/978-3-030-36683-4_11

Tavani, H. (2020). *Ethics and Technology: Controversies, Questions, and Strategies for Ethical Computing*. John Wiley & Sons.

Tavegia, S., Braman, J., Vincenti, G., & Yancy, B. (2019). Enhancing Database Courses through the EDNA Project: A Preliminary Framework for the Extraction of Diverse Datasets and Analysis. *Proceedings of the 21th HCI International Conference on Online Communities and Social Computing*. 10.1007/978-3-030-21905-5_18

Tavera Romero, C. A., Ortiz, J. H., Khalaf, O. I., & Ríos Prado, A. (2021). Business Intelligence: Business Evolution after Industry 4.0. *Sustainability*, *13*(18), 10026. doi:10.3390u131810026

Tempelaar, D. T., Rienties, B., & Giesbers, B. (2015). In search for the most informative data for feedback generation: Learning analytics in a data-rich context. *Computers in Human Behavior*, *47*, 157–167. doi:10.1016/j.chb.2014.05.038

Tennyson, R., Dijkstra, S., Schott, F., & Seel, N. (1997). *Instructional design: International perspectives, theory, research, and models* (Vol. 1). Lawrence Erlbaum Associates, Inc.

Thang, N. D. Y.-K. L. (2010). An improved maximum relevance and minimum redundancy feature selection algorithm based on normalized mutual information. *2010 10th IEEE/IPSJ International Symposium on Applications and the Internet*.

The Campaign for Learning. (2007). *What is learning to learn?* https://www.campaign-for-learning.org.uk/Handlers/Download.ashx?IDMF=07f4cb7b-6f5f-42d2-8831-842c5f189797

The Conference Board. (n.d.). *US Labor Shortages: Challenges and Solutions*. https://conference-board.org/pdfdownload.cfm?masterProductID=20471

Thun, A. (2020). *Matching Job Applicants to Free Text Job Ads Using Semantic Networks and natural Language Inference* [Unpublished MA thesis]. KTH Royal Institute of Technology, Stockholm, Sweden.

Thurstone, L. L. (1947). *Multiple-factor analysis: A development and expansion of The Vectors of Mind*. Academic Press.

Thurstone, L. L. (1932). *The Theory of Multiple Factors*. Edwards Brothers.

Torres, M. A. (2017, November 6). *This is What Powerful Learning Looks Like: Students Share Their Stories* [Blog Post]. Retrieved from: www.digitalpromise.org/2017/11/06/powerful-learning-looks-like-students-share-stories/

Trajkovski, G., Killian, R., & Cohen, S. (2021). Bridging the Gaps between Higher Education, Industry, and the Learner: The Skills First Approach. In S. Ramlall, T. Cross, & M. Love (Eds.), *Handbook of Research on Future of Work and Education: Implications for Curriculum Delivery and Work Design*. IGI Global.

Triantafyllou, I., Drivas, I. C., & Giannakopoulos, G. (2020). How to utilize my app reviews? A novel topics extraction machine learning schema for strategic business purposes. *Entropy (Basel, Switzerland)*, *22*(11), 1–21. doi:10.3390/e22111310 PMID:33287075

Trivedi, S., Pards, Z. A., & Heffernan, N. T. (2015). The utility of clustering in prediction tasks. *arXiv*, (September), 1–11.

Tu, Y. F., & Hwang, G. J. (2018). The roles of sensing technologies and learning strategies in library-associated mobile learning: A review of 2007–2016 journal publications. *International Journal of Mobile Learning and Organisation*, *12*(1), 42–54. doi:10.1504/IJMLO.2018.089233

Tu, Y., Zou, D., & Zhang, R. (2020). A comprehensive framework for designing and evaluating vocabulary learning apps from multiple perspectives. *International Journal of Mobile Learning and Organisation*, *14*(3), 370–397. doi:10.1504/IJMLO.2020.108199

U.S. Bureau of Labor Statistics. (2020). *Data Scientists and Mathematical Science Occupations*. https://www.bls.gov/oes/current/oes152098.htm#nat

U.S. Bureau of Labor Statistics. (2021). *Occupational Employment and Wage Statistics*. https://www.bls.gov/oes/tables.htm#nat

U.S. Census Bureau. (2020). *U.S. Census Bureau Releases New Educational Attainment Data*. U.S. Census Bureau Releases New Educational Attainment Data.

Udacity. (n.d.). *Become a Data Analyst*. https://www.udacity.com/course/data-analyst-nanodegree--nd002

Valk, J.-H., Rashid, A. T., & Elder, L. (2010). Using mobile phones to improve educational outcomes: An analysis of evidence from Asia. *International Review of Research in Open and Distance Learning*, *11*(1), 117–140. doi:10.19173/irrodl.v11i1.794

Van Der Aalst, W. (2012). Process mining. *Communications of the ACM*, *55*(8), 76–83. doi:10.1145/2240236.2240257

Van der Kleij, F. M., Feskens, R. C. W., & Eggen, T. J. H. M. (2015). Effects of Feedback in a Computer-Based Learning Environment on Students' Learning Outcomes: A Meta-Analysis. *Review of Educational Research*, *85*(4), 475–511. doi:10.3102/0034654314564881

van Knippenberg, D., Nishii, L. H., & Dwertmann, D. J. G. (2020). Synergy from diversity: Managing team diversity to enhance performance. *Behavioral Science & Policy*, *6*(1), 75–92. doi:10.1353/bsp.2020.0007

Vandell, D. L., Reisner, E. R., & Pierce, K. M. (2007). *Outcomes linked to high-quality afterschool programs: Longitudinal findings from the study of promising practices*. Policy Study Associates. https://files.eric.ed.gov/fulltext/ED499113.pdf

Vandell, D. L., Reisner, E. R., Brown, B. B., Dadisman, K., Pierce, K. M., Lee, D., & Pechman, E. M. (2005). *The study of promising after-school programs: Examination of intermediate outcomes in year 2. University of Wisconsin*. Wisconsin Center for Education Research., http://childcare.wceruw.org/pdf/pp/year2_executive_summary_and_brief_report.pdf

Vandell, D. L., Reisner, E. R., Brown, B. B., Pierce, K. M., Dadisman, K., & Pechman, E. M. (2004). *The study of promising after-school programs: Descriptive report of the promising programs. University of Wisconsin*. Wisconsin Center for Education Research., http://childcare.wceruw.org/pdf/pp/study_of_after_school_activities_descriptive_report_year1.pdf

Vashishtha, S., & Susan, S. (2020). Fuzzy Interpretation of Word Polarity Scores for Unsupervised Sentiment Analysis. In *2020 11th International Conference on Computing, Communication and Networking Technologies, ICCCNT 2020*. Institute of Electrical and Electronics Engineers Inc. 10.1109/ICCCNT49239.2020.9225646

Walker, M. (2011). *PISA 2009 plus results: Performance of 15-year-olds in reading, mathematics, and science for 10 additional participants*. Acer Press. https://research.acer.edu.au/pisa/1/

Waller, M. A., & Fawcett, S. E. (2013). Data science, predictive analytics, and big data: A revolution that will transform supply chain design and management. *Journal of Business Logistics*, *34*(2), 77–84. doi:10.1111/jbl.12010

Walls, J., & Kemper, S. (2018). Fitting In to Stand Out: How Teachers at Small, Urban "Specialty Schools" Experience Extra-Organizational Influence. *Leadership and Policy in Schools*, 1–27. doi:10.1080/15700763.2018.1453936

Walter, D., & Ophir, Y. (2019). News Frame Analysis: An Inductive Mixed-Method Computational Approach. *Communication Methods and Measures*, *13*(4), 248–266. Advance online publication. doi:10.1080/19312458.2019.1639145

Wang, C., & Blei, D. M. (2009). Decoupling sparsity and smoothness in the discrete hierarchical Dirichlet process. *Neural Information Processing Systems*, *22*, 1982–1989.

Wang, J. (2005). Relationship between mathematics and science achievement at the 8th grade. *International Journal of Science and Mathematics Education*, *5*, 1–17.

Wang, S., Sun, T., Qu, X., & Xu, W. (2021). Online education of atomic physics based on MOOC platform. *Journal of Physics: Conference Series*, *1881*(3), 1–5. doi:10.1088/1742-6596/1881/3/032009

Wang, W., Guo, L., & Wu, Y. J. (2022). The merits of a sentiment analysis of antecedent comments for the prediction of online fundraising outcomes. *Technological Forecasting and Social Change*, *174*, 121070. doi:10.1016/j.techfore.2021.121070

Wang, Y. Y., Wang, Y. S., Lin, H. H., & Tsai, T. H. (2019). Developing and validating a model for assessing paid mobile learning app success. *Interactive Learning Environments*, *27*(4), 458–477. doi:10.1080/10494820.2018.1484773

Wang, Y., Kim, J., & Kim, J. (2021). The financial impact of online customer reviews in the restaurant industry: A moderating effect of brand equity. *International Journal of Hospitality Management, 95*, 102895. Advance online publication. doi:10.1016/j.ijhm.2021.102895

Wang, Y., Norcie, G., Komanduri, S., Acquisti, A., Leon, P. G., & Cranor, L. F. (2011). I regretted the minute I pressed share: A qualitative study of regrets on Facebook. In *Proceedings of the Seventh Symposium on Usable Privacy and Security* (p. 10). ACM. 10.1145/2078827.2078841

Ward, B. (2004). The best of both worlds: A hybrid statistics class. *Journal of Statistics Education: An International Journal on the Teaching and Learning of Statistics, 12*(3).

Weber, L. (2012). Your Résumé vs. Oblivion, Inundated Companies Resort to Software to Sift Job Applications for Right Skills. *The Wallstreet Journal*. http://online.wsj.com/news/articles/SB10001424052970204624204577178941034941330

Weijters, A. J. M. M., van Der Aalst, W. M., & De Medeiros, A. A. (2006). Process mining with the heuristics miner-algorithm. *Technische Universiteit Eindhoven. Tech. Rep. WP, 166*, 1–34.

West, A., & Noden, P. (2000). *School reform in England: Increasing choice and diversity through specialist schools?* Paper presented at the Annual Meeting of the American Educational Research Association, New Orleans, LA. Retrieved from https://files.eric.ed.gov/fulltext/ED445417.pdf

Widyaningrum, P., Ruldeviyani, Y., & Dharayani, R. (2019). Sentiment analysis to assess the community's enthusiasm towards the development chatbot using an appraisal theory. *Procedia Computer Science, 161, 723–730.* doi:10.1016/j.procs.2019.11.176

Winne, P. H., & Nesbit, J. C. (2010). The psychology of academic achievement. *Annual Review of Psychology, 61*(1), 653–678. doi:10.1146/annurev.psych.093008.100348 PMID:19575616

Wolters, C. A., Pintrich, P. R., & Karabenick, S. A. (2005). Assessing academic self-regulated learning. In *What do children need to flourish?* (pp. 251–270). Springer. doi:10.1007/0-387-23823-9_16

World Bank Group. (2011). *Learning for all: Investing in people's knowledge and skills to promote development.* World Bank Group Education Strategy 2020.

Wright, N. (2014). Death and the Internet: The implications of the digital afterlife. *First Monday*. Advance online publication. doi:10.5210/fm.v19i6.4998

Xie, F. M., & Holte, R. (2014). Adding Local Exploration to Greedy Best-First Search in Satisficing Planning. *Twenty-Eighth AAAI Conference on Artificial Intelligence.*

Xuequn, W., & Yanjun, Y. (2015). How individual characteristics influence people's evaluation towards information technology in different contexts. *Behaviour & Information Technology, 34*(3), 286–293. doi:10.1080/0144929X.2014.895045

Yadav, A., Jha, C. K., Sharan, A., & Vaish, V. (2020). Sentiment analysis of financial news using unsupervised approach. In *Procedia Computer Science* (Vol. 167, pp. 589–598). Elsevier B.V. doi:10.1016/j.procs.2020.03.325

Yancey, K. B., McElroy, S., & Powers, E. (2013). Composing, Networks, and Electronic Portfolios. In H. McKee & D. DeVoss (Eds.), *Digital writing assessment & evaluation.* Computers and Composition Digital Press/Utah State University Press. https://ccdigitalpress.org/dwae

Yang, L., Li, Y., Wang, J., & Sherratt, R. S. (2020). Sentiment Analysis for E-Commerce Product Reviews in Chinese Based on Sentiment Lexicon and Deep Learning. *IEEE Access: Practical Innovations, Open Solutions, 8*, 23522–23530. doi:10.1109/ACCESS.2020.2969854

Yi Zhang, S. J. (2014). A Novel Algorithm for the Precise Calculation of the Maximal Information Coefficient. *Scientific Reports, 4*(6662), 1-5.

Yim, W., Yetisgen, M., Harris, W. P., & Kwan, S. W. (2016). Natural language processing in oncology: A review. *JAMA Oncology*, *2*(6), 797–804. doi:10.1001/jamaoncol.2016.0213 PMID:27124593

Yuan Chen, Y. Z. (2016). A New Algorithm to Optimize Maximal Information Coefficient. *PLoS One*, 1–13. PMID:27333001

Yue, L., Chen, W., Li, X., Zuo, W., & Yin, M. (2019). A survey of sentiment analysis in social media. *Knowledge and Information Systems*, *60*(2), 617–663. doi:10.100710115-018-1236-4

Yung, K. W. H. (2020). Comparing the effectiveness of cram school tutors and schoolteachers: A critical analysis of students' perceptions. *International Journal of Educational Development*, *72*, 102141. doi:10.1016/j.ijedudev.2019.102141

Zeelenberg, M., & Pieters, R. (2004). Beyond valence in learner dissatisfaction: A review and new findings on behavioral responses to regret and disappointment in failed services. *Journal of Business Research*, *57*(4), 445–455. doi:10.1016/S0148-2963(02)00278-3

Zehr, M. A. (2009). Study finds mixed success for 'enhanced' after-school lessons. *Education Week*, *29*(6), 5–10.

Zhai, G., Yang, Y., Wang, H., & Du, S. (2020). Multi-attention fusion modeling for sentiment analysis of educational big data. *Big Data Mining and Analytics*, *3*(4), 311–319. doi:10.26599/BDMA.2020.9020024

Zhang, Y., Yu, J., Dong, X., & Zhong, P. (2021). Multi-task support vector machine with pinball loss. *Engineering Applications of Artificial Intelligence*, *106*, 104458. Advance online publication. doi:10.1016/j.engappai.2021.104458

Zhao, W. X., Jiang, J., Weng, J., & Lim, E. P. (2011). Comparing Twitter and traditional media using topic models. In *Advances in Information Retrieval: 33rd European Conference on IR Research, ECIR 2011, Dublin, Ireland, April 18-21, 2011. Proceedings*. Berlin: Springer Verlag.

Zhao, Z., R. A. (2019). Maximum Relevance and Minimum Redundancy Feature Selection Methods for a Marketing Machine Learning Platform. *2019 IEEE International Conference on Data Science and Advanced Analytics (DSAA)*. 10.1109/DSAA.2019.00059

Zheng, B., Warschauer, M., Hwang, J. K., & Collins, P. (2014). Laptop use, interactive science software, and science learning among at-Risk students. *Journal of Science Education and Technology*, *1*(5), 591–603. doi:10.100710956-014-9489-5

Zimmerman, B. (2002). Becoming a Self-Regulated Learner: An Overview. *Theory into Practice*, *41*(2), 64–70. doi:10.120715430421tip4102_2

Zimmerman, B. J. (1989). A social cognitive view of self-regulated academic learning. *Journal of Educational Psychology*, *81*(3), 329–339. doi:10.1037/0022-0663.81.3.329

Zou, D., Xie, H., & Wang, F. L. (2018). Future trends and research issues of technology-enhanced language learning: A technological perspective. *Knowledge Management and E-Learning*, *10*(4), 426–440. doi:10.34105/j.kmel.2018.10.026

About the Contributors

Goran Trajkovski Ph.D., MSML, MSCS, MBA, currently serves as a Senior Lead College Compliance Advisor at Western Governors University. He specializes in program, courseware, and assessmentware design and development for high-demand computing and data-science disciplines, and in the regulatory and accreditation processes in the higher education domain. He has been involved in the eLearning movement since its inception, through the conceptualization, development, and deployment of more than 35 undergraduate and graduate programs in a variety of disciplines for online delivery and leading the development of more than 300 online courses. During his three decades in Higher Education, he has served in a variety of instructional and administration roles, including Dean of the School of Computer Information Systems at Virginia International University, Executive Director of Adult and Graduate Studies at Marian University, and Director of Product Strategy and Development at Laureate Education, Inc.

* * *

Abayomi Akanji is an EdTech researcher and a creative Software Engineer. He has experience leading and building offline and online tech solutions for eLearning, collaborative learning and test-prep. When he was a teenager, he co-founded one of Nigeria's foremost e-testing platforms, PassNG - which has helped over 500K students to achieve success in their college entrance exams. Abayomi holds a Bachelor's Degree in Computer Science (from Ladoke Akintola University of Technology) and a Master's in Education & Technology (from University College London). He is also a winner of the Future Award Africa Prize for Education.

Paul Alvorado is an Educational Data Analyst at EdPlus at Arizona State University. After many years of developing strong business acumen, he decided to up-skill in an area that is invaluable to the success of a business - Data Science. In addition to completing a bachelor's degree in Business Finance with the University of Phoenix, he has spent many years solving problems through collaboration, attention to detail, and determination. Using technology and mathematics to analyze data will aid the pursuit of ideal solutions for the business and customer.

Shaljan Areepattamannil holds a PhD from Queens University, Canada. He is a Professor in the Assessment and School Evaluation Division at Emirates College for Advanced Education (ECAE), Abu Dhabi, United Arab Emirates. He conducts interdisciplinary research at the intersection of social psychology and STEAM education.

Ibrahim Bashir did his Masters in Computer Science in Louisiana State University in 2016, with a focus on Data Science and Machine Learning. Has worked with IBM since 2012 on IBM Watson. Joined Educate Ventures as a researcher and data engineer in 2020.

Canan Blake's research focused on evaluation, computer supported collaborative learning, mobile learning and interactions in massive open online courses (MOOCs) and involved observing the interactions of learners with several technology enhanced learning environments as well as developing an evaluation methodology for these environments. She also contributed to design and evaluation of scenarios for developing digital competencies of secondary and primary students in Europe. Recently she worked with world class academics and London EdTech start-ups to change how EdTech entrepreneurs develop and design their products by applying educational research principles to the development of their products and produce evidence informed designs.

James Braman is an Associate Professor in the Computer Science/Information Technology Department at the Community College of Baltimore County for the School of Business Technology & Law. He has been serving as one of the department coordinators since 2016. He earned a B.S. and M.S. in Computer Science and D.Sc. in Information Technology from Towson University. He is currently pursuing an M.S. in Thanatology from Marian University. From 2009 to 2017 he was a joint editor-in-chief for the European Alliance for Innovation (EAI) endorsed Transactions on E-Learning. Dr. Braman's research interests include thanatechnology, virtual and augmented reality, e-Learning, affective computing, agent-based technologies and information retrieval.

Wendy Chin is an Associate Professor and Computer Science/Information Technology Department Chair in the School of Business, Technology and Law at the Community College of Baltimore County. She has been an educator for the last 24 years with specializations in Microsoft applications, Cisco networking, and cyber security. She holds a BS degree in Computer Science and an MS in Cyber Security. She also holds various networking certifications. Wendy is active in the community as a member of the Cyber Association of Maryland (CAMI) serving on the diversity committee.

Samuel Collins, Ph.D, is a cultural anthropologist interested in information society and globalization, primarily in the United States and Korea. His M.A. and Ph.D. are from American University in Washington, D.C. Before he became a professor at Towson University, he taught at Dongseo University in Pusan, South Korea. During 2006-2007, he spent a Fulbright year at Kookmin University in Seoul, and, during a Fulbright in 2014-2015, at Hanyang University in Gyeonggi-do. He blogs frequently on anthropology, science fiction, and the future at All Tomorrow's Cultures.

Paulette Comet is a Professor in the School of Business, Technology and Law at the Community College of Baltimore County. She has been an educator for the last 25 years and has a special interest in adult learning, distance education and emerging technologies. She holds a B.S. degree in Information Systems from University of Baltimore and M.Ed from Goucher College.

Mutlu Cukurova is an Associate Professor of Learning Technologies at University College London, UK. His research focuses on the design, development and implementation of Artificial Intelligence and Analytics solutions to support human learning. Dr Cukurova is engaged with UNESCO's unit for

Technology and AI in Education, UCL's Grand Challenges on Transformative Technologies, is a chief research advisor at EDUCATE Ventures, an editor of the British Journal of Educational Technology and an AE of the International Journal of Child-Computer Interaction.

Mohammad Daradkeh is an Associate Professor of Business Analytics and Data Science at the College of Engineering & Information Technology, University of Dubai. Prior to joining the University of Dubai, Dr. Daradkeh worked at Yarmouk University in Jordan and Lincoln University in New Zealand. He received his PhD in Software and Information Technology from Lincoln University, New Zealand, and MSc. and BSc. in Computer and Information Science from Yarmouk University, Jordan. His research interests are mainly in the areas of business intelligence, analytics, and data science. He currently teaches undergraduate and graduate courses in data science, business intelligence and analytics, and IT project management. Dr. Daradkeh has published in Int. J. of Decision and Information Sciences, Int. J. of Business Information Systems, Journal of Organizational and End User Computing, Information Technology and People, Int. J. of Information Systems in the Service Sector, and Int. J. of Information and Knowledge Management.

Benedict de Boulay is an Emeritus Professor of Artificial Intelligence in the School of Engineering and Informatics at the University of Sussex, UK. His main research area is the application of Artificial Intelligence in Education, particularly modelling and developing students' metacognition and motivation. He was President (2015-2017) of the International Society for Artificial Intelligence in Education. He has edited/written 11 books and written some 190 papers in the areas indicated above.

Marylee Demeter possesses administrative and academic experience in higher education serving in assessment leadership and adjunct positions at Rutgers University and Middlesex County College. She championed efforts as Chair of the Professional Development Committee for the Student Affairs Assessment Leaders, where she collaboratively developed the MOOC "Developing and Leading Assessment in Student Affairs." She currently serves as a Senior Assessment Developer at Western Governors University.

Morgan Diederich's research focus is understanding student behaviors in technology enhanced learning contexts, combining her passion for data and education. From immersive technologies to online, competency-based education, Morgan seeks to apply learning analytics, educational data mining, and subject matter expertise to help students succeed.

Alfreda Dudley is Professor Emeritus in the Department of Computer and Information Sciences (CIS) at Towson University. She has taught and created courses in the areas of computer ethics, cyberlaw, social informatics, databases, and information technology in the CIS department. Dr. Dudley has published numerous journal articles and book chapters on topics of computer ethics, cyberlaw, computing policy, computing education, cybersecurity, virtual technologies and thanotechnology. She co-edited the IGI book entitled, Investigating Cyber Law and Cyber Ethics: Issues, Impacts, and Practices

Eduard Fabregat, Ph.D., is a researcher at the CritiCC research group at Universitat Pompeu Fabra and an instructor at Universitat Abat Oliba. His research interests include media and immigration, ideology, computational methods, and social media.

Thomas Fikes is Director of Research at the ASU EdPlus Action Lab. His research specializations include social neuroscience, cognitive psychology, learning science, statistical modeling, and data science.

Arthur Fisher, the EDUCATE Company Secretary, has over five years' experience in compliance, corporate liaison and assistance. Proficient in a comprehensive suite of information governance systems, he has a keen eye for specifics. With an academic grounding in politics and history, he demonstrates first-class stakeholder relationship management with his excellent communication skills.

Julie Greenwood, as the Vice Dean for Educational Initiatives, works with the academic units at all ASU campuses, including deans, department chairs, faculty and staff to strengthen online programming and drive course development that transforms student learning experiences. In this role, Julie oversees Instructional Design and New Media, Learning Experience and Student Success, Adaptive and Personalized Learning, Assessment and Compliance, and the EdPlus Action Lab, leveraging data analytics and educational technology to improve and equalize degree completion. In addition, she is the EdPlus liaison to the University Innovation Alliance and the APLU Personalized Learning Consortium. Julie received her Ph.D. from the Neuroscience Program at the University of Alabama at Birmingham and is Associate Professor in the School of Mathematical and Natural Sciences in New College at ASU.

Melissa Hanks is an Assistant Professor in the Computer Science Information Technology Department at the Community College of Baltimore County for the School of Business Technology and Law. Prior to teaching, she worked in the Information Technology field in various information technology positions. She has a certificate in Paralegal Studies and Associates of Science degree in Computer Information Systems from The Community College of Baltimore County, a Bachelor of Science in Information System Management from Walden University, and a Masters in Information System from the University of Phoenix. Her research interest is in mobile app development, artificial intelligence, and ministry in community outreach.

Heather Hayes, PhD, is a psychometrician for the Colleges of Information Technology and Business at Western Governors University. She has been involved in the construction and validation of both cognitive ability and personality assessments for over 20 years. Her research interests center on the conjoint use of cognitive theory and Item Response Theory to aid in the construct validation of test scores as well as to improve the test experience itself through computer adaptive testing and automatic item generation. Her current focus is application of this line of research to developing and validating educational tests for online, competency-based education programs.

Nirali Honest, Ph. D., is an assistant professor at the Chandaben Mohanbhai Patel Institute of Computer Applications, Faculty of Computer Science and Application, Charotar University of Science and Technology where she focuses on research in the domains of Operating Systems, Algorithms, and Data Mining.

Md. Kamal Hossain completed his Masters in World Economy from the school of Chinese Institute for WTO Studies, University of International Business and Economics (UIBE), China in 2019. Currently doing Phd in Management at the Doctoral School of Regional and Business Administration Sciences,

Széchenyi István University, Hungary. His research interests include Investments, Banking, Financial Economics, and Economic growth.

Md. Shamim Hossain is an Associate Professor in the Department of Marketing, Hajee Mohammad Danesh Science and Technology University (HSTU), Bangladesh. In 2019, he received his Ph.D. in Business Management from the University of International Business and Economics (UIBE), Beijing, China. His research interests include operations management, online business, e-marketing, self-service technologies (SSTs), e-commerce, m-banking, online customer behavior, and machine learning in marketing. He has published many researches in top tier journals including Journal of Retailing and Consumer Services, Economic Research-Ekonomska Istraživanja, Management & Marketing. Challenges for the Knowledge Society, & International Journal of Engineering Business Management. He has also experience in publishing book chapters in high quality books published by IGI-Global, USA.

Jennifer Jones is a Senior Project Manager at EdPlus at Arizona State University. Her current focus includes the Data Collective, The goal of the Collective is to create standardized data behavior, using multiple technologies to support EdPlus and ASU Online. The Collective focuses on Peoplesoft, Data Warehouse, Google Marketing and Cloud Platforms, Tealium, and Salesforce, as well as supporting the adoption of ASU data handling standards and data governance policies.

Carmel Kent is a Lecturer, Research Career Development academic lead, at the Institute of Educational Technology, the Open University, UK. Previously, Carmel was the Head of Data Science at EDUCATE Ventures Research and a Senior Research Fellow at UCL. Carmel's research focus is on Artificial Intelligence in Education, Online Learning Communities and Learning Analytics.

David Litz is presently working as an Assistant Professor in the School of Education at the University of Northern British Columbia and as a teacher in School District #52, Prince Rupert, British Columbia. He holds an EdD from the University of Calgary and has several publications; his research interests include comparative education, educational administration and leadership, educational development, as well as educational policy.

Rosemary Luckin is a Professor at UCL's Knowledge Lab. Rose conducts research into the application of Artificial Intelligence (AI) to education and training, in particular how organisations can become 'AI ready.' Her 2018 book: Machine Learning and Human Intelligence: The Future of Education for the 21st Century, stresses the need for AI and Human Intelligence to complement each other. Rose was named as one of the 20 most influential people in Education in the Seldon List 2017. Rose also founded EDUCATE: a hub for EdTech StartUps, researchers and educators to work together on the development of evidence-informed Educational Technology.

Scott Parkman is currently working as the Director of Assessment and Accreditation at New Mexico Highlands University (NMHU). Prior to joining NMHU, he was a lecturer at Emirates College for Advanced Education (ECAE) from 2007-2020 where he taught courses in Applied Linguistics, Technology Education, Mathematics, and Measurement and Assessment in addition to serving as the coordinator of ECAE's online curriculum management system. He has also previously taught in South Korea. He is an educational technology enthusiast and enjoys teaching in technology-rich learning environments. His research interests focus on pre-service teacher education, educational technology, and educational policy.

Atul Patel is the dean and principal at the Chandaben Mohanbhai Patel Institute of Computer Applications, Charusat, India, focusing on Wireless Networks, RDBMS, Data Mining, and Cloud Computing research.

Dharmendra Patel is working as Professor at Smt. Chandaben Mohanbhai Patel Institute of Computer Applications, CHARUSAT, Changa, Gujarat, India. He has received Doctor of Philosophy in Computer Science (Ph.D) from KSV, Gandhinagar, Gujarat. He has more than 17 years of teaching experience. He has published more than 40 research papers in reputed journals/conferences. He has published 4 book chapters in internationally reputed books. He has published 13 technical articles in reputed national/international magazines. He is associated with 26 journals as a member of reviewer board or editorial board.

Mst Farjana Rahman completed her MBA from the Department of Marketing, Hajee Mohammad Danesh Science and Technology University (HSTU), Bangladesh in 2018. Her research interests include online business, e-marketing, online shopping, CRM, and machine learning in marketing. She has published many researches in top tier journals including Journal of Retailing and Consumer Services, Management & Marketing: Challenges for the Knowledge Society, & International Journal of Engineering Business Management. She has also experience in publishing book chapters in high quality books published by IGI-Global, USA.

Alysha Ramirez Hall earned her doctorate degree in Family Studies and Human Development with a minor in quantitative methods and applied developmental science at the University of Arizona, completed a National Science Foundation (NSF) Social, Behavioral and Economics (SBE) Postdoctoral Research Fellowship in the Department of Human Ecology at the University of California, Davis and spent multiple years in the nonprofit sector working closely with community organizations to improve educational outreach programs. She currently is a Senior Research Scientist in the Action Lab at EdPlus at Arizona State University. The Action Lab at EdPlus "strives to achieve new insight into the learning science behind students' learning behavior in a digital world and engage in research that drives instruction design innovation and student success." As a developmental scientist, Dr. Ramirez Hall has centered her research around reducing barriers and enhancing supports for gender and racial minority populations in educational settings. She has served as both a PI and Co-PI on several National Science Foundation grants, most recently an NSF RAPID cycle grant to track college students' transition to remote learning due to the coronavirus pandemic. This quantitative and qualitative daily diary study collected information on academic and wellbeing outcomes, online discrimination, university belongingness and diversity in the times of both coronavirus and historical social justice movements. Intertwined in all aspects of Dr. Ramirez Hall's work are the importance of diversity and people of color achieving equity in education, health and the workplace. She believes that this diversity of ideas and experiences is key in order for progress at any institution to occur.

Sue A. Rodríguez De Jesús is a Senior Research Scientist at The Action Lab at Arizona State University (ASU). She earned her Ph.D. and Master's in Family and Human Development at the T. Denny

Sanford School of Social and Family Dynamics at ASU, and received her Bachelor's in Human Development and Family Studies from The Pennsylvania State University.

Varshita Sher received her Ph.D. in Learning Analytics from Simon Fraser University. Her research is focused on analyzing student learning behavior within technology-enhanced learning environments, using machine learning and data science techniques. Prior to this, she earned her Master's degree in Computer Science from the University of Oxford and was awarded a Distinction for her dissertation in HCI and visual analytics. Passionate about applying state-of-the-art ML and DS technology to problems within the Ed-tech sector, she has published and presented several research papers in reputed journals and conferences. She is a certified Data Carpentry Instructor with pan-global teaching experience and continues to conduct AI/ML workshops for early-career researchers.

Md. Kutub Uddin is a Professor of Management, served as a chairman of Management Department and Dean of Business Studies Faculty at Hajee Mohammad Danesh Science and Technology University (HSTU), Dinajpur, Bangladesh. He has published several full-length research articles in leading journals, presented many research papers in various international conferences, and taught several research-based courses at the undergrad and post-graduate levels. He has also experience in performing several research projects as a Principal Investigator (PI). Professor Uddin has research interests in the field of HRM, Conflict Management, OB, and Machine Learning in Business arena.

Brandon Vaughn joined WGU in 2018 as a course instructor for MSDA, and then as Program Chair revised MSDA to be the first integrated, storied analytics program in the world. He holds a Ph.D. in Statistics and Measurement, and an Ed.D. in Curriculum & Instruction. He is fluent in both data science and psychometrics. He has created a multi-stage k-rank nearest-neighbor rule, as well as a Bayesian hierarchical generalized linear model to detect random effect DIF. His favorite data science models include classification trees, nearest-neighbors, text mining, propensity matching, structural equation, and deep learning.

Pranav Vyas is an assistant professor at the Faculty of Computer Science and Applications with Charotar University of Science and Technology, Changa, Gujarat, India. He has more than 11 years of teaching experience and has published many research papers in reputed journals, conferences, and book chapters.

Tom Wagner is the Director of Learning Analytics at Western Governors University in Utah. In this role, he drives course-level analytics and psychometrics for the largest online university in the United States. Previously, Wagner worked in Product Management, Analytics, and Strategy roles with Ellucian, InsideTrack, and Kuali Inc. Wagner earned an MBA from The Wharton School and a Bachelor's in Quantitative Decision Analysis from the University of California, Berkeley.

Index

A

active learning 176-181, 186, 188, 190-192
app 113-121, 124-126, 128-130, 132
ATS 239, 241-243

B

bias 74, 119, 127, 139, 221, 225, 239, 241-243, 246, 254, 257-258, 264
blended learning platform 113, 115, 117-120, 132
blended learning platform app 113, 115, 117-120
bootcamp 220, 233, 235

C

certificates 161, 173, 220-221, 223-224, 228, 230, 233, 237, 262
Clickstream 1, 4, 23
cluster analysis 11, 17, 23
clustering 1, 8-11, 22, 25, 88, 92, 94, 97-101, 110, 126, 128, 227, 230, 274
collaborative learning 116, 176, 179, 190
Community College 160-161, 164, 174, 190, 260, 270

D

data collection 1, 19, 58, 97, 178, 196, 264-265
data science 20, 23, 71, 93-94, 160-169, 171-175, 197-198, 205, 212, 234
death 177, 260-261, 267-275
degree 2, 7, 66, 77, 79, 85, 91, 99, 143-144, 147, 156, 160-165, 167-169, 172-174, 181, 186, 188, 200, 222, 224-225, 228, 230, 232-235, 240, 242, 244-245, 262-263
diversity 19, 71, 134, 154, 164, 168, 179, 236, 239, 250-255, 257-259, 263

E

education 1-3, 17, 20-22, 27-30, 39, 42-43, 47, 50-55, 67, 85, 94-95, 97, 110-111, 115-116, 127-129, 132, 134, 136, 140, 149-152, 154, 156, 160-161, 163-169, 173-181, 187, 189-196, 201, 220-224, 229-230, 233-234, 236-238, 240-242, 248, 251, 255, 260-262, 264, 266, 268, 271-274
educational offerings 220-221, 224-225, 230-235
elaboration likelihood model 56-57, 59-60, 69, 71
e-learning 111, 131, 264
emotion analysis 132, 153
End of Life 260, 267-268, 273
ePortfolio 239-242, 245, 255-256
exorcism 260-261, 263, 272

F

feature selection 73-76, 79, 83-84, 87-94, 97, 99, 108, 110
filtering technique 73, 90

G

Google Classroom 113, 115-116, 119-125, 127-128
Graduate-level education 176

H

higher education 1-2, 17, 67, 95, 111, 116, 127-128, 161, 174-175, 193-194, 196, 201, 220-224, 236-238, 241, 255, 261, 273-274
high-stakes assessment 194
Hiring Algorithm 239
Hybrid Analysis 1

I

Infranodus 239, 245, 258

innovative cognitive style 56-57, 61, 63

L

Learners' Sentiment 133, 136
Learning Analytics 1-2, 10, 20-22, 94, 111-112, 273
Learning Management System (LMS) 23, 116
Learning to Learn (LTL) 2, 23
lecture-based learning 181
Lexicon-Based Sentiment Analysis 118, 127-128, 132, 152, 155

M

machine learning 68, 73-75, 78, 87, 89-95, 98, 111, 113-114, 116-122, 124-126, 130, 132-133, 136-140, 142-144, 147-151, 155, 162, 166, 171-172, 182, 220-221, 231, 233, 235, 237, 275
M-Learning 115, 132
Multivariate Analysis 73

N

need for cognition 56-57, 60-61, 69
network analysis 220-221, 230, 233, 239, 242, 244-245, 254, 256

O

online 2, 4-5, 15, 18-22, 51-52, 69-70, 94-96, 110-112, 114-116, 119-120, 126-132, 135, 139, 148-155, 157, 161-162, 165, 167-168, 174-177, 179, 181, 188, 193-196, 201, 221, 223-225, 230, 233, 235, 237-238, 240, 242, 256-257, 259, 261-263, 265-266, 268-269, 271-275
ontology 2, 5-6, 8, 18, 23

P

Personalization 94-95, 111
Process mining 8-9, 17, 20, 22-23
program development 160, 162
projects 164, 166, 168, 172-173, 176-179, 186-187, 189-191, 241, 244, 246, 256, 274

R

review 6-8, 11, 18, 20, 22, 25-26, 29, 43, 52-53, 55, 71, 93, 95-96, 110-117, 119-128, 130-133, 135-142, 144, 147-150, 152-157, 161-162, 168, 174, 187, 190, 192, 243-244, 255, 257-258, 264, 266, 275

S

scalable 74, 92, 94-96, 110
scientific literacy 28-29, 38-42, 45-48, 51
self-directed 94-97, 110, 112
self-regulated learning (SRL) 2, 23
self-service business intelligence (SSBI) 56, 58
sentiment analysis 88, 113, 116-118, 120, 124-132, 134-139, 141-142, 147-155, 172
specialty schools 133-134, 136-137, 140, 142, 144, 147-149, 151, 153, 155
statistics education research 176, 191

T

technology evaluation 56-57, 60
text network analysis 239, 242, 244-245, 254, 256
thanatechnology 260, 271-272
Twitter 88, 118, 126, 128-131, 142, 153-154, 220-221, 224-225, 227, 231-233, 235-236, 238

U

Univariate Analysis 73
users review rating prediction 113

V

VADER and AFINN sentiment algorithms 113

W

weak ties 239, 246, 254-255

Recommended Reference Books

IGI Global's reference books are available in three unique pricing formats:
Print Only, E-Book Only, or Print + E-Book.

Shipping fees may apply.

www.igi-global.com

ISBN: 9781522589648
EISBN: 9781522589655
© 2021; 156 pp.
List Price: US$ **155**

ISBN: 9781799840756
EISBN: 9781799840763
© 2021; 282 pp.
List Price: US$ **185**

ISBN: 9781799855989
EISBN: 9781799856009
© 2021; 382 pp.
List Price: US$ **195**

ISBN: 9781799864745
EISBN: 9781799864752
© 2021; 271 pp.
List Price: US$ **195**

ISBN: 9781799875710
EISBN: 9781799875734
© 2021; 252 pp.
List Price: US$ **195**

ISBN: 9781799857709
EISBN: 9781799857716
© 2021; 378 pp.
List Price: US$ **195**

Do you want to stay current on the latest research trends, product announcements, news, and special offers?
Join IGI Global's mailing list to receive customized recommendations, exclusive discounts, and more.
Sign up at: **www.igi-global.com/newsletters.**

Publisher of Timely, Peer-Reviewed Inclusive Research Since 1988

IGI Global
PUBLISHER of TIMELY KNOWLEDGE

Ensure Quality Research is Introduced to the Academic Community

Become an Evaluator for IGI Global Authored Book Projects

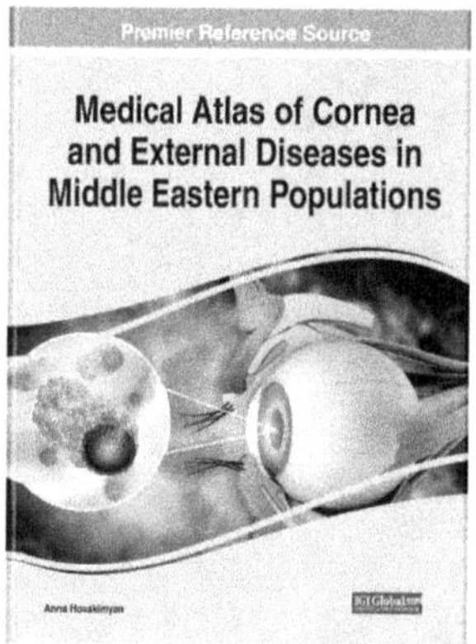

The overall success of an authored book project is dependent on quality and timely manuscript evaluations.

Applications and Inquiries may be sent to:
development@igi-global.com

Applicants must have a doctorate (or equivalent degree) as well as publishing, research, and reviewing experience. Authored Book Evaluators are appointed for one-year terms and are expected to complete at least three evaluations per term. Upon successful completion of this term, evaluators can be considered for an additional term.

If you have a colleague that may be interested in this opportunity, we encourage you to share this information with them.

www.ingramcontent.com/pod-product-compliance
Lightning Source LLC
LaVergne TN
LVHW060421300926
849162LV00006B/1490
* 9 7 8 1 7 9 9 8 9 6 4 4 9 *